Marten Micron

Nederlandse Kerkhistorische Reeks
onder redactie van Erik A. de Boer (Kampen | Utrecht)

In samenwerking met
Henk van den Belt (Amsterdam)
Herman J. Selderhuis (Apeldoorn)
Violet Soen (Leuven)
Mirjam van Veen (Amsterdam)

Deel 8

Eerder verschenen:
Deel 1: Erik A. de Boer, *De macht van de minderheid. Het remonstrantisme in Kampen in de spiegel van de nationale synode te Dordrecht (1618-1619)*
Deel 2: Erik A. de Boer (red.), *De doorstart van de gereformeerde kerk. Kerckboek Campen en correspondentie (1617-1625)*
Deel 3: Gert Leurdijk, *In het voetspoor van Lampe. Gereformeerde piëtisten tussen Bremen en de Republiek in de eerste helft van de achttiende eeuw*
Deel 4: Herman Speelman en Daniël Timmerman, *Gereformeerde getijden. Over vroegmoderne vernieuwing van het spirituele levensritme* (met een bijdrage van Jaco van der Knijff)
Deel 5: Bert Koopman, *Het voorbereidend werk: Een onderzoek naar de invloed van een Engels concept op de theologie in Nederland in de zeventiende eeuw*
Deel 6: Byunghoon Kang, *Guy de Brès on the Lord's Supper as the Focus of his Ministry and Theology*
Deel 7: R.W. de Koeijer, *Concentratie op de passie. Laatmiddeleeuwse, reformatorische en postreformatorische visies op de geestelijke betekenis van Christus' lijden*

H.T. WENDT

Marten Micron (1522/23-1559)

His Reforming Ecclesiology in
Van de weerdicheydt, nutheydt ende noodicheyt der christelicker vergaderinghen

Summum

This study was sponsored by:

Sponsored by **S**TICHTING **A**FBOUW **K**AMPEN

© 2023 Summum Academic Publications – Kampen
www.summumacademic.com

Omslagontwerp: Brainstorm
Opmaak binnenwerk: Gewoon Geertje

ISBN 9789492701541 (gebonden)
ISBN 9789492701558 (paperback)
ISSN 2666-1373
NUR 704

All rights reserved. No part of this publication may be reproduced, translated, stored in a retrieval system, or transmitted in any form by any means, electronic, mechanical, photocopying, recording or otherwise, without prior written permission from the publisher.

To the
Father, the Son and the Holy Spirit,
the triune God
of the covenant,

Who gave
a loving wife,
beautiful children,
devout parents,
brothers and sisters and friends;

Who gave
strength,
perseverance,
faith,
hope
and love;

Who forgave
all my shortcomings
and sins;

Who gave
- gift beyond understanding! -
Himself
in His love,

be given
everlasting
thanks and praise.

To my fellow pilgrim

Bart van Egmond

לְמַעַן אַחַי וְרֵעָי אֲדַבְּרָה־נָּא שָׁלוֹם בָּךְ

Acknowledgments

This study is a slightly revised version of my PhD-thesis, defended at the Theological University of Utrecht (formerly Kampen). Now that this project is finished, there are several people towards whom I should like to express my gratitude.

I sincerely thank my two supervisors, Erik de Boer and Christine Kooi for their time, support and feedback.

I also want to thank the reading-committee, consisting of Mirjam van Veen, Henk van den Belt, Arnd Reitemeier and Sabine Hiebsch, for their insightful remarks and questions.

In my fight against the thorns and thistles of typos and Dutchisms I was assisted by Stephen Quinton and David Fox, for which I heartily thank them. If any errors remain (and I fear that like weeds they are ineradicable) they are completely my responsibility.

Last of all I want to thank all my colleagues, friends and family who supported me during this process.

Harry Wendt

Contents

A Note on Terminology 5

Chapter 1: Introduction to the Research 7
   1.1 Micron-research 9
   1.2 Preliminary Methodological Considerations 19
   1.3 Research Question and Chapter Contents 23

Part 1: Historical 25

Chapter 2: Introduction to Van de weerdicheydt, nutheydt ende noodicheyt der christelicker vergaderinghen 27
   2.1 Description of the book 27
   2.2 Printer 31
   2.3 Authorship 33
   2.4 Structure and Summary of the Book 41
   2.5 Goals of the Book 43
   2.6 Summary and Conclusions 48

Chapter 3: Introduction to the Authors of Van de weerdicheydt, nutheydt ende noodicheyt der christelicker vergaderinghen 49
   3.1 Marten Micron 50
       3.1.1 Early life 50
       3.1.2 Zurich 56
       3.1.3 England 61
       3.1.4 From England to Norden 72
       3.1.5 Norden 77
   3.2 Nicolaus Carinaeus 83
   3.3 Summary and Conclusions 86

Chapter 4: The Second Concentric Circle: The East Frisian Reformation and 'the Reformation of the Refugees' 87
   4.1 The East Frisian Reformation 87
   4.2 The Reformation of the Refugees 99
       4.2.1 Opposing the Paradigm 100
              4.2.1.1 Jesse Spohnholz and Mirjam van Veen 100
              4.2.1.2 Judith Becker 105
              4.2.1.3 Johannes Müller 105

	4.2.1.4 Three Questions	108
4.2.2	The Reformation of the Refugees	109
	A) Continuity between the Churches before and after Emden 1571	110
	B) The Relation between Flight and Theology	116
	C) Was Every Refugee Reformed?	122
	D) Nicholas Terpstra's Religious Refugees in the Early Modern World	123
4.2.3	Evaluation	124
4.3	Summary and Conclusions	129

Chapter 5: Translations — 131
- 5.1 The German Translation by Engelbert Faber — 131
- 5.2 The English Translation of Excerpts from the Book — 136
- 5.3 Summary and Conclusions — 142

Part 2: Theological — 143

Chapter 6: Analysis of the Ecclesiology in Van de weerdicheydt, nutheydt ende noodicheyt der christelicker vergaderinghen — 145

- 6.1 Micron's Method in Van de weerdicheydt — 146
- 6.2 The Purpose of the Church — 148
- 6.3 The Nature of the Church — 155
  - 6.3.1 Gathered out of all People by the Will of God — 156
  - 6.3.2 The Church of God and the World — 158
  - 6.3.3 The Foundation of the Church — 164
- 6.4 The Marks of the Church — 168
  - 6.4.1 The Marks of the Church: Source and Verity — 168
  - 6.4.2 The First Mark of the Church: Doctrine — 172
  - 6.4.3 The Second Mark of the Church: Governance — 175
    - A) Word — 175
    - Excursus: Ministry and Prophecy, Priests and Prophets — 178
    - B) Sacraments — 184
    - C) Christian Discipline — 190
- 6.5 Staying or Seceding — 193
  - 6.5.1 The Command to Join the Church — 193
  - 6.5.2 The Necessity to Secede — 197
  - 6.5.3 Confessional Authenticity and the Pastoral Realism of Broken Life. — 203
- 6.6 Summary and Conclusions — 204

Chapter 7: Micron and Reformed Ecclesiology ... 209
    7.1 Authors and Sources ... 210
    7.2 Purpose and Nature of the Church ... 212
    7.3 The Marks of the Church ... 217
    7.4 Teachers of a Holy Gospel ... 223
    7.5 Unity and Secession ... 231
    7.6 Summary and Conclusions ... 235

Chapter 8: Micron's Reforming Ecclesiology in the Context of the Reformed Reformation – Synthesis and Conclusions ... 237
    8.1 Context ... 237
    8.2 Micron's Ecclesiology within Reformed Ecclesiology ... 241
    8.3 Dissemination ... 245
    8.4 Conclusion ... 251

Bibliography ... 255
  Abbreviations ... 255
  Works by Micron ... 257
  Other primary sources ... 259
  Secondary literature ... 265
  Images ... 295

Appendix A: Schedule of Contents *Van de weerdicheydt, nutheydt ende noodicheyt der christelicker vergaderinghen* ... 297
Appendix B: Edition of *Van de weerdicheydt, nutheydt ende noodicheyt der christelicker vergaderinghen* ... 301
  Method ... 301

Index of Persons and Places ... 425

A Note on Terminology

Since this study addresses the 'Reformation of the Refugees' extensively, a note on the terms used is in order.

The term 'refugee' follows the definition given by Scholz: 'the experience of physical displacement from one's homeland'.[1] When discussing the Reformation of the Refugees we also use the term refugee, in order to avoid confusion.

In addition to the physical displacement, the psychological and theological effect of this displacement are important in this study and the evaluation of the paradigm. The refugees themselves usually refer to this as *peregrinatio*. This term is used to indicate the mental or theological evaluation of the refugees.

The terms 'stranger' and 'exile' are much more difficult. To a certain extent 'stranger' can be used as a synonym for refugee: not being in one's homeland, and hence a stranger. It is, however, also a biblical term (e.g. Hebrews 11:3). The refugees use this biblical language when they refer to themselves as strangers in this world. It would be wrong to change this to 'exiles' or 'pilgrims'. Again, exile is to a certain degree a technical term for someone who has been banished. However, as we will see, Micron also speaks of voluntary exile. Just like 'stranger', 'exile' is also a biblical term. For these terms, then, it is the context that has to make clear whether we are speaking of physical displacement, theology or psychological effect.

When referring to the church led by à Lasco and Micron during the time of Edward VI, Silke Muylaert writes 'Strangers' Church'. Other refugee churches are referred to as 'stranger church(es)'.[2] However, Micron himself also referred to the Strangers' Church as the 'Dutch Church'.[3] We will employ both Strangers' Church and Dutch Church. Since this church was located in London, we sometimes use 'London church'. Moreover, the plural (Churches) is occasionally employed to indicate that the Strangers' church consisted of both a Dutch and French congregation. Where others speak of these churches as *vluchtelingenkerken* we use the translation 'refugee-churches'.

---

1 Scholz, M.M., *Strange Brethren. Refugees, Religious Bonds, and Reformation in Frankfurt 1554-1608* (Charlottesville and London: University of Virginia Press, 2022). xiii.
2 Cf. Muylaert, S., *Shaping the Stranger Churches. Migrants in England and the Troubles in the Netherlands, 1547-1585* (Leiden/Boston: Brill, 2021), 22
3 E.g.: *De Christlicke Ordinancien der Nederlantscher Ghemeinten te Londen.*

Not all refugees fled their home-country, nor did everyone leave for the same reasons. The term flight, however, is used somewhat loosely to indicate emigration. In some cases, to avoid confusion, the term 'displacement' is used.

Where the opinions of others are represented, we use the terms in the way the author uses them, in order to give as fair a representation of their opinion as lies within our abilities.

Chapter 1: Introduction to the Research

If Marten Micron, a Reformed pastor in his mid-thirties, left the Ludgerikirche of Norden through the north door, the edifice of the St. Andreaskirche would tower over him about a hundred meters away. Once this was a glorious church. In Micron's day, however, only ruins were left. The western tower had been set on fire by Balthasar von Esen in 1531, to revenge himself upon the city.[1] What remained was a roofless stump on the west side, two forlorn towers on the east and in between a decaying church where the elements slowly took their toll.[2] The contrast between the ruins to the north and the glorious, solid building the reformer had just left was sharp indeed. One church stood the test of time, whereas the other was in a desperate state of decay. One was a safe place: the forces of nature had no power to trouble the faithful gathering inside. The other was desolate and insecure. Not only could the wind and the rain freely strike anyone walking there, stones and rubble could come loose and hurt the visitor as well. Yet both churches had a solid foundation. Were not the ruins themselves a sign of this? After all, they had not fallen over yet. To be sure, it was not safe, but it was not beyond salvaging. Nonetheless, as time progressed the Andreaskirche fell into increasing disrepair and was at last razed to the ground in 1756.[3] Of course, Marten Micron would have been unaware of this future in the 1550s. In his days there would have been every reason to hope for a reconstruction of the ruined church

---

1 Cremer, U., *Norden im Wandel der Zeiten* (Norden: Heinrich Soltau, 1955), 18. The image, probably by Marten Claessen Eelking (1579-1640) on the cover of the book shows the deplorable state of the building in 1618 (image provided by the Ostfriesisches Landesmuseum Emden).

2 We are not able to ascertain the exact state of decay in the 1550's; however, Cremer summarises from Elsenius' chronicle: 'Am 10. August 1597 wäre die erste Leiche in der alten Kirche begraben, und hätte er dabei die erste Leichenpredigt gehalten, nachdem die Kirche 63 Jahre "desolat und wöste" gelegen hätte. So wurde im Laufe des 17. Jahrhunderts der von den Ruinen gesäuberte Raum für Begräbnisplätze freigegeben.' (Cremer, *Norden*, 20).

3 Louis, C., 'Kunstschätze der Gesellschaft. II. Zwei Zeichnungen der Norder Andreaskirche. Versuch einer Rekonstruktion' in: *Jahrbuch der Gesellschaft für bildende Kunst und vaterländische Altertümer zu Emden* 25 (1937), 146-158, 147. For more on the Andreaskirche, cf. Bärenfänger, R., 'Die Andreas-kirche in Norden' in: Bärenfänger, R. (ed.), *Führer zu archäologischen Denkmälern in Deutschland 35: Ostfriesland* (Stuttgart: Konrad Theiss, 1999), 187-189; Kozok, M. 'Untersuchungen zur Baugeschichte und Rekonstruktion der Andreaskirche in Norden' in: *Jahrbuch der Gesellschaft für bildende Kunst und vaterländische Altertümer zu Emden* 72 (1992), 19-68.

to match the glory of the Ludgerikirche. The contrast between these two buildings was the contrast he would have experienced in his life up to that point. He had left the Roman Catholic church, which he saw as a church in decay, and he had laboured to re-erect the church as a safe bulwark for the faithful.[4] Part of his labour was a steady stream of theological publications.

Thus we move from one historical source to the next. From a building we turn towards a book. Both are a lasting witness to the ideas of people.[5] What people say is said for a moment; when people write, their words become independent objects that can be studied by people of all times.[6] Whether Micron was aware that the two buildings in Norden were a fine illustration of his thoughts we do not know. But we can attempt to follow his thoughts because he wrote them down in his book *Van de weerdicheydt, nutheydt ende noodicheyt der christelicker vergaderinghen* (*On the Worthiness, Benefit and Necessity of Christian Assemblies*). This book is the focal point of our research, since Micron offers his most comprehensive and systematic exposition of his ecclesiology. The Latin manuscript was unfinished when Micron passed away in 1559. Nicholas Carinaeus wrote the last chapters, the first chapters were translated into the vernacular and the book was published in 1561. In it we find Micron's ecclesiology and listen to his views on a subject which has been widely studied.[7]

In this first chapter the theoretical framework is described by summarising four and a half centuries of Micron-research (1.1). In doing so, we will discover what other research-fields intersect with our present study. Secondly, some remarks on historical method will be made (1.2),

---

4 See ch. 6 of this study.
5 Cf. the famous philosophical chapter in Victor Hugo's *Notre-Dame de Paris* where Dom Frollo calls the cathedral one of his books, but also that the book will kill the building ('this will kill that') (Hugo, V., *The Hunchback of Notre-Dame* ed. Walter J. Cobb (New York: Signet Classics, 1964/2010), 169).
6 Cf., e.g., Sikkel, J.C., *De Heilige Schrift en haar verklaring. Inleiding tot de verklaring der Heilige Schrift als het Woord Gods* (Amsterdam: J.W.A. Schaik, 1906), 13. More recently: Vallejo, I, *Papyrus. Een geschiedenis van de wereld in de boeken* ed. Adri Boom (Amsterdam: Meulenhoff, 2021).
7 The *Locus de Ecclesia* has been the subject of many recent dissertations defended at the Theological University of Kampen, e.g. Alten, H.H. van, *The Beginnings of a Spirit-Filled Church. A Study of the Implications of the Pneumatology for the Ecclesiology in John Calvin's Commentary on the Acts of the Apostles* (PhD Theological University Kampen, 2017); Jong, M.J. de, *The Church is the Means, the World is the End. The Development of Klaas Schilder's Thought on the Relationship between the Church and the World* (PhD Theological University Kampen, 2019); Tamminga, K.S., *Receiving the Gifts of Every Member. A Practical Ecclesiological Case Study on Inclusion and the Church* (PhD Theological University Kampen, 2020).

last of all a research question is formulated and an overview of the several chapters is given (1.3).

1.1 Micron-research

Micron, born in 1522 or 1523, passed away in 1559. In 1560 the first historical work reflecting on part of his work and life was published. It is Jan Utenhove's *Simplex et Fidelis Narratio*. Jan Utenhove had been one of Micron's elders in the London Stranger Church and travelled with him to the German Lands. In this apologetic memoir he gives an account of how the London Stranger Church left England after Mary Tudor ascended the throne and how they sought refuge in Denmark and several cities in the north of the German Lands. Utenhove also describes how Micron became a pastor in Norden, East Frisia. In the *Simplex et Fidelis Narratio* Micron is presented as the first among his fellow ministers, under their superintendent, John à Lasco.[8] He was, moreover, an astute theologian in his several disputes with Lutherans and Mennonites[9], during which he does not seem to have been lost for words.[10] Apparently, he was a pastor with a heart for his congregation, opting to travel many miles to be with them.[11] Of course, the *Simplex et Fidelis Narratio* is not a scholarly book; rather, it is the biased account of a friend. As such we cannot take everything Utenhove says for granted. It is, however, also the first account of Micron that presents itself as a historical narrative. Moreover, it is the only lengthy eye-witness account of how he behaved and reasoned.

Utenhove's account shows how Micron was closely linked to John à Lasco and became a pastor in Norden. This means we will have to deal with the course of the East Frisian reformation. The solid stream of important works on the East Frisian Reformation[12] has continued right

---

8   E.g., *SFN*, 35-47; *Bericht*, 17-43.
9   We use the term Mennonites here and elsewhere to indicate that Micron specifically debated with Menno Simons himself and his direct followers.
10 *SFN*, ch. 4-8; *Bericht*, ch. 4-8.
11 See below, 3.1.4.
12 We deliberately say 'East Frisian Reformation' instead of 'the Reformation in East Frisia' because the last term suggests there is a single movement that can be defined as 'the' Reformation(cf., e.g., Eire, C.M.N., *Reformations. The Early Modern World, 1450-1650* (Yale: YUP, 2016, ix-xi). On the other hand, all these reformations are part of a larger movement in the 16th century, bearing many similarities, as such the singular 'Reformation' can still be used as a general term for the many religious changes that occurred in this century (Cf. Kooi, Ch., *Reformation in the Low Countries, 1500-1620* (Cambridge: CUP, 2022), xii). Perhaps it would be advisable to speak of a particular reformation within the age of Reformation (not: *the* Reformation). With this in mind these nomeclatures are used interchangeably.

down to the present time. John à Lasco himself is an important reformer whose relation to Micron cannot be neglected.[13]

In addition we see Micron disputing with both Lutherans and Mennonites. Where necessary we will have to give some attention to this. However, his discussions are either about the Lord's Supper (in the midst of the Second Eucharistic Controversy) or the incarnation. Both, to be sure, are in some way directly or indirectly linked to ecclesiology. However, the research proper deals with neither of these topics directly. Consequently, we will only reflect on these discussions when Micron's ecclesiology demands us to do so.

This summary already shows us many of the subjects we will have to address in this thesis. First of all, Utenhove describes Micron as a religious refugee. The paradigm of the Reformation of the Refugees has been defended and elaborated by several scholars, most famously by Heiko Oberman, Heinz Schilling and Andrew Pettegree.[14] In a recent

---

13 For the East Frisian reformation see: Grochowina, N., *Indifferenz und Dissens in der Grafschaft Ostfriesland im 16. und 17. Jahrhundert* (Frankfurt am Main: Peter Lang, 2003); Janssen, H. E., *Gräfin Anna von Ostfriesland – eine hochadelige Frau der späten Reformationszeit (1540/42-1575). Ein beitrag zu den Anfängen der reformierten Konfessionalisierung im Reich* (Münster: Aschendorff, 1998); Reitemeier, A., *Reformation in Norddeutschland. Gottvertrauen zwischen Fürstenherrschaft und Teufelsfurcht* (Göttingen: Wallstein Verlag, 2017); Smid, M., *Ostfriesische Kirchengeschichte* (Pewsum, 1974); Weerda, J.R., *Der Emder Kirchenrat und seine Gemeinde. Ein Beitrag zur Geschichte reformierter Kirchenordnung in Deutschland, ihrer Grundsätze und ihrer Gestaltung* ed. Matthias Freudenberg & Alasdair Heron (Wuppertal: Foedus, 2000). Further references in 4.1. For John à Lasco, see: Becker, J., *Gemeindeordnung und Kirchenzucht. Johannes a Lascos Kirchenordnung für London (1555) und die reformierte Konfessionsbildung* (Leiden/Boston: Brill, 2007); Jürgens, H.P., *Johannes à Lasco in Ostfriesland. Der Werdegang eines europäischen Reformators* (Tübingen: Mohr Siebeck, 2002); Rodgers, D.W., *John à Lasco in England* (New York: Peter Lang, 1994); Springer, M.S., *Restoring Christ's Church. John a Lasco and the Forma ac ratio* (Aldershot: Ashgate, 2007); Strohm, Ch. (ed.), *Johannes à Lasco (1499-1560). Polnischer Baron, Humanist und europäischer Reformator* (Tübingen: Mohr Siebeck, 2000).
14 Within the framework of a Reformation of the Refugees the following works are of key importance: Bremmer, R.H., *Reformatie en Rebellie. Willem van Oranje, de calvinisten en het recht van opstand. Tien onstuimige jaren: 1572-1581* (Franeker: Wever, 1984); Grell, O.P., *Brethren in Christ. A Calvinist Network in Reformation Europe* (Cambridge: CUP, 2011); Janssen, G.H. *The Dutch Revolt and Catholic Exile in Reformation Europe* (Cambridge: CUP, 2014/2016); Oberman, H.A. [edited by Peter A. Dykema], *John Calvin and the Reformation of the Refugees* (Geneva: Droz, 2009); Pettegree, A., *Emden and the Dutch Revolt. Exile and the Development of Reformed Protestantism* (Oxford: Clarendon Press, 1992); Schelven, A.A. van, *De Nederduitsche vluchtelingenkerken der XVIe eeuw in Engeland en Duitschland in*

overview of Dutch church history Pettegree's view is given as summary of the paradigm: 'this period [of exile] brought new vigor and commitment to the movement, sharpened its ecclesiology, clarified its doctrine and therefore further confessionalised what was gradually turning into the Reformed church.'[15] Recently it has been criticised as 'largely a construction of nineteenth-century neo-Calvinist historians engaged about contemporary debates on religious liberty'[16] as Christine Kooi summarises the critique by, primarily, Jesse Spohnholz and Mirjam van Veen. Judith Becker and Johannes Müller take a more nuanced critical stance.[17] This subject is relevant to the church today, as Christians are once again identifying themselves as strangers in this present secular age.[18]

---

hunne betekenis voor de reformatie in de Nederlanden (The Hague: Nijhoff, 1908); Schilling, H., 'Christliche und Jüdische Minderheitsgemeinden im Vergleich: Calvinistische Exulanten und westliche Diaspora der Sephardim im 16. und 17. Jahrhundert' in: *Zeitschirft für Historische Forschung* 36/3 (2009), 407-444; Selderhuis, H.J. & Nissen, P., 'De zestiende eeuw' in: Selderhuis, H.J. (ed.), *Handboek Nederlandse Kerkgeschiedenis* (Kampen: Kok, 2006); Terpstra, N., *Religious Refugees in the Early Modern World. An Alternative History of the Reformation* (Cambridge: CUP, 2015). For further references, cf. 4.2.2.

15 Kooi, Ch., *Reformation Low Countries, 1500-1620)*, 120. Cf. Selderhuis & Nissen, 'Zestiende eeuw', 283 where they argue the ecclesial model of the Reformed churches implemented in the Republic was prepared in the stranger churches.

16 Kooi, *Reformation Low Countries, 1500-1620*, 120.

17 Key publications are: Becker, J., 'Migration and Confession among Sixteenth-Century Western European Reformed Christians' in: *Reformation and Renaissance Review* 13 (2011), 3-31; Müller, J., *Exile Memories and the Dutch Revolt. The Narrated Diaspora, 1550-1750* (Leiden/Boston: Brill, 2016); Spohnholz, J., *The Convent of Wesel. The Event that Never was and the Invention of Tradition* (Cambridge: CUP, 2017/2020); Spohnholz, J. & Veen, M.G.K. van, 'The Disputed Origins of Dutch Calvinism: Religious Refugees in the Historiography of the Dutch Reformation' in: *Church History. Studies in Christianity and Culture* 86/2 (2017); Veen, M.G.K. van, '"...wir sind ständig unterwegs...": Reformierte Flüchtlinge des 16. Jahrhunderts als Exulanten?' in: *Archiv für Reformationsgeschichte* 109 (2018), 442-458; Veen, M.G.K. van & Spohnholz, J., 'Calvinists vs. Libertines: A New Look at Religious Exile and the Origins of 'Dutch' Tolerance' in: Brink, G. van den & Höpfl, H. (eds.), *Calvinism and the Making of the European Mind* (Leiden: Brill, 2014), 76-99. For further references, see 4.2.1.

18 E.g., Dekker, W., *Marginaal en missionair. Kleine theologie voor een krimpende kerk* (Zoetermeer: Boekencentrum, 2011); Hertog, G.C. den & Peels, H.G.L. (eds.), *Vreemdelingen en bijwoners. Opstellen rond een urgent theologisch thema* (Apeldoorn: Theologische universiteit Apeldoorn, 2012); Paas, S., *Vreemdelingen en priesters. Christelijke missie in een postchristelijke samenleven* (Zoetermeer: Boekencentrum, 2015); Reuver, A. de, 'Verlangen naar het Vaderhuis' in: *Reformatorisch Dagblad* 25-12-2022 (accessed via: https://www.rd.nl/artikel/956507-verlangen-naar-het-vaderhuis [30-9-2022]).

The first more scholarly history that discusses Micron is Menso Alting's[19] *Gründtlicker Warhafftiger Bericht* (1594), an account of the East Frisian Reformation, written from a distinctly Reformed mindset. Alting informs us that the 'important and godly man Marten Micron' became a pastor in Norden in 1554. He speaks highly of Micron's zeal, his books and his obedience to the Word of God, but gives us no other information, though he places Micron in the leading position among his colleagues. Menso Alting does not address Micron's relation to the Dutch churches. This changes with Anthonius Thysius's[20] *Leere ende order* (1615), where he describes the London Strangers' Church with its confessions as the direct predecessor, even mother, of the Dutch churches of his days. He places à Lasco, Micron and Utenhove next to each other as equals.[21] If the London Church was the mother we might therefore say that, in a manner of speaking, Micron, author of many of the works used in the London church, was a midwife to the Dutch churches. Thysius also draws attention to Micron's and Utenhove's experience of exile, underlining the importance to confront ourselves with the Reformation of the Refugees.

Like Menso Alting's history of the East Frisian Reformation, two works in the eighteenth century also discuss Micron. The first, Eduard Meiners'[22] *Oostvrieschlandts Kerkelyke Geschiedenisse* (1738-1739) does so only in passing. He is more concerned with the role John à Lasco played. What he says about Micron is mostly copied from Utenhove's *Simplex et Fidelis Narratio*. We mention his particular attention to East Frisia as a safe haven and his detailed reconstruction of the various

---

19 Menso Alting (1541-1612) was a Reformed pastor, first in Heidelberg, then Emden, where he became the leading pastor. Cf., Onstenk, A.J., 'Alting, Menso' in *Biografisch Lexicon voor de geschiedenis van het Nederlands Protestantisme. Deel 2*, 26-27; Voβ, K-D & Wolfgang, J. (eds.), *Menso Alting und seine Zeit* (Oldenburg: Florian Isensee, 2012).
20 Thysius (1565-1640) studied theology in several places and worked as an assistant minister in Emden from 1594-1596, before becoming professor of theology in Harderwijk in 1601. He wrote his *Leere ende order* in the midst of the debate between remonstrants and contra-remonstrants, being part of the latter group himself. Cf. Lamping, A.J., 'Thysius, Antonius' in: *Bibliografisch Lexicon voor de geschiedenis van het Nederlands protestantisme. Deel 5*, 505-508.
21 Thysius, A., *Leere ende order*, **v.
22 Meiners (1691-1752), born in Emden, studied theology in Leiden. He was a pastor in Grothusen (1712), Westerhusen (1716), Weener (1717) and Emden (1723).Cf. Aa, A.J. van der, *Biografisch woordenboek der Nederlanden. Twaalfde deel* (Haarlem: J.J. van Brederode, 1869), 546-547

catechisms published in Emden.[23] The end of the century saw the extended edition of Peter Fridrich Reershemius'[24] invaluable *magnum opus* titled *Ostfriesländisches Prediger-Denkmahl* (1796), and here we find the first summarising biography of Marten Micron, including an overview of his works. However, apart from his summary of Micron's will, he tells us little of Micron as a person and theologian. He is merely presented as one in the long line of East Frisian pastors. All in all, what we have seen so far, there is no lively debate or much scholarly interest surrounding either his person or his theology. He is merely reckoned as one of the more notable theologians in the earlier history of the Dutch churches.

In the 19th century we come to a new phase. The direction in which the older historiography had moved changed radically due to the work of the Parker Society. This society within the Anglican Church was named after Matthew Parker[25], founded by members of the Anglican church who 'felt the urgent need to make available in an attractive and accessible form the works of the leaders of the English Reformation'.[26] One of the volumes was the *Original Letters Relative to the English Reformation* (1846), published in two parts. It contained letters by many reformers living in England, including Marten Micron's letters to Heinrich Bullinger. Here is a connection which we did not find in any of the earlier sources.[27] The importance of these letters was soon clear and the original Latin letters of Micron and many others were published in the *Epistolae Tigurinae* (1848). Not only do these letters show Micron was closely allied to the Zürich reformation, they also make clear he was a friend of John Hooper. This proved to be a cause for debate. Was Micron, such a notable figure in the history of the Dutch churches, a Calvinist or not? It appears one's conviction in this debate was mainly influenced by one's

---

23 Meiners I, ch. 17 (the catechisms); 363 (Emden as a safe haven).
24 Reershemius (1728-1805) was a Lutheran theologian who served both as pastor and *Kircheninspektor*. Cf. Smid, M. 'Reershemius, Fam..' in: *Biographisches Lexikon für Ostfriesland IV* (Aurich, 2007), 348-350 (for our research we used the digital version on the website of the *Ostfriesische Landschaft*).
25 Matthew Parker was archbishop of Canterbury from 1559-1575. He was heavily influenced by Bucer and 'hailed as one of the chief architects of the Elizabethan religious settlement'. He was also a book collector. (Crankshaw, D.J. & Gillespie, A., 'Parker, Matthew' in: *Oxford Dictionary of National Biography* (accessed via https://doi-org.access.authkb.kb.nl/10.1093/ref:odnb/21327 [2-12-2022])).
26 Cinnamond, A., 'The Reformed Treasures of the Parker Society' in: *Churchman* 122/3 (2008), 221-242. Quotation from 221.
27 Excepting, of course, the *Simplex et Fidelis Narratio*, but this book itself was hard to come by (Pijper, F., 'Inleiding' in: *SFN*, 3-28, 3).

opinion of how strict the churches should be in upholding their confession of divine election. For instance, we read in Antonius Johannes van 't Hooft's[28] *De theologie van Heinrich Bullinger in betrekking tot de Nederlandsche Reformatie* (1888) that Bullinger's milder doctrine was adopted by Micron instead of Calvin's, who 'could think of God's *being* only as despotism'.[29] And Micron, as Bullinger's close friend, wants to be under the Zurich reformer's influence. Van 't Hooft concludes that Utenhove and Micron were not Zwinglians, as Ferdinand Pijper had argued earlier, but Bullingerians[30] – completely in accord with John à Lasco as a Bullingerian trio.[31] That is to say, Van 't Hooft is trying to prove that a confession of divine election does not belong to the original doctrinal foundation of the Dutch churches but came later with staunch Calvinist preachers.

Jan Hendrik Gerretsen[32] was the next to promote a more or less similar view. His work however, deserves more attention. It was, and will remain, an essential work for all who wish to study the life of Marten Micron. In 1895 Gerretsen published the first, and so far only, monograph on Marten Micron: *Micronius. Zijn leven, zijn geschriften, zijn geestesrichting*. As is clear from the title this is a biography, bibliography and assessment of Micron's theology. Especially the biographical part will not lose its value, even though we hope to present a more elaborate and better documented one in this present study. Since Gerretsen's book there has not been anything that comes near to his achievement. However, he sees in Micron the forefather of the *ethischen*,[33] a movement in the Dutch churches at that time. They stressed life and experience above doctrine

---

28 Van 't Hooft (1860-1932) studied theology in Leiden, where he also earned his PhD in 1888. After that he was pastor in the *Hervormde kerk* of Nootdorp (1888), Borne (1896), Meppel (1901), Oosterbeek (1906). Cf. Ponsteen, H.J., 'Hooft, Antonius van 't' in: *Biografisch Lexicon voor de geschiedenis van het Nederlands Protestantisme. Deel 4*, 215.

29 Hooft, A. van 't, *De theologie van Heinrich Bullinger in betrekking tot de Nederlandsche Reformatie* (Amsterdam: Is de Hoogh, 1888), 158.

30 For this opinion compare, also, Büsser, F., *Heinrich Bullinger. Leben, Werk und Wirkung. Band II* (Zurich: TVZ, 2005), 295-296.

31 Hooft, *De theologie van Heinrich Bullinger*, 160-161.

32 Gerretsen (1867-1923) studied theology in Utrecht, where he also defended his PhD on Florens Radewijn in 1891. He was pastor in the *Hervormde kerk* of Lopik (1891), Dedemsvaart (1895) and The Hague (1898). In 1909 he was appointed as court preacher (Antonides, C.F.J., *dr. Jan Hendrik Gerretsen 1867-1923 "Het geluid van een sterke stem"* (Gorinchem: Narratio, 1997), 15-46).

33 Antonides comments: 'Het zijn bovenal de ethische elementen, die Gerretsen uit Micron's theologie zeeft. Het lijkt wel alsof Gerretsen er alles aan gelegen is om toch vooral Micron als ethisch theoloog te karakteriseren.' (*Sterke stem*, 45).

and Bible, though it is better to summarise Gerretsen's view as follows: only the regenerate can understand the meaning of the Bible because their soul understands the mystery the apostles write about.[34] Micron, Gerretsen claims, is anything but legalistic and in this he is radically different from both John à Lasco and John Calvin, especially the latter.[35] Here, then, Micron is seen not as minor figure next to à Lasco, a helpmate, but as a thoroughly distinctive theologian.

This view was opposed within the neo-calvinistic movement. We mention the example of Frederik Lodewijk Rutgers'[36] *Calvijns invloed op de Reformatie in de Nederlanden voor zoveel die door hemzelven is uitgeoefend* (1899), as being a key study by one of the finest scholars in this tradition. The title alone shows this is an addition to Van 't Hooft's dissertation. And indeed, in a lengthy note Rutgers tries to prove that not only were Calvin and Bullinger equally important to Micron, Calvin was in fact the greater influence of the two.[37]

This discussion is relevant to us. In the last twenty-odd years Bullinger research has experienced a revival.[38] Micron's relation to Zurich and

---

34 Cf., e.g., Groenewoud, H.G. 'Ethischen' in: Grosheide, F.W. & Itterzon, G.P van (eds.), *Christelijke Encyclopedie II* (Kampen: Kok, 1957), 652. For an introduction to Gerretsen's theology, see Antonides, *Sterke stem*, p. 47-48.

35 Gerretsen, *Micronius*, 140-142. He writes: 'Ethical, to me, is the opposite of individual, intellectual, juridical, mechanical' (p. 142, translation by HTW). The description runs on for almost half a page before he concludes that of course Micron did not embrace this fully, but certainly moved in this direction.

36 Rutgers (1836-1917) studied theology in Leiden where he also received his doctor's degree. He served as pastor in several churches and ultimately in Amsterdam, where he assisted Abraham Kuyper in founding the *Vrije Universiteit*, where he also became professor of church history, church polity and (temporarily) exegesis of the Old Testament. He was influential as one of the leaders of the Doleantie. Cf. Nauta, D. 'Rutgers' in: Groshcide, F.W. & Itterzon, G.P. van (eds.), *Christelijke Encyclopedie V* (Kampen: Kok, 1960), 696-697.

37 Rutgers, F.L., *Calvijns invloed op de reformatie in de Nederlanden voor zoveel die door hemzelven is uitgeoefend* (Leiden: D.Donner, 1899), 123-126

38 E.g.: Albisser, A. & Opitz, P. (eds.), *Die Zürcher Reformation in Europa. Beiträge der Tagung des Instituts für Schweizerische Reformationsgeschichte 6.-8. Februar 2019 in Zürich* (Zurich: TVZ, 2021); Burnett, A. Nelson, '"It Varies from Canton to Canton": Zurich, Basel, and the Swiss Reformation', in: *Calvin Theological Journal* 44 (2009), 251-262; Burnett, A. Nelson & Campi, E. (eds.), *A Companion to the Swiss Reformation* (Leiden: Brill, 2016), 170-215.Euler, C., *Couriers of the Gospel: England and Zürich, 1531-1558* (Zürich: TVZ, 2006); Campi, E. & Opitz, P. (eds.), *Heinrich Bullinger, Life – Thought – Influence. Zurich, Aug. 25-29, 2004 International Congress Heinrich Bullinger (1504-1575) Volume I and II* (Zurich: TVZ, 2007) (two volumes); Gordon, B. & Campi, E., *Architect of Reformation. An Introduction to Heinrich Bullinger, 1504-1575* (Grand Rapids: Baker Academic, 2004).

Bullinger's theology is something that will need elaborate discussion. What is neglected in all these discussions so far is the role of John Hooper, who fled England for his beliefs and was bishop of Gloucester and Worcester. In 1555, under the reign of Mary Tudor, he was executed for his beliefs. Recent Hooper-scholarship has not had much interest in Micron.[39] This is something we hope to remedy in this research. What we strive to do, is to see Micron as part of the Reformed movement. With Reformed we mean that movement which did not deny paedobaptism, but did deny any form of substantive presence of the body of the Lord in the eucharist. To a large extent this is more or less equal with the Swiss Reformation and the Genevan tradition, though we should not exclude Strasbourg.[40] When, on the other hand, we write reformed, i.e. without the capital, we mean a, e.g., church that has gone through a process of reformation, and not the Reformed movement.

In the twentieth-century editions of some of Micron's works became available. His *Claer Bewijs* and *Een waerachteghe Historie, van Hoste (gheseyt Jooris) vander Katelyne* were published with introduction in respectively volume one (1905) and eight (1911) of the *Bibliotheca Reformatoria Neerlandica*. In 1908, in between these two books, Aart Arnout van Schelven[41] published his dissertation *De Nederduitsche vluchtelingenkerken der XVIe eeuw in Engeland en Duitsland en hunne beteekenis voor de Reformatie in de Nederlanden*, which greatly expanded and enhanced the knowledge and understanding of this period

---

39 Brodie, J.B., *Constructing a Godly Society: The Template for a Reformed Community in the Writings of John Hooper (C. 1500-1555)* (PhD University of Edinburgh, 2016); Dalton, A.J., *John Hooper and His Networks: a Study of Change in Reformation England* (PhD University of Oxford, 2008); Deibler, E.C., *Bishop John Hooper, A Link Connecting the Reformation Thought of Ulrich Zwingli and the Zurich Tradition with the Earliest English Pietistic* (PhD Temple University, Philadelphia, 1970); Primus, J.H., *The Vestments Controversy. An Historical Study of the Earliest Tensions within the Church of England in the Reigns of Edward VI and Elizabeth I* (Kampen: Kok, 1960); Wilson, R.P., *John Hooper and the English Reformation under Edward VI, 1547-1553* (PhD Queen's University Kingston Ontario, 1994).

40 Cf. MacCullough, D., *Thomas Cranmer. A Life* (New Haven/London: YUP, 1996), 173-174; Burnett, A. Nelson & Campi, E. 'Introduction' in: Burnett & Campi (eds.), *Swiss Reformation*, 3-13, 4-5, 9-10; Benedict, Ph., *Christ's Churches Purely Reformed. A Social History of Calvinism* (New Haven/London: YUP, 2002), xxii-xxiv.

41 Van Schelven (1880-1954) studied theology at the *Vrije Universiteit* and defended his PhD there in 1908. He served as Reformed pastor in Maarssen (1909) and Vlissingen (1914) before being appointed as professor of history and philosophy at the *Vrije Universiteit* in 1918. Cf. Roeling, J., 'Schelven, Aart Arnout van' in: *Biografisch Lexicon voor de geschiedenis van het Nederlands Protestantisme. Deel 2*, 387-389.

and Micron himself. Van Schelven sees the stranger churches abroad as refugee-churches. His book has been important in forming the concept of the Reformation of the Refugees, in which the churches abroad were seen as a preparation for the churches in the Netherlands after the Revolt.[42] After Gerretsen, Willem Frededrik Dankbaar[43] is the next scholar to be given special note. Not only did he give an edition of Micron's *Ordinancien* (1956) and *Een waerachtigh verhaal der t'zamensprekinghen tusschen Menno Simons ende Martinus Mikron van der menschwerdinge Iesu Chrisi* (1981), he also wrote the excellent entry on Micron in the *Biografisch Lexicon voor de geschiedenis van het Nederlandse Protestantisme. Deel 2* (1983), which summarised all that was known about Micron at the time and gave an overview of his works and where his letters were published. Dankbaar, after Gerretsen, is the first to deal with Micron as a theologian in his own right. In the same period Willy Otto Richard Willems[44] also studied the life and theology of Marten Micron, focussing especially on his doctrine of the Lord's Supper. Unfortunately his work has gone largely unnoticed. His *licentiaatsverhandeling* is a general study of Micron's life and his views on the Lord's Supper,[45] whereas his dissertation is an introduction, critical edition, summarising translation and analysis of Micron's *Apologeticum Scriptum*,[46] a book aimed against Joachim Westphal[47] and Micron's contribution to the Second Eucharistic Controversy.

---

42 The basic framework of the first chapters creates a rather linear narrative from à Lasco's first work in East Frisia, then to the London Church, then to Emden again.
43 Dankbaar (1907-2001), studied theology in Utrecht and Leiden, defended his PhD on Calvin's doctrine of the sacraments in Leiden (1941). He was pastor in the *Hervormde kerk* of Kuinre (1931), St. Annaparochie (1936), Goes-Wilhelminadorp (1941) professor of church history and the histroy of dogma at the *Rijksuniversiteit* Groningen from 1953-1975. Cf. Knetsch, F.R.J., 'Willem Frederik Dankbaar. Amsterdam 13 september 1907-Oosterwold (Fr.) 15 januari 2001' in: *Jaarboek van de Maatschappij der Nederlandse Letterkunde* 2000-2001, 51-61.
44 Willems (1943) studied theology at the *Universitaire faculteit voor protestantse godgeleerdheid* in Brussels and defenden his PhD there in 1993. He served as pastor of the William Tyndale congregation in Vilvoorde, part of the United Protestant Church in Belgium. Form 1991-2008 he was professor at the *Universitaire faculteit voor protestantse godgeleerdheid*.
45 Willems, W.O.R., *Met Maarten de Kleyne aan het avondmaal* (Licentiate-thesis University for Protestant Theology, 1980,).
46 Willems, W.O.R., *Is is Is?* Apologeticum Scriptorum *van Maarten de Kleyne na een dispuut rondom het "Nachtmael des Heren" met Joachim Westphal in Hamburg anno 1554* (PhD University for Protestant Theology Brussels, 1993).
47 Westphal was a Lutheran pastor in Hamburg, where he and Micron debated about the Lord's Supper. See below, 3.1.4 for further references.

Micron's *Van de weerdicheydt*, our object of study, has gone largely unnoticed. Mirjam van Veen briefly discusses it in her work on Nicodemism.[48] It has received some attention in the discourse on the Family of Love.[49] More recently Jos Schatorjé, in relation to his Faber research, published an article.[50] None of these, however, focus on the actual ecclesiogy that Micron outlines and how this relates to others.

In the last thirty-odd years there have been many books that mention Micron either in passing or more elaborately, for instance by Andrew Pettegree,[51] Judith Becker,[52] Tobias Schreiber,[53] Silke Muylaert[54] and Corinna Ehlers[55]. He is almost always the help 'next to à Lasco'. The work of Gerretsen, Dankbaar and Willems will remain important to all who study Marten Micron. From this overview it is clear we will have to consider Micron's life in relation to the Zurich reformation and Reformed tradition, the Reformation of the Refugees and the East Frisian Reformation in order to understand and evaluate his ecclesiology. It is also clear that this ecclesiology and Micron's last book have not been studied in depth yet. The study of *Van de weerdicheydt* emerges as a desideratum and is hence the focal point of this research.

---

48 Veen, M. van, *'Verschooninghe van de roomsche afgoderye'. De polemiek van Calvijn met nicodemieten, in het bijzonder met Coornhert* (unpubl. PhD thesis VU Amsterdam, 2001), 138-141.

49 Fontaine Verwey, H. de la, 'The Family of Love' in: Quaerendo VI/3 (1976), 219-271, 229-231; Hamilton, A., *The Family of Love* (Cambridge: James Clarke & Co., 1983), 50.

50 Schatorjé, J., 'Engelbert Faber en de Duitse vertaling van het laatste boek van Martin Micron (Heidelberg, 1563)' in: Boonen, U. K. (ed.), *Zwischen Sprachen en culturen. Wechselbeziehungen im niederländischen, deutschen und afrikaansen Sprachgebiet* (Münster/New York: Waxmann, 2018), 19-31.

51 Pettegree, *Foreign Protestant Communities in Sixteenth-Century London* (Oxford: OUP, 1986).

52 Becker, *Gemeindeordnung*; Becker, J., 'Zürich und die Fremdengemeinde in London. Eine entangled history der Reformation' in: Albisser & Opitz (eds.), *Die Zürcher Reformation*, 495-517.

53 Schreiber, T., *Petrus Dathenus und der Heidelberger Katechismus. Ein traditionsgeschichtliche Untersuchung zum konfessionellen Wandel in der Kurpfalz um 1563* (Göttingen: Vandenhoeck & Ruprecht, 2017).

54 Muylaert, S., *Shaping the Stranger Churches. Migrants in England and the Troubles in the Netherlands, 1547-1585* (Leiden/Boston: Brill, 2020).

55 Ehlers, C., *Konfessionsbildung im Zweiten Abendmahlsstreit (1552-1558/59)* (Tübingen: Mohr Siebeck, 2021).

1.2 Preliminary Methodological Considerations[56]

When David Copperfield answers Mr. Dick that Charles II's execution was in 1649, Mr. Dick enquires whether David knows this from a historybook and David answers in the affirmative. Charles Dickens then writes: "'I suppose history never lies, does it?' said Mr. Dick, with a gleam of hope. "Oh dear, no, sir!" I replied, most decisively. I was ingenuous and young, and I thought so.'[57] The implication is that history books and historians cannot always be relied upon. Sometimes history does lie, Dickens tells us. And he was right, for it is a serious threat for historians to mould the facts to tell their own story. A danger all historians should be aware of. For this reason no historian can neglect the important work of Quentin Skinner.[58] He defines the task of the historian as to 'situate the texts we study within such intellectual contexts as enable us to make sense of what their authors were doing in writing them.'[59] The historian gives a representation of what the original author meant, in such a way that the author recognises his views and motivation.[60] What the historian does, then, is to try to understand the context in which a historical person was working on its own terms, in order to understand what he or she was doing.[61] This does not mean that a historian is only interested in the ultimate question: 'what was this person doing in writing this text'. Other areas of attention need to be researched as well. However, neither should it be forgotten that history involves people. When these people write, they are doing something, and we feel it is important to keep this question in mind.

---

56 This position is based on my: Wendt, H.T., 'What Does It Mean to Be a Reformed Church Historian?' in: *Unio Cum Christo* [forthcoming].
57 Dickens, Ch., *David Copperfield* (New York/London/Toronto: Everyman's Library), 249.
58 Skinner, Q., *Visions of Politics I: Regarding Method* (Cambridge: CUP, 2002). Other names from the Cambridge School are J.G.A. Pocock and James Dunn.
59 Skinner, *Visions*, 3; see also, p.4-5; 52-53.
60 Skinner, *Visions*, 77-78.
    Skinner connects his theory to Austin's speech-act theory (Skinner, *Visions*, 3, 103-127). For a short introduction to the speech-act theory see: Cook, G., *Discourse* (Oxford: OUP, 1989), 35-41).
61 Cf. Coffey, J. & Chapman, A. 'Introduction: Intellectual History and the Return of Religion' in: Chapman, A., Coffey, J., Gregory, B.S. (eds.), *Seeing Things Their Way. Intellectual History and the Return of Religion* (Notre Dame, Indiana: University of Notre Dame Press, 2009), 1-23, esp. 1-3; Pocock, J.G.A., 'Working on Ideas in Time' in: Pocock, J.G.A., *Political Thought and History. Essays on Theory and Method* (Cambridge: CUP, 2009), 20-32, esp. 27-29; Bradley, J.E.; Muller, R.A., *Church History. An Introduction to Research Methods and Resources. Second Edition* (Grand Rapids: Eerdmans, 2016), 23-31, esp. 30-31.

This position presupposes objectivity. 'Objectivity arises out of a willingness to let the materials of history speak in their own terms, while the historian, at the same time, exercises a combination of critical judgment and careful self-restraint.'[62] Complete objectivity is not the same as neutrality. No one is neutral or unprejudiced.[63] A necessary degree of objectivity is safeguarded by an intersubjective academic environment of checks and balances. Intersubjectivity is the process in which the community of experts judges a work to be a true representation of the facts and to draw valid conclusions from it.[64] In this way our prejudices are checked. There are many pitfalls when we approach historical data. We might have the prejudice that authors are bound to say something about a certain subject, merely because they are theologians, or that they have well-defined thoughts or a closed system.[65] We should approach a text without such prejudices, but let the data speak for itself. This approach also presupposes that it is possible to communicate and to understand each other. Reading and studying does not necessarily lead to a fusion of horizons, meaning is not contingent,[66] the other can be understood on his or her own terms.[67] These two presuppositions enforce the moral obligation to tell the historical narrative as objectively true as possible.

Church history is unique in that is a *theological* discipline focussed on *historical* data.[68] The church historian is a theologian first, a historian second. The theological viewpoint defines what the church historian

---

62 Bradley & Muller, *Church History*, 47.
63 Schelven, A.A. van, *Wegkruisinging in het landschap der theorie van de geschiedschrijving* (Amsterdam: W. ten Have N.V., 1953), 15 ('De vóóroordeelloosheid der wetenschap...is een fictie. Een onderwerp ter hand nemen zonder dat a priori's van allerlei aard op de behandeling daarvan uitoefenen...is onmogelijk'). Cf. Bradley & Muller, *Church History* 46-50; Kuiper, R., *Uitzien naar de zin. Inleiding tot een christelijke geschiedbeschouwing* (Leiden: J.J. Groen en zoon, 1996), 17.
64 Katerberg, W., 'The "Objectivity Question" and the Historian's Vocation' in: Fea *et al.* (eds.), *Confessing History. Explorations in Christian Faith and the Historian's Vocation* (Notre Dame, Indiana: University of Notre Dame Press, 2010), 101-127, 103. Note that Katerberg opposes objectivity and intersubjectivity more than we do.
65 For this and other pitfalls, cf. Skinner, *Visions*, 59-77.
66 Contra Cadegan, U.M., 'Not All Autobiography Is Scholarship' in: Fea *et al.*, *Confessing History*, 39-59, 49.
67 Gregory, B.S., 'Can we "See Things Their Way"? Should We Try?' in: Chapman, Coffey & Gregory (eds.), *Seeing Things Their Way*, 24-45, esp. 38-39 where he says: 'mine is a deliberately anti-Gadamerian hermeneutic'.
68 Cf. Boer, E.A. de, 'Tolken bij de tijd. Over het hermenautische aspect van de kerkhistorie' in: Bruijne, A. de & Burger, H. (eds.), *Gereformeerde hermeneutiek vandaag. Theologische perspectieven* (Barneveld: De Vuurbaak, 2017), 83-97, 84-89.

looks at. It is 'the church in its history'[69] that is being studied. And that object of study, the 'Christian church', is defined theologically instead of sociologically, since church history is a theological and not a sociological discipline. Theologically, then, the church is the covenantal people that is called and gathered by God through His Word. It heeds this call and makes it heard by proclaiming the gospel. In giving this definition we are doing something that seems and could be decidedly problematic. Before studying the ecclesiology of a historical author we already define what the church is and do so from a Reformed viewpoint that has been influenced by many theological developments since the sixteenth century. Do we not fall into the the very pitfall of not respecting the actual historical and intellectual context that we opposed above? This is not our intention. We merely try to be honest about our own theological prejudices before trying to understand Micron and others on their own terms. In doing so, we strive to facilitate the intersubjective evaluation of how objective the analyses are. For that very reason we do not introduce our definition as a ideal that others have to live up to – i.e. it is not the intention to judge other ecclesiologies. A second reason why a definition is already given, is that we conduct this investigation in the present context and feel it is necessary to validate listening to this particular voice as a voice within the history of the church. In this way the church today can learn from how Marten Micron responded to the gospel concerning the church.[70] Again we stress that this does not mean that the definition can in any way be allowed to become a prejudicial frame to understand or evaluate his ecclesiology or the history of the church. Rather, as said, the (church) historian seeks to tell the historical narrative objectively. In listening to Micron we bracket our own definition. Precisely because the church historian seeks to be objective he or she can give voice to the historical conscience of the church.[71] In order to do so,

---

69 Kamphuis, J., 'Ekklesiologie' in: Douma, J. (ed.), *Oriëntatie in de theologie. Studiegids samengesteld door de hoogleraren aan de Theologische Universiteit van De Gereformeerde Kerken in Nederland te Kampen* (Groningen: De Vuurbaak, 1974), 88-107, 92.

70 Cf. Pol, F. van der, 'Kerkgeschiedenis', in: Bruijne, A.L.Th. de (ed.), *Gereformeerde theologie vandaag* (Barneveld: De Vuurbaak, 2004) , 73-82, 81.

71 Cf. Green, J, 'Public Reasoning by Historical Analogy' in: Fea, J. *et al.* (eds.), *Confessing History*, 262-279, 275. Consequently, studying history is more than 'looking for a usable past'. For this concept, see: Clary, I.H., *Reformed Evangelicalism and the Search for a Usable Past. The Historiography of Arnold Dallimore, Pastor-Historian* (Göttingen: Vandenhoeck & Ruprecht, 2020).

we apply an intentional interpretation, which 'aims to reproduce the argument in the way the author has meant it'.[72]

Church history entails both 'the practice of the church' and the 'thought of the church'.[73] The present study falls in the second category. We seek to analyse Micron's thoughts on ecclesiology as described in his *Van de weerdicheydt*, and in order to do so we also describe the context. Focussing on this one particular book means that we have to limit ourselves to the immediate context insofar as this is needed to understand the book, instead of studying the full context exhaustively. A full analysis of either the networks Micron functioned in, the full discourse on ecclesiology in the sixteenth century or Micron's biography and familial circumstances are beyond the reach of this research. When describing the context, be it intellectual, social or biographical, we are acutely aware that all we have are loose pieces that give evidence to what actually happened. Interpreting these facts into a coherent line of events is the art of history.[74] Here it must be remembered that questions take prevalence over answers and that primary sources take prevalence over secondary sources.

If church history is theology, and if true theology is faith seeking and shaping understanding,[75] then all theology and therefore church history brings the dimension of the divine and of faith into our historical enquiry. The Christian theologian realises that his or her work is done *coram Deo* and hence subject to His good laws. We are therefore to do justice (objectivity) and love kindness (to be fair to the historical person) and to be humble about our personal views, personal capacities and personal knowledge.[76] Last of all it also means that no person in history can be revered as if he[77] were divinely inspired. To love God above all implies that no human being can be given the status of god or demi-god, as has unfortunately all too often been the case.

---

72 Kuipers-Sedee, M., *Chesteron, the New Atheism, and an Apologetics of Common Sense* (Leuven: Peeters, 2022), 5.
73 Bradley & Muller, *Church History*, 5. On the relation between church history, history of dogma and dogmatics, see Wendt, 'Reformed Church Historian'.
74 Kuiper, *Uitzien*, 88; Bradley & Muller, *Church History*, 32-38.
75 Thus not only *fides quaerit intellectum*, as Anselmus' classic dictum says, but also *fides quadrat intellectum*, as Klaas Schilder rephrased it (cf. Schilder, K., 'F.Q.I.' in: *Almanak van het corpus studiosorum in Academia Campensi "Fides Quadrat Intellectum" 1951* (Kampen: Zalsman, 1951), 72-84.)
76 Of course, non-christian scholars also seek to be just, kind and humble. We merely indicate that the confessional church historian also has a spiritual reason to practise church history in this way.
77 'He' is not used here to rule out women, but merely because in church history descriptions of men are more prevalent.

To summarise: The historian seeks to see things their way[78] by mapping the cultural and intellectual environment and re-telling what a historical source offers, partly to understand what a historical figure was doing. The church historian in particular seeks to inform the present-day church by letting the church of the ages speak to us and does so with a humble and receptive attitude in which we esteem the other better than ourselves.[79] This takes place in an intersubjective setting in order to maintain objectivity.

1.3 Research Question and Chapter Contents

By choosing Micron's *Van de weerdicheydt* as its main subject, this study focuses on the historical-theological significance of his ecclesiology, placed within his historical and intellectual environment. Hence, we come to the following research questions:

How can we describe the ecclesiology Marten Micron presents in his *Van de weerdicheydt, nutheydt ende noodicheyt der christelicker vergaderinghen* in relation to its immediate historical and intellectual environment of the Reformed Reformation?

There is a number of sub-questions:
1. What bibliographical information can be discovered concerning *Van de weerdicheydt*?
2. What is Marten Micron's biography?
3. What is the historical environment in which Marten Micron acted, particularly that of Zurich, London, East Frisia and the experience of displacement?
4. Is there any evidence of dissemination of *Van de weerdicheydt*?
5. What is the ecclesiology presented in *Van de weerdicheydt*?
6. How does his ecclesiology compare to that of other Reformed theologians, in particular within the Zurich tradition?
7. What does this analysis of Micron's life and ecclesiology teach us concerning the Reformation of the Refugees?

The research is split into two parts. The first part is historical and takes Micron's last book as its central object. The second part is theological and concentrates on the ecclesiology presented in the book.

In chapter two we will focus on the book *Van de weerdicheydt* itself. What is its physical appearance, who is the printer and how are the contents structured? We will also discuss whether or not the book was

---

78 Chapman, Coffey & Gregory (eds.), *Seeing Things Their Way*.
79 Cf. Phil. 2:3.

really written by Marten Micron and what Micron and the publisher sought to achieve with the book.

There is, to date, no modern edition of *Van de weerdicheydt*, though a reasonably good scan is available through Google Books. We give a transcript in appendix B to facilitate cross-reference and further study. This is preceded by a detailed table of contents of the book in appendix A.

In the third chapter we focus on the authors, the first concentric circle around the book. We describe the course of Marten Micron's life extensively, and that of Nicholas Carinaeus briefly. When we look at Micron's life, we automatically also look at the Zurich Reformation, the English Reformation and (to a lesser extent) the East Frisian Reformation.

Micron's social environment is further discussed in chapter four, the second concentric circle around the book. Micron wrote *Van de weerdicheydt* when he was a pastor in Norden, East Frisia and we therefore look at this history in more detail. Because Micron was a stranger we also look at the Reformation of the Refugees paradigm in this chapter. It will be seen how the current research on the North-German Reformation helps us re-consider the Reformation of the Refugees.

The book was translated into German by Engelbert Faber and two excerpts translated into English were incorporated in John Knewstub's book against the Family of Love. This is the third and last concentric circle. We look at this in chapter five. With this chapter we end the historical part of the book.

The theological part is split into two chapters. Chapter six contains a thorough and meticulous analysis of the ecclesiology Micron gives in the book and places this within the context of his other writings. Chapter seven compares this to the ecclesiologies of other representatives of the Reformed tradition. Here we will see that they are generally in agreement on what they believe concerning the church.

In chapter eight we seek to draw all these lines together by summarising the contents and drawing conclusions. This will also involve a brief discussion on how the ecclesiology of the Dutch Churches after 1572 moved along the same main thoughts as Micron's.

Part 1:
Historical

Chapter 2: Introduction to
Van de weerdicheydt, nutheydt ende noodicheyt der christelicker vergaderinghen

In the previous chapter we selected as our object of study the book *Van de weerdicheydt, nutheydt ende noodicheyt der christelicker vergaderinghen*. In this chapter we want to focus on the book itself before looking at its authors and context. In 2.1 we give a technical description and 2.2 focusses on the printer, Gellius Ctematius. After that we have to confront ourselves with the possibility of the book being a forgery (2.3). In 2.4 we give a summarising structure of the contents and in 2.5 the purpose of the book.

The aim of this chapter is then, to get a feel for the book and its goal.

2.1 Description of the book

The only surviving original copy given in the various catalogues is in the possession of the *Ghent University Library*.[1] However, the 1634 Johan Radermacher sale catalogue and several 19th century catalogues also list the book and these copies may yet be found.[2] In this section we will first describe the book as it currently is, then its known history and we round off with our conclusions.

The surviving copy of *Van de weerdicheydt, nutheydt ende noodicheyt der christelicker vergaderinghen* is a *sammelband* with another book by

---

1 Cf. the *Short-Title Catalogue Netherland* (https://data.cerl.org/stcn/412014564 [9-8-2023]) and *The Universal Short Title Catalogue* (https://www.ustc.ac.uk/editions/405028 [9-8-2023]).
2 The Johan Radermacher sale catalogue of 1634 also lists an edition of *Van de weerdicheydt*. It is unknown whether this copy survived and, if so, where it is (https://www.johanradermacher.net/catalogue/belgici-in-octavo-and-c/ [2-12-2022], entry 11.3). The book is listed in H.C. Rogge's inventory of the books in the Remonstrant Congregation of Amsterdam (*Beschrijvende catalogus der Pamfletten-verzameling van de boekerij der Remonstrantsche kerk te Amsterdam. Stuk II, afdeeling I: Bibliotheek der Contra-Remonstratsche en Gereformeerde Geschriften* (Amsterdam: J.H. Scheltema, 1865) and mentioned in two sales catalogues (*Catalogue de la Bibliothèque Juirdique et Statistique de feu M. le Dr. M. M. von Baumhauer et de la Bibliothèque Théolog., Histor. et Litéraire de M. le Dr. H. C. Rogge* etc. (Leiden: E.J. Brill, 1878), inv. no. 4192, and: *Catalogue de la Bibliothèque Importante de feu M. le Dr. J. G. R. Acquoy* etc. (Leiden: Bugersdijk & Niermans, 1897), inv. no. 1272. To date, these copies have not been found or retrieved.

Marten Micron, *Een Apologie oft verantwoordinghe Martini Micon, op verscheyden Artikelen die Menno Simons teghen het disputacy boecxken van het bespreck met hem over de leer gehouden in druck heeft uutghegeven*, published on the 12th of November 1558, by Gellius Ctematius. The cover consists of two wooden boards and the paste-downs are of laid paper, thicker than the paper used for either of the two publications. One can therefore be reasonably confident that the two books were bound together before 1600,[3] or, as the librarian Frank Vanlangenhove[4] put it, almost certainly from the era of Reformation. Its measurements are 10.5 by 15.6 centimeters, and the depth is 5.5 centimeters including the covers (4.8 excluding them). The wooden boards are covered with decorated leather, of reddish-brown colour. The decorations consist of miniature pictures of scholars[5] and vines (see Image 1)[6]. On the front cover there is a large crack in the leather in the middle of the right-hand edge. The rest of the covering is in fairly good condition, though there are several wormholes in the leather (they do not appear to have gone through the wood) and the spine shows signs of usage. Two decorated metal clasps were originally attached to the back cover of the book. One of these is missing. The clasps show us the binding of the book probably did not take place in either France or England.[7] The pages have been trimmed, and the edges stained.

When opening the book we are confronted with a sign of a 'q' and R attached to each other (see Image 4). It seems to have been made by hand (i.e. not a stamp) and the ink has left a mark on the following pages. It was probably made by a previous owner. Unfortunately, the person behind the initials is as yet unknown.

There is also a sticker 'bibliotheek Snellaert' and several hand-written notes about Marten Micron, all in the same hand.

Both books in the *sammelband* are in octavo format, measuring 9.8 by 14.5 centimeters. The pages are in pristine condition, with the exception of a tear in in fol. 3r. of *Van de weerdicheydt*. Neither book shows any

---

3 Werner, S., *Studying Early Printed Books 1450-1800. A Practical Guide* (Chichester: Wiley Blackwell, 2019), 29; 74.
4 I want to express my sincere gratitude for his help in preparing my visit and for reading this section. And also to Paul Dijstelberge for his comments on this chapter.
5 Further bibliographical research could perhaps shed further light on whether these are pictures of reformers.
6 All images are from the high-quality scan of the book, provided by the University of Ghent.
7 Werner, *Early Printed Books*, 76.

signs of cancels and cancellands. *Een Apologie* runs from A-Ee2.[8] The last two printed pages have been misprinted and are the wrong way around, i.e. what should be on the front of the page is on the back, and the back on the front. There are several handwritten notes ('nota' or a pointing hand)[9] in the margins of *Een Apologie*, which do not need to be discussed here. *Van de weerdicheydt* runs from A-Q8, Q7 and Q8 are blank pages. In this book there are no hand-written notes, excepting several page-numbering corrections (cf. the endnotes of the transcription).

For the title page, see Image 2. It identifies the author of the book as Marten Micron, and declares it to be a translation of his original Latin work. The motto for the book is Hebrews 10:24-25a (And let us consider one another to provoke unto love and to good works: Not forsaking our assemblies, as the manner of some is etc.)[10], however, there is no way of knowing whether this was what Micron intended. The pages have biblical references in the margins. The left-hand page indicates the chapter at the top of the margin, the right-hand page has the folio number. The foreword by Micron starts with an elaborately decorated capital (see image 3), the other sections with a large, undecorated, capital. On fol. 93v we see a clear division in the text, indicated by a pointing hand, to mark where the second author, Carinaeus, continued writing the book. At the end of the book there is a list of errata, followed by an index of the principal contents of each chapter (*Een kort register van hetgene dat een yeghelick capitel in dit boecxken principalicken inhoudt*) and ends with an index of some places of Scripture that are discussed in the book (*Register van sommighe plaetsen der Schriftueren, die hierinne verklaert worden*).

Now that we have looked at the physical appearance of the book, we will look at what this teaches us about its history. The q-R sign at the start was in all likelihood made by a previous, unidentified, owner. The sticker provides us with more information, as it tells us that the book was part of F.A. Snellaert's library. Snellaert (1809-1872), a famous Belgic physician and man of letters, had a large collection of early printed books.[11] The handwritten notes were also made by him. It cannot with certainty be said whether the notes in *Een Apologie* and the corrections of the folio

---

8   Full description: [16], 397, [23], [2 blank], p., A-Z8, Aa-Dd8, Ee2; 8º (Source: https://lib.ugent.be/nl/catalog/rug01:000879208?i=0&q=micron+apologie [18-11-2021]).
9   'Nota' on fol. 225; 257. Pointing hand on fol. 350; 368; 372; 382; 399.
10 Translation based on KJV, which reads 'the assembling of ourselves together'. The given tekst follows the motto on the title page more closely.
11 For more on F.A. Snellaert: Deprez, A., *Kroniek van Dr. F.A. Snellaert* (Brugge: Orion, 1972).

1. Detail of cover

2. Facsimile of title page △

4. q and R sign on paste-down   3. Decorated capital in foreword △

numbers in *Van de weerdicheydt* were made by him, though this seems unlikely.[12] To conclude, then, it seems fairly certain that somewhere between 1561 and 1600 a customer bought both *Een Apologie* and *Van de Weerdicheydt* and had them bound together in either the German Lands or the Low Countries. This shows us the first buyer was assured that both books were authentic works by Micron. At no point were the books rebound, showing it was both little used and not considered to be of major importance. In the 19th century it was acquired by F.A. Snellaert, and after that came in possession of the *Ghent University Library*. A fact unknown to Micron's biographer J.H. Gerretsen, who could find no copy of the book.[13]

Having looked at the physical appearance, let us now turn to what we know about the printer.

2.2 Printer

The very first page of the book immediately presents us with a question. Though the title page gives us the author and the year in which the book was published, it does not provide us with the printer. However, Paul Valkema Blouw identified the printer as Aegidius (or Gellius) Ctematius, or Gillius/Gellius van der Erve(n).[14] In this paragraph we hope to do two things, first a short introduction to the printer, followed by a section on the relationship between Ctematius and the author, Marten Micron.

We do not know anything about Ctematius's youth, except that he came from the city of Ghent in Flanders. He fled to London, probably out of fear for religious persecution, where he became a member of the Dutch Church in 1550.[15] In the Dutch church he served first as a deacon, later as

---

12 The topic of the *Apologie* is more likely to have interested a contemporary reader than a later collector.
13 Gerretsen, J.H., *Micronius. Zijn leven, zijn geschriften, zijn geestesrichting* (Nijmegen: Ten Hoet, 1895), 92.
14 Blouw, P.V., *Typographia Batava 1541-1600. Repertorium van boeken gedrukt in Nederland tussen 1541 en 1600* (Nieuwkoop: De Graaf, 1998), entry 3472. Cf. Pettegree, *Emden and the Dutch Revolt. Exile and the Development of Reformed Protestantism* (Oxford: OUP, 1992), 280 entry 112; Pettegree, A & Walsby, M. (eds.), *Netherlandish Books. Books Published in the Low Countries and Dutch Books Printed Abroad before 1601* (Leiden/Boston: Brill, 2011), entry 21360.
15 This paragraph is largely based on: Tielke, M., 'Gillis van der (Ctematius, Aegidius) Erven', in: *Biographisches Lexikon für Ostfriesland I* (Aurich, 1993), 131-133. (For our research we used the digital version on the website of the *Ostfriesische Landschaft* [https://www.ostfriesischelandschaft.de/fileadmin/user_upload/BIBLIOTHEK/BLO/Erven.pdf [8-5-2020]], this version does not have page-numbers, but does give the original page-numbers in its reference.) For more on Ctematius, see: Hofman, B., *Liedekens vol gheestich confoort. Een bijdrage tot de kennis van de zestiende-eeuwse Schriftuurlijke lyriek* (Hilversum: Verloren, 1993), 59; Isaac, F. 'Egidius van der Erve and His English Printed Books' in: The Library 4/12 (1931-1932), 336-352.

elder. He was married to a woman referred to as 'Anna'. In London Ctematius worked as a printer, though probably not independently. It is likely he co-operated with, or served under, Nicolaas van den Berghe, also known as Nicolas Hill.[16] Ctematius left England in the autumn of 1553, travelling with Utenhove, Micron, à Lasco and many others to Denmark after Mary had succeeded Edward VI. He was one of the small group that travelled over land from Copenhagen to Güdtzöer, after the king of Denmark had denied the refugees the right to observe their own rites. The group, so we read, consisted of Hans Peters, David Symson, Johann Fyns, Bartholemew Husmand, with his wife, one child and a servant, Gillis van der Erven (=Ctematius), with his wife, one boy and one child, Brixius Hecken and Jacob Bytz.[17] From there he travelled on to Emden, where he and Van den Berghe continued their printing company. In 1555 John à Lasco helped him obtain the citizenship of Emden. The Van den Berghe-Ctematius press was one of the two leading printing companies in Emden, the other being the Mierdman-Gaillart press.[18] Though the disastrous publication of Utenhove's New Testament translation almost brought down their company in 1556, they managed to recover.[19] Ctematius became the sole proprietor after Van den Berghe passed away in 1557 and is listed as one of the wealthy citizens in 1562-1563. However, this business success was darkened by personal grief: apparently his first wife, Anna, had passed away, for in the census the name of his wife is given as Katharina.[20] Ctematius remained an influential figure in the Reformed church, once more serving as elder. He was, effectively, the church's printer. The constant stream of prints and reprints of à Lasco's, Utenhove's and Micron's works are almost always from his press.[21] Indeed, Tielke characterises him as 'without the shadow of a doubt a Calvinist',[22] though he was not beyond – secretly – printing Menno Simons's *Een lieffelijcke vermaninghe* (commonly known as his

---

16 Pettegree, A., *Emden and the Dutch Revolt. Exile and the Development of Reformed Protestantism* (Oxford: OUP, 1992), 88.
17 For the list, see: *SFN*, 89n1; Cf. Norwood, F.A., 'London Dutch Refugees in Search of a Home' in: *American Historical Review* 58/1 (1952), 64-72, 68-69.
18 Pettegree, *Emden*, 90-92.
19 Pettegree, *Emden*, 89-90; 93-94. For more on the several bibles printed by Ctematius, cf.: Gillaerts, P. et al. (eds.), *De bijbel in de Lage Landen. Elf eeuwen van vertalen* (Heerenveen: Royal Jongbloed, 2015), chapters 13, 15 and 18.
20 This, at least, is Thielke's opinion ('er war also ein zweites Mal verheiratet'), though one cannot exclude the possibility of 'Anna' as the everyday name for Katharina.
21 Pettegree, *Emden*, 106-107.
22 Tielke, *Dat Rätsel der Emder Buchdrucks (1554-1602)*, (Aurich: Verlag der Ostfriesischen Landschaft, 1986), 11.

'Ban Book').[23] In 1566 Ctematius contracted the plague and passed away. His printing press was taken over by William Gaillart.

So, Ctematius was the household printer of the Reformed church. And, indeed, this is clear from his business relationship with Marten Micron. When we look at his books, we see that they are, in most cases, printed by Van de Berghe and/or Ctematius. Take, for instance, *Claer bewijs*, first printed in 1552 in London by Mierdman; however, the subsequent editions of 1554 and 1560 were printed by Van den Berghe/Ctematius. All editions of the *Kleyne Catechismus* published during Micron's lifetime were printed by Van den Berghe and Ctematius. The same is true for all of Micron's books, the only exception being *Ein kort Undericht*, the short catechism based on the *Corte Ondersoeckinghe*. This is the only book printed by Mierdman during the time Micron lived in East Frisia.[24] What we see, then, is that Micron first was the pastor of the congregation in London where Ctematius served as both deacon and elder, and that Ctematius was Micron's printer. This shows that Micron and Ctematius were well-acquainted with each other, not only having a business relationship, but also the bond of faith.

2.3 Authorship
Having looked at the title page of the book, we turn the page and read the printer's preface. It immediately becomes clear that at the time of publication Marten Micron had already passed away. How then, did Ctematius obtain the manuscript, one might wonder? He claims it was found in, presumably, Micron's house. It was written in Latin by Micron himself: 'in his own hand'[25]. The printer presented it to certain learned men, who all wanted to see it published. To that end it was translated (by whom is unknown) and Carinaeus finished the last chapter. When one reads the printer's preface, one can imagine something along these lines happened: the bereaved family cleared up Micron's study, arranged his papers, and found the manuscript, perhaps even on his writing desk, waiting to be finished. They took it to Ctematius, whom had been their acquaintance in London and during their travels, and handed him the book, asking him to see it published. He, possibly, showed it to several pastors in and around Emden, who were all convinced of the importance

---

23 Blouw, P.V., *Dutch Typography in the Sixteenth Century: The Collected Works of Paul Valkema Blouw* (Leiden: Brill, 2013), 565-567.
   This, in all likelihood, does not mean his own convictions were unorthodox; rather, financial interests sometimes vied with his church membership.
24 The *Apologeticum Scriptum* does not have a printer named in the Short Title Catalogue, however this is provided by Pettegree, *Emden*, 271, entry 73.
25 *VdWNN*, 1v.

of the book. Ctematius ordered someone – could it be Dyrkinus? – to translate the volume. Carinaeus was given the task to finish the last chapter, and Micron's unfinished ecclesiology was published. This reconstruction does justice to the preface in the book, and it has the appeal of making a soothing story after Micron's untimely demise. However, the printer's preface is very little to go on, and the claim of Micron's authorship has to be investigated since it has been challenged by Fontaine Verwey.[26] Moreover, without addressing this the question will cast a shadow of doubt over this research. Could it be, then, that the book is a (partial) pseudepigraphy[27], claiming Micron – who had passed away anyway – as the author in order to increase the authority of the proposed ecclesiology?

Though none of these three options can be proven definitively, yet one can be more likely than the other, and it is our purpose in this paragraph to investigate the likelihood of genuine Micronian authorship. There are several steps in coming to a conclusion. First we will discuss the authorship of Carinaeus's section, second we will look at a theory proposed by Fontaine Verwey, third we present circumstantial evidence for Micron's authorship.

We start, then, with the authorship of Carinaeus. His part of the book is very clearly marked off on folio 93v, where a pointing hand draws our attention to the fact that this is where Micron stopped (*so verre heeftet saligher ghedachten Martinus Micronius ghemaeckt*) (see image 5). The break is as sudden as in Mozart's *Requiem*, with a complete change of subject, abruptly turning to the Family of Love and David Joris.

The theological level also drops severely; for instance, the use of biblical proofs changes from in-depth exegesis to the simple listing of proof texts, indicating that there is indeed another author at work than in the first part. Of course, this argument is based largely on perception and feeling. Nonetheless, the claim is not groundless, as one very clear example shows. On fol. 103r. Carinaeus opposes an argument against secret meetings. His adversaries quote Christ's commandment: 'what I tell you in darkness, that speak ye in the light'.[28] After some counterarguments which are to the point, he concludes by saying that secluded meetings were held by the patriarchs (who gathered in their tents) and even by Christ, Who taught at the seaside, in the mountains

---

26 See below, pp. 37-38.
27 The usage of the term 'forgery' has such malignant overtones that it seems best to avoid it. Even if the book is a forgery, it would appear the intention was good rather than bad. Cf., also, Freeman, A., 'Hoax and Forgery, Whimsy and Fraud. Taxonomic Reflections on the Bibliotheca Fictiva' in: Stephens, W. & Havens, E.A. (eds.), *Literary Forgery in Early Modern Europe, 1450-1800* (Baltimore: John Hopkins UP, 2018), 15-32.
28 Mat. 10:27, KJV.

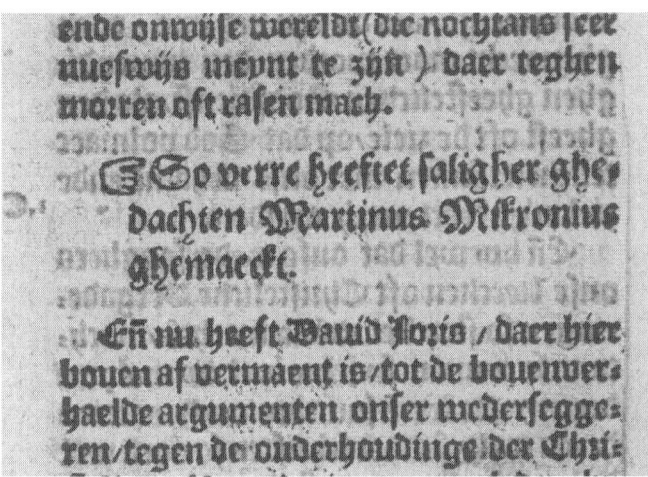

5. Detail of VdWNN, 93v. The point where Micron's part breaks off is clearly indicated, causing a pause in the reading experience.

and the houses to escape the Pharisees and Herodians.[29] This is, indeed, poor theology. Obviously, the example of the patriarchs is completely beside the point and the example of Christ is perhaps even worse. Christ taught openly, for all to hear; moreover, His commandment to speak in the light concerns the next stage in salvation history, after He has gone to heaven.[30] Such exegetical errors are not found in the supposed Micronian part. Moreover, there are more clues which point towards the part beyond 93v to have been written by a second author. The first is the more

---

29 *VdWNN*, 103r.
30 Matthew 10 conflates two foci: the sending out of the twelve during Christ's ministry on earth, but also their apostleship after He has gone to heaven. Verse 27 clearly shows this second focus. Carinaeus could have known this, for Calvin says the same in his commentary on the passage, cf. Calvin, J., *Commentary on a Harmony of the Evangelists Matthew, Mark, and Luke. Volume 1* ed. William Pringle (Grand Rapids: Baker Books, 2005), 448; 461. Bullinger (*In Sacrosanctum Iesu Christi Domini nostri Euangelium secundum Matthaeum (…)* (Zürich: Froschauer, 1542) also draws attention to the two foci when he says that the first instruction (to seek the lost sheep of Israel first) was not perpetual, but for a time only (*non est perpetuum, sed datum ad tempus*), after the resurrection the gospel is to be preached all over the earth (98v) . The warning that the apostles will have to appear before magistrates and kings (verse 18) Bullinger sees fulfilled in the *Acts of the Apostles* (101v). His exposition of verse 26-27 concerns the time from when Jesus is speaking to His glorious return on the last day (103r-v).

substantial usage of references to church fathers and church history.³¹ Secondly, the book was published well within Carinaeus's lifetime, even when he was still living in East Frisia. If he had not been the author of the second part of the book he would have opposed the claim. This also proves there was an unfinished manuscript by an author either living or deceased, be it Micron or somebody else, that was finished by Carinaeus. If it had been a forgery he would have challenged the claim of the book.

Carinaeus could also be the translator of the first part, if it was indeed first written in Latin. The truth of that claim stands or falls with the claim of Micron's authorship. If the book was first written in Latin, however, Carinaeus does not appear to be the translator.³² For instance, he uses the word 'accordeert' on folio 96r, which is not found in the part by Micron. The word is clearly derived from Latin, and one would expect it to be found places where we read, e.g., 'our teaching agrees with the teachings of the prophets and apostles' (*dat onse leeringhe overeenkomt met de leeringhe der propheten ende der apostelen*).³³ Biblical quotations are sometimes just a little bit different from Micron's earlier rendering³⁴ – something that might have to do with the one being translated from the Latin, the other taken from a Bible; be that how it may, it is yet again an argument against seeing Carinaeus as the translator. If there was an original Latin manuscript it will probably be impossible to find out who translated it. We suggested above that it might be the famous Dyrkinus, who would certainly have had the skill to produce a good translation quickly. His work on the translation of Calvin's *Insitutes* would account for the two-year interval between Micron's death and the publication. Godefried van Wingen writes to Utenhove that Dyrkinus translated Micron's *Apologeticum Scriptum*, a polemic work against Joachim Westphal.³⁵ Again, though, it will be nigh impossible to prove this suggestion.

---

31 On fol. 101v. and 102r. Carinaeus lists proofs from Eusebius, Tertulian, and Sozomenus. On fol. 113v. he cites Jerome. In *Een claer bewijs* Micron did cite church fathers to back up his claims. In *Van de weerdicheydt* the supposed Micronian part makes reference to Eusebius's Church history on 75v., this could be either original or a later inclusion.
32 Contra Reershemius, A., *Ostfrieslandisches Prediger-Denkmal. Oder, Verzeichnis der Prediger welche seit der Reformation den Evangelisch-Lutherischen Gemeinen im Ostfries- und Harlinger Lande Evangelium von Christo verkündiget haben* (Aurich: J. Gottlob Luschkn, 1765), 256. His conjecture seems to be based on the printer's preface.
33 *VdWNN*, 82r.
34 E.g. the quotation from 1 Corinthans 13:9-10 on folio 88r and 96v.
35 Van Schelven claims a copy of this translation should be in the Hof- und Staatbibliothek in Munich (Schelven, A.A. van, 'Dyrkinus' in: *Nieuw Nederlandsch Biografisch Woordenboek. Deel 4*, 547-550, 549). However, the library cannot find any reference to it in current or older catalogues.

Even if Dyrkinus known works were compared to this book, any differences or similarities could be due to the original source. At the end of these deliberations, we cannot avoid the conclusion that we will not be able to determine the translator.

Next, we turn our attention to a theory proposed by Herman de la Fontaine Verwey. He claims the book is a revision by Micron, specifically aimed against the Family of Love.[36] Let us read what he says:

> [I]n 1559 a Breda Protestant, Adriaan de Kuiper, travelled to Emden to obtain a judgment from the consistory concerning two little books which he had written against 'Hendrik Claessen van Amsterdam'…The parson Marten Micron offered to revise one of the booklets himself, but died shortly afterwards so that the work was completed by Nicolaas Carinaeus.[37]

If this were true it would be definitive proof that the book is not by Micron. However, how does Fontaine Verwey come to this theory? He refers to the acts of the Emden consistory, his only source. What do we read in the entry for March 18th, 1559?

> Also Adrianus de Kuper from Breda has been here and showed two books, which he desired to publish against the teachings of the Anabaptists

---

[36] The Family of Love has been the object of much study. Important studies are: Fontaine Verwey, H. de la, 'The Family of Love' in: *Quaerendo* VI/3 (1976), 219-271; Hamilton, A., *The Family of Love* (Cambridge: James Clarke & Co., 1983). It has also been studied by Gary K. Waite. The Family of Love was a mystic movement which, even though it found its origins in Anabaptism, was opposed by Reformed and Mennonites alike. The founding father was Henrik Niclaes, who had been influenced by. Key aspects were the belief that one could live perfectly (Hamilton comments on David Joris: 'did David Joris not just mean that he was divinely inspired, that he had accomplished the imitation of Christ which led to spiritual regeneration and to that same redemptive operation in man which God had performed in Christ', *Family*, 18), and 'Vergottung' which was for David Joris 'the descent of God into man' and for Niclaes 'mystical incorporation into the divine being' (Hamilton, *Family*, 8; 25). Both David and Niclaes were megalomaniacs, Joris saw himself as the 'third David' after Moses and even Christ Himself (Fontaine Verwey, 'Family', 224) and Niclaes claimed he had become 'one with God's will and word', and was to reveal this will of God as the Homo Novus (HN). His prophecy was the last chance given to man (Fontaine Verwey 'Family', 228; Hamilton, *Family*, 34). Nicodemism was the common practice within the sect (Fontaine Verwey, 'Family', 249).

[37] Fontaine Verwey, 'Family', 230. The theory is repeated by Hamilton (*Family*, 50) and Schatorjé ('Engelbert Faber en de Duitse vertaling van het laatste boek van Martin Micron (Heidelberg, 1563)' in: Boonen, U. K. (ed.), *Zwischen Sprachen en culturen. Wechselbeziehungen im niederländischen, deutschen und afrikaansen Sprachgebiet* (Münster/New York: Waxmann, 2018), 19-31, 25).

and of Hinderick van Amsterdams; he desires our advice *(tegens de wederdopers und Hinderick van Amsterdams lere)*.

We have referred him *(hebben hem gewyßen)* to Micronium and Feyten, that he would confer with them, whether it would be profitable to publish the books, or not; or whether one should correct and improve them.[38]

The theory Herman de la Fontaine Verwey, despite all his scholarship, extrapolates from this quotation cannot be sustained by it.[39] After all, the minutes prove no more than that there was a man called Adriaan de Kuper who travelled to Emden with two books, and was sent on to both Micron and Feyten. Nowhere does it state that Micron offered anything. Additionally, the Family of Love is mentioned only once in Micron's share of *Van de weerdicheydt*. We can therefore safely say that Fontaine Verwey's theory is not supported by the primary source. The excerpt from the minutes is not without its value, though, for it does show that when it came to theological questions the consistory in Emden considered Micron to be an authority who was to be consulted. Perhaps they knew he was working on a book concerning these questions.

Now that we have seen that the only theory depriving Micron of his authorship is groundless, we can present some circumstantial evidence for the authenticity of the claim.

The first piece of evidence comes from how the book was received. No statement is made that the book has been wrongly attributed to Micron. Indeed, the opposite is true. In 1563, just two years after the book was printed, a German translation was published. The translation had been made by Engelbert Faber, who did not know Marten Micron personally, but had been trained by both Hermes Backerel and Petrus Datheen, who did know Micron personally in London and East Frisia. Datheen, Backerel and Faber were in Frankfurt am Main in 1560.[40] It is certain that both

---

38 *Die Kirchenratsprotokolle der Reformierten Gemeinde Emden 1557-1620. Teil 1: 1557-1574*, ed. Schilling & Schreiber (Cologne/Vienna: Böhlau Verlag, 1989), 78. We have not been able to find any more information on who Feyten was.

39 One cannot avoid a certain feeling of sloppiness either, where the Acta have 'Hinderick van Amsterdams' Verwey has 'Hendrik Claessen van Amsterdam'; moreover, he completely ignores the very clear indication that the books were not only against Hendrik Niclaes, but also against the anabaptists.

40 Schatorjé, J.M.W.C., 'Faber en Venlo. Engelbert Faber en de Reformatie in Venlo (1565-1580)' in: *Venlo's Mozaïek. Hoofdstukken uit zeven eeuwen stadsgeschiedenis* (Maastricht, 1990), 113-142, 116; Schelven, A.A. van, 'Backerel' in: *Nieuw Nederlandsch Biografisch Woordenboek. Deel 2*, 57-58.

Datheen and Faber were still there in 1561 and likely that Backerel had not yet left. *Van de weerdicheydt* having been published in 1561, Frankfurt seems to be the most likely place for Faber to have obtained it (the same goes for Bernard Buwo's *thosamenspreckinge*, which he translated as well).[41] Neither Backerel nor Datheen saw any reason to oppose Micron's supposed authorship. If we follow this strand somewhat further, some extra considerations come to mind. The German translation (1563) was published in Heidelberg, the academic centre of the Kurpfalz, a subject we will return to in chapter 5. Tobias Schreiber has shown that the theology of the London church had a major influence on both the *Heidelberg Catechism* and the *Kurpfälzischen Kirchenordnung*, both published in 1563.[42] One may safely assume that à Lasco, Utenhove and Micron were respected reformers, and a translation of a suspected pseudepigraphy would not be applauded. That the book was indeed generally considered to be by Micron is clear from a cursory remark in Gerardus Nicolai's translation of Bullingers *Von dem vnverschampten fräfel...der selbsgesandten Widertöuffern*. He larded his translation with many interpolations and in one of them says: 'Of the maintenance of Christian meetings, also read Micron's book titled *Van de weerdicheydt* etc.'[43] Nicolai was born in East Frisia and became a pastor in Norden – the very place where Micron served – in 1567. The authenticity was acknowledged, even in Norden. Finally, the only surviving copy, as we have seen, was already bound together with another book by Micron at the time of the Reformation. No one at the time seems to have doubted Micron's authorship.

Another proof is the printer. As was seen above, the book was printed by Ctematius. Micron and Ctematius must have had a special relationship. They had already known each other in London, were together during their travels and Ctematius became the printer of all Micron's books published in Emden. How likely is it that Ctematius, a convinced adherent of the Reformed doctrine, who had been closely allied to Micron, even elected as elder in London and Emden, would willingly publish a book he knew to be a pseudepigraphy? If anyone knew Micron's 'own hand', it would have been him, ruling out the possibility of deceit by a third party.

---

41 For a discussion of Engelbert Faber and his German translation, cf. chapter 5.
42 Schreiber, T., *Petrus Dathenus und der Heidelberger Katechismus. Eine traditionsgeschichtliche Untersuchung zum konfessionellen Wandel in der Kurpfalz um 1563* (Göttingen: Vandenhoeck & Ruprecht, 2017), 89-173; 297-306.
43 [Nicolai, G.], 'Gerardus Nicolai's Inlasschinghen in het vertaalde werk van Bullinger: "Teghen de Wederdoopers" ed. F. Pijper in: Cramer, S., *Bibliotheca Reformatoria Neerlandica 7e deel: Zestiende-eeuwse schrijvers over de geschiedenis der oudste Doopsgezinden hier te lande* (The Hague: Martinus Nijhoff, 1910), (inleiding, 260-289) 290-487, 306.

If it were a 'plot', it would have been one in which at least the translator, the printer and Carinaeus would have been involved. And again, we ask, how likely is it that a Reformed pastor would willingly comply with this? Of course, rules about authorship were different in those days, yet attributing an entire book falsely to a deceased authority would have been frowned upon even then.[44] Additionally, the purpose of conscious forgeries most commonly was to antedate a particular opinion, using Micron's name would in that case hardly prove anything.[45]

A third piece of evidence is the theological consistency of the book. This study will prove (see chapter 6) it is a meticulously crafted book, both in its exegesis and overall theology. It is, moreover, ecclesiologically consistent with Marten Micron's other writings. If the book were a pseudepigraphy, it was made by a very capable theologian who had been steeped in Micron's teachings. There are not many possible candidates who spring to mind to be capable of this.[46]

Fourthly, despite this careful planning the book shows marks of being unfinished and needed brushing up before publication. Indeed, it looks like a 'first version', which would have been altered and smoothed out in several places. The first chapter appears unnecessarily repetitious. For instance, when one reads folios 14r-17v, one gets the feeling this is a repetition of the preceding section. The outline (2.4) shows this is not the case, yet one needs to read closely to pick out the difference between the two sections. The author's preface, also, clearly indicates the concept of four chapters, a framework Carinaeus maintained, even when it would

---

44 For the importance attached to genuine authorship in early modernity see the discussion of Sigonio's *Consolatio* in: Havens, E.A., 'Babelic Confusion: Literary Forgery and the Bibliotheca Fictiva' in: Stephens & Havens (eds.), Literary Forgery, 33-73, 47-49. When Havens discusses religious texts in the early modern context his focus is on the forgeries of ancient sources, not even mentioning possible forgeries assigned to contemporary authors (57-59). That authenticity was important in Reformed circles can be seen when we note how Nicolai (see reference in note above) marked off his interpolations by asterisks. Moreover, Carrie Euler (*Couriers of the Gospel: England and Zurich, 1531-1558)* (Zürich: TVZ, 2006)) in her study of English translations of Reformed literature states that 'close examination of all twenty-one translation revealed only three places where the English translator either inserted or deleted large portions (that is, more than one sentence) of text.' (147) and later: 'Overall, the translators translated literally, diligently striving to preserve the content of the original texts' (154).
45 Stephens W. & Havens, E.A., 'Forgery's Valhalla' in: Stephens & Havens (eds.), Literary Forgery, 1-14, p. 2.
46 Possibilities that do come to mind are Datheen or Guido de Brès; however, there is no reason to suppose they would not have published under their own name. In general one sees that even the most obscure theologians used their own name for their publications (e.g. Carinaeus).

have been wiser for him to create new chapters. Apparently the original concept had to be respected. Two more very clear 'rough edges' can be found on fol. 22r. and 42r. On 22r. the author says he is going to discuss three examples, but he goes on to discuss four (perhaps even five, depending on how one reads the 'body' metaphor), three of which had not been mentioned in the introductory sentence. On 42r. it appears the author switches to the discussion of how Christian discipline is corrupted in the Roman Church. Yet this change is never clearly indicated.

In addition to these reasons it would be helpful if a linguistic analysis could be made. However, we feel this is not possible. What we have before us is a translation of a Latin work. The vocabulary and grammar will bear the mark of the translator. This means a comparison to Micron's other books written in the vernacular will not prove or disprove it was written by him. Without the Latin autograph it will also be impossible to compare it to his Latin works and letters. However, a content analysis is possible and we will compare the contents of this book to Micron's other works when we analyse the ecclesiology of the book.

We have seen that the section by Carinaeus proves there was an unfinished manuscript he finalised. After that we refuted the theory proposed by Fontaine Verwey. Last of all, we presented circumstantial evidence for Micron's authorship: the book is consistently regarded as Micronian by contemporary authors, it was printed by Ctematius, the book is theologically consistent, yet also shows signs that it needed some more editing. All in all this is ample circumstantial evidence to assume the authenticity of Ctematius's claim, though it cannot definitively be proven without the autograph. Nonetheless, the arguments given above show it is much more likely that Micron did write the book. In the absence of any proof to the contrary and the absence of other candidates, it is unnecessary to assume otherwise.

2.4 Structure and Summary of the Book

As was indicated above, the book bears the marks of being an unfinished and unpolished work. This makes the book difficult to read. Sometimes there appear to be unnecessary repetitions, making whole pages redundant at first sight. For that reason it is helpful to give a detailed outline of the book. This will help us see the macro-structure which the authors were trying to fill in. What becomes clear when we look at the structure is that there are two focal points in the book. The first is that Micron is trying to give a biblical theology of the church and the necessity of leaving the false church. The second focal point is the three marks of the church. The page numbers refer to the original folios.

Obviously, the prefaces by the printer and Micron are not part of the theological structure of the book. The printer's preface has been discussed above (2.3). Micron's primary address to the reader is very short. He says that in 'these latter days' (*dese uuterste tijden*) the church has been 'scattered and divided' (*verstroyt ende verdeyst*) all over the world. As a consequence, many doubt whether they should leave the Roman Catholic church in order to join the true church, and if so, what church they should join. To help those who truly seek God's honour and their soul's salvation, Micron has written this book.

Let us now turn to the structure of the ensuing chapters, which also forms a useful summary of the contents of the book; though, it must be added, this will not be a summary of the theological content, for that the reader is referred to chapter 6, where the ecclesiology of the book is examined thoroughly. Based on the prose outline below we have written a more accessible table of contents, which precedes the transcription of the book. The reader is advised to cross reference between the prose and schedulised outline for the corresponding page numbers.

In chapter one Micron's seeks to prove that it is good, useful and necessary to join a visible congregation. He starts by listing biblical-theological[47] evidence to substantiate his claim that God has wanted a church throughout history, even in paradise. Old Testament examples are followed by New Testament examples. In the last category he pays special attention to the images used in the gospels and the letters.

He goes on to claim that the godly honoured and rebuilt the congregation. Again, he lists Old and New Testament examples. To the non-attentive reader this feels repetitive.

In both instances, it must be noted that in the New Testament sections he also uses the 'Word-sacrament-discipline' triad as a framework.

In chapter two the marks of the church are discussed. After having listed what one should not look for, Micron goes on to state what one should look for. This is especially found in the doctrine and as a consequence also in the governance of the church.[48] Again the 'Word-sacrament-discipline' triad comes back.

In chapter three the question whether one may leave the church of Rome is answered. Micron exposes what he perceives to be the errors of

---

[47] Biblical-theological not in its full (and somewhat uncontrolled) contemporary meaning, but as the bridge between exegesis and systematic theology: the analytical summary of biblical data to come to an organised theology (cf. Kwakkel, G. 'Oude Testament', in: Bruijne, A.L.Th. de (ed.), *Gereformeerde theologie vandaag* (Barneveld: De Vuurbaak, 2004) 31-44, 43).

[48] Cf. also, ch. 6.4.

the Roman church. They uphold human tradition, slander Christ's office and His sacrifice. Besides, they tear the governance of the church to shreds: the Word, the sacraments and Christian discipline. This is followed by biblical-theological examples of believers who left the false church. Those who do so can expect their choice to be blessed. Micron knows that many will oppose his opinion, so in the last section of chapter three he addresses the counter-arguments.

Chapter four, the last chapter, states that after leaving the church of Rome, one should join the true church. First, once more, examples from the Bible are presented, followed by an admonition to follow these examples. Micron offers advice to those who wonder what they should do when there is no congregation they can join, before countering the arguments against the necessity to leave one's city or country. Micron's section ends on fol. 93v, while he is still discussing these arguments. Carinaeus continues this, but immediately focuses on the Family of Love and David Joris. He rounds off the book with two sections, the first on why secret meetings should be organised in papistical lands, and the last on how these meetings ought to be organised. In the last pages he quickly opposes the Anabaptist, admonishes princes and governments, then his brothers and sisters.

2.5 Goals of the Book

We round off the introduction to the book itself by looking at the possible goals Micron and Carinaeus might have had in writing the book. This will, once again, force us to re-examine Fontaine Verwey's theory. The best starting point, however, will be to start with what Micron himself states as his purpose in the preface. This automatically leads us into the field of Nicodemism and Fontaine Verwey's theory. After having looked at all these things we will analyse the evidence and give Micron's and Carinaeus's goals.

In his preface to the book Micron states his aim very clearly:

> In this great multitude of opinions, by which the people in these latter days are so grievously scattered and divided, there are yet many in doubt whether a godly and faithful *(godsalich ende gheloovich)* man should necessarily go to any outward ecclesiastical meeting or congregation; and, if this is necessary, which meeting or congregation all *(een yegelick)* should join with a clear conscience, as it is clear that the shape or form of the outward congregations is not the same everywhere in these days, but that they are both in doctrine and in ceremonies different and manifold.
>
> To advise those best who above all and wholeheartedly desire that the honour of God is propagated among men, and who seek their own

salvation seriously, and to bring them to a good easiness of conscience, I have taken it upon me to prove, in a few words and without bitterness that:...[49] (this is followed by the four themes (see appendix A) Micron discusses in the book).

This leaves very little doubt about the audience Micron tried to reach. It is that group of people who are convinced of errors in the Roman Catholic doctrine, yet still live in the areas where the Roman Catholic church was the only legitimate church. Any open profession of their faith might lead to persecution or flight. Hence, they doubted or denied the necessity of leaving the Roman church, or would ask the question which church they should join if they were to leave. In the case of this book, we should probably think of converts in the Low Countries. Micron tried to convince them that it is necessary to join a church, that the Roman Catholic ceremonies are not to be endured and that they should either flee or join a secret church. Two extensive parts of the book refute arguments against this opinion, further underscoring this as the overall purpose of the book. Moreover, this is what the set-up of the book leads up to: from theory, to applied theory, to practice.

This places the book firmly in what are known as anti-nicodemite writings. Nicodemism is the name given to those who adhere to, in this case, the Reformed faith, yet dissemble and still attend the Roman church. In this respect they are like Nicodemus who visits the Lord Jesus by night, supposedly because he feared the other Pharisees.[50] In the Low Countries there was a wide array of sects and groups who in some way sought a type of reform or who did not adhere to the Roman Catholic doctrine, without taking the step of leave.[51] This was perceived as a denial of the cause for reforming the church: could worship be pure when it was mixed with perceived idolatry?[52] The polemic debate between the reformers, especially Calvin, and the Nicodemites spanned several decades and resulted in a long list of books, graced by the names of Bullinger, Vermigli, Melanchthon, Calvin, à Lasco, Bucer and other theologians.[53] By 1559 the

---

49 *VdWNN*, 2v.
50 John 3: 1-21. Note that the gospel itself does not specify the reason why Nicodemus came to Jesus in the night.
51 Cf. Veen, M. van, '*Verschooninghe van de roomsche afgoderye*'. *De polemiek van Calvijn met nicodemieten, in het bijzonder met Coornhert* (PhD thesis VU Amsterdam, 2001), 97-100.
52 Eire, C.M.N., *War Against the Idols. The Reformation of Worship from Erasmus to Calvin* (Cambridge: CUP, 1986), 271
53 The subject of Nicodemism has been studied by many people, to name just a few articles and books: Eire, C.M.N., *War*, 234-275; Overell, M.A., 'Vergerio's Anti-Nicodemite

debate had been going on for over two decades (Calvin's first publication on the subject was *Two Epistles concerning the matters especially worth knowing in this present age* (1537) and in 1554 two of his works against the Nicodemites had been translated into Dutch, i.e. Van *dat scuwen der afgoderie* and *Excuse van Johann Calvinus, tot mijn heeren die nicodemieten*)[54] and it is not surprising that by that time Micron had to challenge many arguments proposed by the Nicodemites. This shows that he was not, above all, concerned with gently leading confused souls, as his preface implies; rather, he sought to convince those who still dissembled by carefully, calmly and rigorously undermining all their arguments. In writing this book Micron stepped onto the battlefield perceived to be crucial in the fight against the Roman Catholic church.[55]

This leads us to the question whether or not Micron had a specific group in mind. We already refuted Fontaine Verwey's theory concerning the authorship of the book. Yet he and Alistair Hamilton might be right about the intended purpose of the book as being specifically against David Joris and the Family of Love.[56] However, careful reading of the book does not corroborate this theory. The theories and doctrines of the Family are never specifically addressed in the first 63 (recto and verso) pages of the book. Only then, on fol. 64v. does the name of David Joris pop up, but even then not in isolation; rather, it is joined to that of the Libertines (presumably Micron's synonym for Nicodemites)[57]. Indeed, for as far as we are able to tell, Micron does not mention David Joris or the Family of Love in any of his other books, nor have we found any reference to them in any of his letters. If he aimed to specifically oppose

---

Propaganda and England, 1574-1558' in: *Journal of Ecclesiastical History* 51/2 (2000), 296-318; Veen, M. van, *Verschooninghe*; White, R., 'Calvin, The Nicodemites and the Cost of Discipleship' in: *The Reformed Theological Review* 56 (1997), 14-27; Woo, K.J., 'The House of God in Exile: Reassesing John Calvin's Approach to Nicodemism in Quatre sermons (1552)' in: *Church History and Religious Culture* 95/2-3 (2015), 222-244; Woo, K.J., *Nicodemism and the English Calvin, 1544-1584* (Leiden: Brill, 2019). It was briefly mentioned by E.A. de Boer in his inaugural oration: Boer, E.A. de, '*Verspreid en verstrooid*'. *Ecclesiologie van de diaspora en de reformatie van de Lage Landen* (Kampen: Theologische Universiteit Kampen, 2016), 15-20.

54 White, 'Calvin', 15; Van Veen, *Verschooninghe, 124*.
55 Overell, 'Vergerio', 297.
56 Fontaine Verwey, H. de la, 'The Family of Love' in: *Quaerendo* VI/3 (1976), 219-271, 230, where he says: 'It was the first writing against Niclaes ever to be published'. Hamilton, repeating Fontaine-Verwey's theory, also claims the book is specifically against David Joris and the Family of Love (*The Family of Love* (Cambridge: James Clarke & Co., 1983), 49-51).
57 Veen, M. van, *Verschooninghe*, 138.

their doctrines at all, it is much more likely he attempted to cut them short in the large sweep of his polemical scythe.[58] However, the complete lack of any reference to David Joris and the Family of Love elsewhere raises the question whether Micron did indeed address them? How is it possible that David Joris and the Family suddenly surface on this page? Why are they not mentioned earlier, nor indeed ever afterwards? Why, for instance, does he not mention them on fol. 83r where he says that one 'finds many who minimise the importance and reject the outward Christian congregation or meeting under the cover (*schijn*) of a 'inward and spiritual (*gheestelicker*) religion"?[59] This leads us to suspect that the reference to David Joris and the Family of Love has been written into the manuscript. The main reason for thinking so is that Carinaeus, when he takes over, suddenly switches from what Micron was discussing (how even the dissemblers do come together) to the Family of Love, polemicizing against them from fol. 94r. to 100r. He, clearly, felt a desperate need to fight them. A need which Micron did not feel, or he would have turned to the subject much earlier and he would have mentioned it somewhere else, in either a book or a letter. If this was the specific goal of his book, why did he not mention that in the title or the preface? He was not afraid to name his opponents in other books (i.e. Menno Simons and Joachim Westphal). The book, then, was not specifically written against David Joris and the Family of Love. Indeed, this might even lead some to have reservations about the genuineness of the lines referring to David Joris and the Family of Love on fol. 64v. The fact that there is a very clear indication where Micron left off tips the scales towards seeing them as genuine. Genuine or not, it is obvious the book was not written specifically against the Family or David Joris.

Nonetheless, Micron might have had a special group in mind when he was writing the book. When the manuscript was found, the publisher alleges, it was written in Latin. Why would Micron write a book like this in Latin? We believe the reason for this is twofold. The first has to do with the aim of the book as it was given in the preface, the opposition of Nicodemism. In the Low Countries Nicodemism was also practised in the upper classes, though it was not limited to this group and was not solely an elitist movement. Decavele, for instance, notes that in Ghent Reformed Protestantism had evolved to a 'drawing room protestantism'

---

58 Mirjam van Veen does not mention Fontaine Verwey's theory when she discusses the book and sees it only as anti-nicodemite (Veen, M. van, *Verschooninghe*, 138-141). Neither does Pettegree in his reference to Adriaan (Pettegree, 'Struggle', 45).
59 *VdWNN*, 83r.

and limited to the 'lettered and wealthy' after 1545.[60] True enough, that is nearly fifteen years before Micron wrote his book; nonetheless, as Marnef shows in his book on Reformation in Antwerp, the practice of Nicodemism certainly did not stop after 1545.[61] Indeed, his study makes it clear that, at least for the city of Antwerp, Micron's book would have hit the mark. After Van Haemstede's public preaching in the city the Reformed party was repressed, yet there seems to have been room for compassion. Marnef comments that the city magistrate was more careful in punishing the Reformed, and that the measures taken against them were less severe (banishment) than those taken against the Anabaptists (often execution). For the respectable tradesman there was good reason to dissemble and practice his Reformed faith in private.[62] There was every reason for Micron to enforce his arguments from *Een claer bewijs* (cf. the biography in chapter 3) by embedding them in a complete ecclesiology which he aimed specifically at that group of educated Nicodemites. However, this reason cannot have been the only one for writing the book in Latin, as there is no convincing reason why he could not have achieved the same purpose by writing the book in Dutch (clearly this was felt by the printer and he therefore printed it in Dutch). The second reason seems to have been that Micron wished to address not only his countrymen, but also a larger European audience. Possibly he meant his book to be more than a polemical work, considering its elaborate ecclesiological expositions. It is not unlike Micron to mention just one of his lesser goals, while having a larger goal behind that. For instance, in *Een clear bewijs* he claims to have written the treatise to educate his simple fellow countrymen,[63] while what he offers is a deep-wrought study of the Lord's Supper and ends with a direct appeal to leave the church of Rome. Likewise, in the *Ordinancien* he states that his goal is an apology for the practices of the London church,[64] while he quite clearly presents a blueprint for a Reformed church order

---

60 Decavele, J. *De dageraad van de Reformatie in Vlaanderen (1520-1565)* (Brussel: Paleis der Academiën. 1975). 322-323.
61 Marnef, G., *Antwerpen in de tijd van de Reformatie. Ondergrond protestantisme in een handelsmetropool 1550-1577* (DBNL, 2007 (ebook of the original published by Amsterdam: Meulenhoff/Antwerpen:Kritak, 1996)), 99.
62 Marnef, *Antwerpen*, 120-123. Opposition to Van Haemstede and his method may have been key in writing this book, in Pettegree (*Emden*, 61) we read: 'But equally irritating was [Van Haemstede's] apparent insistence on his right to conduct seperate meetings for groups of richer citizens, men who sympathized with the gospel but were reluctant to put themselves under the community discipline.'
63 *Claer bewijs*, 441.
64 *Ord.*, 39.

which he himself used in Norden.[65] The last example is *Hoste vander Katelyne*, which he presents as a simple history of Hoste's martyrdom,[66] yet is also a vehicle to present his own views on the doctrine of the Lord's Supper. So, not only did Micron wish to convince his countrymen, he also presented his teachings on the church to an international audience.

This goal was not shared by the printer and Carinaeus. After all, the printer decided to have the book translated to Dutch, in so doing he completely changed the potential readership from a well-educated international readership to those able to read the Dutch language. Carinaeus's part of the book contains an elaborate refutation of the Family of Love and David Joris, followed by two chapters on secret meetings. In this way the book became much more of a handbook for Reformed churches under the cross.[67] Though this last aspect does do justice to Micron's original setup, it is nonetheless the case that at least the first 29 pages (r/v) are solidly ecclesiological, and the following chapters are infused with many ecclesiological arguments as well. All in all one does most justice to the book when the part by Micron is first and foremost seen as an exposition of his convictions in the *locus de ecclesia*.

2.6 Summary and Conclusions

At the end of this first chapter we can summarise what we have found, keeping in mind the two foci we described at the start: to get a feel for the book and how it would have functioned after publication.

We discovered that the book, in all likelihood, is the genuine work of Marten Micron, though he originally wrote it in Latin. It was printed by Ctematius, a refugee from Flanders who had travelled with Micron from London to East Frisia. In this book we come across Micron's final statement concerning the substance and governance of the church. Indeed, this is what was given as the overall goal of the book. Although there is a clear polemical purpose in combating Nicodemism, there is also a clear purpose of offering an overall, solid, foundational ecclesiology, firmly grounded in biblical-theology.

Our aim was to get a feel for the book and to uncover its aims. We now know it is a thorough, though unfinished, ecclesiology, written against Nicodemism and originally intended for an international audience. It presents us with the theology underlying Micron's choices in ecclesiological rites, practices and ordinances.

---

65 *AS*, fol. 6-36 (*Is is is*, 31-61).
66 *Hoste*, 188-191.
67 Schatorjé ('Duitse vertaling', 30) sees this as the primary goal of the book. Cf. 5.1.

Chapter 3: Introduction to the Authors of *Van de weerdicheydt, nutheydt ende noodicheyt der christelicker vergaderinghen*

Having looked at the book itself, we now turn to the authors of the book. We saw that we can accept the claim that the book is Micron's work, finished by Carinaeus. In this chapter we will give a biography of both authors. Since Marten Micron is the main author of the book and his ecclesiology is the focus of this research, his life will be studied more extensively. In doing so we will attempt to place his life in the context in which he lived; however, Micron lived in at least eight countries or cities with their particular history in the sixteenth century. Outlining the precise details and histories of these several contexts is far beyond the possibilities and scope of this thesis, which focusses on the ecclesiology of *Van de weerdicheyt*. Where the context has more importance we will give more details as if painting a still life; where the importance is less, the context will be painted as by an impressionist, or even that of a modern abstract painter, indicating the basic outline and form, not wrong but, rather, generalising.[1] For the same reason the biography of Micron focusses on how he was theologically influenced and his life as a refugee, especially how he himself reflected on it.[2]

Paragraph 3.1 focusses on Marten Micron, 3.2 on the life of Nicolaus Carinaeus.

---

1 We have taken the cue for this comparison from Kooi, Ch., 'The Early Modern Low Countries', in: *Sixteenth Century Journal* 40/1 (2009), 253-255, where she says: 'For the past few decades historians have been producing local studies…the small, highly detailed canvas of the *fijnschilder* being favored over the panoramic sweep of the landscapist.'

2 The given biography is a re-evaluation of previously printed sources and studies and does not include any new archival material. Though this would probably enhance our understanding of Micron, we were unfortunately not able to do so.

3.1 Marten Micron

3.1.1 Early life

Marten de Cleyne, latinised: Micron, was born in the city of Ghent,[3] in the year 1522 or 1523.[4] Little to nothing is known about his youth and education.[5] However, Reershemius does give us an extract of Micron's will, and this sheds some light on his early life.[6] He mentions a brother, Lucas, and a sister who remains nameless. Micron is anxious that his brother and sister only inherit any of his possessions if they have left the church of Rome. This makes it likely that Micron's parents were loyal to the Roman Catholic church and its teachings. Though probably not rich, his parents apparently had sufficient means to give Micron a proper education. The ease with which Micron in later life read and wrote Latin indicates he learnt this early on. In his youth, approximately the first twenty years, Micron was a young man in a mixed environment. Living in Ghent meant that Micron grew up in a wealthy and influential city, where there was an interchange of goods and thought.[7] One might even typify the county Flanders as the commercial and intellectual thoroughfare[8] of Europe and there was a myriad of opinions that might

---

3 The only primary source to support this is the matriculation register of Basel where it says: Martinus Micronius Gandensis (Wackernagel, H. G., *Die Matrikel der Universität Basel. II. Band 1532/3-1600/01* (Basel: Verlag der Universitätsbibliothek, 1956), 51). There is, moreover, no reason to doubt this generally accepted tradition. Cf., also, Gerretsen, J.H., *Micronius. Zijn leven, zijn geschriften, zijn geestesrichting* (Nijmegen: Ten Hoet, 1895), 1-2; Willems, W.O.R., *Met Maarten de Kleyne aan het avondmaal* (Licentiate-thesis University for Protestant Theology, 1980), 13.

4 In the polemic work *Een Waerachtigh verhael* (39) Micron comments that he was 31 years old when he disputed with Menno Simons on February 6th, 1554. In the *SNF*, 138, the same is said in the margin. A simple calculation leads to the conclusion that Micron was born somewhere between February 7th, 1522 and February 7th, 1523. However, one should not take Micron's remark too literally. It may well be he did not know his exact date of birth. On the other hand, neither would he have been so precise if he had only an inkling of his age. All in all the conclusion in the main body seems to be a fair deduction.

5 Johan Decavele, who has read almost all the surviving archives in Ghent, informed me that he did not come across any primary sources relating to Micron.

6 For the will, cf. Reershemius, P.F., *Ostfriesländisches Prediger-Denkmahl (...)* (Aurich: Ben Johann Adolph Schulte, 1796), 226-227. Apparently Reershemius had a primary source to support what he writes about Micron's will.

7 Cf. Woltjer, J.J., *Op weg naar tachtig jaar oorlog. Het verhaal van de eeuw waarin ons land ontstond* ([n.p.] Uitgeverij Balans, 20122), 13-25.

8 The terms 'corridor' and 'thoroughfare' arise from a conversation I had with prof. dr. W.O.R. Willems.

have influenced him. There would have been Roman Catholic influences, next to Luther's works, sacramentarian opinions, Anabaptist thought and the various sects of libertines and freethinkers.[9] '[T]he religious landscape in the Low Countries was complex and fluid.'[10] In the years between 1523 and 1545 there are some aspects which are worth mentioning here. The first is that in Flanders Charles V severely persecuted all heterodox[11] teachings,[12] and in 1536 Micron might have witnessed the burning of Sander Huubert in Ghent. Huubert had sold Lutheran books. Nine years later, if Micron was still in the city, he could also have seen how Joos de Pape, Joos de Vos and Martin Hueriblocq were executed.[13] The numbers of those who were persecuted and killed in Flanders and the Netherlands tell a shocking tale: approximately 1,300 were killed for their heretical beliefs.[14] Obviously, those numbers were unknown to Micron, yet as a young man he would have known that a choice against the doctrines of the Roman Catholic church was dangerous, and potentially life threatening. However, when we look at the second aspect that is important to highlight here, we see that he still had ample opportunity to come across the new teachings. One of the means by which new ideas were spread is

---

9   Arblaster, P. ' 'Totius Mundus Emporium': Antwerp as a Centre for Vernacular Bible Translations 1523-1545' in: Gelderblom, A-J. et al. (eds.), *The Low Countries As a Crossroads of Religious Beliefs* (Leiden: Brill, 2004), 10-31 (especially insightful is his remark that 'readers of each [i.e. readers of 1) Lutheran tracts, 2) Erasmian writings and 3) traditional vernacular works] would by choice consult a different vernacular version.', p.29); Benedict, Ph., *Christ's Churches Purely Reformed. A Social History of Calvinism* (New Haven/London: YUP, 2002), 177-178; Decavele, J. *De dageraad van de Reformatie in Vlaanderen (1520-1565)* (Brussel: Paleis der Academiën. 1975), 70-99; 235-238; 535; 549-550; 596-597; Duke, A. (edited by Pollmann, J. & Spicer, A.), *Dissident Identities in the Early Modern Low Countries* (Farnham/Burlington: Ashgate, 2009), 77-97; Janse, W., 'The Protestant Reformation in the Low Countries: Developments in Twentieth-Century Historiography' in: *Reformation and Renaissance Review* 6/2(2004), 179-202, esp.189-192; Selderhuis, H.J. & Nissen, P., 'De zestiende eeuw' in: Selderhuis, H.J. (ed.), *Handboek Nederlandse Kerkgeschiedenis* (Kampen: Kok, 2006), 216-358, esp. 231-254; Woltjer, *Op weg*, 137-145.
10 Marnef, G. 'Erasmus of Rotterdam and the Protestant Reformation' in: *Erasmus Studies* 36 (2016), 35-52, p.38.
11 This word does not imply any assessment of those teachings. It merely means that they were other than the Roman Catholic dogmas.
12 Albaster, P. 'Totius', 15; Benedict, Ph., *Christ's Churches*, 176-177; Decavele, *Dageraad*, 6-38; Kooi, Ch., *Calvinists and Catholics During Holland's Golden Age: Heretics and Idolaters* (Cambridge: CUP, 2012), 23-24.
13 For the executions see: Decavele, *Dageraad*, 32; 242; 246; Decavele, *De eerste protestanten in de Lage Landen. Geloof en Heldenmoed* (Zwolle: Waanders, 2004), 49.
14 Terpstra, N., *Religious Refugees in the Early Modern World. An Alternative History of the Reformation* (Cambridge: CUP, 2015), 99.

that of plays, especially by the Chamber of Rhetoric. We draw attention to this aspect, rather than books, because we know that Micron attended a play in Antwerp in 1549 and that in Ghent there were at least two moments when Micron may have attended plays that brought him in close contact with heterodox doctrine. The first of these was in a crucial year: 1539. Marten Micron was, at that point in time, sixteen or seventeen years old. In 1539 Ghent's Chamber of Rhetoric, The Fountain (*De Fonteine*), was given consent to organise a feast. The plays staged by the several contributing rhetoricians of other cities had to provide an answer to the question: 'what is the greatest comfort to a dying man?'. Almost all of these plays were critical of the Roman Catholic church, while several openly propagated Luther's doctrines. The printed plays were supressed by the theologians of Louvain in 1540.[15] A few months after the plays were staged in June, the city was in turmoil. The guilds refused to pay Charles V the money he demanded in 1537 to support his wars against France. When the regent, Mary of Hungary, forcefully collected the money it ultimately led to an insurrection. There was chaos and terror, and eventually Charles came over from Spain to supress the rebellion. With thousands of soldiers he entered the city. Of course, there had to be consequences and Ghent was denied all its privileges, including all powers of justice. As a symbol of repression he built a castle on the site of St. Bavo's abbey.[16] Haemers comments: 'With these unprecedented measures, Charles V intended to break the Ghent craftsmen's political power and tradition of resistance decisively (…) [T]he authorities achieved ideological supremacy (…) a situation which still left room for alternative political thoughts, but not for their utterance'.[17] Though the rebellion was primarily for social and economic reasons, religious motives cannot be excluded.[18] There is no proof that Micron was in any way involved in these events. Nonetheless, it is possible that for Micron the two were in some way connected. He had seen or heard how the heterodox believers were executed by a government that now denied the city its rights. Could it be that the persecutions and restrictions played a role in his conversion? Unfortunately, the complete absence of any primary sources deny us the

---

15 Waterschoot, W., *Schouwende Fantasye* (Gent: Academia Press, 2002), 27-36; Erné & Van Dis, *De Gentse Spelen van 1539* 2 vols. (Den Haag: Martinus Nijhoff, 1982) vol 1, 26-30.
16 Decavele, *Dageraad*, 37; 245-246; Haemers, J., 'Social Memory and Rebellion in fifteenth-century Ghent' in: *Social History* 36/4 (2011), 443-463, 460-461; Woltjer, *Op weg*, 74-75.
17 Haemers, 'Social', 461.
18 Decavele, *Dageraad*, 245.

possibilty to draw this conclusion. Another important event that might have played a role, was the play written by Jan Utenhove a few years later. This play is important to note, even if Micron did not attend it. Utenhove would later be an elder in the London Strangers' Church where Micron was a minister, and one of the key-persons in Micron's life.[19] On the 2nd of July, 1543 at the Utenhove estate at Roborst, Jan Utenhove staged a play called *The Evangelical Teacher*. He had written it together with Gillis Joyelx and it was clearly meant to convince people of the new faith. The main character is Unlearnt People, who trusts in his own works for his salvation; however, when he has been taught by 'Evangelical Teacher' and 'God's Servant' he converts to Luther's doctrine of salvation. The staging of this play led to Utenhove's flight and official exile from the city. Several other who contributed to the event were arrested.[20]

Somewhere between 1540 and 1546 Micron went to university. The most likely choice for him would have been Louvain, though we have not yet been able to find any proof that he went there.[21] Neither are we certain of what he studied at university. The tradition has it that he studied medicine, and this does not seem unlikely, given his ready display of medical knowledge in his polemics with Menno Simons.[22] In addition, mention is made of a book titled *In libros de Placitis Hippocratis et Platonis Argumenta*, supposed to have been published in Basel around 1549 by a Marten Micron of Ghent.[23] Though the book has not yet not been rediscovered, there is no reason to doubt it existed. Neither is it likely that two persons with exactly the same name, from exactly the same city were in exactly the same place at exactly the same time. So, even though definite primary proof is lacking, it does not seem unreasonable to state that Micron studied medicine in his late teens or early twenties.

In the second half of the 1540's Micron left his native country and went to Basel. He may have visited other cities along the road, where he

---

19 See below, pp. 65-77.
20 *Een seer schoon Spel van sinnen*, in: Jaarboek de Fonteine 39-40 (1989-1990), 24-94; Coigneau, 'De Evangelische leeraer: Een spel vul heresien', in: *Jaarboek de Fonteine* 39-40 (1989-1990), 117-145; Decavele, *Eerste protestanten*, 69-79. For the identification of the two teachers with Luther, cf. Coigneau, 'Evangelische leeraer, 141, particularly note 83.
21 Willems (*Maarten de Kleyne*, 15) follows up Rahlenbeck's suggestion that it was Louvain. Rahlenbeck also claims Micron got acquainted with à Lasco there; however, there is no primary source for this.
22 Cf. Gerretsen, *Micronius*, 2-3, especially note 2; Willems, *Maarten de Kleyne*, 15.
23 Dewalque, G., 'De Cleene (Martin)' in: *Biographie Nationale 4* (Bussels: Thiry, 1873), 870-871. Cf., also, Sweertius, F., *Athanae Belgicae* (Antwerp: Gulielmum a Tungris, 1628), 551.

stayed for a longer or shorter time. In Basel Micron stayed with De Falais, also known as Jacques de Bourgogne, a correspondent of Calvin.[24] The city was one of the key players during the early years of the struggle between Rome and the Swiss Reformation. But before that Basel had already been important, due to its university and flourishing printing industry. Especially noteworthy is the stay of Erasmus in Basel, where he met and taught, among others, Zwingli and Oecolampadius. The latter of these two would return to the city in 1522, and became professor at the university in 1523 and he was, arguably, the most erudite Reformed scholar before Calvin. Despite Oecolampadius's clear evangelical agenda – even introducing a new liturgy in 1526 – the city would not officially adopt the Reformation until 1529, when the Reformation Ordinance (*Reformationsmandat*) was published. After Oecolampadius passed away in 1531 he was succeeded by Oswald Myconius, who was still the leading figure when Micron arrived in the city. Myconius was not a brilliant theologian, yet he was a well-loved preacher and he built on the foundation laid by Oecolampadius.[25] Nonetheless, the Basel Reformation seems, on the whole, to have influenced Marten Micron only a little.[26] The reason

---

24 We know that Micron lived with de Falais from Utenhove, who mentioned this in a letter to Calvin several years later (*Corpus Reformatorum. Joannis Calvini Opera quae supersunt omnia XIII* ed. Baum *et al.* (Brunswick: Schwetske, 1875), 628.
For more on De Falais, cf. Berg, M. A. van den, *Friends of Calvin* (Grand Rapids: Eerdmans, 2009), 185-195; Gilmont, J-F., 'Les amis de Calvin Originaires des XVII provinces de Charles Quint' in: Cottret, B. & Millet, O. (eds.), *Calvin et la France. Bulletin de la Société de l'Histoire du Protestantisme Français* 155 (2009) (Paris: Droz, 2009), 101-116.

25 This account of the Basel reformation is based on: Burnett, A. Nelson, '"It Varies from Canton to Canton": Zurich, Basel, and the Swiss Reformation' in: *Calvin Theological Journal* 44 (2009), 251-262; Burnett, A. Nelson, ; The Reformation in Basel' in: Burnett, A. Nelson & Campi, E. (eds.), *A Companion to the Swiss Reformation* (Leiden: Brill, 2016), 170-215; Burnett, A. Nelson, *Teaching the Reformation. Ministers and Their Message in Basel, 1529-1629* (Oxford: OUP, 2009), 23-61; Gordon, B., *The Swiss Reformation* (Manchester/New York: MUP, 2002), 108-112.
A fine, though slightly hagiographic, introduction to Oecolampadius is: Poythress, D., *Reformer of Basel. The Life, Thought, and Influences of Johannes Oecolampadius* (Grand Rapids: RHB, 2011).
A modern edition of the Reformation Ordinance is printed in: Campi, E. & Wälchli, Ph. (eds.), *Basler Kirchenordnungen 1528-1675* (Zürich: TVZ, 2012), 13-42.

26 Though influence and the sources of arguments are always difficult to prove, the Zwinglian arguments against the presence of the body of Christ in the Lord's Supper are more easily traced in *Claer Bewijs* than the arguments Oecolampadius uses. For instance the division between matter and spirit (cf., also, Burnett, A. Nelson, A., *Debating the Sacraments. Print and Authority in the Early Reformation* (New York: OUP, 2019), esp. pages 155-157 and 201-203).

for this could be that he was already under the influence of a fiery theologian with a powerful character: John Hooper. It is possible he was first introduced to Hooper by Anne de Tserclaes, a refugee from Antwerp. Micron met Anne in the household of De Falais. She had nursed Hooper back to health when he had fallen ill during his stay with Richard and Anne Hilles in Strasbourg. When Hooper arrived in Basel he married Anne and there can be no doubt that he met Micron during that same visit.[27] Indeed, Hooper was so impressed with Micron that he wrote to Bullinger:

> '[t]here is in [de Falais'] house a certain godly and learned youth, whom I intend to bring down with me to Zurich: I request you, for Christ's sake, if it be possible, to procure him a scholarship (*lectionem*)[28] in some class in your school. He is studious and diligent, and will not shrink from the severest labours; and if he can but meet with some moderate means of subsistence, he will be of service to the church of God.'[29]

Though Hooper does not mention Micron's name, his close alliance in later years, and the fact that we know Micron stayed with De Falais, gives us enough certainty to identify this godly youth as Marten Micron. However, he did not join Hooper when the Englishman moved on to Zurich. From Bullinger's diary we know that Hooper arrived there on the 29th of March, 1547.[30] If Micron travelled with him this would mean

---

There are some instances where the ordinances of the Basel church (*Form der Sacramenten bruch / wie sy zů Basel gebrucht werden / mit sampt eynem kürzen kinder bericht gebessert und gemehrt* (Basel: Erasmus Zymmerman, 1545)) may have influenced the *Ordinancien*, especially in the marriage form.

27 Cf. Deibler, E.C., *Bishop John Hooper, A Link Connecting the Reformation Thought of Ulrich Zwingli and the Zurich Tradition with the Earliest English Pietistic* (PhD Temple University, Philadelphia, 1970), 272-273; Giselbrecht, R.A., 'Religious Intent and the Art of Courteous Pleasantry: A Few Letters from Englishwomen to Heinrich Bullinger (1543-1562)', in: Chappell, J.A. & Kramer, K.A. (eds.), *Women During the English Reformations. Renegotiating Gender and Religious Identity* (New York: Palgrave Macmillan, 2014), 45-68.
Contra Muylaert, S., *Shaping the Stranger Churches. Migrants in England and the Troubles in the Netherlands, 1547-1585* (Leiden/Boston: Brill, 2020), 27.

28 Another possible, though unlikely, translation of *lectionem* is 'teachership'.

29 Hooper to Bullinger (*ET*, 25-27; *OLER*, 40-42 (which reads 'teachership' instead of scholarship)). No date is given, the editors of the Parker society date it shortly after December 12th, 1546.

30 Bullinger, H., *Diarium*, ed. E. Egi (Basel: Basler Buch- und Antiquariatshandlung, 1904), 35.

that he completely wasted the fee he paid when he enrolled at the Basel university. The register shows he matriculated there during the rectorate of Sebastian Münster, running from the 1st of May, 1547 through to the 30th of April, 1548;[31] moreover, whereas Bullinger does mention Hooper's wife, he does not make mention of any other person having joined Hooper. The likeliest option, then, is that Hooper and Anne travelled on, while Micron stayed in Basel until the end of the academic year. Possibly Hooper tried to procure him a scholarship. Another possibility is that Micron worked on the book *In libros de Placitis Hippocratis et Platonis Argumenta* and used the money he obtained in this way to leave Basel after his first year at its university. In that case the question arises what he studied at the university. Was it really medicine, as is generally assumed, or did he prepare for his new calling by studying theology and the languages of Scripture? We consider the second of these options is the more likely one. After all, he intended to follow Hooper to Zurich, where he would start preparing for the work in the church. Spending a valuable year, and valuable money, on medicine would have felt like wasting it. Next to his studies Micron, who would not 'shrink from the severest labours', prepared his book to earn the money necessary for his move to Zurich, which he did in May, 1548.

3.1.2 Zurich

In Zurich Micron became a member of Hooper's household,[32] which had taken residence in the house of one Zingin, to whose wife Micron refers as 'mother Zingin'.[33] There Micron was under the direct influence of Hooper, Bullinger and the other Zurich theologians.[34] It was the period

---

31 Wackernagel, *Matrikel*, 50-51.
32 On March 5th, 1556, Micron wrote to Bullinger that he alone was left 'ex Hoperi familia' (Füslinus, 386). Anne and her daughter had fallen victim to the plague in December 1555, while residing in Strasbourg (Brodie, B.J., *Constructing a Godly Society: The Tamplate for a Reformed Community in the Writings of John Hooper (c.1500-1555)* (PhD University of Edinburgh, 2016), 54; Basch, R., "'Agents of Reformation": Margeret Cranmer, Anne Hooper and Elizabeth Coverdale in: Crankshaw, D.J. & Gross, G.W.C. (eds.), *Reformation Reputations. The Power of the Individual in English Reformation History* ([n.p.]: Palgrave Macmillan, 2021), 245). Micron's remark shows how closely he was allied to Hooper in Zurich. Contra Muylaert, *Shaping*, 32.
33 Micron to Bullinger, March 5th, 1556 (Füslinus, 386). Hooper refers to his stay with host and hostess Zingin in a letter to Bullinger dated April 8th 1549 (*ET*, 35; *OLER*, 55).
34 The extent of this influence, and Micron's self-perception compared to Hooper, can be seen in his later letter to Pellikan in which he trusts that Hooper may prove, by God's grace, England's Zwingli (*Si Dominus Deus dignabitur sua immensa bonitate Hopperum*

which would, above all others, shape his theological thinking. It is therefore necessary to delve more deeply into the environment the young scholar would have found himself and the theological books he would have encountered.[35]

The most important figure in the Zurich Reformation had been Huldrych Zwingli,[36] and his shadow loomed large over the decades that ensued his death.[37] He came to the city in 1519, and started using the *lectio continua* by preaching through the gospel of Matthew. The ultimate breakthrough came in 1523, in which there were two Disputations, the first on January 29th, the second on October 26 through 29. For the first Zwingli wrote his *67 Articles* and it was the city council, rather than the clergy, that would judge who was in the right. Zwingli could not be convicted of being a heretic, and was allowed to preach on as before. The second disputation was the response to increasing tensions, caused by radicals, who demanded the abolition of the mass and took part in bouts of iconoclasm. The result of the second disputation was Zwingli's *Short Christian Introduction*.[38] This was only the start of reorganising the church,[39] and it would take until 1525 before the mass was abolished. One of the most important changes was the Prophecy or *Lectorium*,[40] a Bible school in which large parts of Scripture were translated and explained. When Bullinger became the *Antistes* of Zurich (that is to say, the *primus inter pares* of the pastors)[41] in 1531, aged 27, the *Lectorium*, was turned into one of the finest educational institutions for theology in Europe, and perhaps the finest in the Reformed world. It boasted as its professors

---

inter hostes verbi sui Episcopos tueri, et adaugere spiritum suum in illo, non dubito quin Angliae sit futurus Zwinglius. (Micron to Pellikan, June 26, 1549 in Gerretsen, *Micronius*, v).

35 We refer the reader to chapter 7 for the theological influences. At this point our main interest is to outline, briefly, the overall course of the Reformation in Zurich.
36 A fine short introduction to Zwingli is: Opitz, P., *Ulrich Zwingli. Prophet, Ketzer, Pionier des Protestantismus* (Zürich: TVZ, 2015). A definitive study is: Gordon, B., *Zwingli. God's Armed Prophet* (New Haven/London: YUP, 2021).
37 For a re-evaluation of Zwingli's importance in the the First Eucharistic Controversy, see: Burnett, A. Nelson, *Debating the Sacraments*. In Micron's time, however, Zwingli would have been presented to him as the major theologian and leader of the opposition against Wittenberg-theolgoy.
38 Campi, E., 'The Reformation in Zurich' in: Burnett & Campi (eds.)., *Swiss Reformation*, 59-125, 72-76.
39 Gordon, *Swiss*, 63-68
40 Campi, 'Zurich', 77; Opitz, *Zwingli*, 66; Euler, *Couriers*, 19.
41 Cf. Ainslie, J.L, *The Doctrines of Ministerial Order in the Reformed Churches of the Sixteenth and Seventeenth Centuries* (Edinburgh: T&T Clark, 1940), 101-103.

scholars like Conrad Pellikan and Theodore Bibliander.[42] The art of exegesis, and therefore the mastery of all Scriptural languages (Hebrew, Greek, Latin), was the core of their practice, though natural sciences and ethics were also part of the curriculum.[43] It was in this institution that Micron received his theological education. His most important teacher was Heinrich Bullinger himself: in his letters Micron habitually asks Bullinger for his books and advice.[44] Bullinger's works encompass both exegesis and dogmatics, and in both fields Micron's theological knowledge and skill would have been formed first and foremost by Bullinger. Though there is considerable debate about Bullinger's status as an original theologian, there is no doubt about his incredible knowledge and his immense organising powers, all of which he used to underpin and forward Zwingli's legacy, even if he adapted aspects of it.[45] During Micron's time in Zurich, Bullinger's mind was very much turned towards the issue of the Lord's Supper, leading to the *Consensus Tigurinus* in May, 1549.[46] Micron's stay coincided with the correspondence between Bullinger and Calvin prior to this agreement. This also makes it likely that Micron both knew of, and read works by, John Calvin. Perhaps this situation is the reason why Micron's first book, *Een claer bewijs*, was a very lengthy treatise on the Lord's Supper.[47]

The time of study in Zurich was probably intense and very focussed, for Micron's stay did not even last a year. He arrived, as we have seen, in

---

42 Campi, 'Zurich', 92; 102-104.
43 Maag, K., 'Schools and Education, 1500-1600' in: Burnett & Campi (eds.), *Swiss Reformation*, 520-541, 535.
44 E.g., on October 13th, 1550 he asks for a copy of all Bullinger's sermons. August 14th, 1551 he praises the Decades 'from which we derive no ordinary assistance in edifying the church of Christ'. (*OLER*, 572; 574).
45 Benedict, *Christ's Churches*, 54-56; Campi, 'Zurich', 120; Campi, E., 'Theological Profile', in: Burnett & Campi (eds.), *Swiss Reformation*, 447-488, 450; Chung-Kim, E., 'Advocating for Poor Relief in Zurich: Heinrich Bullinger's Contribution to Religious Ideals and Policy Reforms' in: *Church History* 86/2 (2017). 311-338; Dewey, E., 'Heinrich Bullinger as Theologian: Thematic, Comprehensive, and Schematic' in: Gordon & Campi (eds.), *Architect*, 35-65, 35-36, esp. 36; Euler, *Couriers,* 32; Gordon, *Swiss Reformation*, 141
46 Campi, E., 'Zurich', 106-109. For the *Consensus Tigurinus*, its background and its theology see: *Reformation & Renaissance Review* 18/1 (2016) and Campi, E. & Reich, R. (eds.), *Consensus Tigurinus. Heinrich Bullinger und Johannes Calvin über das Abendmahl. Werden – Wertung – Bedeutung* (Zurich: TVZ, 2009).
47 In chapter 7 we will give more attention to the influence of the *Consensus Tigurinus* on Micron's theology of the Lord's Supper.

May 1548. On March the 24th, 1549 John Hooper and his household left for England. It is not certain whether Micron joined him immediately, though this seems unlikely, for Bullinger does not mention that Micron left, even though he does mention the departure of Hooper, his wife and his daughter Rachel.[48] Moreover, when Hooper writes letters to Bullinger, he habitually salutes him and the other teachers in his own name, and that of his wife and daughter. He does not include Micron until the 8th of April, when he writes from Mainz.[49] It is likely, then, that Micron was among the expected 'worthy and excellent (*bonis ac probis*) companions who are now on their way to the market (*nundinas*)'[50] which Hooper wrote about from Strasbourg on March 31st. Micron may have been joined by Johann Rudolph Stumpf, who went to England to study at Oxford. We suggest, then, that somewhere at the end of March, 1549 Micron left Zurich, and travelled to Strasbourg, probably via Basel, to join the Hooper household soon after March 31st.

So far we have seen that at an early age Micron left his native city and went to two centres of the Reformation. As far as we know, he does not refer to himself as a religious refugee, yet his life is already intertwined with that of other religious refugees. His theological influences are limited to Hooper, the teachers in Zurich and John Calvin. There may have been some influence from Myconius and the particular shape of the Reformation in Basel, yet this seems limited.

---

48 Bullinger, *Diarium*, 37.
49 Hooper to Bullinger, various dates (*ET*, 31-35; *OLER*, 48-55).
50 Hooper to Bullinger, March 31st, 1549 (*ET*, 32; translation adapted from: *OLER*, 50).

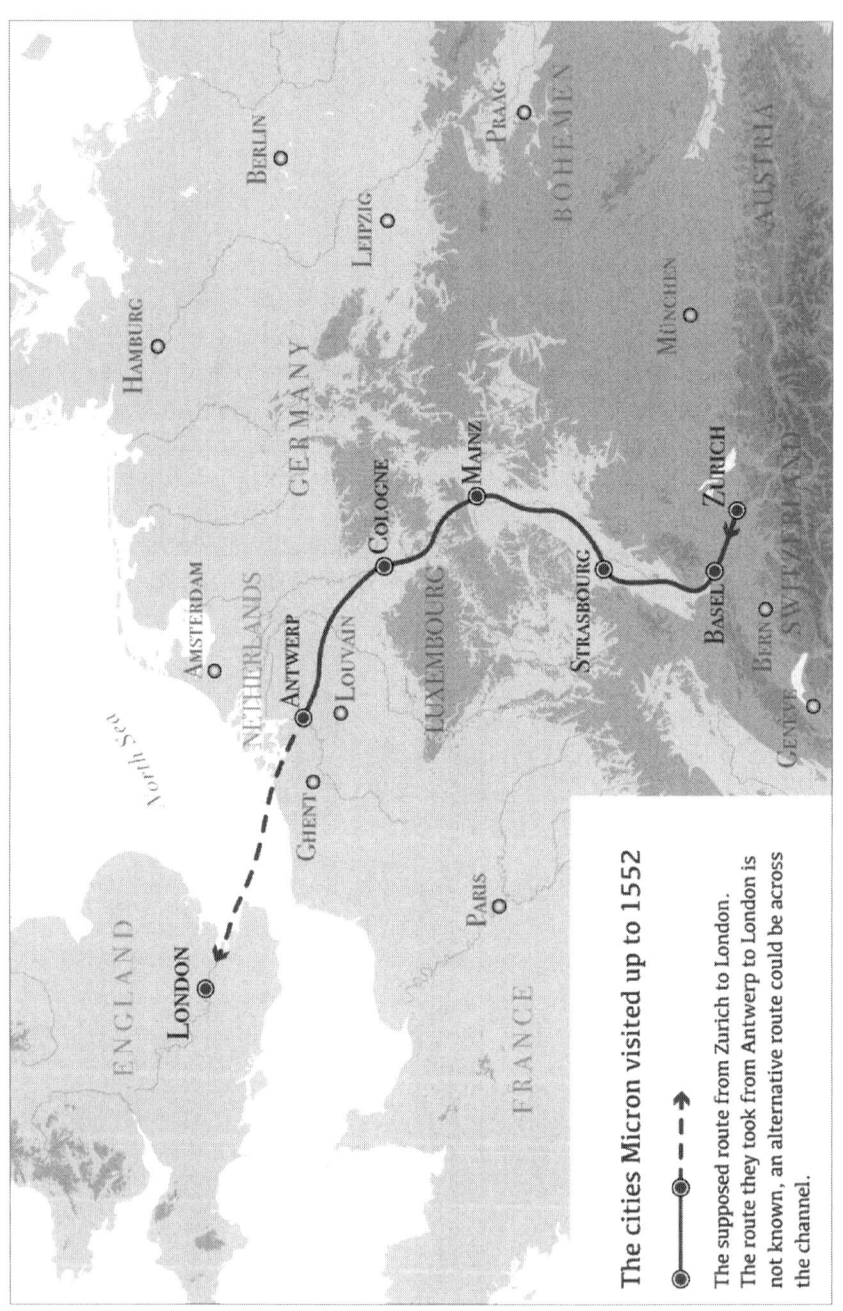

3.1.3 England

From Strasbourg Micron then went on to Mainz, where they arrived no later than April 8th, from thence to Cologne, where they arrived on the 11th of April after poor weather and having witnessed the shipwreck of two other boats. There Micron met, possibly for the first time, Jan Utenhove, who bore the letter Hooper wrote on the 14th. Jan Utenhove was, just like Micron, a native of Ghent and would go on to be the most important elder in the London Strangers' Church. He translated the New Testament and wrote metrical versions of the psalms. Later he published a report relating the journey of the refugees from England to Denmark. The language Hooper uses suggests that his acquaintance with Utenhove goes back several years.[51] On the same day the Hooper household also left the city and went to Antwerp. Micron, Anne and Rachel stayed in that city, while Hooper and Stumpf travelled to Brussels.[52] It was quite a prolonged stay, during which Micron attended a play on the idolatry of Jeroboam.[53] In the light of his quest for a 'pure service' this is an interesting detail. He wrote to Pellikan on May 3rd, and the party cannot have left the city much later, for they arrived in London on the 16th.[54]

In England they found themselves confronted with a completely different environment than the one they had left in Zurich. The history of the Church of England is, at least during its early years under Henry VIII, nothing short of a rollercoaster ride, depending more on the whims of the king, than any profound theological course.[55] However, during the reign of Edward VI the ideal of an evangelical church was being pursued firmly. First by the advisors of the boy-king and later by Edward VI himself. When Micron arrived in 1549, the crucial decisions had already been made. Peter Marshall marks 1548 as 'a tipping point'[56] because the statues were ordered to be removed from churches, the sacrament of confession became optional, and preaching was permitted only to a select few.[57] Those who did not have a license were to use the *Book of Homilies*, a

---

51 Hooper to Bullinger, April 14th, 1549 (*ET*, 35-36; *OLER*, 55-56). Cf. Pijper, F., *Jan Utenhove. Zijn leven en zijne werken* (Leiden: Adriani, 1883).
52 Hooper to Bullinger, April 26th, 1549 (*ET*, 36-37; *OLER*, 57-58).
53 Micron to Pellikan, March 3rd, 1549 (Gerretsen, *Micronius*, III).
54 Stumphius to Bullinger, [n.d.] 1549 (*ET*, 304; *OLER*, 460).
55 It would take us too far afield to give a detailed account of the decades preceding Micron's arrival in England. For more details, cf. MacCulloch, D., *Thomas Cranmer. A Life* (New Haven/London: YUP, 1996), 41-348; Marshall, P., *Heretics and Believers. A History of the English Reformation* (New Haven/London: YUP, 2017), 203-302.
56 Marshall, *Heretics*, 314.
57 Marshall, *Heretics*, 315-321.

collection of sermons, edited and partly authored by Thomas Cranmer, in which the evangelical core dogma of justification through faith featured largely.[58] Moreover, on the 21st of January 1549, the Act of Uniformity had been passed, making the *Book of Common Prayer* the only legitimate service book in the entire kingdom. The first copies were printed in March, and the Prayer book was mandatory by June of the same year.[59] Though Micron, having the Zurich church in mind, thought the reforms that were taking place too few and too superficial,[60] it is nonetheless worth our time to look at the intentions of the Edwardian reforms more closely, as they shed light on the reason the Strangers' Churches were permitted to have their own services. When it comes to the principal motives of Cranmer's approach to the *Book of Common Prayer*, the analyses can be summarised as follows: The language had to be simple and understandable for all hearers, all its rituals and doctrines had to be founded on the Bible, the congregation had to be involved in the worship (rather than being spectators), which radically reduced the rites and mystery of worship.[61] However, Cranmer knew that reform comes slowly. The people should not be pressed, but weaned towards new doctrine.[62] As such the first Prayer book was also a catechetical book, 'teaching people *about* God in the midst of their prayers *to* God'.[63] This is also the view of

---

[58] For more on the *Book of Homilies* cf. Griffiths, J., *The Two Books of Homilies Appointed to be Read in Churches* (Oxford: OUP, 1859); MacCulloch, *Cranmer*, 372-375. A recent critical edition of the homilies is Bray, G., *The Books of Homilies: A Critical Edition* (Cambridge: James Clarke & Company, 2017). For a reading of Cranmer's sermon on the doctrine of salvation within his overall theological development: Null, A., *Thomas Cranmer's Doctrine of Repentance. Renewing the Power to Love* (Oxford: OUP, 2000).

[59] For a general introduction to the *Book of Common Prayer*: Hefling, Ch. & Shattuck, C. (eds.), *The Oxford Guide to The Book of Common Prayer. A Worldwide Survey* (New York: OUP, 2006). Especially part 1, 2 and 6. For a more low-level introduction: Jacobs, A., *The Book of Common Prayer. A Biography* (Princeton: PUP, 2013).

[60] Micron is often decidedly negative about the reforms in England, cf. Micron to Bullinger, May 20th, August 8th and October 13th, 1550 (*ET*, 364-366, 368-373; *OLER*, 558-562, 566-573).

[61] Atherstone, A. 'Reforming Worship: Lessons from Luther to Cranmer' in: *Churchman* summer 2018, 105-122, 144; Davies, H., *Worship and Theology in England. 1. From Cranmer to Hooker 1534-1603* (Princeton: PUP, 1970), 38-39; Dickens, A.G., *The English Reformation* (London/Glasgow: Collins Fontana Press, 19714), 341; Loach, J. (edited by George Bernard & Penry Williams), *Edward VI* (New Haven/London: YUP, 1999), 51. For a more elaborate exposition of Cranmer's approach, see MacCulloch, *Cranmer*, 410-421.

[62] Cf. Marshall, *Heretics*, 325.

[63] Lindsay, M., 'Thomas Cranmer and the *Book of Common Prayer*: Theological Education, Liturgy, and the Embodiment of Prosper's Dictum' in: *Colloquium* 47/2 (2015), 195-207. Quote on p. 207.

Timothy Rosendale. In his book, which is one of the finest on the reforms during Edward's reign, he shows how on the one hand the reform encountered fierce opposition, and on the other hand it was embraced by others. His view is that the *Book of Common Prayer* was the attempt to 'weave a complex textual matrix of identity which held in productive tension both the imperatives of the hierarchical nation and the prerogatives of the evangelical [individualistic] soul.' Or, as he says later on, it sought to stabilise 'by forcibly imposing a degree of uniformity and coherence on a nation of Christian individuals'.[64] That is to say, through the *Book of Common Prayer*. The government sought both to form and to control the people: Shaping the collective identity of the nation anew by offering it a uniform expression of religion. The same can be said about the *Book of Homilies*.[65] Despite these efforts, and – alternatively – due to these efforts, the summer of 1549 was one of insurrection upon insurrection, most famously Kett's Rebellion in Norfolk.[66] The liberty and individualism that came with the reforms should not lead to absolute freedom of thought and the disrespect for authority. Hence the need to form a new identity.[67]

It is doubtful whether Micron knew anything about these considerations when he and his fellow refugees were allowed to form their own church. It is estimated that there were some five thousand speaking the 'German' tongue, and that in the capital the refugee congregation numbered six to eight hundred.[68] Their reasons for emigration were varied:

---

64 Rosendale, T., *Liturgy and Literature in the Making of Protestant England* (Cambridge: CUP, 2007), 2-116. Quotations on 5; 14. Rosendale derives his theory to a large extent from Cranmer's treatise *Of Ceremonies, why some be abolished and some retayned* at the end of the Prayer book (Rosendale, *Liturgy*, 14-15).
  The importance of liturgy in forming the identity and faith of a congregation is currently being re-discovered in the field of practical theology, cf. Schaeffer, H., *Kerk om te vieren* (Kampen: Summum, 2020), especially pages 131-143 and ch.7.
65 MacCulloch, *Cranmer*, 372-373.
66 Marshall, *Heretics*, 328-335; MacCulloch, D. *Tudor Church Militant. Edward VI and the Protestant Reformation* ([n.p.] Penguin Books, 2001), 119; 126; 140. For an account that focusses on the polititcal aspects of the various rebellions, see: Wood, A., *The 1549 Rebellions and the Making of Early Modern England* (Cambridge: CUP, 2007).
67 Rosendale, T., *Liturgy*, 34-57; MacCulloch, *Tudor Church*, 127-130. Note that MacCulloch says that 'there was little sense of any distinctive English ecclesiastical identity' (*Tudor Church*, 79). His point there is the 'internationalism' of the Church of England under Edward VI. That is in itself an identity which had to be created.
68 Pettegree, *Foreign Protestant Communities in Sixteenth-Century London* (Oxford: OUP, 1986), 24; cf. also, Gerretesen, *Micronius*, 8-9. For our account of the Strangers' Church we mostly rely on Pettegree's study, which supercedes Lindeboom, J, *Austin Friars. Geschiedenis van de Nederlandse Hervormde Gemeente te Londen 155-1950* (The Hague: Martinus Nijhoff, 1950) and Schelven, A.A. van, *De Nederduitsche*

it could be either religious, economical or even due to over-population.[69] This group of emigrants already organised their own church services in the summer of 1549. Micron started preaching in these services no later than the spring of 1550.[70]

In April of that year John Hooper, with whom Micron was still living, was offered the bishopric of Gloucester. Let us listen to how Micron tells what happened afterwards:

> The king, as you know, has nominated him to the bishopric of Gloucester, which however he refused to accept, unless he could be altogether relieved from all appearance of popish superstition. Here then a question immediately arises as to the form of the oath, which the bishops have ordered to be taken in the name of God, the saints, and the gospels; which impious oath Hooper positively refused to take. So when he appeared before the king in the presence of the council, Hooper convinced the king by many arguments that the oath should be taken in the name of God alone, who know[s] the heart. This took place on the 20th of July. It was so agreeable to the godly king, that with his own pen he erased the clause of the oath which sanctioned swearing by any creature.[71]

Another issue concerning the vestments to be worn during the confirmation, proved to be more troublesome. After initial success, Hooper saw himself confronted with fierce opposition, leading to what is known as the Vestment Controversy. Wilson suggests this has everything to do with the institution of the Strangers' Churches.[72] To understand this, we have to go back in time a little. On the thirteenth of May, 1550, John à Lasco had arrived in England, and, after staying with Cranmer at Lambeth for a week, he moved on to London. There he pursued the 'right of legal non-conformity', as Rodgers calls it,[73] i.e. the right for foreigners not to be held to the Act of Uniformity, but to organise their own churches to the standards of God's Word. John à Lasco himself would be the superintendent

---

    Vluchtelingenkerken der XVIe eeuw in Engeland en Duitsland in hunne beteekenis voor de Reformatie in de Nederlanden (The Hague: Martinus Nijhoff, 1908).
69 Eβer, R., *Niederländische Exulanten im England des 16. und frühen 17. Jahrhunderts* (Berlin: Duncker & Humblot, 1996), 21-29.
70 Gerretsen, *Micronius*, 10.
71 Micron to Bullinger, August 28th, 1550 (*ET*, 368-369; translation adapted from: *OLER*, 566-567).
72 Wilson, R.P., *John Hooper and the English Reformation under Edward VI, 1547-1553* (PhD Queen's University, Kingston Ontario, 1994), 233-263
73 Rodgers, D.W., *John à Lasco in England* (New York: Peter Lang, 1994), 29.

of the Strangers' Churches.[74] This right was granted in the summer of 1550: first, on June 29, they were given Austin Friars, and on July 24, the Royal Charter, granting them the privilege of following their own ordinances, was issued.[75] Micron was to be one of the ministers of the new church. This non-conformity was not to everyone's liking, and Nicholas Ridley, bishop of London, resented the idea of having non-conformers in his diocese.[76;77] Nonetheless, all seemed well: John Hooper had gone to Somerset to visit his family on June 2 and Micron himself got married to Cecilia on July 1.[78]

Before we proceed to the conclusion of this episode, we address the question why the foreigners were granted the charter. The reasons are similar to the considerations regarding the *Book of Common Prayer*. Here, too, the main reason was to keep a grip on the inhabitants of the isle. It would form the religious thoughts of its attendants as a protection against heretical tendencies among the refugees by their liturgical ordinances (one of them, Joan Bocher, had been burnt for Unitarianism)[79;80] Seeing the *Forma ac Ratio/Ordinancien* as having (politically) the same objective, at least partially, as the *Book of Common Prayer* sheds a new light on their importance in the refugee theology. It was their distinct purpose to, in Rosendale's words, weave a textual matrix of identity. To really value what is being professed in the forms, and consequently shapes the beliefs and identity of the hearers, it is essential to understand the theology underlying the ordinances. It is commonly assumed that the second reason for allowing the Stranger Churches was to have a 'perfect' model of what a Reformed church looked like, as an example for the reforms in the Church

---

74 Rodgers, *John à Lasco*, 27-29.
75 Rodgers, *John à Lasco*, 28.
76 Pettegree, *Foreign*, 24-33;38. Cf., also, Micron to Bullinger, August 28th, 1550 (*ET*, 369-371; *OLER*, 568-570). One of the ways by which the institution of the churches was opposed was delay: the keys to Austin Friars were not handed over because the repairs were not finished. The Strangers' Churches even had to use a diffent building throughout the fall of that year.
77 For an introduction to Ridley, see: Jenkins, D.L., *Whither God Brings Us. Cambridge and the Reformation Martyrs* (Attleborough: Charenton Reformed Publishing, 2018), 223-242. Jenkins judges that Ridley saw a dangerous seperation of church and state, and hence the threat of chaos as in Münster, behind Hooper's opposition (234-235).
78 Micron to Bullinger, June 4th, 1550 (*ET*, 367-368; *OLER*, 565); Utenhove to Bullinger, June 29th, 1550 (Pijper, *Utenhove*, LXVIII); Gerretesen, *Micronius*, 35.
Unfortunately, these sources do not give us any other information than Cecilia's name.
79 MacCulloch, *Tudor Church*, 141; 173
80 MacCulloch, *Cranmer*, 477; MacCulloch, *Tudor Church*, 141 Rodgers, *John à Lasco*, 30-31.

of England.⁸¹ However, this has been challenged by Silke Muylaert.⁸² She thinks à Lasco added this reason later. Though her case seems strong (there is no mention of this goal in the royal charter) there is a question that remains. There was a strong desire for conformity in England, as was seen above. Why would the king allow – indeed, why would Cranmer stimulate – the erection of a non-conformist church if they believed this was a less-reformed church model? It still seems more likely that Cranmer, in his steady pace, encouraged the establishment of a more reformed church, which in turn could not function as anything less than an example. Nicholas Ridley, as we explained, did not like this. The central issue in the fall of that year was this: Should all be forced to conform, or should a freedom of conscience allow for the possibility of non-conformity? The cause of the Strangers' Churches and the outcome of the Vestment Controversy were closely intertwined. Indeed, though the church had been established, and ministers, elders and deacons had been ordained, Micron feared that they would be forced to celebrate the sacraments according to the English liturgy, 'which are intolerable to all godly persons.'⁸³ Yet, Micron and Hooper (who, at that time, no longer lived in the same house) would not allow any popish residues. The struggle between conformity and non-conformity came to a climax at the start of 1551, when Hooper was first held captive at Lambeth, then in Fleetwood prison, before giving in and taking up his office as bishop.⁸⁴ However, despite Hooper's surrender and the Royal Charter, the foreigners would have to wait until the end of the year 1551 before they could put their ordinances into practice.⁸⁵

It is likely that during the period between the summer of 1550 and the end of 1551, the leaders of the Stranger Churches were working on the several forms, catechisms, books and confessions that shaped the liturgical and doctrinal profile of the church and would be published in subsequent years.⁸⁶ Who were these leaders? There is of course John à Lasco, the

---

81 Pettegree, *Foreign*, 35
82 Muylaert, *Shaping*, 35.
83 Micron to Bullinger, October 13th, 1550 (*ET*, 370-373; *OLER*, 570-573).
84 Pettegree, *Foreign*, 42-43; Ross, D.S., *The Role of John Hooper in the Religious Controversies of the Reign of Edward VI in England* (PhD The University of Iowa, 1968), 192-196.
    For detailed accounts of the Vestments controversy, see: Primus, J.H., *The Vestments Controversy. An Historical Study of the Earliest Tensions within the Church of England in the Reigns of Edward VI and Elizabeth I* (Kampen: Kok, 1960), 3-67; Ross, *Role*, 159-196.
85 Pettegree, *Foreign*, 58.
86 Cf. Utenhove's remark in a letter to Bullinger on April 9, 1551: 'Our church, moreover, is going on very favourably, excepting only that the bishops will not yet allow us the

superintendent, Marten Micron and Walter Delenus, the ministers of the Dutch Church, Francis Perussel and Richard Gallus, the ministers of the French church, and Jan Utenhove, elder of the Dutch church. John à Lasco commented on Micron's work attitude: 'I am now engaged in a work on the ceremonies of our Church...I am not writing, however, without a Theseus, I mean our Micron, for whose presence here in our Church I am greatly thankful.'[87] À Lasco refers to Micron as Theseus, the Greek hero who defeated the Minotaur. In Greek mythology Theseus was known for strength, cleverness, wisdom and sense of justice.[88] Not only does this show that à Lasco greatly valued Micron's work, it also suggests he was the one who did a substantial amount of the task at hand. Perhaps it is not too bold a statement to say that when it came to the theological aspects, Micron showed the way out of the maze of possibilities and choices to be made, leading and forming the church with a steady and wise hand.[89] Much has been written about the various documents originating from these churches, and it is not necessary to repeat the discussion here;[90] rather, we will focus on Micron's involvement, which limits it to his three ecclesiological publications: the *Ordinancien*, the *Kleyne Cathechismus* and the *Korte Ondersoeckinghe*. At the same time he was also working on *Een claer bewijs*, a study on the Lord's Supper.

For the liturgical and ecclesiastical documents it is difficult, if not impossible, to ascertain to what extent they flowed from Micron's mind and pen. In all likelihood all of the documents published by the church are works of collaboration, with various 'first authors' who drew up drafts, which would have been discussed, amended, redrafted and going through

---

pure administration of the sacraments. The word, however, is proclaimed in all its purity, with the greatest benefit to the church, by our friend Martin Micronius, who preaches in a popular manner, like the clergy at Zurich, and is at the same time a cautious interpreter of the word, introducing nothing that is forced or trifling, and which does not tend to entire edification. A system of discipline (*disciplina*) is now established by us, as far as we have it in our power; as a part of which is to be considered the catechism which we are now preparing (...)' (*ET*, 381; *OLER*, 586-587

87 Quote from Rodger, *John à Lasco*, 53.
88 Duys-Reitsma, S.J., *Helleense Mythos* (Amsterdam: H.J. Paris, 1956), 149-161.
89 Cf., also, Pettegree, *Foreign*, 73, where he says: 'It is fair to say that Lasco's talent was fundamentally organizational rather than theological: theologically he was heavy-handed and not always clear-headed, and one may suspect the guiding hand of Micron steering the church towards a safe orthodoxy of doctrine.'
90 Studies include: Becker, J., *Gemeindeordnung und Kirchenzucht. Johannes a Lascos Kirchenordnung für London (1555) und die reformierte Konfessionsbildung* (Leiden/Boston: Brill, 2007), 12n34; 36-39; Dankbaar, W.F., 'Inleiding' in:*Ord.*, 1-30, 6-12; Pettegree, *Foreign*, 54-58; 73; Rodgers, *John à Lasco*, 33-36; 51-57; Springer, M.S., *Restoring Christ's Church. John a Lasco and the* Forma ac ratio (Aldershot: Ashgate, 2007), 5; 45-49.

the same process again. This is true especially for the *Ordinancien*. Its relation to à Lasco's *Forma ac Ratio* has been debated.[91] However, both books were published after the refugees left England and were, already, under attack in the Second Eucharistic Controversy, as contemporary scholarship calls it.[92] Neither is likely to be the exact book of ordinances used by the London church. Nonetheless, Micron's is probably closer to the original because his book was published very shortly after leaving England, giving him less time to adapt it. By the time à Lasco published the *Forma ac Ratio*, the Second Eucharistic Controversy was much more heated and à Lasco himself was in the middle of it.[93] Moreover, Micron's book contains the Dutch documents, i.e. the language in which they would have been used in the congregation.[94] The best reconstruction seems to be as follows: in the process of building the church the various theologians devised Latin drafts which were to be discussed and amended, thereafter translated for the use in the churches. Who is the original author of any given form cannot be ascertained. John à Lasco would probably have taken the lead as superintendent, though what we argued above might mean that the overall framework and ecclesiology was framed by Micron, or both together. Possibly, they divided the task of writing the several parts amongst themselves and the other leading men in the church. Whatever the exact origin may be, the *Ordinancien* as we have them, fully represent Micron's own thought, since he was the last 'editor' and they, also, come closest to what the London church would have looked like in practice.[95]

Having started with the last of the ecclesiological documents to have

---

91 See above, note 90.
92 See below, note 133.
93 See below, the description of the Micron's time in East Frisia. Pettegree suggests the *Forma ac Ratio* was published as a contribution to the Controversy (Pettegree, A. 'The London Exile Community and the Second Sacramentartian Controversy, 1553-1560' in: *Archiv für Reformationsgeschichte* 78 (1987), 223-252, 239
94 This is, by the way, a strong argument against Becker (*Gemeindeordnung*, 37), who claims that 1) Micron adapted the *Ordinancien* for use in the Norden congregation, and 2) that à Lasco's *Forma ac Ratio* can easily be used in the congregation. Versus 1), we point towards Micron's adaptation of *Een korte ondersoeckinghe*, which he translated for the use in het Norden congregation. If his aim had been to use the *Ordinancien* he would have published a translated version. Versus 2) we question whether a Latin church order is suitable for use in a vernacular service.
95 This reconstruction suggests they are not a summary (contra Muylaert, *Shaping*, 50) or a translation of the *Forma ac Ratio* (contra Spohnholz, J., *The Convent of Wesel. The Event that Never was and the Invention of Tradition* (Cambridge: CUP, 2017/2020), 262).

been printed, we now turn to Micron's *Kleyne Cathechismus*, printed October 8, 1552. Of this book we can be fairly certain that it is entirely Micron's own.⁹⁶ Obviously, before being adopted it would have been discussed and possibly needed to be corrected in a few places, yet it was well and truly Micron's catechism. The purpose of the catechism was the education of the youth who were not yet old enough to understand the larger catechism written by à Lasco.⁹⁷ The last liturgical work is the *Korte Ondersoeckinghe*. The authorship has been heavily debated. Kuyper named à Lasco as its primary author, Gerretsen opted for Micron, Dankbaar thinks Micron is the more likely option, and in the short title catalogue it is habitually ascribed to Micron.⁹⁸ Another argument greatly in favour of Micronian authorship is the English translation by Thomas Cottesford. However, it also presents us with a problem that asks for an explanation. The English version seems to be based on *Ein kort underricht*, an adaptation of the *Ondersoeckinghe*. Micron published *Underricht* in 1554, when he was a pastor in Norden. Oddly enough, though, the English translation dates the preface, an exact translation of the one in *Ein kurt underricht*, on December 8, 1552.⁹⁹ Of course, it is possible Cottesford or the publisher sought to antedate the publication, yet it is unclear how this would have given the book more authority. We propose the hypothesis that in *Ein kort underricht* and *A short and faythful instruction* we come closer to the original document drafted by Micron in preparation of the *Korte ondersoeckinghe*. This earlier version, possibly in

---

96 When Muylaert says that Micron wrote the catechism 'in cooperation with Jan Utenhove' (*Shaping*, 46) she probably means that Utenhove wrote the original preface.
97 *Ord.*, 67-68. When the children were five years old, their names were written in a book. The first stage in their education was learning the Lord's Prayer, Apostolic Creed and Ten Commandments by heart. When they were able to do so, they started learning Micron's catechism, followed by à Lasco's. When they were fourteen they were expected to publicly profess their faith.
98 Cf. Gerretsen, *Micronius*, 23-27; Dankbaar, 'Inleiding', 4; USTC #408046; 415404; 415405; 421508; 428355; 428356; 428389; 505890; 2212068.
99 Micron, M., *A short and faythful instruction, gathered out of holy Scripture composed in questions and answeres, fort he edifying and comfort of the symple Christianes, whych intende worthely to receyue the holy supper of the Lorde* ([Emden: Ctematius, 1556]).
The short title catalogue ascribes the translation to Thomas Cranmer. The book itself only has the initials T.C. Thomas Cottesford translated Micron's *Antitheses* (Leaver, R., 'A Unique Broadsheet in the Scheide Library, Princeton' in: *PBSA* 83/3 (1989), 337-352), and is the more likely candidate to have translated the *Korte Ondersoeckinghe*. Heijting is of the same opinion (Heijting, W., *De catechismi en confessies in de Nederlandse Reformatie tot 1585. Deel 1: Tekst* (Nieuwkoop: De Graaf Publishers, 1989), 91, 210. Note, however, that Heijting sees both *Ein kort underricht* and *A short and faythful instruction* as translations of the *Een korte ondersoeckinghe* (p. 206-210).

use in the Dutch church and as such translated by Cottesford, eventually evolved into the *Korte ondersoeckinghe*. When he was in Norden, Micron reverted to his original version. This would mean that, even though Micron subscribed to the content of the *Korte ondersoeckinghe*, what we find in *Ein kort underricht* is the purer expression of his own thoughts. Nonetheless, both versions express Micron's line of thought, but they are two distinct works, no matter how much they may have influenced each other.

The last work published by Micron in England is his book on the Lord's Supper, *Een claer bewijs*, his first theological book to have been published. This book truly holds its own among the avalanche of works written upon the subject. It was clearly influenced by Swiss theology and as a whole aligns with the Consensus Tigurinus, though inclining towards a 'Zurich' interpretation of these articles.[100] For our purposes the last pages of the book, chapter 14 of part three, are especially important. It is titled: 'whether the believers are allowed to have any social intercourse with the aforesaid Romish insults (*lachteringen*) of Christ's Supper'. In this chapter Micron refutes the arguments brought forward by Nicodemites and urges his readers to 'flee from Babylon'. The book we are studying in this dissertation may be seen as an elaboration of this chapter after many years of thought and study. Thus, Micron's last book is the conclusion to the ecclesiology set out in his first book.

We linger in England a little while longer, merely to highlight some biographical details, ignoring the various political upheavals, especially around Somerset.[101] Micron's strong friendship with Hooper seems to have become less intense due to the distance and work load. There are no surviving letters between them. It is known that Utenhove visited Hooper in his diocese,[102] but we do not know whether Micron did the same. Micron, however, does write to Bullinger, asking him to advise Hooper to 'unite prudence and Christian levity to the severity of discipline.'[103] Apparently this was something Micron feared might happen. It shows, moreover, that Micron was not rigid in his application of discipline.

---

100 Cf. Willems, *Maarten de Kleyne*; Willems, W.O.R., *Is is Is? Apologeticum Scriptorum van Maarten de Kleyne na een disputu rondom het "Nachtmael des Heren" met Joachim Westphal in Hamburg anno 1554* (PhD University for Protestant Theology Brussels, 1993), 21-23; 133-136; 206-207.
 For a reading of the *Consensus Tigurinus* in relation to Micron, see ch. 7.
101 A fine study of the politics around this time is: Ives, E., *Lady Jane Grey. A Tudor Mystery* (Chichester: Wiley-Blackwell, 2011), 1-30; 96-168.
102 Utenhove to Bullinger, October 12, 1552 (*ET*, 384-385; *OLER*, 591).
103 Micron to Bullinger, November 7, 1551 (*ET*, 375; *OLER*, 577).

However, none of this means they were not still great friends; In his last letter to à Lasco, Hooper says: 'salute my old and godly friend, master[104] Martin'.[105] We get a glimpse of how Micron experienced his time abroad when he writes to Bullinger: 'The multitude of believers [in London] (praised be God!) is increasing every day. Should we be permitted, by God's blessing, to go on in this way for some years, we shall attack our Flanders (*nostram Belgicam*) with fiery darts, and, I hope, take it by storm, that, antichrist being put to flight or at least weakened, our Saviour may reign there.'[106] Clearly he still felt a strong connection to his native country, framed his stay abroad as having religious motives and saw the rule of Charles V as foreign oppression.

In July 1551 à Lasco was hit by the sweating sickness,[107] despite having been invited by Cranmer to Lambeth Palace to avoid getting ill.[108] He survived the disease; however, a year later à Lasco's wife passed away,[109] and when Utenhove fell ill in December 1552 his demise was feared as well.[110] The church was upset by doctrinal debates in 1552, when Walter Delenus wanted the article confessing Christ's descent into hell to be removed from the creed. This storm rapidly blew over and the church was in calm waters again.[111] In April 1553 Micron was unaware of the tempest ahead: he wrote to Bullinger that even though Satan and his episkopoi tried to undermine the church, she was yet stable.[112] Little did he know that Edward VI, the boy king, was suffering from an illness that would cause his death. He passed away on July 6th, the plot to make Jane Grey queen failed, and Mary Tudor acceded to the throne.[113] At first she seemed to be lenient towards the

---

104 In the earlier letters Hooper does not refer to Micron as 'master' (original 'D.'). There is no proof of Micron attending either Cambridge or Oxford, which probably means 'master' was added to Micron's name due to his office in the Church.
105 Hooper to Bullinger, November 25th, 1553 (*ET*, 65; *OLER*, 101-102).
 In 1559 Micron says about Hooper 'sanctae memoriae vir' (Micron to Bullinger February 16, 1559 (Gerretsen, *Micronius*, XIV)).
106 Micron to Bullinger, October 13, 1550 (*ET*, 371; *OLER*, 571).
 Muylaert does not give any attention to this passage in her discussion of Micron's perceived ambivelent stance towards violence and submission to the government (Muyleart, *Shaping*, 128-131).
107 Micron to Bullinger, August 14, 1551 (*ET*, 374; *OLER*, 575-576).
108 MacCulloch, *Cranmer*, 483. On page 487 MacCulloch states à Lasco's wife also fell ill. Micron makes no mention of this.
109 Micron to Bullinger, February 18th, 1553 (*ET*, 378; *OLER*, 581).
110 Pijper, *Utenhove*, 99. Micron to Bullinger, February 18th, 1553 & Utenhove to Bullinger, June 7th, 1553 (*ET*, 378; 385-386; *OLER*, 582; 593).
111 Pettegree, *Foreign*, 51-52; Lindeboom; *Austin Friars*, 18-19.
112 Micron to Bullinger, April 14th, 1553 (Gerretsen, *Micronius*, VII).
113 A fine reconstruction is given in Ives, *Jane Grey*. What is especially interesting is his

protestant cause, but this changed in the fall and many members of the Dutch church, fearing persecution, fled the country. On September 17th John à Lasco, Utenhove and Marten Micron, together with approximately 175 members of their congregation, embarked in two ships, 'The Moor' and 'The Small Crow', and left the country.[114] The refugees were dispersed again.[115]

3.1.4 From England to Norden

How many times will the scattered have thought of Psalm 2, which was sung at their departure by those who stayed behind: The nations rage, yet peace is found by those who kiss the Lord's Son. Peace was eventually found, but not before many hardships were endured. However, this is not the place to give a detailed account of the journey; rather, we will focus on Micron's attitude: both lenient and inflexible. Lenient in what he allowed others, inflexible as to what he would bow under himself. After a storm cast the ships apart, Micron's boat ended up on the isle Flekkerøy from whence they travelled on and were cast upon Marstrandt, where after a few days à Lasco, Micron and Utenhove embarked on a small ship to travel on to Denmark. They arrived in Helsingør (i.e. Elsinore) and from thence the three men travelled on to Koldingen, where King Christian III resided.[116] They reached their destination on November 8, 1553. It was their hope to find favourable circumstances, akin to what they experienced in England; circumstances which would, once more, allow them to erect

---

claim that it was Mary who led a coup against the rightful queen Jane, rather than the other way around. The refugees seem to have been wholly uninvolved.

114 *SFN*, 39-40; *Bericht*, 25.
It is necessary here to make a remark concerning the trustworthiness of the sources. The journey and debates have only been described by Utenhove and Marten Micron. Obviously, when it comes to the attitude of Lutherans, the content of their sermons, the arguments they use, we must be on our guard to believe what Utenhove and Micron say about this. However, we may rely that the facts concerning dates, places and persons involved are accurate. Moreover, the content of what the refugees themselves say is reliable. Generally, then, we can allow their narrations as evidence, albeit we should not uncritically accept what they tell about the occurances in Lutheran areas.
The journey has received considerable attention, yet the authors of various articles do little more than summarise Utenhove's narration (cf., e.g., Norwood, 'The London Dutch Refugees', 64-72; Pettegree, 'London Exile Community', 225-229; Pijper, *Utenhove*, 100-113). Pettegree estimates that the Strangers' Church consisted of some 4000 people around that time, making the 175 who embarked a very small number (Pettegree, 'London Exile Community', 225n8).

115 Micron refers to their state as *dissipationem* (*AS*, fol. 47 (*Is is is*, 72)).

116 The largest part of the group that stayed behind went to Copenhagen (Pijper, *Utenhove*, 110)

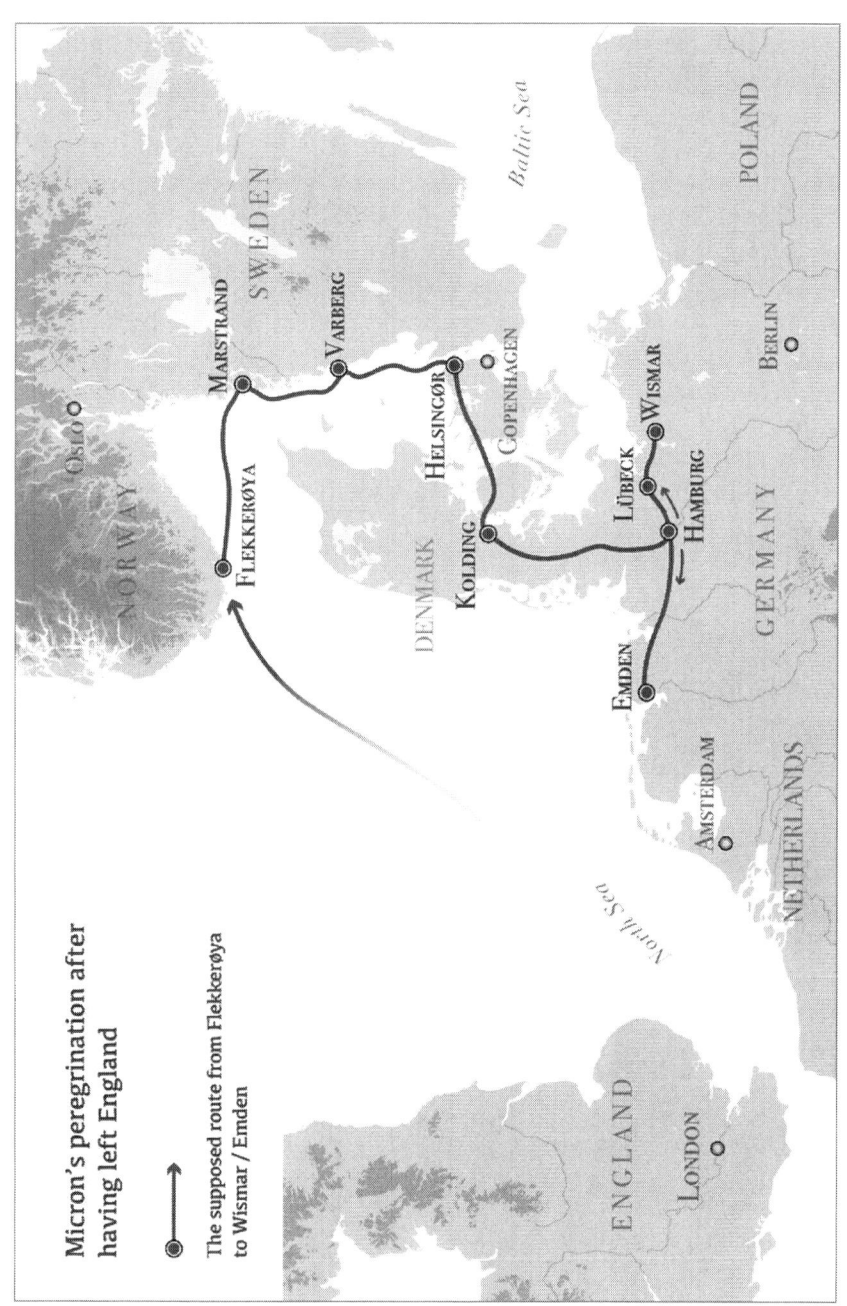

a Stranger Church. Perhaps this was somewhat naïve. The course towards a Lutheran state had been a difficult process in Denmark, not in the least due to a civil war. The outcome was that Lutheranism would be the sole permitted religion. Moreover, Christian III was himself strictly and devoutly Lutheran. The church in Denmark was by no means independent from the government, and Christian III himself intervened in ecclesiastical affairs. Additionally, he 'detested theological debate…the truth…was to be found in the Lutheran understanding of Christianity as expressed in the Lutheran confessional writings, and it was accordingly superfluous or even directly harmful to discuss it.'[117] These, then, were not the favourable circumstances the refugees were hoping for. Even so, they were allowed to appear before the king, whom they presented a letter. Micron subscribed this with: '*dissipata in Anglia Ecclesiae Germanicae minister*', minister of the Dutch Church dispersed in England.[118] On the fifteenth they were given the king's answer: they could not practice their own ordinances, but were to follow the ordinances of Denmark which were according to the Word of God.[119] The three church leaders replied that different ceremonies can be allowed, as they can both be formed by the Word of God in seeking the edification of the church, for which the ceremonies were instituted.[120] It was, however, to no avail, and they were ordered to leave the country forthwith. They could not return to their congregation, which had gone to Copenhagen, but were to leave the country via Holstein. The three men wrote their flock a letter in which they informed them that à Lasco and Utenhove would travel on to Emden, Micron would await them at Lübeck or 'the surrounding area' (*in finitimis eius partibus*).[121] Hence, on their journey south Micron left à Lasco and Utenhove to travel towards Lübeck.[122]

---

117 This account is based on: Andersen, N.K., 'The Reformation in Scandinavia and the Baltic' in: Elton, G.R. (ed.), *The New Cambridge Modern History. Volume II: The Reformation, 1520-1559* 2nd Edition (Cambridge: CUP, 1990), 144-171, 144-152; Grell, O.P., 'From Popular, Evangelical Movement to Lutheran Reformation in Denmark. A Case of Two Reformations' in: *Archiv für Reformationsgeschichte* 102 (2011), 33-58; Schwarz Lausten, M. (translated by Frederick H. Cryer), *A Church History of Denmark* (London/New York: Routledge, 2002), 90-120. Quotation taken from: Schwartz Lausten, *Denmark*, 118.
118 *SFN*, 47. Note that dissipata should be dissipatae.
119 *SFN*, 49 / *Bericht*, 47.
120 *SFN*, 50 / *Bericht*, 49-50. 'Primum, quod varietas ceremoniarum non obstet, quo minus omnes verbo Dei sint consentaneae, modò ut secundum fontes verbi Divini ad aedificationem ecclesiarum instituantur…'
121 *SFN*, 76-77 / *Bericht*, 107-108.
122 *AS*, fol. 48 (*Is is is*, 73). Willems translates the verb *diuellimur* somewhat strongly:

Micron arrived in Hamburg on December 7, where he found a part of his congregation and attended several public lectures and theological introductions (*Theoligicas praelectiones*).[123] In search of his sheep the shepherd travelled to Lübeck and Wismar, but he did not find them, for it was winter and it was supposed they could not leave Denmark in that season. Micron decided to go to Emden, where he arrived on December 28.[124] There he was found by Bartholomeüs Huysman, who told him that Hermes Backerel had been disputing with Menno Simons in Wismar and requested Micron's help. Micron joined him right away, not so much to seek a debate, but because he had also heard that the refugees had been forced to leave Denmark despite the cold and had landed in Wismar and Lübeck after a life-threatening journey. Among them were his wife (and possibly children).[125] In Wismar[126] a confrontation with the Lutheran pastors, Vincentius and Block, ensues. Noteworthy is how Micron talks about himself: 'We are Christians, who, in their voluntary exile for Christ's gospel and name, bear a most heavy cross (*Christianos esse, qui propter Christi evangelium ac nomen, in voluntario suo exilio durissimam crucem sustineant*).'[127] In the meantime they had also had a dispute with Menno Simons, followed by another one on February 15. In the end the Lutheran civic powers expelled them from the city; however, not without accepting a last supplication written by Micron. This is an interesting document, for in it we read how Micron saw himself. He starts the document with '*nos miseri peregrini*'. *Peregrinus* is a difficult word to translate, having various shades of meaning, which range from 'alien' to 'one with no civilian rights' or even 'pilgrim'.[128] It is the term the refugees most commonly used for themselves.[129] We have already seen how Micron spoke of *dissipatio* and *exilium*. Combining that with *peregrini*, the translation of *peregrinus* is

---

'rezen er meningsverschillen'. When the accounts of Utenhove and Micron are put next to each other it is more likely that their seperation was intentional.

123 AS, fol. 49 (*Is is is*, 74).
124 AS, fol. 49-50 (*Is is is*, 74-75).
125 The list of travellers is given in *SFN*, 89n1. It reads 'on the ship to Wismar…Cecilia de Kleyne, with her sister and two children'. Whether the children were Cecilia's or her sister's is unclear. The former is more likely. It could well be that Micron travelled to Wismar first because his wife and children had landed there. Compare Micron's own account in *AS*, fol.50 (*Is is is*, 75).
126 The account of Wismar is given in *SNF*, 92-116 / *Bericht*, 130-176 and summarised by Gerretsen (*Micronius*, 43-52).
127 *SNF*, 98 / *Bericht*, 138.
128 Pinkster, H., *Woordenboek Latijn/Nederlands* (Amsterdam: AUP, 2014[6]), 758.
129 E.g. 'ego home peregrinus' in *AS*, fol. 57 (*Is is is*, 82); 'nostram peregrinationem' in *SNF*, 148; 'Peregrinorum Ecclesiae' (*SNF*, 151).

not exclusivily 'pilgrim'; rather, Micron also indentifies himself as stranger for religion sake, as he testifies in the supplication:

> This we can testify before the Lord, that we diligently seek nothing but that Christ is acknowledged rightly and praised with true piety; that His Church is instituted according to the rules of the Divine Word, rejecting all that is brought forth by the Antichrist to obscure Christ's office of Priest, King and Prophet, and leading back to those things that have Christ's mandate and the apostolic testimony.[130]

This conviction is the reason he had to leave his country, and after that England. What we see is that 'exile' 'scattering' and 'alien' are words that together create an impression of the way he experienced his travels. In London he already expressed his desire to take back Flanders by fiery darts. The following picture arises: Micron thought of himself as an uprooted seed, blown away from his own city, denied living in his own country and many other places, for the sake of Christ, His gospel, His name and the desire to serve Him in accordance with His Word. This pilgrimage included the experience of being a stranger.[131]

Micron went to Lübeck and Hamburg. Just as in Wismar it came to a confrontation with the Luhteran authorities. In Hamburg Micron confronted Westphal,[132] an important occurence, for this confrontation (and in general the presence of the refugees in northern German Lands) was an important moment in the Second Eucharistic Controversy. Westphal had, until then, been a little known theologian, despite having written his *Farrago* against the *Consensus Tigurinus*. His treatment of the refugees, however, was so vexing to Calvin that he decided to oppose him, and this ultimately led to the final rupture between the Lutheran

---

130 *SNF*, 114. 'Hoc enim coram Domino testari possumus, quod omni nostro studio aliud non quaeramus, quam ut Christus recte agnoscatur, et vera pietate colatur, atque ut ipsius Ecclesia, iuxta verbi divini regulam instituatur, iis reiectis quae induxit Antichristus ad Sacerdotale, Regale et Propheticum Christi munus obscurandum: et reductis illis, quae Christi mandatum Apstolicumque testimonium habent.'

131 Cf. Veen, M. van, '"…wir sind ständig unterwegs…": Reformierte Flüchtlinge des 16. Jahrhunderts als Exulanten?' in: *Archiv für die Reformationsgeschichte* 109 (2018), 442-458, 451-452. She, however, stresses the meaning of pilgrim, rather than stranger for religion sake. As she herself says, one should not draw the two aspects too far apart. We would like to add that one should not want to try to specify it too precisely. In the various terms that are employed a pattern can be seen, as we have tried to show.

132 *SNF*, 116-148 / *Bericht*, 176-243; *AS*, fol. 50-68 (*Is is is*, 75-93). Summarised in Gerretsen, *Micronius*, 52-57.

and the Reformed tradition.[133] Micron, to some extent, incited this course of events, though he himself laid all the blame on the Lutheran side, claiming to accept them as brothers in Christ, yet he could not bear to be held to their ceremonies and confessions. He says: 'I have not come to either cause trouble or damn your church, but to defend mine, according to my office, not believing in any knowledge, but in our innocence, on which I hope in the Lord.'[134] What we see is that he was lenient in what he allowed others, he did not seek to uproot Lutheran churches, though he did think they should amend their views; but then again, he was also inflexible, for he would not bow under ceremonies which he believed to be less perfect than those of the London church. He trusted they were innocent, i.e. did not stray from the Bible, in their ordinances, and God would help them.

3.1.5 Norden

On March 7 Micron and his followers left Hamburg, and travelled to Emden. Here, at last, they found rest. Micron preached in Emden several times, and after he entered the service of countess Anna by going to Norden, where he started his work as pastor on May 20th, 1554.[135]

The congregation there had been going through some rough years. In 1551 Johannes Forstius and Johannes Adolphus Fusipedius became colleagues of Wilhelm Lemsius in Norden, who – in Menso Alting's words – still celebrated the Lord's Supper in a 'papistical manner'. Which probably means his rite still bore great resemblance to the mass. Fusipedius, an adherent of Zwingli, sought to introduce the liturgy used in Emden. Lemsius and Forstius, both Lutherans, opposed this. On April 8 1552, the countess Anna ordered them to keep the peace, but after this

---

133 This roughest of sketches is based on: Chung-Kim, E., *Inventing Authority. The Use of the Church Fathers in Reformation Debates over the Eucharist* (Waco: Baylor University Press, 2011), 61-98; Ehlers, C., *Konfessionsbildung im Zweiten Abendmahlsstreit (1552-1558/9)* (Tübingen: Mohr Siebeck, 2021). For Micron see, especially, 249-276; Kuhn, R., *Bekennen und Verwerfen. Westphals Ringen um Luther und Melanchthon* (Göttingen: Vandenhoeck & Ruprecht, 2019), 19-32; 174; 219-221; Mönckeberg, C.V., *Joachim Westphal und Johannes Calvin* (Hamburg: Gustav Eduard Nolte, 1865), 23-34; Pettegree, 'London Exile Community'.

Reiner Kuhn's study is especially significant as it gives a well-balanced analysis of Westphal as a person and a theologian. His expostion of how Westphal brought to the fore Melanchthon's development of thought is an insightful and important contribution to the knowledge of the Second Eucharistic Controversy.

134 'Non enim huc veni ut vestram Ecclesiam aut turbarem, aut damnarum, sed ut meam, pro meo officio, defenderem, non fiducia ullius eruditionis, sed nostrae ut in Domine spero, innocentiae', *AS*, fol. 55 (*Is is is*, 80). Cf. fol. 68-87 (*Is is is*, 93-112).

135 *SNF*, 149 / *Bericht*, 244

proved impossible she arranged a colloquium in Wirdum, led by Gellius Faber de Bouma[136] and Herman Brass[137]. A formula was drawn up which all subscribed.[138] However, a year later the three pastors were at it again, Wilhelm Gnapheus[139] was sent to solve the troubles, but in the end first Fusipedius, and afterwards Forstius and Lemsius were deposed.[140] Micron preached in Norden, the people were willing to have him as their pastor and this consequently happened. His colleagues there were Vincent Frisius and Albert Holtmann.[141] Later that year, in December, Micron and Frisius published *Ein kort underricht*, the vorlage or adaptation of *Een corte Ondersoeckinghe*, already discussed above. It is a sign of Micron's qualities as a pastor that this did not start a second 'Norder Kirchenstreit'. However, there was some opposition to his teachings. In two letters he makes mention of people who, on the pretext of the *Confessio Augustana*, teach 'something monstrous' (*aliquid monstri*) about the Lord's Supper.

---

136 Cf. Nauta, D. 'Bouma, Gellius (Jelle) Faber Smit?)' in: *Biografisch lexicon van de geschiedenis van het Nederlands protestantisme. Deel 2*, 90-91; Heide, J.W. van der, *Gellius Faber. Pastoor in Friesland, predikant in Oost-Friesland* (Amersfoort: [n.p.], 2002).

137 Cf. Schelven, A.A. van, 'Brassius (Hermannus)' in: *Nieuw Nederlandsch Biografisch woordenboek. Deel 1*, 454.

138 The *Formula Wirdumana* can be found in: Beninga, E., *Volledige chronyk van Oostfrieslant: Behelsende niet alleenlik de historie van Oostfriesland, maer ook van alle Nabuirige Volkeren ten Oosten en ten Westen, besonder de allerseldsaemste Geschiedenissen van het oude en gedendaegste Friesland, zoo ten tyde des Heidendoms, als zedert het is gekristent geworden, geschreven* (Emden: Henrich Meybohm, Josua Beek en Hermannus Wolffram, 1723), 823-824; also in: Grochowina, N., *Indifferenz und Dissens in der Grafschaft Ostfriesland im 16. und 17. Jahrhundert* (Frankfurt: Peter Lang, 2003), 142n412.

139 Cf. Graafland, G.J./Trapman, J., 'Gnapheus Guilielmus (Willem Voldersgracht, Willem van Haghen, Fullonius)' in: *Biografisch lexicon voor de geschiedenis van het Nederlands protestantisme. Deel 4*, 142-144. An nice detail is that Gnapheus was the biographer of Johannes Pistorius, who had been educated by Hinne Rode. Hinne Rode marketed Hoen's letter around Europe and became a pastor in Norden (cf. Demoed, V.E.M., *'Wie van gevaar houdt, moet dat met de dood bekopen': De opiniërende strategieën van de toneelschrijver Gulielmus Gnapheus (1493-1568)* (PhD Universteit van Amsterdam, 2011), 38; 74-76; 81-84; Gunst, J.W., *Johannes Pistorius Woerdenis* (Hilversum: De Blauwvoet, 1925), 41-67; 147-149; 210-220) .

140 For the 'Norder Kirchenstreit' see: Alting, M., *Gründtlicker Warhafftiger Bericht: Vond der Euangelischen Reformation der Christlicken Kerkcken tho Embden un[d] in Ostfrieβlandt(...)* (Bremen: Berendt Peters, 1594), 389-399; Gerretsen, *Micronius*, 60-62;I-II; Grochowina, *Indifferenz*, 140-143; Ritter, F., 'Zur Geschichte des Norder Kirchenstreits vom Jahre 1554' in: *Jahrbuch der Gesellschaft für bildende Kunst und vaterländische Altertümer zu Emden* 22 (1927), 329-342.

141 Grochowina, *Indifferenz*, 142-143.

Micron regrets that for many the authority of the *Augustana* supercedes the authority of Scripture. This, he says, is just as bad as popery (*Papistarum*), where councils and traditions lord it over Scripture.[142] The confession, then, should not become a separate norm next to, or instead of, Scripture. Later, in 1557, he thanks the Lord that those attempts have come to nothing, and the church in Norden is stable.[143] The dissent in the congregation did not lead to any major disruptions or arguments, no matter how vexing they were to Micron. This is not only proof of his theological capacities, but also of his organizational capabilities. He was, in modern terms, a good manager. This is underlined by à Lasco's request in 1555, when he asked Micron to come over to Frankfurt and help him with the institution of the Stranger Church there. Micron chose not to stay there, but returned 'to his own' (*ad suos*).[144]

As Micron's time in Norden was generally a peaceful one, there is very little that needs to be mentioned. First we will highlight a few interesting details, after that we will look at the books he wrote during his years in Norden.

In 1556 Micron had some disputes with Mennonite opponents,[145] though he was too busy to accede to the request from Frankfurt to come and help the church in a dispute against the Lutherans. Another aspect worth noting is that during these years there was considerable political unrest. Count Johann II of Rietberg (residing in Esen, twenty-odd miles from Norden) had invaded the lands near the Accumer Deep,[146] part of Eastfrisia. Having a aggressor nearby made Micron uneasy, and he wrote about it several times, sounding concerned. He believed it was the scourge of God. The countess Anna asked the *Reichskammergericht* to intervene, but Johann would not listen. After he also turned against the county of Lippe, he was eventually taken prisoner after his castle Holte (in the county Rietberg, many miles away from Norden) had lain under siege for seven months.[147] A last thing worth noting is that in 1558 Micron writes

---

142 Micron to Musculus, August 24, [1556] (Gerretsen, *Micronius*, IX-X).
143 Micron to Bullinger, March 8, 1557 (Füslinus, 400).
144 *SNF*, 149.
145 Gerretsen, *Micronius*, 66; *WV*, 7; *Apologie*, fol. 17.
146 Count Johann II was also 'Herr des Harlingerlandes', an area surrounded on three sides by Eastfrisian territories, the northern border is the Wadden Sea. Norden lies west of Harlingerland, the Accumer Deep south-east, approximately forty miles from Norden.
147 Behr, H-J., 'Die Exekution des Niederrheinisch-Westfälischen Kreises gegen Graf Johann von Rietberg 1556-1566' in: *Westfälische Zeitschrift* 128 (1978), 33-104, esp. pages 33-78.
Micron mentions these troubles in the following letters:

to Bullinger that an Anabaptist family had joined the church in Norden.[148]

Next we turn to the books Micron wrote during these years. We have already mentioned the first of these, *Ein kort underricht*. A month later, January 1555, he published a translation of Musculus's work *de Juramento*, and added his own exposition on the same theme to it. When the two texts (the translation and Micron's part) are compared, it seems likely that Micron did not translate Musculus's work himself, but was happy to link his own name to that of Musculus. In general Micron's part adds little to Musculus's thorough study.[149] The book probably had a polemical intention in opposition to the Mennonites. Indeed, the ongoing debate between on the one hand the Mennonites and on the other hand the Lutherans, took up much of Micron's time in 1556 and 1557. Against the Mennonites he published his account of the disputes in Wismar, *Een waerachtigh verhaal der t'zamensprekinghen tusschen Menno Simons ende Martinus Mikron van der menschwerdinghe Iesu Christi*. Menno replied by giving his view of the case, which in turn incited Micron's second book on the matter, *Een Apologie of verantwoordinghe Martini Micron op XX. verscheyden Artikelen die Menno Symons teghen het disputacy boecxken van het bespreck met hem over de leere gehouden, in druck heeft uutghegeven*, in 1558. For this second book he asked both Bullinger and Calvin to advise him. Calvin responded with a lengthy letter which later found its way into the *Institutes of the Christian Religion*.[150] While Micron was working on *Waerachtigh verhael* he was also writing two books on the Lord's Supper. The first was finished on June 26 1556, just two weeks after he had finished *Waerachtigh verhael*, and it is an account of the martyrdom of Hoste vander Katelyne (*Een waerachtighe Historie van Hoste (gheseyt*

    Micron to Bullinger, August 24, 1556 (Gerretsen, *Micronius*, VIII-IX).
    Micron to Musculus, August 24, 1556 (Gerretsen, *Micronius*, X).
    Micron to Bullinger, March 8, 1557 (Füslinus, 401).

148 Micron to Bullinger, February 28, 1558 (Gerretsen, *Micronius*, XII).

149 Musculus, W. / Micron, M., *Een claere ende Scriftelicke onderrichtinghe vanden Eedt…waer toeghedaan is een clein anancksel, des selven handel angaende* ([Emden: Ctematius], 1555.

150 For Micron and the Mennonites, see: Balke, W., *Calvijn en de Doperse Radikalen* (Amsterdam: Ton Bolland, 1973), 205-211; Dankbaar, W.F., 'Introduction' in: [Micron, M.], *Een waerchtig verhaal der t'zamensprekinghen tusschen Menno Simons ende Martinus Mikron van der menschewerdinghe Iesu Christi* ed. W.F. Dankbaar, *Documenta Anabaptistica Neerlandica III* (Leiden: Brill, 1981), VII-XXX; Krahn, C., *Dutch Anabaptism. Origin, Spread, Life and Thought (1450-1600)* (The Hague: Martinus Nijhoff, 1968), 241-243; Pettegree, A., 'The Struggle for an Orthodox Church: Calvinists and Anabaptists in East Friesland, 1554-1578' in: *Bulletin of the John Rylands University Library* 70/3 (1988), 45-59.

Jooris) vander Katelyne), which is more or less a vehicle to present his own views on the Lord's Supper.[151] The second book was an answer to calumnies published by Westphal, which he finished in September 1557. It was his only direct contribution to the Second Eucharistic Controversy, titled *Apologeticum Scriptum Martini Micronii(…)*.[152] The first part of this book attests to Micron's usage of the rite of the Lord's Supper as it was described in the *Ordinancien* during his ministry in Norden. The *Apologeticum Scriptum* is the last book Micron finished and the last to have been published during his life. We see in Micron's books and his Norden ministry that the struggle he found himself in was not so much between primarily 'radicals' and also Roman Catholicism, as Pettegree argues,[153] but much more between Lutheran teachings (which he to a certain extent condoned) and Mennonites in an equal degree.

Micron also helped Utenhove with his translation of the New Testament, though to what extent is largely unknown. His involvement was important enough for Utenhove to travel to Norden in 1556.[154]

By the end of his life, Micron, now relatively unknown, was a highly esteemed theologian, considered to be on par with à Lasco, Calvin, Bullinger, and Martyr. For instance, when Adrianus de Kuper came to Emden for advice he was sent on to Micron.[155] Jakob Dieussart named Micron in one sentence with Wycliffe, Huss, Zwingli, Calvin and à Lasco.[156] Mönckeberg presents a remark by Von Eitzen in which Von Eitzen opposes the 'sacramentarians…like Calvin, à Lasco, Ochinus,

---

151 A modern edition is found in *Bibliotheca Reformatoria Neerlandica. Achtste deel*, 177-253. A recent article studying this book is: Selderhuis, H.J., 'A Teachable Death: Doctrine and Death in Marten Micron's Martyrology' in: *Unio cum Christo* 1/1-2 (2015), 119-131.

152 W.O.R. Willems gives a transcription and summarised translation of the book in his *Is is IS?*.
Unfortunately, he does not give much attention to the place of this book in the Second Eucharistic Controversy. Neither is it given any attention by Chung-Kim (*Authority*), Reiner Kuhn (*Westphal*) or Ehler (*Abendmahlsstreit*). Cf., also, chapter 3, footnote 133

153 Pettegree, 'Struggle', 46.

154 Pijper, *Utenhove*, 129-130. This made Smid (*Ostfriesische Kirchengeschichte* (Pewsum, 1974), 196) state that Micron and Frisius were the main driving forces behind this translation. He refers to Meiners I (363), but this reference only proves that in the process of the translation Norden was an important city.

155 See above, 2.3.

156 Recorded in: Haemstede, A.C. van, *Geschiedenis der martelaren (…)* ed. Molenaar & Felix (Arnhem: Swaan, 1868), 723. Cf. Decavele, *Eerste protestanten*, 29. Benedict (*Christ's churches*, 180) gives a translation that is too free.

Bullinger, Micronius, Martyr.'¹⁵⁷ A final, most interesting, example proves that Micron was held in higher esteem than à Lasco, at least by some. In 1563 Christian Mundanum published a German translation of à Lasco's catechism; however, on the title page he asserted that it was the work of Marten Micron.¹⁵⁸ In the subsequent decades his works kept their influence. The *Corte Ondersoekinghe* was printed by Datheen in his church book.¹⁵⁹ Indeed, the many reprints of his catechisms, including the *Corte Ondersoekinghe*, until the start of the seventeenth century show his influence throughout the remainder of the century.¹⁶⁰ His forms, prayers and catechisms influenced the forms and prayers of Datheen's service book and the Heidelberg catechism.¹⁶¹

In 1559 the plague raged through Norden. Micron's wife fell ill and seems to have survived.¹⁶² After Feddo Hommius and Albert Holtmann (Micron's colleagues at the time) passed away at the end of August, Micron also fell victim to the black death and passed away on September 12th.¹⁶³ The manuscript of *Van de weerdicheydt* was found, translated and published.

We have now seen that this is a book by a pastor of international standing, a refugee who was both a superior theologian and church-manager, in which he presented the theology on which his entire ecclesiological work was based. The foundation of the building we see in the *Ordinancien* and the various catechisms, the foundation that directed his course of action during the peregrination, the disputes and his work in the various churches. Truly, to understand the ecclesiology of the refugees, this book cannot be neglected.

---

157 Mönckeberg, *Westphal*, 84.
158 Micron, M. [wrongly asscribed to], *Der grosser Catechismus* (Freyburg: Christianum Mundanum, 1563), title page. Cf. Reu, J.M., *Quellen zur Geschichte des kirchlichen Unterrichts in der evangelischen Kirche Deutschlands zwischen 1530 und 1600. 1/3,1b* (Hildesheim/New York: Georg Olm, 1976), 713.
159 Dathenus, P., *De Psalmen Davids* ed. J.N. IJkel & R. van 't Spijker (Houten: Den Hertog, 1992), 87-109.
160 Dankbaar, W.F. 'Micron (Mikron, Micronius) Marten' in: *Biografisch lexicon voor de geschiedenis van het Nederlands protestantisme. Deel 2*, 327-330, 330.
161 Cf. Schreiber, *Dathenus*, 297-303.
162 Gerretsen, xiv-xv: 'et uxor mea periculose decumbit'.
163 Alting, *Gründtlicker*, 400.
     Micron tot Bullinger, August 14, 1559 (Gerretsen, *Micronius*, XIV). 'Premit nos saeva pestis, quae multos bonos quotidie apud nos Nordanos absumit, et uxor mea periculose decumbit.'
     It follows that Micron could not have become an elder in London in 1560, as Silke Muylaert relates (*Shaping*, 40).

3.2 Nicolaus Carinaeus

We move on to the biography of Nicolaus Carinaeus, who finalised *Van de weerdicheydt,* published in 1561. Very little of his life is known to us, what we do know is presented here. Carinaeus was born in Edam, though the year of his birth is unknown.[164] By the year 1558 he was in East Frisia, for in that year the consistory in Amsterdam asked the Emden consistory for a minister, and they, subsequently, elected Carinaeus. He appeared before the council on the 25th of April, and expressed his doubts about his capabilities to erect a church in such a desolation (*dat het svarlick ys, in sulke vorwoestinge eyn kerke upthorichten*). However, if they decided to send him, he would like to know whether he should baptise children from marriages in which the husband or wife did not leave the Roman church. Another question he had was whether he should condone the members to attend papal services. The council decided to send Carinaeus because the congregation in Amsterdam asked for him, and they themselves did not know a better candidate. As to his questions, they replied that he should counsel them in what is most certain (*und rade hoer nicht, dan dat sekerste*) and to discipline the others (*overst vormane de ande…*).[165] He was to serve in Amsterdam itself, yet it seems likely that he served the area around Amsterdam as well, for the minutes in Emden later admonish both Amsterdam and Alkmaar to pay their pastor, Carinaeus, his wages.[166] The fruit of his work, the amount of work and the exact length of his stay is unknown. There is one important reference to him in the minutes of the Emden consistory. Cornelis Benninck, from the brethren of Holland, asked for someone who can help oppose the Mennonites 'for he says, that Carinaeus is not man enough to stop his mouth.'[167] On the 14th of August 1559 Cooltuyn recorded that he would

---

164 Carinaeus signed his letter to the consistory in London with 'Nicolaus Carinaeus Eda*mensis*' (Hessels II, 191). In all sources his name is given as Carinaeus, it is possible this comes from 'De Bruyne'.
165 *Kirchenratsprotokolle Emden*, 47. The rest of the entry is no longer extant.
166 *Kirchenratsprotokolle Emden*, 58.
167 *Kirchenratsprotokolle Emden*, 78. Interestingly enough Cornelius Benninck is then sent on to Norden to move 'him' to go to Holland. The critical edition by Schilling in a footnote asks 'whom'? (p. 78n15). This could very well refer to Marten Micron. We have no evidence that Micron went to Holland; nonetheless, it is a tantalizing thought that, had he gone, he would have been in Holland while the plague raged through Norden.
From the reference to Carinaeus in the minutes Pettegree concludes that 'The suspicions that Carineus had not proved equal to the demands of the post were confirmed' (Pettegree, *Emden*, 79). This is somewhat harsh. It may very well be that Benninck was a habitual critic of Carinaeus. When it comes to Carinaeus's work in preaching, teaching and pastoral care, little can be derived from this single remark.

ask Jan Arentsz[168] to accept the call to serve the congregations in Holland.[169] This could mean that he either replaced Carineaus or would serve together with him. Be that as it may, by January 1562 the Edam-born minister was back in East Frisia, serving as pastor of Jennelt, part of the lands of squire Christophorus of Ewsum. On the 8th of January, 1562, the consistory in London deliberated about calling another pastor and one of the names that is mentioned was that of Carinaeus.[170] Two deacons, Henrick and Mozes, were sent to East Frisia to talk to the consistory in Emden about the matter, and – if possible – observe the pastors on the shortlist.[171] This eventually led to London extending a call towards Carinaeus, which he declined in a letter written on the first of April 1562, because the squire did not want to let him go. Moreover, again, he said he did not think his gifts were sufficient for such a task. However, the squire's refusal was probably the real reason, which was vexing to him: the work in Jennelt was largely without fruit, for the people were stiff-necked. Additionally, he was only allowed to preach and baptise, but could not administer the Lord's Supper, nor practice Christian discipline.[172] The consistory in London, however, was determined and after a letter by Peter Delenus to the squire, the latter gave in and Carinaeus accepted the call to London,[173] where he arrived on the twenty-ninth of October 1562, together with his wife.[174] It was decided he would start preaching on the eighth of November and lead the prophecy on the subsequent Thursday. The intermittent week (i.e. November 1-8) he was to observe the services led by Delenus.[175] His first sermon in the congregation was on Hebrews 3:12, 'take heed, brethren, lest there be in any of you an evil heart of unbelief, in departing from the living God' (KJV).[176] Midway April 1563,

---

168 On Arentsz see: Itterzon, G.P. van, 'Jan Arentsz (de Mandemaecker) (Johannes Arnoldi)' in: *Biografisch Lexicon voor de geschiedenis van het Nederlands Protestantisme. Deel 2*, 273-275; more elaborately: Vis, G.N.M, *Jan Arentsz, de mandenmaker van Alkmaar, voorman van de Hollandse reformatie* (Hilversum: Verloren, 1992). Note, however, that Vis overlooked the presence of Carinaeus in Amsterdam and Alkmaar (42).
169 *Kirchenratsprotokolle Emden*, 98.
170 *Kerkeraads-Protocollen der Nederduitsche vluchtelingen-kerk te Londen 1560-1563* ed. Van Schelven (Amsterdam: Johannes Müller, 1921), 281.
171 Meiners II, 32.
172 Carinaeus to the London Consistory, April 1st, 1562 (Hessels II, 189-191).
173 Delenus to Eusamanus, May 25th, 1562 (Hessels II, 198-199).
174 *Kerkeraads-Protocollen*, 369.
175 *Kerkeraads-Protocollen*, 371.
176 *Kerkeraads-Protocollen*, 372.
At no point is there anything that suggests Carinaeus was only 'an assisting minister', contra Muylaert, *Shaping*, 58.

there was an argument between Carinaeus and Dorenum, about how Anabaptists should be regarded: are they brothers in Christ or not? Unfortunately, the minutes do neither tell who said what, nor how the matter ended.[177] Of more weight is what transpired a month earlier, on the 18th of March. During the prophecy Justus Velsius, who had joined the congregation in January and was a troublemaker,[178] challenged Carinaeus's views on regeneration and claimed that man could live without sin.[179] Obviously, these opinions could not in any way harm Carinaeus's position, yet it was in all likelihood an unsettling experience. Velsius seems to have renewed his attacks on both Carinaeus and Delenus, for the minutes speak of '*plenum contumeliis adversus Petrum Delenum et Nicolaum Carineum*'.[180] Other than these instances Carinaeus seems to have been a worthy and diligent minister of Christ in the congregation of London. On the nineteenth of August 1563, he takes over the task of writing the minutes of the council. This was a time of severe trouble, for the plague was raging through the streets of London, and it did not pass over the congregation of the refugees. First Peter Delenus fell victim, and on the 5th of September Carinaeus wrote his last entry. The pages he wrote are a grim witness to the disease that killed so many, and in the end caused the death of the man who completed Micron's book, and faithfully served the Reformed churches.[181]

---

177 *Kerkeraads-Protocollen*, 405.
178 *Kerkeraads-Protocollen*, 394 n2. Cf. Rutgers, *Calvijns invloed op de Reformatie in de Nederlanden voor zooveel die door hemzelven is uitgeoefend* (Leiden: Donner, 1899), 73-75; Waardt, J.H.M. de, 'Justus Velsius Haganus: An erudite but rambling prophet' in: Spohnholz, J. & Waite, G. (eds.), *Exile and Religious Identity, 1500-1800* (London: Pickering & Chatto, 2014), 97-109 & 223-227.
179 *Kerkeraads-Protocollen*, 478.
180 *Kerkeraads-Protocollen*, 481.
181 *Kerkeraads-Protocollen*, 487-491. A.A. van Schelven, the editor of the minutes, comments: 'De pestepidemie, tengevolge waarvan straks ook de schrijver dezer notulen, Nicolaus Carinaeus, zou vallen, drukt op deze korte notities wel heel duidelijk haar stempel' (*Kerkeraads-Protocollen*, 487 n1).

3.3 Summary and Conclusions

The primary author of *Van de weerdicheydt* was the Ghent-born Marten Micron. He was formed by the Zurich Reformation, not least by the influence of John Hooper. His theological knowledge and managerial prowess made him a major theologian in his day, ranked among names like à Lasco and Ochino, and even, by some, mentioned alongside Bullinger and Calvin. Moreover, he was an important figure in the church of the diaspora. Not only was he the first minister of the Dutch Church in London, he was also the one who had helped organise both the structure and the theology of the Strangers' Church, fixing its form and doctrine in several publications which would prove to be important in the Dutch churches to the present day. We saw that one of the effects of the Dutch Church in London was to weave a communal identity by creating a shared liturgy. Micron thus left a clear mark on the shape of the churches in their London-period. In the 'reformation of the refugees' there could hardly be a more authoritative author than Micron.

The book was finished by Nicolaus Carinaeus, a relatively unknown author. Indeed, much of his life is obscure. He diligently served several congregations before passing away in London. He, too, was a Netherlandish refugee; however, it seems he had little theological influence or significance.

Chapter 4: The Second Concentric Circle: The East Frisian Reformation and 'the Reformation of the Refugees'

In the preceding chapters we introduced Micron's *Van de weerdicheydt, nutheydt ende noodicheyt der christelicker vergaderinghen* and its authors, Marten Micron and Nicolaus Carinaeus. In this chapter we move to the second concentric circle: the direct environment in which Micron, as the primary author and theological brains behind the book, operated. He was, as the reader will know by now, at that moment pastor of the church in Norden; hence, it is important to briefly outline the East Frisian Reformation in 3.1. More important, however, is Micron's position as a supposed 'founding father' of a Dutch Reformed heritage. This falls within the historiography of 'the Reformation of the Refugees'. The discussion surrounding this paradigm will receive the bulk of our attention in this chapter in 3.2. To be sure, these two subjects are not immediately connected and combined here primarily because they both form the background against which the book was written. As will be seen, however, the description of the East Frisian Reformation helps form a better framework for the Reformation of the Refugees. The chapter ends with a summary and conclusions (3.3).

4.1 The East Frisian Reformation

Though it was stated above that the primary target audience of the book were 'Nicodemites', as they are commonly called, the fact remains that Micron was, at the time of writing, living in Norden, and had been living there for several years. Consequently, then, the situation of East Frisia and its developments in the decades before is important to understand the setting of the book. Indeed, whereas Micron's knowledge of the underground churches in the Netherlands would have been second-hand, his knowledge of the people in East Frisia, their opinions and their views of the church, came from personal experience. In this paragraph we will outline the course of the East Frisian Reformation. Having said that, it is equally true that Micron neither had the specific East Frisian situation in mind, nor was he primarily influenced by the East Frisian Reformation. So, though it is important to come to grips with the broad outline of the East Frisian Reformation, it is not necessary to give a detailed account.

Rather, considering that in the previous chapter we concluded Micron found himself in an environment where he battled Lutherans and Mennonites and was confronted with a church that had just lived through a battle between two Lutheran pastors and a Reformed one, this dynamic between two confessions in his congregation and the ongoing discussion with Mennonites will be the main focus of the following outline. Moreover, whenever there is the chance to highlight more about Norden, at the cost of neglecting other cities or persons, we will not hesitate to do so.

Before focussing too intensely on East Frisia, however, it is better to zoom out, and take the whole of the northern German Lands in view. The course of the several reformations has been sublimely described by Arnd Reitemeier.[1] This is important because the secondary sources describing the East Frisian Reformation are usually somewhat narrow in their scope.[2] First of all, they tend to focus on East Frisia in itself, and not as one of the northern German Lands; and secondly, they become even

---

1 Most comprehensively in his book: Reitemeier, A., *Reformation in Norddeutschland. Gottvertrauen zwischen Fürstenherrschaft und Teufelsfurcht* (Göttingen: Wallstein Verlag, 2017), and more concisely in: Reitemeier, A., 'Zur Einführung der Reformation in Norddeutschland' in: *Jahrbuch der Gesellschaft für niedersächsische Kirchengeschichte* 114 (2016), 7-33

2 The East Frisian reformation has been re-written in almost every century. Names from the past are, to name just a few, those of Menso Alting (*Van der Euangelischen Reformation / der Christlicken Kercken tho Embden und in Ostfriesland (…)* (Bremen: Berendt Peters., 1594)), Peter Friedrich Reershemius (*Ostfriesländisches Prediger-Denkmahl* (Aurich: Ben Johann Adolph Schulte, 1796)), and Ubbo Emmius (*Rerum Frisicarum historia (…)* (Leiden: Elzevier, 1616), a modern translation of this work was provided by Erich von Reeken (*Friesische Geschichte* Band 1-6 (Frankfurt am Main: Wörner, 1980-1982)). However, for our research we used more recent scholarship, starting with the seminal work of Weerda, J.R., *Der Emder Kirchenrat und seine Gemeinde. Ein Beitrag zur Geschichte reformierter Kirchenordnung in Deutschland, ihrer Grundsätze und ihrer Gestaltung* ed. Matthias Freudenberg & Alasdair Heron (Wuppertal: Foedus, 2000) and further: Smid, M., *Ostfriesische Kirchengeschichte* (Pewsum, 1974); Tanis, J. 'East Friesland and the Reformed Reformation' in: *Calvin Theological Journal* 26 (1991), 313-349; Pettegree, A., *Emden and the Dutch Revolt. Exile and Development of Reformed Protestantism* (Oxford: OUP, 1992), Chapter 2: 'Emden'. The most important recent academic contributions are Heiko Ebbel Janssen's analysis of countess Anna's reign (Janssen, H. E., *Gräfin Anna von Ostfriesland – eine hochadelige Frau der späten Reformationszeit (1540/42-1575). Ein beitrag zu den Anfängen der reformierten Konfessionalisierung im Reich* (Münster: Aschendorff, 1998), Henning P. Jürgens account of John à Lasco's early life (Jürgens, H.P., *Johannes à Lasco in Ostfriesland. Der Werdegang eines europäischen Reformators* (Tübingen: Mohr Siebeck, 2002) and Nicole Grochowina's investigation of the lived religion in all of East Frisia (*Indifferenz und Dissens in der Grafschaft Ostfriesland im 16. und 17. Jahrhundert* (Frankfurt am Main: Peter Lang, 2003).

more narrow in their focus by being accounts of reformation in Emden, rather than East Frisia. Accounts of Norden, Aurich and Leer – the other major cities – and the rural parts of the county are scarce.³ Something similar is the case when almost all of the accounts cover à Lasco's work in East Frisia extensively, yet the work and person of Gellius Faber is desperately undervalued.⁴ It is safe to say that generally the focus of the scholarship is somewhat narrow. We therefore start with the wider context of the northern German Lands. Reitemeier describes the course of the several reformations in five phases. These overlap and are of unequal length. Besides, their development and length, and indeed occurrence, were different from area to area. The five phases he gives are[5]:

1. Luther's teachings find their way into the northern regions via books, preachers and hymns.
2. The cities take the lead in furthering developments. They organise disputations and develop new church orders. These actions bring neither unity nor homogeneity. The Roman Catholic church is still strong. This phase takes place from roughly 1520-1540.
3. The princes adopt Luther's teachings. They are firmer in their actions than the cities were. Especially after the peace of Augsburg the princes have a key role in determining the religion in their region. This phase runs from 1527-1569.
4. Further theological developments. The teachings of the Swiss Reformation[6] and the Anabaptists, which were already present, become more widespread than they were. This is roughly in the last third of the 16th century.
5. Return of the Roman Catholic church. This takes place from 1563.

Five phases that can be seen in the northern German Lands, yet East Frisia, though the reader will recognise these stages, is the odd one out from the very start, as Reitemeier himself points out on several occasions.[7]

---

3 Though it must be said that Grochowina's contributions have made a start in filling up this gap. Nonetheless, by taking the several counts as the narrative structure of much of her thesis, Emden features more prominently than other cities and areas.
4 J.W. van der Heide's research into Gellius Faber was cut short by Van der Heide's decease. The results were published in: Heide, J.W. van der, *Gellius Faber. Pastoor in Friesland, predikant in Oost-Friesland* (Amersfoort: [n.p.], 2002).
5 Reitemeier, 'Einführung', 8-10 (phase 1), 12-17 (phase 2), 18 (phase 3), 28-30 (phase 4), 31-32 (phase 5); Reitemeier, *Reformation*, 12-13.
6 Reitemeier speaks of 'adherents of Zwingli and Calvin' (*Reformation*, 12).
7 Reitemeier, *Reformation*, 90; 122-123, 131-133.

Indeed, what we will see is that there were both Lutheran influences and, what is commonly called, 'sacramentarian' influences (i.e. the view in which the corporeal presence of Christ in the Eucharist is questioned) via preachers coming from the Netherlandish lands and educated at Modern Devotion schools.[8] The start of the East Frisian Reformation falls within the reign of Edzard the Great (1492-1528). Little is known about the first men to preach reform, Hinricus Brun and Johannes Stevens van Bulderen.[9] Later preachers were Hinne Rode (the carrier of Cornelis Hoen's letter and teacher of Johannes Pistorius, the first martyr from the northern parts of the Netherlands) who became a pastor in Norden in 1525 or 1526. Obviously, he preached on the Lord's Supper in line with the teachings expounded by Cornelis Hoen.[10] More dramatic was Hinrich Reese, a Norden-based Dominican monk who renounced the papacy and his vows by removing his hood while preaching.[11] Reese supported the most important preacher in the early East Frisian reformation: Georgius Aportanus. Aportanus had been a teacher at the school of the Brothers of the Common Life at Zwolle, when Count Edzard the Great called him to be the tutor of this sons. Aportanus and Reese made a distinct mark on the course of reform by organising disputations in Oldersum in 1526, led by Aportanus, and Norden in 1527, led by Reese.[12] The influence of 'sacramentarian' views was clearly quite strong; nevertheless, Luther's writings were read widely by 1519, and Edzard did nothing to stop this.[13] What this short account shows us is that in the first years many of the reform-minded activities took place outside Emden. Indeed, Heiko Janssen argues that in Emden the resident Roman Catholic clergy fiercely

---

8   The discussion concerning the Modern Devotion as a link towards, forerunner of, or direct cause of reformation is complicated. The secondary literature limits itself to stating that these preachers were taught at Modern Devotion schools, but do not address the extent or content of this influence. One feels that the paradigm of the Modern Devotion as a forerunner of reformation is uncritically taken for granted. For more on this see, e.g.,: Post, R.R., *The Modern Devotion. Confrontation with Reformation and Humanism* (Leiden: Brill, 1968); Van Engen, J., *Sisters and Brothers of the Common Life. The Devotio Moderna and the World of the Later Middle Ages* (University of Pennsylvania Press, 2008); Dijk, M. van, 'The Devotio Moderna, the Emotions and the Search for "Dutchness"' in: *BMNG – Low Countries Historical Review* 129/2 (2014), 20-41. Van Dijk also provides references for further study.
9   Smid, *Ostfriesische Kirchengeschichte*, 118-119; Tanis, 'East-Friesland', 318.
10 Smid, *Ostfriesische Kirchengeschichte*, 119.
11 Tanis, 'East-Friesland', 321.
12 Smid, *Ostfriesische Kirchengeschichte*, 118-131; Tanis, 'East-Friesland', 320-321.
13 Janssen, *Gräfin Anna*, 45-46.

opposed it.[14] It also shows that important preachers were not in line with Luther's sacramental views from the start, creating two different strands in the East Frisian Reformation.

Matters were further complicated by the presence of Anabaptists, who came to East Frisia as early as 1525.[15] Krahn sees the first five years, from 1525-1530, as 'premonitory of coming Anabaptism', and he reckons the work of Melchior Hofmann in 1530, when Hofmann baptised more than 300 adults in the *Große Kirche*, to be the real start of East Frisian Anabaptism.[16] Whether the actual start is in 1525 or 1530 matters little. What it shows is that in the second half of the decade the confessional plurality[17] and the possibility to have a different confession was already present. In subsequent years the county became the headquarters of the Anabaptist movement, and many people form the Low Countries fled to the relatively safe haven of East Frisia, including Norden and its surrounding rural areas.[18]

Though count Edzard neither opposed nor greatly stimulated the new teachings in the county, his son, Enno II, seems to have been more devoted to reform.[19] One of his first acts was the dissolution of several monasteries, among which was the Dominican monastery in Norden, which became his second house.[20] Of special importance here is that he asked Johann Timann and Johann Pelt to write a church order for East Frisia. Timann and Pelt came from Bremen and were influenced by the

---

14 Janssen, *Gräfin Anna*, 19-23. He writes about the clergy: 'es gibt keinerlei Anhaltspunkte dafür, daß aus dem Verband der Kleriker und Mönche Anregungen dazu gegeben werden – im Gegenteil, die ersten reformatorischen Predigten in Emden wurden von einem großen Protest der Kleriker begleitet, der sich bis in die zweite Hälfte der 1520er Jahre hin forstsetzte. (21-22)

15 Smid, *Ostfriesische Kirchengeschichte*, 138-139.

16 Krahn, C., 'Anabaptism in East Friesland' in: *Mennonite Quarterly Review* 30/4 (1956), 247-255, 247-248. Other important sources for the history of East Frisian Anabaptism are: Krahn, C., *Dutch Anabaptism* (The Hague: Martinus Nijhoff, 1968), especially pages 175-182; Visser, P., ' "À Lasco wedder uns" À Lasco und die Täufer und Nonkonformisten' in: Strohm, Ch. (ed.), *Johannes à Lasco (1499-1560). Polnischer Baron, Humanist und europäischer Reformator* (Tübingen: Mohr Siebeck, 2000), 299-313; Zijlstra, S., 'Anabaptists, Spiritualists and the Reformed Church in East Frisia' in: *Mennonite Quarterly Review* 75/1 (2001), 57-73, and chapter 5 of Grochowina's *Indifferenz und Dissens*.

17 Van der Heide (*Gellius Faber*) even calls it a time of anarchy, page 17.

18 Krahn, 'Anabaptism', 249. For a moderate view on how extensive persecution of the Anabaptists was in the low countries, see: Geraerts, J., 'The Prosecution of Anabaptists in Holland, 1530-1566' in: *Mennonite Quarterly Review* 86/1 (2012), 5-47.

19 Janssen, *Gräfin Anna*, 57.

20 Smid, *Ostfriesische Kirchengeschichte*, 137

teachings of Luther. The document they produced, the Bremer Church Order of 1529,[21] was largely based on the church order written by Luther's student Bugenhagen.[22] The effect Enno sought, Jan Remmers Weerda tells us, was for East Frisia to conform to the teachings and order used in the other northern German Lands.[23] However, this was not accomplished due to the count's limited political power. To understand this we have to look at the political history of East Frisia: It was not until 1464 that the house of Cirksena was granted the title of count by the Holy Roman Emperor, before that the areas were controlled by several chieftains (*Häuptlinge*), who remained influential after 1464 too. After a disastrous war in 1514 – the Saxon Strife – the chieftains' power grew.[24] Enno II simply did not have the political power to enforce the church order. Besides, his attention was distracted by the danger of count Balthasar of Esen. Enno II attacked Balthasar. After a quick victory for Enno, Balthasar formed an alliance with Karel of Gelder and retaliated, in his campaign he destroyed the Andreaskirche in Norden in 1531.[25] The Bremer Church Order, then, was not very influential; however, it did force Rode and Reese to leave Norden due their sacramentarianism, but they soon found work somewhere else in East Frisia. In Emden the church order caused an uproar and was never implemented.[26]

A second church order, the Lüneburger, followed in 1535, which was even more distinctly Lutheran than the Bremer and had been more or less forced upon East Frisia by political pressure from Karel of Gelder.[27] Again, as before, preachers in Norden were removed from office due to their views on the Lord's Supper.[28] After these years East Frisian politics were

---

21 This church order is called 'Bremer' merely because its authors came from that city. The document is not to be confused with the *Bremer Kirchenordnung* of 1534. For an introduction to and the text of this later church order, see: Sprengler-Ruppenthal, A., 'Die Bremer Kirchenordnung von 1534' in: *Zeitschrift der Savigny-Stiftung für Rechtsgeschichte: Kanonistische Abteilung* 82/1 (1996), 107-144
22 Smid, *Ostfriesische Kirchengeschichte*, 140.
23 Weerda, *Emder Kirchenrat*, 15.
24 Jürgens, *Johannes à Lasco*, 170-171; Grochowina, *Indifferenz*, 93.
25 Cf. Jürgens, *Johannes à Lasco*, 168-176; 189-190; Grochowina, *Indifferenz*, 93-94; Smid, *Ostfriesische Kirchengeschichte*, 146. Specifically for Norden: Cremer, U., *Norden im Wandel der Zeiten* (Norden: Heinrich Soltau, 1955), 18.
26 Smid, *Ostrfriesische Kirchengeschichte*, 141-143; Janssen, *Gräfin Anna*, 67-68.
27 Smid, *Ostfriesische Kirchengeschichte*, 147; Janssen, *Gräfin Anna*, 71-73; Weerda, *Emder Kirchenrat*, 16. Especially interesting is an article by E.Kochs, who gives a detailed account of the events leading to the church order and its effects (Kochs, E., 'Die Anfänge der ostfriesischen Reformation III (Schluss)' in: *Jahrbuch der Gesellschaft für bildende Kunst und vaterländische Altertümer zu Emden* 20 (1920), 1-125, 85-112).
28 Smid, *Ostfriesische Kirchengeschichte*, 152-153.

strongly influenced by Enno's brother, Johann, who served at the court of Charles V. When Enno II passed away unexpectedly in 1540 Johann tried to seize power, which, however, eventually failed and Anna – Enno's widow – ruled the county, though not without Johann remaining an influential political factor. Jürgens writes that in the first decade Anna's room to act was very limited. Her sovereignty was restricted because Johann's competing claims remained active in the background and the Habsburg Netherlands, as direct neighbours, significantly influenced East Frisian politics.[29]

Still, with Anna's reign an important new phase in the East Frisian Reformation began. Not least by her call upon John à Lasco to become superintendent[30] of the county in 1542, which he accepted.[31] It should be understood that at this time à Lasco was not yet the Reformed church leader he would become in London. Though having been strongly influenced by Erasmus and having married despite his priesthood, he had still hoped to be able to reform the Roman Catholic Church from the inside. He had only just returned from Poland where he had even sworn to a *confessio* that he did not desire to become a sectarian, but rather to stay true to the Roman Catholic Church. The exact reasons for this *confessio* remain unclear and Jürgens detects a sudden break with what happened in Poland when à Lasco returned to Emden.[32] Janssen sees in à Lasco the ideal person for Anna's goals. Belonging to none of the confessional strands, he could create an institution that contained these strands without causing ecclesiological or political unrest.[33] However, à Lasco proved to be too radical for this cause. He soon made it clear that

---

29 Jürgens narrates these political events very extensively and clearly: *Johannes à Lasco*, 177-178; 203-213.
30 According to the Lüneburger church order the superintendent was to be learned man. He had to teach the right doctrine and oppose false doctrine. The superintendent functioned more or less as the pastors' pastor (*upseher syn aver dat ganze land, aver alle pastoren und kerckendeneren des landes*), keeping watch over their doctrine and life. Moreover, he was to examine those who sought an office in church. For this examination he had to lead a board of men, that all things may stand by the testimony of several witnesses. For the tekst of the church order, see: Sehling, E., *Die evangelischen Kirchenordnungen des XVI. Jahrhunderts* 17,2,1, 373-393 (office of superintendent on 383-385). According to V. Goldentstein the examination by a board is unique to this church order and introduced because 'for the entire county only one person was elected for this office, and not, as in other territories, several persons…' (*Die Entstehung des Superintendentenamtes in der Reformationszeit* (Erlangen: FAU University Press, 2015), 315.)
31 Smid, *Ostfriesische Kirchengeschichte*, 158.
32 Jürgens, *Johannes à Lasco*, 147-157.
33 Janssen, *Gräfin Anna*, 86-89.

he would only be led by the Word of God and the honour of God in determining the doctrine and governance of the church.[34] This strict course was opposed in varying degrees by the nobility, the people and both reform and catholic minded preachers. À Lasco threatened to resign and admonished the countess to obey God and lead her people in obeying God. Anna decided to support her superintendent in this view, which Janssen interprets as a sign that she herself sought reform.[35] À Lasco proceeded by re-interpreting the existing structures: he created a consistory in Emden (though this was still dependent on the government) and the *coetus*, where the pastors of East Frisia met to discuss doctrinal issues.[36] According to Weerda these are two important steps, for in à Lasco's view church order and doctrine were closely connected. The church order ensures the doctrine by letting the Word of God rule. There is a large amount of freedom in choosing outward forms, but it is important that the doctrine is not scathed or destroyed by the form. So the church order should follow the rule of faith. This is rooted in the basic fact of the incarnation.[37] This needs some more elaboration, for which we have to turn to the Confession of the Strangers' Church in London.[38] It is stated there that the foundation (*sedem*) of the church is that He who was born of the virgin Mary is the true saviour, the anointed of God, the Son of God.[39] Because He is born of the virgin Mary Jesus shared in the flesh and blood of mankind (Hebrews 2 is quoted here). Without the incarnation there would be no church. Jesus, moreover, is God's anointed, and as such King. The church, to be church, must therefore adhere to His

---

34 Smid, *Ostfriesische Kirchengeschichte*, 160.
35 Janssen, *Gräfin Anna*, 91-93. Anna's attitude and confessional convictions are a matter of debate, Grochowina thinks she let politics rule over religion (*Indifferenz*, 171) Tanis says Anna 'was fully commited to the Protestant position but in a broader form' ('East-Friesland', 329). For the conflict between à Lasco and several groups, especially the monks, cf. Jürgens, *Johannes à Lasco*, 227-229. À Lasco's appeal to Anna's responsibilty to lead her people in matters of religion was not extraordinary, princes saw this as their duty (Reitemeier, *Reformation*, 9).
36 Weerda, *Emder Kirchenrat*, 37; 53; Janssen, *Gräfin Anna*, 96; Jürgens, *Johannes à Lasco*, 281-282. According to Goldenstein these changes found there origin in the Lüneburger church order, but à Lasco radically re-interpreted them and thus created something new (*Die Entstehung*, 317).
37 Weerda, *Emder Kirchenrat*, 28; 57-61 ; cf., also, Tanis, 'East-Friesland', 333.
38 This is anachronistic, of course; however, we do not have an earlier source that clarifies this essential theological presupposition. Moreover, it is the source that most clearly sheds light on how church order is linked to the incarnation, and hence why à Lasco and Micron debated this matter furiously with Menno Simons and other Anabaptists.
39 *London*, 66.

commandments.⁴⁰ He is, in addition, her Prophet, and therefore the church acknowledges Christ's teachings to be eternal.⁴¹ No other Saviour can be sought than Jesus Christ, Who is the Son of God and knowledge of God can only be revealed by Him, Who is in His Father's bosom. His revelation has been written down by the Apostles.⁴² So the link we see is this: Jesus is the anointed Saviour Who must be obeyed, for His teachings are eternal and the only way to know God. These revelations are found in Scripture, from which the church takes her teachings/confession. Church order has to follow the rule of faith. for the church to be true to her King. Hence Weerda's remark that both doctrine and governance are to be cleansed and deepened in continual relation to the incarnation of the Word.⁴³

It can come as no surprise, after this, that there was no place for David Joristen or Mennonites in East Frisia. À Lasco organised disputations in 1544 (one with the Joristen, another with Menno Simons) and this led to the *Polizeiordnung* of 1545, which was above all focussed on discipline. The ordinance ordered all David Joristen to leave the county and Mennonites should receive instruction. They were safe enough, though, if they kept a low profile.⁴⁴ In general, Grochowina remarks, the regulations were more strict on paper than they were in practice and most Mennonites were relatively safe.⁴⁵ This is, partly, due to à Lasco, who persuaded the countess Anna not to be too strict. Consequently, only the spiritualist Batenburgers and followers of David Joris were evicted.⁴⁶ Indeed, it was a time of coexistence, and it was not uncommon that people decided to change their convictions. A situation that lasted until the 1580's when, in Zijlstra's words, 'the religious movements had been institutionalized'.⁴⁷

---

40 *London*, 66.
41 *London*, 68-69.
42 *London*, 70-71. One cannot exclude the possibility that 1 and 2 John played a role in defining the incarnation as the central dogma.
43 Weerda, *Emder Kirchenrat*, 28.
44 Smid, *Ostfriesische Kirchengeschichte*, 170; Jürgens, *Johannes à Lasco*, 251-260; 265-266 (Jürgens further notes that the *Polizeiordnung* did not lead to brotherly admonishment, and the consistory still did not have a role in christian discipline. There was a 'discipline of manners' on behalf of the government, but no 'discipline of sin' on behalf of the church (p. 291-292).).
45 Grochowina, *Indifferenz*, 329-331. See, also, Krahn, *Dutch Anabaptism*, 181.
46 Zijlstra, 'Anabaptists in East Frisia', 59.
47 Zijlstra, 'Anabaptists in East Frisia', 61. Krahn writes that during the interim there was 'a temporary withdrawal of leaders most of whom later returned' (Krahn, *Dutch Anabaptism*, 182).

The opposition against à Lasco reached a new climax in 1546. As we have seen, there had been plenty of preachers in Norden that taught a 'sacramentarian' view on the Lord's Supper. In 1546, however, Wilhelm Lemsius, adhering to Luther's views, was a preacher in the city. When à Lasco wrote a treatise on the Lord's Supper, the *Moderatio Doctrinae*, Lemsius categorically refused this compromise and decided not to attend the *coetus* anymore. In this he was supported by several politically influential men. À Lasco experienced his room to manoeuvre as so limited that he once again threatened Anna he would lay down his office, and, just like a few years earlier, she backed him up. Eventually the *Moderatio Doctrinae* was even read as a sermon from the pulpit in Norden.[48] These events upset both the pastors and the congregation in Norden: the first shadows of the future Norder Kirchenstreit, which was discussed in chapter 3.[49]

Due to the introduction of the Interim of Augsburg in 1548,[50] which was enforced in an adapted form in East Frisia in July 1549,[51] à Lasco left in October of that year and Gellius Faber de Bouma became the most important clergyman.[52] Though he was not officially the superintendent, he was so in practice. In Emden the pastors strongly opposed the Interim, and refused to put it into action. Instead, they were in continual communication with à Lasco, and used every opportunity to preach the Reformed teachings.[53] Things were different in Norden, where Lemsius immediately implemented the demands of the Interim.[54]

After the Interim, when the refugees arrived from England, Anna did not ask à Lasco to resume his office as superintendent, mainly because she still desired to form a church in which several confessional strands

---

48 For these events, see: Weerda, *Emder Kirchenrat*, 31-32 (especially n49); 34; Janssen, *Gräfin Anna*, 93; 120-121; Jürgens, *Johannes à Lasco*, 315-320.
49 Jürgens, *Johannes à Lasco*, 316, especially n113.
50 The Augsburg interim was enforced after the defeat of the Schmalcaldic League; it practically (but for a few points, among which justification) re-introduced Roman Catholicism.
51 Eastfrisia was not part of the Schmalcaldic League; however, Charles V threatened to revoke Emden's *Vorbeifahrtsrecht*, which ensured that alle ships passing through their waters had to moor in Emden first. The economic importance was too great to take the risk of losing it (Pettegree, *Emden*, 35). The text of the adapted interim can be found in Sehling, *Kirchenordnungen* 17,2,1, 328-330 n.51.
52 Weerda, *Emder Kirchenrat*, 92-95; Smid, *Ostfriesische Kirchengeschichte*, 175; Janssen, *Gräfin Anna*, 124-125; Grochowina, *Indifferenz*, 218. Janssen sees the interim as a period in which the balance of the biconfessional coexistence is restored (p. 132-133).
53 Weerda, *Emder Kirchenrat*, 102-103; Jürgens, *Johannes à Lasco*, 344.
54 Weerda, *Emder Kirchtenrat*, 99.

could live together in harmony.[55] This can be seen in the Norder Kirchenstreit, described in the previous chapter: Anna did not support either 'Reformed' or 'Lutheran' doctrine, she supported the pastor who could bring peace. À Lasco's second stay in East Frisia was, nevertheless, of major importance because he managed to prevent publication of Gellius Faber's revised *Emder Katechismus* of 1546. Faber tried to make its teaching of the Lord's Supper less in line with Zurich and more in line with Melanchthon and Bucer.[56] The *coetus* of December 1553 decided that three catechisms would be published: the *Emder Katechismus* of 1546, an adapted version of Faber's catechism and a new catechism for the younger children.[57] Of these three only the *Catechismus, effte Kinderlehre* of 1554 came through the presses and was accepted as the East Frisian confession in 1576.[58] It did not have a unifying effect; rather, it caused the adherents of the several confessional strands to become more divided.[59] In Norden, however, after the Norder Kirchestreit, years of calm ensued, as was seen in the previous chapter. Indeed, so calm were these years, that there is nothing to mention in addition to what was said already. Apparently Micron and his colleagues managed to keep the congregation content and at peace, even though the *Apologeticum Scriptum* and *Ein kort underricht* show they pursued a 'sacramentarian' or 'Reformed' church practice. It appears that the congregation at large was happy as long as their pastors did their work well and did not oppose one another.

This plurality of religious thought and neutrality when it comes to doctrine is the main theme of Grochowina's research. She concludes that already in the 1530's it was difficult to reach confessional unity.[60] Indeed, she characterises the entire 16th century as the age of 'indifference' in East Frisia.[61] Indifference in this case does not mean that people did not care,

---

55 Janssen, *Gräfin Anna*, 138-139.
56 Van der Heide, *Gellius Faber*, 25.
57 Van der Heide, *Gellius Faber*, 26.
58 The authorship and identity of this 1554 catechism in relation to the 1546 catechism is a matter of ongoing discussion, see: Van der Heide, *Gellius Faber*, 25-27; Rauhaus, A., *Untersuchungen zur Entstehung, Gestaltung und Lehre des Kleinen Emder Katechismus vond 1554* (PhD thesis University of Göttingen, 1977); Schreiber, T., *Petrus Dathenus und der Heidelberger Katechismus. Ein traditionsgeschichtliche Untersuchung zum konfessionellen Wandel in der Kurpfalz um 1563* (Göttingen: Vandenhoeck & Ruprecht, 2017), 93-95; Weerda, *Emder Kirchenrat*, 84-85.
59 Smid, *Ostfriesische Kirchengeschichte*, 179; Weerda, *Emder Kirchenrat*, 74; 84-85; Grochowina, *Indifferenz*, 218-220.
60 Grochowina, *Indifferenz*, 16.
61 Grochowina, *Indifferenz*, 163.

but that all confessions were seen as options of equal right.[62] She sees Gellius Faber as a defender of a *via media* polity, defending neutrality.[63] To all effects and purposes there was the 'realism of practical life' in East Frisia,[64] i.e. a pragmatical view towards confessions and their claim to truth. Though one does feel that Grochowina describes early-modern laymen perhaps somewhat too much like 21st century postmodernists when she says that they 'postulated and constructed individual systems of faith that resulted from a combination of all the different influences exerted upon them, which are termed systems of sense'.[65] Having read Grochowina's thesis and reviewing the events in Norden before and during Micron's ministry, the conclusion that forces itself on us is that people were inclined to allow for a measure of freedom in doctrine as long as they could live peacefully in their own city. That, then, is the 'realism of practical life'. Micron becoming a minister in Norden illustrates this realism. Churches in the county had the right to choose their own ministers,[66] and in this case the congregation in Norden called a minister who, though his views were overtly Reformed, managed the congregation in such a way that there was peace in the years he ministered there.[67] How difficult this must have been is clear from the events after Micron passed away. Almost immediately the old feuds were rekindled and the congregation in Norden fell apart. When Cornelis Cooltuyn was sent to Norden from Emden to solve the problems in 1564, violence was used against him and he returned without having been able to solve anything.[68]

When we started this broad outline of the East Frisian reformation we pointed out that the tensions between the Lutheran, Reformed and Mennonite confessions would be our main focus. It was seen that in this

---

62 Grochowina, *Indifferenz*, 54-56.
63 Grochowina, *Indifferenz*, 218.
64 Grochowina, *Indifferenz*, 223. The term 'realismus des praktischen Lebens' comes from Petrus Bartels.
65 Grochowina, N., 'Confessional Indifference in East Frisia' in: *Reformation & Renaissance Review* 7.1 (2005), 111-124, 118.
66 Smid, *Ostfriesische Kirchengeschichte*, 187-188; Grochowina, *Indifferenz*, 130.
67 The extent to which the 'realism of practical life' during Micron's pastorship was practical pragmatism or indifferent (in Grochowina's meaning) pragmatism, and whether this was practiced by the members of the congregation or Micron cannot be known, as there are hardly any primary sources. Micron's letters and publications show little pragmatism.
68 Smid, *Ostfriesische Kirchengeschichte*, 182; Vis, G.N.M., *Cornelis Cooltuyn (1526-1567). De vader van de Hollandse reformatie* (Hilversum: Verloren, 1995), 59-60. Ufke Cremer, in his chronicle of Norden, shows how the dispute between Lutherans and Reformed continued until 1684 (*Norden*, 37; 70-71).

respect East Frisia was different from the other German Lands: from the very start this tension existed. Foreign and domestic political circumstances (which we have only here and there pointed out but played a substantial role throughout these years) made religious reforms a constant balance-act.[69] Within the established church there was a constant struggle between Lutheran and sacramentarian, later Reformed, groups. Especially in Norden where the first preachers were sacramentarians. They had to leave the city due to the Bremer Church Order, and history repeated itself with the Lüneburger. In subsequent years Lemsius caused unrest several times by forcing Lutheran views and practices. Besides this there was the constant presence of Mennonites with whom disputations were organised, and members of either confession crossed confessional boundaries. What we see, then, is that in the direct context of the book we are studying there was tension between confessions, a tension that had lasted for decades by the time Micron wrote the book. This was seen in Micron's biography as well. He opposed strict adherents of the *Confessio Augustana* and rejoiced when an Anabaptist family had been 'won'. On the other hand, though this sounds like the very opposite, there was a tendency to be 'indifferent' about the confession, and to pursue the 'realism of practical life'. We conclude that Micron found himself writing the book in a context where finding good doctrine and governance was one of balance, a balance between right and wrong of course, but more so a balance between peace and unrest, a balance between people who were too hot and those who were too cold, a balance, then, between disruption and cohesion.[70]

4.2 The Reformation of the Refugees

As we indicated in the introductory chapter the (until recently) generally accepted paradigm of the Reformation of the Refugees has come under question. The most obvious way of describing this would appear to first outline the theory, then the criticism and subsequently draw conclusions. However, as we hope to show, there are different strands within the theory which are entangled, and hence often confused, especially in the recent

---

69 Cf. Janssen, *Gräfin Anna*, 12-40; Jürgens, *Johannes à Lasco*, 168-178; Grochowina, *Indifferenz*, 91-95; 170. Additionally: Schilling, H., 'Johannes à Lasco und Ostfriesland. Eine europäische Beziehungsgeschichte am Vorabend der Konfessionaliserung' in: Strohm (ed.), *Johannes à Lasco (1499-1560)*, 1-20.

70 We consciously avoid 'coexistence' because that more or less supposes two different groups, whereas Micron would have had not two, but one congregation sitting in the pews.
For a similar evaluation of Gellius Faber's work, see: Van der Heide, *Gellius Faber*, 84.

criticism. It is therefore best to start with the criticism, because this gives us the opportunity to disentangle the confused strands (4.2.1). Then, in 4.2.2 we outline what several scholars say concerning the Reformation of the Refugees, before we draw our own conclusions and ask questions that need further research in both this thesis and the research of others (4.2.3).

4.2.1 Opposing the Paradigm

4.2.1.1 Jesse Spohnholz and Mirjam van Veen

The most important and most severe criticism of the paradigm is given by Jesse Spohnholz and Mirjam van Veen, sometimes writing together, at other times writing separately from each other.[71] We will start with Spohnholz's article and book on the convent of Wesel,[72] and this will lead us to the other relevant articles in a very natural way.

Spohnholz convincingly argues that the Convent of Wesel, 1568, did not, in fact, take place. He theorises that it was a list of articles drafted by Petrus Datheen (possibly with the help of Herman Moded) in 1568, when William of Orange was combating the duke of Alba, as a model for the soon to be established church(es) in the Netherlands. He actively sought supporters for this model, who expressed their support by subscribing to the document.[73] However, Orange's campaign failed, and – Spohnholz argues – the articles were forgotten until they were rediscovered by Ruytinck who inserted them in the story of the origins of the Dutch Reformed Churches.[74] Spohnholz claims that in those fifty years the articles did not play any role, let alone have any influence on, e.g., the

---

71 Under their supervision three studies have recently seen the light: Muylaert, S., *Shaping the Stranger Churches. Migrants in England and the Troubles in the Netherlands, 1547-1585* (Leiden/Boston: Brill, 2020); Schipper, I, *Across the borders of belief. Netherlandish Reformed migrants and confessional boundaries in the duchy of Cleves, c. 1550-1600* (PhD VU Amsterdam, 2020; and Gorter, P., *Gereformeerde migranten. De religieuze identiteit van Nederlandse gereformeerde migrantengemeenten in de rijkssteden Frankfurt am Main, Aken en Keulen (1555-1600)* (Hilversum: Verloren, 2021). These studies will be discussed sporadically when necessary, mostly in the footnotes. Most of this will take place when we address the three questions we ask in the last part of this chapter.

72 Spohnholz, J., 'Invented Memories. The Convent of Wesel and the Origins of German and Dutch Calvinism' in: Johnson, C.L. *et al.* (eds.), *Archeologies of Confession: Writing the German Reformation, 1517-2017* (New York/Oxford: Berghahn Books, 2017), 284-303; Spohnholz, J., *The Convent of Wesel. The Event that Never was and the Invention of Tradition* (Cambridge: CUP, 2017/2020).

73 Spohnholz, *Convent*, 16-87.

74 Spohnholz, *Convent*, 125.

synod of Emden, 1571.[75] In the second part of his book, and this is also the main argument in his article, he outlines what he believes to be the driving force behind the claimed importance of these articles. Says Spohnholz: 'some orthodox Reformed sought to record the historical foundations of their church and to demonstrate that, from its very beginnings, the Reformed tradition accorded with their current religious views rather than with those of the Remonstrants.'[76] Or, to paraphrase, the historians created a linear history to prove that their convictions were those of the founding fathers of the church. The articles by Datheen were gratefully incorporated in the narrative by both historians and archivists.[77] He unfolds how Guillaume Groen van Prinsterer and Abraham Kuyper followed the same procedure in the 19th century.[78] This story has been repeated over and over again, and thus the memory invented by

---

75 Spohnholz, *Convent*, 99-102. Spohnholz downplays the importance of the fact that ten subscribers of Datheen's/the Wesel articles were delegates at the Synod of Emden, 1571.
76 Spohnholz, *Convent*, 124
77 Spohnholz, *Convent*, 140.
78 There are several mistakes in Spohnholz's exposition which cannot be neglected. For instance ('Invented Memories', 288) he says the Réveil movement had a 'romanticized' vision of the Reformation. What does he mean here? Is it a view that fits with romantic philosophy (as he would appear to mean when compared to *Convent*, pp. 155-161), or does he use the word in its contemporary popular meaning? In either case he misunderstands the confessional presuppositions that underlie Van Prinsterer's thought (cf. Bremmer, R.H., *Er staat geschreven! Er is geschied! Introductie tot het leven en werk van Groen van Prinsterer als getuigend historicus* (Apeldoorn: Willem de Zwijgerstichting, 1981; Zwaag, K. van der, 'De Magnalia Deï. Groen van Prinsterer als historicus' in: Groen van Prinsterer, G., *Handboek der Geschiedenis van het Vaderland* (Veenendaal: G.Kool, 1978), [no pagenumbers]). A second mistake is Spohnholz's claim that when the Dutch church was renamed *hervormd* instead of *gereformeerd* this indicated that 'the church was re-formed without implying that those changes were complete or could be isolated to a specific moment in the past' (*Convent*, 160), i.e. a reforming instead of a reformed church. This is not the case, *hervormd* is simply the 'normal' Dutch for *gereformeerd*, *hervormende* would mean 'reforming'. The supposed difference in underlying philosophy/theology does not exist. A third mistake is Spohnholz's translation of the word *afscheiding*, which he translates with schism (*Convent*, 162). *Afscheiding* means secession. This is important because the leaders of the Secession did not believe they caused a schism, nor started a new church (whether or not one views this sociologically as a new church is another question; the theology behind 'schism' has other implications than 'secession'). Moreover, it is important to carefully distinguish between the Secession, the Réveil and the Doleantie, something Spohnholz neglects to do when he calls Simon van Velzen a neo-calvinist ('Invented Memories', 291). All of this raises the question whether Spohnholz, despite his impressive knowledge, has the (confessional) sensitivity that is needed to evaluate what the (neo-)Calvinists said in the 19th and 20th century.

confessional historians to legitimise their ecclesiology, still determines our interpretation of the sources today.[79]

In a joint article Spohnholz and Mirjam van Veen again question the supposed refugee-origins of the Dutch Reformed churches.[80] Their aim is to show that 'no specific role for religious refugees in the development of Dutch Calvinism can be found in historical writing from the late sixteenth to the mid-nineteenth century'[81], whereas it is commonly assumed that the refugees embraced Calvinism because of its teaching of providence, discipline and a presbyterial governance, leading to volunteeristic[82] and confessional model churches. '[T]here was no coherent exile experience'; rather, the experience, theology and ecclesiastical practice was diverse, Van Veen and Spohnholz claim.[83] Doctrine was toned down, rather than pressed and the refugees 'were ready to accommodate themselves to their environment'. Discipline, moreover, was not unique to the refugees, but shared by all movements.[84] It was not until the nineteenth century that two stories were constructed, an orthodox and a liberal one. The orthodox, with the powerful voices of Groen van Prinsterer and Abraham Kuyper, 'framed their position in the terms of a defence of the Synod of Dordt, the Belgic Confession, and the Heidelberg Catechism. Some with these views began constructing historical narratives that emphasized that the Dutch Reformed Church had been founded in exile in order to stress its independence from state oversight'.[85] This theory of the refugee church as the foundation for Dutch Calvinism is still being repeated today. First advocated by Kuyper, it proved 'resilient' and was 'picked up' by historians like Schilling, Oberman and Pettegree.[86] However, Spohnholz and Van

---

79 Spohnholz, 'Invented Memories', 294.
80 Spohnholz, J. & Veen, M.G.K. van, 'The Disputed Origins of Dutch Calvinism: Religious Refugees in the Historiography of the Dutch Reformation' in: *Church History. Studies in Christianity and Culture* 86/2 (2017), 398-426.
81 Spohnholz & Van Veen, 'Origins', 398. How this can be combined with the argument that Ruytinck in 1618 sought to frame a history that proved the Reformed Church had always been the same (as Spohnholz does in his book about Wesel) needs clarification. One also thinks of Jacobus Trigland's *Kerckelycke Geschiedenissen* and Antonius Thysius who elaborately discusses the London Strangers' Church on page 8 and the influence of Emden on page 9-10 of his introduction in *Leere ende order der Nederlandsche, soo Duytsche als Walsche, Ghereformeerder kercken* (Amsterdam: Pieter Pietersz., 1615).
82 This word seems to have been coined by Spohnholz and Van Veen ('Origins', 400).
83 Spohnholz & Van Veen, 'Origins', 399-402. Quote on p. 401.
84 Spohnholz & Van Veen, 'Origins', 402-404; 411. Quote on p.411.
85 Spohnholz & Van Veen, 'Origins', 417-419. Quote on p.417.
86 Spohnholz & Van Veen, 'Origins', 419, 424.

Veen continue, it does not adequately address the variations within the refugee congregations.[87]

This had already been argued by them several years earlier.[88] There, too, they find fault with the key role historians ascribe to the refugee-churches or stranger churches to 'consolidate this religious movement, theologically, institutionally, liturgically, and even socially'.[89] They list four men (Hubert Duifhuis, Dirck Volckertsz Coornhert, Casper Coolhaes and Herman Herberts) who were decidedly against the course the churches were sailing. Moreover, during the refugee experience many strangers were more than willing to compromise and deemphasise the doctrinal differences.[90]

More or less the same is Spohnholz's key argument in a more recent article, where he carefully outlines exceptions to the rule.[91] The refugee experience did not always lead to confessional Calvinist ideas (i.e. providence, election), or voluntary churches independent from the government.[92] What he subsequently tries to prove is that in Wesel, London, Emden and Frankenthal there were compromises, regarding doctrine and liturgy;[93] that there were refugee theologians, like Herberts, who most decidedly did not embrace Calvinism;[94] that in all of these churches discipline was not always effective (or more effective than other systems), let alone that everyone in the congregation led an exemplary life;[95] and even that the Reformed were quite mild towards the Anabaptists.[96] Hence Spohnholz's conclusion that 'exile did not categorically promote confessional Calvinism and does not explain the nature of Calvinism in the Dutch Republic…Reformed Protestantism proved remarkably flexible and diverse, depending on its environment.'

---

87 Spohnholz & Van Veen, 'Origins', 424.
88 Veen, M.G.K. van & Spohnholz, J., 'Calvinists vs. Libertines: A New Look at Religious Exile and the Origins of 'Dutch' Tolerance' in: Brink, G. van den & Höpfl, H. (eds.), *Calvinism and the Making of the European Mind* (Leiden: Brill, 2014), 76-99.
89 Van Veen & Spohnholz, 'Calvinists', 76.
90 Van Veen & Spohnholz, 'Calvinists', 84-85.
91 Spohnholz, J., 'Exile Experiences and the Transformations of Religious Cultures in the Sixteenth Century: Wesel, London, Emden, and Frankenthal' in: *Journal of Early Modern Christianity* 6/1 (2019), 43-67.
92 Spohnholz, 'Exile Experiences', 43-44.
93 Spohnholz, 'Exile Experiences', 46, 51-52
94 Spohnholz, 'Exile Experiences', 48.
95 Spohnholz, 'Exile Experiences', 49, 56-57, 61-62, 64-65
96 Spohnholz, 'Exile Experiences', 59.

And that 'exile churches [did perhaps not represent] idealised models of a brand of voluanteeristic and morally-pure confessional Calvinism'.[97]

We conclude this paragraph with an article by Mirjam van Veen in which she seeks to evaluate the self-designation of the refugees as *'peregrinus/peregrini'*.[98] She carefully distinguishes between being a refugee and being an exile[99] and concludes that exile did not play a major role in the development of Reformed doctrine or self-perception; rather, being a refugee is part of being an exile on earth – aliens and sojourners on earth – and the mortification of the flesh.[100] In addition, Lutherans and Anabaptists likewise saw persecution (and, consequently, flight) as mark of the true faith.[101] Calvin, moreover, thought that many of the refugees were too strict, and said they should be more willing to compromise.[102] Van Veen concludes that the experiences of flight did not leave a mark on Reformed theology, nor did the refugees see themselves as exiles. All in all the influence of the refugee-experience was on the social level, not the theological level.[103, 104]

When we summarise this, Spohnholz and Van Veen take scholars to task with telling too linear a story from exile to Reformed/Calvinist theology, including ecclesiology, to Dutch Calvinism, which finds its origin in confessional narratives. In reality, they say, it was much more complex, with many exceptions and compromises. Discipline, to them, proves that displacement did not necessarily lead to Reformed religion and moral high

---

97 Spohnholz, 'Exile Experiences', 65-67.
98 Veen, M.G.K. van, "'…wir sind ständig unterwegs…": Reformierte Flüchtlinge des 16. Jahrhunderts als Exulanten?' in: *Archiv für Reformationsgeschichte* 109 (2018), 442-458.
99 Van Veen, 'Reformierte Flüchtlinge', 444. Though she does not here add the more general category of 'migrant', this is done by, e.g., Peter Gorter (*Gereformeerde Migranten*, 14). This is probably due to the focus of Van Veen's article.
100 Van Veen, 'Reformierte Flüchtlinge', 444-447. Cf., also, the precluding sentence on p. 443: 'Im Folgenden wird für die Diversität der religiosen Erfahrung und Begrifflichkeit plädiert und die These vertreten, dass das Exil nicht in uniformer Weise die Identität der Calvinisten beeinflusst hat.'
101 Van Veen, 'Reformierte Flüchtlinge', 445.
102 Van Veen, 'Reformierte Flüchtlinge', 448.
103 Van Veen, 'Reformierte Flüchtlinge', 457-458.
104 Silke Muylaert (*Shaping*) is generally in agreement with this line of thought: 'With the exception of the Strangers' Church under Edward VI the stranger churches in England were not 'paragons of Calvinists [sic!] doctrine' (p.3, cf., also, 48, 60) and they constantly had to consider the wishes of the English government (p.8). Though, as can be seen, she does pay attention to the London church under Edward VI, most of her book deals with the period after Micron's demise, and as a consequence it is not necessary to discuss in detail in addition to Spohnholz and Van Veen.

standards. Moreover, being a refugee was not of major importance to their theology, and had limited importance for their self-perception.

4.2.1.2 Judith Becker

Before Spohnholz and Van Veen started to criticise the paradigm, Judith Becker had already published an article that deals with the theological side of the question.[105] She seeks to test the theory that migration led to a particular theology (in particular the ecclesiology) in which providence, election, discipline and diaconal work are key factors.[106] She has meticulously read the actual confessions of the stranger churches to see whether there are any traces of this and comes to the conclusion that the writers often make no reference to 'exile' at all, nor does predestination play a major role.[107] Discipline, on the other hand, does receive major attention. The congregation is the focal point: this is the group of people that partakes of the Lord's Supper, it is the inner circle. This spiritual definition creates a certain independence from their environment.[108]

So, she asks, is there a refugee theology? She does not think so. On the level of doctrinal standards the experience of displacement receives little attention, just like diaconal work. The only point that is shared by the various confessions is ecclesiology: 'priority was given to making theology practical and observed in congregational life'.[109] Thus, Becker concludes, it is better to speak of an 'ecclesiology of religious exiles' with the Eucharistic community as its main focal point.[110]

4.2.1.3 Johannes Müller

Last of all we turn to the work of Johannes Müller, who has studied the refugee experience very thoroughly. His book on the 'narrated diaspora'[111]

---

105 Becker, J., 'Migration and Confession among Sixteenth-Century Western European Reformed Christians' in: *Reformation and Renaissance Review* 13 (2011), 3-31.
106 Becker, 'Migration', 4.
107 Becker, 'Migration', 17 (especially note 33), 18-19.
108 Becker, 'Migration', 16, 20, 23.
109 Becker, 'Migration', 25.
110 Becker, 'Migration', 23, 25. Quotation on 25. It is a pity that this important article seems to have been overlooked by Spohnholz and Van Veen. It is especially noteworthy that Peter Gorter does not address this article, nor the theology underlying the practice of discipline. His chapter on the practice of discipline would have been more balanced if he had. Now, however, he often states a certain practice is due to pragmatism, though it might just as well be led back to the purpose or intent of discipline (*Gereformeerde migranten*, ch. 4. See, e.g., p. 109).
111 Müller, J., *Exile Memories and the Dutch Revolt. The Narrated Diaspora, 1550-1750* (Leiden/Boston: Brill, 2016).

takes pride of place among his work and we shall outline what he says there first,[112] before moving on to two articles that support his views.

Müller, then, explains how the migrants formed networks that were connected to each other by shared memories and common origin. This led to a shared identity and, in the course of time, this 'created canonic images of the past'.[113] He outlines that the very core of being dispersed is a constantly reinvented narrative of the past that shapes 'bonds and ties between groups in their new host societies'.[114] For the Dutch this all started in the 1550's with the first wave of refugees. Micron was one of this first wave. However, this does not automatically lead to a Reformed confession, for this experience was not unique to those who would turn out to be Reformed, but was also shared by Catholics, Anabaptists and Lutherans. The question arises whether the experience of exile was the primary agent towards shaping a Reformed theology.[115] Above all, Müller later argues, persecution and exile are marks of a true Christian and the true church, because Christians are in the world but not of the world. 'The exile situation is…presented as the spiritual *conditio humana*…[They regard themselves] as homeless travellers on the way to eternity.'[116]

So, though there was perhaps not a refugee-theology as such, the re-telling of the exile-memories did lead to a network of groups who felt connected to each other through shared experiences and common origin. They bore the honorary mark of the true Christian.[117] The presbyterial model they adopted may have led to 'help preserv[e] ties between local congregations', and they ultimately adopted the same doctrinal standards. In that way the refugee-experience may have had influence on the eventual theological and ecclesiological shape of the churches.[118]

The shared religious narrative, then, led to a sense of belonging. A narrative that could be either embraced or not, by refugees and non-

---

112 We cannot give a detailed outline of this valuable book. Our aim is to faithfully represent what Müller says on the connection between flight and refugee-theology.
113 Müller, *Exile Memories*, 5-6.
114 Müller, *Exile Memories*, 9-12.
115 Müller, *Exile Memories*, 33-36.
116 Müller, *Exile Memories*, 46-48. Quote on 48.
117 It would be interesting to examine the martyrologies from the several confessional groups with this in mind. It is also worth noticing that Micron himself wrote a hagiography about the martyr Hoste vander Katelyne. Cf. Selderhuis, H.J., 'A Teachable Death: Doctrine and Death in Marten Micron's Martyrology' in: *Unio Cum Christo* 1/1-2 (2015), 119-131.
118 Müller, *Exile Memories*, 161-162.

refugees who felt attracted to this narrative alike. However, this exile experience does not necessarily lead to a 'confessional narrative'.[119]

This is corroborated by an article in which Müller more or less summarises his views.[120] The refugees had to make theological sense of what was happening to them,[121] but this was not unique to Reformed or Calvinist refugees, rather it was shared by 'virtually all confessional groups'.[122] The image of a church, suffering for the sake of the truth, was created through sermons, letters and other media. In this way 'a collective diasporic consciousness' was created.[123] It was not until later generations re-read the material that they used them to serve as foundation narratives of the Reformed church, representing the ideal example and providing a collective religious identity, even if later generations were no longer refugees – they could still feel like they were defending the truth.[124] Müller concludes that 'the migrant congregations were both subject and object of a collective imagination that provided Post-Reformation societies with meaningful narratives about themselves and their past'.[125]

The last article we want to discuss provides a very general introduction to the discourse on the paradigm of the Reformation of the Refugees. The remark Müller starts off with is, perhaps, the most important of all: the refugee-experience was later used as a viewpoint to legitimise ecclesiastical practice.[126] For, once again, it must be remembered that there were many exceptions: not only were there refugees who did not become staunch Calvinists, there were also refugees from other confessional groups.[127] He summarises the main point that Spohnholz and Van Veen are trying to make as: 'That the influence of exile was not so much confessional unity,

---

119 Müller, *Exile Memories*, 206-207.
120 Müller, J., 'From diaspora to "imagined minority". Memories of persecution and the cross-generational transformation of Protestant migrant networks in early modern Europe' in: *Diasporas* 31 (2018), 21-34.
We used the open access of the article (via OpenEdition Journals) which does not have page-numbers, we will therefore refer to the paragraph-numbers indicated in the margin.
121 Müller, 'diaspora', par. 1.
122 Müller, 'diaspora', par. 2.
123 Müller, 'diaspora', par. 3 & 5. Quote at the end of par. 5.
124 Müller, 'diaspora', par. 9, 13, 18.
125 Müller, 'diaspora', par. 27.
126 Müller, J., 'Eine Reformation der Flüchtlinge? Konfessionsmigranten under der Einfluss des Rheinischen Exils auf die religiöse Landschaft der nördlichen Niederlande' in: Pohle, F., Samp, J. & Roebers, C. (eds.), *Das Ringen um den rechten Glauben. Reformation und Konfessionaliserung zwischen Maas und Rhein. Beitrage zur Tagung Aachen 21./22. April 2017* (Aachen: Centre Charlemagne, 2017), 62-73.
127 Müller, 'Reformation der Flüchtlinge', 66.

but rather the acceptance of diversity'.[128] It is not until after the formation of the Republic that the stranger churches are seen as either foreign ideas or the ideal to be aimed for.[129] So, Müller concludes, though the Reformed churches were shaped and influenced by the experience of flight, this was not unique to them and one should therefore be wary in calling it a 'Reformation of the Refugees'.[130]

Müller's theory is broad and complicated to grasp. We will try to paraphrase the general line of his thought: When a group of people has to leave their country for religious reasons, they have to make sense of what is happening to them. They tell a story of what is going on. Because they can relate to this story through shared experience and common origin, it creates a sense of belonging to that group. In this particular case it was the sense of being part of the true Church, in but not of the world, which is persecuted. The network that was created was further strengthened by the presbyterial church model, which led to the churches adopting the same confessions. When later generations re-read this history they had to relate to these stories in a certain way and subsequently read them as the foundation stories of a church they were also part of: the true believers suffering for the sake of religion. What this means is that the refugee experience came to be read as more or less exclusively Reformed, and the idea that exile was a catalyst for establishing the Reformed confession, whereas now it is clear that these experiences were not limited to the Reformed and did not always lead to Calvinist convictions, even though the ultimate form of the Dutch Reformed churches was influenced by the experiences abroad.[131]

4.2.1.4 Three Questions
Now that the most important criticisms have been outlined it is clear that there are three main strands that are entangled, and therefore often confused.

The first question is the most obvious one: What was the extent of continuity or discontinuity between the stranger churches (be it London under Edward VI, Emden, or any of the others) and the Dutch Reformed

---

128 Müller, 'Reformation der Flüchtlinge', 66n12. (Translation by HTW)
129 Müller, 'Reformation der Flüchtlinge', 69-70.
130 Müller, 'Reformation der Flüchtlinge', 73.
131 Interestingly, Janssen (in: Janssen, G.H. *The Dutch Revolt and Catholic Exile in Reformation Europe* (Cambridge: CUP, 2014/2016)) tells a similar story. The exile was seen as confusing and embarrassing (p. 37) leading to changed lifestyles to understand their experiences (p.55) and later Dutch Catholics crafted a self-image of inner exile that connected them to the 'heroic forebears' (p. 176).

Churches as they started to take shape from 1571 onwards? And if there was continuity, was this so strong that one should say that the foundations for the Dutch Reformed Church were laid in the stranger churches? In this one should make a distinction between the periods before and after the Wonderyear 1566. The experience of being a religious refugee was stronger in the later period.[132] This first question is especially opposed by Spohnholz and Van Veen, and to a lesser extent by Müller. Becker does not address this question.

The second question that arises is about the theological consequences of the refugee experience: Did this inherently lead to a theology that focusses on providence, election and discipline, and a synodal-presbyterial church model? Note that these are two separate aspects, one is doctrinal and the other is ecclesiastical practice, discipline alone falls in both categories. Spohnholz and Van Veen try to disprove this by pointing out that the churches and its members were willing to compromise and were hardly ever independent from the secular government. They weave this into their critique of the stranger churches as being foundational for the Dutch Reformed Church, thus entangling the two questions. Müller, though he also says that one should not talk of a Reformation of the Refugees, does distinguish the two questions more distinctly, but this is mainly because the (dis)continuity between the churches before and after Emden 1571 is not what he is dealing with. Becker clearly only addresses the actual ecclesiology.

The third question is related to the second: If the refugee experience led to a certain theology, was this indeed shared by all refugees? And was it, moreover, adhered to and practised by the actual members of these churches? Connected with this is the extent to which the refugees saw exile or diaspora as fundamental to their identity. Again, Spohnholz and Van Veen seek to oppose this by naming exceptions to the rule and turning to the minutes of consistories to point out that many believers were disciplined. In their work this is, once more, entangled with the other two questions. With all of them they try to re-tell the story of the 'origins' of Dutch Calvinism. Müller also points out the exceptions. Becker does not address this issue.

Now that we have a clearer view of what questions are at stake, we can turn to the expositions of the paradigm itself.

4.2.2 The Reformation of the Refugees
The three questions that have just been presented are the backbone for this section. Starting with the (dis)continuity between the stranger

---

132 Cf. Janssen, *Catholic Exile*, 29-31.

churches and the Dutch Reformed Churches, followed by the supposed theology of the refugees, and concluded by the amount to which this was universally adhered to. Nicholas Terpstra's *Religious Refugees in the Early Modern World*, however, fits in none of these categories and will therefore be addressed separately.

A) Continuity between the Churches before and after Emden 1571
So much has been written about the course of the Dutch Reformation, and especially about the refugee experience and the several synods, that it is difficult to find a place to start. When we look at Spohnholz and Van Veen we see that one of their primary points is that the linear narrative they oppose was constructed by confessional historians who sought to delve arguments from the past to defend their own convictions. Perhaps it is therefore best to start with the book by R.H. Bremmer, *Reformatie en Rebellie*,[133] a thorough study by a confessional theologian. We will follow this up with some articles and/or books by several Dutch Reformed historians and theologians, before moving on to the second major voice, that of Andrew Pettegree, which is again followed by several other opinions.

Bremmer's book, as is clear from the title, does not discuss the period of the churches abroad before 1566. Neither does he go deeply into the refugee experience; nonetheless, he does address this situation briefly before he states that after the Wonderyear 1566 many fled the Low Countries. This wave of refugees, says Bremmer, was received by the churches abroad, who also stayed in touch with the 'churches under the cross'.[134] When he comes to the synod of Emden, 1571, he calls this meeting the 'foundation' for the Dutch Reformed churches, claiming they were anti-hierarchical from the start and very concerned that there should be unity in doctrine between themselves (hence, they subscribed the Belgic Confession)[135] and other Reformed churches (and therefore they also subscribed the Confessio Gallicana).[136] When opportunities arose to go back to the Fatherland churches were slowly established, not without seeking continuity with what had been established in Emden. Says Bremmer:

---

133 Bremmer, R.H., *Reformatie en Rebellie. Willem van Oranje, de calvinisten en het recht van opstand. Tien onstuimige jaren: 1572-1581* (Franeker: Wever, 1984).
134 Bremmer, *Reformatie en Rebellie*, 60-63.
135 Note, in passing, that the *Belgic Confession of Faith*(!) itself speaks of the church as 'spread and dispersed throughout the entire world' (art. 27). Cf., Boer, E.A., 'Verspreid en verstrooid'. *Ecclesiologie van de diaspora en de reformatie van de Lage Landen* (Kampen: Theologische Universiteit van de Gereformeerde kerken, 2016), 12-15
136 Bremmer, *Reformatie en Rebellie*, 73-75

> Several pastors in North Holland had attended the synod of Emden. Now they got to work with the knowledge and experience they had gained in exile (*ballingschap*). They took with them what were immediate necessities for the edification of ecclesial life: their confession, the catechism, the psalter with the forms. Everything was at hand (*Alles was er al*). (…)The new beginning was made in continuity.[137]

This continuity is clear, for instance, in the continued subscription to the Belgic Confession and the very persons who were at that moment working in Holland. The provincial synod of Dordrecht 1574 is a case in point: its chairman was Gaspar van der Heijden, who had also been chairman in Emden. The secretary was Arent Cornelisz., who had been educated in Heidelberg, examined by Datheen and had ministered in Frankenthal. They were assisted by Jean Taffin, who had himself also been a refugee.[138] The strand of continuity throughout the years is what connects the story Bremmer is telling. He points out the same for the synod of Dordrecht 1578 and again for Middelburg 1581. And again, the names of the major representatives are telling: in 1578 Datheen presided, in 1581 Arent Cornelisz. Next to Cornelisz., Michaël Panneel and IJsbrand Trabius (or: Balck) took place in the synodal board. Both had been ministers in the stranger churches abroad.[139] Their major task was to write a church order, which was done by Cornelisz., Trabius, Taffin and Lydius[140]. They were helped by Lambert Daneau, the French professor of Theology in Leiden.[141] Another major issue was the case against Caspar Coolhaes,[142] to which we will return later.

What Bremmer tries to outline is that the churches that were being built up in the period after the return from abroad were to a large extent built up in continuity with Emden 1571, which had itself been a synod

---

137 Bremmer, *Reformatie en Rebellie*, 82. (Translation by HTW)
138 Bremmer, *Reformatie en Rebellie*, 85-90. The decisions of Dordrecht 1574 were also in line with Emden, see pages 92-94, 98
139 For more on Panneel, see: Op 't Hof, W.J., 'Panneel, Michaël' in: *Biografisch Lexicon voor de geschiedenis van het Nederlands Protestantisme. Deel 3*, 291. For Trabius: Pol, F. van der, *Mosterzaad in ballingschap. Over christelijke identiteit en geloofrepressie in de Nederlanden. Het Cleyn Mostertzaet (1590). Auteur, facetten, tekstuitgave* (Kampen: Kok, 2007), 15-43.
140 Lydius was the son of religious refugees. First a Lutheran, he converted to the Reformed faith. Among his influences are Ursinus, Calvin, Beza and Menso Alting. See: Woude, C. van der, 'Lydius, Martinus' in: *Biografisch Lexicon voor de geschiedenis van het Nederlands Protestantisme. Deel 1*, 146-148.
141 Bremmer, *Reformatie en Rebellie*, 122-123; 172-191.
142 Bremmer, *Reformatie en Rebellie*, 191-200.

formed by stranger churches and churches under the cross. Continuity, though, is not the same as dull repetition. Bremmer does not tire of pointing out new articles that are drafted, nor does he neglect the names of those who were not in agreement with the general course.[143]

This change-in-continuity is also clearly the opinion of Jacob Kamphuis: 'In Emden they came to a Reformed church polity out of a Reformed confession, just as they made that church polity instrumental to the dissemination of the Truth which they confessed.'[144] Later synods, he says, built on this foundation: they edited the church order, but did not start from scratch. A not unimportant quotation from a letter by Henrik van de Corput[145] is a direct challenge to the idea that the narrative connecting the Dutch Reformed Churches to the churches abroad and under the cross is relatively late. In 1587 Corput writes: 'the given order (*gestelde ordeninge*) is not new, but has been used under the cross, and that from the very start, and confirmed with (*met*) many synods.'[146] Whether he is referring to the synods under the cross or the synods from Emden 1571 onwards is unclear. Given his biography it is not impossible that he did have the synods under the cross in mind, too. Whichever

---

143 Bremmer, *Reformatie en Rebellie*, 75-76; 92; 95; 187-188
144 Kamphuis, J., *Zo vonden wij elkaar. Het begin van het Nederlandse gereformeerde kerkverband, de synode van Emden, 1571* (Groningen: De Vuurbaak, 1971), 79. (Translation by HTW).
We admit that Kamphuis's booklet is clearly influenced by church political issues within the Liberated churches in the preceding decade (cf. Boer, E.A. de, *De schele dominee. De open brief van 1966 en kerkelijke tucht in de Vrijgemaakte kerken* (Barneveld: De Vuurbaak, 2016); Vries, W.G. de, 'De geschiedenis van de kerken na de Vrijmaking in hoofdlijnen' in: Deddens, D. & Velde, M. te, *Vrijmaking – Wederkeer. Vijftig jaar vrijmaking in beeld gebracht 1944-1994* (Barneveld: De Vuurbaak, 1994), 129-151), it is, nonetheless, a valuable book when one is capable of reading with divided attention: what can I learn about 1571, and what can I learn about 1967 – it is insightful for both eras.
145 Cf. Itterzon, G.P. van, 'Corput (Cornput), Hendrik van den' in: *Biografisch lexicon voor de geschiedenis van het Nederlands protestantisme. Deel 3*, 83-85. Corput had fled from Breda in 1567 and studied theology in Heidelberg, though he had previously studied law in Leuven. Irenic in nature, yet he opposed Coolhaes, Duifhuis and Herberts.
146 Kamphuis, *Zo vonden wij elkaar*, 80. The quotation is taken from Rutgers, *De geldigheid van de oude Kerkenordening*, who refers to *Werken der Marnix-Vereeniging* 3rd series, part 2, p. 281.
Fred van Lieburg points out that during the genesis of the Dutch *Nadere Reformatie* it was considered important to be in line with the piety, doctrine and polity of the reformers 50-100 years before them (Lieburg, F. van, 'Dynamics of Dutch Calvinism: Early Modern Programs for Further Reformation' in: Brink & Höpfl (eds.), *Calvinism*, 43-66, 47-48). Apparently, pietists considered continuity important.

synods he meant, it is clear he saw a continuity between earlier practice and subsequent institutionalization.[147]

Selderhuis and Nissen state that Calvin's influence was mainly through the refugee-churches. Admitting that many emigrated for both economic and religious reasons, the churches abroad nevertheless became 'calvinist' and would continue their polity in the Republic.[148] In another article Selderhuis outlines the importance of Emden for the Dutch Reformed Churches. Next to the synod in 1571 we would like to draw attention to how Selderhuis sees Emden as 'the foreign headquarters of Dutch protestantism'.[149] That is where the churches turned for economical, practical and theological help and that is where the ministers were trained.[150]

Before moving on to Pettegree we round off by briefly glancing at the dissertation of A.A. van Schelven and G. Groen van Prinsterer's seminal work *Ongeloof en Revolutie*. Van Schelven also sees Emden as the 'Mother church' where pastors were educated. She sent out ministers and she gave advice. Indeed, she was so important that Gaspar van der Heijden asked the approval of the Emden consistory before he accepted the call to minister in Antwerp.[151] He also sees the importance of Emden for doctrine and unity, but that is something we will look at when reviewing the

---

147 The minutes of the synods under the cross have been published by N.C. Kist: 'De Synoden der Nederlandsche Hervormde Kerken onder het kruis, gedurende de jaren 1563-1577, gehouden te Braband, Vlaanderen enz.' ed. N.C. Kist in: *Nederlandsch Archief voor Kerkgeschiedenis* 9 (1849), 113-210. Alistair Duke drew up a summary of these minutes, which can be accessed via the 'Dutch Revolt' website, hosted by the University of Leiden (https://dutchrevolt.leiden.edu/english/sources/Pages/15631565.aspx [1-10-2021]).
148 Selderhuis, H.J. & Nissen, P., 'De zestiende eeuw' in: Selderhuis, H.J. (ed.), *Handboek Nederlandse Kerkgeschiedenis* (Kampen: Kok, 2006), 215-496, 279-283. Whether the mix of economic and religious reasons means we have to call the congregations 'migrant churches' rather than 'stranger churches' is interesting. In this summary we use the term employed by Selderhuis and Nissen.
149 Selderhuis, H.J., "Scheepke van Christus' in vreemde haven. De betekenis van Emden voor het Nederlandse calvinisme' in: Hertog, G.C. den, Mulder, M.C., Spanje, T.E. van (eds.), *Acta. Bundel der gelegenheid van het afscheid van prof. dr. T.M. Hofman als hoogleraar aan de Theologische Universiteit Apeldoorn* (Heerenveen: Groen, 2015), 328-337, 333.
Cf., also, Woltjer, J.J., *Op weg naar tachtig jaar oorlog. Het verhaal van de eeuw waarin ons land ontstond* ([n.p.]: Balans, 2012), 285-288.
150 Selderhuis, 'Scheepke', 330; 332.
151 Schelven, A.A. van, *De Nederduitsche vluchtelingenkerken der XVIe eeuw in Engeland en Duitschland in hunne betekenis voor de reformatie in de Nederlanden* (The Hague: Nijhoff, 1908), 118-123.

second question under B). Groen van Prinsterer wrote from the very clear conviction that history is led by God's providence and that, to a certain degree, one can also point out how God has worked in history. Even if this is no longer accepted in academic writing, this does not mean that Groen van Prinsterer can be neglected. As a historian he knew that the fruits of historical knowledge were also harvested in the sweat of one's brow.[152] He states that the ground principle of the Reformation was the freedom to subject oneself but under one yoke: that of God, as He reveals Himself in Scripture. It is Groen's confessional conviction (and therefore, to a certain extent, biased view) that the reformers did so truthfully and that God, Who had allowed the converts to be supressed for some time, rescued them and set them free. In this description Groen sees the churches before and after 1572 in continuance, because he sees the entire movement of Reform as essentially one.[153]

When it comes to the question of continuity between the churches before and after Emden 1571, the most powerful and authoritative academic voice is surely that of Andrew Pettegree. In *Emden and the Dutch Revolt*[154] this is one of his main themes. It is impossible to represent what he says in detail, but the most important points will be outlined. Pettegree opines that the exile was the preparation for a new Dutch Reformed Church.[155] Emden was the Mother Church whose church order influenced many major theologians; she had contact with conventicles (which were by no means joined by all who sympathised with Reformed doctrine) and trained pastors; and Emden was an important printing centre.[156] Those who fled often went to Emden and there it was more and more felt that there should be a stronger structure. This led to the synod of Emden 1571, giving the doctrinal framework of the church. Moreover, 'the guidelines laid down for establishing and regulating congregational life were very largely based on the practice developed in Emden and other exile Churches'.[157] Pettegree, too, outlines the continuity between Emden 1571 and the following synods. However, this does not mean that after Emden 1571 nothing new happened: 'the precise form of the Dutch Reformed Church…was something which would emerge only in the last

---

152 Groen van Prinsterer, G., *Ongeloof en Revolutie* ed. H. Smitskamp (Franeker: Wever [n.d.]), 116.
153 Groen van Prinsterer, *Ongeloof en Revolutie*,114-119.
154 Pettegree, A., *Emden and the Dutch Revolt. Exile and the Development of Reformed Protestantism* (Oxford: Clarendon Press, 1992).
155 Pettegree, *Emden*, vi; 3.
156 Pettegree, *Emden*, 46; 59; 67-85.
157 Pettegree, *Emden*, 176-185. Quotation on 185.

decades of the sixteenth century, and in the course of the next';[158] however, in that development, Emden had played a vital role.[159]

The biographies of Cornelis Cooltuyn and Jan Arentsz., written by Jurjen Vis, show this is more than a paradigm.[160] The position of Emden as Mother Church is obvious when Cooltuyn, after having fled Enkhuizen and Alkmaar, led the 'Holland Mission' from Emden, acting as a 'Paul' to Jan Arentsz. as a 'Timothy'.[161] Cooltuyn himself was active in this mission too and was one of the theologians asked to comment on and approve the Belgic Confession, as were Datheen, Van der Heijden, Taffin, Delenus and Carinaeus – all familiar 'refugee' names by now.[162] Arentsz. was in Amsterdam in the Wonderyear and the description of the Lord's Supper celebrated there shows it was clearly influenced by the rite prescribed in Micron's *Ordinancien*.[163] Arentsz., who had fled to Emden in 1567 (in that year Cooltuyn fell victim to the bubonic plague)[164], was an important church leader in Holland during the early 1570's, defending the importance of confessional subscription in line with Emden 1571 'for the sake of unity'.[165]

In their introduction to the synod of Emden 1571 Freudenberg and Siller call it an 'exile synod'. It was made up of either churches in exile or churches under the cross, and it was their specific aim to establish unity. This unity came into being through the confession and polity, the church order in London being an important source for Emden 1571.[166] Refugees from England and London came to the German Lands, and oftentimes

---

158 Pettegree, *Emden*, 249.
159 Pettegree, *Emden*, 251.
160 Vis, G.N.M, *Jan Arentsz. De mandenmaker van Alkmaar, voorman van de Hollandse reformatie* (Hilversum: Verloren, 1992); Vis, G.N.M., *Cornelis Cooltuyn (1526-1567). De vader van de Hollandse reformatie* (Hilversum: Verloren, 1995).
161 Vis, *Cooltuyn*, 47; 52; Vis, *Arentsz.*, 43.
162 Vis, *Cooltuyn*, 60. Vis bases this on Thysius, *Leere ende order*, 8-9.
163 Vis, *Arentsz.*, 78-85.
164 Vis, *Cooltuyn*, 76.
165 Vis, *Arentsz.*, 99-106.
166 Freudenberg, M. & Siller, A., *Emder Synode 1571. Wesen und Wirkungen eindes Grundtextes der Moderne* (Göttingen: Vandenhoeck & Ruprecht, 2020), 9; 17; 30-31; 39. For the churches represented, the map on p. 12-13 speaks louder than words. Freudenberg and Siller also mention church discipline as a unifying practice on p. 30. Duke sees the *Ordinancien* as one the most important texts in the formation of the Dutch Church (Duke, A., 'Perspectives on European Calvinism' in: Pettegree, A., Duke A., & Lewis, G. (eds.), *Calvinism in Europe, 1540-1620* (Cambridge: CUP, 1996), 1-20, 4.)

their church polity was modelled on à Lasco's church order.[167] Their influence was so large that in greatly affected the theology and formulation of the Heidelberg Catechism and the church order of the Kurpfalz, as has very convincingly been shown by Tobias Schreiber.[168] An influence which was continued in Datheen's *De Psalmen Davids*, which is especially clear in the forms.[169]

After looking at the secondary literature we come to the following conclusion: it is not merely stated that there was continuity; rather, this is shown to be the case by official church documents (minutes), key players and lines of influence (coming mainly from Emden). The pivotal point in the literature is not Wesel 1568, but Emden 1571.[170] The church after Emden was built up under the motto of 'dynamic continuity': though much changed, yet there was a distinct constant core that bound together the churches throughout these years. This is a difference with the period before 1566. Though there are some clear influences, and the London Strangers' Church even functioned more or less as a model church, yet the stress would have to be laid on 'dynamic', rather than 'continuity', though continuity should not be omitted. After 1566 there appears to be an increasing, or even solidifying, continuity. Still dynamic, but less so than before 1566.

B) The Relation between Flight and Theology
Let us move on to the second question: to what extent was the theology of the Reformed Churches after 1571 shaped by the refugee experiences before that time? Did these circumstances lead to that theology automatically, or were there exceptions? And if there were exceptions, what is their importance? The works of Heiko Oberman, Heinz Schilling and Peter Ole Grell push themselves to the forefront when it comes to the actual theology of providence and election, so their works will be discussed first, before we outline what others say about this issue. Then we move on to discipline, and round off with the (in)dependence from the state.

---

167 Ehrenpreis, S., 'Hofcalvinismus und Füchtlingkirchen. Zwei Modelle Reformierter Kirchenorganisation und Politik' in: Reiss, A. & Witt, S. (eds.), *Calvinismus. Die Reformierten in Deutschland und Europa* (Dresden: Sandstein Verlag, 2009), 213-218, 215.
168 Schreiber, T., *Petrus Dathenus und der Heidelberger Katechismus. Ein traditionsgeschichtliche Untersuchung zum konfessionellen Wandel in der Kurpfalz um 1563* (Göttingen: Vandenhoeck & Ruprecht, 2017), 89-174.
169 Schreiber, *Petrus Dathenus*, 299-303
170 In *Een nieuwe tijd, een nieuwe kerk* (Zoetermeer: Meinema, 2009) Mirjam van Veen still seems to defend the classic paradigm. See pages 32; 62; 67; 71; 83-85; 126.

Oberman's thesis about the Reformation of the Refugees has been compiled in *John Calvin and the Reformation of the Refugees*[171]. The doctrine of providence is closely intertwined with the experience of being a refugee, Oberman believes. This experience profoundly influenced the way in which the refugees perceived themselves (we describe this in more detail when we discuss the third question): in their threatened lives, God is the Lord and Protector of the believers.[172] This essential awareness of being on the run for the cause of God's truth, also leads to the conviction that they are the elect 'secret service' in a world where the devil still has a huge amount of influence.[173] The doctrine of election gave assurance that in persecution the believers would be able to persist in faith.[174] However, at no point does Oberman describe a simple 'action-reaction' scheme, as if persecution must of necessity lead to 'calvinist' theology. Says Oberman: 'What we have sketched here [i.e. how Calvinism became dominant] is not an inevitable process, but the tumultuous accumulation of small skirmishes.'[175] This is obvious, because '[g]ood historians are the guardians of contingency. They are aware that it is difficult to understand what actually did happen, if they do not also ponder what might have happened.'[176] Nonetheless, we have seen that Oberman draws attention to the importance of providence and election. The same is done by Heinz Schilling. It is his opinion, too, that the experience of flight has marked the Reformed and their theology, though his articles mainly focus on the development of discipline and church polity, he agrees with Oberman that refugees were profoundly aware of the providence of God in their lives.[177] But again, at no point does Schilling argue that this outcome is a necessity. He acknowledges that there were other refugees, for instance Jews and Lutherans.[178] Nor does he deny that 'refugees seem to have

---

171 Oberman, H.A. [edited by Peter A. Dykema], *John Calvin and the Reformation of the Refugees* (Geneva: Droz, 2009).
172 Oberman, *Reformation of the Refugees*, 58.
173 Oberman, *Reformation of the Refugees*, 192 (cf. p. 46).
174 Oberman, *Reformation of the Refugees*, 86. Cf. Oberman, H.A. [edited by Donald Weinstein], *The Two Reformations: The Journey from the Last Days to the New World* (New Haven: YUP, 2003), 114-115.
175 Oberman, *Reformation of the Refugees*, 85.
176 Oberman, *Reformation of the Refugees*, 75-76.
177 Schilling, H., 'Christliche und Jüdische Minderheitsgemeinden im Vergleich: Calvinistische Exulanten und westliche Diaspora der Sephardim im 16. und 17. Jahrhundert' in: *Zeitschirft für Historische Forschung* 36/3 (2009), 407-444, 434-435.
178 Schilling, 'Minderheitsgemeinden', 412, 436; Schilling, H. 'Calvin und die calvinistische Konfessionskultur' in: *Geschichte im Wissenschaft und Unterricht* 7/8 (2009), 372-386, 378-379; Schilling, H., 'Innovation through Migration: The Settlements of Calvinistic

chosen their new homes primarily according to economic possibilities' and '[a]ctually, the chances of building up and maintaining Calvinistic congregations, and the modalities of their organization, depended on the strength or weakness of the alliance between the mass of native inhabitants and the native clergy, Lutheran or Catholic.'[179] Of course, the same is seen by Ole Peter Grell: there were other refugees besides the Reformed.[180] But their displacement did reinforce 'their sense of belonging…When reading the Old Testament these refugees would construe their experience as a direct consequence of God's Providence…they came to form an international movement, perhaps less through their Calvinism, which often differed in points of doctrine, and their conviction of being God's chosen people, than through their shared experience of displacement and minority existence'.[181] Yet, there is a close link, says Grell, between the diaspora of the Reformed and their belief in providence and election.[182] Not that one led to the other, but that exile 'reinforced' the awareness or reliance on these two points of doctrine. This is more elaborately defended in his book on several Italian refugee-families.[183] There, too, he defends the thesis that flight led to an international network 'underpinned' by a theology strongly aware of providence and election. These two, he claims, 'could not… have emerged without…persecution and subsequent exile.'[184] Though this was not necessarily a strong religious conviction at first, it was nonetheless reinforced by emigration and displacement.[185] The extent to which refugees were willing to compromise appears limited, when Grell describes how refugees living in Nuremberg went to Amberg to attend Reformed services.[186] It is important to draw attention to the words Grell uses. He does not state that in the experience of displacement the theology of special providence and election was born, or thought up, but that it was reinforced. Indeed, without this experience it would have been less prominent, though not absent.[187] One might put it like this: what

---

Netherlanders in Sixteenth- and Seventeenth-Century Central and Western Europe' in: *Social History* 16/31 (1983), 7-33, 9.
179 Schilling, 'Settlements', 16.
180 Grell, O.P., 'Merchants and Ministers: The Foundations of International Calvinism' in: Pettegree, Duke & Lewis (eds.), *Calvinism in Europe*, 254-273, 254.
181 Grell, 'Merchants and Ministers', 257.
182 Grell, 'Merchants and Ministers', 267; 273.
183 Grell, O.P., *Brethren in Christ. A Calvinist Network in Reformation Europe* (Cambridge: CUP, 2011).
184 Grell, *Brethren*, 1-2.
185 Grell, *Brethren*, 5; 7. He provides evidence for this claim on p. 37; 55; 59; 61; 76-77
186 Grell, *Brethren*, 116.
187 Pettegree also sees the refugee experience as a reinforcement of faith (Pettegree, *Emden*, 20).

would have been confessed devoutly – if somewhat absent mindedly – was now confessed fervently with full conviction. At this point it is also interesting to look at the Catholic exile, as described by G.H. Janssen. He, too, sees exile as a 'catalyst for religious radicalisation'.[188] Likewise, the catholics turned to the biblical stories to form their understanding of the exile experience, possibly even adapting well-known protestant arguments to their own advantage.[189] This process, however, is not unavoidable, as if exile automatically leads to this reinforcement. Only under the right circumstances (e.g. media, charismatic leaders and social structures) is exile a unifying experience and the catalyst for confessionalization.[190]

We move on to the practice of discipline. This is dealt with by many more scholars, and indeed it is discipline that takes pride of place in the works of Oberman and Schilling. Let us start with these major academics once more. Oberman states that there was a general longing for moral discipline. Without this practice Calvinism would not have been able to survive. After the reformation of doctrine, there had to be a reformation of life. Moreover, discipline 'ensured fraternal and orderly life'; after all, man's total depravity means that without discipline the believers would fall into sin, and the church might crumble.[191] Schilling points out the same when he says that discipline was the theological core of the Refugee faith: a guard against the world, binding the congregation together.[192] In a world where discipline was stressed by all confessions, this was particularly strong among the refugees to ensure orthodoxy and to have a holy congregation by disciplining sinful behaviour of its members.[193] This sentiment is repeated by Duke.[194] Pettegree sees the articles on discipline in the acts of Emden 1571 as directly influenced by the stranger churches, a practice that was continued later.[195] This sustained practice is evidenced

---

188 Janssen, *Catholic Exile*, 8. One should keep in mind that Janssen takes the refugee thesis for granted. One cannot use Janssen to prove the correctness of the paradigm – that would be a circle. Nonetheless, seeing similar processes going on can corroborate the likelihood of the paradigm.
189 Janssen, *Catholic Exile*, 40; 54.
190 Janssen, *Catholic Exile*, 90; 92; 103; 182.
191 Oberman, *Reformation of the Refugees*, 26-28; 35; 61-62188-189; 192. Cf., also, Bergsma, W., *Gelovigen, dominees en geleerden. Opstellen over Friese en Nederlandse geschiedenis in de vroeg-moderne tijd* (Hilversum: Verloren, 2019), 31; 41-42.
192 Schilling, 'calvinistische Konfessionskultur', 382-383.
193 Schilling, 'Minderheitsgemeinden', 426-427.
194 Duke, 'Perspectives', 13-14. Cf., also, Pettegree, *Emden*, 55.
195 Pettegree, *Emden*, 184-185; 244. Peter Gorter, on the other hand, does not see the practice of discipline in Cologne, Aachen and Frankfurt as 'strict' (e.g. *Gereformeerde migranten*, 183). Perhaps one should conclude that even though elders sometimes

by Bremmer and Vis. In his study on Cornelis Cooltuyn Vis shows that discipline over both life and doctrine was practiced by the church in Emden.[196] Bremmer tells us that action was taken against no less a man than Herman Moded – an influential pastor.[197] He also vividly narrates the case against Caspar Coolhaes. Coolhaes's theology did not align with the Reformed confessions, but ultimately the question was who governed the church: the secular government or the church itself.[198] Let us not forget, moreover, the actions of the synod against Datheen, when he was accused of heresy and his subsequent conversion.[199]

Thus, we arrive at the third aspect of this question seamlessly: that of church polity and its (in)dependence from the secular government. To understand this properly we start with the issue of maintaining the confession. The importance of doctrine in the stranger churches was seen in chapter 3 and it was a practice that continued in the Dutch Churches from Emden 1571 onwards. It was the confession that helped create unity, or perhaps articulated the existing unity, among the Reformed. Confession and church order go hand in hand, they are an expression of faith that binds together and a guard against independent behaviour by churches and persons alike.[200] The germ for this unity lies, so it is argued, in the refugee-character of these churches. Because they were displaced they felt connected to each other and experienced a great need to organise networks of communication. This is the foundation for the presbyterial-synodal system, a church structure that was present in Holland even before Emden 1571.[201] This system created a network of churches in

---

chose to avoid discipline out of pragmatism, they did not consider discipline to be merely an instrument. Note, moreover, that Pettegree speaks of exile churches.

196 Vis, *Cooltuyn*, 58-59.
197 Bremmer, *Reformatie en Rebellie*, 95.
198 Bremmer, *Reformatie en Rebellie*, 191-200. Cf., also, Kamphuis, J., *Kerkelijke besluitvaardigheid. Over de bevestiging van het gereformeerde kerkverband in de jaren 1574 tot 1581/2 ondanks de oppositie van het confessioneel en kerkelijk indifferentisme, zoals deze oppositie inzonderheid vanuit Leiden werd gevoerd* (Groningen: De Vuurbaak, 1970) and Kooi, Ch., *Liberty and Religion: Church and State in Leiden's Reformation, 1572-1620* (Leiden: Brill, 2000) ch. 2-4
199 Nauta, D., 'Dathenus (Daten, Daete, Daets), Petrus (Pieter)' in *Biografisch Lexicon voor de geschiedenis van het Nederlands protestantisme* IV,110-114, 113.
200 Freudenberg & Siller, *Emder Synode*, 30; 39; Kamphuis, *Zo vonden wij elkaar*, 44; 69; 79; Pettegree, *Emden*, 235; Selderhuis, 'Scheepke', 335-336; Bremmer, *Reformatie en Rebellie*, 74; Van Schelven, *vluchtelingenkerken*, 128.
201 The idea of networks as the core from which refugee-theology and practice began is the underlying principle of Grell's study *Brethren in Christ*, see especially pages 5;10-13; 76-77; 119. In addition to Grell, see: Bremmer, *Reformatie en Rebellie*, 84; Vis, *Jan Arentsz.*, 43; Schilling, 'Minderheitsgemeinden, 420; Schilling, H. 'Peregrini und

which they work together, without having dominion over each other. Having a synodal system ensured, so it is said, that the churches could act in relative independence to stand firm in their own faith.[202] Within these structures and power-relations they would sometimes condone errors in others, but they would not compromise when it came to their core beliefs. Freudenberg and Siller, for instance, stress how in Emden the synod of 1571 withstood the pressure exerted by William of Orange and Philips of Marnix to accept the *Augsburg Confession*, a plan mainly driven by political motives.[203] Pettegree sees this as a rite of passage towards ecclesiastical adulthood.[204] For Oberman this independence is rooted in theology: 'Calvin strove to renovate the church and reform society to visibly reflect the glory of God' but the means to do so were not 'in "turning Swiss", the security of Zurich, but in "turning French", opting for organizational self-government'.[205] Interestingly, however, Plasger claims that this quest for independence was rooted in Bullinger's theology, something we might have to look into when we consider Micron's influences.[206] Whatever the source, Schilling informs us that the independence was a matter of principle.[207] However, that does not mean that he neglects the various relationships between the churches and local secular governments: there were local variations due to the fact that governments received refugees differently.[208] A sentiment repeated by Freudenberg and Siller: they had to adapt their way of living to the framework in which they found themselves. This framework included the stipulations by local governments.[209] When the setting conflicted with their conscience, however, they moved on. Thus we return to Groen van Prinsterer's basic statement that the overriding quest of the Reformation

---

Schiffchen Gottes. Flüchtlingserfahrung und Exulantentheologie des frühneutzeitlichen Calvinismus' in: Reiss & Witt (eds.), *Calvinismus*, 160-168, 163; Schilling, 'Konfessionskultur', 379; Ehrenpreis, S., 'Hofcalvinismus', 216; Van Schelven, *vluchtelingenkerken*, 310-312.

202 E.g. Selderhuis/Nissen, 'de zestiende eeuw', 280-283. For further references see the following footnotes.
203 Freudenberg & Siller, *Emder Synode*, 21. Cf., also, Kamphuis, *Zo vonden wij elkaar*, 49-50 and Bremmer, *Reformatie en Rebellie*, 75.
204 Pettegree, *Emden*, 235.
205 Oberman, *Reformation of the Refugees*, 184.
206 Plasger, G., 'The Dynamics of the Reformed Reformation: German Reformed Church Orders in the 16th Century' in: Brink & Höpfl (eds.), *Calvinism*, 67-75, 71.
207 Schilling, 'Minderheitsgemeinden', 421.
208 Schilling, 'Minderheitsgemeinden', 411.
209 Freudenberg & Siller, *Emder Synode*, 18.

was the freedom of conscience to serve God according to His Word.[210]

What we have seen in discussing this second question is that the scholars who defend a more or less linear process from refugee-churches to the Dutch Reformed churches stress the independence from the government and the need for discipline in the congregation. In the experience of emigration and loss the believers sought something to unify them, which was embodied by confessions and a church order. At no point is it said that this was a necessary consequence, for all scholars mention the exceptions. The focus on providence and election is not nearly as strong, and attested by a limited number of scholars. Even if this connection is seen, the relationship is one of reinforcement, not origin. Besides, no one claims any indissoluble knot; rather, they try to show how the experience led to a certain anthropology of fundamental alienation, reinforcing these theological doctrines.

C) Was Every Refugee Reformed?
The last of the three questions will not detain us as long as the other questions did. The first part of the question, indeed, has already been more or less answered. All the sources summarised here pay attention to the fact that there were refugees of other confessions, who – obviously – did not become Calvinists. Within the church itself there was the need to discipline men like Moded, Coolhaes and Datheen. Moreover, many of the exceptions Spohnholz mentions are well-known in the secondary literature that does speak within the framework of the paradigm. Additionally, many of them were 'Libertines', as they are commonly called, a group which is certainly not neglected in the literature.[211]

---

210 Peter Gorter repeatedly highlights that pragmatic considerations were important to local congregations (*Gereformeerde migranten*, 55, 69, 95-96, 143) yet his accounts also show that this pragmatism was not without limits, e.g. the consistories generally refused to act against their consciences (c.f. *Gereformeerde migranten*, 34-35, 38, 46, 53-54, 61, 74, 77, 81, 148).
Opitz, in an analysis of Zwingli's 67 theses of 1523, also argues that 'freedom' for Zwingli is not only freedom from, but also freedom to, i.e. freedom to serve God according to His Word (Opitz, P., *Zwinglis Thesen von 1523 als Manifest christlicher Freiheit*, lecture at the 13th International Emder Tagung *Freiheit im reformierten Protestantismus: Konzepte – Praktike – Diskurse* (2023). This lecture will be published in: Sallman, M. & Zahnd, U., *Emder Beiträge zum Geschichte des reformierten Protestantismus* vol. 13 (Göttingen: Vandenhoeck & Ruprecht, [forthcoming]). I am grateful to prof. Opitz for sharing the written version of his lecture with me.).

211 Coolhaes has already been mentioned in the expositions by Bremmer; For Coornhert see, e.g., Kamphuis, *Zo vonden wij elkaar*, 79; For Herberts, Duifhuis and other groups see, e.g., Selderhuis/Nissen, 'de zestiende eeuw', 299-301; 319-322; 344-348

Pettegree says that in 1566 'there was still a wide variety of experience among those who joined the movement'.[212] True enough, not all refugees held the same convictions, nor did they all go abroad for religious reasons, yet there was in every community of strangers 'a core for whom the religious cause was of overriding importance'.[213] So, no: not all refugees were Reformed, and no, not all members of the stranger churches were faithful and upright in their faith.

We thus move on to the second part of the question, which deals with the extent to which the refugee experience shaped the way in which these people saw themselves. According to Oberman, the experience of exile was a profoundly forming period. Calvin addressed his readers as 'uprooted wayfarers'[214] in exile between heaven and earth.[215] An unsafe place, lacking security on earth, where it is always persecuted, yet safe in the eternal city.[216] In this they are true disciples, for God Himself is given the title of 'fugitive' by Calvin.[217] A sentiment not restricted to Calvin, so Schilling claims: the core of refugee theology is the awareness of *peregrinatio*, being on the road in a world where one is but a sojourner.[218] The believers in North Holland could not have expressed it more clearly than they did, when in 1565 they claimed themselves to be the 'fratres per Hollandiam sparsi'.[219]

D) Nicholas Terpstra's Religious Refugees in the Early Modern World

Before coming to an evaluation we would like to draw attention to a book that is important to the discussion, yet is so broad in its scope, that it needs to be discussed separately. Nicholas Terpstra has taken the element of flight as the strand that knits his narrative of the Reformation-era together. He takes his starting point in the middle ages, where the 'corpus christianum' was the city of God that opposed the city of Man.[220] Each

---

212 Pettegree, *Emden*, 235.
213 Pettegree, *Emden*, 228.
214 Oberman, *Reformation of the Refugees*, 187.
215 Oberman, *Reformation of the Refugees*, 40.
216 Oberman, *Reformation of the Refugees*, 46;58-60; 189; 192.
  Balke has proven this is a key motive in Calvin's works (Balke, W., *Via Vitae. Opstellen over kerk en theologie in het perspectief van de Reformatie* (Apeldoorn: de Banier, 2019), 208-212.)
217 Oberman, *Reformation of the Refugees*, 64.
218 Schilling, 'Minderheitsgemeinden', 435; Schilling, 'Peregrini', 167; Schilling, 'Konfessionskultur', 379.
219 Vis, *Cooltuyn*, 54.
220 Terpstra, N., *Religious Refugees in the Early Modern World. An Alternative History of the Reformation* (Cambridge: CUP, 2015), 21-26.

city on earth had to become a pure and sacred space. This was an important struggle to ward off God's punishments. Heresies and immorality were therefore unacceptable and seen as infections or contagious threats.[221] The 'body' had to be purified through separation, containment or persecution (including discipline). Purgation could be done by either expelling others or expelling oneself.[222] This led, in the end, to a 'map of religious confessions' that shows an 'incredible variety of religious groups co-existing in large communities across Europe'.[223] What was once the city had now become a group in which the experiences of being a fugitive shaped their religion.[224] In time, however, this was 'absorbed' by the 'sacred nation' – the nation as a corpus christianum.[225]

What makes Terpstra's book especially interesting is how he does not only focus on Reformed refugees, or even Christian refugees; rather, Muslims and Jews and atheists are also considered. In doing this Terpstra manages to show that similar experiences led to similar results, even if these results were also shaped by theological prejudices. Moreover, whereas most confessional Reformed scholars can write from the position of 'victors' and where Spohnholz and Van Veen try to acknowledge the voice of the minority or defeated, Terpstra does not so easily step into this pitfall. His study is proof that the vanquished can suddenly become victors, and victors can be defeated. Neither story is a simple straight narrative.

4.2.3 Evaluation

We started this section by summarising how some argued against the paradigm of the Reformation of the Refugees, then we summarised what the scholars who work within this paradigm actually said. Now we will evaluate what we have seen so far and end this by posing some questions, some of which we hope to address in the following chapters.

Spohnholz and Van Veen claimed that the paradigm more or less frames the actual historical data towards a story in which there is a linear process from stranger churches towards the churches after Dordt 1618, in an effort to legitimise their own theology and practices in the 17th, 19th and 20th century. Spohnholz spent a lot of time in showing how this was done with the Convent of Wesel. However, these articles, though they do play a minor role in the secondary literature, are not nearly as important

---

221 Terpstra, *Religious Refugees*, 38; 47; 61; 72.
222 Terpstra, *Religious Refugees*, 74; 76; 99-100; 104-115.
223 Terpstra, *Religious Refugees*, 119.
224 Terpstra, *Religious Refugees*, 151; 157; 289.
225 Terpstra, *Religious Refugees*, 313.

as the several synods in the 16th century, especially Emden 1571 and Middelburg 1581. Within that period of time, this was already seen as 'dynamic continuity'. Spohnholz's work on the Convent of Wesel has done nothing to disprove this so far. Nor indeed does the claim that it is merely a frame to distort the data for confessional purposes have much strength left after we have seen that the churches before and after 1571 were often led by the same persons, used the same documents, and at their synods sailed the same course for at least the first ten to twenty years of their existence. The influence of at least the *Ordinancien* can be seen in the catechism, the forms, and indeed practices. So far, Van Veen and Spohnholz have not yet presented evidence that argues against a large degree of continuity.

Moreover, they criticise the defenders of the paradigm with telling too linear a narrative. Exceptions are, they infer, neglected; churches and persons chose compromises or even radically opposed courses; in no way did discipline or exile lead to a uniform Reformed doctrine and way of life. Though we greatly respect the extensive reading and firm grasp of Spohnholz and Van Veen on the history of the reformations, yet we do feel that in this critique they are the only ones who are actually telling this very linear story. When reading the secondary sources closely, it is clear that they do not tell a linear story, but give plenty of attention to exceptions, compromises, and situational deviations. Not only do Spohnholz and Van Veen claim their summary is the actual content of what is said, they also lump the several strands together, even though these are often carefully distinguished and sometimes even defended by different scholars. When it comes to theology, these scholars, moreover, do not simply state that without exception exile leads to Reformed doctrine; rather they acknowledge exceptions and they show how an environment of exile reinforced certain doctrines. All in all, we get the impression Spohnholz and Van Veen are trying to bring down a mammoth of their own making.

Regarding the aspect of discipline, one wonders whether Spohnholz understands what this in fact implies. He argues that it was not always effective, nor that the members of the congregation led exemplary lives. Of course not, the Reformed refugees would have said, since they believed that every man is prone to sin. The existence of discipline in practice implies that the congregation will also need it. Besides, it seems as if Spohnholz wants to have it both ways. If there is discipline then the believers were apparently not always such staunch believers, and hence exile does not lead to better morality. If there is no discipline, then stranger churches were not concerned about it, and exile does not lead to churches keen on high morality.

When it comes to the examples of exceptions that are mentioned by Spohnholz and Van Veen, we ask the question what they seek to prove. Not only do they list very few exceptions when compared by the sheer mass of refugees; the exceptions they do mention are in their own right to some degree as radical[226] in their views as the Reformed, and in almost all cases already known (like Coornhert, Coolhaes, Duifhuis and Herberts). It is especially remarkable that Spohnholz presents the example of Justus Velsius (though not by name, for some reason)[227], while he should have known that Velsius was a notorious troublemaker – it is said so in a book he himself edited.[228]

Last of all, we get the impression that the strangers are sometimes presented as moderates, led more by pragmatic than religious or confessional considerations.[229] If this is so, one wonders, why did they first leave Flanders, after that England, roamed through Denmark and left several German cities before settling in Emden and other places? If they were willing to compromise, why was it necessary to leave Holland for a period of roughly three decades and why did they enforce disciplinary actions against men like Moded, Datheen and Coolhaes? All of these questions remain to be answered.

This does not mean, of course, that the critique that is offered by Van Veen and Spohnholz is always completely beside the point. It is a necessary correction of a paradigm that is too often presented in too linear a format, especially when it is summarised or used as the framework for further research. Their warning against a simple narrative is important to keep in mind as we progress. However, it would seem that the course Müller and Becker have taken is more fruitful. Asking specific questions to the paradigm, in order to correct it where necessary. Becker's research demands that we look more carefully at whether providence and election were indeed a major theological point among the refugees. Müller's book and articles show the right direction in which to move forward.[230] He

---

226 In this instance radical does not refer to the 'radical reformation', but is used to show that the exceptions, too, had firm convictions which were sometimes intolerant.
227 Spohnholz, 'Exile Experiences', 54.
228 Waardt, J.H.M. de, 'Justus Velsius Haganus: An erudite but rambling prophet' in: Spohnholz, J. & Waite, G. (eds.), *Exile and Religious Identity, 1500-1800* (London: Pickering & Chatto, 2014), 97-109 & 223-227.
229 E.g. Spohnholz, 'Exile Experiences, 67; Gorter, *Gereformeerde migranten*, ch. 4 Cf., also, Spohnholz/Van Veen, 'Origins', 410.
230 Interestingly, Inge Schipper's PhD-thesis, supervised by Van Veen and Spohnholz, takes a more nuanced course as well and is much more convincing (*Across the borders*, see, especially, the conclusion, 225-239).

does justice to the elements in flight and exile that influenced anthropology, ecclesiology and theology, the way in which this was read by subsequent believers and the way in which this experience was shared by others outside the Reformed tradition, without claiming universality or necessity. In the part about the East Frisian Reformation we presented Reitemeier's phase model of reformations in the northern German Lands, to which we now return as we announced at the start of the chapter. It would seem that a similar model in phases could help to add the necessary nuance to the paradigm. In this one should also be attuned to the difference between church history and social history. When outlining the course, growth and development of the Reformed churches in the Netherlands, one looks at the period of the stranger churches and the churches under the cross differently than when one looks at it with the questions of social history. Both viewpoints should complement each other, rather than disputing the difference of outcomes that are due to different questions. Regarding church history (social history would demand slightly altered foci) we tentatively suggest something along these lines:

1. Preparation and first reception of reform in the Netherlands
2. Period of initial emigration and the Dutch Church in London; parallel to this churches under the cross start to be formed.
3. Period of continued emigration, leading to coexistence under different circumstances demanding different degrees of adaptation and flexibility; parallel to this the continued existence of the churches under the cross. In this period one should keep the differences before and after 1566 in mind.
4. Initial process of church formation while abroad (Datheen's (?) articles, Emden 1571)
   Phases three and four overlap to a certain extent.
5. Continued process of church formation in dynamic continuity with earlier phases after the return to the low countries.

There is, interestingly, one consequence of the displacement that all scholars agree on: it led to a fundamental awareness of being a stranger in this world, a sojourner on his/her way to the eternal Fatherland, which we name the *peregrinatio*-experience. The extent to which this influenced theology is debated; however, this is such an essential aspect of self-perception that it is very valuable common ground to start from in rebuilding the paradigm, or constructing a new one.

This leads us to present some thoughts that have to do with the nature of this and other paradigms, which we think are important in evaluating the usefulness of it for academic research in general. It is also necessary because Spohnholz makes this the *finale* of his argument against the paradigm of the Reformation of the Refugees. It is Spohnholz's belief that confessional categories are spectacles that blur our perceptions of ground-level messiness. In a way the confessional categories themselves are paradigms, not only employed by us, but to a certain extent by someone like Micron himself as well. Nonetheless, is a paradigm that neglects the details and messiness a bad paradigm? To us it seems that this is to misunderstand the nature of it. What a paradigm does is to look at the broad scope of historical data and research and seek to define common denominators that help us to develop a useful framework in which we can give significance to the broad sweep of data. Obviously this means 'zooming out'. When we are presented a map of Europe we may complain that Waardhuizen, the residence of the present writer, is not on the map. This would be wrong, for it is all a matter of scale and perspective. When one seeks to tell a basic story of the origins of the Dutch Reformed churches, it makes sense that 'Libertine' exceptions are not given much attention, nor that all details can be addressed. Nonetheless, Spohnholz's argument is important for a detailed research. One does too easily step into the pitfall of working from a paradigm. In a research one would prefer to operate as an agnostic when it comes to paradigms. Since this is not possible, it is good to be very aware of the details a paradigm does not tell, enabling the researcher to ask the right question. What we are suggesting is that we see the paradigm as non-narrative; rather, it should function as the dead colouring of an oil painting, leaving all the necessary liberty to add details and change nuances.

Lastly then, we come to the evaluation that the paradigm has not yet been refuted on the level of a church historical outlook. There does appear to be a dynamic continuity from the stranger churches on to the synod of Dordt 1618. The first period, from the London Strangers' Church through 1566, was more dynamic; whereas the second period, after 1566, shows a solidifying continuity. In most scholarly contributions, the continuity is stressed more than the change. It is therefore good to question what the changes and exceptions are, and where continuity can be seen. In the case of our research this will apply mostly to the theological part, rather than the practical part, of the ecclesiology outlined by Marten Micron. When it comes to the second question we asked above, it would appear that discipline remains unscathed as a mark of the stranger churches. This cannot be said for the doctrine of providence and election. This, then, is something to look out for, as is the independence from the secular government. Lastly, we can work from the common ground that displacement led to a theological anthropology in which the refugees saw themselves as strangers in the world, on their way to the New Jerusalem. In the previous chapter we have seen that Micron saw himself in this manner, too. The influence of this anthropology upon Micron's ecclesiology will certainly demand our attention.

4.3 Summary and Conclusions
In this chapter we looked at the second concentric circle: the direct environment in which Micron wrote the book. There proved to be two relevant backgrounds, i.e. the East Frisian reformation and the so-called 'reformation of the refugees'. The consequence was that the chapter fell apart in two distinct parts; however, the first part proved instructive to adapting the refugee-paradigm.

East Frisia was one of the northern German Lands. Reitemeier sees five phases in the north-german reformations: 1) Reception of Luther's works; 2) cities take the lead; 3) princes adopt Luther's teachings; 4) influence of Swiss reformation and Anabaptists; 5) return of the Catholic church. Though these five phases can roughly be seen in the East Frisian Reformation, too, it nonetheless was more diverse from the start, due to the presence of 'sacramentarian' teachings and the presence of Anabaptists. Lutheran influence increased with the introduction of the Bremer Church Order, and later the Lüneburger Church Order, though their effect was limited. An important new phase is the reign of countess Anna, who called upon John à Lasco to become superintendent in East Frisia. Her aim was to unite the Lutheran and sacramentarian/Swiss Reformation groups in one church. However, the differences between these two confessional strands kept causing unrest, especially so in Norden both before and after the Augsburg Interim. When Micron became a pastor in Norden he was confronted with this plurality of opinions (Reformed, Lutheran, Anabaptist). Overall he seems to have been able to manage this without being disloyal to his own confession. Nonetheless, in this direct historical background to the book we see a tension between confession and the 'realism of practical life', which directly leads to a balance-act between disruption and cohesion.

In the second part of the chapter we reviewed the critique of several scholars on the generally accepted paradigm of the Reformation of the Refugees. Spohnholz and Van Veen were most comprehensive in their evaluation, stating that the history is told in too linear a narrative, neglecting exceptions and compromises. Judith Becker focussed on the theological aspect and Müller offered nuanced critique, questioning specific aspects and highlighting the function of religious narratives of past experiences. This led to three questions: 1) The (dis)continuity between stranger churches and the established churches in the Netherlands; 2) the theological consequences of the refugee experience; 3) did all refugees become Calvinists?

The first question led to the conclusion that there was a dynamic continuity, which became increasingly solid (and therefore increasingly less dynamic) after 1566.

The second question showed that scholars generally see exile as catalyst for certain theological convictions, though this is not a necessity. In the secondary literature discipline and church government were given more weight than the doctrines of providence and election.

The third question led to the conclusion that the experiences of migrants or refugees led to a crucial self-awareness of being a stranger on earth, though not necessarily to becoming Reformed.

All in all we came to the conclusion that the paradigm has not been proven to be wrong, though it nonetheless needs correction. The course Müller and Becker have taken seems the best way forward. We should take the theological-anthropology of being a *peregrinus* as the central point in a less narrative and more framework-like paradigm. This framework can learn from Reitemeier's phases and we suggested something similar. Moreover, on a meta-level, the same tension between confession and the 'realism of practical life'/pragmatism and balance-act between disruption and cohesion can be seen in the *peregrinatio-*experience.

As a general background-conclusion then, we can say that Micron wrote *Van de weerdicheydt, nutheydt ende noodicheyt der christelicker vergaderinghen* in an environment of searching for the limits of confessional strictness in order to prevent disruption, or to accept separation as a consequence of being, existentially, a *peregrinus*.

Chapter 5: Translations

We conclude the first part of this study by looking at the widest historical concentrical circle: the translations of *Van de weerdicheydt*. The first of these is an integral German translation by Engelbert Faber, a pastor serving in the Kurpfalz. This is discussed in 5.1. The second is an English translation of those parts which are against the David Joristen and the Family of Love, which is discussed in 5.2.

5.1 The German Translation by Engelbert Faber

As early as the year 1563, i.e. just two years after the original publication, a German translation was published in Heidelberg by the printer Michael Schirat. The translator was Engelbert Faber. In this paragraph we will first look at the translation, then introduce Engelbert Faber, and finally place the translation in its historical setting, where we also discuss the aim of the translation.

Engelbert Faber, his works and the role of German translations in the Pfalz, have been intensively studied by Jos Schatorjé over a period of at least thirty years. Much of what we will have to say leans heavily on his research. Schatorjé lists three known surviving copies of *Kurtzer und Christlicher bericht Martini Micronii von dem nutz wirdigkeit und nohtwendigkeit der Christlicher versammlung*.[1] One in the *Stiftsbibliothek Xanten*, another in the *Staatsbibliothek Berlin* and the last in the library of the Free University in Amsterdam. The book is in an octavo format, containing 137 pages with a recto and verso side. The last three sides are blank.[2] It was published in Heidelberg by the printer Michael Schirat who had come over from Frankfurt am Main, where he published several works by Datheen, Melanchthon and Beza.[3] In Heidelberg he continued his work, printing works by Bucer, Beza and again Datheen. Moreover, he published Datheen's translation of the *Heidelberg Catechism* and the

---

[1] Schatorjé, J. 'Engelbert Faber en de Duitse vertaling van het laatste boek van Martin Micron (Heidelberg 1563)' in: Boonen, U.K. (ed.), *Zwischen Sprachen* en culturen. *Wechselbeziehungen im niederländischen, deutschen und afrikaansen Sprachgebiet* (Münster/New York: Waxmann, 2018), 19-31, 24.

[2] Interestingly, the copy from the *Staatsbibliothek Berlin* contains a remark in pencil on the last page reading: 'Theologia. Dogmat. II.7. de foedere dei', apparently assigning it to the locus of the covenant.

[3] Cf. the Short Title Catalogue.

actual catechism itself in cooperation with Johannes Mayer.[4] A printer, then, who was clearly bent on publishing Reformed works. In the year 1563 Engelbert Faber published three books, all printed by Schirat. A translation of Bernhard Buwo's *Een frundtlyke thosamenspreckings* (a book on baptism),[5] a translation of the *Belgic Confession*,[6] and the translation of Micron's book. The changes to the text of the book are minimal and overall Engelbert's translation is very loyal and trustworthy. He did add a preface and left out the printer's preface; additionally he made editorial changes, especially in the part by Carinaeus, where he changed the sub-headings into chapters five and six. Throughout the book he added titles in the margins. The indexes are not changed; however, the reference to 2 Corinthians 5:16-17 is missing, probably by mistake. Throughout the book Bible references are fairly loyal to the original, though there is the occasional change. We round off this part by looking at the preface in more detail.[7] The intended audience is the 'cathedral chapter of Köln and the duchy of Jülich'.[8] Faber translated the book because the world is untrue, believing it can serve both God and Belial. Faber sees Micron's book as an antidote against this poison.[9] It looks like Faber considered *Van de weerdicheydt* a powerful means of building up the Reformed church.

Next we turn our attention to the translator, Engelbert Faber.[10] This third generation[11] reformer was born in 1520 in the village of Gustorf in

---

[4] *Catechismus ofte onderwysinge in de christelycke leere, also die in den kercken ende scholen kuervoerstelicken Paltz geleert werdt* (Heidelberg: Michael Schirat, 1563); *Catechesis religionis Christianae, quae traditur in ecclesiis et scholis palatinatus* (Heidelberg: Michael Schirat & Johannes Mayer, 1563).

[5] For this translation, cf. Schatorjé, J.W.M.C., 'Das erste Buch des Reformators Engelbert Faber aus Gustorf' in:Rehm, G. (ed.), *Adel, Reformation und Stadt am Niederrhein* (Bielefeld: Verlag für Regionalgeschichte, 2009), 133-168. For Bernhard Buwo, cf. Hollweg, W., 'Bernhard Buwo, ein ostfriesischer Theologe aus dem Reformationsjahrhundert' in: *Jahrbuch der Gesellschaft für bildende Kunst und vaterländische Altertümer zu Emden* 33 (1953), 71-90.

[6] This translation has received a decent amount of attention, especially by Willem Heijting (Heijting, W. *Profijtelijke boekskens. Boekcultuur, geloof en gewin. Historische studies* (Hilversum: Verloren, 2007), 104-111).

[7] For a full discussion of the preface, cf. Schatorjé, 'Duitse vertaling', 28-29.

[8] *Kurtzer...bericht*, 1r.

[9] *Kurtzer...bericht*, 3r; 5v; 7v-8r.

[10] The description of Faber's life is based on: Schatorjé, 'Faber en Venlo',113-142; Schatorjé, 'Das erste Buch'; Schatorjé, 'Duitse vertaling',19-23. Though Schatorjé is loyal to the earlier biographies by Teschenmacher and Bockmühl, our reading experience was that Schatorjé study surpasses them, even though they are key sources for his own research.

[11] We use this label to indicate the years of his reforming activities, not the year of his birth.

the duchy of Jülich (*Gulik*). Schatorjé suggests he might have been the son of, or a related to, Peter Fabri, who was incarcerated for heresy in 1553. His later life and publications show that he received considerable education. At some point he married Sophie Quadt von Kinkelbach, who sprang from the bastard line descending from Wilhelm Quadt von Wickrath. In 1559 Engelbert and Sophie had Tobias, their youngest son, baptised by Hermes Backerel, the Reformed pastor of the stranger church in Aachen, who had been an elder of the London Dutch Church. This choice quite clearly showed their affinity to the Reformed faith. In 1560 Faber and his family were in Frankfurt am Main, where he was examined by Petrus Datheen before the autumn of 1561 and from there went to Wolfsheim in the Palatinate, which was then governed by Elector Friedrich III.[12] This placed Faber in one of the most important areas and decades in the history of the Reformed confession: near the city of Heidelberg where in 1563 the *Heidelberg Catechism* would be published.[13] On September sixth he finished his translation of Buwo's *thosamensprekings*, though it would not be published until 1563. His first publication was *Sendbrieff an seine liebe Landsleut in dem Stifft Cöln und hertzogthumb Gülich*, the same audience as his translation of Micron's *Van de weerdicheydt*. And indeed, the *Sendbrieff* seems to have been inspired by this book: 'The *Kurtzer und Christlicher Bericht* had many similarities to Faber's *Sendbrieff*, both in intentions and content,'[14] Schatorjé comments. In 1563, as we have seen, he also published his translation of the *Belgic Confession*. The translation of Micron's book was finished on the 20th of March, 1563. Faber would stay in Wolfsheim until 1565, the year in which he published his last book, *Wegfahrt zu dem newen Jerusalem, einem christlichen Ritter nützlich zu wissen*. From that year on a restless life started, travelling to Kempen and Venlo in 1565, preaching in the fields, and returning to Wolfsheim before the winter, he returned to the area the next year. First he went to Köln where he met Datheen, Koenraad Eubulaeo and Johan Zimmerman, and from Köln on to Venlo where he became the pastor of the Reformed congregation during the fall of the Wonderyear. There he organised what may be called a regional synod.[15] However, the victories by Margaret of Parma created a different political

---

12 Note that in doing so Michael Schirat and Engelbert Faber made the same move.
13 In chapter 8 the Heidelberg Catechism is discussed in more detail.
14 Schatorjé, 'Duitse vertaling', 28. For a summary of the *Sendbrieff*: Schatorjé, 'Das erste Buch', 151-160. The *Sendbrieff* itself was republished in the translation of Buwo's *thosamensprekings* and can be found there.
15 The cities represented were Venlo, Aachen, Maastricht, Nijmegen, Roermond, Heinsberg, and Dremmen.

setting,¹⁶ and on the fifth of April 1567 Faber was forced to leave the city and returned to his family in Wolfsheim. He stayed in the Palatinate for several years, where he became the successor of Anastasius Gerardsz. Versteghe as superintendent of Alzey, and then moved to the city of Odernheim where he lived from 1573-1576. After the decease of Friedrich III Faber left for Köln (where one of his sons passed away in March 1577, while Faber and his wife were away in Berleburg). In May 1578 we find him and Datheen in Nijmegen waiting for Jan of Nassau, on their way to the synod of Dordt; however, in the end it turned out that first Datheen and later Faber had to travel on prior to Nassau's arrival. Nonetheless, after the Synod of Dordt (1578) Faber became Jan of Nassau's most important ecclesiastical advisor. The last years of his life he spent most of his time in Venlo, where he served the congregation, but also travelled to Arnhem and Nijmegen. On September eighth, 1580 he passed away after having contracted the plague. He was buried in Venlo, where in 1586 bishop Lindanus ordered the grave to be emptied, and the bones reinterred in an unknown place. The stone over his grave was destroyed. Thus ends the story of a man who started his career relatively obscurely by translating the works of others, and went on to be a key figure in the political and ecclesiastical scene of the lower Rhine valley.

Last of all we turn our attention the historical context in which the book was published, and the possible aims of the translation. In 1563 we are well within the reign of Elector Friedrich III, who steered the Palatinate in a Reformed direction, after he had become convinced of the Reformed faith in the early years of his electorate.¹⁷ This choice was politically dangerous, as the Reformed confession was not legitimate according to the Peace of Augsburg of 1555, even though Friedrich himself claimed to

---

16 Cf. Pettegree, *Emden*, 142-148; Schatorjé, 'Faber en Venlo', 126; Spohnholz, J., *The Convent of Wesel. The Event that Never was and the Invention of Tradtion* (Cambridge: CUP, 2017/2020), 25-27; Stipriaan, R. van, *De Zwijger. Het leven van Willem van Oranje* (Amsterdam/Antwerpen: Querido facto, 2021), 283-284.

17 For a short summary of the early years, cf. Strohm, Ch., 'Politiek, kerk en universiteit in de ontstaanstijd van de Heidelbergse Catechismus' in: Huijgen, A. *et al.* (eds.), *Handboek Heidelbergse Catechismus* (Utrecht: Kok, 2013), 49-60; Gunnoe, Ch. D., 'De Heidelbergse Catechismus in de theologische context van de Palts' in: Huijgen, A. *et al.*(eds.), *Handboek Heidelbergse Catechismus* (Utrecht: Kok, 2013), 61-72. And more elaborately: Hollweg, W., *Der Augsburger Reichstag von 1566 und seine Bedeutung für die Entstehung der Reformierten Kirche und ihres Bekenntnisses* (Neukirchen: Neukirchener Verlag, 1964), 1-30, esp.27-29; Schreiber, T., *Petrus Dathenus und der Heidelberger Katechismus. Eine traditionsgeschichtliche Untersuchung zum konfesionellen Wandel in der Kurpfalz um 1563* (Göttingen: Vandenhoeck & Ruprecht, 2017), 71-81.

be true to the *Confession Augustana Variata*. In the years that followed he sought to instruct his people and to further the Reformed faith by a constant stream of books, which had to be both cheap and short, resulting, among other books, in the publications of the *Confessio Gallicana*, the confession of Beza and the *Belgic Confession*. In his eagerness to impress the Reformed faith on his subjects, this propaganda was essential.[18] Hollweg sees this as the upbeat to Friedrich III's double unifying attempt towards the Diet of Augsburg, 1568. The first focal point was to unite the evangelical princes of the German Lands, both Lutheran and Reformed. The second focal point was to unite all Reformed to churches to a 'large Reformed confessional community'.[19] It is in this light that Heijting discusses Faber's translation of the *Belgic Confession*.[20] We suggest that we should see the other two translations by Faber in the same light. Let us first briefly look at what Schatorjé has to say about this, and after that we will come with some additional comments. Both the *Dialogus* and the *Kurtzer bericht* are specifically addressed to the cathedral chapter of Köln and the duchy of Jülich. Faber's goal was to make these Dutch works available to his compatriots. Schatorjé sees the translation of Buwo's book on baptism as a means to protect them from falling prey to the Anabaptists.[21] When Schatorjé discusses the translation of Micron's ecclesiology he follows Fontaine Verwey's theory that the book was written against the Family of Love, a theory which was already disproved in chapter 2 of this study. However, his conclusions regarding Faber's goals, are to the point: The book supported the minority of Reformed believers who did not want to move, but rather chose to organise secret meetings. Schatorjé concludes that the book was a summary of what the stranger churches learnt and experienced, and thus became a church order, confession and summary of biblical knowledge.[22] In short, it was a handbook for the churches under the cross. This final characterisation of the book is perhaps put somewhat too strongly. After all, the last chapters by Carinaeus are helpful but not sufficient to organise secret meetings. The book cannot be typified as a 'church order' even if there are pages that help towards comprising a church order. Rather, the book is, as was seen above, above all a theological treatise on the church. Even though

---

18 Hollweg, *Augsburger Reichstag*, 156-163. On page 162 he says: 'die Übersetzungen [erwiesen sich]…als unentbehrliche Hilfsmittel'.
19 Hollweg, *Augsburger Reichtstag*, 136. Hollweg talks of a 'großen reformierten Bekenntnisgemeinschaft'.
20 Heijting, W., *Boekskens*, 105-108.
21 Schatorjé, 'Das erste Buch', 161-164; Schatorjé, 'Duitse vertaling', 22-23.
22 Schatorjé, 'Duitse vertaling', 28, 30.

Micron meant to end it with a practical chapter, Carinaeus's conclusion does not serve this purpose satisfactorily. Though we do not want to deny that Schatorjé is right when he says that Faber published the book as a manual for his compatriots, we would suggest that he also had the goal of offering them a treatise summarising Reformed ecclesiology. When we put it like that, the immediate importance of these works for the churches in the Palatinate becomes clear. All three of Faber's books fit within Friedrich III's propaganda campaign. Even if two of them were written for Köln and Jülich, this does not mean they could not and would not also be read in the Palatinate. We suggest the three works are closely connected and together give a very thorough image of what a Reformed church ought to look like and what it ought to confess. One would only expect a fuller treatise on the Lord's Supper to complement these publications. Either Faber could not find the time to do this, or he felt that it was sufficiently discussed in the books he offered to the public. In addition to the missionary aim, there is also a church-edifying aim within the Palatinate.

We have seen in this paragraph that shortly after the publication of the original version, Engelbert Faber published a German translation in the Palatinate, which was at the time being governed by Friedrich III, who had converted to the Reformed faith and used short and cheap editions to spread this religion within his lands. It is reasonable to assume Faber's translation served this purpose, in addition to Faber's stated missionary goal of helping his compatriots in the cathedral chapter of Köln and the duchy of Jülich.

5.2 The English Translation of Excerpts from the Book

Whereas the German translation proved to be of interest in its relation to the Palatinate and the formation of the Dutch churches, the English translation of two excerpts from the book has a more modest place. However, it is not without its own interests. First we will introduce the actual translations, then the author of the book in which the translations are found and last of all we will place it in its proper context.

The translation of the two excerpts is found in John Knewstub's[23] *A Confutation of monstrous and horrible heresies, taught by H.N., and embraced of a number, who call themselues the Familie of Loue*, printed in 1579 by Thomas Dawson 'in London at the three Cranes in the Vinetree...

---

23 Whether Knewstub has only inserted existing translations or translated the two excerpts himself is unknown.

for Richard Sergier'.[24] Knewstub indicates in his dedicatory epistle to Ambrose, the Earl of Warwick[25] that he 'set down the iudgement of some godly & learned, as wel of the Dutch church as our owne, touching these heresies of H.N.'.[26] After the dedicatory epistle comes an address to the reader, appended by the 'iudgement of a godly learned man', bearing the initials of 'W.C.'.[27] This is followed by Knewstub's own opinion, consisting of 173 quarto pages. The translation of *Van de weerdicheydt* follows this. Two passages are cited, the first is from the part supposedly written by Micron, found on folio 64v-67v, starting at '*Daerom en ist gheen gheloove*' and ending at '*der Roomscher kercken af en te wijcken*'. The second excerpt comes from Carinaeus's part. Interestingly this is indicated in the heading, but not in the head margin, where it still reads 'Micronius against the heresies of H.N.'. This could have been the choice of either Knewstub or the printer; however, in both cases it shows that Micron was considered the greater authority. The second passage comes from fol. 93v.-100r., starting at '*Ende nu heeft David Joris*' (i.e. immediately after the mark which indicates where Micron left off), and ending at '*dat men sulcke gheesten ghelooven wilt*'. The translation is generally accurate, and only some important changes have been made. They are: '*In denwelcken grouwelicken kuyl der dwalinghen ghevallen zijn*'[28] has been translated '*Into which gulfe of execrable errour, are fallen…*'[29], where the adjective has been put in another position. On fol. 66r. we read '*als Paulus oock wel gheseydt heeft*', which has become '*according the the prophecie of the Apostle*'.[30] The anonymization and addition of 'prophecy' heighten the eschatological drama of the passage. A substantial theological change is when 'peace' is used for the translation of '*liefde*' and 'love' for '*vrede*'. For instance, Micron speaks of "*'t lant ende 't huys des vredes*', where the

---

24 Knewstub, J., *A Confutation of monstrous and horrible heresies, taught by H.N., and embraced of a number, who call themselues the Familie of Loue* (London: Thomas Dawson, 1579), [sig.*1r]. Fontaine Verwey mentions an earlier English translation of the same two excerpts from the book ('Family of Love', 230). Where he found or heard about this edition is unclear to me, it is not mentioned anywhere.
25 For more on him, cf. Adam, S., 'Dudley, Ambrose, earl of Warwick' in the Oxford Dictionary of National Biography [https://doi-org.access.authkb.kb.nl/10.1093/ref:odnb/8143 (2020-03-20)].
26 Knewstub, *Confutation*, [sig.*7v].
27 Knewstub, *Confutation*, [sig. **7r & **8v].
28 Micon, *VdWNN*, 64v.
29 Knewstub, *Confutation*, 87v.
30 Micron, *VdWNN*, 66r; Knewstub, *Confutation*, 88v. The change of 'Paulus' into 'Apostle' happens on one other occasion.

translation has 'the house and region of love'.³¹ This could have been a mistake, yet such can hardly be the case in the following instance:

> Noch wordt ons in de h[eilige] schrift vermaent dat de warachtighe liefde hare sekere mate heeft, opdat wy met gheen ijdele imaginacie des vredes bedroghen en worden. Want de warachtighe liefde wort met eenen stercken bant tesamen metten gheloove ghebonden.³²

> We are also admonished in the Scriptures, that true <u>peace</u> is enclosed in certayne limites: least we shoulde be deceiued with some vaine shadowe of peace. For true <u>peace</u> is ioyned w[ith] an unspeakable knot to faith <u>and charity</u>.³³

Startling as this difference is, however, it does not seem to greatly change the overall argument of the passage, yet it might show Knewstub (or the anonymous translator) wanted to draw the reader away from the word love, introducing the concept of peace and even replacing 'love' by 'charity'. A further proof for this hypothesis comes from the second excerpt where the word love has been left out of the following sentence: '*Maer de boumeester ende timmerman van het 'huys der liefden' ende 'stadt des vredes', die vergodede werckmeester van den 'Spieghel der gherechticheyt'.* The translation has: 'But a certaine chiefe builder of the house and Citie of peace, and a framer of that same glasse of righteousnesse'.³⁴ However, it must be noted that 'love' is not omitted or changed on all occasions. The conclusion is that Knewstub gives a trustworthy translation of the two excerpts on David Joris and the Family of Love, though not without changes which might have importance in the study of early puritanism. We will now turn to the question of who John Knewstub was.

John Knewstub³⁵ (or Knewstubs) was born in 1544 in Kirkby Stephen, Westmoreland. When he was twenty odd years he received his BA from St. John's College at Cambridge, where he was also given a fellowship in 1567. He proved to be a 'puritan' (though he himself did not use the term,

---

31 Micron, *VdWNN*, 65r; Knewstub, *Confutation*, 87v.
32 Micron, *VdWNN*, 66v.
33 Knewstub, *Confutation*, 88v. Underlings by HTW.
34 Micron, *VdWNN*, 94r; Knewstub, *Confutation*, 90r.
35 This short biography is based on: 'Knewstubs or Knewstub, John (1544-1624)' in: Pastoor, Ch. & Johnson, G.K., *Historical Dictionary of the Puritans* (Lanham/Toronto/Plymouth: The Scarecrow Press, 2007), 175-176 & Bremer, F.J., 'Knewstub [Knewstubs], John (1544-1624)', in the Oxford Dictionary of National Biography [https://doi.org/10.1093/ref:odnb/15713 (2020-03-20)].

as it was still considered derogatory) when he supported a petition against wearing vestments. He was presented the living of Cockfield, Suffolk in 1579 and temporarily suspended three years later on the ground of nonconformity. He joined the earl of Leicester, Robert Dudley, as chaplain on his expedition to the Netherlands. In 1596 he became one of the overseers at Boxford grammar school. Throughout his career he was a prominent and powerful puritan spokesman, especially in Suffolk. His three publications are limited to his early years, in 1577 he published *Lectures upon the twentith chapter of Exodus, and certeine other places of Scripture*, in 1579 the confutation of Henrik Niclaes and also *An aunsweare unto certaine assertions, tending to maintaine the church of Rome to bee the true and catholique church*. In the same year he also published *A sermon preached at Paules Crosse the Fryday before Easter, commonly called good Friday, in the yeere of our Lorde, 1579*. This sermon was incorporated into his work against Henrik Niclaes.[36] John Knewstub passed away in the year 1624.

Though Knewstub is not a well-known theologian,[37] the fierce opposition to the Family of Love by him and others has appealed to the imagination of many scholars.[38] This interest, however, is not due to Knewstub's personage, but rather the appeal of the Family as a sectarian

---

36 The publications are based on the short title catalogue. For the importance of the pulpit at St. Paul's Cross see, e.g.: MacCulloch, *Tudor Church Militant. Edward VI and the Protestant Reformation* ([n.p.]: Penguin Books, 2001), 71-72; Pasquarello III, M., *God's Ploughman. Hugh Latimer: a "Preaching Life" (1485-1555)* (Milton Keynes: Paternoster, 2014), 58; Wabuda, S. *Preaching During the English Reformation* (Cambridge: CUP, 2002), 41-43.

37 For more background to Knewstub as a theologian, see: Winship, M.P., 'Weak Christians, Backsliders, and Carnal Gospelers: Assurance of Salvation and the Pastoral Origins of Puritan Practical Divinity in the 1580's' in: *Church History* 70/3 (2001), 462-481.

38 E.g. Ebel, J. G., 'The Family of Love: Sources of its History in England' in: *Huntington Library Quarterly* 30/4 (1967), 331-343; Moss, J.D., 'The Family of Love and its Critics' in: *The Sixteenth Century Journal* 6/1 (1975), 35-52; Halley, J.E., 'Heresy, Orthodoxy, and the Politics of Religious Discourse: The Case of the English Family of Love' in: *Representations* 15 (1986), 98-120; Martin, J.W., 'Elizabethan Familists and English Separatism' in: *Journal of British Studies* 20/1 (1980), 53-73; Marsh, Ch. W., *The Family of Love in English Society, 1550-1630* (Cambridge: CUP, 1994); Carter, Ch., 'The Family of Love and Its Enemies' in: *The Sixteenth Century Journal* 37/3 (2006), 651-672; Marsh, Ch., '"Godlie matrons" and "loose-bodied dames": heresy and gender in the Family of Love' in: Loewenstein, D. & Marshall, J. (eds.), *Heresy, Literature and Politics in Early Modern English Culture* (Cambridge: CUP, 2006), 59-81; Jones, D.F-H., 'Debating the Literal Sense in England: The Scripture-Learned and the Family of Love' in: *The Sixteenth Century Journal* 45/4 (2014), 897-920.

movement.[39] The seeds of the Family may have been cast out over the English fields as early as the 1550's, yet it did not become a 'popular' movement until the 1570's when Christopher Vittels translated several of Henrik Niclaes's works. It is estimated that by the end of the decade there was a wide network of several Familists, adding up to some 1,000 adherents.[40] It was at this point that several puritan preachers, such as John Roger, John Knewstub and William Wilkinson, started to oppose the movement, a movement which they perceived as a major and obnoxious threat. Knewstub exclaims: 'To conclude this matter, the errours bee so many, so foule and so filthy, as woulde force the very penne in passing to stay & stop her nose.'[41] This, at least, is part of the reason why the preachers opposed this sect. They were so shocked and horrified by what they perceived as heresies in those works, that every Reformed fibre in their body was moved to stop it, even though reading, studying and citing the works of Henrik Niclaes was a gruesome task to them. As if – to mimic the vocabulary the puritans chose in their refutations – the words oozing out of the pages reeked of death. They saw a genuine danger that this doctrine would entice the simple believers. Something that might easily happen as the Familists professed, for those who did not look beyond the surface of their teachings, some affinity to Lollardy and other devotional movements.[42] Knewstub not only used his own authority to challenge Henrik Niclaes's influence. Over against this Dutch foreigner, with his foreign teachings, he placed the authority of that other Dutch church-leader, Marten Micron, who would have been known in Puritan circles – especially through his *Antithesen* and *Ein kort Underricht*, which had been translated by Cottesford (see 3.1.3 above) – and respected as the pastor of the Strangers' Church. To use a metaphor which Knewstub could have used: he fought fire reckoned to be from hell with fire from heaven. In this fight the opinions of many scholars were used, yet only Micron's name is prominently visible, even gracing the head-margin above Carinaeus's opinion. Rogers', Knewstub's, and Wilkinson's opposition was not without success, and it brought Knewstub to the royal court, where he had to investigate Family influences and was ordered to carry letters to several bishops ordering them to investigate the Family in

---

39 Though there is some discussion as to what label should be attached to the Family, even the most unprejudiced serious scholar of their thought can hardly deny it was sectarian and heretical in the sense that it was not in line with biblical teaching.
40 Hamilton, *Family*, 114-122; Marsh, '"Godlie matrons"', 61-62; Carter, 'Enemies', 653-656.
41 Knewstub, *Confutation*, [sig. *5r].
42 Martin, 'Elizabethan Familists', 62-65

their dioceses.⁴³ In 1580 a royal proclamation was issued against the Family, and Knewstub was involved in the preparation of an anti-Familist bill in 1581, which failed and was not heard of again. Indeed, the strong upsurge of opposition to the Family suddenly died down.⁴⁴

This movement to court and the sudden stop to the polemic also brings us to a second goal Knewstub and his allies might have had. This is suggested in a theory forwarded by Carter. He claims that the several publications were part of the campaign to oppose the Roman Catholic influences at court. Says Carter: 'The year 1577 was a turning point…it marked the suspension of Archbishop Grindal, who had sympathised with the reformers, and the beginning of a vigorous struggle between the reforming and conservative factions at court'.⁴⁵ This turned the religious issue into a political one: heretics were traitors. If the Family had its way, Roman Catholicism would reign again in England.⁴⁶ Carter thinks the opposition abated because the conservative faction won, which did not see Familism but nonconformity as the greater threat.⁴⁷ Though this theory is difficult to test because it writes a story based on reading between the lines of facts, it does seem to have a ring of truth to it, and it is certainly true that the political developments at the time would also have had some influence on Knewstub's actions and writings against the Family. Yet, the idea that this is the *actual* reason, rather than the genuine disgust felt by Knewstub and his allies when reading Niclaes's works, has to be toned down somewhat. The writing of Knewstub shows such a genuine shock and abhorrence that the pastoral reason, even if it is mixed up with (church-)political aspects, is the main one. Indeed, this is clear when Carter tries to prove how Knewstub made the matter political. He writes: 'Knewstub sought to make the Family into a political issue…[he] began his *Confutation* by warning that "civil war is always more dangerous than foreign force." … Now Knewstub portrayed the Family of Love as a direct threat to not only the church or the faithful, but to the state as well.'⁴⁸ Yet this is surely more than the words of Knewstub say when read in their proper context. He writes that the harms of the church have been great in every age. Often these harms came by the 'hands of strangers', yet the grief that comes from within is much more grievous. The image of civil war is a metaphor. Of course, there could be a double meaning, a

---

43 Bremer, 'Knewstub'; Carter, 'Enemies', 670.
44 Martin, 'Elizabethan Familists', 58; Bremer, 'Knewstub'.
45 Carter, 'Enemies', 653.
46 Carter, 'Enemies', 666.
47 Carter, 'Enemies', 671.
48 Carter, 'Enemies', 666.

secret appeal to the danger of actual civil war, but the quotation itself cannot serve as proof for Carter's theory. It is safer to conclude that Knewstub perceived the Family as a real doctrinal and pastoral threat which he had to oppose, and that this opposition also had bearing on the larger political issues of his day.[49] In both cases it is noteworthy that he introduces Micron as a major authority in defending the Reformed faith.

To summarise: Knewstub, a puritan preacher, opposed the Family of Love in the years between 1575-1582 and incorporated two sections from *Van de weerdicheydt* into his book against this movement. He perceived the first to be genuinely Micronian and introduced Micron as a father of Reformed doctrine, a definitive authority, in order to defend his flock, the church and possibly the state.

5.3 Summary and Conclusions

The German translation of *Van de weerdicheydt* proved that in the first years after its publication Micron's book was deemed useful for both missionary and church-edifying purposes. It was a faithful translation by a pastor with some influence in the Dutch Reformed Churches in the 1570's. In addition, it was published in the Palatinate where it could have played an important role in Fredrick III's campaign to spread the Reformed faith among his subjects.

The English translation of excerpts from the book also shows that twenty-odd years after its initial publication *Van de weerdicheydt* and especially its author, were still known well enough to find their way into Knewstub's book. Micron is introduced as an authoritative voice from the past. However, *Van de weerdicheydt* is no longer used by Knewstub for its original purposes. He merely takes from the book what serves his own objectives and leaves the rest.

All in all we can conclude that Micron's book exercised a moderate degree of influence in the first decades after publication. Nonetheless, since the book expounds the ecclesiology that guided Micron's decisions, it is still important to analyse its theology. It is to the contents of the book that we turn in the next part of this study.

---

49 The second most important argument Carter presents is how the opposition against the Family stopped after the conservative faction at court won. However, this is proof of the effect political developments had upon the opposition, rather than proof for Carter's theory. After the conservative faction won, Knewstub practically stopped publishing and stayed under the radar. The absence of any sources showing his opposition to the Family does not prove he did not actually oppose it in his pastoral duties.

Part 2:
Theological

Chapter 6: Analysis of the Ecclesiology in *Van de weerdicheydt, nutheydt ende noodicheyt der christelicker vergaderinghen*

In the first half of this research we looked at the historical aspects to *Van de weerdicheydt*. We concluded that Micron is the author of the first part. We also saw that Micron was an important minister in the Netherlandish churches abroad, making him an important theologian to understand for our knowledge of these churches. He wrote the book while serving in Norden, East Frisia, hence we sought to describe the course of reformation in that part of the German Lands. The second part of chapter 4 focussed on, what has come to be known as, 'the Reformation of the Refugees'. This led to questions concerning the relation between the *peregrinatio*-experience and theological convictions, and indeed about certain convictions (election, providence, discipline and the relation to secular government) itself, and also about the balance between disruption and cohesion. To these questions we hope to provide the start of an answer in this chapter.

These answers arise out of a thorough analysis of the ecclesiology of *Van de weerdicheydt, nutheydt ende noodicheyt der christelicker vergaderinghen* and placing it within the whole of Micron's thought, as we know it from his publications. That also means this chapter is the heart of this study. Because we want to highlight Micron's own thought, we will not as yet place him within the broader framework of Reformed theology. That is the subject of the next chapter. The outline of the chapter before us is as follows: First of all, we will briefly discuss Marten Micron's method (6.1), after that the purpose of the church (6.2), followed by the nature of the church (6.3). The fourth section will deal with the marks of the church (6.4) where we will discuss Micron's view on prophecy and ecclesiastical offices as well. Strictly speaking 6.4 is part of the nature of the church; however, for clarity's sake it seems best to devote a separate paragraph to it. When we know what the nature and marks of the church are we can look at the tension between disruption and cohesion by analysing the need to either stay or leave a church (6.5).[1] Because the aim is to analyse

---

1 Another possible structure would have been to use the three words of the title. However, that would mean the meaning of those words is established before the analysis, instead of giving meaning to those words based on the analysis.

Micron's thought, we will not analyse the part written by Carinaeus, who finished the book after Micron's death. In sections 6.2-6.5 we will compare and link the analysis to Micron's other works and biography. This cannot be exhaustive. The mass of data that would have to be incorporated would be superfluous and tedious. Rather, we will cite some examples, sometimes giving more references in the footnotes, and where necessary we will discuss apparent discrepancies. In 6.6 we will summarise the material and draw conclusions, linking this specifically to the questions that arose at the end of chapter 4.

6.1 Micron's Method in *Van de weerdicheydt*

Before starting the actual analysis we would like to draw attention to some of the methods Marten Micron uses in this book. Several aspects are worthy of mention here, of which Micron's biblical-theological[2] approach is the most important, as it is prominent throughout the book. We will consider that aspect first.

When one looks at the outline given in chapter two, it is clear that the bibilical-theoligical data are an essential part of the book. Everything Micron states is proven or defended by using the entire biblical history. In this there is always a linear view of history. He starts with the pre-lapsarian world when showing there has always been a church, and moves to the ante-diluvian times, from there to the times of the patriarchs, Israel and the exilic period.[3] The New Testament, though containing less historical material, receives an equal amount of attention.[4] The lack of histories is made up by the discussion of parables. A similar approach is seen when Micron states that the believers have in all times honoured and rebuilt the Christian congregations.[5] And he does the same when he urges the believers to leave the church of Rome.[6] A final example is given in chapter four, where Micron says it is not enough to just leave: one also has to join a true church.[7] A quick glance at the folio numbers shows the mass of evidence gets shorter as the book progresses. It seems fair to conclude that his main argument can therefore be found in chapter 1, in which he devotes many pages to proving both that God ordained His people to congregate and that believers of all ages have done so. The first chapter is

---

2 For the definition of biblical-theology, see: ch.2 footnote 47.
3 *VdWNN*, 3v-8r.
4 *VdWNN*, 8v-13v.
5 *VdWNN*, 14r-17r.
6 *VdWNN*, 45v-48r.
7 *VdWNN*, 67v-68v.

almost exclusively biblical-theological evidence. All the biblical-theological data together is roughly one-third of the entire book.[8]

The second methodical aspect we turn to is the recurring triad of 'word, sacrament, discipline'.[9] Micron uses this when he states how the church should be governed; however, it can be seen even earlier when in chapter 1 he states that the Lord Jesus ordained them.[10] Thus, when they re-surface in chapter 2, they have the status of a divine ordinance. By that time the reader also knows how beneficial they are. Here we see how the biblical-theological data provides the framework and structure for Micron's ecclesiology: That what has been ordained is how the church should be governed. The governance is embodied by three hubs around which everything in the church is ordered. We will discuss this more elaborately in 4.4.

We already said that Micron discusses the metaphors found in the New Testament. When we look at how he uses them we see something of how he approached them. Two examples are sufficient to see Micron's application. On folio 11r we read:

> The church is called the house of God…and just as one stone – yea, nor many stones strewn about – cannot be called a house, but they have to be joined together appropriately for it to be a house, just so the godly (*godsalighe*) have to be joined together in a Christian congregation by the Holy Spirit and an outward confession of the true religion(…).

And on folio 59v, when he discusses that the bride of Christ must also keep her body pure:

> Nobody among us is so godless, nor so insane (*buyten sinne*) that he would let his housewife or daughter go a-whoring because they can steadfastly claim to have kept a pure, clean and untainted (*suyver, reyn ende onbevleckt*) heart.

---

8   Micron's part of the book is 92 folios (recto and verso). Chapter 1 is 22 folios (recto and verso), the other biblical-theological parts add up to 5 folios (recto and verso). That makes a total of 27 out 92 folios, or 29%. If chapter two is included this percentage would be even higher. That chapter is not included because there Micron does not prove his argument with biblical evidence, rather, he merely references a large number of texts to state his doctrine. However, it is clear that the two approaches, though not identical, are similar.
9   *VdWNN*, 8v-10v; 17v-22r; 28v-30r; 33r-38v; 42r-44v.
10 *VdWNN*, 8v. '[Christ] has given [the church] many things and ordered to uphold [them].

What these examples show us is that Micron thought through the metaphors and their implications. As a consequence, the biblical metaphors no longer serve as 'biblical evidence' to underscore Micron's own opinion. They have become the core of the argument instead, giving them greater authority and making them more persuasive.

A final element we would like to highlight is Micron's pastoral approach. This can be seen, for instance, on folio 30v, where Micron is concerned about those who have left all their possessions behind or whose lives are in peril. His aim is not a dry dogmatic exposition; rather, it is to comfort and encourage his readers: To comfort them in their distress and worries, to encourage them to obey God's will, in a way that would not trouble but ease their conscience.[11]

The conclusion of this paragraph is that the method in the book is a strictly biblical-theological approach in which Micron thinks through the biblical evidence. Additionally, he denotes the 'word, sacrament, discipline'-triad a divine ordinance. All of these have the aim to encourage his readers to leave the church of Rome and join a 'Christian congregation'.

6.2 The Purpose of the Church

In this paragraph we will analyse what Micron says about the purpose or aim of the church. The reader gets an inkling of what the goals are when reading Micron's aim: 'to advise...[those] who above all and wholeheartedly desire (*begeeren*) that the honour of God is propagated (*verbreydet*) among men, and who seek their own salvation (*salicheydt*) seriously.'[12] Apparently those who desire to join the true church seek God's honour and their own salvation. What is stated vaguely here is very clear one page later[13] and even more explicit later on. The church is the 'eternal and steadfast will of God' in which He wants to be 'honoured and served according to His revealed word.'[14] And again, 'if we care a whit (*ons....eenichsins ter herten gaen*) about God's honour and our own salvation, we will esteem and honour the holy meetings of the congregations (*vergaderingen der ghemeynten*).'[15] It can hardly be called surprising that these two elements are considered to be the two main ends of the church. On the very first page of Micron's *Ordinancien* we find that the Roman Catholic church dishonours God and will lead to the

---

11 *VdWNN*, 2r; 30v.
12 *VdWNN*, 2v.
13 We will discuss this page later on in this paragraph.
14 *VdWNN*, 8r.
15 *VdWNN*, 25r.

damnation of the people.[16] Indeed, he writes later on that no office bearer should seek his own glory, their aim should be the glory of God and the edification of the congregation.[17] Therefore, as he says in the book we are studying, one is forced to leave the church of Rome 'for God's honour and our soul's salvation'.[18] However, it is also important to note that this is not explicitly taught in any of the catechetical works. When we investigate these two aims further, we will see that in this we find the answer to the question what Micron means by the 'use' or 'benefit' (*nutheydt*) of the Christian meetings.

The book opens with unfolding these two aims of the church. Let us first focus on how the church honours God. We read that the church was the will of the eternal, just and wise God, 'in which His will and glory… in accordance with His word, would be preached, confessed and praised'.[19] So, the glory of God is that human beings carefully listen to the revelation God has given and proclaim it to all the world. That is, essentially, what preaching and confessing amounts to in this first sentence. The church should strictly adhere to the revealed word and repeat this in her proclamation and confession. The glory and will of God must also be praised or honoured (*ghepresen*). Again, this does not mean anything is added to Biblical revelation; rather, instead of repeating it to the world it is repeated laudatorily to God. The three elements of preaching, confessing and praising are found later on in the book as well. When Micron opposes those who want to serve the Lord in solitude (*eensaemheyt*)[20], he states that God wants the 'public confession of His Name'[21] for it is written: 'I will preach (*prediken*) Thy Name unto my brethren: in the midst of the congregation will I praise Thee.'[22] Here, again, we have these three elements – preaching, confessing and praising – to honour God. These three, then, are like three overlapping circles. The central element in all of them is the glory of God. This end is expressly ordered and willed by God,[23] for it is the answer to God's salvific acts in history. Micron proves

---

16 *Ord.*, 35.
17 *Ord.*, 50, 54, 56.
18 *VdWNN*, 45r-45v.
19 *VdWNN*, 3v.
20 It goes without saying that Micron does not mean you should not *also* serve God in solitude, he addresses those who do not join any church and *only* serve God in solitude.
21 *VdWNN*, 11r.
22 *VdWNN*, 11r; Psalm 22:22. Translation based on the KJV, where 'declare' is used instead of 'preach'.
23 *VdWNN*, 11r.

this with several examples. When God rescued Israel from the house of bondage He ordered them 'certain ceremonies of ecclesiastical service at mount Sinai' (*sekere ceremonien des kerckendiensts aen den berch Sinai*).[24] After the return out of Babel the temple had to be rebuilt.[25] Those whom Christ redeemed from the burden of the Pharisees have to take His yoke upon them.[26] These examples prove it is not enough for a man to leave the church of Rome 'unless he, with his soul (*gheeste*) and the outward confession of his faith,' joins a church.[27] The Spirit and confession bind the 'stones' together that they may be a house, holy unto God.[28] Next to confessing, preaching and praising, God is honoured by the mere fact of obedience, too. The obedient church shows in her behaviour that she acknowledges God as her all-wise sovereign Who 'will not allow His ordinances, when they are used in a Christian manner, to be naked and useless ceremonies or acts (*bloote ende onnutte ceremonien oft handelinghen*).'[29] God does not issue useless commands. Indeed, the obedience itself is useful because 'obedience is a pleasant offering to God.'[30] So, the first aim of the church is the glory of God, which is done by the preaching, confessing, praising and obeying. The first three are overlapping circles. All are strictly bound to the Word of God.

A separate question that arises after this discussion is what Micron means by the terms 'confession' and 'confessing'. Does he mean the simple act of professing God to be your God, to acknowledge Him as He revealed Himself in His word, or does Micron mean the document of a confession? Based on the evidence in *Van de weerdicheydt, nutheydt ende noodicheyt der christelicker vergaderinghen* a division between this seems to be too strict. Paul and the poet of Psalm 116 cannot help themselves, but have to confess: I believed, therefore have I spoken.[31] And let us once more look at the sentence on 11r, where Micron quotes Psalm 22: 'It is clear enough how seriously (*ernstelicken*) God desires the open confession of His Name by all people, yea even in the midst of the congregation, as it is written: "I will preach Thy Name unto my brethren: in the midst of the congregation will I praise Thee."' The outward confession, proclaimed by the individual of Psalm 22, is done among the brethren, connecting the individual

---

24 *VdWNN*, 67v.
25 *VdWNN*, 68r.
26 *VdWNN*, 68r.
27 *VdWNN*, 67v.
28 *VdWNN*, 12r.
29 *VdWNN*, 17r, 20v.
30 *VdWNN*, 17r-17v.
31 *VdWNN*, 58v.

believer to the congregation. Consequently, the confession of one becomes the confession of all. The church repeats the Word of God in her proclamation, this is embraced by faith and subsequently confessed. A written confession is nothing more than the result of the proclamation. This is obvious when we look at the churches Micron served in. The Strangers' Church in London had its confession, and joining that church was equal to confessing one's faith.[32] Those who wanted to partake of the Lord's Supper had to come to the consistory to confess or 'give witness to' their faith. This was done by testing their faith with the *Ondersoeckinghe des gheloofs*, a written statement of the Christian faith.[33] Likewise, the children who wanted to confess their faith had to show their knowledge according to the *Kleyne Cathechismus*.[34] In *Ein kort underricht* the believer shows him- or herself to be a Christian by answering according to that catechism.[35] There does not seem to be a difference between the confession, or testimony, proclaimed by the individual and the written confession of the church. They are both according to God's Word and therefore to God's glory. The confession of all is the confession of the individual. This, indeed, is exactly as it is stated in the confession of the Strangers' Church in London. The public confession of each, is the private confession of the individual.[36] In his answer to Joachim Westphal Micron more or less repeats this when he says that only those who have confessed their faith are allowed to partake of the Lord's Supper: No one is allowed to come with 'unclean hands'[37], for this is grievous in God's sight. Only those who have publicly confessed their faith (*publicè coram Ecclesia palam contestur*) together with subjection to Christian discipline (*disciplinae Ecclesiasticae*) can partake.[38] The same pattern arises: the confession of one goes hand in hand with the confession of the church.[39]

We now turn towards the second goal Micron sees: the salvation of humankind. Or rather, perhaps, the protection of man. For that was the aim of the church, even in paradise. The 'congregation of human beings

---

32 *Ord.*, 83.
33 *Ord.*, 83.
34 *Ord.*, 68-69.
35 *KU*, q+a 1; q+a 14.
36 *London*, 74-75.
37 Probably used metaphorically, though Willems takes it literally (*Is is is,* 155).
38 *AS*, fol. 12 (*Is is is*, 37). Willems translates *disciplinae Ecclesasticae* as 'doctrine of the church (*leer van de kerk*) (*Is is is*, 37).
39 Karlo Janssen comes to exactly the same conclusion in his study on subscription to the confession: Janssen, R.C., *By This Our Subscription. Confessional Subscription in the Dutch Reformed Tradition Since 1816* (PhD Theologische universiteit Kampen, 2009), section 3.3, especially 3.3.4

(*vergaderinghe der menschen*)' was already willed and called into being by God eternally[40], and therefore also present in paradise, before the fall. To Micron this is as clear as day:

> For at that very moment (*alsdoe*) God sanctified the seventh day and planted in paradise two trees, which contained certain holy mysteries, the one of knowledge of good and evil, the other the tree of life. For even though man was at that very moment holy, just, true and immortal, created in God's own image, yet he could fall. He was not free from the tricks (*listen*) of the devil…Therefore, so Adam might be all the more free (*des te vrijer*) of all Satan's tricks, and might protect (*bewaren*) the state of his holy creation wholly and unmarred (*gantsch ende ongheschendt*), God in His endless wisdom prescribed an outward religion in his unspoiled state, and for that reason He ordered the holy meetings to be maintained.[41]

This quote says it all. The church was ordered by God to protect human beings against the devil, who is trying to pull them away from God. Clearly, this would be even more necessary after the fall. For then the nature of man had become corrupt and 'subject to manifold miseries'[42]. His salvation was indeed greatly imperilled, not only because of the opposition between the seed of the serpent and the seed of the woman, but also due to 'the diverse and many commandments of God'.[43] This immediately places the church in a most perilous world. The devil and his seed are constantly trying to draw people away from God, and human beings – with a weak and sinful heart[44] – cannot avoid sin, due to God's many commandments. Her perilous state caused her to come near the brink of extinction in the days before Seth and again in the days of Noah.[45] So, after the flood, God gave the church a further proof of His love and lovingkindness when He showed Noah and his family the rainbow as a sign of the covenant. This would help them against all temptations (*aenvechtinghen*).[46] Yet, the church once more dwindled, until God in His compassion (*ontferminghe*) chose Abraham. This time God rebuilt the church in such a way that she would not lightly fall, because He promised Abraham the Messiah and gave him the sign of circumcision, the sign of

---

40 *VdWNN*, 8r.
41 *VdWNN*, 4r.
42 *VdWNN*, 4r.
43 *VdWNN*, 4r.
44 *VdWNN*, 16r-v; 52v.
45 *VdWNN*, 5r-5v.
46 *VdWNN*, 6r.

rigteousness through faith, which would be a solid foundation.[47] In the church, then, the salvation of humans is guarded by God's love and goodness in which He gave the Messiah. The church builds on Him in faith, and is thus declared righteous. This is the heavenly food for the soul.[48] Truly, the church is God's blessing (*weldaet*), for His will is preached and revealed there.[49] She teaches its people to obey the commandments of the Lord, which are such a peril to man's salvation and she teaches them about Christ, their salvation. In this way the 'one loaf' consisting of 'many seeds' is joined and baked as an 'unleavened bread'.[50] When one does not join the church, not only does one miss out on the spiritual blessings, one is also in danger of being punished for ingratitude.[51] God is a jealous God, who wants us to serve Him with all we have and are.[52] It is, as a consequence, dangerous to serve God in solitude.[53] The human heart is weak and so easily falls asleep, prone to believe the wiles of the devil who only seeks to pull one away from the church.[54] Sinful nature willingly listens to these tricks and neglects the ordinances of God.[55]

How does all of this compare to Micron's other works? We have already seen how the office bearers are to pursue these two goals in their work: the glory of God and the edification of the church. When we read through the letters from the first days of the church in London we find that Micron is eager for this new church 'to guard against the heresies which are introduced by our countrymen.'[56] The church is to make known God's Word. She is under constant threat, for: 'marvellous is the subtlety of antichrist in weakening the churches of Christ.'[57] In another letter the church is called 'the cause of Christ' yet 'the old serpent ceaseth not his stealthy attacks upon the heel of Christ.'[58] Micron, as a minister of the word only wants to labour for God's glory.[59] The church in London is to

---

47 *VdWNN*, 6v.
48 *VdWNN*, 13r.
49 *VdWNN*, 85r.
50 *VdWNN*, 13r.
51 *VdWNN*, 69v.
52 *VdWNN*, 47v.
53 *VdWNN*, 12v-13r.
54 *VdWNN*, 13v; 16r-16v; 52v.
55 *VdWNN*, 69r-69v.
56 Micron to Bullinger, May 20th, 1550 (*ET*, 365; *OLER*, 560).
57 Micron to Bullinger, May 20th, 1550 (*ET*, 365; *OLER*, 561).
58 Micron to Bullinger, May 28th, 1550 (*ET*, 366; *OLER*, 562-563). The constant threat is also clear in the foreword of *Een claer bewijs*, 439-443.
59 Micron to Bullinger, June 4th, 1550 (*ET*, 367; *OLER*, 565).

have 'the pure ministry…according to the apostolic form.'⁶⁰ It is clear from these examples that what was written above is in accordance with what Micron wrote in the letters. We find the same in his East Frisian catechism (q&a 12) where we read that the outward ceremonies are commanded

> for the sake of our weakness, that by them we may be schooled and strengthened in the true religion. And in addition, that we may be the more incited to obediently keep the aforementioned commandments of God.

At the risk of being tedious and straying into what belongs to the discussion of the ministry of the Word, we want to draw attention to the fact that in the several catechisms the 'pure preaching' consists of law and gospel. The law being God's will and the gospel the good tidings of certain forgiveness.⁶¹ Again, we find that this is the same as was read in the analysis of *Van de weerdicheydt*.

Last of all we will attempt to give meaning to the word '*nutheydt*' in the title. That the church must be beneficial is anchored deeply in the doctrine of God, not in the doctrine of the church. That is to say: why the church is beneficial does not flow from what the church is in itself, but it is the necessary consequence of the God's aseity. That God is *God* must mean that what He institutes is beneficial. In some of the most beautiful sentences of the book Micron writes:

> Particularly (*In sonderheydt*), seeing that when these holy congregations of Christians are attended most diligently, they are to each and everyone most edifying (*groote vorderinghe*) and of the utmost spiritual use (*gheestelicke nutheydt*). And in no way can what the holy men of God have always seriously and with full attention driven and upheld, be without use, it being done by the command and law of God, Who at no point (*noyt niet*) ever commanded, instituted or ordained in vain.⁶²

When we read carefully, we can see three steps in this argument. First of all the holy men of God did all they could to uphold the meetings, and therefore it cannot be useless, as their example is to be followed. The second step is that it is the commandment of God to attend those

---

60 Micron to Bullinger, August 28th, 1550 (*ET*, 369; *OLER*, 567-568).
61 *Cathechismus*, q+a 70-74; *OS*, 289 l.14-290 l.3; *KU*, q+a 14.
62 *VdWNN*, 17r.

meetings. We are still on the terrain of ecclesiology, yet in the third step Micron moves to the *locus de Deo*, when he claims that all of God's commandments have their use. This is similar to what we came across earlier: God will not allow His ordinances to be useless.[63] Micron goes on to explain the use of the church. The obedience itself is a great use, yet this is not all. The benefits of the church are shown by discussing the triad of 'word, sacrament, discipline'. They are the proof of Christ's presence, for He is present where two or three gather in His name. 'It is, doubtless, impossible to express in words how good it is to have Christ present with His mercy, Who as a helper and protector defends and rules all our doings (*allen onsen saken voorstaet ende regeert*).'[64] We come, again, to the theme of protection, combined with that of obedience. It returns time and again, for instance on folio 22v-23r, where Micron thinks through the metaphor of the good shepherd: It is most beneficial for the sheep to stay with the shepherd, in order to be guarded against the wolf. Likewise, the godly should attend the church where the pastors protect him or her against wolves, staying within the boundaries of salvation. It is interesting to see the difference between the singular and plural in these two sentences. Christ is the 'one' shepherd, who keeps us safe from the devil – or wolf. The pastors are the many shepherds who guard the flock against the manifold wolves in this world. God's protection is a great comfort to Micron and help him to bear the tribulations patiently[65] even when it is clear from his other works that he felt God's wrath in the persecutions.[66] The church's use, then, is the same as its aim. In it God is glorified and the godly are protected from the wiles and guiles of the devil.

With this we round off the discussion of the aims of the church, which have also proved themselves to be the same as the benefits of the church: The glory of God and the salvation of man by strict adherence to the word in preaching, confessing and praising.

6.3 The Nature of the Church

In this third paragraph we will focus on the nature of the church, or *what* she is. Due to the enormous mass of information it is necessary to create some subparagraphs. First of all we pay attention to how the church is the will of God and gathered out of all people (6.3.1), secondly we analyse Micron's comparison between world and church (6.3.2), thirdly the

---

63 *VdWNN*, 20v. Cf. 8r.
64 *VdWNN*, 17v.
65 *VdWNN*, 48v-49r.
66 E.g. *Ord.*, 36.

foundation of the church (6.3.3), in which we also discuss the obligations to join and secede. Some repetition of what was discussed above cannot be avoided, yet we will try to keep this to the absolute minimum. We would also like to mention that most of what is to be discussed can hardly be divided, because everything is connected. As such, the divisions are sometimes somewhat arbitrary. We strive to make clear how the different aspects are connected when discussing them.

6.3.1 Gathered out of all People by the Will of God
In this subparagraph we will focus on the definition Micron gives us and the underlying commandment of God. Indeed, this last part (God's commandments) is of seminal importance in Micron's ecclesiology and must therefore be discussed before we can move on to the other subparagraphs.

When Micron rounds off his discussion of how God's commands cannot be upheld without a congregation, he concludes: '[the] church or congregation of God is no more than an assembly (*versamelinghe*) of men, called out of the world by the voice of the gospel, and gathered under Christ, the head.'[67] This definition on fol. 11r. already informed all that Micron had written in the preceding pages. By the ministry of the word 'God calls a people out of this world and makes them His own'.[68] Baptism and circumcision set the people of God apart from the world (for more details, see 6.3.2).[69] In the Lord's Supper the believers are one body and one bread, hence they must be joined together.[70] The definition is followed by an elaborate discussion of several New Testament metaphors. Among them is the metaphor of the house, which we came across in 6.1. This house is joined together by the Holy Spirit. Likewise, the one loaf consisting of many grains is baked, the vine consisting of many grapes bears fruit, the flock consisting of many sheep finds food, all by the ministry of word and sacraments. The believers are called to the wedding of Christ, their heavenly bridegroom.[71] It is not necessary to discuss all of the examples Micron gives to support his definition. The church is gathered out of the world by the gospel, to be joined together by the Spirit, by means of the gospel.

In the London church everyone was expected to know this. In the *Ondersoeckinghe des gheloofs* we find:

---

67 *VdWNN*, 11r.
68 *VdWNN*, 8v.
69 *VdWNN*, 9r-9v.
70 *VdWNN*, 9v.
71 *VdWNN*, 11v-13v.

> What do you understand when saying: 'One holy Christian congregation (*ghemeinte*)?
>
> That is, I confess, that Jesus Christ in this wicked world has His certain assembly of believers, of which I confess myself to be a member.[72]

Though the words are not exactly the same, yet the main line of thought is similar. In the *Shorter Catechism*, however, we come across a very interesting difference. In q&a 67 the pupil confesses that Jesus Christ 'in this world has scattered His congregation all over the world'. Note, by the way, the *diaspora* element in this answer. In *Ein kort underricht* this question and answer is completely lacking, though in answer 13 the pupil does note how the ceremonies of the true church separate her from the false sects. So, what we see is that in *Van de weerdicheydt* Micron does not start with the definition, but gives it after more than ten folios in what is almost a cursory remark. In *Ein kort underricht* the definition is not given at all. Based on this evidence it would seem that the definition did not play a major part in Micron's theology.[73]

The same cannot be said about the will of God. It was seen above that the church was ordained and willed by God from the very beginning of the world.[74] That statement is the note on which Micron opens *Van de weerdicheydt*. This could have to do with the aim of the book to convince Nicodemites;[75] however, the same aim could have been reached by starting with the definition. Obeying the will of God and His commandments is, in Micron's theology, an absolutely necessity for the church and her members. A selection of sentences proves this. The ceremonies in the Old Testament were 'commanded' by God and therefore the people were also 'commanded' to uphold them.[76] The children of God 'must' join the church, and it is even 'demanded' (*gheeyscht*).[77] Not attending the meetings would result in guilt, for everyone should obey the will of God.[78] As a direct consequence the true believer is to leave the church of Rome, a theme we will discuss later on.[79] Micron concludes that

---

72 *OS*, 288 l.7-12.
73 Admittedly, the number of two sources on which to build such a conclusion is somewhat slight.
74 *VdWNN*, 3v.
75 See above, ch. 2.6.
76 *VdWNN*, 7v.
77 *VdWNN*, 8r, 11v.
78 *VdWNN*, 13v-14r, 17r, 29r.
79 *VdWNN*, 45v-48v.

God's will is not for a limited time only, but eternal and steadfast. His will must be obeyed.

The theme of obedience is apparent in all of Micron's works, yet it seems more advisable to discuss this when we will look into separate areas where this obedience to God's law is made practical, such as joining and seceding from the church and adherence to the Word.

For now, we conclude that the basic idea of the church as a people collected out of all nations was the basic confession, yet the obedience to the will of God was the key aspect of what defines the true church.

6.3.2 The Church of God and the World

In the previous subparagraph we saw that the church is set apart from the world. We will investigate this statement further in this paragraph. Nicolas Terpstra draws attention to the centrality of Augustine's division between the city of God and the city of man in the Middle Ages and the era of reformations, and we find the same distinction in Micron's book.[80] There are, however, some peculiarities which we will come across. Micron tells us that the church, the assembly or congregation of the holy, started in paradise.[81] The enmity between the seed of the woman and the seed of the devil was the start of the schism (*verscheuringhe*) between believers and non-believers.[82] Interestingly, the translator saw reason to write that Cain erected a church of Satan.[83] So what we have is not a teaching of two kingdoms or cities, but of two churches who serve and adhere to their master, and come together to do his will. The aim of the church of Satan is to shake off the yoke of Christ, just as Esau shook off his brother's yoke,[84] whereas Christ's church takes His yoke upon her. Christ's church thus has signs and laws that separate it from the church of Satan.[85] The division between the two is absolute. Obedience to Belial is irreconcilable

---

80 Terpstra, N., *Religious Refugees in the Early Modern World. An Alternative Histoyry of the Reformation* (Cambridge: CUP, 2015), 26; Augustine, A., *The City of God*, ed. Marcus Dods (Peabody: Hendrickson Publishers, 2011) [*De Civitate Dei contra Paganos*], 430-441.
81 *VdWNN*, 4r.
82 *VdWNN*, 4v.
83 *VdWNN*, 5r. We consciously draw attention to the translator here, for we do not know what word was in the original Latin version. In the rest of this chapter we will interchange church and kingdom of Satan, as is done in *Van de weerdicheydt* (e.g. *VdWNN*, 12v; 82r; 90v).
84 *VdWNN*, 29v-30r; 66r; 68r.
85 *VdWNN*, 11r.

with obedience to Christ.[86] False religion drives out true religion.[87] Just like Cain killed Abel, the kingdom of Satan is constantly trying to fight and destroy the church of God. Therefore Adam and his family 'feared greatly, were diminished and oppressed (*grootelicken beancxt, vercleynt ende benaut*).'[88] This is true for the church of all ages, for the godly have had to deal with 'many perils'.[89] These perils led to the constant rebuilding of the church. We have already mentioned this when we discussed the second aim of the church (the protection of man), yet it is good to repeat it here for it helps us to see that the strength – or constructional integrity – of the church is found not in man, but in God. She is bound to collapse If God does not in His grace constantly rebuild and strengthen her. After Cain's murder the congregation of God was very small and almost entirely gone. To prevent this from happening 'God, by Seth Adam's other son, erected her anew'.[90] Yet, due to man's sin, the church dwindled again and God punished the world with the great flood, saving only Noah and his family. 'And in this way, the godless being taken away by the flood, there was once more a holy assembly of men and congregation of God in the world'.[91] In Abraham 'God…rebuilt anew the fallen church (*in denwelcken Hy de vervallen kercke // also weder opbouwen wilde*).'[92] In the days of the prophets the people of Israel were often disobedient, yet 'God…through certain prophets…let [His congregation] be rebuilt.'[93] Note that in the first three examples God rebuilt the church by electing certain persons, and that later on in history – after the foundation of circumcision – He used prophets to rebuild it. Every time God freed His people He demanded to rebuild His church in the ceremonies and meetings.[94] For Micron that process extends to his own days for, says he, 'we do not introduce a new form of doctrine and church services, but // only return again the old doctrine and religion'. The demand for signs and wonders is unjust, 'because Scripture does not promise anywhere that the collapsed teaching of Christ (*vervallen leere Christi*) would be erected again with signs and wonders.'[95] The work of the reformers,

---

86 *VdWNN*, 11v-12r.
87 *VdWNN*, 46r. Cf. 84v-85r.
88 *VdWNN*, 5r.
89 *VdWNN*, 14v.
90 *VdWNN*, 5r.
91 *VdWNN*, 5v-6r.
92 *VdWNN*, 6r-6v.
93 *VdWNN*, 7v.
94 *VdWNN*, 68r.
95 Both quotations on *VdWNN*, 81v-82r.

indeed of Micron himself, is the same as the work of the prophets in the Old Testament.

If the church has been persecuted by the church of the devil since its very beginning, and if the work of rebuilding the church continued to the days of Micron, then it must needs follow that persecution and cross are part of the nature of the church. We find this is true, for those who want to leave the church of Rome will have to face 'persecution and cross'.[96] A key paragraph is on folio 70v, which we will give in full and analyse afterwards.

> Against all of these [objections to leaving home for the sake of the true religion] it is a good remedy to remember how the Son of God, though He was rich, became poor for our sakes and descended to the lowest regions of the earth, that He might take us, exiles (*ballingen*), to the heavenly fatherland.
>
> Christians should remember that they have to celebrate the feast of tabernacles in this world, until they will be welcomed in the heavenly tabernacles, which were not made by human hands.

We see here that the exile or flight as a consequence of the true religion, is nothing compared to the existential exile before one knows Christ. The believer is rich and found in Him, even if he or she has to become poor and an exile here. Micron poses the question: Is it such a problem to be an exile in the world if you consider that Christ became an exile for you? Is it such a problem to be an exile here, if your existential exile has ended? And he follows this with a most interesting comparison between our lives here and the feast of tabernacles. The Bible speaks about the feast of tabernacles in Leviticus 23: 33-43. Verses 40-43 tell us the purpose of the feast. The Israelites are to 'rejoice before the Lord' and by living in small huts the people of Israel 'may know that [the Lord] made the children of Israel to dwell in tabernacles when [He] brought them out of the land of Egypt'. In Deuteronomy (16:15) we read that the Israelites were to be 'altogether joyful'. Micron expressly calls it the feast of tabernacles. Now the reason for the feast was that God had delivered the people of Israel out of Egypt, just as Christ has redeemed His church from her existential exile. Those who believe in Christ are now, as it were, in the desert, on their way to the promised land. They should not be sorry about this, even if there are hardships; they should rather celebrate the feast of deliverance.

---

96 *VdWNN*, 66r.

What this comparison teaches us is that Micron saw the life of a Christian as fundamentally uncertain. The believers live in tabernacles instead of houses. It is the life of a wanderer, or a pilgrim, on his or her way to the heavenly fatherland. If this involves flight or exile, it should be accepted for God 'loveth the stranger'.[97] Indeed, all Christians have a most troublesome battle against the flesh, the world and Satan. Besides, nothing is so uncertain as the church's peace and the cross may at any time come over her. Indeed, no one is without crosses or persecution:

> For even though Christians may for some time – by God's grace – be free from the teeth of the enemy, yet they are all that time tormented and oppressed (*ghequelt ende beladen*) by many crosses, such as illnesses, poverty, the burden of children etc. They are mocked by their friends, and left altogether. Every day they are subject to the unrighteousness, derision, mocking, insults and threats (*onghelijck, versmaedheyt, lachteringen, bespottinghen ende dreygementen*) of worldly people. Every day they receive news of brothers who were betrayed, taken captive, robbed, drowned, decapitated or burnt at some place or other.[98]

This last quotation gives us a glimpse of Micron's own cross and how he experienced the diaspora, even in the relative calm of Norden.

Before comparing this to Micron's other works, we will quickly summarise what was said. The church and the world are each other's enemies and the aim of the kingdom of the devil is to destroy the church. This would surely happen if God did not in His grace constantly rebuild the church. The struggle between world and church is of all ages and as such the church of Christ suffers persecution and every believer has to bear his or her cross. Yet, they should bear it lightly, celebrating their redemption.

When comparing this to the rest of Micron's output we will follow the same structure of the opposition between world and church, the rebuilding of the church and the tabernacling nature of the church. It is clear in all of Micron's works that he advocates a very strict division between the true church and the church of Satan. It must be remembered that, as already indicated, this was by no means unique. It was a common way of looking at the world in the early-modern period. For Micron the church of Rome is the kingdom of the devil. At no place is this clearer

---

97 *VdWNN*, 71r, where Micron's quotes Deut. 10:18 (here given in the KJV).
98 *VdWNN*, 76r.

than in his *Antithesen*[99], where he compares the mass to the Lord's Supper. The latter he calls the true Christ, the former is the false Masschrist.[100] Indeed, in *Een Claer Bewijs* Micron calls the mass the god 'Maosim', the antichrist from Daniel 11:38.[101] And in the same book he repeatedly condemns the Roman Catholic church as utterly false.[102] A final example from his letters: 'we shall attack our Flanders with fiery darts, and, I hope, take it by storm, that, antichrist being put to flight or at least weakened, our Saviour may reign there'.[103] Let this suffice to make clear that what was analysed above is also found in Micron's other works. It would be impossible to cite all examples, nor would it be satisfactory, for it is a worldview that pervades all that he writes.

The second aspect we saw is how the church is in constant need of repair or rebuilding. We read in the *Ordinancien* that Micron and his fellow ministers 'built' a church.[104] In the letters we hear Micron speak of the London church as being in an 'infant state'[105] and later on 'we feel indeed that we are sometimes assailed by Satan…but the Lord protects us, to whom it belongs to build up the church, and to defend and preserve it when so built up.'[106] Though this is not absolute proof that Micron considered the church as being in a continual process of being rebuilt, it does at least show that he perceived the London church to be a new-born infant, a new building by Christ. Moreover, he often uses the terms 'reform' and reformed church.[107] It is only fair to admit that the aspect of constant repair and rebuilding is, for as far as we could see, not said literally in any other work by Micron. However, neither is his other work alien to this thought, and it must be kept in mind that his other books have other subjects and goals. In the first two pages of the foreword to the *Ordinancien* Micron speaks of the attacks on the church, her fragility, the need of shepherds to lead the flock, God's grace in providing a true church in which His people are fed. Indeed, King Edward is called a 'nurse'

---

99 See: *Hoste*, 235-244. This part of the martyrology was published seperately as well and even translated in English. Cf. Leaver, R.A. 'A Unique Broadsheet in the Scheide Library' in: *The Papers of the Bibliographical Society of America* 83/3 (1989), 337-352.
100 *Hoste*, 235.
101 *Claer Bewijs*, 489
102 *Claer Bewijs*, 448; 524-536
103 Micron to Bullinger, October 13th, 1550 (*ET*, 371; *OLER*, 571).
104 *Ord.*, 37.
105 Micron to Bullinger, August 14th, 1551 (*ET*, 373; *OLER*, 574). The original reads: 'infantia'.
106 Micron to Bullinger, November 7th, 1551 (*ET*, 375; *OLER*, 577-578).
107 E.g. *Ord.*, 36-38; Micron to Bullinger, May 20th, 1550 & March 9th, 1552 (*ET*, 364, 377; *OLER*, 559, 580).

(*Voesterheere*).¹⁰⁸ The congregation is said to be 'erected' (*op te richten*).¹⁰⁹ There is no significant theoretical difference, despite the difference in words.

Last of all, how does the idea of cross and exile feature in other works? When we discussed the definition of the church we looked at the questions and answers from the catechism, where we read that the church was scattered all over the earth. The awareness and impression of the diaspora can be found in all of Micron's works, the only exception being *Ein kort underricht*. In the catechism we read that for the sake of Christ we will gladly bear all disgrace and cross.¹¹⁰ In the *Ondersoeckinghe* the comfort of the doctrine of the church is that the holy people of God will rise again no matter how much they may have been despised here on earth.¹¹¹ Even though the *Ordinancien* hardly ever refer to the experience of exile, there are a few instances, especially in the foreword.¹¹² The book on *Hoste vander Katelyne* reminds us of the cross Micron described: he had heard how his friend had been burnt. That part is solidly founded in his biography. In *Hoste* Micron quotes a letter by his friend, in which Hoste comforts Micron by saying that he 'is glad of this cross…[God wants] us to know we are strangers (*vremdelinghen*) here, without a home…that we may make known Christ to all men in our persecution and pilgrimage (*vervolch ende pilgermage*)'.¹¹³ The experience of existential exile and redemption leading to temporary earthly exile can be found in *Een claer bewijs*, where we read:

> We are nothing but strangers in this world, wherever we may be. (…) Christ came to His own, yet they did not receive Him. And again, God says He loves the stranger, and He gives them food and clothing. And in Christ we are no longer strangers (wherever we may be) but of God's household.¹¹⁴

In this way he links the end of the book to the beginning, for on the very first page he writes to the 'scattered believers' about the long, heavy and perilous battle.¹¹⁵ This leaves us with the cross and tribulation, even in

---

108   *Ord.*, 36.
109   *Ord.*, 36.
110   *Cathechismus*, q&a 61.
111   *OS*, 288 l.20-289 l.6.
112   *Ord.*, 35-37; 64-65; 83.
113   *Hoste*, 209.
114   *Claer bewijs*, 559.
115   *Claer bewijs*, 439.

peace. The clearest example of the constant battle of the Christian can be found in all those places where Micron describes the benefits of the sacraments. Each and every time he also points to the crucifixion of the flesh.[116]

When we combine this with the biography of Micron, the experience of displacement does seem to have affected him and his ecclesiology deeply. He saw he church as being led out of the exile of sin. On her way to the heavenly fatherland, however, she was still in a world alien to her. She is not at home in the world but always in exile. She lives in tabernacles, celebrating the feast of deliverance. This journey means that she has to bear ridicule and mockery, that at many times she will be dispersed. Even when she is safe, God's children have to bear their cross due to their alien status. This all rests on the absolute division between the church of Christ and the kingdom of Satan and his servant, the antichrist.

6.3.3 The Foundation of the Church

If the church is to be constantly rebuilt as was seen in 6.3.2, she must have a foundation. The first time Micron mentions foundations for the church is when he speaks of Abraham. He says:

> God…chose Abraham, in whom He rebuilt the ruined (*vervallen*) church // in such a way that she would not fall so easily again afterwards…[He gave] circumcision…which was a seal of the righteousness of faith to them and gathered all of them in one body, set apart outwardly from all the other unholy congregations of men…By [circumcision] it was always easy to…rebuild [the church] just as one can rebuild a house with less trouble and toil on foundations that have remained intact.[117]

The foundation of the church, in the old covenant, is circumcision. Or, rather, that which is sealed by circumcision: the forensic righteousness through faith. This is exactly the same as saying that the foundation of the church is Christ, Whose righteousness and holiness are declared to be the believer's. It can come as no surprise that Micron literally says this later on, quoting Paul.[118] The church is the church because she builds on Christ and is declared righteous on account of His suffering.

Obviously, this was a commonplace with all the various reformers, yet it seems to have more than common importance for Micron. This is clear

---

116 For references see the discussion of the sacraments below.
117 *VdWNN*, 6v-7r.
118 *VdWNN*, 12r.

when we compare the *Ondersoeckinghe des gheloofs*, which – as we have indicated – was probably a collaborative work, and *Ein kort underricht*, Micron's adaptation of the *Ondersoeckinghe*. The importance of Christ is clear in the very first question and answer. The *Ondersoeckinghe* reads 'that I am a child of God the Father, through Jesus Christ, His Son'[119], whereas the *Underricht* has the pupil answer: 'that I am God's child through Christ alone (*dat ick alleine dorch Christum eind kindt Gades ben*).'[120] The same can be seen in *KU* question and answer 7 and its parallel in the *OS*. The question is how sinners are rescued. The answer in the *OS* is conditional and kept to a bare minimum, whereas the *KU* is more like a doxology: 'Only through pure grace by Jesus Christ'. This is followed by a question and answer not present in the *Ondersoeckinghe*:

> Question: Now that the ground of your faith rests on Jesus Christ alone, explain shortly to us what you believe about Christ?
>
> Answer: That Jesus Christ is in one person both true God of God and true man of man, and therefore my only mediator, high priest, king and prophet, Who took upon Him my curse and damnation and has mercifully given in return His holiness and righteousness to me. Which is summarised in the articles of the Christian faith.[121]

This quotation is even more interesting considering that the *Ondersoeckinghe* goes on to expound on the entire confession, whereas this one question and answer is all that said about the apostolic creed in *Ein kort underricht*. This is, to Micron, the foundation of all other things that can be said in the church. *Ein kort underricht* is less elaborate than the London catechisms, and Micron decided that what the pupil has to know about the articles of faith is the doctrine of Christ. What we find in *Van de weerdicheydt* fits very well with Micron's Norden catechism and it also explains why he had such elaborate discussions with Menno Simons about Christology; for Micron, the very foundation of the church was at stake.[122]

---

119 *OS*, 281 l.6-l.14.
120 *KU*, q+a 1. Underlining HTW.
121 *KU*, q+a 8.
122 Cf. the two publications mentioned above. For the centrality if Christ, cf., also, *Claer bewijs*, 447. The Strangers' Church made the doctrine of Christ's double nature a central point in their confession (*Opera II*, 300-305). Micron extensively proves that Christ was truly man in *Hoste*, 195-207. (Micron attributes this part to Hoste vander Katelyne himself. This may be true, yet it is clear that it serves Micron's purposes as well.) On March 5th, 1556 Micron wrote to Bullinger about Musculus's commentary

We therefore conclude that for Micron the absolute foundation of the church is Christ. By believing in Him, His righteousness and holiness is made that of the church. This means that the church is unholy in itself. She, after all, has to be sanctified by Christ. It also means that the church can never be without fault, as she has to be forgiven by Christ. Micron candidly admits this. On folio 76v-77r he deals with the argument that some do not want to leave their house and join a church because they are afraid they might be contaminated by the sins of that congregation. Micron replies:

> They know, or do not want to know, that the blessed (*saligen*) state of the Christian church has never been completely without sin in this world, nor can it ever be, due to the huge depravity of our nature (*groote verdorventheydt onser nature*).[123]

He proves this by quoting several examples from the Bible. For instance, Judas was among Christ's disciples and the weeds and the wheat grow together.[124] He concludes:

> We all fall in many ways. And even though we have been washed by Christ, yet we greatly need our feet to be washed.[125]

What we see is that Micron calls the church blessed even though there are many sins and faults to be found in her life. This does not mean that the church is not the bride of Christ anymore. This is even true of the church as a *corpus permixtum*, a church in which true believers and hypocrites sit next to each other. Not only does the church as a whole have her faults, the preachers are sinful, likewise. As long as their doctrine is sound one should not leave (*afwijcken*) the church right away. Rather, one should loathe their sinful behaviour, discipline them for it (and when it is necessary try to have them removed) and pray to God for better pastors. Here, as always, he points the reader to his or her own heart. When God sends an untrustworthy pastor 'a Christian shall cry over his own sins and those of the congregation, which God avenges by sending such preachers'.[126] That, of course, is a powerful argument against the initial reason

---

on Genesis, where he perceived Musculus to suggest children were generated by the seed of a man only, thus jeopardizing the human nature of Christs (Füslinus, 384-386). Cf., also, ch. 3.1.5, pp. 77-82.

123 *VdWNN*, 77r.
124 *VdWNN*, 77r-77v.
125 *VdWNN*, 77v.
126 *VdWNN*, 78r-78v.

for not joining. One can never focus on the sins of other, without looking at one's own sins.

When comparing this to the several catechisms, we find that they are in agreement with this. The church is a *corpus permixtum*, for it is not enough to just be a member of the church, one should truly believe. Those who do not believe are chaff.[127] The treasures of this church, despite all its faults, are the communion of saints, forgiveness of sins, resurrection of the flesh and eternal life.[128] Or, to summarise it, a blessed state. This is supported by what Micron says in *Claer Bewijs*,[129] to which we will give attention when we discuss the command to secede (6.5.2).

Thus we come to the end of the analysis of the nature of the church. At the end of the first sub-paragraph we concluded that, for Micron, the church is a people assembled out of all nations, defined by their obedience to the Word of God. In the second sub-paragraph we saw there is an absolute difference between the church of God and the church of the devil. Because the devil constantly tries to attack the people of God, the church is in constant danger of falling to ruins. Yet God, in His good grace, constantly builds her up again, by means of His prophets. Due to the devil's attempts, the life of a believer is always one filled with tribulation. The existential deliverance from the slavery of sin means an existential alienation from the world. Thus, there will always be persecution and a cross, even when the church is at peace. However tough this may be, it can be borne lightly, celebrating the feast of tabernacles. In this last sub-paragraph we looked at the foundation of the church. It is clear as crystal that this foundation is none other than Jesus Christ, God and man, the redeemer of the world, whose righteousness and holiness are imputed to the church and her members. We have seen, when looking at the *Kort underricht*, that Micron loved Christ above all else.

As a general conclusion at the end of this paragraph we say that according to Micron the church confesses Christ to be her foundation, and builds upon this foundation. She is gathered out of all people by the proclamation of the Word, which the Spirit uses to regenerate the heart. This church is alien to this world and must suffer hardships, yet whenever she is destroyed, God builds her up again on that one foundation of Jesus Christ. She is beneficial, because she is a protective barrier against the world, the devil and our own lazy and sinful flesh. She is necessary, because there the Word is proclaimed, the sacraments are administered

---

127 *Cathechismus*, q+a 69; 108; *OS*, 292 l.20-l.26..
128 *OS*, 288 l.14-l.17.
129 *Claer Bewijs*, 560-561.

and Christian discipline is upheld, by which the Holy Spirit renews and regenerates man. She is worthy, because she is holy in Christ.

6.4 The Marks of the Church

Next we turn to the marks of the church. As was already indicated, this should properly be under the heading of the nature of the church; however, for the sake of clarity it is a separate paragraph. In the first sub-paragraph we will tackle two issues. First, the underlying assumption on which the marks are based; then, what are and are not marks of the church. In 6.4.2 we focus on what Micron says about the doctrine of the church. However, that could unfold into an entire systematic theology, and as that is not our aim here and we will limit ourselves to the essentials. In 6.4.3 the government of the church is the subject of our attention. This will be divided into three parts: Word, sacraments and Christian discipline. Though one should try to resist the urge of creating more and more subparagraphs, we feel it is necessary to do so in the analysis of the mark 'Word', and provide an excursus on how Micron looked at ministry, prophecy and priesthood. As it is our goal to describe Micron's ecclesiology it will not be necessary to analyse how Micron opposes the five extra sacraments of the Roman church.

6.4.1 The Marks of the Church: Source and Verity

We start with looking at the source for all religion. A sentence which has been the subject of our attention several times is helpful once more; after presenting biblical theological evidence, Micron concludes on folio 8r:

> It was the eternal and steadfast will of God, that there would be an outward or visible holy congregation of human beings in this world, in which God wants to be honoured and served according to His revealed word.

The source, then, for all true religion is the revelation of God. That what He Himself has ordained and ordered. This is, obviously, not surprising in the age of reformations. In His Word God orders men to serve Him, and how to serve Him. It is of the utmost importance, Micron believes, that these ordinances are kept. In chapter two, where he discusses the marks of the church, he starts with a confessional text, and one of the things he confesses is that:

> The service to this same true and eternal God (*desselven warachtighen ende eewighen Gods*) is not found in the ordinances and commandments of men, with which He is served in vain, neither in any naked ceremony

according to the letter, nor in mouth and lip service, but the body and the heart together, in spirit, truth and love, and this according to the rule of the divine word, as given in the ten commandments.[130]

What we see here is that devotion does not just take place in the service. The entire life of a believer should be shaped according to God's commandments. What is true for everyday life is true for the church too. The ministry of the word, sacraments and Christian discipline are to be conducted 'according to the Lord's command'.[131] When the divine ordinances are mingled with, superseded by or even replaced by human precepts the church will go to ruins.[132] For Micron this was obvious in the Roman Catholic church. He is especially angry that she has slandered both Christ's office as well as His sacrifice.[133] The Bible is the source for how a church should serve God, and as a consequence it is also the source for what the marks of the true church are. This does not mean that every church is exactly the same, but they are all clearly building on the same foundation, and this can be gauged by the marks.

Before saying what the marks of the church are, Micron lists some things which are falsely considered to be marks of the church. These marks are deceptive (*bedriegelicke*). Micron mentions:

- Is the congregation large or small?
- Has its existence been long or short?
- Are the people perfect or imperfect?
- Is the congregation persecuted or at ease?
- Is the congregation prosperous or does it suffer hardships?[134]

This list is not exhaustive, for he ends it with an 'etcetera'. What he means to say is that outward appearances are deceptive. One may think that God either punishes or blesses a congregation, yet you cannot be sure. You would be delving into God's hidden counsel. The only way to know whether a church is true is by measuring it according to what was revealed, not by what is hidden.

Micron believes that the Word of God gives two marks: the doctrine (*leeringhe*) and the governance (*regeringe*).[135] The doctrine of the church

---

130 *VdWNN*, 27v.
131 *VdWNN*, 29r.
132 *VdWNN*, 31r-v; 33v.
133 *VdWNN*, 32v-33r.
134 *VdWNN*, 26r.
135 *VdWNN*, 26v; 28v.

consists of two parts, the knowledge of God and of man,[136] which will be further investigated in 6.4.2. The governance of the church has three pillars: the ministry of the word, the ministry of the sacraments and Christian discipline.[137] A triad which, according to Micron, was ordained by Christ Himself. These three are essential. However, they are only essential in conjunction with doctrine. Word, sacrament and discipline are good and pure when 'they are done according to the Lord's command, and when they work (*strecken*) towards the same end as the abovementioned doctrine works'.[138] Word, sacrament and doctrine are there to make doctrine lived religion. As such the true doctrine is the measure, or the *regula fidei*, for the practices in the church.[139] Moreover, by the means of word, sacrament and discipline Christ proves His strength to us. He proves He is present through the Holy Spirit.[140] God uses these three to assemble and maintain His congregation.[141] So, for Micron, the essential mark of the church is doctrine and the second mark is necessary to live out of this doctrine.[142] Both are based on God's revelation.

This can be visualised in a diagram:

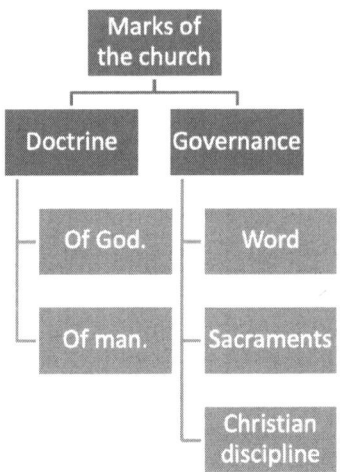

What strikes us, as 21st century readers, is that governance heads what we would call liturgy. One would expect governance to focus on church order, or how the praxis of the church is regulated. But just as the first Dutch 'church order', the *Ordinancien*, is a liturgical book, in the same way the well-governed church is a church in which the governance is an obedient and godly liturgy.

---

136 *VdWNN*, 26v-27r.
137 *VdWNN*, 28v.
138 *VdWNN*, 29r.
139 Cf. *VdWNN*, 28v; 82r.
140 *VdWNN*, 17v.
141 *VdWNN*, 84v.
142 It would be interesting to investigate this in the light of the ancient dictum *lex orandi, lex credendi*. Liturgy is the expression, proclamation, affirmation and education of what is believed. Cf. Lindsay, M., 'Thomas Cranmer and the *Book of Common Prayer*: Theological Education, Liturgy, and the Embodiment of Prosper's Dictum', in: *Colloquium* 47/2 (2015), 195-207, especially pages 200-202.

How does this compare to Micron's other writings? In the *Ordinancien* he says that the builders of the Strangers' Church did not want to accept any superstitious ceremonies, but would only adhere to what was according to God's Word.[143] In his catechism he states that word and sacrament should be administered according to God's Word,[144] and in *Claer Bewijs* he urges his readers to compare what he writes to the Bible, testing all, holding on to what is good. He is certain, though, that they will find his book is true to what the Lord Jesus ordained.[145] If there was any necessity to prove that Micron saw no other authority for the practice, and hence marks, of the church than the Bible, these three examples should be ample evidence.

It is more interesting to compare these marks to what Micron says in his other works. First of all, it is good to look at the confession of the Strangers' Church, for there we find a mark which he called deceptive in *Van de weerdicheydt*. In the confession we read that the marks of the church are: 1) Her antiquity (*vetustas*), 2) her faith (*fides*), 3) her public confession.[146] The first one seems to be in conflict with what Micron wrote: did he not say that we should not look at how long the congregation has been in existence? However, this conflict is only in appearance.[147] For the antiquity of the church is not the same as how a long a particular congregation has been in existence. It is, rather, that the church has existed since the day Adam was called back to God after the fall.[148] Since that time there has ever been a people of God which was called out of the world by the voice of God.[149] Moreover, the faith of the church is the doctrine[150] and her confession entails what Micron denotes as governance.[151] All in all, there seems to be a difference in words, but not in substance between the marks listed in the London confession and in Micron's book. To confirm Micron's constancy we turn to his several catechisms. In the *Kleyne Cathechismus* the pupil has to answer:

---

143 *Ord.*, 37.
144 *Cathechismus*, q+a 68.
145 *Claer Bewijs*, 441.
146 *London*, 65.
147 Note, in passing, that this can be considered as further circumstancial evidence for Micron's authorship. If the book were pseudepigraphical this would have been carefully avoided.
148 That *is* a clear difference. Micron states in *Van de weerdicheydt* that the church existed before the fall.
149 *London*, 65.
150 *London*, 66-74,
151 *London*, 74-77.

> There are two external true marks (*wtwendighe warachtighe teeckenen*) of the outward church. They are the faithful ministry of the word, the orthodox (*rechtsinnighe*) practice of the sacraments, according to Christ's ordinance; to which belongs the diligent use of Christian discipline.[152]

Not a word is said about doctrine here, which would appear to be a difference. However, when the pupil is asked what the ministry of the word is, the answer is 'law and gospel'. In the subsequent answers law and gospel are the summary of true doctrine. Where the doctrine is not faithful, the church is not true.[153] Here we see how the ministry of the word works towards the same aim as the doctrine. By the outward marks of word, sacrament and discipline, the doctrine is born out, and hence they function as marks of the true church. This is also seen in the *Ondersoeckinghe des gheloofs*, where the same marks are listed. Here, too, the ministry of the word is found in law and gospel.[154] *Ein kort underricht* makes no mention of marks at all, yet the triad of word, sacrament, discipline is mentioned. Here, however, they are 'outward practices' to 'train and strengthen us in our faith'.[155] One does not have to stretch the meaning of these words to conclude that the outward practices are there to make doctrine lived religion. In fact, this is said almost literally when the pupil has to answer that the pure ministry of the word lies in the proper (*rechte*) exposition of law and gospel 'as I have confessed so far (*daer ick dusverren nu myne Bekentenisse gedaen hebbe*)'.[156]

All in all, we see that there is a difference, yet this seems to be of a practical nature. In his ecclesiological study Micron shows the theological background of how word, sacrament and discipline can be marks of the church, because they make known what is believed. This is, in fact, in accordance with the confession of the Strangers' Church, where faith and confession correspond to Micron's doctrine and governance.

6.4.2 The First Mark of the Church: Doctrine
Next we turn to the first mark of the church, that of doctrine. We repeat that we will not give a summary of Micron's entire doctrine, for that would entail writing an entire systematic theology. We will indicate the structure he uses and the essential elements within that doctrine.

---

152 *Cathechismus*, q+a 68.
153 *Cathechismus*, q+a 70-75.
154 *OS*, 289 l.7-290 l.3.
155 *KU*, q+a12.
156 *KU*, q+a 14.

Doctrine can be divided into two main points, the knowledge of God and the knowledge of man. The knowledge of God is divided in 'what God is' and 'how one shall serve God'. The doctrine of man has four parts. First, man has a sinful nature, due to Adam's sin. Second, salvation can be found in 'the only Christ'. Third, being justified, believers have to obey God, putting off the old nature (mortification) and putting on the new. Fourth, after this mortal life the godly receive eternal life which has been prepared for them in heaven.[157] This leads to the following diagram:

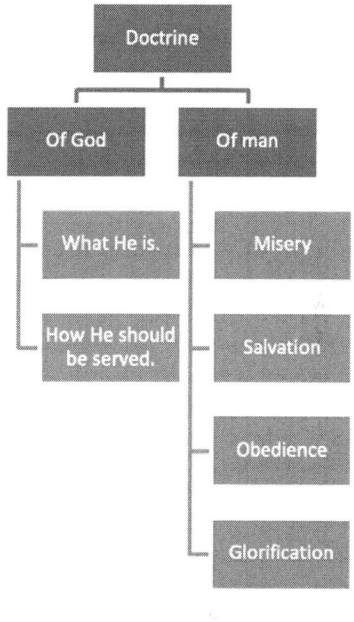

The doctrine of God starts with stating that God is spirit. He is triune. The Father is the creator and ruler of all things. The Lord Jesus Christ is the eternal Son of God who became man. He is king, high priest, prophet, bridegroom, head and foundation of the church. He is our mediator, prays for us in heaven and will return in judgment. The Holy Spirit has inspired the prophets and the apostles and leads us in what is true. He 'enlightens, regenerates, comforts and fills our hearts with the joy of eternal life'. He anoints us to be kings and priests and hands out His gifts. This triune God should be served according to His law and in prayer. In this body and spirit should both be involved.

The doctrine of man receives much less attention. The summary given above is sufficient. However, we will see that the doctrine of man will be fleshed out in the second mark of the church, her governance.

Micron does not make this distinction in doctrine anywhere else. This does not mean, however, that it is a major shift. We have only one other complete confessional text by Micron. It is found in the *Apologeticum*

---

157 *VdWNN*, 26v-28v. (The rev. Stephen Quinton informed us that Thomas Boston's four states of man (in his *The Fourfold state of Man*) correspond to Micron's doctrine of man.)

Scriptorum,[158] which was meant as a defence of his orthodoxy in a Lutheran city. It is not surprising that the structure and stresses are different, especially when there was little time to write it.[159] In the other major works, the *Ordinancien, Claer bewijs* and *Hoste vander Katelyne*, we would not expect a structured confession, nor do we find one. When we look at his *Kleyne Cathechismus*, the first question and answer echoes what we read in *Van de weerdicheydt*. The goal of life is 'know and serve God rightly, and, eventually, life with Him eternally in heaven'. Obviously, the first element of doctrine, that of God, is the same. The doctrine of man is, as it were, summarised, in the doctrine of God. For the catechism goes on to expound the ten commandments,[160] which in turns leads to the depravity of man,[161] his salvation and obedience.[162] The first question and answer adds the outcome of the true confession: eternal life with God. The division of doctrine as outlined above is not found in the other catechisms, though the several aspects, excepting glorification, can be found in all of them.[163] Glorification receives elaborate attention in the *Kleyne Cathechismus*.[164]

As to what is being confessed itself, this is similar to what Micron says in other places. We will limit ourselves here to his *Kleyne Cathechismus* as his most comprehensive doctrinal statement. When the parts on God the Father and the Son are compared, they are similar on a theological level, with an occasional similar turn of phrase.[165] Sometimes the catechism is more elaborate and at other times it is *Van de weerdicheydt* which is more

---

158 This confession is on folios 57-67 (*Is is is*, 82-92). The structure of this work is as follows: The confession is based on the Word of God, not on any human traditions; Christology; soteriology; means of grace (with an elaborate discussion of the Lord's Supper); magistracy.
159 Cf. the biography in chapter 3.
160 *Cathechismus*, q+a 7-36.
161 *Cathechismus*, q+a 37-39.
162 *Cathechismus*, q+a 40-45.
163 OS, 281 l.15-283 l.21 on the commandments, 284 l.4-l.23 on misery, salvation and obedience, 284 l.24-286 l.7 and 287 l.10-288 l.6 on God. KU, q+a 2-5 on the commandments, 6-7 on misery and salvation, 8-11 on God, 20 and 26 on obedience
164 *Cathechismus*, q+a 116-119.
165 For instance, of the Father it is confessed in *Van de weerdicheydt* that He is the Creator and ruler of all things, the Father of our Lord Jesus Christ' (27r), in the catechism it is said that He is 'creator, maintainer and ruler of heaven and earth' (q+a 48). Of the Son it is confessed that He and the Father are equal (*VdWNN*, 27r; *Cathechismus*, q+a 49). On His incarnation, see q+a 56, in which it is said that 'He partakes of the flesh and blood of the children', just as in *Van de weerdicheydt* (27r). After the asecension He is our 'mediator and advocate' in heaven (*VdWNN*, 27r) or, as the *Cathechismus* says, our 'intercessor (*voorspreker*) and mediator' (q+a, 63).

elaborate. A direct dependence of the confession on the catechism cannot be proven, but there is nothing that is dissimilar. When we compare question and answer 66, on the Holy Spirit, we notice that certain words and phrases are virtually the same, though the order is different. In both texts we read that He 'hands out' 'gifts' and He leads 'in all truth'. The Holy Spirit 'regenerates (*eerbaert*) and renews the godly, comforts them and strengthens them in the hope of salvation.' An extra element in the catechism is that the Holy Spirit convicts the world of sin, justice and judgment. There are several other sentences which are not found literally in *Van de weerdicheydt*. Of this the statement that the Spirit is one God with the Father and the Son is the most theologically substantial.[166]

All in all it would appear that the basic confession of God is in accordance with Micron's catechism. The doctrine of man will be compared to his other works when we discuss the sacraments.

6.4.3 The Second Mark of the Church: Governance

After having discussed the doctrine of the true church, as Micron summarised it, we now turn to the more famous triad of word, sacrament and discipline. We will discuss them in that order. Before we do so we draw the reader's attention to the fact that Micron uses 'governance' and 'ceremonies' more or less as synonyms. We read, for instance, that the Roman Catholic church is false in 'doctrine' and in the 'ceremonies'.[167] Ceremonies, moreover, that have been ordered and commanded by Christ. The marks, or ceremonies, are the external practices commanded by Christ. In this model the church only has to do what she has been ordered to do, nothing more. That is how the true church can be recognised.[168]

A) Word

Whereas the Lord's Supper was the major theme of Micron's earlier writings, in *Van de weerdicheydt* the ministry of the word receives more attention than either the sacraments or Christian discipline. We will first look at the aim and importance of the ministry, then its limits and last of all the congregation as the place to receive the word.

---

166 *Cathechismus*, q+a 66.
167 *VdWNN*, 51r. Cf. *OLER*, 573; *ET*, 372.
168 Cf., also, *KU*, q+a 12, 15; *OS*, 289 l.7-l.13, 290 l.4-l.9; *Cathechismus*, q+a, 68, 76; *Ord.*, 37-38; *Claer Bewijs*, 450-451, 464.

First, then, the aim of the ministry. To explain the aim of the ministry Micron reverts to the parable of the net and the fish. We read:

> [By the ministry] many are pulled out of the darkness of deceits (*duysternisse der dwalingen*) into the light of truth, and out of the contamination of sins into a penitent life…Therefore the ministry of the gospel is very aptly compared to a net by Christ. For it is often the case that many are pulled out of the pit of idolatry, ignorance, wanderings, deceits, drunkenness, lusts, lies and all sins into the ship of true godliness (*godfruchticheyt*), and into the kingdom of God's Son.[169]

So, by the ministry of the word people are converted and leave their sin behind them. We have seen how the Spirit uses the preached word to accomplish this. Note that it is not so much about people joining the church, it is about the salvation of their life. By being in the kingdom of God, by hearing the word, they are pulled out of sin and misery into a life of godliness. Just like David was pulled out of the deceit with Bathsheba by Nathan's prophecy. In this way it is the voice of the shepherd that calls his wayward sheep to the right sheepfold.[170] The ministry is the rescue line thrown out of the boat to the man overboard, both to those who believe and who do not or will not. As Micron himself says it: it is the candle lit by the evangelical woman to find the lost coin. It is the harp that silences Saul's evil spirit.[171] It goes without saying, then, that the ministry of the word is of the utmost importance. It is the most important office of the church.[172] Indeed, without it a sinner cannot hope to be saved but will be lost forever and fall into the gravest of sins,[173] for the knowledge of God and salvation is received and confirmed by the ministry. The Holy Spirit uses it for regeneration and to help believers grow in faith and knowledge.[174] To prove this from Scripture Micron uses two texts. Romans 10:17, 'faith cometh by hearing' and Ephesians 4:11-14, the ministers were given 'for the perfecting of the saints'. Whereas Romans is a simple and convincing text, Ephesians 4 is not as clear cut. Micron uses a text which was written to show the aim of ministers (the Greek uses πρὸσ and

---

169 *VdWNN*, 18r. Cf. *VdWNN*, 6868r, where Micron says the Jews and Gentiles assembled by the ministry of the apostles.
170 *VdWNN*, 19r-v.
171 *VdWNN*, 19v.
172 *VdWNN*, 33v. Note, however, that a few pages earlier Christian discipline is called the most important (29v-30r).
173 *VdWNN*, 19v.
174 *VdWNN*, 87v.

εἰς) to prove the necessity of attending the service. However, it is true that Paul[175] says in Ephesians that the effect of the word is the perfecting of the believers. And so it is of the utmost importance that a congregation has a minister of the Word, for 'how will they hear without a preacher'.[176] The preached word is very powerful. By it, the walls of Jericho were demolished. It is even powerful in the godless, for none less than Saul was moved to prophecy when he came amidst the prophets.[177]

Having seen the aim and the strength of the word, we now turn to the limits of the word. The object should always be that Christ is preached.[178] That is the benchmark of whether the sermon is true or false. Christ is found in the Scriptures, and therefore the sermon has to stay within the limits of Scripture.[179] This is not a sign of poverty, for the Scriptures are a 'bottomless treasure of godly wisdom', handed out by the ministers.[180]

The last quote leads us to the final aspect we want to highlight. The word is found in the Bible, the bottomless treasure of godly wisdom; yet, because of this, it is not enough to just read the Bible on your own. Everybody needs the ministry, according to Micron. No matter how much knowledge of Holy Scripture one has, there remains much to be learnt, and this is taught by the ministers in the sermon. Indeed, this has to be done daily for '[w]e are slow and lazy to do what is good, forgetting it quickly, but very eager to do evil (*tot quadt te doen seer snel*) and we remember that very well'.[181] To be truly pulled out of the pit of sin, time and time again, everybody – even ministers themselves – needs to hear the word preached. And so:

> Nobody will excuse himself by saying he has the Bible in his house. I will assume they read it diligently (for there are many houses where a thick layer of dust covers the Bible, or where it is always locked away in a treasury to show it off (*op een tresoyr ghesloten state en pronckt*)), yet the ministry of the word, according to Christ's ordinance, has much more strength and can hit our hearts much better. Because by our nature we are all very blind and admitting too much to ourselves. That is why we cannot, reading the Bible on our own, be admonished of our shortcomings (*onser*

---

175 This is not the place to go into the debate of the authenticity of Ephesians.
176 *VdWNN*, 90r.
177 *VdWNN*, 18v.
178 *VdWNN*, 68v-69r.
179 *VdWNN*, 33v.
180 *VdWNN*, 80r.
181 *VdWNN*, 80r.

ghebreken daer niet so seer mede vermaent worden) so effectively as when we hear another admonishing [us] publicly.[182]

For Micron, then, the ministry of the word took prime position in church.

Can this be proven from his other books, as well? When we turn to the *Ordinancien*, Micron stresses the need for governance. That is why there should be office bearers, including ministers.[183] When he discusses their particular office, he states their first task is to preach the 'true doctrine of the divine word'.[184] Yet, this is still not the same as the discussion above. Neither does he mention this in the catechisms. However, in the letters he does show how Hooper's sermons at King Edward VI's court were very powerful and not without effect. His sermons on Jonah were preached 'with great advantage' and 'stirred up some lazy noblemen and bishops'.[185] In *Hoste vander Katelyne*, moreover, he says that the simple people were tempted by false preachings.[186] This is very scarce evidence, though, to state that what we read in *Van de weerdicheydt* has always been Micron's opinion. It does show, on the other hand, that it is not alien to his earlier texts. Overall, there appears to be a development in his views of the ministry.

Excursus: Ministry and Prophecy, Priests and Prophets
Marten Micron was Bullinger's student. In recent years there has been some discussion on the re-sacralization of the ministry during Bullinger's time as *Antistes* (see below, 7.4). By analysing more fully what Micron says about this, we hope to provide a valuable contribution to the debate. We will start by looking at what Micron says about the biblical priests and prophets, then what he says about prophecy and lastly what he says about ministers. Wherever necessary we will compare this to what Micron writes in his other sources.

First, then, the biblical priests and Levites. He writes of them:

> In addition, the priesthood was installed to teach, offer sacrifices and to pray. The Levites were also dispersed (*verbreydt*) throughout the land, that by their ministry (*dienst*) the people everywhere might be taught God's law more easily and maintained within the holy unity of the body of assemblies (*eenicheyt des lichaems der ghemeynten*).[187]

---

182 *VdWNN*, 80r.
183 *Ord.*, 41.
184 *Ord.*, 43.
185 Micron to Bullinger, May 20th, 1550 (*ET*, 364; *OLER*, 559).
186 *Hoste*, 211.
187 *VdWNN*, 7v.

Their function is fleshed out some more towards the end of the book:

> With these words [i.e. the word is very nigh unto thee][188] all excuses why they would not know God's law are taken away from the Jews, for God has put it in their mouth. That is to say, He has revealed them publicly through Moses. And after that, He let the Levites and priests preach it among them, in such a way that it could always be in their mouth.[189]

Micron uses two texts to prove what he says. For the Levites he refers to Deuteronomy 33:10, 'they [i.e. the Levites] shall teach Jacob thy judgments, and Israel thy law'[190]. In Deuteronomy 33 Moses blesses the several tribes of Israel. What is said there is not a reflection on one or two moments; rather, it is universal statement. Something similar is true for the text Micron uses to prove that the priests were to teach the law. He refers to Malachi 2:7, 'For the priest's lips should keep knowledge, and [the people] should seek the law at his mouth: for he is the messenger of the LORD of hosts'[191]. Again, this is not a general text, but rather a divine statement of what priests ought to be. Micron seems to be correct in seeing the exposition of God's Word as the key aspect of priesthood.[192] By this the people were kept together. Moreover, the priests were to represent the people before God in prayer and by offering sacrifices.

Micron says very little about the biblical prophets. However, the one instance where he does, it is of the utmost importance. The framework is that of the church which is under attack and collapses. She was rebuilt by God in the days of Seth, Noah and Abraham. After God had given His laws He used the prophets for this. The holy ceremonies no longer being kept, the people might be scattered, therefore God used His prophets to re-erect and explain them (*weder oprichten ende verclaren*).[193]

---

188 Deut. 30:14; Rom. 10:8.
189 *VdWNN*, 89v.
190 KJV.
191 KJV.
192 This is underlined by present day Old Testament scholarship, e.g. Block, D.I., *For the Glory of God. Recovering a Biblical Theology of Worship* (Grand Rapids: Baker, 2014), 336-341; Taylor, R.A. & Clendenden, E. R., *Haggai, Malachi* (Nashville: B&H, 2004), 172-173; Boda, M.J., *Haggai, Zechariah* (Grand Rapids: Zondervan, 2004), 143. For the application of the office of Levites and priests to New Testament ministers in the early church, cf. Pelikan, J., *The Christian Tradition. A History of the Development of Doctrine. 1 The Emergence of the Catholic Tradition (100-600)* (Chicago/ London: The University of Chicago Press, 1971), 160.
193 *VdWNN*, 7v.

So it would seem that in Micron's exegesis the priests and Levites were the 'normal' way in which God maintained His congregation and He used prophets to rebuild the church when necessary.

What, then, does this mean for prophecy? For one may assume that the prophets are the ones who prophesy. At first glance what Micron says about prophecy does not seem connected to what he wrote about prophets. On folio 19r we read:

> The prophecy or exposition of the scriptures (*uutlegginge der schrift*) is given to the faithful.

This is the way the prophecy was used in Zurich itself. There the *Profezei* was a daily lecture in which Scripture was translated and explained, rounded off with a sermon. For Zwingli prophecy was the exposition of Scripture.[194] In his *Apologeticum Scriptum* Micron also refers to prophets as 'interpreters of scripture'.[195]

However, this does seem to be at odds with what Micron writes in other places. In the *Ordinancien* he concludes that the prophecy in the London church is a 'public testing of the preacher's doctrine'.[196] Even more important is what Micron writes in *Hoste vander Katelyne*. He tries to prove that Hoste did nothing wrong when he publicly questioned the doctrine preached by a monk. In the church, Micron claims, there is the apostolic ordinance that the doctrine of the preachers can be questioned, and that is the prophecy.[197]

This, then, seems to be a decided difference, whether the prophecy is the exposition of Scripture or the testing of doctrine. However, this cannot be the case. Micron would have attended the prophecies in Zurich, where the Scriptures were expounded. Yet in London he and his co-workers started a prophecy where doctrine was tested. That he did not see a difference can be proven from the *Ordinancien*, for even though the prophecy is the testing of doctrine, this is done by 'a conjoining of places of Scripture (*doer een t'samenvoeginghe der plaetsen der Schriftueren met malcanderen*).[198] In fact, he ends the chapter on the Prophecy by saying

---

194 Cf., e.g., Campi, E. 'Zurich', in: Burnett, A. Nelson & Campi, E., *A Companion to the Swiss Reformation* (Leiden: Brill, 2016), 77-78, 99, 102; Gordon, B., *Zwingli. God's Armed Prophet* (New Haven/London: YUP, 2021), 141-146. For further references see 5.1.
195 *AS*, 100 (*Is is is*, 125).
196 *Ord.*, 72.
197 *Hoste*, 247-248.
198 *Ord.*, 71.

that there is another way of prophecies (*een ander manier der Prophetien*): the exposition of Scripture.[199] The two things which seem so different are placed right next to each other. In the *Apologeticum Scriptum* the same happens, and they even flow into each other. Westphal is to allow the testing of doctrine according to Paul's ordinance that the spirit of the prophets is subject to the prophets. When Westphal mocks Micron for calling himself a prophet, the reply is that he meant it as Paul uses it, 'an interpreter of Scripture'.[200]

When one considers this, it is not strange. It is through the exposition of Scripture, carefully listening to the revelation of God, that the doctrine which is taught in the pulpit can be tested. Based on Scripture, questions are asked to prove that the doctrine taught is Scriptural. In a general way Micron says that 'prophecy edifies the congregation'.[201] This is the office of all believers, especially of ministers and elders.

However, when the doctrine is no longer sound and the people are scattered, it is the special office of prophets to prophesy. That is, to draw the people back to the Word of God by explaining God's ordinances and questioning the doctrine taught by others. One might say that the office of particular prophets is to prophesy when the prophecy has stopped.

We conclude this excursus by drawing these lines together regarding the office of the minister. However, we will find that strict conclusions cannot be drawn, and perhaps Micron thoughts had not crystallised definitely yet.

First we will look at what Micron says about this in *Van de weerdicheydt*. He calls the ministers those who hand out the mysteries of God, as found in Scripture.[202] In this he sees a direct parallel between the priests and Levites of the Old Testament and the ministers in the New Testament. The priests and Levites were the means by which God made sure the 'word was nigh' the people of Israel, 'in their mouth'. This sentence is repeated by Paul where he strongly affirms the necessity for the ministry of the word, for how will they hear of the gospel without a preacher?[203] Why, Micron asks in another place, would Christ have instituted the ministry of the word if ministers were not necessary? They are necessary, because God uses them to teach others the gospel.[204] Micron uses Ephesians 4: 11-12 to prove his argument. He quotes this text, without a

---

199 *Ord.*, 73.
200 *AS*, 100 (*Is is is*, 125). Cf. *AS*, 64-65 (*Is is is*, 89-90).
201 *VdWNN*, 19v.
202 *VdWNN*, 79v-80r.
203 *VdWNN*, 90r.
204 *VdWNN*, 80v.

reference to the apostles and prophets. Micron says: 'ministers of the word (*dienaers des woordts*), item, pastors and teachers'.[205] Now, 'item' could mean 'that is'; however, everywhere else in the book it means 'and also'.[206] So, God gave ministers of the word *and* pastors and teachers. 'Ministers of the word' thus becomes Micron's translation of evangelists.[207] The punctuation seems to indicate Micron saw 'pastors and teachers' as one group. Whatever the ministers are, they are certainly not apostles and prophets, and probably not exactly the same as pastors and teachers.

Earlier in the book Micron writes about the Roman Catholic priests. This part of the book is rather unclear and every conclusion from it can only be drawn tentatively after very careful reading. Micron writes:

> The office of the priests was that they would help the pastors (*pastooren*) to practice and maintain the governance of the congregation and Christian discipline well and properly in good doctrine (*behoorlijcke wijse in een goede leeringhe*).[208]

He goes on to sketch the profile Paul gives of a true 'bishop or pastor'.[209] Paul writes about this in the letter to Titus (1:6-9) and the letters to Timothy (1 Tim. 3:2-3; 2 Tim. 2:24-25). All of these texts are quoted by Micron, of which the one from Titus is certainly about elders (the Greek has πρεσβύτερος). 1 Timothy 3 is probably about elders (the Greek has ἐπίσκοπος) and the text from 2 Timothy is probably about a minister, as Paul addresses Timothy directly. In the *Ordinancien* Micron uses these texts when describing the type of man, a minister of the word should be.

So, the priests are to help the pastors, and the profile of the pastors is taken from texts which are about elders. In the *Ordinancien* these texts are used for the ministers of the word. The careful conclusion is that the Roman Catholic priests are seen by Micron as elders who help the pastor, or minister of the word. Or could it be that Micron had the office of superintendent in view here? That might be the reason why this text does not seem to conform with what we have already seen, where ministers of the word and pastors were separate categories.

---

205 *VdWNN*, 80v.
206 Cf., e.g., folio 27r. However, as Micron does not give a list here (there is even some gapping between the terms) it could mean 'that is'. Nonetheless, based on the rest of the book, 'also' seems the more likely option.
207 This was not common. Utenhove's edition of the New Testament has *euangelisten*.
208 *VdWNN*, 40r.
209 *VdWNN*, 40v.

This reading seems to be in accordance with what is said about elders and ministers in the *Ordinancien*. Micron calls the ministers 'bishops, pastors and teachers'.[210] The other elders assist the ministers of the word, that the congregation may be governed in all 'godliness, holiness, peace, order and honour (*eerbaerheit*)'.[211]

Yet, this still leaves us with the difference between the two texts in *Van de weerdicheydt*. Are ministers of the word pastors and teachers or not? It would appear they are. Yet, perhaps, we should not want to be able to define the office of the minister, and the difference between elders, ministers and the superintendent too tightly. According to the *Ordinancien* the office of the minister and the elder are 'entirely one (*ganschelick een*)'.[212] The office of the priests and Levites, by whom the Scriptures were taught and unity kept, is replaced by the ministers and the elders, who cooperate in their office as preachers, pastors and teachers of Christ's flock. This seems to be the interpretation that does justice to all the texts.

Yet, are not the ministers prophets too? We think we could say that this is true when they rebuild or reform the church. We already explained how Micron called the work of the reformation the rebuilding of Christ's church.[213] When we look at the office of the prophet in this way it explains why Micron sometimes calls the ministers of the word 'prophets'. In the prayer for the congregation and her needs he asks the Lord that the people of England will listen to their 'prophets'.[214] The church of England was, at that time, in need of further reform. This way of looking at the office of prophet seems to be the only way of making sense of a startling expression in one the letters, too. On November 7th, 1551 he writes to Bullinger that à Lasco is a '*vir…plane divinus*'.[215] Now, surely Micron did not mean that à Lasco comes close to being like God. It seems best to interpret *divinus* here as prophet, which is perfectly valid translation. À Lasco, after all, was the one who built the Strangers' Church, and in this way may be said to have fulfilled a prophetic office in the Micronian view.

What we have seen is that, according to Micron, God used the priests and Levites in the Old Testament to teach the people of Israel God's law, to pray and sacrifice for them, and to keep them one people. This office has been replaced by that of the ministers of the word and the elders, who govern the church and teach the Scriptures. The prophets were special

---

210 *Ord.*, 41.
211 *Ord.*, 41, 44.
212 *VdWNN*, 44.
213 *VdWNN*, 82r.
214 *Ord.*, 64.
215 Micron to Bullinger, November 7th, 1551 (*ET*, 375; *OLER*, 578).

men who drew back the people to the Word of God, who rebuilt the church when the people were scattered and the church in ruins. That office was not superseded and some men Micron believed to be prophets, perhaps including himself. Prophesying, however, is not unique to the prophets; rather, it is done by all believers. There is both a priesthood and prophethood of all believers. They read scripture, explain it and use it to test the doctrine of the ministers. In this way the entire congregation is edified. Though this should be done by all, it is especially asked of those who are ordained office bearers. In no way does this make the ministers 'holy' because they replace the priests. Their office is completely one with that of the elders, and their doctrine should always be proven from and corrected by Scripture, if necessary by a prophet.

B) Sacraments

Next, we turn to Micron's doctrine of the sacraments. We will focus on what he says in this book and how it compares to what he says in his other publications. This means we will not analyse his entire doctrine of the Lord's Supper as it is given in *Een claer bewijs*, *Apologeticum Scriptorum* and the *Ordinancien*; however, what he says in the book we are studying is sufficient material to know what Micron thought about both baptism and the Lord's Supper. First we discuss baptism, afterwards the Lord's Supper.

Baptism, Micron states, was ordained by Christ and it is a sign that the congregation is the body of Christ, which is edified by the ministry of the word. Just like circumcision, baptism is the mark that separates the people of God from the world. Those who are baptised belong to the people of God.[216] In the New Testament those who were *won* by the ministry were baptised and joined the congregation without delay.[217] Baptism has an effect on those who undergo the rite and on those who observe it being administered. We read:

> For every time they see baptism being administered, when they themselves or their children are baptised, they immediately remember (*denken sy in henselven*)…first, how great our depravity (*verdorventheyt*) is in Adam, due to sin – yea, great enough for them and their children to be worthy of eternal damnation. Therefore they also remember how great the lovingkindness (*goedertierentheydt*) of the heavenly Father is towards them, by the communion of His Holy Spirit. By which [lovingkindness],

---

216 *VdWNN*, 9r-v.
217 *VdWNN*, 68r-v.

as truly as they are baptised, He mercifully saves them from damnation by His Son, giving them the righteousness and eternal life...Third, he remembers, how we, by the mortification of the old man and the taking up of the new man, bind ourselves to an eternal holiness of life.[218]

So, to summarise, baptism shows us three things: Our depravity, our salvation, our sanctification. It is immediately clear that these three are the same as what was seen in the doctrine of man. The only element that is missing is glorification. In baptism the baptised is a participant in Christ's death and resurrection.[219] In this the same elements can be seen. Depravity leads to death, resurrection is both justification and the start of a new life. The effect of baptism is put very strongly in the quotation, for the salvation is given 'as truly as they are baptised'. However, this cannot be read as an *ex opere operato* doctrine. On the very same page Micron states that baptism 'truly and powerfully shows (*voorghebeeldt*) and seals (*beseghelt*)' the gift of salvation.[220] This shows that baptism does not work automatically, even though it is a sure affirmation and, indeed, proclamation. Last of all, the effect of baptism is unlimited by time. It is not necessary to use holy water for daily sins, in fact, this practice 'minimises the worthiness of baptism'.[221] The sign, when given, is enough for life.

Let us compare this to what Micron says elsewhere about baptism. In the *Ordinancien* it is taught that those who are members of God's covenant have to be baptised. Baptism testifies that the entire congregation has fellowship with God, having been cleansed by the blood of Christ. He goes on to teach that baptism shows us our depravity and cleansing. This cleansing is the deepest mystery in death, for in baptism the baptised has joined Christ in His death and has put on Christ. Thirdly, baptism also admonishes us to be grateful, mortifying our old flesh and putting on the new life.[222] This doctrine is repeated in the several catechisms.[223] So, we see that the doctrine of man, as taught by Micron in *Van de weerdicheydt* agrees with his earlier works. In the catechisms we also find that baptism has a lifelong effect, for it is a constant source of comfort, even though 'I, out of weakness, may fall [into sin] as long as I live'.[224] In these questions and answers Micron seems to be more nuanced about how the baptised is

---

218 *VdWNN*, 20r-v.
219 *VdWNN*, 35v.
220 *VdWNN*, 20r.
221 *VdWNN*, 35v.
222 *Ord.*, 74-76.
223 *Cathechismus*, q+a 84, 86, 87; *OS*, 290 l.14-291 l.10; *KU*, q+a 18-20.
224 *KU*, q+a 19.

to live afterwards. In *Van de weerdicheydt* we read that salvation is 'as truly as they are baptised', whereas in the several questions and answers he continually draws attention to the mortification of the flesh and putting on of the new man. The sign of baptism admonishes the baptised to act out his or her baptism in life. Nonetheless, in the *Ordinancien* Micron repeats that all who are baptised have entered the salvific fellowship with God.[225] Micron can say it like this for two reasons. First of all, because that is what he read in the Bible, where Paul calls baptism the bath of regeneration, the baptised have put on Christ and have been baptised in Christ's death.[226] Secondly, he can assign the 'thing signified' to the sign by speaking sacramentally. The Holy Spirit, Micron says in *Een claer bewijs*, calls the sign by the thing signified to make known the mystery of the sacrament and to help us remember that mystery. The sign is called by that name figuratively.[227] What the sacraments seal outwardly, the Holy Spirit seals inwardly. The sacraments embrace the outward man who opposes the promises of God, leading him to God's grace, but the Holy Spirit works in the heart.[228] So, what is said in *Van de weerdicheydt* is fully in line with what Micron says elsewhere.

The second sacrament is that of the Lord's Supper, what does Micron say about that in his last work? He focusses on sin and forgiveness. In fact, when he discusses the worth and use of the sacrament (which, he says, no tongue can utter)[229], the first thing he says is that all should remember that those who eat unworthily are guilty of the Lord's body and blood. The Lord's Supper then leads to penitence, one examines his or her shortcomings (*ghebreken*), cries over his or her sins, and tries to avoid sin more and more in the future. True examination will also lead to reconciliation with one's neighbour. What we see here is that Micron believed self-examination to be very important. Without it, eating the Lord's Supper worthily is impossible.[230] After self-examination, however, the Lord's Supper is an endless source of joy:

> [B]ecause by the strength of the Holy Spirit they are sealed in the salvific fellowship of Christ and His benefactions (*weldaden*). Then they are awakened to gratitude, they are tied to each other with the bond of

---

225 *Ord.*, 75.
226 Titus 3: 5; Gal. 3:26; Rom. 6: 3. Micron mentions these texts in the *Ordinancien*.
227 *Claer bewijs*, 477.
228 *Claer bewijs*, 456. Cf., also, *AS*, fol. 92.
229 *VdWNN*, 20v.
230 *VdWNN*, 20v-21r.

brotherly love more tightly, and are more fiery to adhere to all godliness of life.[231]

This is, surely, much more than a mere 'remembrance-meal'. The Lord's Supper itself actually does and works something. For Micron it was an emotional moment that made him face his own sin, feel deep gratitude and a strong bond of Christian love with his fellow-believers. Indeed, this last aspect can hardly get enough attention. No one really enjoys a meal being on his or her own. The joy lies in fellowship, so the congregation has to come together to celebrate this meal, as they are one bread.[232] Hence, one should not avoid the Lord's Supper, with the caveat of being able to partake purely and unspoiled (*onvervalscht*).[233] This last sentence is somewhat unclear. Does Micron mean one has to examine oneself, or does he mean that the administration of the sacrament has to be according to God's Word? He refers to 1 Corinthians 11:24, where Paul tells how the sacrament was instituted by Christ. It seems most likely that Micron meant the administration had to be according to Christ's command. However, it might also be the case that he had both in mind, as Paul presses the need for self-examination only three verses later. Last of all, Micron believes the administration should always be linked to the Word. When the sacrament is administered it is necessary to explain what the sign signifies, for the death of the Lord has to be given witness to, until He comes.[234]

For that reason, among many others, Micron strongly opposes the Roman Catholic celebration of the mass: The people are not told what the sacrament means. Nowhere is Micron so fiery and offensive as when he attacks the Roman mass. The doctrine of transubstantiation is the origin of a 'new and heinous idolatry', for it lets people kneel and bow to a 'baked Christ'. This 'new Christ' is given all veneration. Micron brands this as idolatry and the god Maosim, the antichrist of Daniel 11:38.[235] The reason for Micron's strong language here is not difficult to gauge. Nowhere did he find such an endless joy as in the Lord's Supper, nowhere did he experience God's grace and love more than at the table when eating bread and wine. When this is tarnished he flares up, especially when – in his perception – Christ is replaced by an antichrist. His strong language wells up out of deep love.

---

231 *VdWNN*, 21r.
232 *VdWNN*, 9v-10r.
233 *VdWNN*, 20v.
234 *VdWNN*, 36v.
235 *VdWNN*, 36v-38v.

Micron wrote several books on the Lord's Supper, next to giving it attention in his catechisms. It would be tedious to cite comparisons from all of these works, we will therefore make small selections of evidence. In all of the works we come across the need to examine oneself. Three examples will suffice. In the *Ordinancien* it is explained that fourteen days before the Supper was celebrated the congregation was admonished to examine themselves.[236] Willy Willems reads this admonition in such a way that *all*, whether they find themselves worthy or not, are to celebrate.[237] This would seem to be at odds with what was seen above. Though it is true that Micron repeatedly urges all to come,[238] this does not mean he would force people to load greater guilt on themselves by eating unworthily. Only a few pages later does he warn those who are stubborn sinners to stay away from the Lord's Supper.[239] The sole purpose of his last catechism, *Ein kort underricht*, was to help his congregation partake of the Lord's Supper worthily, as the title indicates. All of this can be found in *Een claer bewijs*, as well. On pages 507-514 Micron educates the congregation how to examine themselves. Here, too, he urges all to come. Especially those who seek to avoid the Lord's supper as a license to sin are corrected: sin will always lead to guilt, whether you partake or not. The focus in self-examination is, as we have seen, on sin. This is clear in a striking passage of the *Apologeticum Scriptum* as well, where it is said that the minister admonishes (*monet*) the partakers that they should come with hungry souls. To whet their appetite he gives a gruesome picture of sin, that the hearers may examine themselves.[240] At the table the partakers are reminded that Christ died for their sakes and they have full forgiveness of sins. In *Een claer bewijs* Micron clearly says the Lord's Supper is a remembrance-meal,[241] yet the other, mystic, element is also present. This is clear from his vehemence in the books on the Lord's Supper. The same emotion as in *Van de weerdicheydt* can be read in the other books, for instance:

> ...it was ordained and commanded by our Lord and master Jesus Christ for our spiritual use and profit. For we are not only powerfully admonished

---

236 *Ord.*, 81.
237 Willems, W.O.R., *Met Maarten de Kleyne aan het avondmaal* (Licentiate-thesis University of Protestant Theology Brussels, 1980), 92.
238 e.g. *Ord.*, 96.
239 *Ord.*, 98-99. Strangely enough Willems notices this too (p. 94), yet it did not lead him to change the statement on page 92.
240 *AS*, fol. 20 (*Is is is*, 45).
241 *Claer bewijs*, 468.

and bound to true love, unity (*eendrachticheyt*), humility, patience, fleeing from idolatry, confession of the name of Christ, the mortification of the old man, and all manner of godliness, but, what is greatest, our consciences – when they, gravely downcast and oppressed by sin, rest in Christ – are comforted beyond all limits, being assured by the strength of the Holy Spirit(…).[242]

With Willems we conclude that for Micron the Lord's Supper was more than a remembrance-meal. There was a deep mystery in which the partaker truly receives what is signified.[243] At the table Christ feeds us spiritually, to *refresh* us it is placed before us to eat, he says the *Apologeticum Scriptum*.[244] Though the elements do not change, eating them goes together with spiritual eating. The sacrament shows outwardly what the Spirit does inwardly. Though the body and blood of Christ are not physically present, the body and blood of Christ are eaten spiritually.[245] This meal is eaten together with the entire congregation. In both the *Ordinancien* and *Een claer bewijs* Micron says he wants the supper to be celebrated at the table, while the congregation is sitting down, to show their peace with God. They eat together, because they are bound by Christian love, they are one bread.[246] We immediately think of the extended metaphor of the Christian congregation consisting of many grains, which are winnowed, ground, mixed and baked together. A metaphor given in both the *Ordinancien* and *Een claer bewijs*.[247] To every aspect Micron assigns a spiritual dimension. We have to be ground by the mill of God's Word and deny ourselves. The flour is purified, i.e. set apart from the unbelievers. With water it is mixed into a dough, as the congregation is bound by the Holy Spirit. The congregation is baked in the world, full of tribulation.[248]

In this extended metaphor we see almost all of the aspects of the doctrine of man: The sinful nature of man, justification and mortification. Again, the only element which is lacking is glorification. However, in the *Ordinancien* Micron does draw attention to this after the celebration of the Lord's Supper.[249] Having looked at the doctrine of man several times

---

242 *Hoste*, 216.
243 Cf. Willems, *Met Maarten de Kleyne aan het avondmaal*, 103; *Is is is*, 163.
244 *AS*, fol. 17-18 (*Is is is*, 42-43).
245 *KU*, q+a 25.
246 *Ord.*, 81; *Claer bewijs*, 496.
247 *Ord.* 104-105; *Claer bewijs*, 496-498.
248 *Claer bewijs*, 496-497. Cf., *Ord.*, 104-105
249 *Ord.*, 103.

now, it is a good moment to draw attention to a particular aspect within this doctrine. Most modern-day Reformed believers are familiar with the triad misery-salvation-gratitude. It strikes us that Micron constantly uses the terms mortification and the putting on of the new man. This sounds more severe and more active than gratitude.[250]

The last element we saw was Micron's tirade against the Roman mass. The simple mention of a small treatise within *Hoste vander Katelyne* should be enough to prove that the same emotion could be felt in the earlier works. In a series of 75 antitheses Micron sharply opposes the true Christ to the 'false mass-christ' in scornful and emotional language. In theses 54, 60, 63 and 75 he calls the host the antichrist of Daniel 11. In the last thesis we see that it is out of deep love for Christ as his only saviour that Micron uses such sharp language: having rejected the mass, the believer is to cling (*aanhanghen*) to the only Bridegroom Christ in faith, love, and true obedience.[251]

With this we round off the discussion of the sacraments. In baptism Micron saw three elements: depravity, salvation, sanctification. The effect of baptism is for life. It is the sign that the baptised belongs to God's people. He or she is admonished by baptism to live out what was signified.

In the Lord's Supper attention was also drawn to the community over against the world. The congregation comes together to give witness to Christ's work. No one can come without proper self-examination, and as a consequence Micron emphasises the aspect of sin and forgiveness. In the Lord's Supper he had strong spiritual experiences. From a focus on sin, the Lord's Supper led him to new obedience and love for his fellow Christians. The deep emotion he felt in this caused him to write in the strongest terms against the Roman Catholic mass.

C) Christian Discipline

The third aspect of governance is Christian discipline. This is necessary, because the congregation can never be without sin. Therefore, one should

---

250 This also means the origin of the misery-salvation-gratitude triad in the Heidelberg Catechism and the Church Order of the Pfalz is more complicated than a more or less direct dependance on Micron/the London tradition, as suggested by Schreiber (Schreiber, T., *Petrus Dathenus und der Heidelberger Katechismus. Eine traditionsgeschichtliche Untersuchung zum konfessionellen Wandel in der Kurpfalz um 1563* (Göttingen: Vandenhoeck & Ruprecht, 2017), 165-169. He admits the likelihood of Bucer's *Einfältiges Bedenken* as a *vorlage*, but states the indepence of this triad in self-examination before the Lord's Supper, becoming, ultimately, a structuring element for the entire doctrine.

251 *Hoste*, 235-244.

admonish the sinner and pray for him or her.[252] Indeed, at one point Micron even calls this the most important of all God's ordinances.[253] It is wise to take this with a grain of salt, the book is unfinished and a translation, yet it does show how important Christian discipline was for Micron. So, why is Christian discipline so important? Micron outlines this on folio 21v:

> [Christian discipline] is a bridle (*toom*) against everything untoward (*alle ongheschicktheyt*), against wildness, and careless living (*sorgheloosheyt des levens*). She urges (*verweckt*) the fallen brothers by healing admonitions to return to the straight way and she is a very good remedy against many offenses (*ergernissen*).[254]

When one withdraws him/herself from the congregation one endangers one's soul. The fallen sinner, living on one's own, is not so easily pulled out of sin as when he or she is part of a congregation. Moreover, it is detrimental to the congregation itself.[255] So, there are three uses: it is a bridle to keep brothers and sisters from sinning, it is a remedy against offenses, and it is a means to pull back the sinner on the road towards eternal life. The first and last are clear, but what does Micron mean by the second? The apostle Paul and Christ speak of sins which cause others to stumble and fall away, they are offending.[256] One of the uses of Christian discipline is that it warns against these offenses. With it, the congregation helps and looks after each other. It is for that reason that it is detrimental for the congregation when someone does not join but decides to live on one's own: not only can it be an offense, there is also one person fewer to warn against offenses. The practice of Christian discipline itself should not offend true believers. In discipline the ministers and others only put the yoke of Christ on someone's shoulders. To throw off this yoke is similar to Esau shaking off Jacob's. Those who do so seek freedom for the flesh, instead of Christ's kingdom of glory, righteousness and humility.[257] What Micron says here is that those who refuse Christian discipline do not build Christ's kingdom but the kingdom – or church, as he called it before – of satan. True believers are happy to receive the admonition and to mend their lives when necessary. Christian discipline makes clear

---

252 *VdWNN*, 77r-v.
253 *VdWNN*, 30r.
254 *VdWNN*, 21v.
255 *VdWNN*, 21v.
256 Rom. 14; 1 Cor. 8; Mat. 18.
257 *VdWNN*, 29r-30v.

there are two kingdoms.[258] The very essence of Christian discipline is the essence of the church: to be a people called out of the world to serve God, having been cleansed by Christ, mortifying the flesh and putting on the new man, in the hope of glorification.

Once more we turn to Micron's other works to see how they compare to *Van de weerdicheydt*. In the *Ordinancien* we read a definition which returns almost verbatim in all of the catechisms.

> Christian discipline is a certain ordinance given by the Lord, which He instituted in His congregation by His Word, by which every member of the congregation is bound to Christianly admonish his neighbour in good order (*oerdentlick*) and from God's Word. And also to receive admonitions from him. Those who are stubborn rejecters of these adomonitions will be thrown out of the congregation, given over to the devil, that by this ordinance the entire body and all members will be kept in their office.[259]

Christian discipline is only administered to those who are members of the congregation. The goal is salvation of the body and its members, for it is a bridle (*breidel*) and bond of love.[260] In the catechism Micron mentions several other uses: 1) That all godliness is maintained in the congregation; 2) that God's name does not suffer infamy; 3) that the sinner is saved; 4) that others are not led on to sin by the example of one; 5) that the congregation is saved from temporal judgment, for the entire congregation can be judged with tyranny and heresy when sin is given a free hand.[261] We see that the catechism mentions more uses of discipline than *Van de weerdicheydt*, whereas the *Ordinancien* name fewer; however, there are no discrepancies between them. The bridling of sin, the salvation of sinners and the edification of the congregation are present in all. The extra element of God's honour is not absent in the *Van de weerdicheydt*, though one needs to read between the lines to see this.

In *Van de weerdicheydt* we read that it is important to receive discipline, not just to discipline others. The definition drew attention to that and in the *Ordinancien* Micron devotes four entire folios to this aspect.[262] In those pages he warns against offenses. Those who do not admonish others are guilty of their sins, for they should have won them, whereas

---

258 *VdWNN*, 10r-v.
259 *Ord.*, 105-106; cf., *Cathechismus*, q+a 103; *OS*, 292 l.7-l.13; *KU*, q+a 28.
260 *Ord.*, 106.
261 *Cathechismus*, q+a 106.
262 *Ord.*, 109-110.

now they are lost. They fill the entire congregation with offenses, which they should have warded off. Micron refers to Matthew 18. This proves the conclusion drawn above was correct. The sins which cause others to stumble are to be rooted out by Christian discipline.

6.5 Staying or Seceding

In the previous chapter we concluded that an important background and an important question in the discussion concerning the refugee-paradigm, is that of the tension between disruption and cohesion, the balance between confessional strictness and the realism of practical life. A discussion of what Micron says about the necessity of staying true to, or leaving a false church will shed further light on this. We start the discussion with looking at the command to join the church (6.5.1) and subsequently the necessity of leaving a false church (6.5.2) before reflecting on the balance between the two (6.5.3).

6.5.1 The Command to Join the Church

The command to join the church rests firmly in the conviction that an outward and visible church is God's eternal and steadfast will,[263] a claim we have already looked at. Indeed, the entire biblical-theological part stresses the outward church, which is especially clear in the Old Testament examples and the discussion of the metaphors and parables. It is a visible church because God's people have to be one body 'joined by holy bonds'.[264] For that reason God gave the people of Israel the ceremonies and offerings.[265] In the New Testament, the church is edified by the offices. She is gathered by the proclamation of the Word. Her unique status as God's people sealed by baptism and the Lord's Supper; it is guarded by Christian discipline.[266] They are, furthermore, bound together by a common confession and the Spirit,[267] as was seen above. All of this leads to the conclusion that the people of God have been gathered together.[268] That should be familiar by now, but here we want to draw attention to the word 'together'. For the church to be a building, the individual stones have to be joined together. For the many grains to make a bread, they have to be baked together. For the grapes to be a bunch, they have to be together.[269]

---

263 *VdWNN*, 8r.
264 *VdWNN*, 7r.
265 *VdWNN*, 7r-7v.
266 *VdWNN*, 8v-10v.
267 *VdWNN*, 12r.
268 *VdWNN*, 11r.
269 *VdWNN*, 12r-13r.

Micron exclaims, at one point, 'and if there were no church or congregation of Christ to be gathered, the little word 'church' or 'congregation' would have been used in Scripture to no purpose whatsoever (*heel te vergeefs ghestelt zijn*).'[270]

There were people who claimed they did not have to leave the church of Rome in order to adhere to the Reformed confession. According to Micron they separated body and soul when they claimed that even though the body was present, their soul did not partake in nor was it infected by the faults and sins.[271] Micron does not admit any room for a separation of body and soul. Micron, of course, admits that God looks at the heart. However, God also looks at the body. For Micron the inward religion is the source for outward piety. Outward piety is nothing without inward piety, yet inward piety must – as a necessity – lead to outward confession, for: 'I have believed, and therefore I have spoken'.[272] Not only the tongue should serve God:

> in holy Scripture it is lavishly said (*overvloedelicken genoech gheseyt*) that all our words and deeds; item, all our members, such as knees, tongue, mouth, flesh and body, have to be appropriated to the service of one God (*eenen God te dienen moeten toegheeygent worden*).[273]

The outward deeds are the touchstone for the inward affections. These two are inseparable, for 'love is bound, with a strong bond, to faith. Item, she is found in good works only (*alleen in goede dinghen geleghen*)'.[274] It is very important to delve into this non-dualistic theology of 'inward' and 'outward' more deeply to understand the reason for seceding. Inward and outward cannot be divided from each other, and inward piety leads to outward deeds. However, the opposite is also true. The outward religion, the word being preached, has an effect on regeneration. We will first present some of the things Micron says about that:

> The outward religion (*godsdienst*) moves the outward man, and…the Holy Spirit touches, moves, pulls up and bends inwardly the heart, thus causing (*makende*) the outward man to be touched and moved by the outward ceremonies and religion with (*met*) multiplication of godliness.'[275]

---

270 *VdWNN*, 11r.
271 For more details, see the summary.
272 *VdWNN*, 58r-60v; 61v-62v; 68r. Quotation of psalm 116 on 58v.
273 *VdWNN*, 58v.
274 *VdWNN*, 65r.
275 *VdWNN*, 85v

Here on earth, the soul and body of man are joined together. And considering that the same is with outward means awakened and pulled towards sin by the outward senses, God has - in His wisdom accommodating Himself to this human weakness – ordained (*inghestelt*) outward remedies and means…by which man is pulled away from sin and pulled up towards godliness (*tot de godslicheyt…verweckt*). For God, by His Spirit, causes the outward pieties (*godsdiensten*) to be so powerful in the heart of man, that they feel…their hearts are inwardly pleased and made glad (*vermaect ende opghetoghen worden*). The outward pieties, then, and the inward aspiration (*aenblasinghe*) of the Holy Spirit work together in man.[276]

[T]he outward exposition of the word (*leeringhe*) cannot be beneficial to worldly men (*vleeschelicke menschen*), no matter how sharp they are, unless they are taught inwardly by God, pulled and moved by the Holy Spirit.[277]

[In the practices ordained by God] we are pulled up towards and awakened to the sweet vision and reflection of heavenly thing, at all times, more and more.[278]

True Christianity…is found in regeneration and the renewal of the mind (*gemoets*) by the Spirit of God. This renewal does not exclude the outward service, yea, what is more, she desires // the same to be driven more and more, seeing that we are to a certain extent regenerated and renewed by it.[279]

What we see is that the Holy Spirit, in Micron's theology, has, to a certain extent, bound Himself to the outward religion to work regeneration by it. So the ceremonies, entering the body by the outward senses, are used by the Holy Spirit to move the heart inwardly, to renew and regenerate it. The heart which has been renewed, the person that has an inward piety, will then show his/her piety by joining a church and hear the Word, in order to be pulled away from sin and be renewed to God's image more and more.[280] Because the Spirit works in the hearts by means of outward

---

276 *VdWNN*, 85v-86r.
277 *VdWNN*, 91v.
278 *VdWNN*, 91v-92r.
279 *VdWNN*, 92r-92v.
280 This is a deep vision of how Word and Spirit are connected and cannot be captured in the terms '*per verbum*' and '*cum verbo*'. (For a brief introduction to this, see: Velema/Van Genderen, *Beknopte gereformeerde dogmatiek* (Utrecht: Kok, 2013), 695-697 and Wentsel, B., *Hij-is-er-bij. Handboek bijbelse geloofsleer II* (Kampen: Kok, 2006), 423-426.)

ceremonies it is perilous to stay on one's own.²⁸¹ Solitary believers follow the will of the flesh, trying to avoid Christian discipline.²⁸² They do not join the flock, which is protected by the Shepherd.²⁸³ Just how perilous it is to stay on one's own is made clear by the examples of Eve and Thomas. Eve sinned when she was alone. Thomas, who did not join the other disciples at first, could not believe the resurrection of Christ until he once more attended the congregation.²⁸⁴ All of this makes it clear that one should join the outward church, to confess one's faith together with her, and be edified by the ceremonies. The church is not just a building, it is God's house: 'based on God's Word, we think there are places and times… where there is a house and church of God…Not for the sake of the outward place…but because of the boon (*weldaet*) that God's will is revealed and preached [there]'.²⁸⁵ Notice how Micron reverses it: The church is God's house not by anything human beings do, it is His house because of His blessing.

It is almost unnecessary to prove that this is not at odds with what we know from Micron's life and other writings. After all, he was so convinced of the necessity to join a true church that he fled Flanders and England, Denmark and Lutheran cities, just so he could practice the outward religion in accordance with his inward convictions.²⁸⁶ The entire last section of *Claer bewijs*, twenty pages in the modern edition, are devoted to the obligation to secede from the Roman church and join a reformed church. There he says that one should go to a place where one can 'heartily serve God without the taint of superstition, the more so because God commanded it'.²⁸⁷ There they are to confess their faith, subject themselves to Christian discipline and attend the services.²⁸⁸ In these pages Micron talks about the inward and outward, the spirit and the body, in similar terms as in *Van de weerdicheydt*. For if we truly mark the worth of our bodies we would not contaminate them with idolatry, according to Micron.²⁸⁹ God sees what the body does.²⁹⁰ Soul and body should not be

---

281 *VdWNN*, 10v; 12v-13r.
282 *VdWNN*, 25v; 29v; 69r.
283 *VdWNN*, 22v.
284 *VdWNN*, 24r. Whether this is a correct exegesis of Genesis 3 does not concern us here.
285 *VdWNN*, 85r.
286 Cf. the discussion of Nicodemism in Ch.2.5 (with references) and the biography in Ch.3, especially 3.1.3 and 3.1.4.
287 *Claer bewijs*, 561. A similar remark is on page 555
288 *Claer bewijs*, 562.
289 *Claer bewijs*, 547.
290 *Claer bewijs*, 548.

divided from each other.²⁹¹ Fleeing superstition with the spirit should be followed by fleeing from it with the body.²⁹² In this light it interesting to, once more, look at the act of confession. It was seen that Micron quoted psalm 116:10. In *Van de weerdicheydt* this means that inward piety should be joined to outward religion, soul and body are one and should serve God as one. So, it urges the reader to go join a church. In that church the faith is confessed, as in the Strangers' Church in London, where psalm 116:10 returns in the confession. There it is the private confession which flows out of the public confession of the entire church.²⁹³ The text once more returns in *Ein kort underricht*, as the motto on the cover.²⁹⁴ There it is the public confession which is taught to the pupil and thus make it his own, private, confession. Again, as above, we see that there is no distinction between the written, public confession of the church, and the private, inward confession of an individual. The one flows from the other, the inward piety seeks the public confession, the public confession feeds the inward religion. So we see that here, too, *Van de weerdicheydt* offers a theology firmly in accordance with Micron's other books.²⁹⁵

6.5.2 The Necessity to Secede

So now we turn to the other command, the command to secede or leave a false church. First we will see that this should not be done lightly; then when and why one must; lastly, where one should go to.

When Micron has concluded that one should leave the church of Rome, one of the counter-arguments he discusses is the following:

> It is not lawful to leave any church or congregation for the sake of some abuses, as long as the foundations of salutary doctrine (*heylsamer leere*), of God and His word, are yet kept.²⁹⁶

---

291 *Claer bewijs*, 549.
292 *Claer bewijs*, 554.
293 *Opera II*, 324-325.
294 *KU*, [2].
295 For more evidence, though slightly more circumstantial, cf. Micron to Bullinger, May 20th, 1550 (*OLER*, 560-561; *ET*, 365); *KU*, q+a 10, 15; *Cathechismus*, q+a 69, 71-73, 76; *Ord.*, 35-36, 41, 67-70.
296 *VdWNN*, 49v.

To which Micron replies:

> We certainly confess that one should not lightly leave or avoid any congregation (*uutscheyden noch afwijcken*) for the sake of some abuses, or for the sake of some shortcomings of men, when the godly doctrine of God and His Son are kept and driven purely.[297]

Here we see that Micron believes nobody should leave the church for just any reason. Indeed, as long as the foundations are still kept, much may be wrong in the building, yet one does not have to leave it. The church where word, sacrament and discipline are upheld and directed to the central teaching of man's sinful nature, the redemption by Christ, and true thankfulness, can be joined with a clear conscience.[298] Even when the pastor, upright in doctrine, is sinful in his deeds, the church should not be left; rather, the pastor should be disciplined.[299] From which one may derive the general rule that discipline comes before secession.

However, even though one should not easily secede, there comes a time, according to Micron, when one must. On folio 50v-51r he names several aspects when one should secede.

- When the salutary teaching is openly mocked and tampered with (*ghelastert ende vervalscht wort*).
- Where God's ordinances are publicly turned upside down.
- Where many heathenish and idolatrous corruptions invade.
- Where it is not allowed nor hoped that the doctrine and God's ordinances are Christianly improved in accordance with God's Word.
- Where Christians are tyrannically forced to uphold or claim as right all abuses.

It is unclear whether Micron means that all of these should be present before one must secede or that one of them is enough. This is probably thinking too strictly. Micron had the Roman Catholic church in mind, in which he saw all of these things, and therefore wrote them down. They should therefore not be used as in inflexible rule, or a list of demands which have to be met before one secedes; rather, they should be seen as a plumb line, to measure the depth of a church's orthodoxy. When the water is too shallow one should 'cut himself off (*afsnijden*)' from the false church. Being

---

297 *VdWNN*, 50v.
298 *VdWNN*, 29r-30r.
299 *VdWNN*, 78r-78v.

forced into upholding abuses is of special importance to Micron. On folio 54r-v he repeats that where one is forced to take part in unholy ceremonies, one should leave. This is even rooted in the ten commandments: Thou shalt have no other gods before me.[300] What we see, then, is that one must leave the church when the abuses are so manifold and inescapable that all who stay cannot help being contaminated with them.

That is also the reason why one really *must* leave that false church. For no one can eat a rotten apple and stay healthy. First, the rotten part has to be cut out. In the same way, Micron says, the church of Rome has to be reformed before it is safe to go there.[301] Contamination is the key word here. A word we saw in Terpstra's study of religious refugees as well. The safety within the city of God, which is the *nutheydt* of the Christian assembly, is endangered when a church is so corrupt that it has left the foundation of Christ and the justification through faith and God's ordinances, which she publicly and privately confesses. That is why all true believers have no other option than to leave the Roman Catholic church. This does not make them schismatics, Micron counters Roman Catholic opponents, for the abuses are too many and too severe to bear with.[302] To some degree, then, this argumentation has an apologetic nature as well.

When the Roman Catholic church has been left, Micron explains, the converts should join a reformed church. If this is not possible they should start a secret church or leave their birthplace to join a reformed church abroad, as Micron himself had done.[303] However, then and now, the much heard objection is: where should one go? There are so many churches![304] Let us look at Micron's reply:

> Yet tell me, rather, whether they would not be obliged to have and follow a certain and assured (*sekere ende ghewisse*) opinion of religion if they were living on their own? For every christian is demanded to be wise, not unwise, in what the Lord's will is and to be perfect in understanding. And, so as to take the most certain out of these manifold opinions, would it not be better and more assured to live in a holy Christian congregation (to which Christ promised His presence, and in which the spirit of the prophets is subjected to the prophets), than to live solitarily, which is forbidden?[305]

---

300 *VdWNN*, 45v.
301 *VdWNN*, 54v.
302 *VdWNN*, 49v-55r.
303 *VdWNN*, 70r.
304 *VdWNN*, 76v.
305 *VdWNN*, 76v.

This answer is not so easy to understand. What Micron means is this: yes, there are many opinions, and how can you choose which church you should join? Whatever you do, do not try to figure it out by yourself, which is forbidden. You should join a holy and Christian congregation, which at least is true to the foundation of faith, and there perfect yourself in the knowledge of the will of God and become perfect in understanding. A church where, as Micron said earlier, the sinful nature of man, the redemption in Christ, and the sacrifice of gratitude is taught.[306] Though every church has its mistakes, even in doctrine, yet Christ has promised His presence to them. Moreover, the pastors of that church subject their teaching to the examination of the congregation, which means that individual believers can ask the pastors to prove their doctrine from Scripture. With an anachronistic conclusion we might say that Micron advises to at the very least join a protestant church, even when there are faults, as long as one leaves the church of Rome and does not join radical sects. Mirjam van Veen, in her book on Calvin and Nicodemites, paid some attention to the argument above. She claims that Micron does not adequately answer the argument because, Van Veen says, Micron states 'it is more certain to live in a congregation…than to live alone.'[307] However, Van Veen probably misunderstood the sentence because she does not note that Micron is not talking about certainty in general, but about certainty and assuredness of the right opinion of doctrine/religion. For we must note that Micron repeats the words 'certain' and 'assured' (*seker; ghewis*). First he says that all are obliged to have a certain and assured opinion of doctrine. To choose the most certain doctrine, to have a most assured opinion, it is better to join a church than to be alone. So, Micron does not bluntly state: just join one. He guides as a true pastor those who are already unsure to a place where they may grow in their knowledge.

To prove that Micron's other works also professed his strong belief that one should secede from the Roman church would merely be a repetition of arguments, and it will suffice to refer in general to *Hoste vander Katelyne* and the fourteenth chapter of *Claer bewijs*.[308] It is more to the purpose to investigate what seems like un-Micronian leniency in condoning other churches. However, before we do so we will show that obedience is a key word in Micron's theology.

When it comes to obedience, the *Kleyne Cathechismus* is very telling. The first question and answer draws attention to serving God. The sixth

---

306 *VdWNN*, 29r.
307 Van Veen, *Verschooninghe*, 140.
308 *Claer bewijs*, 543-563; *Hoste*, 220-225.

defines the right disposition towards God: 'That is, that we obey Him by keeping His commandments.'[309] This leads to a discussion of the ten commandments, which is rounded off by stating that all God's institutions are perfect and therefore cannot be replaced or appended.[310] De Ondersoeckinghe states that all people are bound to the commandments, even on pain of damnation.[311] As a consequence the church and service has to be conformed to God's commandments, for this was ordained by Christ.[312] In London Micron and his co-workers sought the implement what was according to God's Word, and nothing more. 'Superstitious ceremonies' were carefully avoided, even though that would have meant temporary comfort and safety.[313] Obedience to God's Word, then, is key in Micron's beliefs.

Let us move on and look at whether Micron is more lenient in *Van de weerdicheydt* than he was in other works. In his letters we see that he often lashes out at the Anglican reformation, led by Thomas Cranmer. For instance, in its (to use a Micronian phrase) infant state Micron was still expecting a 'more complete reformation'.[314] He declares the original oath Hooper had to take 'in the name of God, the saints and the gospels' an 'impious oath'.[315] The Strangers' Church is free from all superstition, which cannot be said of the Anglican church, where they 'will not depart a nail's breadth from their prescribed form of consecration, which is manifestly superstitious'. Here Micron refers to the vestments-controversy, which we touched upon in the biography. Micron condemns the bishops and says they prefer their own credit to that of Christ.[316] In a postscriptum to this letter he adds that 'the privileges of our German church are in the greatest danger…[we are] to be fettered by the English ceremonies, which are intolerable to all godly persons.'[317] However, it should not be overlooked that all of these remarks are from before the second prayer book of 1552. Nonetheless, Micron is very severe. A severity that we see, moreover, when he moved from England to Denmark and travelled along the northern coast of the German Lands. Wherever he and his colleagues came they disputed about the presence of Christ in the Lord's Supper and

---

309 *Cathechismus*, q+a 1 & 6.
310 *Cathechismus*, q+a 37.
311 *OS*, 281 l.15-282 l.22, 283 l.22-284 l.3.
312 *KU*, q+a 12
313 *Ord.*, 38.
314 Micron to Bullinger, May 20th, 1550 (*ET*, 364; *OLER*, 559).
315 Micron to Bullinger, August 28th, 1550 (*ET*, 368; *OLER*, 566).
316 Micron to Bullinger, October 13th, 1550 (*ET*, 371-372; *OLER*, 571-572).
317 Micron to Bullinger, October 13th, 1550 (*ET*, 372-373; *OLER*, 573).

had to leave.[318] This surely does not agree with how Micron urged his readers to join a church, even if it were faulty and not to secede when the foundations were still in order. It is our suggestion that the reason for this can be found in the unity of outward behaviour and inward conviction. Those two have to be in agreement with each other. Micron cannot publicly confess a Lutheran doctrine which he does not inwardly believe, even if that church builds on the foundation of Christ. However, this does not universally apply to each and every one in any given circumstance, for one is to consider that no church is perfect. There can, moreover, be no doubt that Micron saw other 'protestants' as true brothers and sisters. In the *Apologeticum Scriptum* he asks his readers to listen with Christian love to what he is about to say. He greets all of his readers as 'brothers in Christ'. However, the book, especially the pages that follow this cordial greeting, is aimed at Joachim Westphal, the Lutheran pastor of Hamburg.[319] Though Micron can have had little love for Wespthal, yet he addresses him as a brother in Christ. Micron claims to have said in Hamburg that he did not come to condemn the Lutheran church there.[320] Especially folios 86-88 are of the utmost importance here. He says he does not want to condemn Luther or Zwingli to hell, yet their doctrine should be weighed and tested. However, neither should be condemned, for teachers who have Christ, professing Him to be both God and man, as the foundation of their work, will be saved.[321] This opinion is repeated in other places. In the *Ordinancien* he is quick to add, at the end of the introduction, that he does not condemn other reformed churches, as long as they have the foundation of Christ – truly God, truly man, the redeemer of the world – and desire to build with gold and precious stones. For 'it is not possible that all congregations should have the same outward appearance: The gifts are manifold, the circumstances are manifold, shortcomings, too, are everywhere, in this our great weakness and illness of marred human nature'.[322] Last of all, the conclusion in *Claer Bewijs* underlines what we have seen so far:

> '[One] should understand that there is a great difference between the faults in the churches. Some do not have the right foundation of Christ Jesus. For they go astray (*dwalen*) when it concerns His Person, either in His divine or human nature, or in His strength and the glory of His

---

318 Cf. the biography in chapter 3.1.
319 *AS*, fol. 11 (*Is is is*, 36); Ch. 3.1.4 of this study.
320 *AS*, fol. 55 (*Is is is*, 80).
321 *AS*, fol. 86-88 (*Is is is*, 111-113).
322 *Ord.*, 39-40.

kingdom, priesthood or prophethood. All such must be shunned, like the Jewish, Turkish and papist and all such churches. The others, holding on to the foundation of Christ in His person, natures and office, are true churches of Christ, even though they have built upon this true foundation with wood, straw or stubbles, as far as this is known it is punished by the Word of God. These churches are without spot or wrinkle through Christ. Such a one was the church in Corinth. And such churches God, in His unspeakable grace, planted in our days in Germany, Switzerland, Savoy and England.'[323]

So we see that Micron had very strong opinions as to what was the pure doctrine. Yet, he was not so absolute as to condemn each and every church that did not fully agree with his views. He even calls the Lutherans his brothers, in the firm faith they build upon the same Christ. He sought to live alongside them, as long as he was able to practice his faith according to his own Reformed thought. And where he does condemn the Roman church and David Joris,[324] he does, at first, not condemn Menno Simons. After their first meeting they even ate together.[325] Though, of course, we should add, Micron strongly urges his readers to beware of Menno's teachings.[326]

6.5.3 Confessional Authenticity and the Pastoral Realism of Broken Life.
What does this analysis mean for the balance between pragmatism and radicalism? It was seen that the nature of the Church is defined by her foundation: she should build on Jesus Christ as her one foundation. For Micron all churches who do so are true churches and in everyday life a degree of leniency, or realism, is possible, so long as this does not mean that one dissembles. There is, if you will, a pastoral realism to Micron's guidance in *Van de weerdicheyt*, which is based on the doctrinal belief that every church is sinful due to man's depravity. One may with a good conscience join the Anglican church, for instance, as his friend John Hooper did, either to grow in knowledge or to pursue its further reform. However, what is not possible is that body and soul are divided, that there is no agreement between outward act and inward conviction. That is where Micron, in his own life, draws the line: he would not stay in Lutheran cities if this meant he could not lead his congregation in

---

323 *Claer bewijs*, 560-561.
324 *VdWNN*, 66v-67r.
325 *Waerachtigh*, 102.
326 *Waerachtigh*, 159-160.

accordance with their convictions. He shunned confessional playacting and sought confessional authenticity. The difference of outward forms between the churches, and even the differences in doctrine, did not imperil their faith-unity if they could practise their religion in one and the same city.

So there is the demand of confessional authenticity: Micron would not accept anything that forced him to believe less or confess otherwise than what he inwardly knew to be true. If necessary one has to flee, preferring the temporary tabernacles to worldly comforts. And at the same time there is a degree of pastoral realism, which admits that other churches are true, and can be joined with a free conscience if circumstances demand it. Both these aspects should be given equal weight, and stressing one at the cost of the other endangers our proper understanding of it and the overall theology of the Reformed.

6.6 Summary and Conclusions

Thus we come to the end of this chapter in which we analysed the ecclesiology given in *Van de weerdicheydt, nutheydt ende noodicheyt der christelicker vergaderinghen* and compared it to Micron's other works. In the comparison we did not find any major contradictions between the book we are studying and the other books, and it may therefore be taken as a trustworthy source for Micron's ecclesiology. We will summarise the several paragraphs.

In 6.2 it was seen that the purpose of the church is the glory of God and the salvation of man. The glory of God is sung in the confession, which also binds the several members of the church together. The church serves the salvation of man by protecting those within her from the wiles of the devil.

In 6.3 we looked at the nature of the church. She is a kingdom in direct opposition to the kingdom of the devil. She was called out of the world by God and Christ is her only foundation. the two kingdoms are enemies and the devil seeks to destroy the church, and indeed she often does collapse. However, God always sends His servants to rebuild the church. In Christ the church is holy and she proclaims His mighty deeds in Word, sacrament and Christian discipline.

In 6.4 we turned towards the marks of the church. The source for the marks are God's revelation, and as such the marks are God's ordinances. There were two: doctrine and governance. Doctrine consisted of the knowledge of God and the knowledge of man. Governance divided itself into Word, sacraments and discipline. The two diagrams given in the chapter lead to the following full diagram:

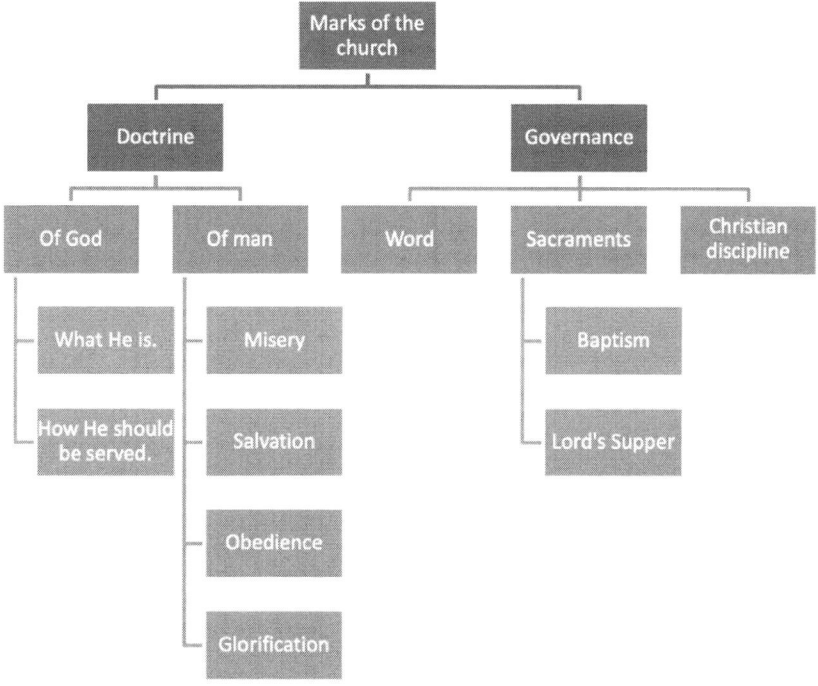

The ministry of the Word is the proclamation of Christ by which people are pulled out of the world into the kingdom of God, and built up to a holy life. The ministers of the Word take up the role of priests and Levites in the Old Testament, though prophesying should be done by all Christians. Prophecy is the exposition of Scripture in order to test doctrine. When the church is in a state of disrepair there may be prophets whose special task it is to rebuild the church on the foundation of Christ.

Baptism and the Lord's Supper are sacraments that turn our attention to our sins and the salvation by Jesus Christ. They admonish us to live a sanctified life. They are, moreover, truly congregational feasts. The baptised becomes a member of the church. The Lord's Supper binds us together in Christian love.

Christian love leads to Christian discipline, in which all of the threads outlined in this summary come together. The sinner is warned by the Word of God to turn away from sin. In this way he or she is pulled inside the kingdom, and stopped from building the kingdom of the devil. In this way he or she is protected and admonished to glorify God. Those two aspects are, after all, the purpose of the Church: the protection of God's people and the glory of God's name by the people He redeemed through Christ.

In 6.5 Micron's views on the balance between disruption and cohesion were analysed. Though it is necessary to join the church, there can be a point at which one has to leave it due to its many sins. Dissembling is not an option: body and soul are one, and outward behaviour should agree with inward conviction. At the same time there was pastoral realism that acknowledges other churches to be true churches of Christ, despite their sins.

That was an important discovery in the course of finding an answer to the questions at the end of the last chapter. It was seen how the status of a being a *peregrinus* on an existential level was fundamental in urging others to leave the Roman Catholic church, even if this meant exile or migration. This analysis showed that Micron thought of himself as a man on the way to the promised land, living in tabernacles, and as a stranger in this world. To what extent this was caused by his leaving Flanders cannot be ascertained; however, what is clear, is that the two are closely linked and the theology seems to have been strengthened by experience, confirming the idea that flight, exile or migration worked as a catalyst for theological convictions.

This brings us to the question of what theological convictions it strengthened. In his book Micron does not reflect on the independence of the church. Indeed, this very idea seems to be absent, and he simply takes it as a given that either a government does or does not give room to a Reformed church. Though discipline is clearly present in the book, it is not necessarily strongly linked to the refugee experience. Absence of evidence is, however, not evidence of absence. The centrality of discipline is so strong that it is essential in remaining faithful to Christ. Moreover, trying to avoid it is equal to throwing off Christ's yoke and leaving the true church. The weight given to discipline makes it one of Micron's reasons to leave the Roman Catholic church and seek a true church.

The doctrines of providence and election were not addressed independently. Does this mean they did not play a role? It does not. The entire biblical-theological section makes clear that God providentially kept His church in existence to the present day, and that He elected men in order to achieve this. There can be little doubt, based on Micron's ecclesiology, that he believed God had providentially led His church to the forms adopted in London and that many of his direct colleagues, and perhaps he himself, had been elected by God as prophets. The call to lead the church also meant that he was strict in his confessional authenticity, even if this meant exile.

The perfect summary of Micron's ecclesiology is given in the three words of the book's title. The church is *worthy*, because she is Christ's bride and God is in her midst. She is *necessary* to protect the true believers against the devil and the world. She is *beneficial*, because there the Word, sacraments and discipline are ordered according to God's Word. By these outward means, God regenerates, saves and edifies His congregation.

Chapter 7: Micron and Reformed Ecclesiology

Having analysed Micron's ecclesiology in detail, it is now time to zoom out again. For after all, Micron was just one of the many theologians in the constantly changing and adapting movement which is called 'Reformed'[1]. How his ecclesiology fits within this larger movement is the question that occupies us in this chapter. However, we need to limit the extent of this discussion. First of all, we will not go beyond the better-known theologians. In addition, we will only study those persons and works that we can be fairly certain influenced Micron. We will see in 7.1 that this was direct and personal with Heinrich Bullinger, John Hooper and John à Lasco whereas with John Calvin, Wolfgang Musculus[2] and Peter Martyr Vermigli[3] it was via letters or books. These six, then, are the theologians we will study in this chapter. However, Bullinger cannot be seen as a stand-alone figure. Micron studied theology in Zurich, and was thus confronted with the entire Zurich Reformation. In addition to Bullinger we will also use works by Huldrych Zwingli and the Larger and Shorter Catechism written by Leo Jud.

Even with these limitations, the field of research is still too large. First of all, to study exhaustively the full ecclesiology of all these reformers is the work of a lifetime, rather than that of one supporting chapter. Secondly, there is the danger of getting entangled in all sorts of theological debates, especially concerning the marks of the church. These marks are

---

1 Cf. ch. 1.1 above.
2 Wolfgang Musculus (1497-1563) was a monk who, under the influence of Luther's works, left the monastery. He was assistant to Matthäus Zell and Martin Bucer in Strasbourg, from 1531-1548 he worked in Augsburg until the Augsburg interim. After leaving that city he ended up in Bern. (Cf. Selderhuis, H.J., *Oecumenische Ecclesiologie. Ideale kerk en ideale overheid in de theologie van Wolfgang Musculus* (Apeldoorn: Theologische Universiteit Apeldoorn, 1999), 7n1; Dellsperger, R., 'Wolfgang Musculus (1497-1563). Leben und Werk' in: Dellsperger, R. *et al.* (eds.), *Wolfang Musculus (1497-1563) und die oberdeutsche Reformation* (Berlin: Akademie Verlag, 1997), 23-36.)
3 Peter Martyr Vermigli (1499-1562) was an Italian monk who, under the influence by works of Bucer and Zwingli, left the monastery. Ultimately he fled, stopping in Zurich and Basel, and accepted a teaching position in Strasbourg, where he worked closely with Martin Bucer. In 1547 the Augsburg Interim forced him to move on and he went to England. In 1553 he went back to Strasbourg. In 1556 he accepted a teaching position in Zurich. (Cf. Taplin, M., 'Vermigli, Pietro Martire [Peter Martyr] (1499-1562)' in the Oxford Dictionary of National Biography [https://doi-org.access.authkb.kb.nl/10.1093/ref:odnb/28225 (2022-01-23)].

not at all the main focal point of Micron's book. He focusses on what the church is and why one should join it. We will have to keep this in mind, even to the extent of neglecting interesting debates. A third pitfall is the amount of secondary literature available. The list of works on Calvin and Geneva is endless and quite often of a sociological, rather than a theological, nature. To place Micron's work within the Reformed movement it is much more important to use key primary sources. This does not mean we will neglect secondary sources; what it does mean is that they will be seen for what they are: secondary. So, with these limitations in place, what we will present here is how Micron's thought compares to the broader Reformed movement as this was expressed by reformers he knew, in influential books they published before Micron's death, focussing especially on what the church is and why one should join it, and giving more importance to men of whom we know they played a large part in Micron's life.

The outline for the chapter will follow the previous chapter, though with fewer divisions. In 7.1 we will explain the choice of authors and sources. In 7.2 we look at the purpose and nature of the church, in 7.3 the marks of the church, a separate paragraph will be devoted to the re-sacralisation thesis put forward by Pamela Biel (7.4). In 7.5 we look at unity and secession, before ending with a summary and conclusions.

7.1 Authors and Sources

The introduction to this chapter mentioned six reformers. It is our goal here to explain both this choice and the selection of sources.

Chapter three described how Marten Micron studied in Zurich under Bullinger, while living with John Hooper. He even reckoned himself to be part of Hooper's household. There can be little surprise, then, that they are chosen as major theological influences. The same must surely be said for John à Lasco. However, the selection of the other three theologians needs some defending. Calvin, as a major theologian in the second half of the sixteenth century, cannot be neglected. Especially since we know Micron corresponded with him on the issue of the Mennonites.[4] We must assume therefore, that Micron considered him an authority. Regarding Musculus we know that Micron was familiar with his *Proskairos* and

---

4 Dankbaar, W.F., 'Introduction' in: [Micron, M.], *Een waerchtigh verhaal der t'zamensprekinghen tusschen Menno Simons ende Martinus Mikron van der menschewerdinghe Iesu Christi* ed. W.F. Dankbaar, *Documenta Anabaptistica Neerlandica III* (Leiden: Brill, 1981), VII-XXX, pageVIII.

commentary on Genesis, which he studied thoroughly.[5] Vermigli, last of all, was asked for advice by Micron.[6] Though it does not prove major influence, it does mean Vermigli cannot be neglected.

The key sources for these reformers are as follows.[7] Bullinger's *Decades*[8] backed up by Jud's catechisms and Zwingli's *Confessio Fidei* and *De Vera et Falsa religione*, give us a good summary of the Zurich ecclesiology. Hooper's ecclesiology is found in his *Jonah* sermons,[9] visitation articles and *A godly Confession*. When it comes to à Lasco, things are more difficult. After all, the truly ecclesiological works were written, or at least designed, in cooperation with Micron. Differences between, for instance, the *Forma ac Ratio* and the *Ordinancien*, may not have been seen as theological differences by the authors themselves. This means we depend on secondary sources more heavily. Calvin's theology is, of course, outlined in the *Institutes*; however, we cannot assume that Micron was familiar with the edition published in 1559. We will therefore use the Latin edition published in 1554. Concerning Musculus we have seen that Micron was familiar with both his *Proskairos* and commentary on Genesis, these two works will therefore be used to discover his thought. Vermigli, last of all, wrote an exposition of the Apostle's Creed with a long section on the church. Moreover, we think it is likely Micron would have been aware of Vermigli's disputation on the Lord's Supper, held at Oxford and subsequently published. Vermigli's early thought has been exquisitely analysed by Klaus Sturm, so this will prove to be an invaluable source as well.

Let us now look at the theology put forward by these reformers.

---

5 *ET*, 372; *OLER*, 527: 'The Πρόσκαιρος of Musculus is published in French'. Micron wrote to Bullinger about Musculus' commentary on Genesis, asking him to write to Musculus and make corrections (Füslinus, 384-385), he also wrote to Musculus (addressing him as 'my father in the Lord') about it (Gerretsen, *Micronius*, ix-xi). (Cf. Bodenmann, R., *Wolfgang Musculus (1497-1563). Destin d'un autodidacte lorrain au siècle des Réformes. Etude basée sur la biographie établie pas son fils, la correspondance personelle, et de nombreux autres documents d'époque* (Geneva: Droz, 2000), 560.)
6 Gerretsen, *Micronius*, xi.
7 For full titles, please see references in the footnotes below.
8 For the importance of the *Decades*, see: Opitz, P., 'Bullinger's *Decades*: Instruction in Faith and Conduct' in: Gordon, B. & Campi, E. (eds.), *Architect of Reformation. An Introduction to Heinrich Bullinger, 1504-1575* (Grand Rapids: Baker Academic, 2004), 101-116, esp. 111-112.
9 Brodie, J.B., *Constructing a Godly Society: The Template for a Reformed Community in the Writings of John Hooper (C. 1500-1555)* (PhD University of Edinburgh, 2016), 44: 'In it, he could outline his true desires for reform'.

7.2 Purpose and Nature of the Church

Concerning the purpose and nature of the church, we will see that among the selected reformers there was basic unity of thought. It goes without saying that their thought was not uniform,[10] but when it comes to the doctrinal core they were very much in agreement. This would make it unnecessarily repetitive to discuss them separately. Since this is a comparison with Micron's thought, we choose to discuss the purpose of the church before the nature of the church. That was the order that forced itself upon us in *Van de weerdicheydt* and that is the order we hold on to for the comparison.

The purposes of the church Micron gave were the honour of God and salvation of man. This was also very clearly believed by his colleague John à Lasco: all Christians should flee from what might diminish the glory of Christ and hinder their salvation.[11] Micron's friend John Hooper, confessed that 'the people of God be those that with heart and mind, know, worship, honour, praise, and laud God after the doctrine of the apostles and the prophets',[12] and: 'let [confessors] embrace only Christ and His doctrine, and worship God in spirit and verity, as his word teacheth'.[13] Likewise, Bullinger says that the church is the house of God where He receives the service done unto Him.[14] That is what the church is: the house of God. And what the church does is sing His praise. Indeed, according to Calvin, breaking the unity of the church is so terrible because it is a violation of God's authority, and therefore of God's honour.[15]

We saw how Micron sang God's honour in the confession. The reformers we are studying are all convinced of the necessity to confess the faith. The church consists of those who confess and believe that Jesus Christ is God, Leo Jud explains in the Larger Catechism.[16] Bullinger and Calvin are likeminded.[17] Profession and true faith belong together, for: 'Thinkeste thou that faith is anydle thing and without facte, and that she

---

10 This is made clear, for instance, in: Vind, A. & Selderhuis, H.J. (eds.), *'Church' at the Time of the Reformation. Invisible Community, Visible Parish, Confession, Building...?'* (Göttingen: Vandenhoeck & Ruprecht, 2021).
11 Lasco, J. à, *(...) Of het den christenen, na dien zij het word Godes ende de godloosheit des Pauwstdoms bekent hebben, eenighszins verorloft is, dat zy sick in den Pauwstlicken godsdiensten, ende in zonderheit inder Misse, vinden laten* ([n.p.]: 1557), f.3. Cf. f.2 and 5.
12 *Later Writings*, 71.
13 *Early Writings*, 469.
14 *Decades (Teilband 3.2)*, 787-788 / *Fifth decade*, 82-83. Cf. Zwingli, who says that in baptism children are dedicated, devoted, consecrated to God (*De Vera et Falsa Religione* ed. C.N. Heller, *The Latin Works of Huldreich Zwingli*, iii (Philadelphia, 1929), 196).
15 Calvin, *Institutio Christianae religionis* (Geneva: Riverios, 1554), 316-317.
16 Jud, L., *Der grössere Katechismus* ed, O. Farner (Zurich: Max Niehan, 1955), 143.
17 *Decades (Teilband 3.2)*, 742 / *Fifth decade*, 7; Calvin, *Institutio*, 314. Note that Calvin explicitly links profession to glorifying God.

maye be so hyd in the harte, that she cannot appeare out wardly? Fayth is a fyre: it is impossible ether to hyde her, or inclose her, but that she wil ether cast forth flame or smoke ... the faith of the harte is not dombe, but her violence breaketh the barres of the mouth.'[18] For the church to be truly church, in Vermigli's opinion, she must be a community that confesses, has a doctrine of faith (*sensus fidei*), and glorifies God in her worship.[19] The true church sings God's glory by professing the faith.

The second purpose of the church Micron defined was the salvation of sinners. The reformers surrounding him all see this purpose as well. Bullinger defends the maxim that there is no salvation outside the church,[20] and even calls ministers saviours[21] because in their preaching the bountiful blessing of having been made children of God is laid open.[22] This is fully in line with the larger Zurich tradition.[23] A line Hooper defended, for in his visitation articles he opened with the command that 'none (…) do teach or preach any manner of thing to be necessary for the salvation of man other than that which is contained in the book of God's Holy Word.'[24] And we have already seen how à Lasco named the same purposes as Micron. Calvin says: '[The church] is the mother of us all, where our Lord wants to hand out His treasures of grace.'[25] Note, however, that this does not mean that the church in and of itself possesses these treasures of grace. They are God's treasures, the grace handed out by the church is Christ's. As Vermigli says: the church receives 'the grace, righteousness, holiness, blessings and the other bounties Christ gives'.[26] Vermigli and Jud, like Micron, believe that a commandment of God must

---

18 Myone, Eutychio [= Wolfgang Musculus], *Proscaerus (…)* ([Basel.:Jakob Kündig], 1549), [C7v] / [Musculus, W.], *The Temporisour (…)* ([Wesel: Singleton?], 1555), [D5r].
19 Sturm, K., *Die Theologie Peter Martyr Vermiglis während seines ersten Aufenthalts in Straßburg 1542-1547* (Neukirchen-Vluyn: Neukirchener Verlag, 1971), 183.
20 *Deacdes (Teilband 3.2)*, 769 / *Fifth decade*, 51. Cf. Opitz, P., *Heinrich Bullinger als Theologe. Eine Studie zu den <<Dekaden>>* (Zurich: TVZ, 2004), 422, where he says 'Das traditionelle 'extra ecclesiam nulla salus' wird von Bullinger als 'extra Christum nulla salus' interpretiert.'
21 *Decades (Teilband 3.2)*,795 / *Fifth decade*, 95.
22 *Decades (Teilband 3.2)*, 938 / *Fifth decade*, 322.
23 Zwingli, *Vera et falsa*, 172; Jud, *Grössere*, 152: 'Wer in dieser Kirche und Versammlung ist und bleibt, der wird selig.'
24 *Later writings*, 120.
25 Calvin, *Institutio*, 310-311. For the church as the mother of all believer's in Calvin's thought, cf. Kim, Y., *The Identity and the Life of the Church. John Calvin's Ecclesiology in the Perspective of His Anthropology* (Eugene, Oregon: Pickwick Publications, 2014), ch. 4, especially pages 104-105; 109.
26 [Vermigli, P.M.], *Ik geloof. Een eenvoudige verklaring van de Apostolische geloofsbelijdenis door Petrus Martyr Vermigli* ed. C.L. Freeke (Apeldoorn: De Banier, 2018), 95.

have a purpose and benefit, because it is a manifestation of God's will.[27] This shows that there was a broader sentiment in which it was believed that God's commandments are never in vain. Micron, then, seems to be in accord with the other reformers; however, we did not discover the notion of the church as a protective establishment against our sinful nature and the devil – so important to Micron – among these six influences. This idea could be a trace of *corpus Christianum*-thought in Micron's theology. The body of Christ, Terpstra explains, was seen in statues, the eucharist and the community of local believers. This third form became a civic religion where the city was a holy community. There was safety within the walls of this city. In this way an individual city was to be a *civitas dei contra paganos*.[28] Terpstra states this concept was absorbed by that of the sacred nation, moving from a local *corpus* to a national one.[29] Micron's ecclesiology seems to suggest something different from either of these two concepts: the congregation as a safe haven, functioning as a community within the community. Even if this is not the case, it does show us something of Micron's own psychology. He desired the protection of the church.

Let us now move on to the nature of the church. That she is the people of God, the assembly of the faithful, called by the gospel, gathered under Christ as their head is the universal belief of the reformers we have studied.[30] It is interesting to highlight how in the Zurich tradition the church is called under the yoke of Christ,[31] an expression Micron also used. Of course, this is a biblical metaphor, and certainly not absent in the writings of the other reformers;[32] however it would be worth investigating whether it was more prevalent in the Zurich tradition.

---

27 Sturm, *Theologie*, 225; Jud, *Grössere*, 160.
28 Terpstra, N., *Religious Refugees in the Early Modern World. An Alternative History of the Reformation* (Cambridge: CUP, 2015), 22-29.
29 Terpstra, *Religious Refugees*, 313.
30 *Decades (Teilband 3.2)*, 741-741 / *Fifth decade*, 4-5; Jud, *Kürzere*, 315; Zwingli, *Vera et falsa*, 178; *Later Writings*, 87; Calvin, *Institutio*, 310; Musculus, *Proscaerus* C3r / *Temporisour*, [C8r-v]; Vermigli, *Ik geloof*, 90-91.
31 Jud, *Kürzere*, 302; *Later Writings*, 124; Hooper, *Whether Christian Faith maye be kepte secret (…)* ([London: John Day?],1553), [p.2].
32 Especially in Bucer's thought. Cf. Burnett, A. Nelson, *The Yoke of Christ: Martin Bucer and Christian Discipline* (Kirksville: Sixteenth Century Essays and Studies, 1994). (This study, as the title indicates, focusses primarily on discipline. Especially interesting in relation to Micron are pages 1, 9, 73, 121 and 211.) Also: Spijker, W. van 't, ' "…Den hals buygende onder het jock Jesu Christi…" Oorsprong en zin van een uitdrukking in art. 28 en 29 van de Nederlandse Geloofsbelijdenis' in: *Bezield verband. Opstellen aangeboden aan prof. J. Kamphuis bij gelegenheid van zijn vijfentwintig-jarig ambtsjubileum* (Kampen: Van den Berg, 1984), 206-219.

We have seen that for Micron the church started in paradise. It is not entirely clear how this was seen in the broader Reformed field. Bullinger, for instance, seems to say the church did not start until after the fall of man,[33] yet he does call the covenant eternal,[34] and also says that Adam was a priest and prophet, though he does not state this was already the case in paradise.[35] For Jud the vocation of man in creation and the vocation of the church are the same,[36] and he says: 'from the first to the last day there is only one church of all the faithful'.[37] Calvin also says the church consists of all the elect 'since the commencement of the world'.[38] Only with Musculus can we be fairly sure that he saw the start of the church after the fall of man, when the Adamites started to call upon God's name after Enosh's birth.[39] A careful conclusion would be that most did not take quite so linear a view as Micron, but generally agreed that both before and after the fall there was the people of God, called to live with God.

The church of God stands in opposition to the church of the devil, so Micron believed. This was not strange to the ears of other reformers. Hooper believed 'all the people of the world to be either the people of God, either [sic!] the people of the devil.'[40] For the devil also has his church on earth, Bullinger taught in the *Decades*.[41] Calvin and à Lasco state the same.[42] Out of this dualism arose the *peregrinatio*-experience: being a stranger on earth was an essential aspect of Reformed ecclesiology and anthropology.[43] This is an existential alienation: far from home, awaiting the eternal city, Christians sigh in the flesh. The church is always a church dispersed.[44] Micron seems to have taken his exegesis of the feast of

---

33 So Moser, Ch., *Die Dignität des Ereignisses. Studien zu Heinrich Bullingers Reformationsgeschichtsschreibung* (Leiden/Boston: Brill, 2012), 21.
34 Opitz, *Bullinger als Theologe*, 321.
35 Bullinger, H. *Schriften II* ed. Barbara Braune-Krikau *et al.* (Zurich: TVZ, 2006), 159; 161.
36 Jud, *Kürzere*, 251; 253-254; 355.
37 Jud, *Grössere*, 157.
38 Calvin, *Institutio*, 314.
39 Musculus, *In Mosis Genesim (…) expendentur* (Basel: Johannis Hervagij. 1565), 154.
40 *Later Writings*, 71. Cf. *Early Writings*, 457-458 and Brodie, *Constructing*, 98.
41 *Decades (Teilband 3.2)*, 744/ *Fifth decade*, 10-11. Cf. Moser, *Dignität*, 23.
42 Calvin, *Institutio*, 327; Lasco, *of het den christenen*, F.23.
43 Note that Augustine in his *Civitate Dei* opens with this: 'The glorious city of God is my theme…a city surpassingly glorious, whether we view it as it still lives by faith…and sojourns as a stranger.' (Augustine, *The City of God* ed. Marcus Dods (Peabody: Hendrickson, 2011), 3) [*De Civitate Dei contra Paganos*].
44 Cf. *Decades (Teilband 3.2)*, 742 / *Fifth decade*, 7; Jud, *Grössere*, 169; Jud, *Kürzere*, 314; 365; Zwingli, *Vera et falsa*, 374; Vermigli, *Ik geloof*, 91. For Calvin, cf. Kim, *Identity*,

tabernacles directly from Pellikan, who explains that this feast should be a reminder of 'our '*peregrinationis*' ' in which we travel towards eternity, knowing we do not have an eternal city here, but seeking the future city.[45] Musculus explains that for this very reason the descendants of Seth did not build a city. All the saints, he says, have lived on this earth as pilgrims far from home (*in morem peregrinorum*). Not until they have reached heaven will believers stop being strangers (*peregrini*).[46] Later in the commentary in Genesis we find a lengthy exposition of how miserable it is to be a stranger. Being a stranger is like living in the dark, because the language and customs are strange to you and even if one has lived in a foreign city a long time, one still feels alienation. In this present age God's children are strangers (*peregrini*) and under this affliction they are moved to longing for the eternal rest and freedom of the heavenly fatherland. In this way God wants His people to be educated, as in a school, before they inherit the earth, just as a son is educated by his father before he gets the inheritance.[47] What we see here is that the theological concept of being a stranger underpins the actual experience. One does not take prevalence over the other; rather, the theology informs the experience and vice versa.

Last of all we look at how the church is built upon the foundation of Jesus Christ, and that the church can fall to ruins. Bullinger gives a metaphor of the church as a house which is so elaborate that we might almost call it a conceit.[48] The church, he says, is presented to us in the image of a house. Of this house God is the builder, the foundation is Jesus Christ, who keeps the house together. Christ is also the roof (i.e. head) that protects and rules. The stones used for the building are the believers.[49] It is Calvin who, like Micron, observes how the church can be ruined and

---

72n14; 73; 158-159; 163-164. For Bullinger, also: Opitz, *Bullinger als Theologe*, 42n21. In Hooper we did not read anything about this. For à Lasco it is more difficult. Documents like the confession of the London church do pay attentation to dispersement and the *peregrinatio* experience, but were written together with Micron.

45 Pellikan, K., *Commentaria Biblia (…) Tomus Primus in quo continenter v. libri Mosis* ([Zurich]: Chr. Froschauer, [1536]), 228v.
46 Musculus, *Genesim*, 151.
47 Musculus, *Genesim*, 378-379.
48 A conceit is the term used for 'usually ingeniously elaborate' metaphors. Technically this is neither a Petrarchan conceit (since it is not a love poem) nor a mataphysical conceit (since it does not combine dissimilar images). We use the term to highlight the elaborate and complex comparison Bullinger makes (cf. Abrams, M.H. & Harpham, G.G., *A Glossary of Literary Terms. Ninth Edition* (Boston: Wadsworth Cengage Learning, 2009), 52-53).
49 *Decades (Teilband 3.2)*, 785-788 / *Fifth decade*, 79-83. Cf. Opitz, *Bullinger als theologe*, 423.

needs to be rebuilt on the foundation of Christ.[50] We will see later on how obedience to the Word of God is taught by all of these reformers, a matter closely related to this issue.

In the secondary literature considerable attention is given to the two aspects of the church as the mother of all believers or the church as the assembly of all believers (i.e. the body of Christ).[51] It is our careful proposition that this is more or less similar to the twofold purpose of the church.[52] She exists to praise God in accordance with His Word, as such she is the communion of saints, built upon the rock Jesus Christ. At the same time she offers, in Micron's words, protection against the devil as the church of God. She is the mother of all believers, where the treasures of grace are distributed. This is mentioned here because Judith Becker regards the *communio corporis Christi* as seen in the Lord's Supper the unique moment in à Lasco's theology: the community as community is central, united in her head, Christ. The epitome and essence of this is seen in the Lord's Supper. She, furthermore, sees a distinct theological difference between à Lasco and Micron, especially when it comes to pastoral sensitivity and the extent to which the church order itself is theological.[53] The above exposition suggests, however, that Micron was fully in line with Reformed thought. He, too, sees the community as a community in Christ, that is the twofold purpose of the church.[54] Perhaps Micron and à Lasco did not experience a theological difference between their respective ecclesiologies; rather, there was a difference in nuance within the general acceptance that the church has a twofold identity and purpose.[55]

7.3 The Marks of the Church

Next we turn to the marks of the church. Again, instead of discussing the reformers separately, it will be better to follow the line of thought presented in the last chapter.

---

50 Calvin, *Institutio*, 324; 332.
51 E.g. Kim, *Identity*, ch. 4 and 5; Sturm, *Theologie*, 151-152; 176-177; 181.
52 Cf. also, Musculus, *Proscaerus* C2v-C3r / *Temporisour*, [C8r-v].
53 Becker, J., *Gemeindeordnung und Kirchenzucht. Johannes a Lascos Kirchenordnung für London (1555) und die reformierte Konfessionsbildung* (Leiden/Boston: Brill, 2007), 32; 38-39; 45-47.
54 We agree with Becker that Micron's view of the church's governance is functional, though we are hesitant whether this means it is less theological.
55 To some degree this thought is present in Becker's study itself. On p.39n64 she says: 'So schrieb a Lasco ein Vorwort für Microns kleinen Katechismus, in dem er den kleinen dem großen Katechismus der Gemeinde beiordnete, ohne zu erwähnen, dass der kleine Katechismus eine andere Theologie vertrat als er selbst.' and on page 133 she unfolds how little influence à Lasco's thought exerted on the Emden church ordinations.

There we saw that the only source for both doctrine and governance is the Bible. In a way it could be said that, for Micron, the only mark of the church is obedience to the Word of God. The very opening of Bullinger's *Decades* shows the importance of the Word of God, too, for it is the subject of the first three sermons.[56] Jud likewise says that if the servants of the church have God's honour, the wellbeing of the church and the salvation of the flock in view they will take as their guideline nothing but the Word of God.[57] Hooper, true to character, says we are admonished to 'offer none other obsequy and religion unto God than he himself by his word requireth: if we do, we offer an idol of our own head, and honour the devil under the person and name of God.'[58] Rodgers and Becker conclude that for à Lasco there had to be clear directives from the Word of God.[59] Over against this Vermigli wrote to Hooper during the vestments controversy that it is not necessary to prove all things directly from Scripture, indifferent things can be used without burdening the conscience.[60] Clearly, Micron's thought is the same as that of Hooper and à Lasco, not that of Vermigli. But they would all have agreed with Calvin, that the true mark of the church is that it is governed by God's Word to which she listens.[61]

This automatically leads us to the next section. For it was surprising to discover that for Micron there were two marks: doctrine first and governance working towards the same goal, both resting on obedience to God's Word. Now we have just seen that Calvin in fact says the same. How did the reformers that surrounded Micron see this? For Bullinger the church shows itself in unity of faith and doctrine and the partaking of the sacraments.[62] Doctrine and rite stand next to each other, even if rules

---

56 *Decades (Teilband 3.1)*, 29-55. Cf. Opitz, *Bullinger als Theologe*, 31-77, especially p. 63-67. In Opitz's analysis the church is a 'hearing community' in Bullinger's thought (p. 419-425).
57 Jud, *Grössere*, 170. For the place of the Bible in Zwingli's thought, cf. Stephens, W.P., *Zwingli. An Introduction to his Thought* (Oxford: OUP, 1992), 31-36.
58 *Early Writings*, 457. Cf. Deibler, E.C., *Bishop John Hooper, A Link Connecting the Reformation Though of Ulrich Zwingli and the Zurich Tradition with the Earlies English Pietistic* (PhD Temple University Philadelphia, 1970), 339-340.
59 Rodgers, D.W., *John à Lasco in England* (New York: Peter Lang, 1194), 29; Becker, *Gemeindeordnung*, 69.
60 In: *A briefe examination for the tyme* (London: Richard Jugge, [n.y.]), C2r.
61 Calvin, *Institutio*, 327; 333. Cf. Kim, *Identity*, 105; Mannion, G. 'Calvin and the Church: Trajectories for Ecumenical Engagement Today – Volume Introduction' in: Mannion, G. & Borght, E. van der (eds.), *John Calvin's Ecclesiology. Ecumenical Perspectives* (London/New York: Bloomsbury T&T Clark, 2013), 1-30, 8.
62 *Decades (Teilband 3.2)*, 741 / *Fifth Decade*, 5.

and traditions should be kept to a minimum.⁶³ And though Leo Jud explains a church order is temporary and local, ⁶⁴ Bullinger also says that the church should, in word and sacrament, 'embrace, retain, and determine the true sense and that which is agreeing with the articles of faith,'⁶⁵ which is basically the same as what Micron means when he places doctrine before governance. With Hooper things are clearer. He believed the church of God 'to have a certain doctrine, [that] never was, is, or hereafter shall be, violated'⁶⁶ If it is the doctrine that defines the church, then its governance should aim at maintaining this. We find this is exactly what Hooper strived for in his visitation articles.⁶⁷ Springer says that à Lasco's *Forma ac Ratio* presented a worship service that was crafted to engage the audience [i.e. making them partakers rather than just hearers], convey doctrinal lessons and teach about God's promise of salvation.'⁶⁸ The liturgy, part of governance, was formed to teach doctrine. The three Dutch scholars Selderhuis, Van 't Spijker and Speelman all make clear how for Calvin the ordinances are aimed towards the proclamation of God's Word, i.e. doctrine.⁶⁹ Clearly, then, it was commonly held in the Reformed churches that what the church does should be modelled on what she believes, and this is taken from the Word of God. The only true mark is biblical doctrine in both doctrine and governance.

Let us now turn to what are usually called the marks. Micron clearly defined three, and even though among the studied reformers there is some disagreement, it is Ballor and Littlejohn's opinion that the difference between two (word, sacraments) and three (word, sacraments, discipline) is overstated and by most reformers understood to be dependent on local circumstances.⁷⁰ This opinion is corroborated by the primary sources.

---

63 *Decades (Teilband 3.2)*, 1042; 1070 / *Fifth Decade*, 478; 525.
64 Jud, *Grössere*, 169.
65 *Decades (Teilband 3.2)*, 750 / *Fifth Decade*, 21. The quote comes from the English translation. The original reads: 'sensum quoque nativum et fidei articulis congruum simul amplectamur, retineamus et tueamur'.
66 *Later Writings*, 71.
67 *Later Writings*, 120-129.
68 Springer, M.S., *Restoring Christ's Church. John a Lasco and the* Forma ac Ratio (Aldershot: Ashgate, 2007), 77.
69 Selderhuis, H., '1.a. Kerkorde, kerkrecht en kerkverband' in Selderhuis, H. (ed.), *Handboek gereformeerd kerkrecht* (Heerenveen: Groen, 2019), 11-14, 12; Spijker, W. van 't, '2.c.1. Luther, Zwingli en Bucer' in: Selderhuis (ed.), *Handboek gereformeerd kerkrecht*, 91-103, 100-101; Speelman, H., '2.c.2. Calvijn' in: Selderhuis (ed.), *Handboek gereformeerd kerkrecht*, 104-125, 105.
70 Ballor, J. & Littlejohn, W.B., 'European Calvinism: Church Discipline' in: *European History Online (EGO)*, published by the Leibniz Institute of European History (IEF),

For instance, though Hooper only called the word and sacraments the marks of the church[71] because discipline was never perfect anywhere,[72] yet he also fully believed discipline to be an essential part of the church, and named it right next to word and sacraments in his visitation articles.[73] À Lasco has all three,[74] and so does Vermigli.[75] In the Zurich tradition, however, only word and sacraments are named. Discipline, as the keys, is part of preaching, whereby the gates of heaven are opened,[76] whereas for Micron discipline flows from the right administration of the sacraments.[77] The gap between Bullinger and Micron widens when we see that according to Bullinger admonition is indeed the task of elders, yet actual discipline is the task of the government.[78] Calvin's opinion agrees with Hooper's. He did not consider discipline a mark of the church, yet it was so essential that there is very little difference between calling it a mark or not.[79] We can therefore conclude that Micron, probably under the guidance of à Lasco and possibly Vermigli, was moving away from the Zurich tradition where the power of the keys were an aspect of the preached Word. However, this did not lead to a real difference between him and Hooper.[80]

Mainz 2013-03-25. URL: http://www.ieg-ego.eu/ballorj-littlejohnw-2013-en URN: http://nbn-resolving.de/urn:nbn:de:0159-2013032507 [2021-12-24], 1; 32.

71 *Later Writings*, 87.
72 Brodie, *Constructing*, 158-159.
73 *Later Writings*, 125. Cf. Wilson, R.P., *John Hooper and the English Reformation under Edward VI, 1547-1553* (PhD Queen's University Kingston Ontario, 1994), 305-306; Deibler, *Bishop John Hooper*, 341.
74 Springer, *Restoring*, 61.
75 Sturm, *Theologie*, 185.
76 *Decades (Teilband 3.2)*, 748; 825 / *Fifth Decade*, 17; 146. Cf. Zwingli, *Vera et falsa*, 167. For the discussion between Bullinger and Jud on autonomous church discipline, cf. Campi, 'Theological Profile' in: Burnett, A. Nelson & Campi, E., *A Companion to the Swiss Reformation* (Leiden/Boston: Brill, 2016), 447-488, 468-469. Bullinger goes on to list the inward marks of the church, which make the outward marks fruitful (*Decades (Teilband 3.2)*, 751 / *Fifth decade*, 23. Cf. Opitz, *Bullinger als Theologe*, 427-432.
77 *Cathechismus*, Q+A 68.
78 *Decades (Teilband 3.2)*, 1059-1060 / *Fifth Decade*, 507-508. Consequently, we are not convinced by Plasger's suggestion that the quest for an independent church is rooted in Bullinger's theology (sse above, ch. 4.2.2 *sub* B).
79 Calvin, *Institutio*, 451-452. Cf., especially, Kingdon, R.M. & Lambert, T.A., *Reforming Geneva. Discipline, Faith and Anger in Calvin's Geneva* (Geneva: Droz, 2012), 13; also: Mannion, 'Calvin and the Church', 10; Fulop, T.E., 'The Third Mark of the Church? – Church Discipline in the Reformed and Anabaptist Reformations' in: *The Journal of Religious History* 19/1 (1995), 26-42, 35; 41.
80 This, though, might be an example of what Ballor and Littlejohn call the dependence on local circumstances and it begs the question whether the difference between the keys as connected to the Word or the sacraments was in fact perceived as a real difference, since the sacraments were seen as appendices to the Word.

The mark of the preaching of the word is best left to the next section, when we look at the re-sacralisation thesis. So we will now turn to the sacraments. However, what was said before should be kept in mind here. It is not the aim to confront ourselves with the entirety of Reformation thought on the subjects of baptism and the Lord's Supper;[81] rather, we want to see how Micron fits within the Reformed world. The *Consensus Tigurinus*, as a Reformed confessional agreement, accepted by all the major Reformed theologians, is therefore taken as the key text.[82] In the *Consensus*[83] we read that sacraments are supplements to the gospel,[84] they are annexed to the Word. Just like Micron said that the sacraments should be joined to proclamation. In article five attention is drawn to how the congregation is one body.[85] Micron's insistence on the importance of the community echoes this article, though the *Consensus Tigurinus* does not see community as an effect of the sacraments. The sacraments themselves are 'marks and tokens of Christian profession and community or fraternity, that they may be incitements to gratitude (…) But the goal that is preeminent among others is that through them God may testify, represent, and seal his grace to us.'[86] Here we see the triad of 'sin, salvation,

---

81 There are several studies covering these subjects. For the Lord's Supper, see: Burnett, A. Nelson, *Debating the Sacraments. Print and Authority in the Early Reformation* (Oxford: OUP, 2019); Wandel, L. Palmer, *The Eucharist in the Reformation. Incarnation and Liturgy* (Cambridge: CUP, 2006), especially ch. 4. On baptism, e.g., Spierling, K.E., *Infant Baptism in Reformation Geneva. The Shaping of a Community, 1536-1564* (Aldershot: Ashgate, 2005); Fesko, J.V., *Word, Water, and Spirit: A Reformed Perspective on Baptism* (Grand Rapids: Heritage Books, 2010), ch. 2-4. For discipline the article by Ballor and Littlejohn cited above (footnote 54) and Kingdon's *Reforming Geneva* (see footnote 62). All of these subjects are addressed in: Karant-Nunn, S.C., *The Reformation of Ritual. An interpretation of early modern Germany* (London/New York: Routledge, 1997), ch. 2 and 4.

82 For an introduction to the *Consensus Tigurinus*: Campi, E., 'Consensus Tigurinus: Werden, Wertung und Wirkung' in: Campi, E. & Reich, R. (eds.), *Consensus Tigurinus. Heinrich Bullinger und Johannes Calvin über das Abendmahl. Werden – Wertung – Bedeutung* (Zurich: TVZ, 2009), 9-41 (see, especially, pages 35 and 37 where we read that, among others, Musculus, Vermigli, à Lasco and Hooper consented to the agreement); Campi, E., 'The Consensus Tigurinus: origins, assessment, and impact' in: *Reformation & Renaissance Review* 18.1 (2016), 5-24; Burnett, A. Nelson, 'From Concord to Confession: The Wittenberg Concord and the Consensus Tigurinus in Historical Perspective' in: *Reformation and Renaissance Review* 18.1 (2016), 47-58.

83 We have used the edition given in: Campi & Reich (eds.), *Consensus Tigurinus*, 127-142 (English translation: 259-267)

84 *Consensus Tigurinus*, 127. Cf. *Later Writings*, 90; Sturm, *Theologie*, 216.

85 *Consensus Tigurinus*, 128. The metaphor between the body and the congregation is also explored by Jud (*Grössere*, 233) and Zwingli (*Vera et falsa*, 232).

86 *Consensus Tigurinus*, 129 (translation taken from 261).

gratitude' Micron also offered.[87] There are differences in nuance, but the same key thoughts are present. With the administration of the sacraments God truly offers what the sacraments figure, viz. righteousness and salvation. Hence, the truth must not be separated from the sign, but by faith Christ and His spiritual gifts are received spiritually.[88] Compare this to what Micron said: [baptism] truly and powerfully shows and seals the gift of salvation,[89] and in the Lord's Supper the believers are 'sealed in the salvific fellowship of Christ and His benefactions' by the Holy Spirit.[90] The signs themselves do not accomplish this, as if they worked automatically; rather, 'it is Christ alone who truly baptises inwardly, Christ alone who makes us partakers of himself in the Supper'[91] and 'the Spirit alone is properly the seal'[92]. Like Micron, Calvin and Bullinger say in the *Consensus* 'the benefit of baptism is accessible throughout life'.[93] And the Lord's Supper is to be preceded by self-examination.[94] It goes without saying that in the *Consensus* transubstantiation is denied.[95] What we see is that regarding the doctrine of the sacraments, what Micron expresses is – consciously or not – in accordance with the *Consensus Tigurinus*. The only thing that is omitted in the *Consensus* is how baptism makes the baptised part of God's people. This, however, is explained by Bullinger in his *Decades*.[96] All in all, there is hardly anything 'unique' in Micron's exposition of the sacraments; rather, he expounds them within the bandwidth of Bullinger's and Calvin's agreement, endorsed by the major reformers in Micron's theological milieu.

Last of all we return to discipline.[97] This was briefly addressed when looking at the number of marks, where we have already seen how essential

---

87 Micron seems to have taken the triad directly from Bullinger, cf. *Decades (Teilband 3.2)*, 1039-1040 / *Fifth Decade*, 474-475.
88 *Consensus Tigurinus*, 129-130. Vermigli says that partakers truly become one with Christ (*The Oxford Treatise and Disputation on the Eucharist* ed. Joseph C. McLelland (Moscow, ID: The Davenant Press, 2018), 122-124. For Hooper true eating is believing (*Early Writings*, 530). Cf. Wandel, L. Palmer, *The Eucharist*, 153.
89 *VdWNN*, 20r.
90 *VdWNN*, 21r.
91 *Consensus Tigurinus*, 132-133 (translation taken from 262).
92 *Consensus Tigurinus*, 133 (translation taken from 262).
93 *Consensus Tigurinis*, 136 (translation taken from 263).
94 *Consensus Tigurinus*, 135.
95 *Consensus Tigurinus*, 152-153. For à Lasco the entire sacramental action signifies the communion with Christ (Rodgers, *John à Lasco in England*, 104-118.
96 *Decades (Teilband 3.2)*, 946; 977-978 / *Fifth Decade*, 334; 372. Cf. Jud, Grössere, 222; Zwingli, *Vera et falsa*, 196. For Calvin, cf. Spierling, *Infant Baptism*, 47.
97 Karant-Nunn sees discipline as the Reformed re-invention of the Roman Catholic sacrament of confession (*Reformation of Ritual*, 101).

it was to all the reformers under consideration. Nonetheless, since the Zurich tradition saw discipline as a task of the government, we will not take this tradition into consideration.[98] Micron listed four goals: 1) a bridle against sin, 2) a guard against offenses, 3) the salvation of the sinner, 4) the honour of God's name. Though Hooper does not, to our knowledge, actually mention these goals anywhere, his entire theology is a call to repentance in order to save men and honour God, as was seen above. Says Wilson: 'When Hooper published his Jonah sermons, he placed on the title page a scripture verse, "Except ye repent, ye shal pearish." This verse not only conveys the emphasis of that one work, but might be taken as an epithet for his entire corpus and career.'[99] According to Becker, à Lasco saw the community of saints as both the foundation and the goal of discipline, aimed towards the edification of the entire church.[100] The parallels between this and Micron are clear: it is done by the community, it has the community as its objective and the goal of the community is to honour God. Calvin, lastly, names three purposes: 1) a pure church to God's honour, 2) protecting the righteous from being tainted by sin, 3) the salvation of the sinner.[101] Likewise, for Vermigli, discipline is like a medicine against illnesses, and to bring sinners back to Christ.[102] It was given to the church by Christ in His high wisdom and endless goodness.[103]

Regarding the marks, then, there was greater diversity between the reformers. Especially when it came to Christian discipline, Micron's views on this issue were more in accordance with à Lasco, Calvin and Vermigli than with the Zurich tradition. On the other hand, however, we also saw how obedience to the Word of God was universally seen as the true mark of the church, which reveals itself in the practices of word, sacraments and discipline. Regarding the sacraments it was seen how Micron stayed within the bounds of the *Consensus Tigurinus*.

7.4 Teachers of a Holy Gospel

The governance of the church consists of the preaching of the Word, the administration of the sacraments and the application of Christian

---

98   For expositions of church discipline in Zurich, see: Campi, 'Theological Profile', 463-470; Euler, C., *Couriers of the Gospel: England and Zurich, 1531-1558* (Zurich: TVZ, 2006), 45-51; Gordon, B., *Clerical Discipline and the Rural Reformation: The Synod in Zurich, 1532-1580* (Bern: Peter Lang, 1992).
99   Wilson, *John Hooper and the English Reformation*, 101.
100 Becker, *Gemeindeordnung*, 57; 64-66.
101 Calvin, *Institutio*, 454-455. Cf. Kim, *Identity*, 178-180.
102 Vermigli, *Ik geloof*, 104
103 Vermigli, *Ik geloof*, 104.

discipline. The task remains to see how Micron's exposition of the first of this trio fits within Reformed thought. Here, however, we stumble across a fairly recent discussion in Bullinger scholarship: the re-sacralisation thesis. First we will look at this discussion, then compare Micron to Bullinger and Hooper (as another Bullinger student) and conclude by presenting the opinion of Calvin and Vermigli.[104]

The re-sacralisation thesis was developed by Pamela Biel in the early 1990s.[105] Bullinger, she says, made the ministry such a high office in the Zurich community that it was in effect a holy office, since only the ministers were called to criticise and advise the magistrate. Moreover, the exacting standards of knowledge and lifestyle created a sacral aura.[106] Reading Biel's case, it appears she does not pose that Bullinger claimed the ministerial office to be sacred on a theological-doctrinal level; rather, she seems to say that the sociological effect of Bullinger's reforms was a re-sacralisation. The ministers functioned as God representatives on earth.[107] Says Biel: 'the minister as preacher was a conduit for the Word of God. His words were where heaven and earth met.'[108] Not theologically a mediator, yet in effect a mediating agent between God and humanity.[109] Biel's thesis has been backed up by Jon D. Wood.[110] He, however, lays a greater stress on the theological shift from the prophet to the priest as the model for the minister[111] and claims that Bullinger actually sought a re-sacralisation[112] in order to transform the society into a godly society.[113]

---

104 In the sources we studied, Musculus does not discuss this topic to such an extent as to be able to draw conclusions. Since Micron's practice of the ministry was formed in close alliance with à Lasco, he is also left out of consideration.
105 Biel, P., *Doorkeepers at the House of Righteousness. Heinrich Bullinger and the Zurich Clergy 1534-1575* (Bern: Peter Lang, 1991).
106 Biel, *Doorkeepers*, 27; 41; 43.
107 Biel, *Doorkeepers*, 43.
108 Biel, *Doorkeepers*, 106.
109 Biel, *Doorkeepers*, 107.
110 Wood, J.D., *Reforming the Priesthood in Reformation Zurich. Heinrich Bullinger's End-Times Agenda* (Göttingen: Vandenhoeck & Ruprecht, 2019).
111 In this regard he also claims that the ministry derived, ultimately, from the priestly order of Melchizedek (page 85) (cf. also, Biel, *Doorkeepers*, 123). Our research however, does not corroborate this claim. Wood refers us to the *Decades*. There Bullinger refutes the necessity for apostolic succession by showing that Christ was ordained in the order of Melchizedek, and likewise the apostles were ordained by Christ, outside of Levitical succesion. If this is what Bullinger meant, the order of Melchizedek is reserved for Christ alone. Based on the letter to the Hebrews, this is the more likely reading (*Decades*, 756 / *Fifth Decade*, 30).
112 Wood, *Reforming*, 83-84; 88.
113 Wood, *Reforming*, 89.

Clearly Wood takes Biel's thesis to another level by claiming a deliberate theological choice on Bullinger's part.

Biel's thesis has not been universally accepted. Two scholars, Daniel Bolliger and Daniel Timmerman, are the major voices here.[114] Bolliger goes so far as to say that the very creation of the office of *Antistes* was 'an extension of the process of *desacralisation* and the removal of hierarchy: the principal authority of the *Antistes* was to guarantee the *collegial authority* of the ministers'.[115] In the process of coming to grips with ultimate authority, Bullinger decentralised power, laying it in the community of ministers, not individual ministers.[116] Indeed, the ministers are nothing special, but God, Who chooses to deploy their gifts in a particular church office.[117] Timmerman has made a major contribution to this discussion by giving us a meticulous reading of Bullinger's works from 1523-1538. He states that the primacy of a prophetic model in the earlier thought of Bullinger should not be overstated,[118] even if it does move to the background.[119] This is not due to a *de facto* changed theology, but a more mature, multi-layered reading and application of the Bible.[120] Timmerman refutes the re-sacralisation thesis because 1) 'when Bullinger calls the preaching minister a priest (*sacerdos*) he understands this designation in terms of the New Testament presbyter' and 2) 'both the prophet and the priest serve to emphasise the central kerygmatic function of the ministry'.[121] What we see is that Bolliger denies the sacral *effect* Bullinger's theology might have had and Timmerman refutes the sacral *theology* Wood sees in Bullinger's later works.

Now that the discussion is clear, we can compare Bullinger to his students. Micron's thought, as we saw, can be summarised as follows: The task of the priests and Levites was to teach the law. This task is now that of the ministers: they teach the gospel. Their office is one with that of the elders, who help the ministers of the Word in their calling. Prophecy is the exposition of Scripture in order to test teaching. This is to be done by

---

114 Bolliger, D., 'Bullinger on Church Authority: The Transformation of the Prophetic Role in Christian Ministry' in: Gordon, B. & Campi, E. (eds.), *Architect of Reformation. An Introduction to Heinrich Bullinger, 1504-1575* (Grand Rapids: Baker Academic, 2004), 159-177; Timmerman, D., *Heinrich Bullinger on Prophecy and the Prophetic Office (1523-1538)* (Göttingen: Vandenhoeck & Ruprecht: 2015).
115 Bolliger, 'Church Authority', 176 [italics mine].
116 Bolliger, 'Church Authority', 176.
117 Bolliger, 'Church Authority', 172-173.
118 Timmerman, *Prophecy*, 272.
119 Timmerman, *Prophecy*, 240.
120 Timmerman, *Prophecy*, 274.
121 Timmerman, *Prophecy*, 256.

everyone in the congregation, especially the office bearers. There is, however, as special calling for some to be prophets when the church has collapsed and needs to be reformed. What follows is an attempt to read Bullinger in accordance with Micron's thought. In his *Decades* Bullinger says that the ministers are chosen to teach only what has been given by Christ.[122] The Bible and nothing but the Bible is their source for doctrine, as it was with the Levites.[123] In this they are like the prophets, and those ministers who stray beyond the Word are false prophets (*pseudoprophetae*).[124] In *De episcoporum institutione et functione* he defines a prophet as God's spokesman for the people and a priest as a man ordained and sanctified to perform the sacred service to God.[125] Adam and Abraham were both priest and prophet.[126] Later, however, the Levites only had a priestly office, not a prophetic one. Their task was to be guardians of the law, to teach it, to bless and pray for the people and to maintain the outward institution of religion.[127] In the new covenant the Levites were replaced by teachers of the gospel.[128] Paul calls them 'evangelists' in Ephesians. The 'shepherds' are the watchmen and overseers/bishops (*vigiles & episcopi*) who protect the flock against wolves and practise Christian discipline.[129] Based on the word '*episcopi*' it would

---

[122] *Decades (Teilband 3.2)*, 764 / *Fifth Decade*, 44.
[123] *Decades (Teilband 3.2)*, 827 / *Fifth Decade*, 149. Here Bullinger quotes, among other texts, Maleachi 2.
[124] *Decades (Teilband 3.2)*, 827-828; 770 / *Fifth Decade*, 150; 53.
[125] Bullinger, H., *De scripturae sanctae authoritate, certitudine, firmitate et absoluta perfectione, deque Episcoporum, qui verbi dei ministri sunt, institutione et functione, contra superstitionis tyrannidsque Romanae antistes (…)* (Zurich: Forschauer, 1538), 66r–66v /Bullinger, H. *Schriften II* ed. Barbara Braune-Krikau *et al.* (Zurich: TVZ, 2006), 159-160.
[126] Bullinger, *De scripturae*, 67r-68r / *Schriften II*, 161-163.
[127] Bullinger, *De scripturae*, 68v-69r / *Schriften II*, 164-165.
[128] Bullinger, *De scripturae*, 78v / *Schriften II*, 185.
[129] Bullinger, *De scripturae*, 79r / *Schriften II*, 186. This seems to be how Micron interpreted Bullinger's *De episcoporum* on page 80v of *VdWNN* (see above, pp. 181-182). In the *Decades* (*Decades (Teilband 3.2)*, 802 / *Fifth Decade*, 109) Bullinger says that the office of evangelist was only for a time. This is in line with Calvin, as we shall see later on. Micron, in his writing process, either did not notice this difference, or did not think it mattered much. Likewise, in *De episcoporum* pastors and teachers are separate categories, whereas in the *Decades* they are more or less the same. Again, either Micron did not notice, remember or care. The evolvement from *De episcoporum* to the *Decades* explains the differences in Micron's text we wrestled with on pp. 181-184. It is likely he had both of Bullinger's texts on his desk, and was not overly meticulous in his definitions. This underscores the conclusion that we should not be overly meticulous either. Micron's thought probably was not entirely coherent here.

appear that Bullinger has superintendents in view here.[130] Because ministers are teachers of the gospel they may well be called 'saviours' (*salvatores*): they speak not their own words, but the Word of God.[131] Here, where Bullinger comes closest to actually re-sacralising the ministers, he immediately de-sacralises what he just stated by saying 'let the ministry indeed be beautified (*Ornetur*) and kept in authority, but let it be done without the dishonouring of God'.[132] For it is Christ, not the minister, who is the Saviour, and He alone can give the Holy Spirit Who regenerates.[133] The ministers, then, are the continuation of the Levitical priesthood, giving witness to (not handing out) grace. They are to be assisted by elders or priests (*presbyter*) 'that the church of God may the better and more conveniently be governed.'[134] Prophets, on the other hand are rarer. Their task, as was seen, was likewise to be God's spokesman. However, this was on a different level. The king, for instance, wants to learn from the priest, Bullinger says. Prophets are different. For the priest was not above the king, neither does the king despise the prophet.[135] The prophet was, as it were, outside the normal structure. Such persons were Luther and Zwingli, who in the spirit of Elijah sought to 'restore the true faith' (*religione vera restauranda*) and fought against antichrist to 'reform the church' (*reformanda ecclesia*).[136] The prophet is a special person who can oppose the powers that be, in order to renew, reform, rebuild the church according to the Word of God.[137]

This reading of Bullinger's work accords with Micron's views in *Van de weerdicheydt*. In discussions surrounding Bullinger's theology it is helpful to look at his writings through the eyes of his students. Let us now turn, then, to John Hooper, Micron's friend and fellow student in Zurich. For the bishop of Gloucester the only authority a preacher could ever have

---

130 Cf. *Decades (Teilband 3.2)*, 802 / *Fifth Decade*, 106.
131 *Decades (Teilband 3.2)*, 795 / *Fifth Decade*, 95.
132 *Deacdes (Teilband 3.2)*, 796 / *Fifth Decade*, 96.
133 *Decades (Teilband 3.2)*, 796-797 / *Fifth Decade*, 96-97.
134 *Decades (Teilband 3.2)*, 802-803 / *Fifth Decade*, 106-107. Quotation taken from the English translation, p. 107.
135 Bullinger, *De scripturae*, 71v-7[2]r / *Schriften II*, 170-171. The various prophetic gifts are to excel in singular revelation, to predict the future and to have a special gift in explaining Scripture, cf. *Decades (Teilband 3.2)*, 802 / *Fifth Decade*, 105. In our reading the later text of the *Decades* serves as an exegetical key to the definition of prophets as expositors of Scripture in *De scripturae* (79r / *Schriften II*, 186).
136 Bullinger, *De scripturae*, 157r / *Schriften II*, 361-362.
137 Cf. *Decades (Teilband 3.2)*, 804 / *Fifth Decade*, 109: 'God even at this day is able to raise up apostles, evangelists, and prophets.'

comes from the Bible. The Bible alone should be taught,[138] even to such an extent that the preacher can say: 'My doctrine is not my doctrine, but his that hath sent me'.[139] And therefore, 'a bishop or pastor...must walk abroad there, and cry out the commandment of the Lord'[140]. For this very reason a pastor has to, as it were, soak himself in the gospel message, that his flock may have consolation and comfort at his hands.[141] Besides preaching, they are also to pray for the people and to discipline them when necessary,[142] for the bishop is to rule their soul.[143] When Hooper uses the word 'bishop' he means an overseer, a guardian. Not hierarchically above the pastors, but the *primus inter pares*, like a superintendent, all functioning in the one office under Christ as the pastor and shepherd of souls.[144] In the environment of the English Reformation, however, he had little choice but to accept the offices of deacon, priest and bishop as they were defined in the *Book of Common Prayer*.[145] In practice, Hooper, as can be seen in his sermons on Jonah, saw priest and bishop as basically the same office. Their task was to teach the congregation what the apostles and prophets had taught.[146] This, though taking authority away in theory, might yet have a self-authenticating effect, i.e. the congregation would see them as the ones in authority. In his visitation book Hooper seemed to be aware of this danger. He started a thorough visitation of the diocese, which was also undertaken most vigorously.[147] In it, Hooper sought to re-educate the entire clergy and laity in his diocese, thus creating a society that by their knowledge of the gospel-truth was able to judge all that is

---

138 *Later Writings*, 120.
139 *Early Writings*, 509.
140 *Early Writings*, 511.
141 *Later Writings*, 129.
142 *Early Writings*, 504; 507.
143 Cf. Brodie, *Constructing*, 109. In the same context Hooper says the magistrate is the guardian of the body, a thought common in Zurich theology (cf. Biel, *Doorkeepers*, ch. 1).
144 Cf. *Decades (Teilband 3.2)*, 802 / *Fifth Decade*, 106. In the *Forma ac Ratio* à Lasco identified the ἐπίσκοπος as the superintendent or office of overseer (*Opera II*, 57). Later, Guido de Brès (educated in the London church) also links bishop to superintendent in his *Baston de la foy* (Boer, E.A. de, 'De katholieke ecclesiologie van de Confessio Belgica in het licht van *Le Baston de la foy*' in: *Theologia Reformata* 55/3 (2012), 264-277, 269-271).
145 *The First and Second Prayer Books of Edward VI* ed. E.C.S. Gibson (London: J.M. Dent & Sons / New York: E.P. Dutton & co.: 1910/1960), 292-317.; cf. Leggett, R.G., 'Anglican Ordinals' in: Hefling, Ch. & Shattuck, C. (eds.), *The Oxford Guide to The Book of Common Prayer. A Worldwide Survey* (Oxford: OUP, 2006), 528-537.
146 *Early Writings*, 460; cf. also page 448, 480.
147 Cf. Wilson, *John Hooper and the English Reformation*, 333-334.

said and done.¹⁴⁸ Nor were ministers to lead the congregation by themselves. Hooper demanded the churchwardens to take part in correcting the people and the ministers themselves. They also had to help defend biblical doctrine.¹⁴⁹ In doing so, Hooper moves far beyond the churchwardens' ordinary tasks¹⁵⁰ and it seems he tried to give them the position of elders. The evidence in the visitation book is on the whole too little to claim this with absolute certainty, but that is the direction in which his injunctions are moving.

The office of deacon has been strangely absent in this discussion, mostly because Micron does not pay any attention to it in *Van de weerdicheydt*, nor does he deal with relief of the poor in any way. Though we cannot be sure this area meant little to him, and it might be because Micron was not able to finish the book himself, yet it does show it was not the first thing that came to mind. This was different for Bullinger and Hooper. The Zurich reformer said in his *Decades* that what is given to the poor is given to God, and when the money is held back it leads to disasters and punishment of individuals and the society because it is a sacrilege. Despising the poor is the same as despising God in the poor.¹⁵¹ Hooper also says that collections are necessary, because they have been commanded by Christ.¹⁵² Almsgiving is among the sacrifices that Christians still have to offer up to the Lord.¹⁵³ The bishop turned this into practice by organising meals for the poor in his own house every day.¹⁵⁴

We return to the question of whether the term re-sacralisation is appropriate. At a theological level we must say that Bullinger, Micron and Hooper tried hard to de-sacralise the ministry. After all, the minister's

---

148 Cf. *Later Writings*, 131-133.
149 *Later Writings*, 134-135.
150 Henry VIII charged churchwardens to provide arms for soldiers, relief for maimed veterans and to enforce local conformity (Carlson, E., 'The origins, function, and status of the office of churchwarden, with particular reference tot he diocese of Ely' in: Spufford, M. (ed.), *The World of Rural Dissenters 1520-1725* (Cambridge: CUP, 1995), 164-207, p. 170-171). This was already a move away from their historical task as ecclesiastical representatives of the parish (Drew, Ch., *Early Parochial Organisation in England. The Origins of the Office of Churchwarden* (London: St. Anthony's Press, 1954), 5-6).
151 *Decades (Teilband 3.2)*, 1052-1053 / *Fifth Decade*, 495-496. Cf. Chung-Kim, E. 'Advocating for Poor Relief in Zurich: Heinrich Bullinger's Contributions to Religious Ideals and Policy Reforms', in: *Church History. Studies in Christianity and Culture* 86/2 (2017), 311-338.
152 *Later Writings*, 127.
153 *Early Writings*, 488.
154 Wilson, *John Hooper and the English Reformation*, 332-333.

only authority lies in the Word of God, which he is to preach. Moreover, he does not have this authority on his own; rather, it is shared with both the overseer (who is not above the minister, but a *primus inter pares*) and the priests, or presbyters. This short review supports Bolliger's and Timmerman's assessment. However, it cannot be denied that in the theologies presented here, the minister is more or less seen as the conduit of God's Word. The sociological effect of this could still be that the congregation saw the minister as more sacred. The expressions used come close to re-sacralisation, for instance when the clergy are called the bishops of the soul or when ministers are called saviours. Whether or not the council of elders, churchwardens, other ministers or an overseer effectually de-sacralised the minister in the eyes of the laity, is beyond the scope of this research. Theologically speaking, the Reformed aim was to minimise the importance of the preacher and maximise the importance of the Word preached.[155] And this was in fact common in Reformed theology.[156] Vermigli, likewise, sees the church as the mediator of grace, because in the church the Word of God is preached.[157] The sermon is merely the means by which the Word, infinitely higher, is brought to the congregation.[158] Because the sermon is out of God's Word it is the Word of God, but only so long as it is true to God's Word in the Bible.[159] Calvin, too, sees the church – the Mother of all believers – as the mediator of grace.[160] This grace is handed out by means of servants.[161] This ministry is both useful and necessary, for through the ministers God Himself governs the church.[162] Because it is the LORD who governs, there is no authority outside what He has spoken in the Bible.[163] This teaches all ministers humility, for only by staying true to God's Word can peace and

---

155 Cf. Biel, *Doorkeepers*, 204.
156 Contra Biel, *Doorkeepers*, 204.
157 See, especially, Sturm, *Theologie*, 216, where it is said: 'Die Bedeutung des >>externum ministerium<< der Wortverkündigung wird hervorgehoben, Christus will die Wirkung des Geistes nich anders bei den Glaubenden zum Ziel kommen lassen als durch das äussere Wort, das Wort ist >>promissio<<. Durch die Predigt wird >>remissio peccatorum<< geschenkt, Vergebung wird den Glaubenden >>per Christum<< >>gratis<< zuteil. Die Sakramente sind >>verba visibilia<<.' See, also, pages 175; 185.
158 Sturm, *Theologie*, 219.
159 Sturm, *Theologie*, 220.
160 Cf. Kim, *Identity*, 104; 107.
161 Calvin, *Institutio*, 317-318.
162 Calvin, *Institutio*, 333-336 (= ch. VIII.34-36).
163 Calvin, *Institutio*, 420. In discussing this Calvin, like Bullinger and Micron, draws attention to Malechi 2 (*Institutio*, 418).

unity be maintained.¹⁶⁴ In his exposition of Ephesians 4:11-12 Calvin claims the offices of apostles, prophets and evangelists are no longer the normal means by which God governs the church, though in exceptional situations God can send them. The shepherds function more or less as apostles (whose task is to preach and administer the sacraments) and the teachers as prophets expound Scripture.¹⁶⁵ Though Micron did not follow this exegesis, it does not lead to a major difference. Again we see that, despite different accents, the overall framework within which these reformers thought about the ministry was the same.¹⁶⁶ The Word preached, not the preacher, was the mediator of grace and in the dissemination of the Zurich tradition, as with Bullinger and Calvin, the ministry was a collegial, not a solitary calling.

7.5 Unity and Secession

Last of all we seek to compare whether Micron's views on unity and secession were consonant with those of other reformers. This is not so much a review of how they wrote for or against Nicodemism;¹⁶⁷ rather, we look at the theological presuppositions that underlie calls for unity or secession.

Unity was firmly bound to the demand to join the church, necessary for the salvation of the sinner and the harmony of body and soul. When we look at the Zurich tradition it is almost as if Micron has merely given an exposition of what Jud wrote on the necessity of joining the church:

> Who seeks and loves truth, and does not want to move away from it, looks in all things at God's ordinances, not at his own battles. God does nothing without cause. If it had been enough [to stay alone], then He would not have pointed Cornelius, who believed already, to Peter, nor Paul to Ananias. God, however, wants there to be such a big and exuberant love among His own, that they recognise, love and consider one another fellow members [of Christ]. (…) He has fixed this ordinance, that the one will obey and serve the other, and He wants that the one is taught, admonished, comforted and disciplined by the other[.] (…) Who, then, is

---

164 Calvin, *Institutio*, 333-334; 424-425.
165 Calvin, *Institutio*, 336-338 (= ch. VIII.37-39).
166 For more on the office in Reformed theology, see: Ainslie, J.L., *The Doctrines of the Ministerial Order in the Reformed Churches of the 16th and 17th Centuries* (Edinburgh: T&T Clark, 1940); Spijker, W. van 't, *De ambten bij Martin Bucer* (Kampen: Kok, 1970).
167 Cf. ch. 2.5 and the literature given there.

elected of God and inwardly called by Him, will not despise this outward ordinance of the Church.[168]

Truly, all that we distilled on the necessity to join the church is given here in a nutshell. The church, in Zurich thought, is one,[169] and this is revealed in her being gathered visibly.[170] Outward ceremonies, which differ from place to place are therefore not a reason for secession, nor are the faults in ministers and others, even if unworthy persons partake of the supper. Neither is faulty doctrine a reason to secede, as long as it does not corrupt the core of the simple teachings of the apostles.[171] The believers belong to each other and their goal is, Bullinger says, to grow in unity in Christ.[172] Again, then, we see that Micron disseminated the Zurich tradition. When we look at à Lasco's pamphlet on whether one must secede, we see very little on the necessity of joining the church,[173] but he does say that 'this is not the least part in our confession of the Gospel, that we leave popery and join a public (*opentlicke*) congregation of Christ'[174] For Calvin, indeed, the unity of the church is so sacred that being schismatic is as bad as being apostate.[175] The unity of the church, however, is not man-made, for it rests in her election in Christ, and He will not allow the believers to lose their faith, nor that the church is torn into pieces.[176] Last of all, we saw that when it comes to unity Micron sought harmony between the inward and outward man, and the Spirit uses outward means to reach the inward man. We were struck most of all by the similarity between Micron's and Vermigli's thought. He says, for instance, that by signs and means men are admonished to do their duty, and the sacraments are instituted

---

168 Jud, *Grössere*, 160-161.
169 *Decades*, 767-768 / *Fifth Decade*, 49
170 Jud, *Kürzere*, 315.
171 *Decades (Teilband 3.2)*, 770-775 / *Fifth Decade*, 53-61. The core teaching Bullinger gives is: The apostolic confession, original sin, regeneration, justification by faith, Christ was sacrificed once, good works are necessary, receiving the sacraments, prayer. (*Decades,* 770 / *Fifth Decade,* 53-54). Compare, moreover, what was written above about a minimalist church order by Bullinger and Jud.
172 *Decades (Teilband 3.2)*, 799 / *Fifth Decade*, 101.
173 Cf. however, Becker's exposition of the congregation as the *communio corporis Christi*. Seeing the church in this way makes joining it non-negotiable (Becker, *Gemeindeordnung*, 35; 45-47).
174 Lasco, *of het den christenen*, f.12.
175 Jowers, J.D., 'In What Sense Does Calvin Affirm 'Extra Ecclesiam Nulla Salus'?' in: Mannion/Borght (eds.), *Calvin's Ecclesiology*, 50-68, 50.
176 Calvin, *Institutio*, 313-314.

that the external senses move man inwardly.[177] The means by which sins are forgiven is not only the promise proclaimed, but also the inward working of the Spirit by which the promise is grasped: 'The words of Scripture, that the minister merely preaches, have the effect that Christ's Spirit and grace flow to the heart "through eager ears, as through a straw"'.[178] If this is how the Spirit works, going to church to hear the gospel becomes vital and separating oneself from it is dangerous. However, there are times when this is deemed necessary, to which we now turn.

Our main interest here will be Calvin, for here it seems as if Micron has written his book with Calvin's *Institutes* on his desk. Before that, however, we look at the others. Bullinger says that one must separate when not only the sacraments are corrupted, but the doctrine is adulterated too.[179] A schismatic tears the unity of the church by separating from it; the Reformed however, Bullinger says, have left the fellowship of darkness, by abstaining from the horrible Roman Catholic heresies, and are now gathered together again with Christ.[180] In short, secession happens when it is necessary to disobey men, in order to obey Christ.[181] Micron believed one would be contaminated by the inexcusable sins of others if one stayed. Hooper likewise says 'let us praye to [God] that we pollute not ourselves, with any rites, ceremonies or usages, not instituted by [G]od.'[182] And one has no business to be present where God's name is dishonoured, for why would one's body be present when one's mind abstains?[183] So, rather than leading the weak to sin by a poor example, one should show them the right course to take.[184] But what are the things that should lead to separation? Musculus explains that in religion there are things necessary and of necessity (the core of the Christian faith), things indifferent and lawful and things unlawful and prohibited. The third

---

177 *A briefe examination*, C1v-C2r.
178 Sturm, *Theologie*, 218-220. Quotation on 220.
179 *Decades (Teilband 3.2)*, 770 / *Fifth Decade*, 53. The English translation gives 'altogether corrupted' for '*prorsus (…) adulterata*'. However, it is not necessary to translate *prorsus* as altogether. *Prorsus* commonly means 'straightforward, simply' and one could imagine a translation like 'where doctrine is directly/wilfully adulterated.' This last translation accords better with Micron, when he says that one should secede when God's Word is openly mocked and tampered with (*VdWNN*, 50v).
180 *Decades (Teilband 3.2)*, 775-777; 785 / *Fifth Decade*, 63-65; 66; 78. Cf., also, Stephens, W.P., 'The Understanding of the Church in Heinrich Bullinger's Ecclesiology' in: *Zwingliana* 41 (2014), 57-84.
181 Jud, *Grössere*, 162. For Zwingli: cf., Stephens, *Zwingli*, 114.
182 Hooper, *kepte secret*, [a.vi v].
183 Hooper, *kepte secret*, [a.iii v].
184 Hooper, *kepte secret*, [a.iv v].

category is so grievous that one cannot be present bodily without sinning against God.[185] Not even when the church or government demands presence should one go, for man's conscience is subject only to God and cannot be compelled to any unlawful thing.[186] Musculus believes these unlawful and prohibited things to be present in the Roman Catholic church. So does à Lasco: God's law is trespassed, Christ is mocked, as are His merits and teachings. The people are led astray from the true road to salvation.[187] In short: if nothing that Christ commanded remains,[188] one should leave.[189]

Although it is easy to note the similarities, all of this is rather abstract. Calvin is in accordance with this line of thought when only looking at the broad scope of things: unity should be kept, even when there are human failings, as long as the essentials of the Christian faith are adhered to. Unity can only exist in truth, the last is the foundation of the first.[190] It is strictly forbidden to secede from a true church.[191] But when does a church becomes false? Calvin does not easily say a church is false: even though the Roman Catholics maintain an untrue form of being church, there are still traces of the church, due to God's faithfulness.[192] Those who go before it is absolutely necessary are heavily condemned by Calvin: it is a sign of *hubris* and contempt of others.[193] For this reason, then, the prophets, the apostles and Christ did not separate themselves from the people of Israel. Could it be that Micron directly challenges Calvin (or perhaps persons using what Calvin wrote for their own ends) when he says that 'the prophets have always and without ceasing despised and most earnestly scolded and condemned [the godless ceremonies that were in the Israelite church]'.[194] True enough, Calvin admits this later on,[195] but he also said that the prophets did not leave the community of the church, not even when the confession was wrong.[196] Micron on the other hand paints a clear opposition between the righteous and the superstitious. The

---

185 [Musculus], *Proscaerus* Cr-v; C3v-C5r. / *Temporisour*, [C.vi v – C.vii r]; D.i r-D.ii r.
186 [Musculus], *Proscaerus*, [A7v]; B3v. / *Temporisour* B.iv v; B.viii v.
187 Lasco, *of het den christenen*, f.6.
188 Lasco, *of het den christenen*, f.13.
189 Lasco, *of het den christenen*, f.23.
190 Calvin, *Institutio*, 317-318.
191 Calvin, *Institutio*, 317; 327.
192 Calvin, *Institutio*, 331-332.
193 Calvin, *Institutio*, 321.
194 *VdWNN*, 51r.
195 Calvin, *Institutio*, 330-331. The prophets were not forced to take part in supersticious rites and they cried out against the profane assemblies.
196 Calvin, *Institutio*, 323.

righteous meticulously obey God's law and God's law only. When they do stay among the idolaters they only do this in so far as it does not contaminate them.[197] It asks for some reading between the lines, but on the whole Calvin does not fear contamination with error so much as Micron and consequently Micron seems to draw the lines more rigidly in his exegesis than Calvin.

So, we round off the last area of comparison. In general, again, we see that Micron offered a view widely accepted within the Reformed church. It is necessary to go to church, for that is where the body of Christ assembles to hear the gospel preached. The actions of the body should be in harmony with the convictions of the inward man. Unity must be maintained, faults in morals and even doctrine are not reasons to separate, as long as the core-doctrines are maintained. Micron seems to oppose Calvin's leniency, and to be more in line with Hooper: let us pray that we do not pollute ourselves.

7.6 Summary and Conclusions

In this chapter we sought to place Micron's ecclesiology in the context of the Reformed milieu in which he wrote and fulfilled his office. It was seen that, despite several minor differences, there was in fact a fundamental agreement in doctrine. The honour of God and salvation of man was universally seen as the purpose and even identity of the church: she is the communion of saints *and* the mother of all believers. This twofold identity comes together in the confession. Since the creation of the world there has been a people of God, and ever since the fall of man the church of Christ and the church of the devil stand opposite each other, leading to a fundamental *peregrinatio*-experience with all believers on this earth. The only true mark of the church is her obedience to the Word of God and the marks of word, sacrament and discipline are expressions of the true doctrine taken from the Bible. The preacher or minister, has no authority per se. His only claim to authority comes from speaking what the Bible says. In this, however, the servants of the church act as 'saviours', for it is through the church that Christ offers His treasures of grace. Albeit this led to a theological de-sacralisation, yet it might have caused a sociological re-sacralisation of the clergy. Last of all, all reformers stress the demand for church unity. Schism is strictly forbidden. The only reason for separation is when the actual core of faith is being corrupted. Regarding rites, some reformers were stricter than others, yet all agreed that a degree of flexibility is necessary in order to be able to adapt to local circumstances.

---

197 See above, 6.5.2

This general agreement does not mean that there were no disagreements. First and foremost, the importance Micron attached to the church as a safe haven against the tricks of the devil and the weakness of sinful nature, was not seen in the work of the other reformers. Here, then, we have an element which is unique to Micron. Another major difference was the position of church discipline. Though all reformers stressed the importance of discipline in general, they did not universally include this as a mark of the church, and in the Zurich tradition the secular government – not the church – was responsible for upholding it. Micron moved away from Bullinger and Hooper and moved towards à Lasco, Vermigli and Calvin in including discipline as a mark of the church. The last difference we saw was the degree to which disobedience to the Word of God can be condoned. Calvin and Micron seemed to disagree. Micron drew much stricter lines than Calvin. Whereas Calvin suggested that even when the confession is contrary to the Bible one could still stay without any danger and that even Christ and the apostles did not separate themselves from the people of Israel, Micron would not accept that the holy men in the Bible had any dealings with the sinful rites and practices of the apostate, indeed they separated from them.

We can safely conclude that Micron has written a thoroughly Reformed ecclesiology. Moreover, we can say that among the reformers the framework of what the church was and should do was not in discussion. The discussions were often minor points which entailed the practical application of the doctrine rather than doctrine itself. The exception to this is Micron's insistence on the church as protector of the people. We suggested this is a re-interpretation of the *corpus Christianum*, which with Micron has developed into a community within the civic community. It is in the congregation where the Word is obeyed that one finds protection against the flesh, the world and the devil.

Chapter 8: Micron's Reforming Ecclesiology in the Context of the Reformed Reformation

Synthesis and Conclusions

In this last chapter we present a summary of this research and thus come to a synthesis. First we look at the context in which Micron lived and wrote his *Van de weerdicheydt* (8.1), then we summarise his theology in relation to other reformers (8.2). In 8.3 we look at the possible dissemination of Micron's ideas. In 8.3 we start by looking at the translations, which opens a vista beyond the time-span of this research and see the contours of Micron's ecclesiology in the Low Countries by focussing on a case study of Arent Cornelisz., Reformed pastor in Delft. In 8.4 we present our conclusions in answer to the main question: How can we describe the ecclesiology Marten Micron presents in his *Van de weerdicheydt, nutheydt ende noodicheyt der christelicker vergaderinghen* in relation to its immediate historical and intellectual environment of the Reformed reformation?

8.1 Context

In 1531 Balthasar von Esen set fire to the western tower of the St. Andreaskirche in Norden, destroying an important landmark for sailors at sea. The church was on fire. And perhaps we can say that this was symbolic for that century. What is commonly known as 'the Reformation' set the church (do we dare say: the western tower of the church?) ablaze and it started a new phase in religious history.[1] This was no different in Norden or the rest of East Frisia. In chapter 4 we looked at the East Frisian Reformation and followed the framework provided by Arnd Reitemeier. He outlined five phases: 1) the first spread of Lutheran teachings, 2) cities take the lead in furthering developments, 3) princes adopt Luther's teachings, 4) further theological developments, 5) return of the Roman Catholic church. We saw that in East Frisia there was a sacramentarian influence from the very start and that, especially in Norden, there arose

---

[1] Cf., e.g., the title of a recent overview: Leeuwenberg, H., Slechte, H., Staalduine, T. van, *De Reformatie. Breuk in de Europese gescheschiedenis en cultuur* (Zutphen: Walburg Pers, 2017).

fierce conflicts between Lutheran preachers and sacramentarians. Countess Anna sought to appease these conflicts and tensions by appointing John à Lasco as superintendent, who was to form a church in which these two confessional strands worshipped together. However, à Lasco quickly coursed a more radical route in which church governance should be in agreement with the professed faith. This conviction was deeply rooted in à Lasco's view on the incarnation of Christ: without Him there would not have been a church and as He is her King and Prophet, He must be obeyed as well as believed. Consequently, worship should follow the rule of faith. John à Lasco's work was cut short by the Augsburg Interim in 1548. When Micron became a pastor in Norden the same tensions were still present there and had resulted in the Norder Kirchenstreit. Micron, then, found himself in a situation where reform was a balancing act between disruption and cohesion, theologising with a pastoral realism of sinful and broken life.

Micron's own life was a witness to this brokenness. Born in Ghent in 1522 or 1523, he saw the consequences of choosing for the Reformed faith in the burning of both books and people. It is possible he linked political suppression to religious suppression. However, we do not know this for sure. What we do know is that in the second half of the 1540's he had joined the Reformed movement and we met him in Basel, in the household of De Falais, where he befriended John Hooper. In 1548 he followed Hooper to Zurich to study theology under Bullinger and the other Zurich scholars. A year later he went to England as part of the Hooper household. In London he became one of the pastors of the Strangers' Church, of which John à Lasco was the superintendent. Thomas Cranmer led the English Reformation at a moderate pace, taking no more than one step at the time, seeking to form the religious beliefs people held through liturgy. A similar goal was pursued in granting the foreigners their own form of church. It was a way of getting a grip on the foreign inhabitants of the isle. Moreover, it appears Cranmer encouraged the formation of a thoroughly Reformed church as a template to which the English Reformation could conform slowly. To this end Micron cooperated with the other officers of the Strangers' Church and they wrote many liturgical documents, which to a large degree have a confessional aspect to them. Confession and liturgy are, after all, related, as we have already summarised. With the ascent of Mary Tudor in 1553 the ground became too hot under the strangers' feet and they left, travelling via Denmark – where they were not allowed to practice their religion – to, in the end, East Frisia. There Micron became the pastor of Norden. It was a life full of travel and hardships, a life that Micron himself described as voluntary exile for Christ's sake. He gave words to what we have consistently called the *peregrinatio*-experience. We will return to a definition of this concept later in this chapter.

It is clear that Micron can be placed squarely in what is commonly called the Reformation of the Refugees. In this paradigm he is an important figure. He was the leader of the first Strangers' Church, one of the drafters of its liturgy, leaving his mark via various publications and personal influence on persons such as Petrus Datheen and Hermes Backerel.[2] However, were the *peregrini* churches indeed the place where the future church model of the Reformed churches in the Netherlands was formed? This has been questioned by several scholars, most notably by Spohnholz and Van Veen. In our analysis of their critique we discovered that there are three basic questions being asked: 1) what is the extent of continuity or discontinuity between the stranger churches and the Dutch Reformed Churches in the Republic, 2) was Reformed doctrine (especially providence, election, discipline, autonomous church polity) a necessary consequence of the refugee experience, 3) was every refugee Reformed? We concluded that, though condensed versions of the narrative are too linear, the more detailed studies by advocates of the paradigm show a dynamic continuity between the stranger churches and the later churches, acknowledging the changes and differences between the two. The experience of exile did not inherently lead to Reformed doctrine, but it worked as a catalyst, reinforcing the confession of several doctrines. Spohnholz and Van Veen rightly argue that refugees subjected to the government and in this often practised a large degree of pragmatism; nonetheless, at no point was this beyond what their conscience allowed. We suggested that Groen van Prinsterer's essential summary – the freedom to bow only under the yoke of God's Word – was perhaps not the worst point of view. Where displacement is the stimulus rather than the cause of doctrine, it goes without saying that not all refugees were Reformed. Indeed, almost all scholars give liberal attention to the exceptions. The critique offered by Spohnholz and Van Veen held a degree of truth, but in general we decided that it was put too forcefully, without enough nuance, and preferred the stance taken by Johannes Müller, who questioned specific aspects of the paradigm and gave more attention to the actual effect of being refugees together: The refugees shared experiences and the narration of their history led to a shared identity. For Reformed refugees, and for refugees adhering to other

---

2 See ch. 2.3 and 5.1.

confessions, displacement or flight worked as a catalyst. On a general level, then, we concluded that the paradigm still stands, though in need of corrections, and we suggested a framework, rather than a narrative, based on the phase-model provided by Reitemeier. In the first phase the preparation for reform and first reception, in the second initial immigration and the Dutch Church in London, the third phase is that of continued emigration, in the fourth phase the initial steps towards a more solidified church federation took place, but in dynamic continuance with the past, in the fifth phase the process of church formation continued in the Low Countries, becoming less dynamic. Micron's life and work falls within the first three of these phases. In addition to the phase model, scholars from both sides can work from the common ground of the *peregrinatio*-experience. This is the ever-stronger existential awareness of being a stranger in the world: Christians are sojourners on their way to the eternal Fatherland. However, there were many who did not share in the physical refugee-experience. They preferred to stay where they were and not leave the Roman Catholic church, practising the Reformed faith secretly. It would appear one of Micron's aims was to convince the 'Nicodemites' and 'Libertines', as they were pejoratively called, to leave the false and join the true church. This debate forms the brackets around his work, since in his first book, *Een claer bewijs*, he devoted the last chapter to it and it was his final word.

It was within this context, then, that Micron wrote his book on the church. A context where he sought to balance between disruption and cohesion and was acutely aware of being in exile for the sake of Christ, a mere sojourner, living in tabernacles here, awaiting the city that has foundations.[3] It was with this book that we started our research, researching wider circles as we progressed. In the conclusion we have worked our way back to the centre. When confronting ourselves with *Van de weerdicheydt*, the first question we had to answer was whether the book was written by Micron at all. Several reasons – e.g., the unfinished state, the un-challenged reception, the theological level and consistency – led us to the conclusion that it is an authentic work by Micron. We also refuted the theory that the book was a spin-off from an earlier manuscript by Adrianus de Kuper against the Family of Love. The acts of the Emden consistory did not support this reading, nor was Micron's book primarily aimed against the Family of Love and David Joris at all; rather, it was aimed against Libertines, as they were called by the Reformed, and Nicodemites. Micron chose to embed his polemic in an encompassing

---

3 Cf. Hebr. 11: 8-10.

biblical-theological discourse on the doctrine of the church. By drafting his manuscript in Latin he sought to present his views on the church to an international audience. His aim was to write an encompassing Reformed ecclesiology in order to convince believers to join and build the true church. However, he was unable to finish the book and the manuscript was completed by Nicolaus Carinaeus, an Edam native who served as a pastor in East Frisia, afterwards in Amsterdam, Jennelt and London. His addition to the book focusses on the Family of Love and he also gave some advice on how to organise secret meetings, which turned the book into something of a handbook for churches under the cross. This practical advice was part of Micron's original set-up. In *Van de weerdicheydt* we come across the doctrinal foundations underlying Micron's church-formational work. Here, then, we can hope to find how he balanced between disruption and cohesion and how the experience of being a *peregrinus* influenced his ecclesiology.

8.2 Micron's Ecclesiology within Reformed Ecclesiology

And so we turn from the first part of the research to the second, in which we analysed Micron's ecclesiology and compared it to that of other reformers whom we know influenced him in various degrees.

We have seen that Micron embedded his argument to join a true church in a firm biblical-theological framework, i.e. he constantly grounded his opinions in all of Scripture. The triad of Word, sacrament and discipline keeps recurring throughout the work. These three together are in fact what make the church worthy, beneficial and necessary. Why the church is both beneficial and necessary is the overture of the book. The purpose of the church is the honour of God and the salvation of people. God is glorified by preaching, confessing and praising His truth obediently. It is by faithfully acknowledging God's salvific acts that we praise Him. This is done in 'the midst of the congregation': the confession of one is the confession of all – it is the confession of the church. The church in turn teaches this confession to her members, who give witness to God's truth both individually and together. If people acknowledge God's saving grace, they also acknowledge His righteousness and seek to praise Him in obedience to His laws.

When we compared Micron's thought to that of other reformers we saw that they, too, see the church as the house where God is honoured and His gospel confessed. Confessing this truth is not optional, but an intrinsic necessity for all believers.

The second purpose of the church is the salvation of humankind. In our analysis we saw that for Micron there is a strong protective element to this. Through the institution of the church, including the commandments, God protects His people from sin and the wiles of the devil. This was already the case in paradise. Though the church fell to ruins due to people's weakness in resisting evil, God rebuilt her upon the foundation of forensic righteousness through faith. He protects by having His gospel and will proclaimed. Not only is this beneficial, it is necessary, for due to the sinful human heart solitude would endanger one's salvation. It is also a sign of ingratitude to neglect the church.

How was this seen by the other reformers? They, too, see the church as the place where God's salvation is proclaimed and in this way ministers can even be called saviours, according to Bullinger. The church hands out God's treasures of grace and expounds His beneficial commandments. Micron was unique, however, in casting this second purpose in the mould of the church as a protective institution. We suggested this might be a re-interpretation of the *corpus Christianum* ideology: no longer the city, but the congregation as a safe haven.

We have consistently adopted Micron's order of addressing *why* the church is before considering *what* she is. It is part of the nature of the church to be an assembly of people. These people have been called out of the world by the Word, set apart as a group by circumcision/baptism. The New Testament church celebrates this in the Lord's Supper.[4] As said, the church is called out of the world, and is therefore the enemy of the world. Against the church of God is the church of satan. The latter seeks to shake off the yoke of Christ, whereas the first wants to bow under it. Under this opposition the church constantly dwindled or was even ruined. But God rebuilt her. Not only in the time of the patriarchs and prophets, but also in the New Testament, right up to Micron's own time. The rebuilding of the church is done upon her foundation: Jesus Christ, through Whom the church is holy – or worthy – despite her sins and the hypocrites within her. We followed Micron through several of his documents and found that his dependence on Christ alone was the pinnacle of his ecclesiological thought. This opposition between world and church also means that persecution and the *peregrinatio*-experience are part of the identity of the church. This should be borne gladly, celebrating the feast of tabernacles, because the existential exile from God has ended: Christ redeemed His people. After the exodus out of sin, the faithful are in the desert on their way to the promised land. Facing fundamental uncertainty and battling against sin, believers are strangers in this world, wherever they may be.

---

4 Micron does not explicitly draw a parallel between the Lord's Supper and the Old Testament Passover.

Yet they are not strangers, wherever they are, for they are of God's household. We concluded that the church is *worthy* because she is holy in Christ, *beneficial* as a protective barrier against the world, our flesh and the devil, *necessary* because through Word, sacrament and discipline the Spirit renews and regenerates humans.

We have seen that basically all of this is in full accordance with Reformed ecclesiology at large. The minor nuances are just that: nuances. At the end of our discussion we thought it likely that the twofold purpose of the church corresponds with the church as the mother of all believers (salvation) and the church as the assembly of all believers (glorify God). Differences in nuance between reformers, stressing one of these two aspects more than the other, should not lead to the conclusion that they advocated a unique or different ecclesiology.

After the *why* and the *what* we come to the *how*: when is a church truly a church? Micron described that it is essential for the church to be obedient to the Word of God. Whether this is the case is seen in doctrine. Doctrine consists of two parts: 1) the confession of the triune God and His work and 2) the confession of humankind's misery, salvation, obedience and glorification. However, it is not enough for a church to have the right doctrine, her governance should work towards the same end as doctrine. To achieve this the church should strictly adhere to what Christ Himself ordained. Micron believed that the triad Word, sacrament, discipline is Christ's own institution and these three are the backbone of obedient governance. The preached Word is the net in which the fish are caught. Baptism is the sign that the congregation is the body of Christ. It reminds the faithful of their depravity and salvation, it also urges them to mortify the old nature and take up the new. The Lord's Supper likewise reminds the congregation of these three aspects of the doctrine of man. But here Micron stresses the need for self-examination before attending and receiving the endless joy that goes with it. It was much more than a remembrance meal to him, it was a moment of a deep spiritual unity with Christ and the congregation. Discipline, thirdly, is necessary as a bridle against sin and offenses. It serves to keep the congregation holy and to rescue sinners. Again we see the twofold purpose: God's glory and salvation of people.

Was this vision of how the church should be shared by the other reformers? They too, see obedience to the Word of God as the *conditio sine qua non* for the marks of the church. Nor was it in fact an aberration to see doctrine as the essential mark and governance as working towards to same end. Careful reading of primary and secondary sources revealed that Reformed ecclesiology shapes what the church does after what she believes. The Reformed reformers also agreed that this is seen in Word and sacrament. Discipline was not always denoted as an actual mark, but it was always seen as unmissable. The relation between discipline and the other marks was also diversely interpreted. Was it part of preaching or did it flow forth from the need to keep the Lord's Supper table holy? In addition, who is responsible? Should the government or the church punish offenders? This was variously interpreted and we concluded that Micron moved away from the Zurich tradition in this respect, giving the church a more autonomous role. Though these differences are not unimportant, one should not overstate the differences either.

In connection with the mark of the Word we also looked at Micron's view on the several offices and the re-sacralisation thesis. We had to conclude that Micron's thought was not always clearly defined, nor did it at all times seem to be consistent. But the general outline was that the offices of the priests and Levites were replaced by that of ministers of the Word and elders. Together they govern the church and teach Scripture. These two offices, together with that of superintendent, are one. Only by seeing them as basically one office in different forms can the several texts be streamlined. The Old Testament prophets are a different category. Prophets do still, sporadically, occur. Their task is to rebuild the ruined church when she has collapsed. In normal circumstances, however, the prophethood of all believers serves to expound doctrine and test preaching.

The identification of the ministers with priests raised the question of re-sacralisation. On a theological level this seems to have been the case neither with Bullinger or his followers: the authority of the minister is not his own, it is the authority of the message he proclaims. Moreover, the collegial governance should prevent autocracy by ministers. Was the sociological effect of this theological de-sacralisation the same? We were not able to examine this but we thought it unlikely, since the minister was still seen as the conduit of God's Word.

This, then, is the church one should join. Like a sheep is safe with the shepherd, even so a believer is safe in the stable of the church, where the good Shepherd guards his flock. Solitude is, in fact, an impossibility. Inward religion must lead to outward religion, for body and soul are connected and it is through the outward means that the Spirit touches the heart. The place where one should be safe, however, can also become dangerous. Especially when one is forced to uphold abuses it is necessary to leave the false church forthwith. When the abuses are so numerous that they cannot be evaded contamination is, likewise, inescapable and the same conclusion follows. After leaving an unsafe church it is necessary to join a safe one to grow in the knowledge of true doctrine. We saw that

Micron was not rigid in his definitions. He acknowledged the Lutheran churches as building upon the true foundation. It seems he did not see their separate institutions and rites as a division, even though he could not join them in their service for his conscience's sake. The inward and the outward religion should agree with each other, but since every church is sinful there can be a degree of leniency towards each other. This is the pastoral realism in his book and how he sought the balance between disruption and cohesion. However, this realism could never lead to confessional inauthenticity: what is believed has to be confessed and worship should conform, though this did not mean that the confession was a fixed entity; rather, it was always subordinate to the Bible.

It was not surprising that the need to join the church was universally taught in Reformed doctrine. Concerning the outward and inward man we noted a strong resemblance of Micron's words in Vermigli's thought. Concerning the necessity to secede, however, we saw that Micron was stricter than Calvin. The Frenchman appeared to condone many more and grosser faults in the church. Likewise, he seems to have been less afraid of contamination by errors. Micron was more in line with John Hooper's radical opposition to all that is not instituted by God.

What we see is that generally speaking the Reformed doctrine concerning the church was the same, though it was not always uniform. Micron is neither Bullingerian or Calvinist, but Bullinger, Calvin, Micron and others are Reformed, with their own particularities. Micron stressed the church as a protective establishment. Moreover, his continual focus on obedience and a view of (church) history as a cycle of destruction and rebuilding merit the designation of his thought as a reforming ecclesiology. Reforming also, because obedience will always be incomplete. The foundation is not the fidelity of the church, but the work of Jesus Christ, whose holiness and righteousness is attributed to her. She therefore always reforms herself onto this foundation. Reforming, last of all, because she awaits her glorification when her abode will be reformed from tabernacles in exile to the eternal city in the Fatherland.

8.3 Dissemination

This chapter and research would not be complete if we did not also look beyond Micron to the last two phases of the 5-phases framework suggested for the Reformation of the Refugees above. Is there any correlation between Micron's ecclesiology and the formation of the Reformed Churches in the Low Countries? And indeed, the reception of *Van de weerdicheydt* gives us ample reason to do so. By summarising the chapter on the translations of *Van de weerdicheydt* we find ourselves in the environment where we almost automatically look ahead to the developments in the second half of the 16th century.

We start, however, with the English translation of two excerpts from the book, which John Knewstub inserted in his book against the Family of Love. The research showed that apparently Micron was still considered an authority in 1579. However, the actual ecclesiology set forward by Micron does not play any role in the choice for these excerpts. The book by Knewstub and his use of Micron is more important for the study of early-puritan thought than for our research.

A German translation of the entire book was published in 1563 in Heidelberg by Engelbert Faber. We placed this publication within the wider campaign, started by Elector Friedrich III, to disseminate the Reformed faith among inhabitants of the Palatinate. To a limited extend it could also serve as a handbook for the churches under the cross. Faber published no fewer than three translations in that year. Most notably, for our present goal, a translation of the Belgic Confession, written by Guido de Brès. In 1571 the Synod of Emden decided that all office bearers should subscribe to this document. Subsequent synods pursued the same course.[5] Engelbert Faber saw the Belgic Confession and *Van de weerdicheydt* as setting forth the same doctrine. Is this in fact true? Though we cannot prove direct influence (which, the confession having been written between 1559-1561,[6] is almost impossible), the similarity of thought in the doctrine of the church is striking, especially when we consider where the Belgic Confession differs from its direct source, the *Confessio Gallicana*. In article twenty-seven we read that the church has been in

---

5 Rutgers, F.L., *Acta van de Nederlandsche Synoden der zestiende eeuw* (Dordrecht: J.P. van den Tol, 1980²), 55-57 (Emden), 134 (Dordrecht 1574), 247 (Dordrecht 1578), 390 (Middelburg 1581), 498-499 (The Hague 1586). Cf. Harten-Tip, A. van, *De Dordtse Kerkorde 1619. Ontwikkeling, context, theologie* (Utrecht: KokBoekencentrum Academic, 2018). Pol, F. van der, 'De vroege receptie van de *Confession Belgica* in Nederland' in: Pol, F. van der (ed.), *Geloofstaal trekt haar spoor. 450 jaar Nederlandse Geloofsbelijdenis* (Utrecht: Kok, 2012), 71-86. The definitive text of the confession was established during the National Synod of Dordt 1618/1619 (Bakhuizen van den Brink, J.N., *De Nederlandse belijdenisgeschriften in authentieke teksten met inleiding en tekstvergelijkingen* (Amsterdam: Ton Bolland, 1976²), 26-27). In 1566, for instance, the exultant climax that God is 'the fountain of all good' was added (Baars, A., 'In God geloven en Hem beleven. Over artikel 1, 8 en 9 van de Nederlandse Geloofsbelijdenis' in: Van der Pol, *Geloofstaal*, 127-141, 132). Gootjes (Gootjes, N.H., *The Belgic Confession. Its History and Sources* (Grand Rapids: Baker, 2007), 150-158) rightly argues that the changes did not lead to a revised doctrine.
6 Gootjes, *Belgic Confession*, 17. Cf. Braekman, E. & Boer, E.A. de (ed.), *Guido de Bres. Zijn leven, zijn belijden* (Utrecht: Kok, 2011).

existence since the beginning of the world (the *Gallicana* does not mention this). In the same article we read that Christ as King cannot be without subjects, closely resembling Micron's text.[7] Again, in article twenty-nine we read that the ultimate mark of the church is conformation to the Word of God, rejecting all things that oppose it.[8] And therefore, the church does not accept a church order opposing God's law, but only what serves to feed and preserve harmony and unity and to keep all in obedience to God.[9] This does not mean there are no differences between the Belgic Confession and Micron's ecclesiology. The church as a protective establishment is absent in the confession. Moreover, when De Brès talks about the *diaspora* of the churches he stresses the essential unity without presenting a *peregrinatio*-experience. All in all, there is certainly a telling degree of correlation between the two documents,[10] just as there is with Reformed theology at large, but it would be a stretch to see the Belgic Confession as an implementation of exclusively Micronian ecclesiology.

The synod of Emden 1571 not only subscribed to the Belgic Confession, it also cemented the place of the Heidelberg Catechism, which had been translated by Petrus Datheen – Micron's former church member in London. Frank van der Pol says the catechism played a central role in defining the Reformed identity in the northern Netherlands.[11] But it is not so much the document itself that shows any significant influence by Micron. The dynamic continuity before and after 1571 is best seen in how the several synods sought to form the church is such a way that she was faithful to the doctrine she confessed. When we read the acts of the Synod of Emden 1571 we constantly see how they strove to protect the

---

7 'aenghesien dattet blijckelick is, dat Christus een koninck zijnder ghemeynten is, so moet daer oock wel nootsakelicken uut volghen dat de kercke oft ghemeynte die hier noch op dese werelt leeft, zijn rijck zy (*VdWNN*, 11v.); 'dat Christus een eeuwich Coninck is, de welcke sonder onderdanen niet zijn en kan' (BC, art. 27).
8 Bakhuizen-van den Brink, *Belijdenisgeschriften*, 125.
9 Bakhuizen-van den Brink, *Belijdenisgeschriften*, 129-131 (article 32),
10 It is no surprise, then, that my father, who served as a Reformed pastor for more than forty years, commented that reading *Van de weerdicheydt* feels like reading the *Belgic Confession*.
11 Pol, F. van der, 'De receptie van de Heidelbergse Catechismus in de noordelijke Nederlanden' in: Huijgen, A., Fesko, J.V., Siller, A. (eds.), *Handboek Heidelbergse Catechismus* (Utrecht: Kok, 2013), 123-133. For an introduction to the Heidelberg Catechism, see: Bierma, L.D. et al., *An Introduction to the Heidelberg Catechism. Sources, History, Theology* (Grand Rapids: Baker, 2005); Bierma, L.D., *The Theology of the Heidelberg Catechism: A Reformation Synthesis* (Louisville: Westminster John Knox Press, 2013).

confessional identity of the church.[12] The principle set out by Micron (though not solely by him) that governance works towards the same end as doctrine was firmly pursued in the Reformed Churches. This is clear when we read that the Emden synod ordered particular synods to first address matters of doctrine, then of governance and lastly particular matters, just as Micron placed doctrine before governance.[13] This was repeated during the synod of Dordt, 1578.[14] This synod, by the way, had Petrus Datheen as its chairman and Engelbert Faber was one of the delegates. Its first clerk was Arent Cornelisz.

In Arent Cornelisz. we have a pastor who was influential in the Netherlandish churches,[15] with output that shows us something of his lived religion and who, moreover, lived, studied and worked in places where Micron's influence could have been felt. This makes it interesting to investigate whether we see any agreement in thought between Micron and him. Cornelisz. had been Datheen's colleague in Frankenthal from 1571-1573 and his first theological studies were in Heidelberg in 1565, not long after Faber's translation of *Van de weerdicheydt* was published.[16] In 1573 he became a pastor in Delft and played a major role in drafting the church order of Middelburg 1581.[17] When we zoom in on him and his work, we see that the correlation which we noted between Micron's thought and the official documents of the Reformed Churches, is more pronounced in the life and work of Arent Cornelisz., to such an extent even, that one at times suspects utilisation of Micron's works.[18] In 1573, for instance, he wrote a liturgy for how the names of new members were

---

12 Rutgers, *Acta*, 56-58 (art. 2 and 5), 63 (art. 16), 86 (art. 51). Cf. Van Harten-Tip, *Dordtse kerkorde*, 50-52; 98
13 Rutgers, *Acta*, 111.
14 Rutgers, *Acta*, 244. Instead of *regimente* the word *Kerckenordeninghe* is used. The synods of 1581 and 1586 do not repeat the expression. A possible reason for this is that stipulations concerning practical execution were removed (Van Harten-Tip, *Dordtse Kerkorde*, 60). Minutes from provincial synods should be examined to highlight if and how this was practised.
15 Not only in hindsight, but also affirmed by primary sources (Wouters, A.Ph.F. & Abels, P.H.A.M., *Nieuw en ongezien. Kerk en samenleving in de classis Delft en Delfland 1572-1621. Boek 1: De nieuwe kerk* (Delft: Eburon, 1994), 145-146).
16 Jaanus, H.J., *Hervormd Delft ten tijde van Arent Cornelisz (1573-1605)* (Amsterdam: Nordemann's Uitgevers Maatschappij, 1950), 97, 100-101.
17 Bremmer, *Reformatie en Rebellie. Willem van Oranje, de calvinisten en het recht van opstand. Tien onstuimige jaren: 1572-1581* (Franeker: Wever, 1984),184-191.
18 Cf., also, Wouters & Abels, *Nieuw en ongezien 1*, 316; Abels, P.H.A.M. & Wouters, A.Ph.F., *Nieuw en ongezien. Kerk en samenleving in de classis Delft en Delfland 1572-1621. Boek 2: De nieuwe samenleving* (Delft: Eburon, 1994), 32-33.

to be declared from the pulpit.[19] In it we read that the 'poor servants and handmaidens' have gathered to make public confession of the faith.[20] And God is prayed to raise up love for His holy ordinances. Those who confess the faith should not do so inwardly only, but one should also confess it openly, especially when one hears the truth is mocked. The document is written specifically against those who did not want to be publicly known as professors of the Reformed religion. Cornelisz. asks them whether they truly seek the glory of God and the edification of the church. A twofold purpose that echoes Micron's. We remember how Micron wrote that those who do not join give offense and hinder the salvation of church members. Erik de Boer comments: 'Confessing the faith is equal here to openly joining the Reformed Church'.[21] We do not know, however, whether Micron's *Corte Ondersoeckinghe* played any role in the admission of new members, though we do know this short catechism remained influential until at least 1610.[22] Nearly ten years later Arent Cornelisz. assisted his colleague Reinier Donteclock, who wrote a book against Dirck Volkertsz. Coornhert.[23] In the very title we read the dynamic continuity we are looking for: 'and, on the contrary, how *beneficial* and *necessary* it is, that one joins the true visible congregation of God, *through the means that God ordained*'.[24] It is far beyond our scope to highlight all the instances where we almost hear Micron speak through these pages. But this book likewise sets out with pointing out that the glory of God

---

19 Jaanus, *Hervormed Delft*, 249-253
20 Cf. *Ord.* 83.
21 Boer, E.A., '[Hubrecht Duifhuijs], *Vande wterlyke kercke Godes* [1581] en het debat over de aard van de kerk' [forthcoming]. On the relation between confession and membership, cf. Wouters & Abels, *Nieuw en ongezien 1*, 198-202; 212-214.
22 Wouters & Abels, *Nieuw en ongezien 1*, 213-214; Nauta, D., *Twee geschirften uit de begintijd van de Gereformeerde Kerk in Nederland* (Amsterdam: Buijten & Schipperheijn, 1974), 21. Cf. the list of reprints in Heijting, W., *De catechismi en confessies in de Nederlandse Reformatie tot 1585. Deel 1: Tekst* (Nieuwkoop: De Graaf Publishers, 1989), 198-207.
23 On him, see: Veen, M. van, *Dirck Volckertszn Coornhert* (Kampen: Kok, 2009).
24 *Teghenbericht op eenen brief over een wijle ghedruckt achter een boeckxken vande wterlicke Kercke Godes, sonder den naem des autheurs, waer in hy antwoordt op een vraghe hem by een goet vriendt voorghestelt: Of hy hem soude behegeven inde Ghemeynte der Ghereformeerden etc. Aenwijsende hoe onghegrondt ende onchristelick dien raedt des Autehurs is dear mede de menschen vande wterlicke oeffeninghe der Religie afghetrocken werden, ende hoe nu ende noodich ter contrarie is datmen hem door de middelen van Godt gheordonneert begheve tot de ware sichtbare Ghemeynte Godts. Geschreven door de dienaren der Kercke Christi tot Delft* (Delft: Aelbert Hendricxz., 1582). Italics by HTW.

and the salvation of the soul is the foundation of all other things.[25] This is done in the church, which has existed since the beginning of the world.[26] The church obeys Christ's commandments, and those who do not are not truly His disciples.[27] One of His commandments is that it is our debt to join the church – and a commandment of Christ is never useless.[28] In church you hear the gospel and increase in knowledge and understanding and believers should also ask the ministers to educate them from God's Word.[29] Through hearing the truth is known, for inward and outward man are connected and should be in agreement,[30] therefore the truth should also be confessed.[31] In fact, in order to prove the necessity of education Donteclock cites the same three examples as Micron: Philip and the eunuch, Peter and the Roman centurion, Ananias and Paul.[32] It is the living voice of the preached word that wakes up those who are forgetful in doing what is right.[33] Clearly, we are here in the same sort of ecclesiology as Micron set out. To be sure, it has solidified due to further institutionalization; nonetheless, it is a church that confesses and brings to confession. It does so for the glory of God and the salvation of humankind.[34]

---

25 *Teghenbericht*, 1.
26 *Teghenbericht*, 4-5.
27 *Teghenbericht*, 13, 46.
28 *Teghenbericht*, 14, 38.
29 *Teghenbericht*, 18, 41, 54.
30 *Teghenbericht*, 63, 22.
31 *Teghenbericht*, 65. Confessing and confession was important tot Arent Cornelisz. (cf. Wouters & Abels, *Nieuw en ongezien 1*, 91-92.)
32 *Teghenbericht*, 67; *VdWNN*, 80v.
33 *Teghenbericht*, 71. For the relation between hearing and believing, cf. Wouters & Abels, *Nieuw en ongezien 1*, 196; Abels & Wouters, *Nieuw en ongezien 2*, 307-308.
34 In the archive of Arent Cornelisz. there is another intriguing document titled 'XXIX propositien van der Kercke' (Stadsarchief Delft, archief 445 (Hervormde Gemeente te Delft), inv. nr. 635). We have not been able to date this document with any certainty. It could be somewhere between 1578-1582 as the content bears resemblance to the discussion on whether Roman Catholic children should be baptised (Wouters & Abels, *Nieuw en ongezien 1*, 200). However, it is written primarily against those who doubt the necessity of leaving the Roman Catholic Church and indeed doubt the legitimacy of the Reformed Churches. Here, too, we read that the church always was and always will be (pr. 2), that it is Jesus Christ Who builds the church (pr. 4) and He Himself is the foundation as is seen in baptism (pr. 13). Churches can be more or less true, depending on how they build upon this foundation (pr. 9). What the church should do is follow Christ's ordinances, because He is her Bridegroom and Head (pr. 27). Cornelisz. is more lenient when he says that false churches are still catholic in those parts that are built upon the true foundation (pr. 17, 18, 21, 25). He

It is fair to say that there is no hard line between the ecclesiology Marten Micron described and the ecclesiology practised in the Low Countries after 1572. True enough, there are differences. But just as Reformed ecclesiology at large was substantially the same throughout the Reformed Reformation, the Reformed ecclesiology of the Reformed Churches shows significant signs of dynamic continuity with Micron's reforming ecclesiology: The need for a visible church, where the faithful gather for confession and salvation. We suggest that in this the subscription to the confession was not a solidifying tendency, but rather a means to constantly reform, since doctrine was to be established before form.

8.4 Conclusion

In the above synthesis we have answered the sub-questions stated in chapter one. We can now answer our main question: How can we describe the ecclesiology Marten Micron presents in his *Van de weerdicheydt, nutheydt ende noodicheyt der christelicker vergaderinghen* in its immediate historical and intellectual environment of the Reformed Reformation? First and foremost the ecclesiology presented here is the *foundational* theology behind Micron's work as a pastor in the Strangers' Church and the church in Norden. We saw that his was a truly *reforming* ecclesiology. One that always urges to conform to the Word of God, that reforms itself upon the foundation of justification and sanctification in Christ alone, that awaits the ultimate reformation on the last day. We analysed that this makes it a *peregrinatio*-ecclesiology. The Christian is a stranger in this world. This is also how Micron saw himself. However, other reformers addressed the same topic. Indeed, when we compared Micron to other reformers we had to conclude that their theology of the church was the same, with a few exceptions. The contours of Micron's ecclesiology are visible in the confession, governance and lived religion of the Reformed Churches in the Netherlands. Micron's *reforming* theology was therefore also a thoroughly *Reformed* theology. His unique moment was his insistence that the church is a protectress, constantly rebuilt by God for the good of His people. Micron's ecclesiology is therefore a *corpus Christianum* ecclesiology, i.e. the church as the city of God with walls protecting the faithful gathering inside. Consequently, it is a *providential* ecclesiology, that is to say, the belief that this history of the church and its members is not contingent, but guided by God. Last of all, his is a *confessional* ecclesiology. Not in such a way that the confession can rule it

---

therefore sees hope for those in the adulterate Roman Catholic church, but not, we must unfortunately add, for the Arabians and Jews as breakers of the covenant (pr. 15).

over the Bible; rather, a church where the mouth joins the heart, where the believer confesses together with the church, where the church in her worship lives her confession – if need be in exile.

Historically, also, we can see Micron as a representative of the broader Reformed movement. I.e., the movement within the time of reformations that reject substantial presence of Christ's body in the Eucharist, but adhered to paedobaptism. Micron's life and work did not solely disseminate Bullinger's teachings, but Micron also used works of, and cooperated with other theologians. Micron is a link between Bullinger and the Dutch Reformed churches, to be sure; however, he is also a link between them and Calvin, Hooper, à Lasco, Musculus and Vermigli, and probably others that we have not had the opportunity to study. Micron's theology, we have discovered, was continued in both the confessional documents and the lived religion. This means that his foundational ecclesiology also functions as, partly at least, the foundation on which the Dutch Reformed churches rested. I.e. the churches as they developed in the Netherlands after 1572 are a dynamic continuance of the work Micron and others started. It should be clear that we cannot mark out Micron as *the* church father of the churches in the Netherlands, that would be to start or continue a myth, but he was certainly one of her primary teachers. For large parts of the Reformed tradition Micron remains one of her teachers to the present day through the several liturgical forms and confessions that show traces of his thought and work. Just as the *Book of Common Prayer* was written to form the beliefs of the English people, so Micron's liturgical and catechetical work helped form the confession of the Dutch churches. There was, and even is, dynamic continuance. Regarding the Reformation of the Refugees, Micron's life and work is of key importance to understand how displacement works as a catalyst, not source, for the theological convictions analysed above. In the second phase we proposed, that of the Strangers' Church, Micron is one of the few key-players and deserves equal attention, both historically and theologically, as John à Lasco. Micron's position in the Strangers' Church means we can describe his ecclesiology as archetypal for refugee ecclesiology; hence, it plays an important role in re-evaluating this paradigm. The *peregrinatio*-experience should not and cannot be seen as a separate 'reformation'; however, we can say that with Micron this experience left a distinguishable mark on his ecclesiology, causing it to have different accents within the same basic beliefs. This gives the historian the right to study the *peregrinatio*-experience as a phenomenon, but not to study in in isolation from the movement of which the representative was a part. On several occasions we looked at the tension between disruption and cohesion. The years Micron served in Norden were peaceful, despite different views on the Lord's Supper being present in the congregation. On the other hand, during his travels and in his works Micron is often fiercely polemic and was involved in the Second Eucharistic Controversy. Micron's ecclesiology, then, caused both disruption and cohesion. To summarise: From a historical perspective, Marten Micron's ecclesiology is foundational and it enlightens the correlation between social circumstances, theological convictions and lived religion of the Reformed in those circumstances. Moreover, this correlation between events and theology unearths the freedom of conscience and submission to the Word of God in serving Christ as essential convictions in the development of the Reformed Reformation.

Perhaps Micron once walked among the ruins of the St. Andreaskirche after he left the Ludgerikirche. It was a striking image of how the church can burn, dwindle, collapse, even be razed to the ground by satan's fierce opposition. The foundations, however, were intact, and just as the magnificent Ludgerikirche was a safe haven for those who gathered there to hear, see, taste and confess the gospel, in the same way this church could be rebuilt. Just as the church as the body of Christ had been rebuilt so often in history through God's providence. He led her, that His people might find protection within her walls for the salvation of their life and to laudatorily confess: all glory be to God.

Bibliography

Abbreviations
(For full references the reader is referred to the literature section).

AS	Micron, *Apologeticum Scriptum* [ed. Willems].
Bericht	Utenhove, *Kurzer, einfältiger und waarhafter historischer Bericht*.
Cathechismus	Micron, *De kleyne Cathechismus* [ed.Lang].
Clear bewijs	Micron, *Een clear bewijs, van het recht gebruyck des Nachtmaels Christi, ende wat men van de Misse houden sal* [ed.Pijper].
Decades	[Bullinger], *Heinrich Bullinger Werke (...) Sermonum Decades* [ed. Opitz].
Early Writings	[Hooper], *Early Writings of John Hooper* [ed. Carr].
ET	*Epistolae Tigurinae.*
Fifth Decade	[Bullinger], *The Decades of Henry Bullinger* [ed. Harding].
Füslinus	*Epistolae ab ecclesiae Helveticae.*
Hessels II	Hessels, *Ecclesiae Londino-Batavum Archivum. Tomus secundus.*
Hoste	Micron, *Waerachteghe historie van Hoste (gheseyt Jooris) vander Katelyne* [ed.Pijper].
Is is s	Willems, *Is is Is? Apologeticum Scriptorum van Maarten de Kleyne.*
KU	Micron, *Ein kort underricht.*
Later Writings	[Hooper], *Later Writings of Bishop Hooper* [ed. Nevinson].
London	*Niederländer Bekenntnis, London 1550/1551* [ed. Mühling].
Meiners I; II	Meiners, *Oostvrieschlandts kerkelyke geschiedenisse*
OLER	*Original Letters Relative to the English Reformation.* [Part 1 pp.1-376; part 2 pp.377-784].
Opera II	Lasco, J. à, *Opera.*
Ord	Micron, *De christlicke ordinancien* [ed. Dankbaar].
OS	[Micron], *Een corte undersouckinghe des gheloofs* [ed. van Ravenswaay].
SFN	Utenhove, *Simplex et Fidelis Narratio* [Ed. Pijper].
VdWNN	Micron, *Van de weerdicheydt, nutheydt ende noodicheyt der christelicker vergaderinghen* [see appendix B].

Works by Micron[1]

Micron, M., *A short and faythful instruction, gathered out of holy Scripture composed in questions and answeres, fort he edifying and comfort of the symple Christianes, whych intende worthely to receyue the holy supper of the Lorde* ed. T[homas] C[ottesford?] ([Emden: Ctematius, 1556]).

[Micron, M.,], *Antithesen, oft, teghensettinghen, des waren Christi, ende des valschen Mischristi* (Emden: Gellius Ctematius, 1564).

[Micron, M], *Apologeticum Scriptum*, ed. Willems, W.O.R., *Is is Is? Apologeticum Scriptorum van Maarten de Kleyne na een dispuut rondom het "Nachtmael des Heren" met Joachum Westphal in Hamburg anno 1554* (PhD University for Protestant Theology Brussels, 1993).

Micron, M., *De Christlicke Ordinancien der Nederlantscher Ghemeinten te Londen (1554)*, ed. W.F. Dankbaar,K.S. VII (The Hague: Martinus Nijhoff, 1956).

Micron, M. [wrongly ascribed to], *Der grosser Catechismus* (Freyburg: Christianum Mundanum, 1563).

Micron, M., *De kleyne Cathechismus, oft Kinderleere der Duytscher Ghemeynte van Londen* ed. A.Lang, *Der Heidelberger Katechismus und vier verwandte Katechismen (Leo Jud's und Micron's kleine Katechismen, sowie die zwei Vorarheiten Ursins) mit einer historisch-theologischen Einleitung* (Leipzig: A. Deichert, 1907), 117-149.

[Micron, M.], *Een clear bewijs, van het recht gebruyck des Nachtmaels Christi, ende wat men van de Misse houden sal* ed. F. Pijper, *Bibliotheca Reformatoria Neerlandica. Geschriften uit den tijd der hervorming in de Nederlanden. Eerste deel: Polemische geschriften der Hervormingsgezinden* (The Hague: Martinus Nijhoff, 1903), 437-563.

[Micron, M.], *Een corte undersouckinghe des gheloofs (1553) inder Fassung von 1555* ed. J. Marius J. Lange van Ravenswaay in: *Reformierte*

---

1 As many of the works have been consulted in modern editions, the books are given in alphabetical order.

Bekenntnisschriften Bd. 1/3 1550-1558 (Neukirchen-Vluyn: Neukirchener Verlag, 2007), 277-294.

[Micron, M]. *Een Waerachteghe Historie, van Hoste (gheseyt Jooris) vander Katelyne, the Ghendt om het vry opentlick straffen der Afgodischer Leere, ghebrandt ten grooten nutte ende vertroostinghe aller Christenen gheschreven* ed. F. Pijper, *Bibliotheca Reformatoria Neerlandica. Geschriften uit den tijd der hervorming in de Nederlanden. Achtste deel* (The Hague: Martinus Nijhoff, 1911), 187-253.

[Micron, M.], *Een waerchtigh verhaal der t'zamensprekinghen tusschen Menno Simons ende Martinus Mikron van der menschewerdinghe Iesu Christi* ed. W.F. Dankbaar, *Documenta Anabaptistica Neerlandica III* (Leiden: Brill, 1981).

[Micron, M.,], *Eene Apologie of verantwoordinghe Martini Micron, op XX. verscheyden Artikelen die Menno Symons teghen het disputacy boecxken van het bespreck met hem ouer de leer gehouden, in druck heeft wtghegeuen* (…) (Emden: Ctematius, 1558).

[Micron, M]. & [Phrisius, V.], *Ein kort undericht voor den eenfoldigen Christen , de desz Heren Hillich Aventmahl werdiglicken willen geneten* (…) *Gedrukt na het Original van 1554* ([Emden?: Steven Mierdman?).

Micron, M. & Carineus, N., *Van de weerdicheydt, nutheydt ende noodicheyt der christelicker vergaderinghen* ([Emden: Ctematius], 1561).

Musculus, W. / Micron, M., *Een claere ende Scriftelicke onderrichtinghe vanden Eedt…waer toeghedaan is een clein anhancksel, des selven handel angaende* ([Emden: Ctematius], 1555).

Other primary sources

Augustine, A., *The City of God,* ed. Marcus Dods (Peabody: Hendrickson Publishers, 2011) [*De Civitate Dei contra Paganos*].

Bakhuizen van den Brink, J.N., *De Nederlandse belijdenisgeschriften in authentieke teksten met inleiding en tekstvergelijkingen* (Amsterdam: Ton Bolland, 1976²).

Bray, G., *The Books of Homilies: A Critical Edition* (Cambridge: James Clarke & Company, 2017).

Bullinger, H., *De scripturae sanctae authoritate, certitudine, firmitate et absoluta perfectione, deque Episcoporum, qui verbi dei ministri sunt, institutione et functione, contra superstitionis tyrannidsque Romanae antistes (…)* (Zurich: Forschauer, 1538).

Bullinger, H., *In sacrosanctum Iesu Christi Domini nostri Euangelium secundom (…)* (Zurich: Froschauer, 1542).

Bullinger, H., *Diarium*, ed. E. Egi (Basel: Basler Buch- und Antiquariatshandlung, 1904).

[Bullinger, H.], *The Decades of Heinrich Bullinger* ed. Thomas Harding (Grand Rapids: Reformation Heritage Books, 2004).

Bullinger, H. *Schriften II* ed. Barbara Braune-Krikau *et al.* (Zurich: TVZ, 2006).

[Bullinger, H.,], *Heinrich Bullinger Werke 3.3: Sermonum Decades quinque de potissimis Christianae religionis capitibus (1552) Teilband 1 & 2* ed. Peter Opitz (Zurich: TVZ, 2008).

Calvin, J. *Institutio Christianae religionis* (Geneva: Riverios, 1554).

Calvin, J., *Commentary on a Harmony of the Evangelists Matthew, Mark, and Luke. Volume 1* ed. William Pringle (Grand Rapids: Baker Books, 2005).

Catechesis religionis Christianae, quae traditur in ecclesiis et scholis palatinatus (Heidelberg: Michael Schirat & Johannes Mayer, 1563).

Catechismus ofte onderwysinge in de christelycke leere, also die in den kercken ende scholen kuervoerstelicken Paltz geleert werdt (Heidelberg: Michael Schirat, 1563).

Campi, E. & Wälchli, Ph. (eds.), *Basler Kirchenordnungen 1528-1675* (Zürich: TVZ, 2012).

[Cornelisz., A.], 'XXIX propositien van der Kercke (Stadsarchief Delft, archief 445 (Hervormde Gemeente te Delft), inv. nr. 635).

Corpus Reformatorum. Joannis Calvini Opera quae supersunt omnia XIII ed. Baum *et al.* (Brunswick: Schwetske, 1875

Dathenus, P., *De Psalmen Davids* ed. J.N. IJkel & R. van 't Spijker (Houten: Den Hertog, 1992).

'De Synoden der Nederlandsche Hervormde Kerken onder het kruis, gedurende de jaren 1563-1577, gehouden te Braband, Vlaanderen enz.' ed. N.C. Kist in: *Nederlandsch Archief voor Kerkgeschiedenis* 9 (1849), 113-210.

Die Kirchenratsprotokolle der Reformierten Gemeinde Emden 1557-1620. Teil 1: 1557-1574, ed. Schilling & Schreiber (Cologne/Vienna: Böhlau Verlag, 1989).

Een seer schoon Spel van sinnen, in: Jaarboek de Fonteine 39-40 (1989-1990), 24-94.

Epistolae ab ecclesiae Helveticae reformatoribus vel ad eos scriptae. Quibus multa Theologica, Historica, Politica, & maxime Ecclesiastica continentur ed. J.C. Füslinus (Zurich: Heidegger, 1742).

Epistolae Tigurinae de rebus potissimum ad Ecclesiae Anglicanae Reformationem, pertenibus conscriptae A.D. 1531-1558 (Cambridge: CUP, 1848)

Form der Sacramenten bruch / wie sy zů Basel gebrucht werden / mit sampt eynem kürzen kinder bericht gebessert und gemehrt (Basel: Erasmus Zymmerman, 1545).

Griffiths, J., *The Two Books of Homilies Appointed tob e Read in Churches* (Oxford: OUP, 1859).

Haemstede, A.C. van, *Geschiedenis der martelaren (...)* ed. Molenaar & Felix (Arnhem: Swaan, 1868).

Hessels, J.H., *Ecclesiae Londino-Batavum Archivum. Tomus secundus: Epistulae et tractatus cum reformationis tum ecclesiae Londino-Batavae historiam illustrantes (1544-1622)* (Cambridge: CUP, 1889).

Hooper, J., *Whether Christian Faith maye be kepte secret (...)* ([London: John Day?],1553).

[Hooper, J.], *Early Writings of John Hooper, D.D. Lord Bishop of Gloucester and Worcester. Martyr, 1555* ed. Samuel Carr (Cambridge: CUP, 1843)

[Hooper, J.], *Later Writings of Bishop Hooper, together with His Letters and Other Pieces* ed. Charles Nevinson (Cambridge: CUP, 1852).

Jud, L., *Der grössere Katechismus* ed, Oskar Farner (Zurich: Max Niehan, 1955).

Jud, L., *Der Kürzere Katechismus* ed. Oskar Farner (Zurich: Max Niehan, 1955).

Kerkeraads-Protocollen der Nederduitsche vluchtelingen-kerk te Londen 1560-1563 ed. Van Schelven (Amsterdam: Johannes Müller, 1921).

Klockhohn, A., *Briefe Friedrich des Frommen Kurfürsten von der Pfalz mit verwandten Schriftstücken. Erster Band* (Braunschweig: Schwetschke und Sohn, 1868).

Knewstub, J., *A Confutation of monstrous and horrible heresies, taught by H.N., and embraced of a number, who call themselues the Familie of Loue* (London: Thomas Dawson, 1579).

Lasco, J. à, *(...) Of het den christenen, na dien zij het word Godes ende de godlooszheit des Pauwstdoms bekent hebben, eenighszins verorloft is, dat zy sick in den Pauwstlicken godsdiensten, ende in zonderheit inder Misse, vinden laten* ([n.p.]: 1557).

Lasco, J. à, *Opera tam edita quam inedita. Volumen II* ed. Abraham Kuyper (Amsterdam: Frederic. Muller & The Hague: Martinus Nijhoff, 1866).

[Musculus, W.], *The Temporisour (...)* ([Wesel: Singleton?], 1555).

Musculus, W., *In Mosis Genesim (...) expendentur* (Basel: Johannis Hervagij. 1565).

Myone, Eutychio [= Wolfgang Musculus], *Proscaerus (...)* ([Basel.:Jakob Kündig], 1549).

[Nicolai, G.], *Gerardus Nicolai's Inlasschinghen in het vertaalde werk van Bullinger: "Teghens de Wederdoopers"* ed. S. Cramer, Bibliotheca Reformatoria Neerlandica. Zevende deel: Zestiende-eeuwsche schrijvers over de geschiedenis der oudste Doopsgezinden hier te lande (The Hague: Martinus Nijhoff, 1910), 267-487.

Niederländer Bekenntnis, London 1550/1551 ed. Andreas Mühling in: *Reformierte Bekenntnisschriften Bd. 1/3 1550-1558* (Neukirchen-Vluyn: Neukirchener Verlag, 2007), 59-77.

Original Letters Relative to the English Reformation, Written During the Reign of King Henry VIII., King Edward VI., and Queen Mary: Chiefly from the Archives of Zurich. Part 1 & 2 ed. Hastings Robinson (Cambridge: CUP, 1546-1547).

Pellikan, K., *Commentaria Biblia (...) Tomus Primus in quo continenter v. libri Mosis* ([Zurich]: Chr. Froschauer, [1536]).

Rutgers, F.L., *Acta van de Nederlandsche Synoden der zestiende eeuw* (Dordrecht: J.P. van den Tol, 1980^2).

Sehling, E., *Die evangelischen Kirchenordnungen des XVI. Jahrhunderts* 17,2,1 (Tübingen: Mohr Siebeck, 1963).

Sprengler-Ruppenthal, A., 'Die Bremer Kirchenordnung von 1534' in: *Zeitschrift der Savigny-Stiftung für Rechtsgeschichte: Kanonistische Abteilung* 82/1 (1996), 107-144.

Teghenbericht op eenen brief over een wijle ghedruckt achter een boeckxken vande wterlicke Kercke Godes, sonder den naem des autheurs, waer in hy antwoordt op een vraghe hem by een goet vriendt voorghestelt: Of hy hem soude behegeven inde Ghemeynte der Ghereformeerden etc. Aenwijsende hoe onghegrondt ende onchristelick dien raedt des Autehurs is dear mede de menschen vande wterlicke oeffeninghe der Religie afghetrocken werden, ende hoe nu ende noodich ter contrarie is datmen hem door de middelen van Godt gheordonneert beghove tot de ware sichtbare Ghemeynte Godts. Geschreven door de dienaren der Kercke Christi tot Delft (Delft: Aelbert Hendricxz., 1582).

The Johan Radermacher Sale Catalogue 1634. Libri Belgici in Octavo & Duodecimo accessed via: https://www.johanradermacher.net/catalogue/belgici-in-octavo-and-c/ (2-12-2022]).

Utenhove, J., *Kurzer, einfältiger und waarhaftiger historischer Bericht* etc ed. Bartholomeus Rhodingum (Herborn, 1608).

Utenhove, J., *Simplex et fidelis narratio de instituta ac demum dissipata Belgarum, aliorumque peregrinorum in Anglia, Ecclesia: et potissimum de susceptis posteà illius nomine itineribus, quaeque eis in illis euenerunt* ed. F. Pijper, *Bibliotheca Reformatoria Neerlandica. Negende deel* (The Hague: Martinus Nijhoff, 1912), 29-186.

Vermigli, P.M., *A briefe examination for the tyme* (London: Richard Jugge, [n.y.]).

Vermigli, M.P., *The Oxford Treatise and Disputation on the Eucharist* ed. Joseph C. McLelland (Moscow, ID: The Davenant Press, 2018).

[Vermigli, P.M.], *Ik geloof. Een eenvoudige verklaring van de Apostolische geloofsbelijdenis door Petrus Martyr Vermigli* ed. C.L. Freeke (Apeldoorn: De Banier, 2018).

Wackernagel, H. G., *Die Matrikel der Universität Basel. II. Band 1532/3-1600/01* (Basel: Verlag der Universitätsbibliothek, 1956).

Zwingli, H. *De Vera et Falsa Religione* ed. C.N. Heller, in: *The Latin Works of Huldreich Zwingli*, iii (Philadelphia, 1929).

Secondary literature

Aa, A.J. van der, *Biografisch woordenboek der Nederlanden. Twaalfde deel* (Haarlem: J.J. van Brederode, 1869).

Abels, P.H.A.M. & Wouters, A.Ph.F., *Nieuw en ongezien. Kerk en samenleving in de classis Delft en Delfland 1572-1621. Boek 2: De nieuwe samenleving* (Delft: Eburon, 1994).

Abrams, M.H. & Harpham, G.G., *A Glossary of Literary Terms. Ninth Edition* (Boston: Wadsworth Cengage Learning, 2009).

Adam, S., 'Dudley, Ambrose, earl of Warwick' in the Oxford Dictionary of National Biography [https://doi-org.access.authkb.kb.nl/10.1093/ref:odnb/8143 (2020-03-20)].

Ainslie, J.L, *The Doctrines of Ministerial Order in the Reformed Churches of the Sixteenth and Seventeenth Centuries* (Edinburgh: T&T Clark, 1940).

Albisser, A. & Opitz, P. (eds.), *Die Zürcher Reformation in Europa. Beiträge der Tagung des Instituts für Schweizerische Reformationsgeschichte 6.-8. Februar 2019 in Zürich* (Zurich: TVZ, 2021).

Alten, H.H. van, *The Beginnings of a Spirit-Filled Church. A Study of the Implications of the Pneumatology for the Ecclesiology in John Calvin's Commentary on the Acts of the Apostles* (PhD Theological University Kampen, 2017).

Alting, M., *Van der Euangelischen Reformation / der Christlicken Kercken tho Embden und in Ostfriesland (…)* (Bremen: Berendt Peters., 1594).

Andersen, N.K., 'The Reformation in Scandinavia and the Baltic' in: Elton (ed.), *The New Cambridge Modern History. Volume II*, 144-171.

Antonides, C.F.J., *dr. Jan Hendrik Gerretsen 1867-1923 "Het geluid van een sterke stem"* (Gorinchem: Narratio, 1997).

Arblaster, P. ' 'Totius Mundus Emporium': Antwerp as a Centre for Vernacular Bible Translations 1523-1545' in: Gelderblom, A-J. et al. (eds.), *The Low Countries*, 10-31.

Atherstone, A. 'Reforming Worship: Lessons from Luther to Cranmer' in: *Churchman* summer 2018, 105-122.

Baars, A., 'In God geloven en Hem beleven. Over artikel 1, 8 en 9 van de Nederlandse Geloofsbelijdenis' in: Van der Pol, *Geloofstaal*, 127-141.

Balke, W., *Calvijn en de Doperse Radikalen* (Amsterdam: Ton Bolland, 1973).

Balke, W., *Via Vitae. Opstellen over kerk en theologie in het perspectief van de Reformatie* (Apeldoorn: de Banier, 2019)

Ballor, J. & Littlejohn, W.B., 'European Calvinism: Church Discipline' in: *European History Online (EGO)*, published by the Leibniz Institute of European History (IEF), Mainz 2013-03-25. URL: http://www.ieg-ego.eu/ballorj-littlejohnw-2013-en URN: http://nbn-resolving.de/urn:nbn:de:0159-2013032507 [2021-12-24].

Bärenfänger, R., 'Die Andreas-kirche in Norden' in: Bärenfänger, R. (ed.), *Führer zu archäologischen Denkmälern*, 187-189

Bärenfänger, R. (ed.), *Führer zu archäologischen Denkmälern in Deutschland 35: Ostfriesland* (Stuttgart: Konrad Theiss, 1999).

Basch, R., ' "Agents of Reformation": Margeret Cranmer, Anne Hooper and Elizabeth Coverdale in: Crankshaw & Gross (eds.), *Reformation Reputations*, 223-253.

Becker, J., *Gemeindeordnung und Kirchenzucht. Johannes a Lascos Kirchenordnung für London (1555) und die reformierte Konfessionsbildung* (Leiden/Boston: Brill, 2007).

Becker, J., 'Migration and Confession among Sixteenth-Century Western European Reformed Christians' in: *Reformation and Renaissance Review* 13 (2011).

Behr, H-J., 'Die Exekution des Niederrheinisch-Westfälischen Kreises gegen Graf Johann von Rietberg 1556-1566' in: *Westfälische Zeitschrift* 128 (1978), 33-104.

Bekelaar, G.A.M. et al., *Richtlijnen voor het uitgeven van historische bescheiden* (Den Haag: Nederlands Historisch Genootschap, 1988).

Benedict, Ph., *Christ's Churches Purely Reformed. A Social History of Calvinism* (New Haven/London: YUP, 2002).

Beninga, E., *Volledige chronyk van Oostfrieslant: Behelsende niet alleenlik de historie van Oostfriesland, maer ook van alle Nabuirige Volkeren ten Oosten en ten Westen, besonder de allerseldsaemste Geschiedenissen van het oude en gedendaegste Friesland, zoo ten tyde des Heidendoms, als zedert het is gekristent geworden, geschreven* (Emden: Henrich Meybohm, Josua Beek en Hermannus Wolffram, 1723).

Berg, M. A. van den, *Friends of Calvin* (Grand Rapids: Eerdmans, 2009).

Bergsma, W., *Gelovigen, dominees en geleerden. Opstellen over Friese en Nederlandse geschiedenis in de vroeg-moderne tijd* (Hilversum: Verloren, 2019).

Biel, P., *Doorkeepers at the House of Righteousness. Heinrich Bullinger and the Zurich Clergy 1534-1575* (Bern: Peter Lang, 1991).

Bierma, L.D. et al., *An Introduction to the Heidelberg Catechism. Sources, History, Theology* (Grand Rapids: Baker, 2005).

Bierma, L.D., *The Theology of the Heidelberg Catechism: A Reformation Synthesis* (Louisville: Westminster John Knox Press, 2013).

Block, D.I., *For the Glory of God. Recovering a Biblical Theology of Worship* (Grand Rapids: Baker, 2014).

Blouw, P.V., *Typographia Batava 1541-1600. Repertorium van boeken gedrukt in Nederland tussen 1541 en 1600* (Nieuwkoop: De Graaf, 1998).

Blouw, P.V., *Dutch Typography in the Sixteenth Century: The Collected Works of Paul Valkema Blouw* (Leiden: Brill, 2013).

Boda, M.J., *Haggai, Zechariah* (Grand Rapids: Zondervan, 2004).

Boer, E.A. de, 'Geloof onder woorden. Over de betekenis van en het theologisch onderzoek naar belijdenis en dogma' in: *Radix* 10/2 (1984), 68-102.

Boer, E.A. de, *'Verspreid en verstrooid'. Ecclesiologie van de diaspora en de reformatie van de Lage Landen* (Kampen: Theologische Universiteit Kampen, 2016).

Boer, E.A. de, *De schele dominee. De open brief van 1966 en kerkelijke tucht in de Vrijgemaakte kerken* (Barneveld: De Vuurbaak, 2016).

Boer, E.A. de, 'Tolken bij de tijd. Over het hermenautische aspect van de kerkhistorie' in: De Bruijne & Burger (eds.), *Gereformeerde hermeneutiek vandaag*, 83-97.

Boer, E.A., '[Hubrecht Duifhuijs], *Vande wterlyke kercke Godes* [1581] en het debat over de aard van de kerk' [forthcoming].

Bolliger, D., 'Bullinger on Church Authority: The Transformation of the Prophetic Role in Christian Ministry' in: Gordon & Campi (eds.), *Architect*, 159-177.

Boonen, U. K. (ed.), *Zwischen Sprachen en culturen. Wechselbeziehungen im niederländischen, deutschen und afrikaansen Sprachgebiet* (Münster/ New York: Waxmann, 2018).

Bradley, J.E.; Muller, R.A., *Church History. An Introduction to Research Methods and Resources. Second Edition* (Grand Rapids: Eerdmans, 2016).

Braekman, E. & Boer, E.A. de (ed.), *Guido de Bres. Zijn leven, zijn belijden* (Utrecht: Kok, 2011).

Bremer, F.J., 'Knewstub [Knewstubs], John (1544-1624)', in the Oxford Dictionary of National Biography [https://doi.org/10.1093/ref:odnb/15713 (2020-03-20)].

Bremmer, R.H., *Er staat geschreven! Er is geschied! Introductie tot het leven en werk van Groen van Prinsterer als getuigend historicus* (Apeldoorn: Willem de Zwijgerstichting, 1981).

Bremmer, R.H., *Reformatie en Rebellie. Willem van Oranje, de calvinisten en het recht van opstand. Tien onstuimige jaren: 1572-1581* (Franeker: Wever, 1984).

Brink, G. van den & Höpfl, H., *Calvinism and the Making of the European Mind* (Leiden: Brill, 2014).

Brodie, B.J., *Constructing a Godly Society: The Template for a Reformed Community in the Writings of John Hooper (C.1500-1555)* (PhD University of Edinburgh, 2016).

Bruijne, A.L.Th. de, *Gereformeerde theologie vandaag* (Barneveld: De Vuurbaak, 2004).

Bruijne, A. de & Burger, H. (eds.), *Gereformeerde hermeneutiek vandaag. Theologische perspectieven* (Barneveld: De Vuurbaak, 2017).

Burnett, A. Nelson, '"It Varies from Canton to Canton": Zurich, Basel, and the Swiss Reformation' in: *Calvin Theological Journal* 44 (2009), 251-262.

Burnett, A. Nelson, *Teaching the Reformation. Ministers and Their Message in Basel, 1529-1629* (Oxford: OUP, 2009).

Burnett, A. Nelson & Campi, E. (eds.), *A Companion to the Swiss Reformation* (Leiden: Brill, 2016).

Burnett, A. Nelson, 'From Concord to Confession: The Wittenberg Concord and the Consensus Tigurinus in Historical Perspective' in: *Reformation and Renaissance Review* 18.1 (2016).

Burnett, A. Nelson, ; The Reformation in Basel' in: Burnett & Campi (eds.), *Swiss Reformation*, 170-215.

Burnett, A. Nelson, *Debating the Sacraments. Print and Authority in the Early Reformation* (New York: OUP, 2019).

Büsser, F., *Heinrich Bullinger. Leben, Werk und Wirkung. Band II* (Zurich: TVZ, 2005).

Cadegan, U.M., 'Not All Autobiography Is Scholarship' in: Fea *et al.*, *Confessing History*, 39-59.

Campi, E. & Opitz, P. (eds.), *Heinrich Bullinger: Life, Thought, Influence Volume 1* and *Volume 2* (Zurich: TVZ, 2007).

Campi, E. & Reich, R. (eds.), *Consensus Tigurinus. Heinrich Bullinger und Johannes Calvin über das Abendmahl. Werden – Wertung – Bedeutung* (Zurich: TVZ, 2009).

Campi, E., 'Consensus Tigurinus: Werden, Wertung und Wirkung' in: Campi & Reich (eds.), *Consensus Tigurinus*, 9-41.

Campi, E., 'The Consensus Tigurinus: origins, assessment, and impact' in: *Reformation & Renaissance Review* 18.1 (2016), 5-24.

Campi, E., 'The Reformation in Zurich' in: Burnett & Campi (eds.), *Swiss Reformation*, 59-125.

Campi, E., 'Theological Profile', in: Burnett & Campi (eds.), *Swiss Reformation*, 447-488.

Chappell, J.A. & Kramer, K.A. (eds.), *Women During the English Reformations. Renegotiating Gender and Religious Identity* (New York: Palgrave Macmillan, 2014).

Carter, Ch., 'The Family of Love and Its Enemies' in: *The Sixteenth Century Journal* 37/3 (2006), 651-672.

Chapman, A.; Coffey, J., Gregory, B.S. (eds.), *Seeing Things Their Way. Intellectual History and the Return of Religion* (Notre Dame, Indiana: University of Notre Dame Press, 2009).

Chung-Kim, E., *Inventing Authority. The Use of the Church Fathers in Reformation Debates over the Eucharist* (Waco: Baylor University Press, 2011).

Chung-Kim, E., 'Advocating for Poor Relief in Zurich: Heinrich Bullinger's Contribution to Religious Ideals and Policy Reforms' in: *Church History* 86/2 (2017). 311-338.

Cinnamond, A., 'The Reformed Treasures of the Parker Society' in: *Churchman* 122/3 (2008), 221-242.

Clary, I.H., *Reformed Evangelicalism and the Search for a Usable Past. The Historiography of Arnold Dallimore, Pastor-Historian* (Göttingen: Vandenhoeck & Ruprecht, 2020).

Coffey, J. & Chapman, A. 'Introduction: Intellectual History and the Return of Religion' in: Chapman, Coffey & Gregory (eds.), *Seeing Things Their Way*, 1-23

Cook, G., *Discourse* (Oxford: OUP, 1989).

Cottret, B. & Millet, O., *Calvin et la France. Bulletin de la Société de l'Histoire du Protestantisme Français* 155 (2009) (Paris: Droz, 2009).

Coigneau, 'De Evangelische leeraer: Een spel vul heresien', in: *Jaarboek de Fonteine* 39-40 (1989-1990).

Crankshaw, D.J. & Gillespie, A., 'Parker, Matthew' in: *Oxford Dictionary of National Biography* (accessed via https://doi-org.access.authkb.kb.nl/10.1093/ref:odnb/21327 [2-12-2022]).

Crankshaw, D.J. & Gross, G.W.C. (eds.), *Reformation Reputations. The Power of the Individual in English Reformation History* ([n.p.]: Palgrave Macmillan, 2021).

Cremer, U., *Norden im Wandel der Zeiten* (Norden: Heinrich Soltau, 1955).

Dalton, A.J., *John Hooper and His Networks: a Study of Change in Reformation England* (PhD University of Oxford, 2008).

Dankbaar, W.F., 'Inleiding' in: *Ord.*, 1-30.

Dankbaar, W.F., 'Introduction' in: [Micron, M.], *Een waerchtigh verhaal der t'zamensprekinghen tusschen Menno Simons ende Martinus Mikron*, VII-XXX.

Dankbaar, W.F. 'Micron (Mikron, Micronius) Marten' in: *Biografisch lexicon voor de geschiedenis van het Nederlands protestantisme. Deel 2*, 327-330.

Davies, H., *Worship and Theology in England. 1. From Cranmer to Hooker 1534-1603* (Princeton: PUP, 1970).

Decavele, J. *De dageraad van de Reformatie in Vlaanderen (1520-1565)* (Brussel: Paleis der Academiën. 1975).

Decavele, *De eerste protestanten in de Lage Landen. Geloof en Heldenmoed* (Zwolle: Waanders, 2004).

Deddens, D. & Velde, M. te, *Vrijmaking – Wederkeer. Vijftig jaar vrijmaking in beeld gebracht 1944-1994* (Barneveld: De Vuurbaak, 1994).

Deibler, E.C., *Bishop John Hooper, A Link Connecting the Reformation Thought of Ulrich Zwingli and the Zurich Tradition with the Earliest English Pietistic* (PhD Temple University, Philadelphia, 1970).

Dekker, W., *Marginaal en missionair. Kleine theologie voor een krimpende kerk* (Zoetermeer: Boekencentrum, 2011).

Demoed, V.E.M., *'Wie van gevaar houdt, moet dat met de dood bekopen': De opiniërende strategieën van de toneelschrijver Gulielmus Gnapheus (1493-1568)* (PhD Universteit van Amsterdam, 2011).

Deprez, A., *Kroniek van Dr. F.A. Snellaert* (Brugge: Orion, 1972).

Dewalque, G., 'De Cleene (Martin)' in: *Biographie Nationale 4* (Bussels: Thiry, 1873), 870-871.

Dewey, E., 'Heinrich Bullinger as Theologian: Thematic, Comprehensive, and Schematic' in: Gordon & Campi, *Architect*, 35-65.

Dickens, A.G., *The English Reformation* (London/Glasgow: Collins Fontana Press, 1971[4]).

Dickens, Ch., *David Copperfield* (New York/London/Toronto: Everyman's Library).

Douma, J. (ed.), *Oriëntatie in de theologie. Studiegids samengesteld door de hoogleraren aan de Theologische Universiteit van De Gereformeerde Kerken in Nederland te Kampen* (Groningen: De Vuurbaak, 1974).

Duke, A., 'The Reformed Churches under the Cross: extracts from the so-called Walloon Synods, 1563-1565 (accessed via: https://dutchrevolt.leiden.edu/english/sources/Pages/15631565.aspx [1-10-2021]).

Duke, A., 'Perspectives on European Calvinism' in: Pettegree, Duke & Lewis (eds.), *Calvinism in Europe*, 1-20

Duke, A. (edited by Pollmann, J. & Spicer, A.), *Dissident Identities in the Early Modern Low Countries* (Farnham/Burlington: Ashgate, 2009).

Duys-Reitsma, S.J., *Helleense Mythos* (Amsterdam: H.J. Paris, 1956).

Dijk, M. van, 'The Devotio Moderna, the Emotions and the Search for "Dutchness"' in: *BMNG – Low Countries Historical Review* 129/2 (2014), 20-41.

Ebel, J. G., 'The Family of Love: Sources of its History in England' in: *Huntington Library Quarterly* 30/4 (1967), 331-343.

Ehlers, C., *Konfessionsbildung im Zweiten Abendmahlsstreit (1552-1558/59)* (Tübingen: Mohr Siebeck, 2021).

Ehrenpreis, S., 'Hofcalvinismus und Füchtlingkirchen. Zwei Modelle Reformierter Kirchenorganisation und Politik' in: Reiss & Witt (eds.), *Calvinismus* (Dresden: Sandstein Verlag, 2009), 213-218

Eßer, R., *Niederländische Exulanten im England des 16. und frühen 17. Jahrhunderts* (Berlin: Duncker & Humblot, 1996).

Eire, C.M.N., *War Against the Idols. The Reformation of Worship from Erasmus to Calvin* (Cambridge: CUP, 1986).

Eire, C.M.N., *Reformations. The Early Modern World, 1450-1650* (Yale: YUP, 2016).

Elton, G.R. (ed.), *The New Cambridge Modern History. Volume II: The Reformation, 1520-1559 2nd Edition* (Cambridge: CUP, 1990).

Emmius, U., *Rerum Frisicarum historia (...)* (Leiden: Elzevier, 1616).

Erné & Van Dis, *De Gentse Spelen van 1539* 2 vols. (Den Haag: Martinus Nijhoff, 1982).

Euler, C., *Couriers of the Gospel: England and Zurich, 1531-1558* (Zürich: TVZ, 2006).

Fea, J. et al. (eds.), *Confessing History. Explorations in Christian Faith and the Historian's Vocation* (Notre Dame, Indiana: University of Notre Dame Press, 2010).

Fesko, J.V., *Word, Water, and Spirit: A Reformed Perspective on Baptism* (Grand Rapids: Heritage Books, 2010).

Fontaine Verwey, H. de la, 'The Family of Love' in: Quaerendo VI/3 (1976), 219-271.

Freeman, A., 'Hoax and Forgery, Whimsy and Fraud. Taxonomic Reflections on the Bibliotheca Fictiva' in: Stephens & Havens (eds.), *Literary Forgery*), 15-32

Freudenberg, M. & Siller, A., *Emder Synode 1571. Wesen und Wirkungen eindes Grundtextes der Moderne* (Göttingen: Vandenhoeck & Ruprecht, 2020).

Fulop, T.E., 'The Third Mark of the Church? – Church Discipline in the Reformed and Anabaptist Reformations' in: *The Journal of Religious History* 19/1 (1995), 26-42.

Gelderblom, A-J. et al. (eds.), *The Low Countries As a Crossroads of Religious Beliefs* (Leiden: Brill, 2004).

Geraerts, J., 'The Prosecution of Anabaptists in Holland, 1530-1566' in: *Mennonite Quarterly Review* 86/1 (2012), 5-47.

Gerretsen, J.H., *Micronius. Zijn leven, zijn geschriften, zijn geestesrichting* (Nijmegen: Ten Hoet, 1895).

Gillaerts, P. et al. (eds.), *De bijbel in de Lage Landen. Elf eeuwen van vertalen* (Heerenveen: Royal Jongbloed, 2015).

Gilmont, J-F., 'Les amis de Calvin Originaires des XVII provinces de Charles Quint' in: Cottret & Millet (eds.), *Calvin et la France*, 101-116.

Giselbrecht, R.A., 'Religious Intent and the Art of Courteous Pleasantry: A Few Letters from Englishwomen to Heinrich Bullinger (1543-1562)', in: Chappell & Kramer (eds.), *Women During the English Reformations*, 45-68.

Goldentstein, V., *Die Entstehung des Superintendentenamtes in der Reformationszeit* (Erlangen: FAU University Press, 2015).

Gootjes, N.H., *The Belgic Confession. Its History and Sources* (Grand Rapids: Baker, 2007).

Gordon, B., *Clerical Discipline and the Rural Reformation: The Synod in Zurich, 1532-1580* (Bern: Peter Lang, 1992).

Gordon, B., *The Swiss Reformation* (Manchster/New York: MUP, 2002).

Gordon, B., *Zwingli. God's Armed Prophet* (New Haven/London: YUP, 2021).

Gordon, B. & Campi, E. (eds.), *Architect of Reformation. An Introduction to Heinrich Bullinger, 1504-1575* (Grand Rapids: Baker Academic, 2004).

Gorter, P., *Gereformeerde migranten. De religieuze identiteit van Nederlandse gereformeerde migrantengemeenten in de rijkssteden Frankfurt am Main, Aken en Keulen (1555-1600)* (Hilversum: Verloren, 2021).

Graafland, G.J./Trapman, J., 'Gnapheus Guilielmus (Willem Voldersgracht, Willem van Haghen, Fullonius)' in: *Biografisch lexicon voor de geschiedenis van het Nederlands protestantisme. Deel 4*, 142-144.

Green, J, 'Public Reasoning by Historical Analogy' in: Fea, J. *et al.* (eds.), *Confessing History*, 262-279.

Gregory, B.S., 'Can We "See Things Their Way"? Should we try?' in: Chapman *et al.* (eds.), *Seeing*, 24-45.

Grell, O.P., 'Merchants and Ministers: The Foundations of International Calvinism' in: Pettegree, Duke & Lewis (eds.), *Calvinism in Europe*, 254-273

Grell, O.P., *Brethren in Christ. A Calvinist Network in Reformation Europe* (Cambridge: CUP, 2011).

Grell, O.P., 'From Popular, Evangelical Movement to Lutheran Reformation in Denmark. A Case of Two Reformations' in: *Archiv für Reformationsgeschichte* 102 (2011), 33-58.

Grochowina, N., *Indifferenz und Dissens in der Grafschaft Ostfriesland im 16. und 17. Jahrhundert* (Frankfurt: Peter Lang, 2003).

Grochowina, N., 'Confessional Indifference in East Frisia' in: *Reformation & Renaissance Review* 7.1 (2005), 111-124.

Groenewoud, H.G. 'Ethischen' in: Grosheide & Itterzon, *Christelijke Encyclopedie II*, 652.

Groen van Prinsterer, G., *Ongeloof en Revolutie* ed. H. Smitskamp (Franeker: Wever [n.d.]).

Groen van Prinsterer, G. van, *Handboek der Geschiedenis van het Vaderland* (Veenendaal: G.Kool, 1978).

Grosheide, F.W. & Itterzon, G.P van (eds.), *Christelijke Encyclopedie II* (Kampen: Kok, 1957).

Grosheide, F.W. & Itterzon, G.P. van (eds.), *Christelijke Encyclopedie V* (Kampen: Kok, 1960)

Haemers, J., 'Social Memory and Rebellion in fifteenth-century Ghent' in: *Social History* 36/4 (2011), 443-463.

Halley, J.E., 'Heresy, Orthodoxy, and the Politics of Religious Discourse: The Case of the English Family of Love' in: *Representations* 15 (1986), 98-120

Hamilton, A., *The Family of Love* (Cambridge: James Clarke & Co., 1983.

Harten-Tip, A. van, *De Dordtse Kerkorde 1619. Ontwikkeling, context, theologie* (Utrecht: KokBoekencentrum Academic, 2018).

Havens, E.A., 'Babelic Confusion: Literary Forgery and the Bibliotheca Fictiva' in: Stephens & Havens, (eds.), *Literary Forgery*, 33-73.

Hefling, Ch. & Shattuck, C. (eds.), *The Oxford Guide to The Book of Common Prayer. A Worldwide Survey* (New York: OUP, 2006).

Heide, J.W. van der, *Gellius Faber. Pastoor in Friesland, predikant in Oost-Friesland* (Amersfoort: [n.p.], 2002).

Hertog, G.C. den & Peels, H.G.L. (eds.), *Vreemdelingen en bijwoners. Opstellen rond een urgent theologisch thema* (Apeldoorn: Theologische universiteit Apeldoorn, 2012).

Hertog, G.C. den, Mulder, M.C., Spanje, T.E. van (eds.), *Acta. Bundel der gelegenheid van het afscheid van prof. dr. T.M. Hofman als hoogleraar aan de Theologische Universiteit Apeldoorn* (Heerenveen: Groen, 2015).

Heijting, W., *De catechismi en confessies in de Nederlandse Reformatie tot 1585. Deel 1: Tekst* (Nieuwkoop: De Graaf Publishers, 1989).

Heijting, W. *Profijtelijke boekskens. Boekcultuur, geloof en gewin. Historische studies* (Hilversum: Verloren, 2007).

Hofman, B., *Liedekens vol gheestich confoort. Een bijdrage tot de kennis van de zestiende-eeuwse Schriftuurlijke lyriek* (Hilversum: Verloren, 1993).

Hooft, A. van 't, *De theologie van Heinrich Bullinger in betrekking tot de Nederlandsche Reformatie* (Amsterdam: Is de Hoogh, 1888).

Hugo, V., *The Hunchback of Notre-Dame* ed. Walter J. Cobb (New York: Signet Classics, 1964/2010).

Hollweg, W., 'Bernhard Buwo, ein ostfriesischer Theologe aus dem Reformationsjahrhundert' in: *Jahrbuch der Gesellschaft für bildende Kunst und vaterländische Altertümer zu Emden* 33 (1953), 71-90.

Hollweg, W., *Der Augsburger Reichstag von 1566 und seine Bedeutung für die Entstehung der Reformierten Kirche und ihres Bekenntnisses* (Neukirchen: Neukirchener Verlag, 1964).

Huijgen, A. et al. (eds.), *Handboek Heidelbergse Catechismus* (Utrecht: Kok, 2013).

Isaac, F. 'Egidius van der Erve and His English Printed Books' in: *The Library* 4/12 (1931-1932), 336-352.

Itterzon, G.P. van, 'Jan Arentsz (de Mandemaecker) (Johannes Arnoldi)' in: *Biografisch Lexicon voor de geschiedenis van het Nederlands Protestantisme. Deel 2*, 273-275.

Itterzon, G.P. van, 'Corput (Cornput), Hendrik van den' in: *Biografisch lexicon voor de geschiedenis van het Nederlands protestantisme. Deel 3*, 83-85.

Ives, E., *Lady Jane Grey. A Tudor Mystery* (Chichester: Wiley-Blackwell, 2011).

Jaanus, H.J., *Hervormd Delft ten tijde van Arent Cornelisz (1573-1605)* (Amsterdam: Nordemann's Uitgevers Maatschappij, 1950).

Jacobs, A., *The* Book of Common Prayer. *A Biography* (Princeton: PUP, 2013).

Janse, W., 'The Protestant Reformation in the Low Countries: Developments in Twentieth-Century Historiography' in: *Reformation and Renaissance Review* 6/2(2004), 179-202.

Janssen, G.H. *The Dutch Revolt and Catholic Exile in Reformation Europe* (Cambridge: CUP, 2014/2016).

Janssen, H. E., *Gräfin Anna von Ostfriesland – eine hochadelige Frau der späten Reformationszeit (1540/42-1575). Ein beitrag zu den Anfängen der reformierten Konfessionalisierung im Reich* (Münster: Aschendorff, 1998).

Jenkins, D.L., *Whither God Brings Us. Cambridge and the Reformation Martyrs* (Attleborough: Charenton Reformed Publishing, 2018).

Johnson, C.L. et al. (eds.), *Archeologies of Confession: Writing the German Reformation, 1517-2017* (New York/Oxford: Berghahn Books, 2017).

Jones, D.F-H., 'Debating the Literal Sense in England: The Scripture-Learned and the Family of Love' in: *The Sixteenth Century Journal* 45/4 (2014), 897-920.

Jong, M.J. de, *The Church is the Means, the World is the End. The Development of Klaas Schilder's Thought on the Relationship between the Church and the World* (PhD Theological University Kampen, 2019).

Jowers, J.D., 'In What Sense Does Calvin Affirm 'Extra Ecclesiam Nulla Salus'?' in: Mannion/Borght (eds.), *Calvin's Ecclesiology*, 50-68.

Jürgens, H.P., *Johannes a Lasco in Ostfriesland. Der Werdegang eines europäischen Reformators* (Tübingen: Mohr Siebeck, 2002).

Kamphuis, J., *Kerkelijke besluitvaardigheid. Over de bevestiging van het gereformeerde kerkverband in de jaren 1574 tot 1581/2 ondanks de oppositie van het confessioneel en kerkelijk indifferentisme, zoals deze oppositie inzonderheid vanuit Leiden werd gevoerd* (Groningen: De Vuurbaak, 1970).

Kamphuis, J., *Zo vonden wij elkaar. Het begin van het Nederlandse gereformeerde kerkverband, de synode van Emden, 1571* (Groningen: De Vuurbaak, 1971).

Kamphuis, J., 'Ekklesiologie' in: Douma (ed.), *Oriëntatie in de theologie*, 88-107

Karant-Nunn, S.C., *The Reformation of Ritual. An interpretation of early modern Germany* (London/New York: Routledge, 1997).

Katerberg, W., 'The "Objectivity Question" and the Historian's Vocation' in: Fea *et al.* (eds.), *Confessing History*, 101-127.

Kim, Y., *The Identity and the Life of the Church. John Calvin's Ecclesiology in the Perspective of His Anthropology* (Eugene, Oregon: Pickwick Publications, 2014).

Kingdon, R.M. & Lambert, T.A., *Reforming Geneva. Discipline, Faith and Anger in Calvin's Geneva* (Geneva: Droz, 2012).

Knetsch, F.R.J., 'Willem Frederik Dankbaar. Amsterdam 13 september 1907-Oosterwold (Fr.) 15 januari 2001' in: *Jaarboek van de Maatschappij der Nederlandse Letterkunde* 2000-2001, 51-61.

Kooi, Ch., *Liberty and Religion: Church and State in Leiden's Reformation, 1572-1620* (Leiden: Brill, 2000).

Kooi, Ch., 'The Early Modern Low Countries', in: *Sixteenth Century Journal* 40/1 (2009), 253-255.

Kooi, Ch., *Calvinists and Catholics During Holland's Golden Age: Heretics and Idolaters* (Cambridge: CUP, 2012).

Kooi, Ch., *Reformation in the Low Countries, 1500-1620* (Cambridge: CUP, 2022).

Kozok, M. 'Untersuchungen zur Baugeschichte und Rekonstruktion der Andreaskirche in Norden' in: *Jahrbuch der Gesellschaft für bildende Kunst und vaterländische Altertümer zu Emden* 72 (1992), 19-68.

Krahn, C., 'Anabaptism in East Friesland' in: *Mennonite Quarterly Review* 30/4 (1956), 247-255.

Krahn, C., *Dutch Anabaptism. Origin, Spread, Life and Thought (1450-1600)* (The Hague: Martinus Nijhoff, 1968).

Kuhn, R., *Bekennen und Verwerfen. Westphals Ringen um Luther und Melanchthon* (Göttingen: Vandenhoeck & Ruprecht, 2019).

Kuiper, R., *Uitzien naar de zin. Inleiding tot een christelijke geschiedbeschouwing* (Leiden: J.J. Groen en zoon, 1996).

Kuipers-Sedee, M., *Chesteron, the New Atheism, and an Apologetics of Common Sense* (Leuven: Peeters, 2022).

Kwakkel, G. 'Oude Testament', in: De Bruijne (ed.), *Gereformeerde theologie vandaag* , 31-44

Lamping, A.J., 'Thysius, Antonius' in: *Bibliografisch Lexicon voor de geschiedenis van het Nederlands protestantisme. Deel 5*, 505-508.

Leaver, R., 'A Unique Broadsheet in the Scheide Library, Princeton' in: *PBSA* 83/3 (1989), 337-352.

Leeuwenberg, H., Slechte, H., Staalduine, T. van, *De Reformatie. Breuk in de Europese gescheschiedenis en cultuur* (Zutphen: Walburg Pers, 2017).

Lieburg, F. van, 'Dynamics of Dutch Calvinism: Early Modern Programs for Further Reformation' in: Brink & Höpfl (eds.), *Calvinism*, 43-66.

Lindeboom, J, *Austin Friars. Geschiedenis van de Nederlandse Hervormde Gemeente te Londen 155-1950* (The Hague: Martinus Nijhoff, 1950).

Lindsay, M., 'Thomas Cranmer and the *Book of Common Prayer*: Theological Education, Liturgy, and the Embodiment of Prosper's Dictum' in: *Colloquium* 47/2 (2015), 195-207.

Loach, J. (edited by George Bernard & Penry Williams), *Edward VI* (New Haven/London: YUP, 1999).

Loewenstein, D. & Marshall, J., *Heresy, Literature and Politics in Early Modern English Culture* (Cambridge: CUP, 2006).

Louis, C., 'Kunstschätze der Gesellschaft. II. Zwei Zeichnungen der Norder Andreaskirche. Versuch einer Rekonstruktion' in: *Jahrbuch der Gesellschaft für bildende Kunst und vaterländische Altertümer zu Emden* 25 (1937), 146-158

Maag, K., 'Schools and Education, 1500-1600' in: Burnett & Campi (eds.), *Swiss Reformation*, 520-541.

MacCulloch, D., *Thomas Cranmer. A Life* (New Haven/London: YUP, 1996).

MacCulloch, D. *Tudor Church Militant. Edward VI and the Protestant Reformation* ([n.p.] Penguin Books, 2001).

Mannion, G. & Borght, E. van der (eds.), *John Calvin's Ecclesiology. Ecumenical Perspectives* (London/New York: Bloomsbury T&T Clark, 2013).

Mannion, G. 'Calvin and the Church: Trajectories for Ecumenical Engagement Today – Volume Introduction' in: Mannion, G. & Borght, E. van der (eds.), *John Calvin's Ecclesiology. Ecumenical Perspectives* (London/New York: Bloomsbury T&T Clark, 2013), 1-30.

Marnef, G., *Antwerpen in de tijd van de Reformatie. Ondergrond protestantisme in een handelsmetropool 1550-1577* (DBNL, 2007 (ebook of the original published by Amsterdam: Meulenhoff/Antwerpen:Kritak, 1996)).

Marnef, G. 'Erasmus of Rotterdam and the Protestant Reformation' in: *Erasmus Studies* 36 (2016), 35-52.

Marsh, Ch. W., *The Family of Love in English Society, 1550-1630* (Cambridge: CUP, 1994).

Marsh, Ch., '"Godlie matrons" and "loose-bodied dames": heresy and gender in the Family of Love' in: Loewenstein & Marshall (eds.), *Heresy, Literature and Politics*, 59-81.

Marshall, P., *Heretics and Believers. A History of the English Reformation* (New Haven/London: YUP, 2017).

Martin, J.W., 'Elizabethan Familists and English Separatism' in: *Journal of British Studies* 20/1 (1980), 53-73.

Meiners, E., *Oostvrieschlandts kerkelyke geschiedenisse (…)* 2 vols. (Groningen: Laurens Groenewout en Harmannus Spoormaker, 1738-1739).

Mönckeberg, C.V., *Joachim Westphal und Johannes Calvin* (Hamburg: Gustav Eduard Nolte, 1865).

Moser, Ch., *Die Dignität des Ereignisses. Studien zu Heinrich Bullingers Reformationsgeschichtsschreibung* (Leiden/Boston: Brill, 2012).

Moss, J.D., 'The Family of Love and its Critics' in: *The Sixteenth Century Journal* 6/1 (1975), 35-52.

Müller, J., *Exile Memories and the Dutch Revolt. The Narrated Diaspora, 1550-1750* (Leiden/Boston: Brill, 2016).

Müller, J., 'Eine Reformation der Flüchtlinge? Konfessionsmigranten under der Einfluss des Rheinischen Exils auf die religiöse Landschaft der nördlichen Niederlande' in: Pohle, Samp & Roebers (eds.), *Das Ringen um den rechten Glauben*, 62-73.

Müller, J., 'From diaspora to "imagined minority". Memories of persecution and the cross-generational transformation of Protestant migrant networks in early modern Europe' in: *Diasporas* 31 (2018), 21-34.

Muylaert, S., *Shaping the Stranger Churches. Migrants in England and the Troubles in the Netherlands, 1547-1585* (Leiden/Boston: Brill, 2020).

Nauta, D., *Twee geschirften uit de begintijd van de Gereformeerde Kerk in Nederland* (Amsterdam: Buijten & Schipperheijn, 1974).

Nauta, D., 'Dathenus (Daten, Daete, Daets), Petrus (Pieter)' in *Biografisch Lexicon voor de geschiedenis van het Nederlands protestantisme. Deel 4*,110-114

Nauta, D. 'Gellius Faber de Bouma' in: *Biografisch lexicon van de geschiedenis van het Nederlands protestantisme. Deel 2*, 90-91.

Nauta, D. 'Rutgers' in: Grosheide & Itterzon, *Christelijke Encyclopedie V* , 696-697.

Norwood, F.A., 'London Dutch Refugees in Search of a Home' in: *American Historical Review* 58/1 (1952), 64-72.

Null, A., *Thomas Cranmer's Doctrine of Repentance. Renewing the Power to Love* (Oxford: OUP, 2000).

Oberman, H.A. [edited by Donald Weinstein], *The Two Reformations: The Journey from the Last Days to the New World* (New Haven: YUP, 2003).

Oberman, H.A. [edited by Peter A. Dykema], *John Calvin and the Reformation of the Refugees* (Geneva: Droz, 2009).

Onstenk, A.J., 'Alting, Menso' in *Biografisch Lexicon voor de geschiedenis van het Nederlands Protestantisme. Deel 2*, 26-27.

Op 't Hof, W.J., 'Panneel, Michaël' in: *Biografisch Lexicon voor de geschiedenis van het Nederlands Protestantisme. Deel 3*, 291.

Opitz, P., *Heinrich Bullinger als Theologe. Eine Studie zu den <<Dekaden>>* (Zurich: TVZ, 2004).

Opitz, P., *Ulrich Zwingli. Prophet, Ketzer, Pionier des Protestantismus* (Zürich: TVZ, 2015).

Opitz, P., *Zwinglis Thesen von 1523 als Manifest christlicher Freiheit*, lecture at the 13th International Emder Tagung *Freiheit im reformierten Protestantismus: Konzepte – Praktike – Diskurse* (2023).

Overell, M.A., 'Vergerio's Anti-Nicodemite Propaganda and England, 1574-1558' in: *Journal of Ecclesiastical History* 51/2 (2000), 296-318.

Paas, S., *Vreemdelingen en priesters. Christelijke missie in een postchristelijke samenleven* (Zoetermeer: Boekencentrum, 2015).

Pastoor, Ch. & Johnson, G.K., *Historical Dictionary of the Puritans* (Lanham/Toronto/Plymouth: The Scarecrow Press, 2007).

Pasquarello III, M., *God's Ploughman. Hugh Latimer: a "Preaching Life" (1485-1555)* (Milton Keynes: Paternoster, 2014).

Pelikan, J., *The Christian Tradition. A History of the Development of Doctrine. 1 The Emergence of the Catholic Tradition (100-600)* (Chicago/London: The University of Chicago Press, 1971).

Pettegree, *Foreign Protestant Communities in Sixteenth-Century London* (Oxford: OUP, 1986).

Pettegree, A. 'The London Exile Community and the Second Sacramentartian Controversy, 1553-1560' in: *Archiv für Reformationsgeschichte* 78 (1987), 223-252.

Pettegree, A., 'The Struggle for an Orthodox Church: Calvinists and Anabaptists in East Friesland, 1554-1578' in: *Bulletin of the John Rylands University Library* 70/3 (1988), 45-59.

Pettegree, *Emden and the Dutch Revolt. Exile and the Development of Reformed Protestantism* (Oxford: OUP, 1992).

Pettegree, A., Duke A., & Lewis, G. (eds.), *Calvinism in Europe, 1540-1620* (Cambridge: CUP, 1996).

Pettegree, A & Walsby, M. (eds.), *Netherlandish Books. Books Published in the Low Countries and Dutch Books Printed Abroad before 1601* (Leiden/Boston: Brill, 2011).

Pinkster, H., *Woordenboek Latijn/Nederlands* (Amsterdam: AUP, 2014[6]).

Plasger, G., 'The Dynamics of the Reformed Reformation: German Reformed Church Orders in the 16th Century' in: Brink & Höpfl (eds.), *Calvinism*, 67-75.

Pocock, J.G.A., *Political Thought and History. Essays on Theory and Method* (Cambridge: CUP, 2009).

Pohle, F., Samp, J. & Roebers, C. (eds.), *Das Ringen um den rechten Glauben. Reformation und Konfessionaliserung zwischen Maas und Rhein. Beitrage zur Tagung Aachen 21./22. April 2017* (Aachen: Centre Charlemagne, 2017).

Pol, F. van der, 'Kerkgeschiedenis', in: De Bruijne (ed.), *Gereformeerde theologie vandaag*, 73-82.

Pol, F. van der, *Mosterzaad in ballingschap. Over christelijke identiteit en geloofrepressie in de Nederlanden. Het Cleyn Mostertzaet (1590). Auteur, facetten, tekstuitgave* (Kampen: Kok, 2007), 15-43.

Pol, F. van der (ed.), *Geloofstaal trekt haar spoor. 450 jaar Nederlandse Geloofsbelijdenis* (Utrecht: Kok, 2012).

Pol, F. van der, 'De vroege receptie van de *Confession Belgica* in Nederland' in: Van der Pol, *Geloofstaal*, 71-86.

Pol, F. van der, 'De receptie van de Heidelbergse Catechismus in de noordelijke Nederlanden' in: Huijgen *et al.* (eds.), *Handboek Heidelbergse Catechismus*, 123-133.

Ponsteen, H.J., 'Hooft, Antonius van 't' in: *Biografisch Lexicon voor de geschiedenis van het Nederlands Protestantisme. Deel 4*, 215.

Post, R.R., *The Modern Devotion. Confrontation with Reformation and Humanism* (Leiden: Brill, 1968).

Poythress, D., *Reformer of Basel. The Life, Thought, and Influences of Johannes Oecolampadius* (Grand Rapids: RHB, 2011).

Primus, J.H., *The Vestments Controversy. An Historical Study of the Earliest Tensions within the Church of England in the Reigns of Edward VI and Elizabeth I* (Kampen: Kok, 1960).

Pijper, F., *Jan Utenhove. Zijn leven en zijne werken* (Leiden: Adriani, 1883).

Pijper, F., 'Inleiding' in: *SFN*, 3-28.

Rauhaus, A., *Untersuchungen zur Entstehung, Gestaltung und Lehre des Kleinen Emder Katechismus vond 1554* (PhD thesis University of Göttingen, 1977).

Reershemius, A., *Ostfrieslandisches Prediger-Denkmal. Oder, Verzeichnis der Prediger welche seit der Reformation den Evangelisch-Lutherischen Gemeinen im Ostfries- und Harlinger Lande Evangelium von Christo verkündiget haben* (Aurich: J. Gottlob Luschkn, 1765).

Reformation & Renaissance Review 18/1 (2016) *Reformation Debates over the Lord's Supper (1536-1560): Sources and Impact of the Consensus Tigurinus.*

Rehm, G. (ed.), *Adel, Reformation und Stadt am Niederrhein* (Bielefeld: Verlag für Regionalgeschichte, 2009).

Reiss, A. & Witt, S. (eds.), *Calvinismus. Die Reformierten in Deutschland und Europa* (Dresden: Sandstein Verlag, 2009).

Reitemeier, A., 'Zur Einführung der Reformation in Norddeutschland' in: *Jahrbuch der Gesellschaft für niedersächsische Kirchengeschichte* 114 (2016), 7-33.

Reitemeier, A., *Reformation in Norddeutschland. Gottvertrauen zwischen Fürstenherrschaft und Teufelsfurcht* (Göttingen: Wallstein Verlag, 2017).

Reu, J.M., *Quellen zur Geschichte des kirchlichen Unterrichts in der evangelischen Kirche Deutschlands zwischen 1530 und 1600. 1/3,1b* (Hildesheim/New York: Georg Olm, 1976).

Reuver, A. de, 'Verlangen naar het Vaderhuis' in: *Reformatorisch Dagblad* 25-12-2022 (accessed via: https://www.rd.nl/artikel/956507-verlangen-naar-het-vaderhuis [30-9-2022]).

Ritter, F., 'Zur Geschichte des Norder Kirchenstreits vom Jahre 1554' in:*Jahrbuch der Gesellschaft für bildende Kunst und vaterländische Altertümer zu Emden* 22 (1927), 329-342.

Rodgers, D.W., *John à Lasco in England* (New York: Peter Lang, 1994).

Roeling, J., 'Schelven, Aart Arnout van' in: *Biografisch Lexicon voor de geschiedenis van het Nederlands Protestantisme. Deel 2*, 387-389.

Rosendale, T., *Liturgy and Literature in the Making of Protestant England* (Cambridge: CUP, 2007).

Ross, D.S., *The Role of John Hooper in the Religious Controversies of the Reign of Edward VI in England* (PhD The University of Iowa, 1968).

Rutgers, *Calvijns invloed op de Reformatie in de Nederlanden voor zooveel die door hemzelven is uitgeoefend* (Leiden: Donner, 1899).

Schaeffer, H., *Kerk om te vieren* (Kampen: Summum, 2020).

Schatorjé, J.M.W.C., 'Faber en Venlo. Engelbert Faber en de Reformatie in Venlo (1565-1580)' in: *Venlo's Mozaïek. Hoofdstukken uit zeven eeuwen stadsgeschiedenis* (Maastricht, 1990), 113-142.

Schatorjé, J.W.M.C., 'Das erste Buch des Reformators Engelbert Faber aus Gustorf' in: Rehm (ed.), *Adel, Reformation und Stadt am Niederrhein*, 133-168.

Schatorjé 'Engelbert Faber en de Duitse vertaling van het laatste boek van Martin Micron (Heidelberg, 1563)' in: Boonen (ed.), *Zwischen Sprachen en culturen*, 19-31.

Schelven, A.A. van, *De Nederduitsche Vluchtelingenkerken der XVIe eeuw in Engeland en Duitschland in hunne beteekenis voor de Reformatie in de Nederlanden* (The Hague: Martinus Nijhoff, 1908).

Schelven, A.A. van, 'Backerel' in: *Nieuw Nederlandsch Biografisch Woordenboek. Deel 2*, 57-58.

Schelven, A.A. van, 'Dyrkinus' in: *Nieuw Nederlandsch Biografisch Woordenboek. Deel 4*, 547-550.

Schelven, A.A. van, 'Hermannus Brassius' in: *Nieuw Nederlandsch Biografisch woordenboek. Deel 1*, 454.

Schelven, A.A. van, *Wegkruisinging in het landschap der theorie van de geschiedschrijving* (Amsterdam: W. ten Have N.V., 1953).

Schilder, K., 'F.Q.I.' in: *Almanak van het corpus studiosorum in Academia Campensi "Fides Quadrat Intellectum" 1951* (Kampen: Zalsman, 1951), 72-84.

Schilling, H., 'Innovation through Migration: The Settlements of Calvinistic Netherlanders in Sixteenth- and Seventeenth-Century Central and Western Europe' in: *Social History* 16/31 (1983), 7-33.

Schilling, H., 'Johannes a Lasco und Ostfriesland. Eine europäische Beziehungsgeschichte am Vorabend der Konfessionaliserung' in: Strohm (ed.), *Johannes a Lasco (1499-1560)*, 1-20.

Schilling, H. 'Calvin und die calvinistische Konfessionskultur' in: *Geschichte im Wissenschaft und Unterricht* 7/8 (2009), 372-386.

Schilling, H., 'Christliche und Jüdische Minderheitsgemeinden im Vergleich: Calvinistische Exulanten und westliche Diaspora der Sephardim im 16. und 17. Jahrhundert' in: *Zeitschirft für Historische Forschung* 36/3 (2009), 407-444.

Schipper, I., *Across the borders of belief. Netherlandish Reformed migrants and confessional boundaries in the duchy of Cleves, c. 1550-1600* (PhD VU Amsterdam, 2020).

Scholz, M.M., *Strange Brethren. Refugees, Religious Bonds, and Reformation in Frankfurt 1554-1608* (Charlottesville and London: University of Virginia Press, 2022).

Schreiber, T., *Petrus Dathenus und der Heidelberger Katechismus. Eine traditionsgeschichtliche Untersuchung zum konfessionellen Wandel in der Kurpfalz um 1563* (Göttingen: Vandenhoeck & Ruprecht, 2017).

Schwarz Lausten, M. (translated by Frederick H Cryer), *A Church History of Denmark* (London/New York: Routledge, 2002).

Selderhuis, H.J. (ed.), *Handboek Nederlandse Kerkgeschiedenis* (Kampen: Kok, 2006).

Selderhuis, H.J., 'A Teachable Death: Doctrine and Death in Marten Micron's Martyrology' in: *Unio Cum Christo* 1/1-2 (2015), 119-131.

Selderhuis, H.J., "Scheepke van Christus' in vreemde haven. De betekenis van Emden voor het Nederlandse calvinisme' in: Hertog, Mulder, Spanje (eds.), *Acta. Bundel der gelegenheid van het afscheid van prof. dr. T.M. Hofman*, 328-337.

Selderhuis, H. (ed.), *Handboek gereformeerd kerkrecht* (Heerenveen: Groen, 2019).

Selderhuis, H., '1.a. Kerkorde, kerkrecht en kerkverband' in: Selderhuis, (ed.), *Handboek Gereformeerd kerkrecht*, 11-14.

Selderhuis, H.J. & Nissen, P., 'De zestiende eeuw' in: Selderhuis (ed.), *Handboek Nederlandse Kerkgeschiedenis*, 215-496.

Sikkel, J.C., *De Heilige Schrift en haar verklaring. Inleiding tot de verklaring der Heilige Schrift als het Woord Gods* (Amsterdam: J.W.A. Schaik, 1906).

Skinner, Q., *Visions of Politics I: Regarding Method* (Cambridge: CUP, 2002).

Smid, M., *Ostfriesische Kirchengeschichte* (Pewsum, 1974).

Smid, M. 'Reershemius, Fam..' in: *Biographisches Lexikon für Ostfriesland IV* (Aurich, 2007), 348-350.

Speelman, H., '2.c.2. Calvijn' in: Selderhuis (ed.), *Handboek gereformeerd kerkrecht*, 104-125.

Spierling, K.E., *Infant Baptism in Reformation Geneva. The Shaping of a Community, 1536-1564* (Aldershot: Ashgate, 2005).

Spohnholz, J., 'Invented Memories. The Convent of Wesel and the Origins of German and Dutch Calvinism' in: Johnson *et al.* (eds.), *Archeologies of Confession*, 284-303

Spohnholz, J., *The Convent of Wesel. The Event that Never was and the Invention of Tradition* (Cambridge: CUP, 2017/2020).

Spohnholz, J., 'Exile Experiences and the Transformations of Religious Cultures in the Sixteenth Century: Wesel, London, Emden, and Frankenthal' in: *Journal of Early Modern Christianity* 6/1 (2019), 43-67.

Spohnholz, J. & Veen, M.G.K. van, 'The Disputed Origins of Dutch Calvinism: Religious Refugees in the Historiography of the Dutch Reformation' in: *Church History. Studies in Christianity and Culture* 86/2 (2017), 398-426.

Spohnholz, J. & Waite, G. (eds.), *Exile and Religious Identity, 1500-1800* (London: Pickering & Chatto, 2014).

Springer, M.S., *Restoring Christ's Church. John a Lasco and the* Forma ac ratio (Aldershot: Ashgate, 2007).

Spijker, W. van 't, '2.c.1. Luther, Zwingli en Bucer' in: Selderhuis, *Handboek gereformeerd kerkrecht*, 91-103.

Stephens, W. & Havens, E.A. (eds.), *Literary Forgery in Early Modern Europe, 1450-1800* (Baltimore: John Hopkins UP, 2018).

Stephens, W. & Havens, E.A., 'Forgery's Valhalla' in: Stephens & Havens (eds.), *Literary Forgery*, 1-14.

Stephens, W.P., *Zwingli. An Introduction to his Thought* (Oxford: OUP, 1992).

Strohm, Ch. (ed.), *Johannes a Lasco (1499-1560). Polnischer Baron, Humanist und europäischer Reformator.* (Tübingen: Mohr Siebeck, 2000).

Strohm, Ch., 'Politiek, kerk en universiteit in de ontstaanstijd van de Heidelbergse Catechismus' in: Huijgen *et al.* (eds.), *Handboek Heidelbergse Catechismus*, 49-60.

Sturm, K., *Die Theologie Peter Martyr Vermiglis während seines ersten Aufenthalts in Straßburg 1542-1547* (Neukirchen-Vluyn: Neukirchener Verlag, 1971).

Sweertius, F., *Athanae Belgicae* (Antwerp: Gulielmum a Tungris, 1628).

Tamminga, K.S., *Receiving the Gifts of Every Member. A Practical Ecclesiological Case Study on Inclusion and the Church* (PhD Theological University Kampen, 2020).

Tanis, J. 'East Friesland and the Reformed Reformation' in: *Calvin Theological Journal* 26 (1991), 313-349.

Taylor, R.A. & Clendenden, E. R., *Haggai, Malachi* (Nashville: B&H, 2004).

Terpstra, N., *Religious Refugees in the Early Modern World. An Alternative History of the Reformation* (Cambridge: CUP, 2015).

Thysius, A., *Leere ende order der Nederlandsche, soo Duytsche als Walsche, Ghereformeerder kerkcken 1: Corpus Doctrinae (…)* (Amsterdam: Pieter Pietersz, 1615),

Tielke, *Dat Rätsel der Emder Buchdrucks (1554-1602)*, (Aurich: Verlag der Ostfriesischen Landschaft, 1986).

Tielke, M., 'Gillis van der (Ctematius, Aegidius) Erven', in: *Biographisches Lexikon für Ostfriesland I* (Aurich, 1993), 131-133.

Timmerman, D., *Heinrich Bullinger on Prophecy and the Prophetic Office (1523-1538)* (Göttingen: Vandenhoeck & Ruprecht: 2015).

Vallejo, I, *Papyrus. Een geschiedenis van de wereld in de boeken* ed. Adri Boom (Amsterdam: Meulenhoff, 2021).

Van Engen, J., *Sisters and Brothers of the Common Life. The Devotio Moderna and the World of the Later Middle Ages* (University of Pennsylvania Press, 2008).

Veen, M. van, '*Verschooninghe van de roomsche afgoderye'. De polemiek van Calvijn met nicodemieten, in het bijzonder met Coornhert* (unpubl. PhD thesis VU Amsterdam, 2001).

Veen, M. van, *Dirck Volckertszn Coornhert* (Kampen: Kok, 2009).

Veen, M. van, '"…wir sind ständig unterwegs…": Reformierte Flüchtlinge des 16. Jahrhunderts als Exulanten?' in:Archif für die Reformationsgeschichte 109 (2018), 442-458.

Veen, M.G.K. van & Spohnholz, J., 'Calvinists vs. Libertines: A New Look at Religious Exile and the Origins of 'Dutch' Tolerance' in: Brink & Höpfl, *Calvinism*, 76-99.

Vind, A. & Selderhuis, H.J. (eds.), *'Church' at the Time of the Reformation. Invisible Community, Visible Parish, Confession, Building…?'* (Göttingen: Vandenhoeck & Ruprecht, 2021).

Vis, G.N.M, *Jan Arentsz, de mandenmaker van Alkmaar, voorman van de Hollandse reformatie* (Hilversum: Verloren, 1992).

Vis, G.N.M., *Cornelis Cooltuyn (1526-1567). De vader van de Hollandse reformatie* (Hilversum: Verloren, 1995).

Visser, P., ' "A Lasco wedder uns" A Lasco und die Täufer und Nonkonformisten' in: Strohm (ed.), *Johannes a Lasco (1499-1560)*, 299-313.

Voβ, K-D & Wolfgang, J. (eds.), *Menso Alting und seine Zeit* (Oldenburg: Florian Isensee, 2012).

Vries, W.G. de, 'De geschiedenis van de kerken na de Vrijmaking in hoofdlijnen' in: Deddens & Velde (eds.), *Vrijmaking – Wederkeer*, 129-151.

Waardt, J.H.M. de, 'Justus Velsius Haganus: An erudite but rambling prophet' in: Spohnholz & Waite (eds.), *Exile and Religious Identity*, 97-109 & 223-227.

Wabuda, S. *Preaching During the English Reformation* (Cambridge: CUP, 2002).

Wandel, L. Palmer, *The Eucharist in the Reformation. Incarnation and Liturgy* (Cambridge: CUP, 2006).

Waterschoot, W., *Schouwende Fantasye* (Gent: Academia Press, 2002).

Weerda, J.R., *Der Emder Kirchenrat und seine Gemeinde. Ein Beitrag zur Geschichte reformierter Kirchenordnung in Deutschland, ihrer Grundsätze und ihrer Gestaltung* ed. Matthias Freudenberg & Alasdair Heron (Wuppertal: Foedus, 2000).

Wendt, H.T., 'What Does It Mean to Be a Reformed Church Historian?' Unio Cum Christo [forthcoming].

Werner, S., *Studying Early Printed Books 1450-1800. A Practical Guide* (Chichester: Wiley Blackwell, 2019).

White, R., 'Calvin, The Nicodemites and the Cost of Discipleship' in: *The Reformed Theological Review* 56 (1997), 14-27.

Willems, W.O.R., *Met Maarten de Kleyne aan het avondmaal* (Licentiate-thesis University for Protestant Theology Brussels, 1980).

Willems, W.O.R., *Is is Is? Apologeticum Scriptorum van Maarten de Kleyne na een dispuut rondom het "Nachtmael des Heren" met Joachim Westphal in Hamburg anno 1554* (PhD University for Protestant Theology Brussels, 1993).

Wilson, R.P., *John Hooper and the English Reformation under Edward VI, 1547-1553* (PhD Queen's University, Kingston Ontario, 1994).

Winship, M.P., 'Weak Christians, Backsliders, and Carnal Gospelers: Assurance of Salvation and the Pastoral Origins of Puritan Practical Divinity in the 1580's' in: *Church History* 70/3 (2001), 462-481.

Woltjer, J.J., *Op weg naar tachtig jaar oorlog. Het verhaal van de eeuw waarin ons land ontstond* ([n.p.] Uitgeverij Balans, 2012²).

Woo, K.J., 'The House of God in Exile: Reassesing John Calvin's Approach to Nicodemism in Quatre sermons (1552)' in: *Church History and Religious Culture* 95/2-3 (2015), 222-244.

Woo, K.J., *Nicodemism and the English Calvin, 1544-1584* (Leiden: Brill, 2019).

Wood, A., *The 1549 Rebellions and the Making of Early Modern England* (Cambridge: CUP, 2007).

Wood, J.D., *Reforming the Priesthood in Reformation Zurich. Heinrich Bullinger's End-Times Agenda* (Göttingen: Vandenhoeck & Ruprecht, 2019).

Woude, C. van der, 'Lydius, Martinus' in: *Biografisch Lexicon voor de geschiedenis van het Nederlands Protestantisme. Deel 1*, 146-148.

Wouters, A.Ph.F. & Abels, P.H.A.M., *Nieuw en ongezien. Kerk en samenleving in de classis Delft en Delfland 1572-1621. Boek 1: De nieuwe kerk* (Delft: Eburon, 1994).

Zijlstra, S., 'Anabaptists, Spiritualists and the Reformed Church in East Frisia' in: *Mennonite Quarterly Review* 75/1 (2001), 57-73

Zwaag, K. van der, 'De Magnalia Deï. Groen van Prinsterer als historicus' in: Groen van Prinsterer, *Handboek der Geschiedenis van het Vaderland*, [no pagenumbers])

Images

Front cover: Marten Claessen Eelking (1579-1640) (?), 1618. Provided by the *Ostfriesisches Landesmuseum Emden*.

Image 1-5 taken from the high-quality scan provided by Ghent University Library.

Maps provided by Buro Glaap Cartografie en Vormgeving.

Appendix A: Schedule of Contents *Van de weerdicheydt, nutheydt ende noodicheyt der christelicker vergaderinghen*

- Chapter 1: How good, useful and necessary it is that one joins a visible congregation. [3v]
    - Biblical-theological evidence that God wanted a church throughout history. [3v] Old Testament examples. [3v]
        - Paradise.
        - Post-lapsarian; pre-diluvian.
        - Noah.
        - Babel.
        - Abraham.
        - Egypt and Israel.
        - Post-exilic.
    - New Testament examples.[8v]
        - Jesus Christ.
            - Word.
            - Sacraments.
            - Christian discipline.
        - Images used in the New Testament.
            - King & kingdom.
            - House.
            - Bread.
            - Vine.
            - Flock.
            - Body.
    - Biblical-theological evidence that the godly honoured and rebuilt the congregation. [14r]
        - Old Testament examples. [14v]
            - Abel.
            - Noah.
            - Patriarchs.
            - Pre-exilic period (including Tobit).
            - Exilic and post-exilic.
            - New Testament examples.

- Apostles.
    - Matthias.
    - Paul.
- The benefits (*nutheden*) of the Christian congregation. [17r]
    - Word. [17v]
    - Sacraments. [20r]
    - Christian discipline. [21r]
    - [Three][1] examples of the benefits of the Christian congregation. [22r]
        - Kingdom.
        - Corn.
        - Flock.
        - Body (in combination with wedding).
    - All bodies and groups come together. [24v]

- Chapter 2: The Marks of the True Church. [25v]
    - Introduction: What not to look for. [25v]
    - Doctrine. [26v]
        - God. [27r]
            - The Father.
            - The Son.
            - The Holy Spirit (including devotion to God).
        - Man. [28r]
            - Misery.
            - Salvation.
            - Mortification / thankfulness.
            - Eternal life and last judgment.
    - Governance. [28v]
        - Word.
        - Sacraments.
        - Christian Discipline.

---

1 This is one of the clearest examples that the book needed brushing up before being published. In the 'heading' three examples are mentioned: kingdom, house and family. In the exposition Micron discusses four examples: kingdom, corn, flock, body (in combination with wedding).

- Chapter 3: May a Christian Leave the Church of Rome? [30r/v²]
    - The many errors in the Roman Church. [31r]
        - In general. [31r]
            - Human tradition.
            - They slander Christ's sacrifice.
            - They slander Christ's office.
        - The entire governance of the church is torn to shreds. [33r]
            - Word. [33v]
            - Sacraments. [35r]
                - Baptism. [35r]
                - Lord's Supper. [35v]
                - The other five so-called sacraments. [38v]
        - Christian Discipline.(?)³ [42r]
    - Conclusion: A Christian must leave the church of Rome. [45r]
        - Biblical-theological examples and commandments to leave. [45v]
            - Paul.
            - Patriarchs.
            - Moses.
            - Tobit.
            - Elijah and Elisha.
            - Exile.
            - Maccabees.
            - New Testament.
        - Grace in secession and persecution. [48v]
            - Abraham.
            - Ruth.
    - Counter-arguments and answers. [49v-67v]

---

2 The chapter title is on 30r whereas the actual chapter starts on 30v.
3 Micron does not actually say that he discusses church discipline here. He switches from the five Roman sacraments to how the Roman Catholic Church allows for sin and uncertainty in everyday life. Because he was going to discuss how the governance of the church was being torn apart one would expect a paragraph on Christian discipline. This seems the most obvious place to let it start, though it could also start one page later after Micron has addressed the issue of purgatory. This is another example that the manuscript was not finished.

- Chapter 4: After Leaving the Church of Rome it is Necessary to Join a Public or Secret Meeting of the Christian Congregation. [67v]
    - Biblical-theological examples. [67v]
        - Israel in the desert.
        - Post-exilic temple.
        - Christ.
        - The apostles.
    - Admonition to join the church. [68v]
    - Counsel: what should one do when there is no congregation? [69v]
        - Leave city/country to join one.
        - Start a secret meeting.
    - Counter arguments to leaving the city/country and answers. [70r-93v]

-- Here ends the original manuscript. The remainder of the book was written by Nicolaus Carinaeus --

- Continues the answers to counter-arguments, yet switches from general counter-arguments to David Joris and the Family of Love. [93v]
- ¶ [New sub-chapter][4] On the Secret Meetings in Papist Lands. [100r]
    - Counter-arguments and answers. [100r-110v]
- ¶ [New sub-chapter] How One Should Start and Maintain (*aenrichten ende oock onderhouden*) the Secret Meetings. [110v/111r]
    - Is there a church which may yet be reformed? [111r]
    - Call a Minister of the Word. [112v]
    - The practical issues of conducting the meetings. [113v]
    - In case of imprisonment. [115v]
    - Against the Anabaptists [115v]
    - Admonitions to several groups. [118r]

---

4 It looks like Carinaeus felt constrained to stay loyal to the four chapters outlined in the foreword, yet felt a need to impose his own structure on the last part of the book. The German translation has, quite sensibly, created two new chapters.

Appendix B: Edition of *Van de weerdicheydt, nutheydt ende noodicheyt der christelicker vergaderinghen*

Method

In 1988 the Dutch Historical Society published the guidelines for the publication of historical texts.[1] In this text two methods of presenting the text are outlined: The critical method and the diplomatic method. The critical method aims at legibility to unlock the contents of the text. The diplomatic method aims at precise transcription for the purpose of linguistic study. Not surprisingly, one can also choose a mixed method. Though the aim of this publication is to enable the reader access to Micron's ecclesiology, we have decided to use a mixed method. This is, in part, because language and content cannot easily be separated. Moreover, it brings us closer to the environment and culture of Micron and his readers. Our aim is to come as close to Micron as possible, while offering the reader an easily legible text.

For these reasons we have decided to make the following changes:

Letters have been normalised. The long ſ has been changed to a normal s. The letters u, v, w, i and j are always given as either present-day vowel or consonant signs.

Capitals, small letters and punctuation have been normalised when necessary.

Words that are combined have been separated (e.g. 'moetmen' becomes 'moet men') except when the spelling had to be changed in order to do so (e.g. 'datter' or 'alsser' does not become 'dat er' or 'als er'). Likewise, words that in contemporary Dutch would not have spaces have been combined (e.g. 'daer omme' becomes 'daeromme'). Furthermore, abbreviated articles were apostrophised (e.g. 'tghene' becomes ''tghene'). Other abbreviations were changed when necessary.

---

[1] Bekelaar, G.A.M. *et al.*, *Richtlijnen voor het uitgeven van historische bescheiden* (Den Haag: Nederlands Historisch Genootschap, 1988).

There are endnotes and footnotes.

The endnotes are indicated by capital letters. They provide original readings, meaning of outdated words, comments on syntax, comparisons to the German translation and references to modern editions of classical works. Corrections of obvious mistakes and corrections based on the errata are not mentioned in the endnotes.

The footnotes give the references to bibletexts taken from the margin. They have also been changed to contemporary usage. Since it is a Dutch text, the Bible books are given in Dutch too. Sometimes the reader wil see brackets around the verse-numbers. The reasoning behind this is as follows (We take John 1:1 as and example): When both chapter and verse are given in the orginal the reader will see Joh. 1:1. When there is a general indication where to look in the chapter by means of a letter, only the verse number is between brackets, like this: Joh. 1:[1]. When only the chapter is given the double colon is between brackets too, like this: Joh. 1[:1]. Obvious mistakes have been corrected silently. Sometimes the reference is unclear, for example on 6v, where Micron refers to Genesis 17, whereas it would appear he means chapter 18. In those cases the original reference is given first, then our suggestion with a question mark and between square brackets.

The original page numbers are given in square brackets in the text. In the indeces at the end the references were given to a folio number with either 'a' or 'b', we changed this to 'r' and 'v'.

The text is according to the copy in the *Ghent University Library*, published in 1561 by Gellius Ctematius (cf., for further details, chapter 2.1 and 2.2 of the study).

The text of the German text is according to the copy owned by the *Staatsbibliothek Berlin*, published in 1563 by Michael Schirat (cf. chapter 5.1 of the study).

Text

VAN
DE VVEER-
dicheydt, nutheydt
ende noodicheyt der Christelicker
Vergaderinghen.

Eerst in den Làtyne gheschreuen door
Marten Micron, ende nu tot stichtinghe der eenuuldigher in
nederduytsch trouvve-
lick ouergheset.

Hebr. 10.c.24.
Laet ons deen den anderē waernemen/
met verwecken ter liefden ende goede
wercken: ende onse Vergaderinghe
niet laten/ als sommighe
een wijse hebben &c.

Ghedruckt Anno
1561.

[1ᵛ] Nadien dat van sommighe gheleerde ende godsalighe mannen zeer gepresen is dit tegenwoordige boecxken Martini Microni saligher gedachtenisse, 'tselve der kercken Christi nut ende profijtelick te zijn (ghelijck in de voorrede des autheurs 'tselve in 't korte te sien is), so heeft ons oock goet gedocht 't voorbenoemde boecxken, d'welck in 't latijn by den voor ghenoemden autheur met zijnder eyghener hant gheschreven, na zijn doot bevonden is, in Nederduytsche sprake over te setten ende in druck te laten uut gaen, niet sonder advijs ende raet der voorghenoemde geleerden. Ende also het voor ghenoemde boecksken van den autheur ten eynde toe niet volbracht zijnde, so is van Nicolao Careneo, des autheurs goede vriendt, daerby ghevoecht 'tghene dat tot de perfectie of volmaeckheyt des boecxkens begeert mochte worden, d'welck wy oock in duytsch overghe<levert^A> de een van des anders werck onderscheyden hebbende. Ende also ons propoost bysonder in desen gheweest is der kerkcen Christi dienst te doen met communiceren derselver den arbeyt des ghetrouwen dienaers Christi in syner tijt Micronii, so bidde wy den goetwillighen leser desen onsen kleynen arbeyt in danck te willen nemen.

[2ʳ] Martinus Micronius, den christelicken leser ghenade ende vrede.

In dese groote menichfuldicheyt der opinien, door welcke de menschen in dese uuterste tijden des wereldts so jammerlicken verstroyt ende verdeyst^B worden, zijnder vele noch in twijffel oft een godsalich ende gheloovich mensche hem nootsalicken tot eenighe uutwendighe kerckelicke vergaderinge oft ghemeynte begeven moet, ende in dien sulcx van nooden is, tot welcke vergaderinge of gemeynte een yegelick met goeder consciencien hem voegen sal, aengesien dattet blijckelick genoech is dat de gestaltenisse oft forme der uutwendigher ghemeynten hedensdaechs niet eenderley over al en is, maer dat se, so wel in de leere, als in [2ᵛ] ceremonien, seer verscheyden ende menigherley bevonden wort.

Om nu denghenen ten besten te raden, ende tot een goede gerusticheydt der consciencie te brenghen, die boven al ende van gantscher herten begeren, dat de eere Gods onder den menschen verbreydet worde, ende die haer salicheydt ernstelicken soecken, so hebbe ick voor my genomen, met korte woorden, ende sonder eenighe verbittertheyt, te bewijsen:

Ten eersten dattet eenen yegelicken godfruchtigen mensche van nooden is, dat hy hem tot eenighe sichtbaerlicke kercke oft ghemeynte voeghe.

Ten tweedden, door wat teecknen men sal moghen de ware ende rechte kercke of ghemeynte van de valsche onderscheyden.

Ten derden, oft men hedensdachs rechtelick van de roomsche kercke afwijct.

Ten vierden, dattet den christenen nadat se den grouwel der roomscher kercken ghekent ende verlaten hebben, [3ʳ] van noodt is, dat se hen tot eenige sonderlinge openbare of heymelicke kercke of christelicke gemeynte begeven. Waer in verklaert wort, wat men van de heymelicke christelicke vergaderingen in de papistische landen gevoelen, ende hoe men deselve aenrichten ende onderhouden sal.

Gemerct nu dat alsulcken handel in dese onse verdorvene tijden seer nut ende noodich is te weten ende te onderhouden, so eyscht de billicheydt van allen godfruchtigen, dien de vreese des Heeren voor ooghen is, dat se dit vlijtichlicken ende sonder eenighe partijdicheydt lesen willen. Want van de wereldts ghesinde spotters,[1] die na haer godloose begeerlicheden wandelen, en is niet te verhopen dat se door dit boecxken yet sullen ghevordert worden, aenghesien dat hen over lange tevoren van andere tevergheefs tot danssen ghepepen, ende tot weenen gheklaecht is.[2]

[3ᵛ] Hoe [h]eerlick, nut ende noodich dattet zy, dat hem yemant tot de sienlicke ghemeynte Christi voeghe.
Dat eerste capittel

Men kan niet versaecken dat de eewighe, rechtveerdige ende wijse God van den beghinne des werelts af ghewilt heeft datter een vergaderinghe der menschen in dese werelt wesen soude, in dewelcke synen wille ende heerlicheydt van deselfde menschen, na zijn geopenbaerde woort, gepredict, bekent ende ghepresen mochte worden. Waer af wy een klaer exempel in Adams huysghesin hebben, oock voor den val des menschelicken geslachts. Want God alsdoe des sevenden dach geheylicht[3] ende twee boomen die sekere heylighe verborgentheden vervaten, den eenen des wetenschaps goets ende quaets, ende den anderen des levens, in den paradijse gheplantet hadde.[4] Want hoewel dat de mensche alsdoe heylich, rechtveerdich, warachtich ende onsterffelick na den beelde Gods gheschapen was, so konde hy nochtans wel vallen.[5] Hy en was niet vrij van des duyvels listen,[6] ende was aen de ghehoorsaemheyt des gebots des

---

1 Jud.:18.
2 Mat. 11:17.
3 Gen. 2:3.
4 Gen. 2:9.
5 Pred. 7[:29]; Eph.4[:22-27?]; Gen.1:27; Gen. 5[:1]; Gen. 9[:6]; Sap.2[:23]; Syrach.17[:1-24].
6 Gen. 3[:1-7].

eenigen Gods verbonden, ende met de straffe des doots ge[4ʳ]dreycht, waer 't dat hij 't overtrade: 'Tot wat dage,' seyde de Heere, 'dat ghy daer af etet, sult ghy den doot sterven.'[1] Opdat dan Adam des te vrijer mochte wesen van alle listen des Satans, ende den standt zijnder heyligher scheppinghe gantsch ende ongheschendt bewaren soude, so heeft God nadat se syne oneyndelicke wijsheyt eenen uutwendighen godsdienst, hem noch onverdorven zijnde, voorgheschreven, ende daerom oock de heylighe vergaderinghe te onderhouden gheboden. Ende als hy nu na den val weder in genaden aengenomen was, so is hem dese remedie des te meer van nooden geweest, tot de bescherminge zijnder zielen salicheyt; mitsdien dat zijn nature verdorven ende veelderhande ellendicheden onderworpen was, ende hy oock (om de gheduerighe vyantschap tusschen de vrouwe ende 't serpent, ende haerder beyden zaet; item, om de verscheydenheyt ende veelheyt der godlicker gheboden), in meerder ende grooter perijckel zijnder salicheyt begost te leven.[2]

Dat nu God de Heere, nadat de mensche weder in ghenade aenghenomen was, gewilt heeft datter in de werelt eenige heylighe vergaderinge der godsaligen wesen soude, dewelcke door [4ᵛ] sekere Godlicke teeckenen onderscheyden oft onderkent soude worden van andere menschen die naderhandt oft den naem Gods door valsche religie ontreynighen, oft onder haer hooft den duyvel sorgheloos na des werelts wellusten leven souden, is blijckelick genoech uut de heerlicke prophecie in de eerste beloftenisse van het vrouwen zaet, aldaer God opentlick ende klaerlick van tevoren te kennen gheeft die groote vyantschap die daer sonder ophouden tusschen der vrouwen ende 't serpent, tusschen der vrouwen ende des serpents zaet wesen soude.[3] Ende uut sulcken vyantschap volcht een verscheuringe of deylinge der vergaderingen, als terstont daerna metterdaet wel ghebleken heeft.

Metten eersten was Adams gantsche huysgesin (nadattet de beloftenisse der salicheyt in Christo ontfangen hadde) een heylighe ende eendrachtighe kercke oft ghemeynte Gods in dewelcke den naem Gods niet alleen metter herten ende metten monde, maer oock met uutwendighe sacrificien gheeert ende gepresen werde, als uut de historie van Cain ende van Abel goedt te verstaen is.[4] Maer desen standt der eendrachtiger gemeynten Gods en bleef niet lange [5ʳ] staende, want sy terstont verstoort wert door Cain, die synen broeder Abel versloech, diewelcke na de

---

1 Gen. 2:17.
2 Gen. 3[:8-24].
3 Gen. 3:15
4 Gene.[4]:4; Hebr. 11:4.

grousame moort zijns broeders van de kercke oft ghemeynte Gods afgheweken is, als daer staet dat hy van den aenghesichte Gods uutghegaen is.[1] Alsdoen begost die warachtige kercke in Adams familie grootelicken beancxt, vercleynt ende benaut te worden, insonderheyt daerom dat haer wederpartijdighe kercke des Satans, door Cain opghericht, grootelicken toenam, ende van daghe te dage stercker ende gheweldigher wert.[2]

Maer opdat nu de ware gemeynte Gods, welcke doe in Adams familie seer cleyn was, ten lesten niet gheheelick te niete gebracht en werde, so wert sy van God door Seth den anderen sone Ade wederom opgerecht, ende daerom seyt de Schriftuere dat men alsdoen heeft begonnen des Heeren Naem aen te roepen.[3] Ende sommighe andere godvreesende mannen, die na den voorschreven Seth ghekomen zijn[4] (onder dewelcke Enoch de principaelste was,[5] van denwelcken gheschreven staet, dat hy met God ghewandelt ende Gode aenghenaem gheweest heeft[6]) hebben dese heylighe vergaderinge Gods seer neerstichlick ghe[5v]eert ende onderhouden: ende alle de leden dier heylighe vergaderinghe werden doe ghenaemt kinderen Gods.[7] Maer dewijle alle dinghen van daghe te daghe booser werden (als ghemeynlick die menschen meer totten quaden gheneghen zijn), so was de boosheyt der menschen onder den patriarche Noe so seer ghewassen, dat men nauwelicx erghens eenen schijn der heylighe vergaderinghe ghesien konde. Want de kinderen Gods vermengden hen met kinderen der menschen.[8] De aerde was verdorven voor den Heere ende met boosheyt vervult, alle vleesch hadde synen wech vervalscht, also dat doe de werelt een werelt der godloosen was, als de apostel Petrus scrijft[9]. Van der oprechter kercken wasser doetertijt noch een seer kleyn hoopken overghebleven; te weten, die kleyne familie oft ghesinne des rechtveerdighen ende onverdorven Noe,[10] die voor den Heere wandelde, denwelcken God zijn achtster in de arcke bewaert heeft, ende alle de andere menschen, die 120 jaren lanck door Noe den prediker der gherechticheyt tot boete waren gheroepen gheweest[11] (hoewel

---

1 Gen. 4[:1-24].
2 Gen. 4:17[-24].
3 Gen. 4:26.
4 Gen. 5[:1-32].
5 Gen. 5:24.
6 [Sirach] 44[:16]; Hebr. 11[:5-6].
7 Gen. 6:2.
8 Gen. 6:3-4.
9 2 Pet. 2[:4-10?].
10 Gen. 6:8.
11 Gen. 7[:11?]; 1 Pet. 3:[19-20]

tevergheefs)¹, zijn door de diluvie verdroncken.² Ende aldus alle godloosen door de [6ʳ] diluvie wech ghenomen zijnde, was daer wederomme in de werelt een eenighe heylighe vergaderinghe der menschen ende gemeynte God; te weten, Noe met zijn huysghesin, dewelcke God teghen alle aenvechtinghen met een nieu teecken zijns verbondts ende goetwillicheyts (te weten, met de reghenboghe) gheconfirmeert ende bevesticht heeft.³ Maer desen saligen standt der gemeynte Gods en bleef niet langhe daerna ongheschendt, want daer gheschiedde terstont eenen afbrueck in den eersten door den dertelen bespotter zijns vaders, Cham, die de vader was van Canaan.⁴ Daerna oock door de onghehoorsamighe stichters des torrens Babel,⁵ welcke God al de werelt door verstroyt heeft. Ende binnen korte jaren daerna heeft die afgoderije over al so grootelicken de overhant genomen, datter nauwelicx eenighe vergaderinghe opentlick ghevonden en werdt in dewelcke den rechten dienst ende de uutwendighe religie Gods onvervalscht ghehouden wert.

Daerom God over de ellende der menschen Hem ontfermende, heeft ten laetsten synen knecht Abraham verkoren, in denwelcken Hy de vervallen kercke [6ᵛ] also weder opbouwen wilde dat se daerna niet so lichtelicken meer vallen en soude, noch dat voortaen de godsalighe haer niet so lichtelick in de religie met de anderen vermenghen en souden. So heeft dan God Abraham uut Ur der Chaldeen gheroepen⁶ ende hem de beloften van Messias,⁷ dat Hy uut synen zade soude gheboren worden, vernieut, ende de besittinghe des lants Chanaan beloeft,⁸ ende tot de gewoonlicke offerhanden der voorgaender tijden oock de besnijdinghe toeghevoecht,⁹ dewelcke in de lichamen der huysgenooten Abrahe ghedruckt zijnde, hen eenen seghel der gherechticheyt des geloofs zijn soude¹⁰ ende hen allen in een lichaem der ghemeynte vergadert zijnde, van aller anderer menschen onheylige vergaderinghen uutwendichlicken verscheyden souden. Ende opdat dese heylige ende van God vernieude vergaderinghe die nu alle menschen ter aenschouwinge ghestelt ware, teghen alle periculen der verstooringhen dies te bestandigher staen

---

1 2 Pet. 2[:5 & ?] [Original: 2 Petr. 2 a.b.]
2 Gen. 6[:1-8?].
3 Gen. 9[:8-17]
4 Gen. 9[:22-29]
5 Gen. 11[:1-9].
6 Gen. 11[:27-32]; Gen. 12[:1-5] Gen. 15[:7]; Hand. 7:[2-5].
7 Gen. 12[:2-3?]; Gen. 18[?] [17:19-21?]; Gen. 21[?] [22:14-18?].
8 Gen. 12[:7]; Gen. 13[:14-18]; Gen. 15[:7; 16; 18-20].
9 Gen. 17[:9-14; 23-27].
10 Rom. 4[:11].

mochte, so heeft hen God een bevel ghegeven, dat se oock haer manlicke kinderkens ten achtsten dage besnijden souden.¹ Uut dewelcken het tot den tijt Messie toe altijts licht was de ghemeynte [7ʳ] die door eenich gheval in Abrahams huysghesin mochte vervallen zijn, wederom op te richten, ghelijckerwijs als men ghemeynlick op de fundamenten die noch heel ghebleven zijn, met veel minder moeyten ende swaricheyt de huysen wederomme opbouwen kan.

Dese heylighe vergaderinghe dan, aldus in Abrahams huysghesin opghericht, heeft God ghewilt dat se in de nakomelingen Abrahe neerstelick onderhouden ende bewaert soude worden.

Ende opdat alle het volck, d'welck van dien tijt af in Egypten wonderlicken vermenichfuldicht was,² soude in een lichaem der ghemeynte vereenighen, ende met heylighe banden ghebonden blijven, so en heeft se God niet alleen uut Egypten in 't beloefde landt Chanaan ghebracht, maer heeft hen oock veelderhande heylige ceremonien ende offerhanden voorgeschreven ende gheboden. Want tot de besnijdinghe is noch byghevoecht geweest het jaerlicx eten des paeschlams.³ Ende voort meer, veelderley andere ende verscheydene sacrificien ende ceremonien. Tot den sabbath, die alle weke ghehouden wert, zij noch toegheboden de nieuwe maenden,⁴ ende sommighe andere hooge [7ᵛ] jaerlicxsche feestdaghen, op dewelcke de ghemeynte by een geroepen wert.⁵ Voort was dat priesterdom ingestelt, om te leeren, offerhande te doen ende te bidden.⁶ De Leviten⁷ waren oock al het lant door verbreydt,⁸ opdat door derselver dienst het volck over al des te lichtelicker in de wet Gods onderwesen⁹ ende in de heylighe eenicheyt des lichaems der ghemeynten onderhouden mochte worden.¹⁰ In gelijcken was daer oock een sekere heylighe plaetse den gantschen volcke tot ghemeyne vergaderinge verordent;¹¹ te weten, by de arcke des Heeren in den tabernakel, ende in den heylighen tempel Gods binnen Jerusalem. Welcke dinghen alle so neerstelicken van God den volcke Israël bevolen ende inghestelt, geven

---

1 Gen. 17[:9-14].
2 Exod.1[:7].
3 Exod. 12[:1-20].
4 Num. [2]8[:9-15].
5 Lev. 23.
6 Exod. 28[:4]; Lev. 8[:1-13].
7 Num. 18[:2].
8 Deut. 24[:8?].
9 Deut. 17[:8-13].
10 Deut. 12[13-19?] ende 14[:22-29].
11 Exod. 25[:1-9]; Exod. 40[:1-38]; Num. 9[:15-23]; 1 Kon. 8[:6-11].

opentlicken te kennen dat de onderhoudinghe der heyligher vergaderinghe seer ernstelicken den volcke van God bevolen gheweest is. Oock so wanneer de heylighe ceremonien tot verstroyinghe der heyligher vergaderinge onder den volcke bestont te vervallen, so heeft se God altijt door eenighe propheten met seer grooten arbeyt laten wederoprichten ende verclaren, als klaerlicken ghenoech blijckt uut de wederopbouwinghe der [8ʳ] stadt ende tempels van Jerusalem na de Babylonische ghevanckenisse door Esdram,ᶜ Aggeum,ᴰ Malachiam ende andere heylige mannen van Gode uutghesonden, welcke niet afghelaten en hebben de opbouwinghe des huys des Heeren te drijven, totdat het ghemaect was, om de heylige vergaderinge daer in te onderhouden. Welcken sijnen uutwendighen dienst God wonderlick in menigerley perioden, tot de tijden Messie toe, onderhouden ende bewaert heeft.[1]

Nu kan een yeghelick dan wel claerlicken hier uut mercken dattet den eewighen ende bestandigen wille Gods is, datter eenighe uuterlicke oft sienlicke heylighe vergaderinghe der menschen in dese werelt zy, in dewelcke God na zijn gheopenbaerde woort gheeert ende ghedient wilt wesen, ende tot dewelcke hen alle de kinderen Gods toevoeghen moeten. Ten waer dat yemant vermetelicken seggen wilde, dat God, die alleen wijs is, van den beghinne des werelts af, yet tevergheefs onder zijn volck inghestelt oft onbedachtelick een sake tot allen tijden so ernstelicken bevolen ende ghedreven hadde; d'welck niet en kan sonder groote sonde ende boosheyt ghedacht worden.

[8ᵛ] Van desen wille des hemelschen Vaders, aengaende heylighe vergaderingen te maken ende te onderhouden, is Christus de Sone Gods gheenssins gheweken, maer heeftse selve door veel redenen bevesticht ende versterckt. Hy heeft hemselven discipulen door den dienst des doops vergadert.[2] Ende opdat niemant van de syne tot eenighen tijde soude de vergaderinge verachten ende de eensaemheyt verkiesen, so heeft Hy haer veel dinghen ghegheven ende bevolen te onderhouden, tot welcke dinghen ghemeynschap ende vergaderinghen noodich zijn.

Het eerste is den dienst des woorts allen apostelen ende ghetrouwe pastooren ernstlick bevolen, door d'welck ons God uut de werelt tot eenen volcke roept ende Hem eyghen maect. Waerom dat hetselve woordt oock wel terechte by een nette geleken[3] wort door dewelc de menschen uut de zee oft golven deser werelt in 't schip der kercken oft ghemeynten Gods ghetrocken worden. Hier toe dient oock het woort 'discipulen

---

1 Ezra 3[:1-13]; Neh. 2[11-20]; Hagg. 1[:1-11].
2 Johan. 3:22; 4:1.
3 Matt. [4?]:19; 13:47.

maken', d'welck Christus ghebruyct (Mat. in 't 28. cap.). Ende Paulus schrijvende tot de Ephesien, getuycht dat van Christo ghesettet werden apostelen, pro[9ʳ]pheten, evangelisten, pastooren ende leeraers, tot opbouwinghe der heylighen, totten wercke des ampts, waerdoor het lichaem Christi ghebouwet wort.[1] Hier toe doet oock den doop van den Heere Christo ingestelt,[2] diewelcke oock dese selfde gemeynschap in deselve vergaderinghe der ghemeynten klaerlicken ghetuycht te wesen.[3] Want wy alle heeten ghedoopt te worden in Christum, in den Naem des Vaders, des Soons ende des H[eylighen] Gheests, ende in een lichaem.[4] Ick verswijghe noch dat in de h[eylighe] schriftuere de arcke, besnijdenisse, wolcke ende de zee by den doop vergeleken worden,[5] met welcke h[eylighe] teeckenen voortijden in 't oude testament uutghedruckt wert een onderlinge ghemeynschap die onder de Godsalighe gheweest is. Want in de arcke was begrepen alleen de familie Noe, alle andere menschen daer buyten gesloten ende met de diluvie verdroncken.[6]

De besnijdenisse maecte een onderscheyt tusschen de familie Abrahe ende de onbesneden heydenen.[7] De wolcke deylde den heyrlegher pharaonis van den volcke Israels. Ende de zee, dewelcke alleen het gantsche volc Israels door heeft laten trecken, datselfde heeft pha[9ᵛ]raonem metten synen verslonden.[8]

Daerenboven de insettinge van des Heeren nachtmael, diewelcke tot de wederkoemste des Heeren onderhouden moet worden, is een klare bevestinghe des bevels van de christelicke vergaderinghe te onderhouden.[9] Want de Heere heeftet selve in de vergaderinghe zijnder discipulen ingestelt.[10] Ende de apostel Paulus straft die van Corinthen scherpelicken, omdat sommighe van dat ghemeyn ghebruyck des nachtmaels haer eyghen avontmael maeckten, drijvende met dappere woorden dat de gantsche ghemeynte tesamen tot het recht gebruyck desselfs vergaderen soude. 'Als ghy tesamen koemt,' seyt hy, 'in de gemeynte.'[11] Item: 'Myne broeders, als ghy tesamen komt om te eten, die eene vertoeve den anderen.'[12]

---

1 Ef. 4:11 etc.
2 Matt. 28:19; Mar. 16:[16].
3 Rom. 6:3.
4 Matt. 28:19; 1 Kor. 12: 13; 1 Petr. 3:20-21; Kol. 2: 11-12.
5 1 Kor. 10:1-2.
6 Gen. 7[:11-24].
7 Gen. 17[9-14].
8 Exod. 14[:15-29].
9 1 Kor. 11: 26.c.26
10 Mat. 26: [26].
11 1 Kor. 11: 20.
12 1 Kor. 11: 33.

Ende aenghesien dat den gantschen handel des nachmaels van den apostel des Heeren tafel genoemt wort,[1] so is 't daeruut wel blijckelick dat alle degene die deser tafelen mede deelachtich worden, een heylige ghemeynschap onder malcanderen (als den huysghenooten Christo toebehoort) onderhouden moeten. Want oock wereltswijse te spreken, wat vermaeck kan yemandt ghenemen [10ʳ] in 't nutten der spijsen so hy alleen is, ende met d'ander gasten gheen gheselschap noch ghemeynschap en heeft?

Hier moet men oock wel neerstelicken aenmercken dat op een ander plaetse de apostel schrijft dat wy alle, die eens broots medeedelachtich zijn, een broot ende een lichaem zijn.[2] So is dan wel klaer blijckende uut de instellinghe van des Heeren nachtmael, door Christum inghestelt, dat de godsalighe menschen met een sekere sichtbare ghemeynschap by malcanderen t'samengevoecht, ende van andere wereltsghesinde menschen afghedeylt moeten zijn.

Ten lesten, so wort oock alsulcx wel klaerlicken bewesen door het recht ghebruyck der christelicker straffen, van Christo inghestelt. Diewelcke ghelegen is in goede christelicke vermaningen onder malcanderen ordentlicken te doene ende aen te nemen, ende in 't verbannen oft uutsluyten der menschen die met opentlicke ergernisse der gantscher gemeynten hardtneckelicken tegen de wet Gods sondighen. Want hoe soude anders die ghevallen broeder, oft deghene die de bysonderlicke oft particuliere vermaningen veracht, na het bevel Christi der ghemeynten aengebracht, ende [10ᵛ] van deselve (is 't dat hy obstinaet ende hardneckich blijft) eendrachtelicken als een heyden ende publicaen uutghesloten worde, waer 't datter gheen uutwendighe kercke oft gemeynte der godsaliger en ware, maer dat een yeghelick op hemselven in eensaemheydt leven wilde?

De apostel Paulus van de uutsluytinghe oft verbanninge sprekende, stelt een merckelick onderscheyt tusschen deghene die buyten der gemeynten zijn ende deghene die broeders ghenaemt worden.[3] D'welck gantschelicken onnoodich zijn soude, waer 't dat een yeghelick na zijn goetduncken buyten de uutwendighe ghemeynschap der kercken leven mochte.

Alle deghene dan, die hen van de ghemeynte oft christelicke vergaderinghe afsonderen ende aftrecken, willende op henselven in eensaemheyt leven ende sterven, die selve versmaden ende verkrencken opentlicken die bovenghenoemde insettingen Christi, als namelicken des

---

1 1 Kor. 10: 21
2 1 Kor. 10: 17.
3 1 Kor. 5: 10-12.

woorts, des doops, des nachtmaels ende des diensts der sleutelen; het welck hoe grouwelicke sonde dat hetzy, gheve ick allen godvruchtighen te bedencken.

[11ʳ] Het is oock blijckelick ghenoech hoe ernstlick dat God van allen menschen die opentlicke belijdinge zijns Naems, ja oock in 't midden zijnder vergaderinghen, hebben wilt,[1] als daer gheschreven staet: 'Ick sal dynen naem prediken mynen broederen, ick sal dy in 't midden der ghemeynten prijsen.'[2] Deghene dan die hen tot ghene uutwendighe ghemeynte Gods voeghen en willen, die en konnen metter waerheyt niet ghesegghen dat se Gode een volkomene belijdinghe zijns Naems bewijsen.

Ende waer 't datter gheen kerckce oft ghemeynte Christo te vergaderen en ware, so moeste dan dit woordeken 'kercke' oft 'ghemeynte'ᴱ in de heylighe schrift heel te vergeefs ghestelt zijn; dewelcke kercke oft ghemeynte Gods anders niet en is dan een versamelinghe der menschen, uut de gantsche werelt door de stemme des evangeliums gheroepen, ende onder het hooft Christo by een vergadert.

Daerom is 't dat wy den Naem Gods (als ons bevolen wort) in syne ghemeynte door een standtvaste belijdinghe eeren, ende den naem der kercken oft ghemeynten niet ijdel noch te ver[11ᵛ]gheefs maken en willen, so sullen wy onsselven vlijtelicken begheven tot de onderhoudinge der vergaderinghe der ghemeynten Gods.

Noch so vindt men in de heylighe schrift veelderley namen der ghemeynten Christi waer uut wel klaerlicken te merkcen is, dattet van den kinderen Gods gheeyscht wordt dat se haer tot een uutwendighe heylighe vergaderinghe oft ghemeynte Gods voeghen sullen.

In den eersten, aenghesien dattet blijckelick ghenoech is, dat Christus een koninck zijnder ghemeynten is,[3] so moet daer oock wel nootsakelicken uut volghen dat de kercke oft ghemeynte die hier noch op dese wereldt leeft, zijn rijck zy. Ghelijckerwijs dan de wereltlicke koninghen haer eygen volck hebben, met sekere teeckenen ende wetten van andere volcken verscheyden, also moet oock het rijcke Christi hier opter aerden zijn volck hebben, hetwelcke met sekere teeckenen ende wetten van denselven inghestelt, onder malcanderen vereenicht ende van den Satan ende van syne ondersaten verscheyden zy, aenghesien datter gheen ghelijckenisse noch vereeninghe des [12ʳ] rijcx Christi ende Satans ghesijn en kan. Hoe koemt Christus over een met Belial?[4]

---

1 Mat. 10: 32; 2 Tim. 2:12.
2 Ps. 22[: 23]; Hebr. 2:12.
3 Ps. 2.
4 2 Kor. 6: 15.

Daerom al deghene die alle uutwendighe heylighe ghemeynschap der vergaderinghen Gods hardtneckichlicken schouwen, dieselve en doen niet anders, dan dat se oft bedecktelicken, oft opentlicken den heyrlegher des duyvels, die teghen de ghemeynte strijdt, verstercken oft vermeerderen.

De kercke wort oock ghenaemt het huys Gods, hetwelcke ghebouwt is op het eenighe fundament der apostelen ende der propheten, hetwelcke is Christus.[1] Ende ghelijckerwijs eenen steen – ja, noch oock vele steenen verscheyden ligghende – gheen huys en konnen ghenaemt worden, maer moeten behoorlicke wijse byeenghevoecht wesen soude 't een huys zijn, also moeten oock de godsalighe in een christelicke vergaderinghe door den Heylighen Gheest ende door een uutwendighe belijdinghe der warachtigher religien vereenicht wesen, soude 't een bouwinge Christi zijn (als Paulus spreect), ende souden sy levende ende nutte steenen zijn, om een alsulcke heylighe bouwinghe te volmaken ende te vercieren.[2] [12ᵛ] Daerenboven, ghelijckerwijs een huys ghemeynlicken opghetimmert wordt opdatter deghene dien 't toebehoort inne woonen mach, also is 't oock wel betamelick dat de kinderen Gods, denwelcken alle gherechticheden des huys Gods in Christo toebehooren (want in Hem behoort ons al toe)[3], in 'tselve gheestelick huys woonen door een heylige onderhoudinghe der godsaligher vergaderinghen, ende alle die sulcx doen worden in de heylighe schrift 'huysghenooten des gheloofs' ghenoemt, ende de ander worden 'vreemdelinghen' oft 'die buyten zijn' gheheeten. Daerom so vervreemden dese haerselven van den huyse Gods (ymmers so vele als in hen ghelegen is) die alle heylighe vergaderinghen sorghelooselicken verachten oft versuymen, ende dat oft om op henselven in eensaemheyt te leven, oft uut een plompe verachtinge der religie, oft om eenigherhande andere dierghelijcke oorsaecken wille.

Ende als wy hooren dat de christgheloovige in de h[eylighe] schrifture by den broode;[4] item, by de wijngaertrancken in den waren wijnstock Christo;[5] ende by de schapen in den eenighen schaepstal [13ʳ] onder den eenighen oppersten herder Christo vergadert gheleken worden,[6] ende dattet wel blijckelick is dat het broot niet van een, maer van vele ghemaelne ende tesamen ghebackene koornkens ghemaect wert; ende dat de wijngaertsrancken nemmermeer alleen op en groeyen, noch gheen een besie alleen voort en brengen, maer vele tesamen in een trosken; ende dat

---

1 1 Tim. 3:[15]; Ef. 2:19; 1 Kor. 3:11; Mat. 16:18.
2 1 Kor. 3:9; Ef. 2:21.
3 1 Kor. 3:22.
4 1 Kor. 10:17.
5 Joh. 15:1.
6 Joh. 10:16; Hebr. 13:20; 1 Pet. 5:4.

de schapen niet alleen, maer met kudden gaen, denwelcken de eensaemheydt gantsch periculoos is; so is ontwijffelicken daeruut goedt te mercken dat van ons gheeyscht wert, so verre wy het broot, de wijngaertsrancken, ende de schapen Christi gheachtet zijn willen, dat wy onsselven tot syne heylighe vergaderinge begeven, in dewelcke wy door den dienst zijns woorts ende der sacramenten, door den Gheest ende door 't geloove tot ongeheefde brooden ghebacken, in den wijstock Christo overvloedelicken vruchten voortbrengen, ende met de andere schapen Christo door de hemelsche spijse der zielen altijt ende ghenoechsaemlicken ghespijst worden moghen.

Item, de kerkce wert oock in de heylighe schrift by een lichaem gheleken, waer af Christus 't hooft is.[1] Nu weet [13ᵛ] een yeghelick wel dat een lichaem gheen verscheydene, maer tesamengevoechde leden heeft. Daerom is 't dat wy voor de oprechte leden des lichaems Christi willen gherekent worden, so en moghen wy onsselven van de ghemeynschap der christenen gheenssins afsnijden noch afscheyden.

Noch so behooren wy hier inne aen te mercken, dat Christus selve het rijck der hemelen, oft den teghenwoordighen standt zijnder kerckcken hier opter aerden, by een koninklicke bruyloft ghelijckt,[2] tot dewelcke Hy alle manieren van menschen door syne knechten doet roepen, ende die traech zijn, doet dwinghen. Waermede klaerlicken ghenoech beteeckent wordt, dat alle de christgheloovige, die tot de gheestelicke bruyloft ons hemelschen bruydegoms Christi gheroepen worden,[3] dickwijls by malcanderen, tot onderhoudinge der heyliger vergaderingen, by een komen mochten. Want ghelijck de eensaemheydt den bruydegom, die zijn bruyloft [h]eerlick houden wilt, gheensins en betaemt, also betaemt oock veel min denghenen die genoodt zijn, dat se alleen ende in eensaemheyt blijven.

Uut alle welcke voorgaende rede[14ʳ]nen eenen yeghelicken openbaer zijn kan dat alle godsalighe schuldich zijn hen tot de heylighe uutwendighe ghemeynte oft vergaderinghe Christi des Heeren te voeghen, teghen de sotte wijsheydt deser wereldt, sonder hen eenichsins daeraf, door eenighe swaricheden des vleesches die de duyvel sonder ophouden voorwendet, nemmermeer te laten aftrecken oft verleyden, so verre sy (als 't behoorlick is) den eeuwighen wille Gods onderdanich zijn, den dienst des woordts ende der sacramenten ghebruyck terechte aenmercken, de kerckelicke straffe oft discipline, van den Heere Christo selve inghestelt, ghetrouwelicken

---

1 Rom. 12:5; 1 Kor. 12:27; Ef. 1:23; 4:12, 16, 23; Kol. 1: 24; Ef. 1:22; 4:15; 5:23; Kol. 1:18.
2 Matt. 22: 1-2; Luk. 14:16.
3 Joh. 3:[29?].

onderhouden, den Naem Gods opentlicken ende volkomelicken eeren, den naem der kercken onghequetst laten ende onderhouden, ende Christo haren Heere ende koninck ghetrouwelicken onderworpen zijn wille. Ja, is 't dat se warachtighe steenen tot opbouwinge der kercken Christi, item, oock brooden, wijnrancken, schapen ende medegenooten syner gheestelicker bruyloften begheeren te wesen.

In de heylighe schrift, so wel in het oude als in het nieuwe testament, vindt men veel treffelicke exempelen [14ᵛ] der heyligher menschen, dewelcke desen godsalighen raedt navolghende, de heylighe vergaderinghen, na de ordinancien van God inghestelt, in veelderhande perijckelen seer neerstelicken onderhouden ende gheeert hebben, deselve weder oprechtende wanneer dat sy se eenchsins vervallen saghen.[1]

In den ghesinne oft familie ons eersten vaders heeft de rechtveerdige Abel door den gheloove Gode gheoffert.[2]

Noe uuter arcken ghegaen zijnde, bouwede den Heere eenen altaer, ende offerde op tenselven brandtoffer Gode den Heere.[3]

Abraham, alder ghelooviger vader, eenen altaer by Bethelᶠ opgericht hebbende, heeft hy aldaer des Heeren Naem aengeroepen, ende eenen opentlicken godsdienst ingestelt.[4] Hetselve heeft hy ooc daerna in Hebron ende in Beerseba ghedaan.[5]

Ende als hem bevolen werdt dat hy hemselven ende alle syne sonen besnijden soude, heeft hij 't terstondt ende sonder eenich vertreck volbracht.[6] Ende niet alleen heeft desen heylighen man zijn uuterste beste gedaen dat den reynen onvervalschten godsdienst in zijn familie zijn leven lanck mochte onderhouden [15ʳ] worden, maer hy heeft oock op synen nakomelingen ghedacht, als God de Heere van hem oock ghetuycht heeft, met dese woorden: 'Ick weet, hy sal 't bevelen syne kinderen, ende synen huyse na hem, dat sy des Heeren wegen houden ende doen wat recht ende goedt is.'[7] Daerom wilde hy dat zijn sone Isaac gheen Cananeesche, maer eene godvreesende vrouwe uut zijn gheslachte tot eender huysvrouwen nemen soude.[8] Siet in hoe grooter weerden dien heylighen man de onderhoudinghe der heyligher vergaderinghen ghehouden heeft. Van des vaders godfrutichheyt en heeft de sone Isaac

---

1 Mat. 23:34
2 Gen. 4:4; Hebr. 11:4.
3 Gen. 8:20.
4 Gen. 12:8.
5 Gen. 13:18; 21:33.
6 Gen. 17:10, 23.
7 Gen. 18:19.
8 Gen. 24:3[?].

oock niet gheweken, want als hy eenen altaer in Beerseba opgericht hadde,[1] heeft hy aldear des Heeren Naem aengeroepen, ende zijns vaders Abrahams exempel navolghende, opdat hy den warachtighen ende oprechten godsdienst op syne nakomelingen brenghen soude, heeft hy ghewilt dat synen sone Jacob een van de dochteren Laban zijns ooms tot eener huysvrouwen name,[2] ende niet een van de dochteren Heth, als Esau gedaen hadde, waer in syne ouders seer bedroeft waren.[3] Ende Jacob was der godfruchticheydt so seer toeghedaen dat hy beloefde God een [15ᵛ] huys op te bouwen, mochte hy eens gesont uut Mesopotamien weder in zijn lant komen.[4] D'welck hy oock daerna (soo 't hem de Heere beval) ghetrouwelicken volbracht heeft.[5]

Hoe neerstich dat Moyses, Aaron, Josue, Samuel, David, Josaphat, Ezechias,[G] Josias ende andere mannen Gods, hier voortijden gheweest hebben in 't onderhouden, aendrijven ende wederoprichten der heyliger vergaderingen, en behoeft men nu hier niet te verhalen, ghemerckt sulcx allesins in de boecken Moysi, der koninghen, in de psalmen ende propheten overvloedelicken genoech aengheteeckent staet.

Den overtreffelicken propheet David, dewijle hy uut den lande zijn moeste, en konde niet droeffelicker geschieden dan dat hy terwijlen van de heylighe vergaderinghe ende van den huyse Gods moeste afghescheyden wesen.[6] Also dat hij 't wel voor d'alder grootste ghelucksalicheydt achtede in 'tselve huys oft ghemeynte te zijn,[7] ende dat, sonder twijffel, om de ghemeynschap wille der vergaderinghen ende dienst des Heeren. De godvreesende Tobias heeft hemselven den perijckelen ende swaricheden der reysen onderworpen, opdat [16ʳᴴ] hy tot Jerusalem in de vergaderinghen der godsalighen komen mochte.[8]

Ende de godvreesende Israeliten, dewijle sy in de Babylonische gevanckenisse noch waren, en hebben sy ter wereldt niet so bitterlicken beweent als de verstroyinghe haerder vergaderingen. 'Hoe souden wy,' spraken sy, 'Gode lofsanck singen in een vreemdt lant?'[9] Ende nadat haer de vrijheydt weder door Cyrus ende andere koninghen van Perssen ghegheven was den tempel van Jerusalem te moghen weder opbouwen,

---

1 Gen. 26:25.
2 Gen. 27:46; 28:1.
3 Gen. 26:35.
4 Gen. 28:22.
5 Gen. 35:6.
6 1 Sam. 26[:25?]; 2 Sam. [15:30-37].
7 Ps. 5:8; 11:1; 22:23; 23:6; 26:8; 27:4; 84:2; 122:1.
8 Tob. 1:6.
9 Ps. 137:4.

om aldaer haer ghemeyne heylighe vergaderingen t'onderhouden, als weleer in voorgaende tijden, so isser een groote blijschap onder alle de godsaligen opgeresen; dewelcke alle swaricheden des reysens kleyn achtende, zijn sy weder tot Jerusalem ghekomen, aldaer sy met grooter blijschappen ende vlijticheydt begonnen den tempel weder op te bouwen.[1]

Ende dewijle sy daerna slapper ende versuymelicker begonnen te worden (want in 't vorderen ende promoveren der warachtiger religien ende des waren godsdiensts werden wy lichtelicken moede ende slaperich), so werden sy door Aggeum,[2] Zachariam ende andere mannen van [16ᵛ] God ghesonden wederom vermaent, dat se het begonnen werck des huys Gods volmaken souden; overmits dien dat de heylighe vergaderinghen onder hen anders niet wel bequamelicken en konden onderhouden worden.

Dese selfste vlijticheydt in de onderhoudinge der heyligher vergaderingen is oock ghebleven by de heylighe apostelen Christi. Want na de verrysenisse Christi leest men dat se dickwils by een vergadert gheweest hebben.[3] Ende nadat de Heere Christus ten hemel ghevaren was,[4] so zijn de discipulen tesamen binnen Jerusalem gebleven,[5] aldaer sy de broeders tesamen vergadert zijnde, Matthiam tot eenen apostel verkoren hebben.[6] Korts daerna, als sy oock desghelijcx byeen vergadert waren, is de Heylighe Gheest in hen ghedaelt.[7] Denwelcken ontfanghen hebbende, zijn se daerna veel dickwijlder ende met meerder menichte tesamen gekomen. Ende dat oock niet alleen binnen Jerusalem, maer oock by na alle de werelt door, als uut d'werck der apostelen ende uut de brieven van den apostelen gheschreven, klaerlicken ghenoech te mercken is. De apostel Paulus, nadat hy van een vervolgher een apostel [17ʳ] Christi gheworden was, heeft hy hem terstont by de andere discipulen vlijtichlicken gevoecht. Ten eersten binnen Damasco,[8] ende daerna oock binnen Jerusalem.[9] Ende dat wy hare goede exempelen met alder vlijticheydt behooren na te volghen en kan niemandt gheloochenen, hy en moeste wel gantsch godloos wesen. In sonderheydt, ghemerct dat so wanneer dese heylige vergaderingen der christenen op het alder vlijtichste

---

1 Ezra 1:2, 3 ende 3:6 ende 6[:13-22].
2 Hag. 1[:1-11].
3 Luc. 24:32; Joan. 20:19,26.
4 Hand.1:4; 1 Kor. 15:6.
5 Luc. 24:48, 52.
6 Hand. 1: 14, 25.
7 Hand. 2:1.
8 Hand. 9:19.
9 Hand. 9:26.

onderhouden worden, so geschiet alsulcx eenen yegelicken tot groote vorderinghe ende gheestelicke nutheyt. 't En kan oock gheenssins onnut wesen 't ghene dat de heylighe mannen Gods altijt seer ernstlicken ende met alder aendacht ghedreven ende onderhouden hebben, ende dat uut bevel ende door 't ghebot Gods, dewelcke noyt niet tevergheefs bevolen, inghestelt noch geordineert en heeft.

Ende oft nu alle de heylighe mannen gheen ander vrucht noch nutheydt uut hare heylighe vergaderinghen en hadden, dan dat sy Gode gehoorsaemheyt bewesen hebben, so ware dit noch al genoech om deselve vergaderingen nemmermeer te versuymen noch achter te laten. Aenghesien dat ghehoorsaemheyt [17ᵛ] Gode een aenghenaem offerhande is. Maer gemerckt nu dat noch veel ander groote nutheden den christenen daeruut komen, so behooren wy oock in dese sake – aller godvreesender exempel navolgende – den wille Gods des te meer goede ghehoorsaemheyt te bewijsen.

In den eersten, hoe nuttelic dattet zy in de heylighe vergaderingen der ghemeynten daghelicks te zijn, kan men klaerlicken genoech uut de heerlicke belofte Christi verstaen, als hy seyt: 'Waer datter twee oft dry in mynen naem vergadert zijn, daer ben Ick in het midden van hen.'[1] Het is ontwijffelicken een onuutsprekelicke groot goet Christum met zijn ghenade teghenwoordich ende met ons te hebben, dewelcke als eenen hulper ende beschermer allen onsen saken voorstaet ende regeert. Oock so bewijst Christus in zijn heylighe ghemeynte wonderlicke krachten zijnder teghenwoordicheyt door synen H[eylighen] Gheest in den dienst des woordts, der sacramenten ende der christelicker straffe, d'welck ons hier met korte woorden de bewijsen staet. Ende in den eersten sullen wy handelen van de kracht oft werckinghe die den dienst des woorts in hem heeft, d'welck so wanneer dattet suyver [18ʳ] in de christelicke vergaderinge verkondicht wort, so wordender veel uut de duysternisse der dwalingen tot het licht der waerheit, ende uut de besmettinge der sonden tot een boetveerdich leven ghetrocken. 'Want 't gheloove koemt door 't gehoor, ende 't gehoor door d'woort Gods.'[2] Waerom dat oock den dienst des evangeliums seer wel by een nette van Christo geleken wordt.[3] Want door 'tselve wordender dickwils veel uut den diepen kuyl der afgoderijen, des onwetenschaps, der dwalingen, des bedrochs, des dronckenschaps, der wellusten, der leugenen ende aller sonden in 't schip der warachtiger godfruchticheyt, ende in 't rijck des Soons Gods op getrocken, als men

---

1 Mat. 18:20.
2 Rom. 10:17.
3 Mat. 13:[47].

met dagelicxsche experiencien ende met veel getuygenissen der h[eyligher] schrift wel klaerlicken bewijsen kan.

Deghene die Christum ghecruyst hadden, werden door de predicacie Petri bekeert.[1] De knechten die uutghesonden waren om Christum te vanghen keerden weder tot de oversten ende phariseen, seggende: 'Noyt en heeft er mensche ghesproken als dese.'[2]

De Samaritanen dewelcke Simon de Toovenaer tevoren verleydt hadde, door de predicacie Philippi beweecht zijnde, ontfinghen het woort Gods.[3]

[18ᵛ] Ende Lydia, neerstelicken de predicacie Pauli hoorende, werdt totten gheloove bekeert.[4] 'Want dat woordt Gods is levendich ende krachtich, ende scherper dan eenich tweesnijde sweert, ende doordringhet totdat scheydet ziele ende gheest, oock het merch ende beenen, ende is een richter der ghedachten ende meyninghen des herten, ende daer en is gheen creatuere voor hem onsienlick.'[5] Waerom oock de apostel op een ander plaetse van de kracht ende werckinghen des woordts sprekende, seydt aldus: 'Waer 't dat sy alle propheteerden, ende daer quame dan een ongeloovighe oft ander leecke in, die soude van alle denselven ghestraft worden, ende van allen gheoordeelt worden, ende also sal dat verborgen zijns herten openbaer worden, ende sal also op zijn aensicht vallen, God aenbidden, ende belijden dat God warachtich in u is.'[6] Want des Heeren woort is gelijck een vyer, ende gelijck eenen hamer die de steenrotzen in stucken slaet.[7]

Die stercke mueren van Hiericho en vallen niet neder, dan door 't gheluyt der evangelischer basuynen.[8] Ende Saul in 't midden der propheten gekomen zijnde, begint oock te propheteren.[9] So krachtich is d'woort, ja oock in de godloose, [19ʳ] om dieselve te beweghen. Diewelcke kracht in de godsalighe ende gheloovige noch veel krachtelicker werct, so lange sy hier op dese wereldt zijn, gemerct dat dieselve door de dagelicksche oeffeninge des woorts in der gemeynten meer ende meer in de warachtige kennisse Gods ende in de godsalicheyt bevesticht worden, daer in oock van dage te daghe toenemende, wantter niemant en is, hoe

---

1 Hand. 2:37.
2 Joh. 7:[46].
3 Hand. 8:5, 6, 11, 13.
4 Hand. 16:14.
5 Hebr. 4:12[-13].
6 1 Kor. 14:24-25.
7 Jer.23:29.
8 Joz.6:20.
9 1 Sam.19: 23[-24].

godvreesende ende gheschict in de h[eylighe] schrift dat hy oock zijn mach, hem en gebreect noch al veel aen de volmaectheyt. Daerom seyt de apostel wel terechte: 'Wie propheteert, die sticht de gemeynte.'[1] Want de prophecie of uutlegginge der schrift is den geloovigen ghegeven, als hy op een ander plaetse seyt.[2] Die selve getuycht oock dat Christus sommige tot apostelen geset heeft, sommighe tot propheten, sommige tot evangelisten, sommighe tot herders ende leeraers, daer mede de heyligen opgebout souden worden.[3] Want de christgheloovighe struyckelen seer dickwils ende vallen in den swaren slaep der sonden, also dat se qualicken opstaen konnen, dan door de openbare oft heymelicke verkondinghe des woorts.

Laet ons alleen David ons tot een exempel voor nemen, dewelcke hoewel [19ᵛ] hy een man was na Gods herte, ende die veel aenstoots geleden hadde, nochtans bleef hy sorgheloselicken in de sonden der onkuysheydt ende dootslach by na een heel jaer lanck steken, totdat hy van Nathan vermaent werdt.[4] Want alleen de predicacie des evangeliums is de stemme, door dewelcke de herder zijn verloren schaep totten rechten schaepstael roept ende wederbrengt.[5] Het is de keersse die de evangelische vrouwe ontsteect om haren penninc, die sy in 't huys verloren hadde, weder te soecken.[6] Het is 't gheluyt der herpen, door d'welck Saul metten boosen gheest ghequelt zijnde, gestilt wert.[7]

Summa 't en is niet om uut te spreken hoe groot de vruchten des woorts zijn, wanneer dattet reyn ghepredickt ende ghehoort wort, so wel by de ongheloovighe als by de gheloovige menschen. Daerom moeten deselve wel jammerlicken verloren gaen, in seer grove sonden ende leelicke dwalingen vallen, oft haer tot een sorgheloos leven begeven, de de reyne evangelische leere noyt gehoort en hebben, of die daer een walginghe van ghekreghen hebben. Also dat de wijse man oock wel terechte geseydt heeft: 'Als de prophccic uut is, so [20ʳ] wordt dat volck wildt ende woest.'[8]

Nu en hebben de godsaligen in de christelicke vergaderingen t'onderhouden niet alleen nutheit uut den dienst des woorts, maer oock der sacramenten, als namelicken des doops ende des nachtmaels. Want telcken als sy daer den doop sien uutreycken, dat sy of haer kinderen

---

1 1 Kor. 14:4.
2 1 Kor. 14:22.
3 Ef. 4:11, 12.
4 2 Sam. 12:6.
5 Ezech. 34; Luc. 15:4; Joh.10:3.
6 Luc. 15:8.
7 1 Sam. [16:14-23]
8 Spr. 29:18.

gedoopt worden, terstont denken sy in henselven (so verre daer ymmers eenich voncxken der godvreesentheit in is) in den eersten, hoe groot onse verdorventheyt door de sonde in Adam is – ja, so groot dat se om dier sonden willen t'samen met hare kinderen der eewiger verdoemenissen weerdich zijn. Daerom dencken sy wederom, hoe groot de goedertierenheydt des hemelschen Vaders tot henwaerts is, door de ghemeynschap zijns H[eylighen] Gheests. Door dewelcke, so waer als sy daer ghedoopt worden, Hy[1] deselve genadelicken door synen Sone van de verdoemenisse verlost, gevende hen de gerechticheydt ende het eewighe leven. Want alsulcke weldaet Gods wort der ghemeynten door den doop warachtichlicken ende krachtichlicken voorghebeeldt ende beseghelt.

Ten derden overdenct hy oock, hoe wy door het afsterven des ouden mensches ende des nieuwen mensches aenneminge, [20ᵛ] ons verbinden tot een eewighe heylicheydt des levens. Ende wanneer men alle dese dinghen wel ernstelicken overdenct, daer men den doop na den bevele des Heeren siet uutreycken, oft een alsulck overdencken nuttelick ende vruchtbaer in de herten der christgeloovigher is worden sy selve dagelijcx in hare consciencie wel ghewaer. Want God en gedoocht nemmermeer dat syne insettinghen, wanneer die christelicken ghebruyct worden, yemmermeer bloote ende onnutte ceremonien oft handelinghen zijn.

Hoe groote nutheyt ende vruchten dat oock een christgheloovighe neemt uut het oprecht ghebruyck des nachtmaels ons Heeren Jesu Christi, en is met ghene tonge uut te spreken. In den eersten, wanneer sy overdencken, dat alle degene die des Heeren nachtmaels onweerdelicken nutten, henselven noch niet terechte beproeft hebbende, aen des Heeren lichaem ende bloedt schuldich zijn.[1] Item, dat se oock sien, dat se des Heeren nachtmael om het expres bevel Christ wille niet versuymen en moghen, so verre zij 't puer ende onvervalscht bekomen konnen.[2] In alsulcke gedachten staende, moeten sy alle dese dinghen met een [21ʳ] oprechte boetveerdicheyt beteren, waer sy hen eenichsins inne schuldich kennen. Dus worden sy beweecht metten naesten hen te versoenen, daer gaet men dan rekenschap des voorgaenden levens in henselven houden, men examineert er syne ghebreken, men beschreydt er de sonden, ende daer wort men dan des te voorsichtigher om de sonden in toekomende tijden te schouwen.

Ende tot de tafel des Heeren komende, worden sy daer oock met een sonderlinghe vreuchde des gheests vermaect, na dien dat se door de kracht des H[eylighen] Gheests, in de heylsame ghemeynschap Christi

---

1   1 Kor. 11:27.
2   1 Kor. 11:24.

ende alle syner weldaden krachtelicken besegelt worden. Alsdan so worden sy tot danckbaerheyt verwect, sy worden des te vaster met den bandt der broederlicker liefden aen een gebonden, ende worden des te vyerigher alle Godsalicheyt des levens na te komen. Van alle welcke ende meer diergelijcke gheestelicke goeden sy henselven berooven, alle die henselven lichtveerdichlicken van de uutwendighe vergaderinge der ghemeynten aftrecken, ende lust hebben om alleen ende op henselven te leven.

Noch so vernemen de godsalighe [21ᵛ] een seer groote nutheyt ende profijt uut de christelicke straffe ende discipline, wanneer die wel ende terechte toegaet. Om dewelcke discipline in de ghemeynte te vercrijgen ende te onderhouden alle ghetrouwe dienaren Gods, ende bysonder in dese boose tijden, haer grootelicken bekommeren. Want sy is eenen toom teghen alle ongheschicktheyt, woestheyt, ende sorgheloosheyt deses levens. Sy verweckt de ghevallen broederen door de heelsame vermaninghen weder totten rechten wech te keeren, ende is een seer goede remedie tegen veel erghernissen.

Alle deghene dan die uut een hoochmoedighe verachtinghe, oft om eenigherhande diergelijcke ander oorsaken wille henselven van de christelicke vergaderinghe afsonderen, die versuymen oock een alsulcke goede insettinghe Christi,[1] niet alleen tot haerder schaden, maer oock tot schaden des naesten, ende der gantscher ghemeynten.[2] Want als sy in eenighe sonden ghevallen zijn, so en worden se daer niet so lichtelicken weder af ghetrocken, in eensaemheyt levende, alsoft sy van der ghemeynten waren.[3] In dewelcke de een broeder den anderen gevallenen broeder na de ghe[22ʳ]leghentheydt, ende na de graden van Christo inghestelt, christelicken vermaent, soeckende remedie teghen de erghernissen der gemeynten. Hetwelcke buyten der ghemeynten oft christelicker kercken also niet onderhouden en wort. Daerom so is 't seer profijtelick om den dienst wille des woorts, der sacramenten, ende der christelicker straffen dat men hem vlijtelicken tot een christelicke ghemeynte voeghe. Hetwelcke oock wel klaer blijckelick is uut de ghelijckenisse der dinghen, daer den teghenwoordighen standt der gemeynten in der schriftueren by geleken wort.

De kercke is het rijcke Christi, sy is zijn huys, ende zijn huysghesin.[4]

---

1 Mat. 18:15.
2 1 Kor.5:3, 8.
3 Mat. 18:16, 17.
4 Ps. 2; 1 Tim. 3:[15].

Alle deghene dan die van syne konincklicke insettinghen, ende van de uutwendighe gemeynschap zijns rijcx ende huysghesin een walginghe hebben, noch en willen oock synen huyse niet toeghevoecht worden, ick en kan niet verstaen hoe die eenichsins der koninclicker beschermingen sullen moghen ghenieten, oft hoe dat se onder des konincx huysghenooten oft gheestelicke steenen zijns huys sullen gherekent moghen worden.

[22ᵛ] Ende ghelijckerwijs het koren alsdan eerst tot des menschen voedtsel bequam is wanneer dat het ghemalen, tot een deech gheknedet, ende daerna tot broot ghebacken wort; desgelijcx dat de wijngaertrancken alsdan vruchten dragen, ende tot meerder vruchtbaerheyt ghesnoeyt worden, wanneer sy in den wijstock blijven,[1] also oock en konnen wy onsen naesten nemmermeer beter met eenige sake ghedienen tot de eere Gods, noch en worden oock nemmermeer beter verwect heylige vruchten der godsalicheyt voort te brengen, dan so wanneer wy in de ghemeynschap der vergaderinghen, onder het hooft Christo, na zijn voorgheschreven reghelen ende wetten simpelicken ende eenvuldichlicken wandelen. Daerenboven so is de kercke Christi eenen schaepstal[2] in denwelcken syne schapen vergadert worden. Ende ghelijckerwijs dattet nu d'aldersekerste ende nutste voor 't schaepken is dattet niet alleen en gae dolen, maer dat het metter gheheelder kudden blijven ende weyde onder de bescherminghe zijns ghetrouwen herders, door wien dattet van den wolf beschermt vrijelicken in zijn perck mach blijven, also oock is 't den godsalighen alderbest dat hy hem [23ʳ] by der christelicker ghemeynten houde, opdat hy aldaer met de hemelsche spijse des godlicken woorts ghespijst, ende door de neersticheyt der pastooren teghen de wolven beschermt worde, ende also binnen de palen der salicheyt blijve.

Ende ghemerckt dat de kercke in de heylighe schrift by een lichaem ende by een koninklicke bruyloft gheleken wort, so kan men daer wel lichtelicken uut verstaen in hoe grooter weerden dat de christelicke vergaderinghe te houden is.[3] Want gelijckerwijs de leden tot haerder baten den lichame t'samenghevoecht zijn, ende die mede van der koninklicker bruyloften is, die is metten anderen der blijschappen medeelachtich die daer bedreven wordt. Also oock de christgheloovighe in 't lichaem der ghemeynten zijnde, ghebruycken met den anderen vele gheestelicke goeden door de onderlinghe leeringen, vermaninghen ende liefde. Ja, sy worden oock in de heylighe byeenkoemsten haers bruydegoms Christi met zijn gheestelicke spijsen, tot grooten vermake des gheests,

---

1 Joh.15:1, 2.
2 Joh.10:16.
3 Rom. 12:5; Luc. 14:16.

overvloedelicken ghespijst ende vermaect, also dat se dickwils ghedronghen worden met den propheet David te segghen: 'Du maeckst mijn [23ᵛ] hooft vet met olye ende schenckst my vol in.'¹ Ende wederomme: 'Siet, hoe fijn ende lieflick is 't dat broeders met malcanderen woonen.'²

Nu hopen wy ghenoechschaemlicken bewesen te hebben, hoe nut dat het den godsalighen is heylighe vergaderinghen te onderhouden.

Ja, oock in wereltlicke dingen, niet soseer in goede als in quade, is de kracht ende werckinghe der vergaderingen so groot datter gheen insettingen anders dan door sekere gemeynten ende vergaderingen in haren standt gheblijven en konnen. Gheen politisch regiment noch ghemeynte en salder konnen onderhouden worden, tenzy dat se haer burgherlicke vergaderinghen gestadelick onderhouden. Desghelijcx oock de bontwerckers, schippers, backers, brouwers, kleermakers ende andere ambachtslieden onderhouden haer gilden ende daghen der vergaderinghen, om also haer ambacht ende neeringe in eeren ende in weerden te houden. Ja, oock alle deghene die in eenighe boosheyt den Satan moetwillichlicken dienen, die onderhouden oock haer gemeynten ende vergaderingen, als de dronckaerts, tuysschers, hoereerders, afgodendienaers, [24ʳ] ende dierghelijcke duyvels ghespuys. Siet, hoe grootelick der ghemeynten oft vergaderinghen ghebruyck in alle dinghen van nooden is. Daerom en is 't oock niet wel betamelick dat de godsalighe haer heylighe vergaderinghen, die so [h]eerlick ende nut zijn, eenichsins versuymen. Want derselver versuyminghe ende verlatinghe plach altijt veel quaets na te volghen, aengesien dat deghene diese hoochmoedichlicken verlaten om op henselven buyten der ghemeynten te leven, van alle de bovengenoemde goeden haerselven berooven.

Ende de Heere Christus van deghene sprekende, die hen weygerden ter bruyloften te komen, seyt in deser manieren: 'Ick segghe u, datter niemandt van de mannen die daer ghenoot waren, mijn avontmael smaken en sal.'³ Ende Eva alleen zijnde, wert van het serpent bekoort ende verwonnen.⁴ Cain oock, van des Heeren aensicht voortvluchtich, heeft eenen hypocritischen ende geveynsden godsdienst ingevoert.⁵ Ende Thomas, by de heylige vergaderinghe niet zijnde, heeft swaerlick – dan alleen daerna in de vergaderinge – des Heeren verrijsenisse konnen ghelooven.⁶

---

1 Ps. 23:5.
2 Ps. 133:1.
3 Luc. 14:24.
4 Gen. 3:6.
5 Gen. 4[:16-24].
6 Joh.20:24-28.

Gemerct dan dattet seer klaerlicken [24ᵛ] blijckt, dattet seer [h]eerlick ende nut is dat hem iemant niet alleen metten gheest ende gheloove, maer oock met cerimonien ende uutwendighe belijdinghe der religien in de christelicke vergaderinghe te voeghen, ende de eensaemheyt also een schadelicke plage van herten te schouwen ende te vervloecken. Ende wel terechte heeft ons die prediker Salomo gheleert, segghende: ''t Is beter twee tesamen zijn dan een alleen, want sy ghenieten doch haers arbeyts wel. Valt haerder eene, so helpt hem zijn ghesellle op. Wee denghenen die alleene is, want als hy valt, so en is daer gheen ander die hem op helpe. Ooc als twee by malcanderen ligghen verwarmen sy malcanderen, hoe kan een alleen warm geworden? Een mach verweldicht worden, maer twee moghen wederstaen. Want een drijvoudich snoer en breeckt niet lichtelicken in twee.'[1] Ende de apostel Paulus, wel wijsselicken overleggende de onuutsprekelicke noodicheyt ende nutheyt der heyligher vergaderinghe, vermaent ghetrouwelicken alle godvreesende tot de onderhoudinge derselver, met dese woorden: [25ʳ] 'Latet ons onder malcanderen onsselfs waernemen tot een verweckinghe der liefden ende der goeder wercken, onse vergaderinghe niet verlatende, so de sommighe doen, maer onder malcanderen vermanen.'[2] Ende opdat Paulus syne vermaninghe des te stercker maken soude, so doet hy daer noch tweederhande verweckingen by. Het een is, dat den dach by is, oft dat ons leven rasschelicken wech vloeyt ende haestelicken na de doot ende na den dach des oordeels loopt.[3] De tweede verweckinghe oft aendrijvinge Pauli is dese: 'Want is 't dat wy moetwillichlicken sondigen, na dien dat wy de kennisse der waerheyt ontfangen hebben, so en is ons gheen offerhande meer achtergelaten, maer een vervaerlicke verwachtinghe des oordeels ende des vyers wreetheyt, die de vyanden verteeren sal.'[4]

Daerom, is 't sake dat ons de eere Gods ende onse salicheyt eenichsins ter herten gaen, so sullen wy de heylighe vergaderingen der ghemeynten groot achten ende in eeren houden, ons daerby voeghende ende in deselve alle ons leven lanck volherdende, sonder ons eenchsins daer af te laten trecken om sorghelooselicken op onsselven in eensaemheyt te willen leven. Amen.

---

1 Pred. 4[:9-12].
2 Heb. 10:24, 25.
3 Heb. 10:25.
4 Heb. 10:26[-27].

[25ᵛ] Van de teeckenen, waerdoor men de ware kercke oft gemeynte van de valsche onderscheyden sal.
Dat II. capittel.

Hetghene dat wy tot nu toe van de weerdicheyt, nootsakelickheyt ende nutheyt der heyliger vergaderinghen der gemeynten gheseyt hebben, wort van veel menschen voor goet ende warachtich ghehouden, ende sy en souden oock niet schoonders wenschen dan dat se in eenighe christelicke ghemeynte leven mochten. Maer sy zijn gheheelicken in twijffel tot welcke kercke oft ghemeynte zy haer met goeder consciencien keeren oft begeven sullen, ghemerckt datter hedensdaechs tot allen kanten so veel ende verscheyden opinien zijn. Ende so sy noch niet sekers ghevinden en konnen, so blijven sy by henselven in eensaemheyt, hetwelcke den vleesche in sonderheyt wel behaecht. Oft sy begheven hen onbedachtelicken tot een alsulcke ghemeynte, aldear sy der eeren Gods niet bequamelicken soecken, noch oock haerder sielen salicheyt wel terechte ghedienen konnen.

Opdat wy dan alsulcken menschen in haer twijffelachticheden ghenoech doen, sullen wy hier metten kortsten [26ʳ] eenvuldichlicken bewijsen hoe een godvreesende mensche die gheerne de waerheyt moeten ende navolghen soude, hem in dese sake regeren ende een onderscheyt tusschen d'een ende d'ander vergaderinghe maken sal.

In den eersten, wie in 't onderscheyden der ghemeynten een recht oordeel gheven wil, die moet eerste ende voor al vrij zijn van alle haet, nijdicheyt, partijdich[eyt], eygengoetdunckelicheyt, ende van alle diergelijcke blinde affectien. Daerna moet hi wel toesien, om de gemeynte te onderscheyden, dat hy gheen bedriegelicke teeckenen na en volghe, als het ghemeyn volck te doen plach; te weten, dat hy niet en sie oft de menichte groot oft kleyn is, oft alsulcke ghemeynte langhe oft onlanghe ghestaen heeft, oock niet op de volmaectheyt noch onvolmaectheyt der menschen, niet op vervolginge noch gerustheyt in derselver gemeynten, niet op voorspoet, tegenspoet noch ander dierghelijcke dingen, aengesien dat hem satan ook wel in eenen engel des lichts verstellen kan.[1] Maer hy sal alleen hetgene aenmercken dat warachtich is, ende daer men gheensins aen en twijffelt, als Christus ons oock leert, seggende: 'En oordeelt niet na het aensien, maer oordeelt [26ᵛ] een gherecht oordeel.'[2] Ende alsulcke warachtighe teeckenen en sal men nergens dan in de heylighe schrift soecken, tot dewelcke de Heylige Gheest ons altijt sendet, telcken alsser

---

1 2 Kor. 11:14.
2 Joh. 7:24.

eenigen twist in de sake der religien is. De propheet Jesaias wijst ons tot de wet ende ghetuyghenisse.[1] Ende Christus spreect: 'Sy hebben Moysen ende de propheten.'[2] Ende noch op een ander plaetse: 'Ondersoeckt de schrift.'[3] So sal men dan de sekere ende onb[e]drieghelicke teeckenen, waeraen men een christelicke ghemeynte sal weten te kennen, in de heylighe schrift soecken, ende niet sien op den waen des ghemeynen volcx, noch oock op dat goetduncken ende besluyt der princen ende vorsten.

Dewelcke teeckenen wy hier oock op d'alder kortste stellen sullen, opdat een yeghelick sekerlicken weten mach tot welcker ghemeynten oft kercken hy hem voor het alder sekerste sal moghen ende moeten toevoeghen.

In den eersten moet men hier aenmercken de leeringhe, ende ten tweeden de regeringe derselver kercken oft ghemeynten. De principaelste capitelen oft hooftstucken der leeringen zijn dese, als namelick, van God ende van den [27ʳ] mensche. Van God, te weten, wat God is ende hoe men God dienen sal.

ᴵGod is een gheest.[4] Te weten, de almachtighe eewige Vader, Schepper ende regeerder aller dinghen, de Vader ons Heeren Jesu Christi. Item, de Sone des eewigen Vader,[5] den Vader ghelijck,[6] die in de volheydt des tijts mensche ghewordten is,[7] een sone des menschen uuten mensche na den vleessche door de medede[e]lachtich[eyt] des vleesch ende bloets der kinderen. Hy heeft de ghedaente des knechts aengedaen,[8] also dat de eenige Heere Jesus Christus is God ende mensche. Diewelcke daerenboven is der kercken Gods eenige ende eewighe koninck,[9] opperste priester,[10] propheet,[11] bruydegom,[12] hooft[13] ende fundament;[14] ghelevert om onse sonden ende verresen om onser rechtveerdichmakinge.[15] Dewelcke als

---

1 Jes.8:20.
2 Luc. 16:29.
3 Joh. 5:[39]; Hand.17:11.
4 Joh. 4:24.
5 Heb.7:3; Micha 5:[1-]2; Spr.30:4.
6 Joh. 5:18; 10:22; Fil. 2:6.
7 Gal.4:4; Joh.1:14; Mat.1:1; Hand.2:30; Rom.1:3; 9[:5, ?] [original: b.c.]; Hebr.2:14.
8 Fil. 2:7.
9 Ps. 2; Luc.1:[32].
10 Hebr. 5:6.
11 Deut.18:18; Hand.3:22.
12 Joh.3:29.
13 Ef.1:22.
14 1 Kor. 3:11.
15 Rom. 4:25.

onse eenighe middelaer ende advocaet, nu in den hemel in der eewicheyt voor ons bidt,[1] ende sal hier na weder in der wolcken komen om te oordelen de levende ende de dooden.[2]

Item, des eewighen Vaders ende Soons is een eewige Heylige Gheest.[3] Door wiens inghheven altijt ghesproken hebben de heylige mannen Gods, [27ᵛ] de propheten ende apostelen.[4] Die selve leydt ons in alle waerheyt: Hy verlicht, wederbaert, troost ende vervult onse herten met de blijschap des eewigen levens.[5] Hy salft ons Gode tot gheestelicke koningen ende priesteren, Hy voecht ons aen Christum onsen hoofde ende maect ons met Hem een lichaem, dat wy ware ende levende leden zijns lichaems zijn.

Ten laetsten, wy worden door Hem met heylsame gaven verciert, dewelcke Hy eenen yeghelicken mededeylt, als 't Hem belieft.[6]

De eere ende dienst desselven warachtighen ende eewighen Gods is ghelegen, niet in menschen insettinghen ende geboden, waermede men Hem tevergheefs dient,[7] noch in eenige bloote ceremonien na de letter, niet in den mont ende lippen,[8] maer t'samen in den lichaem ende in 't herte, in den gheest, waerheyt ende liefde, ende dat na den reghel des godlicken woorts,[9] cortelicken in de thien gheboden vervaet.

Noch so wilt dese onse hemelsche Vader in onse gebeden also ghedient ende gheeert wesen, als dat Hy van ons aengheroepen wilt zijn in den naem zijns Soons, door den H[eylighen] Gheest,[10] niet door de creatueren, noch uut eenige vleeschelic[28ʳ]ke affecten. Dit is hetghene datter van God ende van zijnder eeren, ende dienst in zijn ware kercke oft vergaderinghe gheleert wort.

Van den mensche wort er gheleert, in den eersten, dat hy na der gedachten, herten ende lichame van zijnder natueren wegen door de sonde in Adam verdorven is.[11]

Ten tweeden, dat alle zijn salicheyt ende heyl alleen door de genadenrijcke barmherticheyt Gods, in den eenighen Christo gheleghen is.[12]

---

1   1 Tim. 2:5; 1 Joh.2:1; Hebr.7:24.
2   2 Tim 4:[8]; Mat. 26:[64].
3   Heb. 9:14.
4   Mar.12:36; Hand. 1:16; 2 Pet. 1:21.
5   Luc.12:12; Joh.3:5; 14:17, 26; 15:26; 16:26; 1 Kor. 2:10; Ef. 3:5; 1 Joh. 2:27.
6   1 Kor.12: 4, 8, 11.
7   Jes.29:13; Mat.15:9.
8   Mat.15:8; 2 Kor.3:6.
9   1 Kor.6:20; 2 Kor. 7:1; Joh.4:23; Jac.1:27.
10 Joh. 14:13, 16, 23; Rom. 8:26-27.
11 Gen.6:[5], [11]; Jer.17:9; Ps. 51; Spr.20:6; Ezr. 4:[19?]; Rom. 5:12; Ef. 2:3.
12 Rom: 3:24-25; 5:9-10; Ef. 2:5-8.

Ten derden, dat de mensche door het geloove in Christus, door den H[eylighen] Gheest gerechtveerdicht zijnde, Gode gehoorsaemheyt na zijn ghebot ende bevel schuldich is te bewijsen, door het afsterven des ouden menschen ende door het aennemen des nieuwen menschen, ende dat na eens yegelicx beroep, hetzy dat hy een openbaer oft een particulier persoon zy, nadat hem God geroepen mach hebben.[1] Want gelijck de overheyt haer bysonder ampt oft officie heeft, also heeft ooc de dienaer des woorts, desgelijcx oock de huysvader. Ten laetsten,[2] dat allen alsulcke godvreesende menschen terstont na dit leven te verwachten staet het eewige leven, hetwelcke hen in den hemel by Christo bereydt is. Ghelijc[28ᵛ]kerwijs oock den anderen, die oft door opinien der eyghener gerechticheyt opgeblasen zijnde, van yemant anders dan van den Heere Christo haer salicheyt verwachten ende hopen, oft die haer tot gheen boetveerdicheyt begheven en willen, maer leven gantsch sorgheloselicken, nemende in haer sonden een welbehaghen ende sterven also ten lesten henen, sonder eenich berou oft leetwesen, niet anders te verbeyden en staet, dan na dit leven die eewighe verderffenisse, na de rechtveerdige strenghicheyt Gods, aldaer sy in eewiger pijnen wesen sullen.[3K] Dese is de leere, die alle de propheten ende apostelen drijven ende beschermen, also dattet klaer genoech is dat men na luydt derselver, de heylighe vergaderinghe der ghemeynten afmeten sal.

Het oprecht regiment der kercken, hetwelcke metten woorde Gods overeenkoemt ende hetwelcke men alletijt wijsselicken van het wereltlick regiment behoort te onderscheyden, is ghelegen in de reyne ende onvervalschte predicatie des woorts Gods, in 't oprecht ghebruyck der sacramenten (als namelicken, des doops ende des nachtmaels), ende in de behoorlicke onderhoudinghe der christelicker straffen.

[29ʳ] Ende alsdan so is de predicacie des godlicken woorts voor goedt ende suyver, 't ghebruyck der sacramenten voor oprecht, ende de christelicke straffe voor behoorlick te houden, wanneer alle dese dinghen uutgericht worden na des Heeren bevel, ende wanneer sy alle strecken na het eynde tot welck de bovengenoemde leeringhe streckt. Te weten, dat wy, door dese onser ellendicheden in Adam ende der godlicker ghenaden tot onswaert door Jesum Christum ernstlicken vermaent zijnde, tot een rechte gehoorsaemheyt ende tot een boetveerdighe godvreesentheyt verweckt worden. In wat ghemeynten dan alle dese dinghen also gheleert, ghehandelt ende gedreven worden; item, daer alle andere questien ende

---

1 Rom. 6:12; Ef.2:[10]; 4:17, 20-21; 1Pet.4:2-3.
2 Joh.5:24.; 14:3; 17:24; Fil.1:23.
3 Mat.3:10-11; Mar. 16:16; Rom 2: 5, 8; 2 Thes.1:8; 1 Kor. 6:10; Ef. 5:5; Gal. 5:21.

handelinghen der religien soberlicken, manierlicken ende sonder eenighen lust tot twisten tot de bovenghenoemde leeringhe gherefereert worden, alleen tot heylsame stichtinghe der gantscher ghemeynten, tot een alsulcke ghemeynte, segghe ick, mach hem een yeghelick wel met goeder consciencien begheven. Ende ghemerckt dat wy na den voorseyden regel der h[eyligher] schrift onse christelicke ghemeynte, so wel opentlicken als heymelicken, also [29ᵛ] vergaderen ende onderhouden (als wy des oock in onse consciencie wel gherust zijn), ende ghelijck wy by alle billicke richters alle tijdt tot noch toe bereyt hebben gheweest sulcks met een christelicke liefde ende vriendelicheydt te bewijsen, so en kan nu gheen godvreesende mensch langher in twijffel staen maer sal hem wel goeder ende gheruster consciencien tot een alsulcke ghemeynte moghen voeghen als tot noch toe van onse broederen vergadert zijn, oft noch alle daghen door de hulpe Gods teghen alle poorten der hellen vergadert moghen worden.

Maer hier hebben wy noch met korte woorden deghene te vermanen die in het verkiesen der christelicker ghemeynten also voortvaren, dat se deselve ghemeynte haten ende schouwen in dewelcke de christelicke straffe wat scherpelicken onderhouden wort, ende willen hen alleen tot een alsulcke kercke oft ghemeynte begheven daer alsulcks wat slappelicker toegaet. Want alsulcke menschen zijn van de gemeynte des hooveerdighen ende rebellighen Esau, die zijns broeders jock van synen hals schuddede.[1] Men kan oock van sulcke menschen anders niet ghesegghen [30ʳ] dan dattet gheve[n]ysde hypocrijten zijn. Want sy willen van de gemeynte Christi wesen, nochtans verworpen sy moetwillichlicken van haer het voorneemste deel der insettinghen Christi, te weten, de christelicke straffe. Ende in het rijcke Christi soecken sy een vleeschelicke vrijheyt, d'welck nochtans een rijck der heerlicheyt, der ghcrcchticheyt ende der ootmoedicheyt is, in d'welc alle vrijheyt tot sonden scherpelicken gestraft wort. Sy en overlegghen niet hoe swaerlick een yeghelick van alle, in sonderheyt in een sulcke verderffenisse der natueren, tot godvreesentheyt te trecken is,[L] ende dat om sulcx te beteren onder de insettinghen Christi d'alder krachtichste is de onderhoudinghe der christelicker straffe, dewelcke anders niet en is dan een behoorlicke openbare oft heymelicke bestraffinge der sonden, ende dat na den regel der apostelen. Waer uut volcht, dat degene die sulcx verachten, alleenskens meer ende meer in de sorgeloose vrijheyt tot sondigen ende in groote perijckelen haerder zielen vallen. Want als de wijse man seyt: 'Wie de straffinge hatet, die sal sterven.'[2]

---

1 Gen. 27:40.
2 Spr. 15:10.

Oft een christen oock wel van de Roomsche kercke afwijcken mach.
Dat iii. capittel.

[30ᵛ] Tot nu toe hebben wy op d'alder vlijtichste verklaert hoe dat men de heylighe vergaderinge der gemeynten onderhouden moet. Daerna oock, welck de teeckenen zijn by dewelcke men de christelicke van de valsche ghemeynten onderkennen sal. Nu hebben wy voorder te verklaren of de christenen wel moghen afwijcken van alsulcke vergaderingen als hedensdaechs in 't pausdom ghehouden worden.

Nu willen wy den godvreesenden leser vriendelicken ende om Christus wille gebeden hebben, dat hy dit navolghende goedertierlicken ende sonder eenighe partijcheyt lesen wil, ende dat principalick in een so twistige sake, om dewelcke daghelicks tot vele plaetsen so veel turbacien komen. Om dewelcke, segge ick, so menigen mensch van al zijn goet berooft, so menigen mensch so jammerlicken om d'leven ghebracht wort. Aengaende van ons, wy sullen simpelicken ende sonder eenighe bewimpelinge (als 't behoort) voor God onse meyninge verklaren, hoe wel dat wy des al versekert zijn dat wij er by de werelt seer kleynen danck mede behalen sullen.

Wy bekennen wel, ende danckender oock God onsen hemelschen Vader af, [31ʳ] datter in de Roomsche kercke noch veel goede leeringhen na de letter over ghebleven ende behouden zijn, als te weten, van God, van synen Sone, van den H[eylighen] Gheest, ende van noch sommighe andere hooftstucken der christelicker religien. Maer onder dese is so veel suerdeechs der phariseen vermengt, so veel grouwelicke dwalinghen bygheset, ende daer zijn so groote misbruycken des kerkelicken dienst toe gekomen, om d'welck al tesamen te verantwoorden ende te verdedigen zy dapperlick ende hardtneckelick strijden, den volcke hare beuselinghen voor Gods woordt voorhoudende, dat so wie eenichsins godsalich is ende God vreest door de kennisse der waerheydt verlicht zijnde, die moet er niet alleen een schroemen af hebben, maer wordt oock in zijn consciencie ghedronghen van alle gheselschap ende conversacie der Roomscher kercken af te wijcken.

In den eersten hebben sy in veelderhande manieren vervalscht, verandert ende gecorrumpeert den waren godsdienst, diewelcke gheleghen is in den Gheest, waerheydt ende oprechte ghehoorsaemheyt des wille Gods, na uutwijsinghe zijns woordts.[1] Want sy ver[31ᵛ]sieren ende maken den volcke wijs dat men God wel terecht met sommighe koude menschelicke insettinghen ende vonden dienen mach. Als daer

---

1 Joh. 4:24; Rom.12:1-2; 1 Thes.4:2.

zijn, het hooren of aensien der missen, het koopen der missen; item, onderscheydt der spijsen, eenigherhande versierde monickerije, het murmelen oft babbelen van sommighe ghebedekens, altaren ende capellekens oprichten, ende dieselve met renten begaven, ende andere diergelijcke beuselkens sonder ghetal door des menschen verstandt ghevonden ende also onder het volck ghebracht. Ende hiermede niet tevreden zijnde, hebben syer noch sommighe grove afgoderijen mede onder ghemenghet. Sy leeren het aenroepen van sommighe ghestorvene menschen, dewelcke sy tot patroonen, maerschalcken ende beschermers over sieckten, kranckheden, ambachten, gilden, landen, steden ende dorpen stellen ende ordineren.

Ende ter eeren van alsulcke ghestorvene stichten sy vastedaghen, vyerdagen, verscheydene sacrificien, missen, vesperen, mettenen ende dierghelijcke meer. Sy sweeren by alsulcker heylighen namen, ende niet alleen by den naem Gods.[1] Noch so maken sy, tegen [32ʳ] dat opentlicken bevel Gods,[2] ter eeren van dese geschilderde, gulden, silveren, steenen ende houten beelden, die sy heymelicken in hare huysen ende openbaerlicken in tempelen ende op andere plaetsen hooghe verheffen, die selve met kleederen, wasse, keerssen, ghebedekens, kussen, knyen buygen ende meer andere diergelijcke heydensche raserijen verrieren. De treffelickste ende principaelste beelden (want so wel onder de papisten als onder de heydenen isser noch hedensdaechs een onderscheydt der afgoden) worden by hen met grooter weerden ende met groote processien omghedraghen teghen allerley manieren van ellendicheden, als tegen krijch ende oorloch, peste ende dieren tijdt, droochte ende andere diergehelijcke. Alsulcken beelden werden beloftenissen gedaen, men koemt se van verren landen in pelgrimagien besoecken. Daerenboven so dragen sy een houten cruys om, d'welck by hen quansuys[M] d'beeldt des ghecruysten Christi is, ende daer zijn dan de papistische priesteren so onverschaemt dat sy hen niet en ontsien voor 'tselve cruys te roepen: 'Weest ghegroet h[eylig] cruys, onse eenighe hope, in desen tijdt des lijdens. Vermeerdert in den godvreesenden [32ᵛ] de gherechticheydt ende vergheeft den sondaren hare schulden.' Uut alle welcke dinghen klaerlicken ghenoech te mercken staet hoe grousamelicken den warachtighen godsdienst by de papisten vervalscht is.

Daerenboven so wordt noch door haer leeringhe de sacrificie des doodts Christi (die met een eenighe offerhande de geheylichde in der

---

1 Jes. 45:23.
2 Exo. [20]:4; Deut. 5:8; Lev. 26:1; Ps. 96:5; Jes. 44:17; Wijsh.13:[10]-19; 1 Joh.5:21.

eewicheyt volkomen ghemaeckt heeft)[1] een groot lachter ende oneere aenghedaen, aenghesien dat sy de menschelicke verdiensten, den uutwendighen ghebruyck der sacramenten, dat mommelen der missen, hare salvingen, pauselicken aflaten ende bullen; item, de oorbiechte, den veghevyere, den wijwatere, roosekranskens, der papen ghesangen, vereeringhen der heylighen, neffens hare reliquien ende beelden, der moniken oordenen, hare be[de]vaerden, ende voort meer andere beuselinghen sonder ghetal, niet en schamen de verghevinge der sonden toe te rekenen.

Noch so willen sy Christum schandelicken berooven van zijn ampt oft officie waermede Hy der gheloovigen eenighe middelaer ende advocaet by den Vader is,[2] hebbende een eewich prie[33ʳ]sterdom,[3] waerom Hy oock volkomelicken salich maken kan degene die door Hem tot God komen, ende leeft altijt om voor haer te verbidden; want den gestorvenen heyligen schrijven sy de eere toe dat se onse middelaers ende verbidders zijn. Hier van koemt dat se tot Marian roepen: 'Weest ghegroet koninghinne der barmherticheyt, ons leven, onse soeticheyt ende onse hope.'

Ghemerckt nu dat uut de h[eylighe] schrift wel blijct dat Christus een hoogepriester der barmhertichenden is,[4] alle degene van selfs tot Hem roepende, die daer arbeyden, belast ende beladen zijn,[5] dat Hy gheenen medehulper en behoeft om medemiddelaer te wesen, aenghesien dat Hy des Vaders wel beminde Sone is, in denwelcken de Vader een welbehagen heeft,[6] so volcht daer nootsakelicken uut dat Christus van de papisten zijnder eeren des middelaerschaps berooft wort, dewelcke leeren dat het voorbidden der heylighen ons voor Christum, oft met den middelaer Christo voor den Vader van nooden zy.

Hierenboven, so hebben sy noch jammerlicken verscheurt ende vervalscht het geheel regiment der christelicker kercken van Christo ingestelt ende van den [33ᵛ] apostelen in grooter weerden onderhouden. Want men siet dat byna al haer kercken regiment in beuselingen ende versierde supersticieuse ceremonien gelegen is.

Het predickampt in der kercken, d'welck een seer heerlick ende excellent ampt is, d'welck ooc alletijt in de christelicke vergaderinghen

---

1 Hebr. 10:14.
2 Gal.3:[20]; 1Tim. 2:5; Heb. 9:15; 1 Joh. 2:1.
3 Heb.7:24.
4 Heb. 2:[17]; 4:15.
5 Mat. 11:28.
6 Mat. 3:17; 17:5; Col. 1:13; 2 Pet. 1:17

voor het principaelste behoort gheacht te wesen,[1] hebben sy so kleyn gheachtet ende so verworpen dat sulcx nemmermeer oft seer selden vant hare bisschoppen oft pastoren uutghericht, maer meestendeel somghe moniken opgeleyt wort, dewelcke en [ont]deden hare kappen ende berderen[N] aenghesichten, sy souden dickwils bequamer zijn om achter den ploech te gaen, om een spiesse opten hals te draghen, om Venus oft Bacchus te dienen, dan om opten predickstoel te klimmen. Ende wanneer se eens bestaen den volcke te prediken, so en beghinnen sy niet met aenroepinghe des godlicken naems (als 't wel behooren soude), maer beginnen heydensche wijse van de aenroepinghe Marie. Ende mitsdien dattet ghesworene pausslaven zijn, so en blijven se met hare predicacien niet binnen de palen der prophetischer ende apostolischer leeringhen[2] (als den ghetrou[34ʳ]wen dienaren Christi toebehoort), maer om de afgoderijen, tyrannijen ende grouwelicke misbruycken der Roomscher kercken te bevestighen, so brengen sy alle weghen haerder doctoren schriften voort, die selve also hooge achtende als de heylighe schrift selve. Dickwils verdrayen sy de ghetuyghenissen der heyligher schrift in een heel verkeerden sin, sy brenghen voort hare versierde miraculen, de pauselicke aflaten ende indulgencien op sekere plaetsen ende tijden te verdienen. Sy storten hare ghebeden voor de zielkens in 't veghevyer, wanneer men hen daer gelt voor geeft. Sy lachteren, belieghen ende bedraghen schandelicken de warachtige puere leeringhe Christi, met alle deghene diese prediken ende beschermen willen. Ende hare eyghen leeringhe en willen sy van gheenen godvreesenden laten oordeelen. Maer so wie daer een woordeken teghen seggen wilt, denselven beschuldighen sy terstont voor eenen ketter, sy brenghen hem aen, ende so veel in hen is, sy maken dat deselve aen eenen staeck verbrandt wort. 'Want wie quaet doet, die hatet dat licht, ende hy en koemt niet totten lichte, opdat syne wercken niet ghestraft en worden.'[3]

[34ᵛ] Noch so ghebruycken sy in alle hare godsdiensten een vreemde ende onbekende sprake, sonder eenighe stichtinghe des ghemeynen volcx, daer men aldermeest in de vergaderinge der ghemeynte op behoorde te letten, als Paulus ghebiedt, ende hadde om dier oorsaken wille liever vijf woorden te spreken door synen sin, opdat hy oock den anderen onderwese, dan anders thienduysent woorden in een vreemde sprake, die der ghemeynten onbekent ware.[4] Maer de papisten wel

---

1 Mat. 28:19-20; Mar. 16:15; Luc. 24:[47]; 2 Tim. 4:2.
2 Ef. 2:[20].
3 Joh. 3:19.
4 1 Kor.14: 5, 12, 17, 19.

wetende dat 't gheheel fundament ende steunsel haerder tyrannijen ende afgoderijen in des ghemeynen volcx onverstandt ende der godlicker dinghen onwetenheydt ghelegen is (want het grove plompe volck wort lichtelicken herwaerts ende derwaerts gedreven), so en gebruycken se niet alleen vreemde sprake in hare vergaderingen, teghen de leeringhe Pauli[1] ende tegen het gebruyck alder vaderen, maer verbieden oock den leecken (als sy se noemen) de bybel te lesen, gevende hen tot boecken ende meesters de geschilderde, houten of steenen beelden, dewelcke nochtans in de h[eylighe] schrift onderwijsingen der ijdelheden ende valstricken voor de voeten der onwijser ghenaemt worden.[2]

[35ʳ] Den doop, die na de insettinghe Christi ende exempel der apostelen eenvuldichlicken behoorde uutghereyckt te wesen,[3] hebben sy met vele eensdeels onnutte, ende eendeels supersticieuse ceremonien schandelicken vermenghet, als namelicken met sout in den mont te steken, met smeeren, besweeren ende dierghelijcke beuselinghen meer. Ende de gheestelicke mijsterien oft verborghentheden des doops, dewelcke begrepen worden in een klare ende ghetrouwe uutlegginghe oft verklaringhe onser verdoemenissen in Adam, ende onser salicheydt uut ghenaden weder in Christo verkreghen; item, onses ghehoorsaemheydt d'welck wy Gode ende onsen naesten schuldich zijn door het afsterven des ouden menschen ende aenneminghe des nieuwen menschen, en bedie[n]en sy nemmermeer wanneer sy doopen, ymmers dat ick noch gheweten kan.

Hierenboven maken sy noch den lieden wijs dat de kloosterlicke professie also veel is alsof het den anderen doop ware; item, dat de sonden (die sy daghelicksche sonden noemen) door het besprenghen des ghewijden waters afgesuyvert worden. Met alle [35ᵛ] welcke droomen ende beuselinghen sy de weerdicheit des doops grootelicken verkleynen.

Ende ten laetsten, opdatter aen hare lasteringhe ende vervalschinghe des doops niet ontbreken en soude, so doopense oock de klocken, door een godloose ende seer schandelicke supersticie. Dewelcke klocken gheen ghemeynschap met Christo in zijn doot totten eewighen leven en konnen ghehebben.

Des Heeren heylighe nachtmael, d'welck een sacrament onser gheestelicker spijsinghen in Christo is, hebben sy oock seer jammerlicken mishandelt ende verontreynicht. Want hoewel dattet een openbaer werck ende oeffeninge der gantscher ghemeynten behoorde te wesen, na de

---

1 1 Kor. 14: 2, 4, 6-9, 11, 13, 16-17, 19, 21, 23, 28.
2 Jer. 10:8; Wijsh. 14:11.
3 Mat. 28:19; Mar.16:16; Hand. 8:37; Ef. 5:26.

insettinghe Christi ende het exempel der apostelen,[1] so is 't van hen verandert in een particulier miswerck eens mispaeps, d'welck sy meestendeel met gheldt daer toe ghekocht zijnde in een onbekende sprake afweven, ende dat met groote verwonderinghe der omstanders, met wonderlicke kleederen ende ghewandt vermomt zijnde, veel ende verscheyden belachelicke faxienᵒ oft grillen bedrijvende die der mysterien des nachtmaels gheens[36ʳ]sins aen en gaen. Als nu slapen sy, alsdan waken sy weder, dan mommelen sy wat heymelick by henselven, dan laten se hen weder hooren, sy wasschen, sy drooghen, sy laten hen alsnu van voren sien, alsdan van achter. Wie soude dese ongheschickte handelinghen ende dit apenspel al konnen beschrijven? Noch maken sy den menschen wijs dat dit miswerck, so men het van hen koopt, een seer goede recepte is teghen alle quaden ende ghebreken, so wel des lichaems als der zielen. Item, dattet een offerhande zy door dewelcke Christus synen hemelschen Vader wederomme gheoffert wordt, om de salicheydt so wel der levender als der dooden met een alsulc werck te verwerven. Welck alles recht teghen is ende strijdet met de voornemelickste ende besonderlickste gheheymenisse ende verborgentheydt des nachtmaels onses Heeren,[2] ende oock met de weerdicheyt der hoogher offerhanden d'welck onse opperste, eewighe ende eenighe hooghepriester Christus eens in den cruyce voor ons opgheoffert heeft.[3] Christus heeft ghewilt, dat dit sacrament des nachtmaels tot zijnder gedachtenissen soude ghehouden worden. 'Sulcx doet,' seyde [36ᵛ] Hy, 'tot mijnder gedachtenissen.'[4] Maer dese lesen haer missen oock tot ghdachtenisse der heylighen, de heylighen daerin aenroepende, ende dat meer is, hen bysondere missen ter eeren onderhoudende. Ende wanneer sy eens quansuys een openbare uutreyckinghe des nachtmaels willen houden, als gemeynlicken ontrent paesschen by hen te gheschieden plach, so en konnen sy alsdan daer toe oock niet ghekomen dat zij 't onvervalscht uutreycken. Want de rechte bereydinghe[5] ende proeve om het nachtmael weerdichlicken te ontfangen stellen sy in hare versierde oorbiechte ende absolucie. Daerna so benemen sy den volcke den beecker tegen de opentlicke instellinghe Christi, ende teghen het ghebruyck der gheheelder eerster kercken.[6] Daerenboven aengaende de vrucht ende weldaet des doots Christi, dewelcke men den volcke alle tijdt klaerlicken ende

---

1 Mat. 26:[26]; Mar.14:22; Luc.22:14;Hand. 20:7; 1 Kor. 10:17; 1 Kor. 11: 20-22. 33-34.
2 1.Co.10.b.16.
3 1 Kor. 10:16; Hebr. 7: 23[24?]; 10:14.
4 Luc. 22:19; 1 Kor. 11:24-25.
5 1 Kor.11:28.
6 Mat. 26:26; Mar. 14:23; 1 Kor. 11:25-29.

beduydelicken behoorde in te beelden telcken als men het nachtmael uutreyckt (als daer staet: 'Ghy sult des Heeren doot verkondighen, totdat Hy koemt')[1] oft sy laten sulcx gantselicken achter, alleen sommighe latijnsche woorden binnensmonts sprekende, wanneer sy den volcke [37r] het broot gheven. Oft sy rueren de voorschreven weldaet des doodts Christi so luttel aen dattet jammer is – ja, oock nemmermeer gelijck dattet wel behooren soude. Ende dit haer jaerlicx ontfangen des sacraments maken sy meer een bewijsteecken des afgodischen gheselschaps met den paus ende met zijnder afgoderijen, dan des heylsame ghemeynschaps met Christo in zijn lichaem voor ons ghegheven ende in zijn bloet voor ons vergoten. Want waerom souden sy anders op groote straffe ende onghenade des overheyts de arme menschen tot haer onheylich ende vervalscht nachtmael so strengelick dwingen? Waerom souden sy anders deselve doen vangen, die om der consciencien wille van haer sacrament blijven ende met grooten trecke van herten begheeren datselfde reyn ende onvervalscht te gebruycken.

Ten laetsten oock, het broot dat in het oprecht gebruyck des nachtmaels 'het lichaem Christi voor ons ghegheven', sacramentsch wijs, ende warachtelicken na des h[eylighen] schrift meyninghe genoemt wort, omdattet een krachtelick ende seker teecken van de ghemeynschap des lichaems Christi is, na des Heeren insettinge, oft dat zijn lichaem eens voor [37v] ons in den cruyce warachtelicken tot verghevinge onser sonden ghelevert ende opgheoffert is,[2] dit broot, segghe ick, imagineren sy door de kracht der vijf woorden verandert te worden in 't wesentlicke lichaem Christi, dat metten vleeschelicken monde totten eewighen leven moet gheten worden.[3] Het welck een beghinsel ende oorspronck is van een nieuwe ende grouwelicke afgoderie. Want daeruut koemt dat deghene die het broot consacreert, als sy sggen, nadat hy de vijf woorden op het alderstilste over het broot gesproken heeft, so is hy de erste die 't met gebuychde knyen aenbidt, daerna met de handen hooghe opheffende, thoont hij 't den volcke oock te eeren ende aen te bidden. Ende opdat nu desen nieuwen ende den oudtvaderen onbekenden god Maosim[4] gheen dinc ter vereeringe ontbreken en soude, so klinct men de bellekens, men schuyft er de gardijnen op, een yegelijck slaet voor zijn borst. Ende als nu de misse wat hoogher ende heerlicker is, so ontsteect men de keerssen ende tortsen, men worpt er het wieroock, men speelt er met orghelen,

---

1 1 Kor. 11:26.
2 1 Kor. 11:24.
3 1 Kor. 10:[16].
4 Dan. 11:38.

met trect er de klocke om van den torren af den volcke te kennen te geven dat den nieuwen Christus nu al gemaect ende [38ʳ] tusschen des priesters vingeren om aenghebeden te worden, den volcke voorgehouden is. Hiermede en neemt dese afgoderie noch gheen eynde, maer daerna wort dit geconsacreert broot, so zij 't noemen, het welck het arme verdoolt volc meynt Christum te wesen, nauwelicken bewaert, opghesloten oft opghehangen in een kasken oft huysken besloten, om van den volcke aengebeden te worden; ende dat door de decreten van sommige pausen, die niet oudt en zijn. Daerna vereert men dit besloten broot met keerssen, met knyebuygen, met bloemkens ende met sekere ghebedekens, hoewel dattet nochtans hemselven van de muysen, wormen ende eyghen verdervinge niet beschermen en kan. Hetselve wort oock tegen alle onweder, geruchte van oorloghen, ende alle andere tegenspoeden opentlicken ende met groote processie ommeghedraghen. Ter eeren van dit broot sticht men altaren, capellen, besondere missen; ende deselfde is van den paus Urbanus de vierde van dien name, ontrent den jare ons Heeren 1264, eenen jaerlicxschen feestdach ingestelt, opten welcken dach het verblinde volc door den afgodischen gheest ghedreven zijnde, doet hem groote eere, met meerder pomperie [38ᵛ] ende praele dan oyt ten tijde Nabuchodonosoz, oft oock in Perssen is ghesien gheweest.[1] Ende dat meer is, gheen hooghe feestdaghen, noch treffelicke vergaderinge en kan van hen gheviert ende ghehouden worden oft dese gebacken Christus, in een silvere oft gulden ciborie besloten, moet er altijt by wesen. Alle welcke dinghen gheschieden gheheelicken teghen de insettinghe ende weerdicheyt des nachtmaels, sonder eenich exempel der apostelen ende oudtvaderen der eerster kercken, als den genen die in de historien ervaren is ghenoech blijcken mach. So wie nu alle dese ende dierghelijcke grillen die de papisten by des Heeren nachtmael ghebruycken neerstelicken insien, ende terechte met de ware instellinghe Christi ende de onderhoudinghe der apostelen ghelijcken wilt, die sal klaerlicken mercken dat de papisten de rechte sacramentschenders zijn, welcken naem sy ons tot noch toe valschelick ende onrechtelick naghegeven hebben.

Hetghene dat se voorts leeren van de andere vijf sacramenten (als sy se valschelicken noemen), als namelicken van de confirmatie oft vorminge, penitencie, oordens, houwelicken staet ende [39ʳ] uuterste olysel, datselve is ooc al met veel beuselinghen ende grouwelicke dwalingen vermengt. Want aengaende de confirmacie oft vorminghe, die in ouden tijden niet anders en is geweest dan een nutte oeffeninghe der jonge jeucht die nu in haer kintsheyt ghedoopt waren in 't leeren ende

---

[1] Dan. 3:7.

van buytens by de ghemeynte teghen de bisschoppen op te segghen de hooftstucken des christelicken gheloofs, dese hebben de papisten verandert in een maniere van een guychelspel, eerst de kinderen wat besmeerende, ende daerna met de hant aen de kinnebacken slaende. Nochtans willen sy een alsulcken spel een sonderlinghe kracht toeschrijven, te weten, dat daerdoor de wortel ende den brandt der sonden die na den doop uut de erfsonde den vleesche by ghebleven is, gantschelicken wech ghenomen wort, het welck des doops ende der sacrificien Christi weerdicheyt gheheel contrarie is ende opentlick teghenstrijdt. De boete oft belijdinghe, die hier voortijden in de apostolische kercke anders niet gheweest en is dan een hertelicke belijdinghe der sonden voor God, oft ooc voor de verergherde broederen,[1] om alsulcke erghernisse alsser geschiet was wech te [39ᵛ] nemen, hebben de papisten verandert in een vertellinghe oft verhalinghe der sonden met alle haer circonstancien ende ommestanden, ende dat in de oorbiechte, dewelcke biechte sy den volcke wijs maken ghenoechsaem te zijn om daerdoor volkomen verghevinghe der sonden te vercrijgen. Siet, so groote kracht schrijven sy toe der absolutien, dewelcke van hen al heymelick, sonder van den volcke verstaen te worden, binnensmonts ghesproken wort, ende dat ten grooten achterdeele ende tot oneere der verdiensten Christi, ende tot groot misbruyck der Evangelischer absolutien ende des ghewelts der sleutelen. Ick verswijghe noch dat door alsulcken misbruyck het recht ghebruyck der christelicker straffen buyten der ghemeynten ghesloten wort. Item, dat alsulcke oorbiechte een schole ende een decsel is van veel sonden ende eenen sleutel waermede de paus van Roomen in aller menschen – keyseren, koningen, ende princen – herten ende secrete raden getreden kan, ende dat oock met seer kleynder moeyten, om also zijn antichristische tyrannie des te beter teghen alle aenstoot te houden staende.

De oordene (als sij 't noemen) oft der kercken dienst hebben sy oock in veel[40ʳ]derley manieren ommgehedraeyt ende verkeert. Want buyten den woorde Gods hebben sy sommighe nieuwe graden der kerckendienaren ingevoert, sommighe gantsch onnut ende sommighe der kercken schadelick: als die se noemen exorcisten, acoluthos, subdiakenen, cardinalen ende dierghelijcke. Andere dienaren die haer namen in de heylighe schrift hebben, behouden sy alleen voor so veel als den naem aentreft ende misbruycken dieselve tot dingen die haer ampten oft officien gheenssins aen en gaen. Want by hen hebben sy diakenen, priesteren, pastooren ende bisschoppen. Der diakenen officie was na de

---

1 Mat. 18:15; Luc. 17:3-4; Jac. 5:16.

apostolische insettinghe, dat se in de ghemeynte de aelmoessen ghetrouwelicken ende neerstelicken vergaderden ende den behoeftighen uutdeylden.[1] Der priesteren ampt was dat se den pastooren behulpelick waren om wel ende behoorlicke wijse in een goede leeringhe ende heylige conversacie de regeringe der ghemeynten ende de christelicke straffe te oeffenen ende te onderhouden. Maer hoe luttel dat hen de papistische diakenen moeyen met der ghemeynten aelmoessen te vergaderen ende deselve weder uut te deylen; item, hoe [40ᵛ] weynich de paussche priesteren beneerstigen dat de christelicke ghemeynte in de rechte godvreesentheyt onderwesen worde, is eenen yeghelicken wel so klaer dat men daer niet veel woorden om en behoeft te maken. Daerna so siet men hedensdaechs oock wel hoe de papistische pastooren ende bisschoppen haer ampt genoech doen: De apostel Paulus vermaent dat een bisschop oft pastoor met dese gaven ende deuchden behoort verciert te wesen, als dat hy zy onstraffelick, eender vrouwen man, gheloovighe kinderen hebbende, niet groots van hemselven houdende, niet toornich, gheen wijndrancker, niet bijtich, niet ghierich na schandelick ghewin maer gastvrij, goedertieren, sober, rechtveerdich, godvreesende, kuysch, vasthoudende de leeringe des getrouwen woorts opdat hy machtich zy te vermanen door de heylsame leeringhe ende te verwinnen de tegensprekers.[2] Item, hy behoort rechtveerdich te wesen, zijn eygen huys wel voorstaende, een goede ghetuygenisse hebbende van dien die daer buyten zijn, vriendelick tegen alle man, leerachtich, die de quade verdraghen kan, met saechtmoedicheyt straffende de wederspannighe.[3] Maer nu stellen alle dese [41ʳ] hoopen der papistischer bisschoppen, pastooren ende ander mispapen al haer weerdicheyt ende heylicheyt in haer kruynen, scheeren, smeeren ende in dierghelijcke droomen, alle de bovenghenoemde deuchden ten meesten deele achter rugghe stellende. Door symonie ende menschelicke gonste klimmen, ja breken sy in tot haer kercken ampten. Haer schandelicke hoererien willen sy boven den houwelicken staet verheffen, liever hebbende schandelicken met veel concubijnen tegen den wille Gods, dan [h]eerlicken ende lieflicken met een christelicke huysvrouwe na den wille Gods, ghemeynschap te houden. Haer hoererie koopen sy met ghelt af, ende dat een priester een wettelicke huysvrouwe hebben soude, dat achten sy des brandts weerdich te zijn. Sy en zijn niet vasthoudende der leeringhen des getrouwen woorts, maer het valsch twijffelachtich menschenwoort willen sy met al haer macht ende

---

[1] Hand. 6:3.
[2] Tit.1:6-9.
[3] 1 Tim. 3:2-3; 2 Tim. 2:24-25.

ghewelt beschermen. Ende denselven tijt dien sy met heylighe opentlicke predicacien ende met goede heymelicke vermaninghen te doene behoorden te besteden, brenghen sy omme met singen, met missen te doen, met besweeringhen ende dierghelijcke onnutte ver[41ᵛ]sierde beuselingen. Uut alle welcke dinghen klaerlicken blijckt dat der kercken ordinancien niet door ons, maer door onse wedersprekers schandelicken verstoort ende verwoestet wort.

Daerna so besmetten sy seer leelicken ende schandelicken den houwelicken staet, die van eenen yeghelicken heylich ende eerweerdich behoorde gheacht te worden.[1] Want haer eensaem leven (als zij 't noemen), hoewel dat het vol oncuysheyts is, noemen sy een gheestelick leven, ende den reynen houwelicken staet heeten sy een vleeschelick ende wereltlick leven te wesen, waerom dat se oock het trouwen oft huysvrouwe te nemen verbieden, te sommige tijden, die daer veel te heylich toe zijn, als sy meynen. Ende dwingen oock tyrannisch om de ongodlicke gheloften wille by na een ontallicke menichte van menschen – die noch van haers moeders lichaem af, noch door menschen, noch oock om het rijcke der hemelen wille gesneden en zijn[2] – dat se in eensaemheyt buyten den houwelicken staet blijven moeten, ende dat (so sy wijs maken) om het eewich leven te verdienen. Ende hebben liever tegen de apostolische leere dat dese bernen, dan dat se trouwen,[3] ende dat om haerder insettingen wille derwelcker onderhoudin[42ʳ]ghe dese geveynsde gheesten meer achten dan het volbrengen des willen Gods.[4]

De uuterste salvinghe oft olysel (so sy 't noemen), dewelcke van Christo ingestelt was alleen om de ghesontheyt des lichaems te vercrijgen,[5] ende die naderhant met de ander miraculen der eerster kercken achter gelaten is, willen sy nu oock met alle ghewelt ende hardneckicheyt behouden. Ende gemerct dat se nu niet meer en derren seggen dat se bequam is tot ghesontmakinghe des lichaems, so maken sy den volcke wijs dat het seer nut is tot de verghevinge der sonden te vercrijghen, ende tot der zielen salicheyt. Ende als sy de lieden smeeren segghen sy: 'Ick salve u met de heylighe olye, opdat ghy door dese heylighe salvinge de volle verghevinge der sonden ontfangt'.

In alsulcker manieren trecken sy de ellendighe menschen tot de bloote elementen deser werelt, tot grooter lasteringhen des bloets Christi,[6]

---

1 Hebr. 13:4.
2 Mat. 19:12.
3 1 Kor. [7]:9.
4 Mat. 15:3, 6.
5 Mar. [16:18]; Jac. 5:14.
6 Kol. 2:20.

diewelcke sy met de blijde vercondinge des evangeliums behoorden te salven ende te vertroosten.

Noch en is 't desen tyrannen der consciencien niet ghenoech dat se de menschen dewijle sy leven aldus quellen maer sy willen oock haer wreetheyt aen [42ᵛ] hen als sy doot zijn bewijsen. Want sy leeren in alder obstinaetheyt dat de zielen, ja oock van de aldergodsalichste menschen, uuten lichame verscheyden zijnde, eerst in 't veghevyer moeten ghepurgeert ende ghesuyvert wesen eer sy ten hemel inne ghelaten moghen worden. Ende daerna maken sy den menschen wijs dat der levender menschen wercken, als aelmoessenen, offerhanden – insonderheyt die men den monicken ende den mispapen gheeft –, item, de bedevaerden, sielmissen, vigilien, psalmen lesen, ghewijdt water ende dierghelijcke meer, den brant des vegevyers uutblusschen konnen. Met welcke valsche leeringe sy de geheele weerdicheyt der offerhanden Christi gantsch te niete maken ende de heerlickheyt der christelicker religie verswacken ende besmetten ende, ten lesten, den rijcken groote oorsake gheven om vrij ongheschickt te leven ende den armen een oorsake om mismoedich ende desperaet te worden. Wie soude konnen gelooven (hy en moeste gantsch betoovert zijn) dat alsulcken brant des veghevyer (so daer anders een veghevyer waer, als nu niet en is) door der ontuchtiger mispapen bleeten dat sy om 't ghelt in haer sielmissen ende vigilien doen; [43ʳ] item, door het besprenghen des wijwaters op der dooden graven ende door dierghelijcke meer ander leurenᵖ soude konnen uutgheblusscht oft ghemindert worden? Onse sonden zijn voorwaer voor de ooghen Gods veel grouwelicker ende verschrickelicker dan dat se met sulcke beuselingen mochten uutgewischt worden. Tot een so groote ende treffelicke sake moet men sonder twijffel eenen den alderkostelicxsten prijs der verlossingen hebben by welcke gheen ander mach vergelecken worden, als namelic het bloet des onbevlecten lams, het bloet Christi, d'welck ons van allen sonden reynicht.¹

Noch so hebben de papisten met haer suerdeech den reghel des christelicken levens seer vervalscht ende verdorven. Want de aldervolmaeckste ende eenige religie Christi, die den minsten so wel als den aldermeesten, eenen yegelicken na zijn ampt ende beroep in 't ghemeyn bevolen is, hebben sy in verscheyden ende supersticieuse secten der monicken seer godlooselicken verdeylt na veel ende verscheyden reghelen die van menschen gevonden zijn. Van haer tempelen hebben sy koophuysen gemeact in welcken bullen, missen, verdiensten, gesanghen, beneficien, vicarien, pastoor[43ᵛ]schappen, bisdommen, ja oock den

---

1 1 Pet. 1:19; Heb. 9:14; 1 Joh. 1:7; Op. 1:5.

hemel veyl gebracht worden. Ende dat, na de prophecie des apostels Petri van de valsche doctoren daer hy seyt: 'Door ghiericheyt met versierde woorden sullen sy met u koophandel drijven.'[1] Oock seggen sy veel van haer verdiensten ende wercken die sy 'opera supererogationis' noemen, te weten, die hen ter salicheyt overloopen, door dewelcke sy met een onverschaemde stouticheyt ende met een phariseeusche opgheblasenheyt niet so seer voor henselven als voor anderen (so sy hen slechs ghelt gheven willen) den hemel aennemen te bestormen.

Daerenboven so stellen sy de summe der godsalicheyt in de onderhoudinge van sommighe supersticieuse menschelicke insettinghen, als in cruynen, smeeren, gesangen, keerssen, beelden, phariseeusche vasteldaghen, popelen^Q, bedevaerden, oorbiechten, kappen, eensaem leven ende onderscheydt der spijsen meer ghelegen te zijn dan in de ghehoorsaemheyt der godlicker gheboden, daeruut oock koemt dat se de overtredinghe eens menschelicken ghebots veel swaerder straffen dan het overtreden van veel godlicke gheboden. De dronckaerts, hoerejaghers, [44^r] overspeelders ende diergelijcke, dewelcke na klare ghetuyghenisse der heyligher schrift uut de erffenisse des hemelrijcx ghesloten worden,[2] tracteren sy veel lieffelicker dan denghenen die om zijnder consciencien wille zijn onbehoorlicke belofte om eensaem sonder wijf te leven gebroken hebbende, hem totten heylighen houwelicken staet van God inghestelt begeven heeft, ofte dan denghenen die met dancksegghinghe op eenighen verboden dach vleesch ghegeten heeft. Also dat Paulus van hen wel terechte geseyt heeft: 'De Gheest seyt openbaerlicken dat in den laetsten tijden sommighe sullen van den gheloove af treden ende aenhanghen den dwalenden gheesten ende der leeringhen der duyvelen, door deghene die door gheveynstheydt leughensprekers zijn ende een brantteecken in haer conscience hebben ende verbieden te trouwen ende ghebieden te schouwen de spijsen die God gheschapen heeft te nutten met danckbaerheyt den ghelovigen ende denghenen die de waerheyt bekent hebben, aenghesien dat het goet is wat God gheschapen heeft ende datter niet verworpelicx is wanneer dat het met dancksegghinge ghe[44^v]nuttet wort, want het door den woorde Gods ende door dancksegghinge gheheylicht is. Is 't dat du de broederen van dese dinghen vermaendet, so salt due een goet dienaer Jesu Christi wesen.'[3]

Maer wie soude alle de corruptien ende vervalschinghen, alle de dwalingen, misbruycken, supersticien ende afgoderien der Roomscher

---

1 2 Pet. 2:3.
2 1 Kor. 6:10; Gal. 5:21; Ef. 5:5; Kol. 3:6; Op. 22:15.
3 1 Tim. 4:1[-6a] (cf. Rom. 14: 6 & 1 Kor. 10:30).

kercken konnen vertellen, daer sy der menschen salicheyt noch aen derren^R verbinden ende daer oock gheen hope af en is dat se alsulcx ymmermeer beteren sullen? Want om die te verwen^S ende te bevestighen versieren sy dagelicx veel nieuwe konsten ende sophisterien, ja oock dickwils tegen haer eyghen consciencie. Want hoewel sy door bedwanck moeten belijden (oft sy willen oft niet en willen) datter veelderhande misbruycken in der kercken inghedronghen zijn, nochtans en laten sy niet af deselve sterckelicken te beweeren ende te verantwoorden. Want aenghesien dat se haer niet en schamen haer opentlicke kerckrooverie te beschermen, waerdoor sy den volcke in des Heeren nachtmael den kelck gestolen hebben,[1] hoe souden se dan in haer andere dwalingen, die wat bedecter zijn, konnen ghewijcken? Ende wanneer sy schoon een con[45^r]silium^T beroepen, om aldaer van der kercken reformacie te handelen, daer en tracteren sy niet ernstelicken van derselver reformacien na Gods woordt maer doen veel meer haer uuterste beste om alle hare afgoden diensten een nieuwe verwe te gheven ende oock tyrannische wijse te behouden, als oock de consilien van sommighe voorledene tijden sulcks wel klaer te kennen gheven. Oock is 't by hen gantsch in de ghewoonte gekomen dat so wie sy met woorden tot het aennemen haerder afgoderijen niet gebrenghen en konnen, denselven dwinghen sy met ghewelt daer toe. Want aenghesien dat sy hare dwalinghen met der schrift niet en konnen beschermen, so nemen sy de wereltlicke overicheyt tot haerder baten, ghebruyckende alle manieren van wreedtheydt teghen den christgheloovighen, als bannen, confiscacien der goeden, ghevanckenissen, banden, pijnighen, onthalsen, hangen, raeybraken, bernen, sieden ende diergelijcke tormenten.

Aenghesien dan dattet eenen yegelicken klaer ghenoech is dat de Roomsche kerckce hedensdaechs door veel grouwelicke ende onghcneselicke afgoderijen ende dwalinghen aengaende den [45^v] godsdienst ontreynicht is, so hope ick dat de goede ende onpartijdighe lesers wel sien, ja oock wel tasten, dat wy niet door eenighe lichtveerdicheydt, noch godloosheydt, maer alleen om der eeren Gods ende om onser zielen salicheydts wille ghedwonghen worden van deselve af te wijcken. Want het is doch des Heeren eewige ghebot: 'Ghy en sult gheen andere goden beneffens My hebben.'[2] Nu heeft men so veel vreemde goden als men valsche godsdiensten ende afgoden behoudt. Met des Heeren gebot komen ooc over een de apostolische vermaningen: 'Weest gheen dienders der

---

1 Mat. 26:[27]; Mar.14:23; 1 Kor. 11:25-29; 1 Kor. 10:16.
2 Ex. 20:4; Deut. 5:8.

afgoden.'[1] 'Hoedt u voor de afgoden.'[2] 'En trect gheen vreemt jock aen metten ongeloovigen.'[3] 'Wijct, wijct, trect uut van daer ende en ruert niet onreyns aen.'[4] Daerom is 't dat ons bevolen wort uut Babel te trecken,[5] ende de valsche propheten te schouwen die ons tot vreemde goden verwecken[6] ende sprecken de ghesichten haerder herten ende niet uuten monde des Heeren.[7] Ooc so biddet Paulus de geloovighe so hertelicken: 'Ick bidde u,' seyt hy, 'ghy broeders, dat ghy opsiet op deghene die daer secten ende ergernisse aen richten beneven de leere die ghy gheleert hebt ende wijct van denselven.'[8] [46ʳ] Ende wederom tot Timotheum: 'Is 't dat yemant anders leert ende niet en blijft by den heylsamen woorden ons Heeren Jesu Christi ende by der leere van de godsalicheyt, die is opgheblasen ende en weet niet. Scheyt dy van sulcken.'[9] 't En is ooc niet sonder oorsake dat de H[eylighe] Gheest in de heylige schrift ons so sorchfuldelicken van den valschen godsdienst ontraedt, want den waren ende den valschen godsdienst zijn malcanderen so contrarie dat se nemmermeer beyde t'samen voor God bestaen en konnen, maer waer den valschen godsdienst is, daer moet den oprechten wijcken. Want als de apostel seyt: 'Ghy en kondt niet tesamen deelachtich zijn des Heeren tafel ende der duyvelen tafel.'[10] 'Want wat mededeel heeft gherechticheydt met de ongherechticheyt? Wat ghemeynschap heeft het licht met de duysternissen? Hoe koemt Christus overeen met Belial? Oft wat deel heeft de geloovige met de ongeloovige? Wat ghelijckenisse heeft den tempel Gods met de afgoden?'[11] 'Niemant en kan twee heeren dienen, want oft hy sal den eenen haten ende den anderen lief hebben, oft hy sal den eenen aenhangen ende den anderen versmaden.'[12] Ende ghemerct dat niemant t'samen God gedienen kan ende [46ᵛ] den mammon, so en kan ooc voorwaer niemant twee so ongelijcke heeren als God ende de afgoden zijn, t'samen gedienen.[13]

---

1 1 Kor. 10:7.
2 [1] Joh. 5:21.
3 2 Kor. 6:14.
4 Jes. 52:11.
5 Op. 18:4.
6 Deut.13:1-3.
7 Jer. 23:16.
8 Rom.16:[17].
9 1 Tim. 6:3, 5.
10 1 Kor. 10: 21.
11 2 Kor. 6:14-16.
12 Luc. 16:13.
13 Mat. 6:24.

Daerom hebben de alderheylichste mannen Gods altijdt van den beginne des werelt af de onreyne godsdiensten seer vlijtichlicken geschouwet, dickwils tot grooten perijckel haerder goeden ende levens. Abraham, verlatende zijn vaderlandt, is van Ur der Chaldeen lant in een lant ghereyst dat hem onbekent was.[1] Wiens godvreesentheyt in den reynen godsdienst te beschermen, Isaac, de sone, ende daerna oock Jacob seer volstandichlicken alle tijdt na ghevolcht hebben.[2] In alsulcker manieren zijn de kinderen van Israël door Moysen uut Egypten ghevoert geweest, opdat se van de valsche goden der Egyptenaren verlost zijnde, God puerlicken na zijn woordt ende bevel dienen mochten.[3] Ende opdat se oock in de warachtighe religie hen van God ghegheven voortaen blijven souden sonder met haerder nagebueren afgoderijen te besmetten, so wert hen bevolen dat se alle de afgoden der heydenen totten gronde uutroeyen souden,[4] d'welck de heylige mannen ende overste onder 'tselve volck [47ʳ] als Moses,[5] Josue,[6] Samuel,[7] Josaphat,[8] Ezechias,[9] Josias[10] ende andere deser ghelijcke alletijt getrouwelicken gedaen hebben. Ende nadat Jerobeam ende de andere koninghen van Israël die na hem ghekomen zijn den warachtighen godsdienst door hare afgoderijen vervalscht hadden, so hebben de heylighe mannen hen alletijt van een sulck afgodisch gheselschap seer neerstelicken ghewacht ende afghesondert.

Tobias noch jonck zijnde, achterlatende den dienst die Jerobeam op gherichtet hadde, is na Jerusalem na des Heeren bevel ghereyst.[11]

Elias ende Eliseus[U], die dappere propheten Gods, hebben met hare predicacien grootelicken ghearbeydt om het volck van den dienst Baal af te trecken, den genen scherpelich bestraffende die aen beyden zijden hinckeden. 'Hoe langhe,' seyde Elia, 'hinckt ghy op beyde zijden? Is de Heere God, so wandelt hem na, maer is 't Baal, so wandelt hem na.'[12] Desghelijcx oock hebben alle de andere propheten de valsche godsdiensten op d'alder grouwelickste bestormt. Ende terstont als Naaman van Syrien

---

1 Gen. 11:31; 12:1; Heb. 11:8.
2 Gen. 25 and 26 [original: Gen. 25 c. 26, e, f. It is unclear to which verses Micron is referring]; Gen. 28[:10-21]; 35:6.
3 Deut. 4[:1-21, 25-40]; Lev.18:3; Num. 33:53.
4 Deut.7[:1-11]; Lev. 20:23.
5 Ex. 32:20.
6 Joz. 22:10-34(?); 23:8-16(?).
7 1 Sam. 7:3.
8 2 Kron. 17:6.
9 2 Kron. 31:1, 2.
10 2 Kron [34:1-13]; [2 Kon. 22: 13-20; 23:1-20?] [original: 3. Reg. 12. f,g; 13.a.]
11 Tob. 1:6.
12 1 Kon. 18:21.

tot der Israeliten godsdienst bekeert was heeft hy wel geweten ende bekent [47ᵛ] dat hy van synen ghewoonlicken valschen godsdienst wijcken moeste om den God Israels puerlicken ende vrijelicken te dienen.¹

Item, de dry jonghers, daer Daniel af vermaent, hebben so bestandich gheweest in het wederstaen des Babylonischen afgods, dat se liever gehadt hebben in den gloeyenden oven geworpen te worden dan dat se hen met den valschen godsdienst souden besmet hebben.²

Oock is de stercmoedicheyt Eleasari in de belijdinge des warachtigen godsdiensts eenen yeghelicken ghenoech bekent, dewelcke liever hadde te sterven dan dat men van hem vermoeyt hadde dat hy vercken vleesch ghegeten soude hebben.³ Dit en hebben oock de heylige mannen aldus niet lichtveerdichlicken noch tevergeefs gedaen. Want sy hebben wel verstaen dat onse Heere onse God een yelours God is, die gheen goden beneffens hem hebben en wilt,⁴ ende die wilt dat wy hem uut geheelder zielen, uut geheelder herten, ende uut alle onse krachten lief hebben sullen.⁵ Die in den Gheest ende in der waerheit van ons wilt gheeert ende aenghebeden wesen,⁶ die oock de ontheyliginge zijns godsdienst door de afgoderijen nemmermeer ongestraft en laet. [48ʳ] De heydenen zijn in eenen verkeerden sin geworpen omdat se God, dien sy uut de geschapene dingen kenden, niet terechte gheert en hebben.⁷ Ende die van Corinthen, omdat se de weerdicheydt van des Heeren nachtmael gheschendet ende misbruyct hadden, so zijnse van den hant Gods swaerlicken gestraft geweest.⁸ Hoe meynen dan noch degene ongestraft te ontkomen die uut de h[eylighe] schrift de waerheyt des evangeliums gekent hebbende, noch niet af en laten henselven tegen hare eygen consciencie noch dagelijcx met godloose diensten ende afgoderijen te besmetten? Willen wy God tot gramschap verwecken? Sijn wy oock wel stercker dan Hy?⁹ Moghen wy er niet veel in onsen tijden vinden, dewelcke, nadat se d'licht des evangeliums aengenomen hadden, om harer ondanckbaerheyt wille, door het rechtveerdich oordeel Gods in een libertijnschⱽ oft in een godloos ende sorgeloos leven, of ooc in grove duysternissen der Roomscher afgoderijen seer schandelicken wederom gevallen zijn? God en kan niet bespottet

---

1 2 Kon. 5: 9-19.
2 Dan.3:13-30
3 2 Mak. 6:18-31.
4 Ex. 20:5; Jes. 42:8; 48:11.
5 Deut.6:5, ende 10:12, ende 30:6; Mar. 12:30.
6 Joh. 4:[24].
7 Rom. 1:21-24.
8 1 Kor. 11:30.
9 1 Kor. 10:22.

worden,¹ dewelcke in de h[eylighe] schrift spreect: 'Gaet uut van haer mijn volck, dat ghy niet deelachtich en wort haerder sonden, opdat ghy niet van hare plaghen wat en ontfangt.'²

[48ᵛ] Daerom is 't dat wy de geboden Gods (als 't wel behooren soude), de heerlicke exempelen der heyliger mannen ende onse salicheyt eenichsins ter herten nemen willen, so sullen wy ons van alle afgoderijen der Roomscher kercken gheelicken afsnijden. Ende is 't dat wy daerom verachtet, bespottet, verdreven ende met veelderhande vervolginghen aenghevochten worden (als ghemeynlicken gheschiet, dat terstont na het verlaten der godloosheyt ende der afgoderijen het cruys ende lijden navolghen), so en sullen wy ons alsdan daer niet alleen in vertroosten dat wy der straffen ontslaghen zijn die de Babylonische hoere onderworpen is,³ maer oock daermede dat ons God getrouwelicken ende vaderlicken in zijn beschuttinghe ende bescherminghe ontfanghen sal. 'Gaet uut van haer,' seyt Hy, 'ende scheydt u af, spreeckt de Heere, ende en roert niet onreyns aen, so wil ick u aennemen ende uwe vader zijn, ende ghy sult myne sonen ende dochteren zijn, spreeckt de almachtighe Heere.'⁴

Also oock Abraham, nadat hy uut het Chaldeesche landt ghetrocken was, so is hy wonderlicken van God gheseghent gheweest.⁵ Ende de godsalighe [49ʳ] vrouwe Ruth wort oock daerom grootelicken ghepresen ende van den Heere rijckelicken begaeft, omdat se de goden Moab verlatende, tot den warachtighen God van Israël gehaen was.⁶ Ende sonder twijffel en hadde God ons, die verdreven zijn, in synen vaderlicken schoot niet so goedertierenlick ontfanghen ende na zijn beloftenisse niet so lieflick getroost, wy en hadden nemmermeer den saechten nest der Roomscher kercken konnen verlaten, noch wy en souden ooc noch ter tijt so veel aenstoots ende benautheden so gheduldelicken konnen verdragen die ons dagelijcx aenkomen, omdat wy sulcx verlaten hebben.

Ende hoewel dat wy nu klaerlicken ghenoech bewesen hebben dattet allen christgheloovighen die met de ware bekentenisse Christi verlichtet zijn, niet toeghelaten en is dat se met de onreyne godsdiensten der Roomscher kercken eenighe ghemeynschap hebben sullen; nochtans, aenghesien datter sommighe zijn die daer meynen sulcx gheoorloft te wesen, so moeten wy hier hare principale argumenten kortelicken verhalen ende wederlegghen, opdat se door haren schoonen schijn den simpelen niet en verleyden.

---

1 Gal.6:7.
2 Op. 18:4.
3 Op. 18:4.
4 Jes. 52:11; 2 Kor. 6:17-18; Op. 18:4.
5 Gen.12.
6 Ruth 1:16-22; 2:8-18.

[49ᵛ] In den eerste dan, so argumenteren sommighe in deser manieren: 't En is niet gheoorloft van eenighe kercke oft ghemeynte af te wijcken om sommiger misbruycken wille, so ve[r]reᵂ de fundamenten der heylsamer leere, van God ende van zijn woort, daer noch in behouden zijn. Daerom het oock onbehoorlick is van de Roomscher kercke af te wijcken, omdatter sommighe misbruycken in ghekomen zijn, ghemerckt de principale hooftstucken der christelicker religien – van God, van Christo, van de sekerheyt der h[eyligher] bijbelscher schrift ende diergelijcke meer – noch getrouwelicken in derselver kercken behouden worden. Want, segghen sy, hoe wel dat der joden ghemeynte met veel misbruycken in leere ende in ceremonien bedorven was, nochtans en zijnder de propheten Gods daerom noch niet afgheweken. Item, hoewel dat ten tijden der phariseen den tempel in eenen moordtkuyl verandert was,[1] ende datter veel menschelicke insettingen boven den bevele Gods ghedreven worden,[2] nochtans en zijnder de godsalighe noch niet afgheweken maer hebben in denselven met de andere haren godsdienst noch blijven doende: Zacharias heeft in den tempel [50ʳ] gerooct,[3] Maria heeft haer kint te Jerusalem gebracht opdat zij 't voor den Heere stellen ende voor hem offeren soude,[4] Anna de propheterssse en ghinck niet uut den tempel,[5] Maria ende Joseph gingen alle jaren na Jerusalem op dat paeschfeest ende 't kint Jesus leerde in den tempel onder de doctoren,[6] Ende Christus heeft synen jongheren bevolen te houden ende te doen al wat de schriftgeleerde ende phariseen gheboden.[7] Ende daerna, de apostelen selve waren altijt in den tempel, God lovende ende prijsende.[8]

Petrus ende Joannes klommen t'samen op in den tempel ter uren der bedinghen, ontrent den neghen uren.[9]

Paulus haeste hem dat hy opten pinxterdach te Jerusalem wesen soude.[10]

Ende deselve daerna, door den ghemeynen raedt van de andere broeders binnen Jerusalem, is gereynicht in den tempel met de andere broederen gegaen aldaer den offer ghegheven wert.[11]

---

1 Mat. 21:13.
2 Mar. 7:3, [13].
3 Luc. 1:5.
4 Luc. 2:[22].
5 Luc. 2:37.
6 Luc. 2:41.
7 Mat. 23:1.
8 Luc. 24:53.
9 Hand. 3:1.
10 Hand. 20:[16].
11 Hand. 21:23, 25-26.

In ghelijcken segghen sy, hoewel dat in de kercke oft ghemeynte van Corinthen groote twisten om des doops wille, groote vleeschelicke tweedrachten der broederen, hoererijen, groot misbruyck van des Heeren nachtmael ende valsche opinien van de verijsenisse [50ᵛ] der dooden waren, nochtans en beval de apostel noch niet dat men daerom van deselve ghemeynte afwijcken soude.¹

Wy bekennen seer wel dat men niet lichtveerdichlicken uutscheyden noch afwijcken en sal om sommiger misbruycken, oft oock om sommigher menschen ghebreken wille, van eenighe gemeynte in dewelcke de godsalighe leeringe van God ende van synen Sone noch puer ghehouden ende ghedreven wort. Want om des oncruyts wille en behoort men de weyte oft tarwe niet te verworpen. Noch het huys dat met gulden ende silveren vaten verciert is en behoort om sommigher snooder vaten wille niet ijdel noch woest verlaten te worden. Maer daer de heylsame leere opentlicken ghelastert ende vervalscht wort, daer de insettinghen Gods openbaerlicken omghekeert worden, daer veel heydensche ende afgodische corrupcien by komen ende daer gheen christelicke beteringhe der leeringhen ende der godlicker insettinghen na den woorde Gods noch toeghelaten noch verhoept en wordt, maer daer de christenen tyrannichlicken ghedwonghen worden alle misbruycken, hoe grouwe[51ʳ]lick dat se zijn, te onderhouden, oft ymmers voor goedt te houden, van een alsulcke ghemeynte behoort men hem voorwaer af te snijden ende deselve te verlaten. 'En hebt gheenen ghemeynschap,' seyt de apostel, 'met de onvruchtbare wercken der duysternissen, maer straftse veel meer.'²

Daerom behooren de christgeloovige ende die tot de waerheyt Christi gekomen zijn, sonder eenich vertreck van de Roomsche kercke oft ghemeynte, so sy hedensdaechs is, af te wijcken, aengesien dat uut de boven verhaelde redenen klaer ghenoech blijct dat deselve kercke so seer vervalscht is, so wel in de leeringe als in de ceremonien, dat de christenen in deselve gheen reyn noch christelick ghebruyck der leeringhen noch der ceremonien ghehebben, noch oock ghehopen en konnen.

Onse wedersegghers en sullen oock niet konnen metter waerheyt doen blijcken dat de heylige godvreesende mannen ten tijden der propheten eenighe ghemeynschap gehadt hebben met de godloose ceremonien, die in de Israelitische oft in de jootsche kercke zijn inghevoert gheweest. Ja dat meer is, de propheten hebben sulcx altijt sonder ophou[51ᵛ]den verachtet ende seer ernstelicken ghescholden ende verdoemt, als oock uut Samuelis, Elie, Esaie, Jeremie, Osee ende andere

---

1 1 Kor. 1: 11, 12; 6: 1, 8; 5:1; 11:18, 20-22; 15:34.
2 Ef. 5:11.

propheten heerlicke predicacien goedt te mercken is. Souden sy dan selve ghedaen hebben hetghene dat se so dapperlicken in de anderen scholden? Oft souden sy sulcx wel van de andere hebben laten gheschieden, die doe ter tijdt ghemeynlicke de kinderen der propheten ghenaemt werden?[1] Tobias, verlatende de kalveren der Israelitischer kercken[X] oft ghemeynten, is na Jerusalem ghereyst opdat hy aldaer den Heere na uutwijsen zijns woordts terechte offeren mochte.[2] Ende als Elias de prophete hem beklachde datter so luttel in de Israelitische kercke gebleven waren, so antwoordde hem de Heere: 'Ick hebber my noch seven duysent in Israël bewaert die de knyen voor Baal niet ghebuycht, noch synen mont niet ghekust en hebben.'[3] Ende ofter nu noch sommighe heylighe mannen onder de afgodische koningen Juda in den tempel te Jerusalem gheoffert hebben (want door des Heeren bevel waren [*]y[k]en[Y] een sekere plaetse ende Levitische priesteren gebonden,[4] van dewelcke diensbaerheydt der plaetsen, persoonen ende [52ʳ] tijden wy door Christum verlost zijn[5]), so en kan men noch daermede niet bewijsen dat se hem met eenighe afgoderije besmettet oft de offerhanden teghen de wet Gods in hare insettinge, forme oft wesen eenichsins vervalscht hebben. Want daer was gheboden van God dat de overtreder des wets Gods uuten midden des volcks uutgheroeyt soude worden,[6] ghelijckerwijs oock Ophni ende Pinehas om dier oorsaken wille van den Heere gestraft werden. Ende voort noch alle d'andere, die hen onder de koningen door afgoderijen besmettet hadden, werden grouwelicken geplaecht.[7] Desgelijcx oock dat de godvreesende mannen in der phariseen kerckce oft ghemeynte in den tempel gheoffert hebben, dat hebben sy ontwijffelicken gedaen alleen na uutwijsinghe ende bevel des wets, sonder eenige ghemeynschap te hebben met de supersticieusche menschen ceremonien. Want men leest van Zacharias den priester, die in den tempel roockte, dat hy een rechtveerdich man voor God was, levende na de gheboden ende bevele Gods onberispelick.[8] Ende daer staet gheschreven dat de ouderen Jesu het kint Jesum brachten in den tempel, opdat sy hem [52ᵛ] voor den Heere stelden, als gheschreven staet in de wet des Heeren.[9] Christus en heeft oock synen

---

1 2 Kon. 4:38.
2 Tob. 1:6.
3 1 Kon. 19:18; Rom. 11:4.
4 Deut.12:18; 17:[10]; 24:8; Joz. :21, 23(?); 1 Cor.1.d.
5 2 Kor. 1:20(?); 1 Tim. 2:8.
6 Lev.17.
7 Ez.8:18; 9: 1, 5-7.
8 Luc. 1:6.
9 Luc. 2: 22-23, 39.

apostelen gheen afgodische vergaderinge gepresen, noch oock gheen supersticieuse insettinghen der schriftgeleerden onderworpen als hy hen geseyt heeft: 'Op Moyses stoel sitten de schriftgeleerden ende de phariseen, al watse u seggen dat ghy houden sult, dat houdt ende doet.'[1] Want met dese woorden heeft hy se alleen willen vermanen dat se om des boosen levens wille der schriftgheleerder ende der phariseen van de gehoorsaemheyt des wets Gods nemmermeer afwijcken en souden. Want natuerlicken zijn de menschen daer toe gheneycht dat se lichtelicken om der leeraren ghebreken wille de Godsalighe ende hemelsche leere verachten. Ghelijck men hier voortijden gesien heeft dat om de ongheschickte giericheyt wille der kinderen Eli de menschen verachtet hebben des Heeren sacrificien.[2]

Dus heeft dan Christus met dese woorden synen jongheren willen inbeelden de ghehoorsaemheydt, niet tot menschelicke insettinghen, maer alleen tot de wet Gods, die door Moysen gegheven was, in dewelcke de phariseen [53r^Z] dickwils het volck onderrichteden (want Moses hadde van ouden tijden af in allen steden die hem predicten ende wert alle sabbathen in der scholen gelesen).[3] Daerom seyde hen Christus oock dat se opten stoel Moses gheseten hadden.[4] Hoe kleyn dat Christus alle der phariseen supersticien gheacht heeft ende oock van syne discipulen gantschelicken heeft willen veracht hebben, dat heeft Hy in menigerhanden manieren te kennen ghegeven. Want de leere des wets, dewelcke door haer glosen ende uutlegghingen seer verduystert ende besmet was, heeft Hy door zijn autoriteyt wederom gesuyvert.[5] Uut haren tempel heeft Hy tweemael de koopers ende verkoopers gedreven.[6] Hy heeft zijn apostelen neerstelicken vermaent dat se hen voor der phariseen suerdeech hoeden souden.[7] Ende teghen de phariseen ende schriftgheleerde, omdat se de menschelicke insettinghen so seer dreven, heeft Hy dapperlicken gestormt met alsulcke woorden: 'Waerom overtreedt ghy Gods ghebot om uwer insettinghen wille?'[8] 'Tevergheefs dienen sy My, dewijle dat sy leeren sulcke leeringhen, die niet anders dan menschen geboden en zijn.'[9] Ende wederom seyt Hy van hen tot zijn [53^v] jongheren: 'Alle plantinge die

---

1 Mat. 23:1.
2 1 Sam. 2:17.
3 Hand. 15:21.
4 Mat. 23:1.
5 Mat. 5:20 etc.
6 Joh. 2:14-16; Mat. 21:12; Mar. 11:15; Luc. 19:45.
7 Mat. 16:6; Luc. 12:1.
8 Mat. 15:3.
9 Mat. 15:9.

Mijn hemelsche Vader niet gheplant en heeft sal uutgheroeyt worden. Laet se varen, sy zijn blinde ende leyders der blinden. Wanneer de een blinde den anderen leydt, so vallen sy beyde in den gracht.'¹

Christus dan die een so groot vyant der menschelicker insettinghen was en heeft noyt alsulcke afgodische supersticien oft sacrificien die in het wesen vervalscht waren, ofter eenighe gheweest hadden, door de vingheren willen sien. Want so doende soude hy de swacke gheerghert ende de hardtneckicheyt der priesteren in 't overtreden der gheboden Gods grootelicken ghesterct hebben.

Daerna oock wanneer de apostelen in den tempel te Jerusalem ghebeden oft gheoffert hebben, so en hebben sy in haer ceremonien niet bedreven dat der wet des Heeren contrarie was, want doetertijt en wasser noch gheenen afgodischen waen, noch eenighen schijn van valschen godsdienst gemengt onder ende met alsulcke sacrificien die na den eysch des wets noch gheheel ende onverdorven onderhouden werden. Want Christus ghetuycht selve dat de phariseen den uutwendighen godsdienst so nauwe onderhouden hebben dat se de [54ʳ] munte, dille ende comijn vertienden.² Ende Paulus getuyct van de joden die binnen syne tijden waren, dat se eenen grouwel voor de afgoden hadden.³ Daerenboven de apostelen, in de christelicke kercken oft gemeynten zijnde gaven een openbaer getuygenisse van henselven dat se de jootsche kercke verlaten hadden, voor also veel als sy se doe sonder ergernisse der swacker verlaten konden.

Ten is oock gheen wonder dat Paulus niet en ghebiedt, noch oock niet en readt, af te wijcken van de gemeynte die binnen Corinthen was, niet tegenstaende dat se haer in veel stucken vergrepen hadde, want de ghebreken derselver kercken en waren noch niet al het lichaem door gekomen. Den meesten hoop gaf noch der vermaningen Pauli goet ghehoor ende regeerden hen noch na de insettingen des Heeren. Niemant en wasser ghedwonghen eenich quaet noch misbruyck voor goet te houden, noch oock daermede eenighe ghemeynschap te hebbene. De vermaninghen ende de straffe warender noch in weerden ghehouden, ende die obstinaet oft opentlicken boos blijven wilden werden bevolen den sathan overghelevert te worden.⁴ Van alsulcke kercken oft gemeynten [54ᵛ] en leeren wy oock niet af te wijcken, hoe wel datter noch wel sommighe fauten oft ghebreken moghen gevonden worden. Maer wat

---

1 Mat. 15:13-14.
2 Mat. 23:23; Luc. 11:42.
3 Rom. 2:22.
4 1 Kor. 5:3.

gaet dit der Roomscher kerkcken aen, in dewelcke alle stucken des kerckendienst met so veel supersticien ende afgodische dwalingen besmet ende vervalscht blijven, dat een christen gheen van deselve ghebruycken en kan sonder hem daer in te besmetten. Ende ghelijck niemant eenen verrotten appel ghesondelicken eten en kan, tenzy dat de verrotheyt uutghesneden worde, also en kan oock niemant de papistische ceremonien sonder groote besmettinge zijnder consciencien ghebruycken, tenzy dat se eerst na den reghel des godlicken willes ghebetert ende ghereformeert worden.

Aenghesien dan datter een so groot onderscheyt is tusschen de kercken van dien tijden, als namelicken tusschen de kercken oft ghemeynten der Israeliten, der phariseen ende der Corintheren, ende tusschen de Roomsche kercke van onsen tijden, voor also veel als de vervalschinghe ende der kerckendiensten aengaet, so en kan men niet de comparacie oft ghelijckinghe van alsulcke kercken oft ghemeynten teghen een [55r^AA] noch niet gheconcluderen, dat men van de papistische kercke niet afwijcken en mach.^AB

Ende dat sommighe nu seggen willen: 'Het misbruyck en kan de substancie of het wesen eens dincx niet te niete maken,' sy en aenmercken niet datter onder de misbruycken een groot onderscheyt te maken is. Want de misbruycken die den insettinghen Gods oft de weerdicheyt Christi tegen zijn, die selve maken oock de substancie oft het wesen der dinghen teniete. Ghelijckerwijs de waerheyt door de leughen ende de hitte door de koude teniete ghemaect wort. Also en konden de offerhanden die Jeroboam in Dan ende in Bethel oprichtede gheen oprechte noch godlicke offerhanden genoemt worden.[1] De besnijdinghe van die van Sichem en was oock voor het sacrament der besnijdinge niet te rekenen.[2] Ende het nachtmael dat de rijcke binnen Corinthen hielden, de arme niet verwachtende maer veel meer versmadende ende rijckelicken op henselven levende, en konde niemant voor het rechte nachtmael gehouden.[3] Ende ghemerct dat byna alle de misbruycken der leeringhen ende der sacramenten in 't pausdom de godlicke insettinghe te niete [55v] maken oft verduysteren de heylsame leeringhe der weldaden Christi, so worden de godsalighe ghedwongen van haerder gemeynschap ende vervalschte sacramenten gantschelicken af te blijvene.

Ende oft nu de substancie oft het wesen der insettingen Christi door der papisten misbruyck niet wech ghenomen en ware, noch en soude

---

1 1 Kon. 12:28-29
2 Gen. 34:24.
3 1 Kor. 11:20.

men haer sacramenten niet moghen gebruycken aenghemerct dat niemant by haer tot deselve toegelaten en wort, tenzy dat hy deselve misbruycken mede prijst, oft te minsten schijnt te prijsen, ende voor goet te bekennen.

Maer nu zijnder noch andere die haer veynsinghe met de strenghe gheboden ende decreten haerder princen beschermen ende verontschuldighen willen, seggende dat se door dese tot de ghemeynschap der Roomscher kercken tegen haren danck gedwongen worden. Ende om haer excusacie een verwe te gheven, so brengen sy veel argumenten by van de autoriteyt ende weerdicheyt des overheyts in wiens handen, ende niet in de macht des ghemeynen volcx, gheleghen is het wechnemen ende de vernielinghe der misbruycken. Sy seggen dat Elizen schijnt Naaman van Syrien [56ʳ] toegelaten te hebben dat hy om synen koninck te behaghen in der afgoden tempel bidden mochte,[1] ende dat den joden in Babel ghevanghen zijnde van den propheet Jeremias gheraden is dat so wanneer sy aldaer gulden, silveren ende houten goden van den volcke souden sien aenbidden – ghemerckt dat hen anders niet ghebeuren en mochte om der tyrannije wille des konincx van Babylonien – so souden sy in hare herten segghen: 'Dy Heere, moet men aenbidden.'[2]

Maer nu weten alle godsalige seer wel dat alle overheyt, hoe hooge dat se oock wesen kan, alleen een dienersse Gods is ende dat se ooc hare mate heeft; item, dat se oock veel minder dan den wille Gods te achten is.[3] Daerom, als oock de apostelen ghetuyghen, 'men moet Gode meer ghehoorsaem zijn dan den menschen,'[4] wanneer principalicken dat se wat bevelen dat den wille Gods contrarie is. Het is wel behoorlick dat de minste overheyt der opperster overheyt onderworpen zy.

Het is wel waer dat de overheyt de openbare afgoderien behoort wech te nemen, hetwelcke, aenghesien dat het in de macht eens particulieren mensches niet ghelegen en is, so wort hem noch[56ᵛ]tans bevolen deselve te schouwene. Waer 't dat men na het believen der princen alderley religien oft gelooven uutwendichlicken belijden ende ghebruycken mochte, so souden alle religien haest schadelicken ondereen vermengt ende verwerret worden, ende oock en soude de kercke noyt met eenige martelaren verciert ende bevesticht geweest zijn. Daerom wanneer ons eenige princen tot een valsche religie oft tot eenighe verdorven misbruycken in de ware religie met haer decreten ende gheboden

---

1 2 Kon. 5:19-19.
2 Baruch 6:5.
3 Rom. 13:4.
4 Hand. 4:19; 5:29.

dwinghen willen, dan sullen wy meer op des Heeren gebot dencken, dewelcke also seyt: 'En roert niet aen dat onreyn is.'¹

Ende dat nu onse wederseggers van Naaman van Syrien bybrenghen willen, daermede en konnen sy noch haer veynsen ende simuleren in de valsche godsdiensten niet verontschuldighen. Want de propheet Elizeus heeft sulcx alleen toeghelaten eenen mensche die in de oprechte religie eerst inghetreden was; dat hy om zijns dienst wille (dien hy synen koninck schuldich was) met hem in den tempel Rimmon gaen mochte ende niet dat hy des konincx afgoderie eenichsins toestandich wesen oft [57ʳ] daer mede simuleren souden moghen. Want Naaman selve hadde hem daer tevoren by den propheet Elizeus daer af ontschuldicht, seggende: 'En mocht dynen knecht niet eenen last van deser aerden ghegeven worden, so veel als twee muylen draghen moghen? Want dijn knecht en wilt niet meer andere goden offeren ende brantoffer doen dan alleen den Heere.'² Daerom misbruycken sy leelicken het exempel deses heyligen mans ende oock den vrede hem van den propheet gewenscht,³ alle deghene die langen tijt ende veel in de kenisse der christelicker religien gheoeffent gheweest hebben ende henselven nu tot de papistische ghemeynte begeven niet om eenighe politische sake uut te richten, maer alleen om in de warachtighe religie wat te veynsen ende te dissimuleren sonder byna ergens eenich teecken oft ghetuyghenisse haers gheloofs te laten blijcken.

Jeremias en laet oock den joden die in Babylonien ghevangen waren niet toe dat se hen tot den uutwendighen afgodendienst begheven souden,⁴ d'welck tegen het klaer ghebot Gods van gheen beelden te eeren ende te dienen;⁵ item, teghen het exempel van de drye kinde[57ᵛ]ren, daer Daniel af vermaent, opentlick strijden soude.⁶ Maer de propheet heeft se vermaent dat se haer door het quaet exempel der babylonischer mannen met gheen afgoderie – noch uutwendich metterdaet, noch inwendich metten gedachten – besmetten en souden, aengesien dat wy, van onser verdorvener natueren weghen, alle daer toe seer gheneghen zijn.

Oock en doogen hier gheenssins de excusatien der ghener die seggen dat sy gheen afgoderie en doen maer de mispapen; want onse teghenwoordicheyt, daer wy een alsulcke godloosheyt mede vereeren,

---
1 Jes. 52:11; 2 Kor. 6:17.
2 2 Kon. 5:17.
3 2 Kon. 5:19.
4 Baruch 6:5.
5 Ex. 20:5.
6 Dan. 3:12.

maect dat wy oock derselver sonden mede deelachtich worden. Daerom heeft de apostel oock denghenen van Corinthen bevolen dat se hen by den afgodendienst niet en souden laten tegenwoordich vinden.¹ Ende Christus en heeft niet alleen de verkoopers, maer oock de koopers met gheesselen uut den tempel ghejaecht.²

D'anderen segghen dat God daer niet op en siet tot welcke uutwendige kercke oft gemeynte yemant hem voecht, so verre hy den gheestelicken godsdienst oft religie – dewelcke in den gheloove, lijdtsaemheyt ende diergelijcke deuchden ghelegen is – vastelicken in zijn herte be[58ʳ]houdt. Hier sullen wy met korte woorden op antwoorden.

Wy bekennen van herten ende nemen oock in alder eeweerdicheyt^AC aen alle hetghene dat yemandt uut de heylighe schrift bybrenghen kan om den gheestelicken ende inwendigen godsdienst te verstercken ende te bevestighen, want deselve is den oorspronck ende den gheest des uutwendigen godsdiensts, sonder denwelcken dattet anders niet en is dan vleesch ende doodende letter.³ Maer wy en laten dat niet toe, dat yemant bewijsen kan, dat desen inwendigen godsdienst daerom sulcx is dat hy eenige uutwendighe belijdinghe ende vermenghinghe met eenigen valschen godsdienst by hem lijden oft toelaten soude. Want van eenen goeden boom en konnen niet dan goede vruchten ghekomen ende van den goeden schat des herten en kan niet dan goet ghekomen.⁴ Waerom so wie God warachtichlicken, van herten ende metten gheeste dienen wilt, die sal hem van de afgoderie afsnijden, diewelcke van Paulus onder de wercken des vleeschs gerekent wort.⁵ Ende als Christus getuycht: 'God wilt ghedient zijn in den gheest ende in de waerheyt'⁶ – maer wat waerheydt des godlicken [58ᵛ] dienst kan daer wesen daert lichaem van 't herte door hypocrisie ende geveynstheyt verscheyden ende gedeylt is? Daerom worden wel terechte gheest ende waerheyt van Christo t'samengevoecht in de ware aenbidders Gods. Waer uut goet te verstaen is dat de uutwendighe beveynsinge des valschen godsdiensts seer verre van den gheestelicken ende warachtighen godsdienst verscheyden is. Daerom schrijft Paulus van hemselven uut den propheet David: 'Ick hebbe gelooft ende daerom hebbe ick ghesproken.'⁷ Desghelijcx wort er oock in de heylighe schrift overvloedelicken genoech gheseyt dat alle onse woorden

---

1 1 Kor. 10:7, 20..
2 Mat. 21:12.
3 Rom. 2:27; 2 Kor. 3:6.
4 Mat. 7:18; 12:33-35.
5 Gal. 5:20.
6 Joh. 4:23-24.
7 Ps. [116]:10; 2 Kor. 4:13.

ende wercken; item, alle onse leden, als knyen, tonge, mont, vleesch ende lichaem eenen God te dienen moeten toegheeygent worden, als wel uut de nabeschreven ghetuygenissen blijcken mach:

'Al wat ghy doet, met woorden oft met wercken, dat doet altemael in den naem des Heeren Jesu.'[1]

'Hetzy dat ghy eet oft dat ghy drinckt, oft wat ghy doet, dat doet altemael totter eeren Gods.'[2]

'Laet also u licht voor den menschen schijnen dat se uwe goede wercken sien ende dat se uwen Vader prijsen, die in den Hemel is.'[3]

'Gelijck als ghy uwe leden begheven hebt tot [59ʳ] dienst der onreynicheyt ende van der eender ongherechticheyt tot de andere, also begheeft oock nu uwe leden tot dienst der gerechticheyt, dat sy hylich worden.'[4]

'Ick sweere by my selven, seyt de Heere, een woort der gherechticheyt gaet uut mynen monde, daer sal 't by blijven, te weten: Alle knyen sullen haer voor My buyghen ende alle tonghen My sweeren.'[5]

'Metter herten ghelooft men tot de gherechticheyt ende metten monde belijdt men totter salicheyt.'[6]

'Mijn alderliefste, laet ons van alle bevleckinghe des vleeschs ende des gheests ons reynigen ende voortvaren met de heylighinge in de vreese Gods.'[7]

'Ghy zijt dier gecocht, daerom so prijst God aen uwen lichame ende in uwen gheest, die daer God toebehooren.'[8]

Uut alle welcke getuygenissen der heyligher schrift neerstelicken ondersocht ende byeen gheleken klaerlicken blijct dat oock alle onse uutwendighe wercken die door eenighe leden onses lichaems geschieden konnen, behooren den eenighen God toegheeyghent te worden ende daerom sullen sy oock suyver wesen van alle supersticieusicheyt ende afgoderie, is 't dat wy God gheestelicken ende warachtichlicken na synen wille begheeren te dienen. Daer[59ᵛ]om is 't oock dat de apostel Paulus (denwelcken seer wel bekent was hoe men God terechte behoort te dienen) met veel argumenten van de Corintheren begeert dat se hen met gheen afgodische vergaderingen vermengen en souden,[9] hoewel dat se

---

1 Kol. 3:17.
2 1 Kor. 10:31.
3 Mat. 5:16.
4 Rom. 6:19.
5 Jes. 45:23; Rom. 14:11; Fil. 2:10.
6 Rom. 10:10.
7 2 Kor. 7:1.
8 1 Kor. 6:20.
9 1 Kor. 10:7, 14, 19-20.

wel weten dat den afgod niet met allen en is.¹ Ende in der waerheyt, aengesien dat onse lichamen leden Christi zijn,² ende tempelen Gods³ ende des Heylighen Gheests,⁴ hoe sullen wy die noch derren met supersticieuse afgoderien besmetten?⁵ Ende aenghesien dat wy suyvere maechden zijn, Christo ondertrout, hoe sullen wy onse lichamen met gheestelicke hoererie derren besmetten?⁶ Niemant onder ons en isser so godloos, noch so buyten sinne, dat hy zijn huysvrouwe oft zijn dochter daerom wel soude willen laten hoereren omdat se wel stantvastelick souden konnen seggen dat se noch een suyver, reyn ende onbevleckt herte ghehouden hadden. Daerom sullen wy ons metter herten ende metten lichame neerstelicken voor alle valschen godsdienst hoeden, na den mate dat ons van den apostel Paulus bevolen wort dat wy allen boosen schijn mijden sullen.⁷ Want waer 't sake dat wy onder den schijn des gheestelicken gods[60ʳ]dienst allerley supersticien ende afgoderien drijven mochten, so soudender ontallicke veel christenen seer sot ende dul gheweest hebben die van den tyrannen ende hypocryten groote tormenten hebben moeten lijden omdat se de valsche godsdiensten verlaten hadden. D'welck te dencken groote sonde ware, aenghesien dat alsulcke menschen in de heylige schrift grootelicken gepresen worden; gelijck ter contrarien, die swaerlick ghestraft werden die de bekende waerheyt verloochent ende versaeckt hebben. Aldus worden de overste der joden van de evangelist ghescholden (omdat se om der phariseen wille niet en dorsten belijden denghenen daer sy aen ghelofden, opdat sy niet in den ban gedaen en werden): 'Want sy hadden liever de eere by den menschen dan de eere by Gode.'⁸ Ende: 'Is 't dat wy versaken,' seyt Paulus, 'so sal Hy ons versaken.'⁹ Ende Christus seyt: 'So wie My versaect voor de menschen, Ick sal hem versaken voor mynen Vader die in den hemel is.'¹⁰ Maer dat de opentlicke veynsinghe eens valschen godsdienst een specie oft maniere van de waerheyt te verloochenen ende te verraden zy en kann niemant gheloochenen.

1 1 Kor. 8:11.
2 1 Kor. 6:15.
3 1 Kor. 3:16-17.
4 1 Kor. 6:19.
5 2 Kor. 6:17.
6 2 Kor. 11:2.
7 1 Thes. 5:22.
8 Joh. 12:42-43.
9 2 Tim. 2:12.
10 Mat. 10:33.

[60ᵛ] Wie nu alle dese dingen wel terechte overlegghen wilt, die sal wel lichtelicken verstaen dattet al tevergeefs is dat yemant onder den schijn des gheestelicken godsdiensts hem noch uutwendichlicken met der afgodendienst vermenghen wilt ende dat deghene die sulcx doen willen haren acker met tweederhande zaet beseayen, met eenen ezel ende met eenen osse ploegen, een wullen ende lijnen kleedt draghen;[1] item, dat se in den godsdienst – diewelcke so hy anders Gode behaghen soude, heel ende gantsch moeste onderhouden wesen – seer grouwelicken hincken.

Noch zijnder vele binnen onsen tijden dewelcke meynen dat hen alle uutwendighe belijdinghe ende vermenghinghe der valscher godsdiensten vrij zijn, omdat haer ghemoedt gantsch vrij is van alle ghedachten ende gevoelen der afgoderijen. Want sy en achten gheen sonde noch gheen onreynicheyt te wesen dan hetghene dat yemant voor sulcx in zijn herte houdt ende acht. Ende om dese haer grouwelicke dwalinghen te verbloemen ende te bevestighen, so brenghen sy dese spreucken der h[eyligher] schrift by:

'Den reynen zijn alle dinghen reyn.'[2]

'Ick wetet ende bens gewisse in den Heere [61ʳ] Jesu datter niet onreyn en is aen hemselven dan alleen die 't voor onreyn rekent, denselven is 't onreyn.'[3]

'Hebt ghy het geloove, so hebbet by u selven voor God. Salich is deghene die hemselven gheen consciencie en maect in hetgene dat hy aenneemt.'[4]

'De gherechtighe sal uuten gheloove leven.'[5]

Door d'welck geloove sy hen so vastelicken in haer ghemoet voorstellen ende duncken laten van duyvel, helle ende alle sonden so volkomelicken bevrijdt te zijn dat hen dese – ja, watse ooc uutwendichlicken doen konnen – gheenssins hinderen en mogen. Ghelijck daer gheschreven staet: 'Daer en is gheen verdoemenisse denghenen die in Christo Jesu staen.'[6] Item, 'wy weten dat denghenen die God lief hebben alle dinghen ten besten dienen.'[7]

Maer onse wedersegghers de libertijnen – willende de spreucke Pauli ('den reynen zijn alle dinghen reyn')[8] uutlegghen ende verklaren – sondigen in tweederhande manieren tegen de waerheyt der h[eyligher]

---

1 Lev. 19:19; Deut. 22:10-11.
2 Tit. 1:15.
3 Rom. 14:14.
4 Rom. 14:22.
5 Hab. 2:4; Rom. 1:17; Gal. 3:11; Heb. 10:38.
6 Rom. 8:1.
7 Rom. 8:28.
8 Tit [1]:15.

schrift. In den eersten, omdat sy dit woordeken 'alle' sonder eenich onderscheyt tot alle goede ende quade woorden ende wercken strecken willen. Ten tweedden, omdat se by dat woordeken 'reynen' deghene verstaen die [61ᵛ] in hare herten ende ghemoeden gheen sonde en ghevoelen, hoewelse uutwendichlicken de wet des Heeren overtreden. Daer nochtans by den apostel Paulus met dit woordeken 'alle' verstaen wort alle creature welcke na de ordinancie Gods terechte ghebruyckt wort. Ende dat woordeken 'reyne' beteeckent de oprechte christenen die door den Gheest Christi vernieut ende herboren zijn, denwelcken, om Christus wille, het behoorlick gebruyck aller creatueren van God vrij toeghelaten is, als daer gheschreven staet: 'God heeft de spijsen geschapen om te ontfanghen met dancksegginghe den gheloovigen ende dien dien de waerheyt bekennen. Want alle creature Gods is goet, ende niet verworpelick, dat met danckseggingge ontfangen wort, want het wort geheylicht door dat woordt Gods ende dat ghebet.'[1] Want waer 't sake dat door dit woordeken 'alle' te verstaen waren alle uutwendige wercken hoe quaet dat se oock wesen mochten; item, dat het woordeken 'reyne' te verstaen ware van alle deghene die in haer ghemoet gantsch gheen ghevoelen der sonden en hebben, so hadde Adam wel vrijelicken van den appel moghen eten die hem van God verboden was.[2] Het [62ʳ] overspel met doodtslach vermengt en hadde David, sonder ghevoelen zijnder sonden seer sorgeloos levende, niet mogen hinderen.[3] Het gegoten kalf en hadde Aaron gheen sonde gheweest,[4] noch oock Petro zijn veynsinghe ende verloocheninge.[5] Ja, de moorderijen, dieverijen, valsche eeden, hoererijen ende andere schandelicke stucken en souden gheen sonden meer zijn denghenen die, onder den schijn des geloofs, quansuys hen beroemen souden met allen gheen gevoelen der sonden in haer ghemoet te hebben. Voorwaer, niet erghers noch grouwelickers ter werelt en mochte satan versiert noch ghevonden hebben om gantsch te niete te brenghen ende uut te roeyen, niet alleen alle de religie, maer oock alle goede policijen, so wel in burghelicke saecken als in de huyshoudinghe.

Also jammerlicken moeten se verblindet worden die, om haer begheerlicheden met eenige verwe te bedecken, hen niet en schamen de heylighe schrift so valschelicken ende opentlicken te draeyen. Maer nu willen wy desen oock voorstellen hetghene dat de schrift allessins seydt:

---

1 1 Tim. 4:3-5.
2 Gen. 3:6.
3 2 Sam.11:4, 15.
4 Ex. 32:4, 22-24.
5 Gal.2:13-14; Mat. [25]:70.

dat men na de uutwendighe woorden oft wercken van de in[62ᵛ]wendige affectie des herten, sy zy goed oft quat, richten sal.

'Aen de vruchten,' seyd Christus, 'kent men den boom.'[1]

Ende: 'Een goet mensche treckt goede dinghen uut den goeden schat des herten, ende een quaet mensche uut eenen quaden schat treckt quade dinghen.'[2]

Item: 'Uut dyne woorden salt du gheoordeelt worden.'[3]

Ende op een ander plaetse leert Christus klaerlicken dat alle uutwendige sonden den mensche onreyn maken; te weten, omdat se uut een onreyn herte komen: 'Hetghene,' seyt Hy, 'dat uut den monde gaet dat koemt uuter herten ende dat is 't dat den mensche besmettet. Want uuter herten komen quade ghedachten, dootslagen, overspel, hoererijen, dieverijen, valsche ghetuyghenissen, achterklap. Dese zijn 't die den mensche besmetten.'[4]

Daerom kan nu niemant meer getwijffelen oft deghene is onreyn die uut sorgheloosheydt de wet Gods uutwendichlicken overtreedt, alhoewel hy hooghelick van de reynicheyt zijns gemoets oft weerdicheyt ende kracht zijns geloofs hemselven beroemt. Daerom werden alle christgheloovige neerstelicken van Paulo vermaent dat se hen van alle besmettinge des vleesch hoeden,[5] God met hare lichamen eeren[6] ende [63ʳ] also alle boosen schijn schouwen souden.[7] Die van Corinthen wisten wel dat den afgod niet met allen en was, nochtans en laet hen Paulus niet toe dat sy met den uutwendigen afgoden dienst eenighe gemeynschap hebben souden maer noemt alsulcx afgoderije te wesen, hen bevelende daer af oock uutwendichlicken te blijven.[8] 'En weest,' seyt hy, 'gheen afgodendienaers…schouwet afgoderije.'[9] 'Ick en wil niet dat ghy in der duyvelen ghemeynschap zijn sult. Ghy en kondt niet ghedrincken den kelck des Heeren ende den kelck der duyvelen. Ghy en kondt niet deelachtich zijn der tafelen des Heeren ende der tafelen der duyvelen.'[10] Dus en maeckt de apostel alle sonden niet vrij als hy seyt dat den reynen alle dingen reyn zijn, maer hy aenwijset alleen met een woordeken dat aller creatueren

---

1 Mat.12:33.
2 Mat. 12:35.
3 Mat. 12:37; Jac. 3:11-12.
4 Mat. 15:18-19; Mar. 7:20-23.
5 2 Kor. 7:1.
6 1 Kor. 6:20.
7 1 Thes. 5:22.
8 1 Kor. 8:4.
9 1 Kor. 10:7, 14.
10 1 Kor. 10:20[-21].

middelmatich gebruyck den christgheloovighen reyn ende heylich is, ende dat door Christum.

Desghelijcx oock dat de disputacie Pauli totten Romeynen in 't veerthinde niet van sommighe wercken van Gode verboden, maer alleen van den gebruyc der spijsen ende van andere dierghelijcke middele dinghen te verstaen zy brengt de text so klaer mede dat men daer niet [63ᵛ] veel woorden af en behoeft te maken. Ende dit woordeken 'gheloove' in dese sentencie ('hebt ghy 't geloove, so hebbet by u selven voor Gode' etc.)[1] en wort hier niet genomen voor de gheheele christelicke religie, maer alleen voor de gherusticheyt des gemoets, door welcke yemant hem laet voorstaen dat hy alle goede creatueren Gods ende alle middelmatige dinghen, met vrijer consciencien om Christus wille, wel gebruycken mach. Welck geloove oft voornemen des herten van den geoorlofden gebruycke der middelmatiger dinghen Paulus gebiedt dat eenen yegelicken by hemselven voor God hebben sal; item, dat se niemant teghen den wille Gods tot ergernisse des naesten misbruycken en sal.[2]

Ende met dese woorden, 'salich is degene die hemselven niet en verdoemt' etc., en wilt Paulus anders niet seggen dan dat niemant de middelmatighe dinghen met een twijffelachtighe consciencie en behoort te ghebruycken, oft dattet anders sonde is. Want wie daeraen twijffelt ende eet doch even wel, die is verdoemt.[3]

So verdraeyen dan de libertijnen seer schandelicken de geheele disputacie Pauli als sy deselve verstaen ende draeyen willen oock tot dingen die grootelicken [64ʳ] van God verboden zijn. D'welck sy niet seggen en souden en hadde de God deser werelt hare sinnen niet verblindt.[4]

Item, het levende christelick geloove in d'welcke rechtveerdighe leeft en is sulcks niet dattet den christenen vrij maeckt eenich werck dat van Gode verboden is, als dese luciaensche^AD gesellen godlooselicken seggen willen. Want daerom seyt de schrift dat de rechtveerdige zijns geloofs leeft, omdat hy door 'tselve gheloove ons leven, Christum Jesum, aenneemt, door wiens verdiensten hy van de straffe der sonden verlost wort, opdat hy voortaen der gherechticheyt leve, gelijck oock Paulus (Rom. 6) ende voort de gantsche h[eylighe] schrift overvloedelicken ghenoech ghetuycht. Daerom en heeft Paulus niet absolutelicken geseyt 'daer en is nu niet verdoemelicx denghenen die in Christo Jesu zijn,' maer

---

1 Rom. 14:22.
2 Rom. 14:22.
3 Rom. 14:23.
4 2 Kor. 4:4.

daer volcht terstont na: 'die niet na den vleesche wandelen maer na den Gheest.'[1] 'Want so wie seyt dat hy in Hem blijft, die moet,' als Joannes seyt, 'wandelen gelijck Hy ghewandelt heeft.'[2] Ende met dit woordeken 'wandelen' wordt principalick beteeckent een uutwendighe wandel ende conversacie des levens.

[64ᵛ] Ende dat nu de apostel seyt 'den genen die God lief hebben dienen alle dinghen ten besten,'[3] dat moet principalicken van alle haerder tribulacien verstaen worden. Want dat hen de sonden somtijts ooc wel ten besten dienen, dat gheschiet alsdan uut sonderlinghe weldaet Gods, teghen de natuere der sonden, dewelcke uut hare eyghen natuere de eewighe verdoemenisse verdienen. Ja, sy worden oock wel dickwils hier op deser aerden seer scherpelicken aen de godsalighe ghewroken ende met groote straffe ghecastijt. Daerom en is 't gheen gheloove, maer is een vermetene ende ontrouwe afwijckinge van God – ja, 't is een enckel bedroch – dat men den menschen wijs maeckt dat afgoderije, supersticie ende alle andere uutwendighe sonden denghenen vrij ende puer zijn die het gheloove quansuys hebben, ende die hen beroemen konnen, dat se in hare consciencie gheen ghevoelen der sonden en hebben. In denwelcken grouwelicken kuyl der dwalinghen ghevallen zijn niet alleen de ghemeyne libertijnen ende die daer navolghen David [J]oris (welcke Jesum Christum verworpende, hemselven seer dwaeslicken wijs ghemaeckt hadde dat hy onsterffelick [65ʳ] hier opter aerden zijn soude, welcke aerde hy tevergheefs – gemerct hy nu doot ende begraven is – den synen beloeft hadde metten sweerde t'onder te brengen), maer oock de quade kiekenen die uut 'tselve quade ey ghebroedet zijn ende die onder den lieflicken tijtel oft naem des vredes hedensdaechs de wereldt so jammerlicken bedriegen, hen beroemende dat se 't lant ende 't Huys des Vredes ghevonden hebben, in d'welck achterlatende alle onderscheydt des goets ende des quaets, alle dinghen behalven de liefde vrij ghelaten zijn. Uut d'welck Huys des Vredes sy versieren ende maken hen wijs dattet den haren vrij is tot de andere landen ende deelen des wereldts weder te keeren ende deselve vrijelicken te doorwandelen, als sy spreken. Dat is te seggen, dat se hem wel, 'tsy geveynsdelic oft andersins, tot alle gebruycken ende manieren van leven van andere menschen die totten huyse des vredes noch niet en hooren toevoeghen mogen. Daeruut koemt dat se alle deghene bespotten die hen van de grousame afgoderijen der Roomscher kercken aftrecken – ja, oock degene die eenich geloove oft

---

1 Rom. 8:1.
2 1 Joh.2:6.
3 Rom. 8:28.

religie ernstelicken beschermen oft belijden willen; item, dat se hen tot alderley religien ende quade [65ᵛ] wercken uutwendichlicken begeven, tenzy dat se door vreese van eenich perijckel oft door hope van eenich ghewin daeraf afghetrocken worden.

Hoe grouwelicke dwalinghe dat dit is, hoe schadelick (niet alleen der ghemeynten Gods, maer oock allen goeden policyen ende ordinancien in burghelicke saecken ende huyshoudinghen), die gantschelick teghen den wille Gods is, als door dewelcke de Heere Jesus van syne koninklicke, prophetische ende opperste bisschops ampte ende weerdicheyt berooft wort; alle godsalicheyt verdreven; allen boosheden, leugenen, bedriegerijen, hoererijen, dieverijen, afgoderijen, gierichheden etc. eenen grooten toeganck gegheven; de hope des eewigen levens ende de vreese der eeuwigher verdoemenissen na dit tijdtlicke leven uut der menschen herten ghenomen wordt, kan een yegelick wel ghemercken die ymmers een voncxken godvreesentheyts by hem heeft, sodat wy daer gheen woorden meer om en behoeven toe seggen. Nochtans, so veel moet ick er toe seggen, dattet gheen wonder en is datter hedensdaechs so veel menschen in dese grove en grouwelicke dwalingen vallen. Want in een so groote oneenicheyt ende twist van de [66ʳ] ware religie, de menschen des pausdoms afgoderije bekennende (welcke een yeghelick, hoe plomp hy oock is, lichtelick met handen tasten kan) ende nochtans uut vreese des vervolchs ende des cruyces de ware religie niet belijdende ende navolghende, oft uut hooveerdicheydt hare schouderen den jocke Christi ontreckende, so vallen sy lichtelic in dese grouwelicke dwalinghe, nadenmael sy met so sueten naem des vredes ende der liefden verciert is, ende om haerder vrijheyt wille diese medebrengt ende hare navolgeren beloeft, seer aengenaem is. Desgelijckx is oock God rechtveerdich, dewelcke de onverdragelicke ondanckbaerheydt des wereldts teghens synen Soon Jesum Christum ende zijn woort met so grove dwalinghen wreeckt, als Paulus oock wel gheseydt heeft: 'Omdat se de liefde der waerheydt niet en hebben aengenomen dat se salich werden, daerom sal hen God krachtighe dwalinghen senden dat se der leugenen ghelooven. Opdat gheoordeelt werden alle die der waerheyt niet en gelooven maer hebben lust aen de ongherechteydt.'[1]

Ende wie de apostolische prophecijen die [in] 2 Tim. 3 ende 2 Pet. 2 [ende] 3 ende [66ᵛ] wederom in den brief Jude van de laetste tijden gheschreven staen neerstelicken overlesen wilt, die sal hem daeruut teghens dese duyvelsche vrede genoechsaem moghen wapenen.

---

1 2 Thes. 2:10-12.

Noch wordt ons in de h[eylighe] schrift vermaent dat de warachtighe liefde hare sekere mate heeft, opdat wy met gheen ijdele imaginacie des vredes bedroghen en worden. Want de warachtige liefde wort met eenen stercken bant tesamen metten gheloove ghebonden. Item, sy is alleen in goede dinghen gheleghen ende dat oock na Christum, als uut de navolgende spreucken Pauli wel te mercken is:

'Nu blijven geloove, hope ende liefde, dese dry.'[1]

Ende: 'Een yeghelick van ons behage synen naesten in 't goede tot stichtinge.'[2]

Item: 'Den God des ghedults ende des troosts gheve u dat ghy onder malcanderen eensgesint zijt, ende dat na Christum Jesum. Opdat ghy eendrachtelicken met eenen monde moecht prijsen God ende den Vader ons Heeren Jesu Christi.'[3]

Dese nieuwe vrede dan – de op 't gheloove noch op de hope niet en achtet, die oock in quade dingen die van God verboden zijn gheleghen is ende sluytet Jesum Christum buyten – die zy vervloect met haer gantsche huys [67ʳ] ende boumeester des vredes. Want nademael dattet Aaron verontschuldicht en heeft dat hy vrede sochte in 't gieten des gulden kalfs,[4] noch Saul in 't offeren,[5] noch ooc Petrum in 't veynsen,[6] so en sullen voorwaer dese, die onder des schijn des vredes alle eerbaerheydt ende religie verdraeyen ende omkeeren, van den Heere niet ongestraft blijven. Insonderheydt, aenghesien dat de propheten hier voortijdts teghen alle voornemen des valschen vredes so dapperlicken geroepen hebben.[7] Ooc roept Jesaias: 'Wee denghenen die dat quaet goet, ende dat goet quaet heeten. Die uut duysternisse licht, ende uut licht duysternisse maken, die uut suer suete, ende uut suete suer maken.'[8] Van alsulcken vloeck des propheets en kan dit volck des vredes (so sy ghenoemt willen wesen) niet vrij ghewesen, dewijle sy onder hen hetghene vrij maken dat God so grouwelicken in zijn woort ghestraft ende verdoemt heeft.

Nu hopen wy breedelicken ende genoechsaemlicken uutgheleyt te hebben hoe grootelicken men alle deghene behoort te schouwen dewelcke segghen willen dattet den christenen, die tot de kennisse des evangeliums gekomen zijn, [67ᵛ] niet gheoorloeft en is van de onreyne gemeynten

---

[1] 1 Kor. 13:13.
[2] Rom.15:2.
[3] Rom. 15:5-6.
[4] Ex.32:22.
[5] 1 Sam. 13:9, 13.
[6] Gal. 2:14.
[7] Jer. 8:11; 23:17; Ezech. 13:10.
[8] Jes. 5:20.

ende supersticien der Roomscher kercken af te wijcken. Nu laet ons wijder to andere dinghen voortvaren.

Dattet den christenen, nadat se den grouwel der Roomscher kercken gekent ende verlaten hebben, van nooden is dat se hen tot eenige sonderlinghe openbare oft heymelicke vergaderinge der christelicker gemeynte begheven.
Dat iiii. capittel.

Niemant en sal hem laten voorstaen dattet eenen christen genoech zy de supersticieuse misbruycken ende afgoderijen der Roomscher kercken te kennen ende deselve te vervloecken ende te verlaten, tenzy dat hy hem oock metten gheeste ende met de uutwendige belijdinghe zijns geloofs tot eenige heylighe vergaderinge der gemeynte voege, in dewelcke hy 't recht ende behoorlick ghebruyck des woorts ende der sacramenten ghenieten mach.

In alsulcker manieren en heeft het Gode in voortijden niet ghenoech gheweest dat Hy de kinderen van Israël uut den diensthuyse van Egypten verlost hadde, maer Hy heeft hen sekere ceremonien des kercken diensts aen den berch Sinai voorgheschreven.[1] Gelijckerwijs Hy oock ghewilt heeft dat deselve Is[68ʳ]raeliten daerna, als sy weder uut de Babylonische ghevanckenisse ghekomen waren, den tempel van Jerusalem wederomme opbouwen souden om haer ghewoonlicke vergaderinghen daer in te onderhouden, straffende swaerlicken denghenen die hier in luye ende traech waren ende hen ernstlicken door den mont zijnder propheten vermanende, dat se den begosten tempel voort op maken souden.[2] Ende denselven die Christus van den last der phariseen verlost hadde en heeft Hy niet ledich ghelaten, maer heeft hen neerstelicken vermaent dat se zijn jock op hen nemen souden. 'Neemt,' seydt Hy, 'mijn jock op u.'[3] Alle deghene oock die de apostelen door het verkondighen des woordts uut de Jodenschap oft heydenschap hebben konnen vergaderen, deselve – terstont alse gedoopt waren – hebben sy voort der geloovigen vergaderingen toegevoecht.[4] Ende Paulus, bekeert zijnde, heeft hem terstont by de christelicke gemeynte gevoecht, eerst binnen Damasco, daerna ooc te Jerusalem.[5] In dewelcke christelicke vergaderinge de geloovige neerstelicken ende volstandich bleven, als Lucas van hen is tuygende: 'Sy

---

1 Ex. 25:1; 26:1.
2 Ezra 1: 3-5; Hag. 1:3; 3 Ezra 6: 1-2; Hag.1:2, 4, 6.
3 Mat.11:29.
4 Hand. 2: 42, 47; 10:48; 16: 15, 33.
5 Hand. 9: 19, 26.

bleven,' seyt hy, 'volstandich in der apostelen leere, ende in de [68ᵛ] gemeynschap, ende in 't breken des broots, ende in den ghebede.¹ Ende daerna: 'Sy waren dagelijcx ende ghestadelick eendrachtelicken by malcanderen in den tempel.'² Ende de apostel Paulus vermaent seer ernstelicken allen christenen hetselve na te volghen, daer hy seyt: 'Laet ons onder malcanderen onsselven waernemen met verwecken totter liefden ende goede wercken ende niet verlaten onse vergaderinghe, als sommige pleghen.'³ Daerom, is 't dat wy willen wijselicken handelen ende onse salicheyt waernemen, so sullen wy neersticheit doen dat wy, het pausdom verlaten hebbende, ons nu by eenige christelicke vergaderinge oft gemeynte onbewegelicken houden ende dat wy in de oeffeninge des woorts, der sacramenten ende der christelicker straffen totten eynde ons levens toe heylichlicken voortvaren ende bestandich blijven. In welcke sake, ghemerct datter hedensdaechs hen veel in versondigen, so worden wy gedrongen tot stichtinge der godvreesender daer af noch wat breeder te handelen.

Is 't sake dan dat yemant in een alsulcke plaetse woone daerdoor Gods ghenade een openbare christelicke ghemeynte oft vergaderinge is in dewelcke Christus onvervalschtelicken verkon[69ʳ]dicht wort, ende de sacramenten na des Heeren insettinghe uutgereyct, ende de menschen tot een boetveerdich ende tot een deuchdelick leven (item, tot de onderhoudinge der christelicker straffen) van de predicanten ernstelicken vermaent worden, tot een alsulcke ghemeynte behoort een godvreesende mensche hem gheerne ende sonder eenich vertreck te begheven. De onderhoudinghe ende vorderinge derselver ghemeynten te soecken ende dat om de redenen die wy hier boven in 't eerste capittel aengeteeckent hebben. Ende so wie door onachtsaemheyt ende versuymenisse, oft om na des vleeschs lust vrijelicker te leven, oft door opgeblasenheid des gheests, oft oock om eenige andere diergelijcke oorsake hem van een alsulcke christelicke gemeynte af houdet, dien sal God ontwijffelicken van alsulcke ondancbaerheyt niet ongestraft laten. Als Christus selve ghetuycht wanneer Hy in een prekinge sommiger steden groote ondancbaerheyt scheldet, daer Hy aldus seyt: 'Wee dy Chorazin! Wee dy Bethsaida! Want waren de daden in Tyro ende Sidon gheschiet die by u geschiet zijn, sy hadden in voortijden in sacken ende in der asschen gheseten ende boete ghedaen. Doch [69ᵛ] het sal Tyro ende Sidon verdrachelicker vergaen in 't uuterste oordeel dan u. Ende du Capernaum,

---

1 Hand. 2:42.
2 Hand. 2: 46.
3 Heb. 10:24-25.

du die tot aen den Hemel verheven zijst, du salt tot in der hellen nederghestooten worden.'[1]

Een dierghelijcke dreyghinge wort er van Christo uutgesproken tegen deghene die ter bruyloft gebeden zijnde, niet en wilden komen, oft omdat se eenen acker oft ossen ghekocht, oft een huysvrouwe ghenomen hadden. 'Ick segghe u,' seyt Christus, 'dat niemandt van den mannen die gheroepen waren mijn avontmael smaken sullen.'[2]

Daerom, is 't dat wy de schult ende de straffe der ondanckbaerheyt schouwen willen ende is 't dat wy begheeren met veel gheestelicke weldaden in de ghemeynte Christi ghespijst te worden, so sullen wy ons met alder vlijticheyt ende ootmoedicheydt des herten tot zijnder ghemeynte begeven ende door gheen listicheden des satans nimmermeer daer af laten trecken.

Maer is 't dat yemandt in alsulcke plaetsen woondt daer den openbaren godsdienst also vervalscht is dat hy dien met goeder consciencien niet ghebruycken en kan, als ontwijffelicken den papistischen godsdienst is, so is daer [70ʳ] tweederhande raet toe. De eerste is dat de godvreesende tot alsulcker plaetsen vertreckt daer den reynen godsdienst – oft opentlick oft heymelick – is ende gebruyckt wort. Den anderen raet is dese: so verre alsulck vertrecken oft verreysen gheenssins oft ymmers seer qualicken gheschieden soude konnen, so sullen sy daer se woonen onder haer christelicke vergaderinghen maken ende onderhouden. Ende aenghesien dat beyde dese raden den vleesche seer swaer vallen, so pleech men ghemeynlicken veel dingen hier teghens op te worpen, dewelcke wy hier ordentlicken by een stellen ende elck bysondert examineren sullen.

In den eersten: Teghen het vertrecken van d'een plaetse in d'ander om de reyne leere ende der heyliger vergaderingen willen soect men veel uutweghen ende excusatien. Ende insonderheyt wenden se voor veel periculen, swaricheden ende moeyelicheden die alsulcke reysen ende vertrecken in haer hebben, als namelicken het verlaten van ouders, vrienden, maghen, vaderlant ende diergelijcke; versmaedtheyt in een ander landt; een ander maniere van leven aen te nemen; ende (dat het meeste is) vreese van groote armoede te lijdene.

[70ᵛ] Teghen alle welcke verschrickingen een seer goede remedie is dat wy overdencken hoe dat de Sone Gods, hoewel Hy rijck was, om onsentwille arm gheworden is ende is neder ghedaelt in de nederste

---

[1] Luc. 10:13; Mat. 11:21.
[2] Luc. 14:18-20, 24.

plaetsen der aerden, opdat Hy ons ballingen wederom in 't hemelsche vaderlant brenghen mochte.¹

Noch so behooren de christenen te dencken dat se so lange de feest der tabernaculen in dese werelt houden moeten, totdat se in de eewighe hemelsche tabernaculen, die niet met menschen handen ghemeackt en zijn, ontfanghen worden. 't En is oock niet nieus dat yemant om der religion wille sal reysen, want Abraham de vader aller gheloovighen, opdat hy hem met de afgoderie der Chaldeen niet besmetten en soude, is door Gods bevel in een lant ghereyst dat hem onbekent was.²

Sommige godsalige vrouwen zijn Christum uut Galileen tot Jerusalem nagevolcht om syne predicatien te hooren.³ De christenen binnen Jerusalem ten tijden der vervolghinghen Stephani werden verstroyt door de landen van Judeen ende Samarien.⁴

Ende ghemerct dat het den kooplieden niet verdrietelick en is te reysen te [71ʳ] water ende te lande, door menigherley periculen, alleen om den schamelen kost te winnen; item, ghemerckt dat vele supersticieuse menschen dicwils seer sware ende onnutte pelgrimagien aen nemen (als na Roomen, S[t]. Jacobs, Jerusalem etc.) met groote oncosten ende schade haerder goederen alleen uut supersticien, hoe sullen wy het ons dan verdrieten laten om der warachtiger religien wille een reyse aen te nemen. Insonderheyt daer wy wel weten datter in de christelicke ghemeynte eenen so grooten schat der gheestelicker goeden te vinden is, ende dat wy oock van uuterlicken bystant nemmermeer van den Heere en sullen verlaten worden? 'Want Hy heeft de vreemdelinghen lief, Hy gheeft hen spijse ende kleederen.'⁵ 'De godsalicheyt is tot alle dinghen nut ende heeft de beloftenisse deses ende des toekomenden levens.'⁶ Ende de Heere roept: 'Gaet uut van het midden van haer ende scheydt u af, spreeckt de Heere. Ende ruert niet onreyns aen, so wil Ick u aennemen ende uwe Vader zijn, ende ghy sult mijn sonen ende dochteren zijn, spreect de almachtighe Heere.'⁷

Op dese manieren seyt Christus ooc: 'Daer en is niemant in dien hy verlaet [71ᵛ] huys, oft broeder, oft suster, oft vader, oft moeder, oft wijf, oft kinderen, oft ackers om Mynen ende des evangeliums wille, die niet

---

1 2. Kor. 8:9; Ef. 4:9.
2 Gen. 12:[1]; Hand. 7:3.
3 Luc.8:2.
4 Hand. 8:1.
5 Deut. 10:18.
6 1 Tim. 4:8.
7 2 Kor. 6:17-18; Jes. 52:11.

hondertfout weder en ontfangt, nu in dese tijt huysen, ende broederen, ende susteren, ende moederen, ende kinderen, ende ackeren met de vervolghinge, ende in de toekomende werelt dat eewighe leven.'[1]

Ende dat dese beloftenissen warachtich ende seker zijn kan men met veel exempelen der h[eyligher] schrift bewijsen.

Abraham is in een vreemt lant rijck gheworden.[2] De kinderen van Israël, in der woestijne dolende, werden van den Heere met hemelsch broot gespijst ende haer kleederen en sleten niet van oudtheyt, noch haer schoenen aen haer voeten, veertich jaren lanck.[3] Ruth, diewelcke Naomi ghevolcht was,[4] verlatende der Moabiten lant om der religien wille, kreech eenen seer rijcken man, Booz den ouden grootvader van David den propheet.[5] Het volck dat Christum om Zijn woort te hooren in der wildernissen naghevolcht was, wert tot verscheyden tijden seer wonderlicken ghespijst.[6] Ende dat tot onser alder eewigher vertroostinghe, als Christus selve oock wel te kennen ghegeven heeft, daer Hy [72ʳ] syne discipulen, die om den buyck bekommert waren, met dese woorden berispt, segghende: 'Wat bekommert ghy u doch, ghy kleyngheloovige, dat ghy gheen broot met u ghenomen en hebt? En verstaet ghy noch niet? En denckt ghy niet op de vijf brooden onder de vijf duysent menschen ende hoe veel korven ghy doe op naemt? Noch oock op de seven brooden onder de vier duysent ende hoe veel korven ghy doen opnaemt?'[7]

Wanneer wy dan om des woordts wille eenige reyse aennemen, so en sullen wy van de sorghe ende goetwillicheyt Gods t'onswaert gheenssins twijffelen. Ende al is 't daerentusschen datter somtijts eenighe swaricheden in vallen ende ons overkomen (want Christus heeft den synen voorspoet beloeft die met tribulacien vermengt is, opdat se in den voorspoet haer niet te seer verheffende, de hemelsche goeden vergeten en souden),[8] so wy nochtans volstandichlicken in den gheloove ende godvreesentheyt na onse beroepinge neerstelicken volherden, ende in gheduldicheyt hulpe van den Heere verwachten, so en sullen wy niet verlaten worden, maer sullen gewisselicken des Heeren hulpe ende bystant ghewaer worden. Ten alderminsten sal ons God [72ᵛ] so in der consciencien vertroosten dat wy

---

1 Mar. 10:28-30.
2 Gen.13:2.
3 Deut. 8:4.
4 Ruth 1:16; 2:11.
5 Ruth 4:10.
6 Mat. 14:19; 15:36; Joh. 6:13.
7 Mat. 16:8-10.
8 Mar. 10:30.

oock andere menschen, in hoe groote bedrucktheyt dat se zijn moghen, sullen konnen eenen goede troost gheven.¹

Daerom en behoort ons gheen vreese der moeyelickheyt noch der armoede af te trecken, noch te beletten van so een heylighe reyse ende vertrecken tot de heylighe vergaderinghe des Heeren, maer behooren altijt te dencken op het woort des propheten Davids: 'De aerde hoort den Heere toe, ende wat daer in is.'² Ende op een ander plaetse seyt hy: 'De Heere is met my, daerom en vreese ick niet. Wat konnen my de menschen doen?'³

Nu willen sommighe voorwenden dat se in haer vaderlant met geveynsen by veel menschen veel vruchten konnen ghedoen, ende bysondert by den genen die in de religie noch niet wel ghefundeert en zijn. Wel, ick neme nu dat sommige van haer, hoewel seer weynich,^AE uut goeder herten also spreken ende gevoelen (want ick vreese datter veel zijn die onder desen schoonen mantel van haren naesten te helpen ende te onderrichten, haer eyghen mistrouwen op God ende de sorghe haers buycx bedecken), nochtans en is 't niet anders dan enckel menschelicke wijsheyt, dewelcke by God [73ʳ] sotheyt ende teghen denselven vyantschap is.⁴ Want [zo]als Paulus seyt: 'Men behoort gheen quaet te doen opdatter goet uut volge.'⁵ Ende alsulcke menschen willen aldus de kracht Gods een mate stellen, alsoft Hy anders niet dan door haer gheveynsheyt zijns naems heerlicheyt by de menschen verbreyden, oft [alsoft God niet] oock om den eenvoudighen te leeren veel bequamer ende gheschickter leeraers dan sy zijn verwecken ende uutschicken en konde.

Maer is 't dat se nu so groote begeerte hebben (als sy seggen) haren naesten met woorden ende met wercken te stichten, so laet sy dat veel liever bewijsen ende doen met haer vertrecken om des woorts wille, dan met haer huychelen ende guychelen. Want met haer vertrecken sullen sy alle afgoderijen opentlicken verdoemen ende sullen de kennisse der waerheydt ende de lust tot de oprechte religie in veler menschen herten verwecken. Ende alletijt sullen sy wel goede oorsaken hebben om haren naesten te stichten, te troosten ende hulpe te doen in der plaetse daer se sullen vertrocken zijn, so verre sy aldaer heylichlicken ende ghetrouwelicken handelen ende wandelen. Maer willen sy in haer papisti[73ᵛ]sche huychelijen blijven volherdende, so sullen sy met sulcx te doen de

---

1 2 Kor. 1:4.
2 Ps. 24:1.
3 Ps. 118:6; Hebr. 13:6.
4 1 Kor. 2:14; Rom. 8:7.
5 [Rom. 3:8.]

tyrannen in de gheloovigen te vervolghen noch bitterer ende hardtneckigher maken, ende de afgodische menschen meer ende meer in hare supersticien verstercken, tot groote droeffenisse der godsalighen ende erghernisse derghener die noch swack zijn. Ende sullen al hetgene met één hant om verre smijten dat se met de ander hant ghesticht sullen moghen hebben, henselven terwijlen in groot perijckel haerder zielen stellende. Want 't is te beduchten dat alsulcke veynsers ende huychelaers ten laetsten door het rechtveerdich oordeel Gods also sullen verharden dat se – in de papistische blintheit wederom ghevallen zijnde – doodelicke vyanden der waerheyt worden, oft dat se – heel godloos ende libertijnsch ghewurden zijnde – der waerheydt ende godsalicheyt (diese tevoren bekent hebben) bespotters ende belachers worden, als wy, leyder, des rechtveerdigen oordeels Gods veel exempelen in veel overheden, mispapen ende kooplieden daghelijcx sien ende ghewaer worden.

Sommighe anderen worpen voor dat men alsulcken vertreck tot alsulcke plaetsen daer men de rechte evangeli[74ʳ]sche leere wel vrijelicken ende met vreden drijven ende belijden mach, behoort te schouwen omdattet alsdan te beduchten staet dat men uut sulcke rusten ende vrijicheyt een sorgheloos leven aennemen sal. 'Want,' seggen sy, 'men vindt er veel die, in 't pausdom in haer vaderlant onder het cruyce ende vervolginghe levende, in de religie Christi seer vyerich waren, ende daerna tot plaetsen gekomen zijnde daer se met vreden leven mochten, zijn se heel koel ende slaperich gheworden.' 'Ghelijckerwijs Loth,' segghen sy, 'die in Sodoma rechtveerdichlicken gheleeft heeft, opten berch ghekomen zijnde, heeft hy hem aldaer in dronckenschap aen syne dochteren besondicht.'[1]

Hoe wel dat wy met groote droeffenisse onser herten belijden moeten datter veel in alsulcke vrede des te onachtsamer ende sorghelooser gheworden zijn, nochtans en is sulcx niet door de vrede oft gherusticheydt by ghekomen maer alleen door der menschen boosheyt. Gelijckerwijs dat Lot opten berch sondichde, zijnder sorgeloosheyt, ende niet zijnder vreden toe te schrijven is. Ende dat nu sommige in 't pausdom door het cruyce ende de vervolginghe, de waer[74ᵛ]heydt verloochenen oft gheveynstlick verswijgen, wie en soude dat niet meer des menschen verdorventheyt toe rekenen dan den cruyce oft der vervolginghen? Maer dat nu de vrede oft gerusticheyt der kercken in haerselven goet ende nut is om een godsalich leven aen te richten ende te leyden wordt daer ut klaer ende blijckelick genoech dat ons in de h[eylighe] schrift bevolen wordt God om de vrede der kerckken te bidden. Want also heeft de Heere

---

1 Gen.19:30-31.

ghesproken tot de joden die in Babylonien ghevangen waren: 'Soeckt der stadt vrede oft welvaert, daer Ick u hebbe laten wech voeren. Ende biddet voor haer tot den Heere, want als 't haer wel gaet, so gaet het u oock wel.'[1] Ende Paulus heeft bevolen dat de dienaers der kercken bidden souden voor de koningen ende voor alle overicheyt, opdat wy een gherustelick ende stil leven leyden moghen, in alder godsalicheyt ende eerbaerheydt.[2] 'Want sulcx,' seyt hy, 'is goet, daer toe ooc aenghenaem voor God onsen Vader.'[3] Hier toe dienen oock de heerlicke prophecijen des propheten Esaias van den standt der christelicker kercken: 'De koningen sullen uwe voesterheeren ende hare vorstinnen uwe voestervrouwen [75ʳ] zijn. Sy sullen voor u neder vallen ter aerden op 't aensicht ende dat stof uwer voeten lecken.'[4] Ende op een ander plaetse: 'Ghy sult melck van den heydenen suyghen ende de vorsten der koninghen sullen u soogen.'[5] Desghelijcx ghetuycht oock Lucas dat de christelicke ghemeynte de vrede tot groote voorderinge der godsalicheyt ghebruyct heeft, daer hy seyt: 'De gantsche gemeynte hadde vrede door gantsch Judea ende Galilea ende Samaria, ende wert gesticht, ende wandelde in de vreese des Heeren, ende wert vervult met troost des H[eylighen] Geests.'[6]

Uut alle dese boven ghenoemde ghetuyghenissen blijckt wel dat de vrede der kercken een sonderlinghe weldaet Gods is, seer nut ende bequaem om de godsalicheydt opentlick in 't ghemeyn ende by een yeghelick in 't particulier te vorderen; so verre dat men deselve niet schandelicken en misbruyckt. Ende om het misbruyck te schouwen zijn dese remedien:

1. In den eersten, dat een yeghelick in alsulcke uutwendige vrede der kercken by hemselven dencke dat hy noch eenen seer sorghelicken strijdt te voeren heeft tegen de gheestelicke vyanden, als namelicken teghen het vleesch, de werelt [75ᵛ] ende den satan. In denwelcken strijdt hy alletijt, ende sonder eenich bestandt te maken, totter doot toe te kempen heeft, wilt hy de eewighe kroone verkrijgen.
2. Ten tweedden, dat hy neerstich zy in 't onderhouden al 'tghene dat men in de christelicke gemeynte schuldich is te onderhouden.
3. Ten derden, dat hy dencke, datter niet onghestadighers noch verandelickers en is dan de uuterlicke vrede ende gherusticheydt der kercken, na dewelcke dickwils het cruys onverhoets over den

---

1 Jer. 29:7.
2 1 Tim. 2:1-2.
3 1 Tim. 2:3.
4 Jes. 49:23.
5 Jes. [60]:16.
6 Hand. 9:31.

hals koemt, insonderheyt wanneer de menschen den vrede oft gherusticheydt schandelicken tot een sorgeloosheyt des levens misbruycken. Waer af men een seer heerlick exempel vindt by Eusebium (Lib[er] Eccles[iastica] Hist[oria] 8, cap[ut]1[AF]). So wie nu dese dingen in de vrede oft gherusticheyt der kercken wel terechte overdenckt, die sal sonder twijffel uut de vrede een groote vorderinghe der godsalicheydt verkrijghen.

Maer wanneer nu yemant van den vrede oft gherusticheydt der kercken hoort vermanen, so en sal hy niet meynen dattet hier opter aerden also vaste vrede in der ghemeynten zijn sal, dat der christgheloovigher leven ghehee[76r]licken sonder cruys oft vervolginghe zy. Want hoe wel dat den christenen door een sonderlinghe ghenade Gods gegundt wort eenen tijt lanck vrij van der tyrannen tanden te leven, so wordense nochtans daer en tusschen met veelderley cruyce – als kranckheden, armoede, last van kinderen etc. – ghequelt ende beladen. Sy worden van hare vrienden versmaedt ende gantsch verlaten. Sy moeten daghelicks alle onghelijck, versmaedtheyt, lachteringhen, bespottinghen ende dreygementen van de wereltsche menschen onderworpen zijn. Ende daghelicx ontfangen sy tijdingen van broederen die op andere plaetsen verraden, ghevangen, berooft, verdroncken, onthooft oft verbrant zijn. Also dat het woort Pauli warachtelicken in alle de leden Christi (ja, oock als de gemeynte aldermeest in vreden ende gherusticheyt is) na zijn mate volbracht wordt, daer hy seyt: 'Alle die godsalicken willen leven in Christo Jesu, die moeten vervolginghe lijden.'[1] Uut alle welcke redenen wel te verstaen is dat men wel sonder eenich perijckel der salicheyt na alsulcke plaetsen trecken mach, daer de christelicke ghemeynte met vreden leven mach.

[76v] Sommighe menschen nemen oock haer onschult hierin datter binnen onsen tijt so veelderhande opinien in de werelt zijn, dat se na het afwijcken van de papisterije niet en weten (so sy segghen) tot welcke uutwendighe kercke oft gemeynte dat se hen begheven sullen. Maer segt my doch lieve[r][AG] oft se alleenlick ende op henselven bleven levende, souden sy dan niet schuldich zijn een sekere ende ghewisse gevoelen van der religie te hebben ende te volghen? 't Is doch eenen yeghelicken christen bevolen niet onverstandich maer verstandich te syne wat des Heeren wille zy,[2] ende dat se in den verstande volmaeckt zijn[3]. Ende, om nu uut dese menichfuldicheyt der opinien het aldersekerste te nemen, is

---

1 2 Tim. 3:12.
2 Ef. 5:17.
3 1 Kor. 14:17.

't niet beter ende ghewisser in een heylighe christelicke ghemeynte te leven (dewelcke Christus zijn tegenwoordicheydt belooft heeft,[1] ende in dewelcke de gheest der propheten denselven propheten onderworpen is)[2] dan in een eenichlick particulier leven, d'welck doch verboden is?

Sommighe anderen klaghen dat se met andere lieden sonden oock souden mogen besmet worden waer 't dat se hen tot eenighe ghemeynte begaven, ge[77r]merckt dat men nerghens gheen so wel gheschickte ghemeynte en vindt in welcke altijt niet wat ghebreect, oft in 't leven ende conversacie der pastoren oft des ghemeynen volcx. Maer alsulcke lieden en konnen, in eensaemheydt levende, van deselve sonde noch niet gevrijdt worden, tenzy dat hen sulcx van herten leet zy ende trachten daerna van herten dat alsulcx ghebetert mach worden: niet so seer andere lieden als hare eyghen sonden verheffende ende groot makende. Want is 't dat se in de gemeynte hen alleen daer toe begheven willen [om] andere lieden gebreken aen te mercken ende haere eyghen gebreken te laten onghemerckt henen gaen; mitsdien, dat se andere lieden ghebreken so hooghe achten, so en bewijsen sy daer mede gheen maniere van godvreesentheydt maer gheven met sulcx te doen haer hooveerdighe hypocrijticheyt te kennen. Sy weten wel, oft sy en willens niet weten, dat den saligen standt der christelicker kercken noyt op dese wereldt gantsch vrij van sonden geweest en heeft, noch en kan oock niet ghewesen, overmidts de groote verdorventheydt onser natueren.

Christus heeft in zijn heylich ghesel[77v]schap gehadt Judam die een dief,[3] een murmureerder,[4] een verrader[5] ende een duyvel[6] was.

De h[eylighe] schrift getuycht dat het onkruyt t'samen met 't koren opwast ende dat 't kaf altijt met de tarwe in de kercke Christi sal t'samen gemengt blijven totten eynde des werelts toe.[7] Het evangelische net vangt goede ende quade visschen.[8] In den wijnstock Christo zijnder vruchtbare ende onvruchtbare rancken.[9] In 't rijcke Gods zijnder wijse ende onwijse maechden.[10] In de konincklicke bruyloft wordt er oock gevonden die

---

1 Mat. 18:20.
2 1 Kor. 14:32.
3 Joh 12:6.
4 Joh.12:4.
5 Marc. 14:10-11.
6 Joh. 6:70-71.
7 Mat.13:30, 40; Mat. 3:11.
8 Mat. 13:47-48.
9 Joh. 15:2.
10 Mat. 25:2.

gheen bruyloftskleet aen en hebben.¹ Wy vallen alle in veelderley manieren.² Ende hoewel wy van Christo gewasschen zijn, so behoeven wy noch grootelicken dat onse voeten ghewasschen worden.³ Van andere lieden ghebreken sullen wy voor God wel vrij blijven in de christelicke ghemeynte, is 't dat wy ons wachten van de ghemeynschap, van de daet ende wille der sonden; ons by godvreesende mannen voegende; andere lieden sonden beterende (so veel in ons ghelegen is); ende God den Heere biddende dat Hy andere lieden de sonden verghheven wil.

Ende oftet nu ghebeurde dat der [78ʳ] predicanten leven in alle deelen niet so heylich en ware, daerom en sal men noch so terstont van de gemeynte niet afwijcken, so verre sy by de predicacie ende belijdinghe des onvervalschten woorde Gods blijven. Want alsdan behoort van weerden ghehouden te worden hetghene dat Christus gheseydt heeft: 'Op Moyses stoel sitten de schriftgheleerde ende Phariseen, al wat sy u seggen dat ghy houden sult, dat houdt ende doet. Maer na hare wercken en doet niet, want sy segghen ende en doen 't niet.'⁴ Item, 'tgene dat Paulus seyt: 'Wat dan? Nochtans wort Christus allesins, hetzy door een decksel, hetzy door de waerheyt, verkondicht; ende ick verblijde my daer in ende sal my oock verblijden.'⁵

Maer daerentusschen aenghesien dat niemant gheloochenen en kan daer kan wel groot perijckel van alsulcke predicanten komen, so behoort een christen mensche hier wijsselicken in te handelen. Haer gebreken sal hy tot een walginghe hebben ende niet navolghen, noch oock met deselve syne gebreken verontschuldighen, alsoftet hem al geoorloft ware wat de predicanten doen. Men behoort neersticheydt te doen, dat se vermaent worden ende dat se hen [78ᵛ] beteren. Willen se hen niet beteren, so sal men daerna arbeyden dat se af geset worden; ende en wilt dat noch niet gheluckken, so sal alsdan een christen zijn eyghen ende der ghemeynten sonden beschreyen, dewelcke God wreken wilt met alsulcke predicanten te senden. Hy sal den Heere des oogsts aenroepen, Hem biddende dat Hy goede ende ghetrouwe wercklieden uutsenden wil. Den goeden Herder sal ten laetsten het suchten zijnder schapen verhooren. Siet wat Ezech[iel] seyt (cap. 34).

Ende deghene die tot dienaers der ghemeynten ghekoren zijn, die sullen ten eersten neersticheydt doen dat se de ghemeynte met gheen quade exempelen ergheren, opdat de h[eylighe] insettinghen door haer quaet leven van den ghemeynen volcke niet veracht en worden.

---

1 Mat. 22:11.
2 Jak. 3:2.
3 Joh. 13:10.
4 Mat. 23:2-3.
5 Fil. 1:18.

Is 't sake dat de Heere 'wee' over hen seyt, prononcerende deselve weerdich verdroncken te worden, [deselve] die eenen van den minsten erghert die in Hem gelooven,[1] wat straffe sal dan deghene te verwachten hebben die de gheheele ghemeynte (over dewelcke hy van zijnder officien oft ampts wegen behoorde te waken)[2] met zijn schandelick leven noch dagelicx erghert. Ghelijckerwijs [79ʳ] Ophni en Pinehas, die door hare onversadelicke ghiericheydt deden dat de offerhanden des Heeren van den volcke verachten werden,[3] metten doot in den slach van God ghestraft werden,[4] also sullen dese oock de wrake Gods in 't eewich vyer ghevoelen. Ende ghelijck haer vader Eli de opperste priester van achterover uut synen stoel vallende den hals brack, omdat hy syne kinderen die so boos waren in den dienst der kercken geleden heeft,[5] also sullen ooc voorwaer seer grouwelicken van den Heere ghestraft worden alle deghene die tot kercken dienaers aennemen so danighe mannen, van welcker vromicheydt ende godsalicheydt gheen menschen goedt ghetuyghenisse gheven en konnen; oft die alsulcke kerkcken dienaers door haer autoriteydt van haren dienst niet af en setten – ja, houden se dickwils daer in, teghen alle klachten der christennen. Ende meestendeel wordt er in deser manieren ghesondicht van alsulcke princen, edelen ende potentaten, die onder den schoonen tijtel van beschermheeren de heerlicheydt ende ghewelt over de kercke nemen. Ende dese sullen in den dach des oordeels rekenschap geven van alle de zielen die door [79ᵛ] alsulcke boose predicanten, die sy ingevoert oft tegen der gemeynten danck in haren dienst behouden hebben, tot de verdoemenisse gekomen zijn, d'welck uut dese vermaninghe Pauli seer wel te mercken is, daer hy seydt: 'En legt niemant haest de hant op en maect dy ooc niet deelachtich vreemder sonden, houdt dyselven reyn.'[6]

Dat sommige nu haer onschult soecken willen, seggende dat se haer tot geen christelicke kercke oft gemeynte voegen en konnen om haer rijckdommen, edeldom, weerdicheyt haerder beroepinghe ende wetenschap der heyligher Schrifts wille, dat koemt gemeynlick al uut een hooveerdich herte; te weten, dat se hen Christi ende syner kercken schamen, die na de werelt verachtet ende versmaedt wort.

---

1 Mat. 18:6-7.
2 Heb. 13:17.
3 1 Sam. 2:13-17, 24.
4 1 Sam. 4[:11].
5 1 Sam. 4:[18].
6 1 Tim. 5:22.

En heeft Christus niet eenen yeghelicken sonder onderscheyt geseyt: 'Neemt mijn jock op u'?¹ Is hy niet onser alder Meester, Koninck ende Heere? Wat vertoeven wy dan noch synen gheboden onderdanich te zijn?

Niemant en isser so verre in de kennisse der h[eyligher] schrift ghekomen, hy en heeft noch al veel te leeren. Want de h[eylighe] schrift is eenen ongrondelicken schat [80ʳ] der godlicker wijsheyt, dewelcke door de dienaren des woorts (die uutdeylers zijn der verborgentheden Gods) dagelicx in de gemeynte uutgedeylt worden. Wy zijn oock seer traech ende luye tot wat goets te doen, hetselve haestelicken verghetende, maer tot quaedt te doen seer snel, ende dat blijft ons seer vast in de memorie hangende, so dat wy wel behoeven daghelijcx goede vermaninghen te hooren.

Niemant en sal hem oock daer mede soecken te verontschuldigen dat hy de bijbel binnen synen huyse heeft. Want ick neme dat men dien seer vlijtelicken overleest (men vindt wel veel huysen daer de bijbel wel dick van stoffe bedect leyt, oft daer hy alletijt op een tresoyr ghesloten staet en pronckt), nochtans so is den dienst des woordts na de insettinghe Christi van veel meerder krachten ende kan oock veel beter het herte treffen. Want van natueren zijn wy alle seer blindt ende onsselven wat te veel toeghevende. Daeromme en konnen wy, de bijbel by onsselven lesende, onser ghebreken daer niet so seer mede vermaent worden, als wanneer wy eenen anderen openbaerlicken hooren vermanen.ᴬᴴ

[80ᵛ] 't Heeft Gode oock belieft de menschen door andere menschen te leeren, opdat also onsen hoo[g]moet ghebroken, ende wy metten bant der liefden aen malcanderen ghevoecht souden worden. Den kamerlinck, die de schriftuere niet en verstondt die hy las, werdt Philippus tot eenen uutleggher toeghevoecht.²

Paulus wert van Christo tot Ananiam gesonden, om van hem met de levende stemme onderwesen te worden.³

Cornelio wert bevolen Petrum tot hem te roepen, die hem segghe wat hy doen sal.⁴

Ende den raet van de broederen binnen Jerusalem bestemde ende besloot dat t'samen met de brieven aen de ghemeynte van Antiochien gesonden, Paulus, Barnabas, Judas ende Silas mede trecken souden, om oock met woorden 'tselve te verkondighen.⁵ Ende waertoe soude Christus dienaers des woordts inghestelt hebben, item, 'pastoren ende leeraers, tot

---

1 Mat.11:29.
2 Hand. 8:30-31.
3 Hand. 9:6.
4 Hand. 10:5-6..
5 Hand. 15: 23, 25, 27..

toerichtinghe der heylighen, totten wercke des ampts, daerdoor het lichaem Christi gesticht soude worden'[1] als Paulus seyt, waer 't dat den leere onnoodich ware, daer men de bloote schrift by hemselven lesen mochte?

Ende opdat nu niemant ter wereldt [81ʳ] de uutwendige ghemeynschap oft vergaderinghe der godsaligher, om syne heerlicke gaven wil, versmaden en soude, Christus selve die onse koninck ende Heere is (in denwelcken all schatten der wijsheyt ende kennisse verborghen zijn)[2] heeft dickwils in verscheyden manieren met syne teghenwoordicheyt de vergaderinghe vereert. Een kindt acht daghen oudt zijnde is Hy besneden gheweest.[3] Als de daghen der reyninghen Marie volbracht ware, is Hy te Jerusalem in den tempel voor Gode gestelt.[4] Hy is met syne ouders opten feestdach van paschen na Jerusalem getrocken.[5]

Twaelf jaren oudt zijnde satt Hy in 't midden der doctoren, toehoorende ende vraghende.[6]

Tot synen jaren ghekomen zijnde hoorde Hy Joannem prediken in de ghemeyne vergaderinghe des gantschen volcx ende is met d'ander van hem ghedoopt ghweest.[7] Daerom en behoort oock niemant door eenighe wereltlicke weerdicheyt oft meyninghe der eyghener wijsheyt beweecht te worden van de christelicke vergaderinghe afghesundert te blijven. Maer dese wereldt en heeft gheene ooren, also dat wy wel terechte met Paulo roepen mochten: [81ᵛ] 'Waer is de wijse? Waer is de schriftgeleerde? Waer is de kloecksinngihe deser werelt? Siet aen, lieve broeders, uwe roepinghe: Niet veel wijsen na den vleessche, niet veel gheweldighe, niet veel edelen en zijn geroepen. Maer wat dwaes is voor de werelt, dat heeft God verkoren opdat Hy de wijse te schande make; ende wat swac is voor de werelt, dat heeft God verkoren opdat Hy te schande make wat sterck is; ende wat onedel is voor de werelt, ende dat verachte, heeft God verkoren, ende dat daer niet en is, opdat Hi te niete maeckte wat yet is. Opdat hem[AI] gheen vleesch voor Hem en beroeme.'[8]

Sommige wenden voor dat niemant eenighe kerckelicke vergaderinge, die van de Roomsche kercke verscheyden zijn, maken en mach sonder miraculen, wonderwercken ende sonderlinge beroepinghe. 'Ghelijckerwijs,'

---

1 Ef. 4:11-12.
2 Kol. 2:3.
3 Luc. 2:21.
4 Luc. 2:21.
5 Luc.2:42.
6 Luc. 2:46.
7 Mat. 3:13-14.
8 1 Kor. 1:20 [&2-29].

seggen sy, 'hier voortijden Moses, de propheten ende apostelen, die eenen nieuwen kerckendienst ingestelt hebben, die hebben alsulcx ghedaen in een sonderlinge beroepinghe ende oock met wonderlicke teeckenen ende miraculen.'

't Is wel waer, dan dewijle wy gheen nieuwe forme der leeringhe ende kerckendiensten inne en voeren, maer bren[82ʳ]ghen slechs weder terechte de oude leere ende religie (die hier voortijden van Christo ende van de apostelen ingestelt, met ontallick veel miraculen bevesticht, ende in 't pausdom vervallen is), so eyscht men t'onrechte van ons dat wy onse beroepinge met wonderwercken bevestigen sullen; bysonderlicken, aengesien datter nergens in der schriftueren gheen beloftenisse ghevonden en wort dat de vervallen leere Christi wederomme met uutwendige miraculen ende wonderteeckenen opgericht soude worden. Maer Paulus seyt klaerlicken dat de boosachtige van den Heere sal verdoemt worden met den Gheest zijns monts.[1] Dat is, metten woorde. Daerom sal dat by ons voor een sonderlick mirakel wesen, te weten, dat onse leeringhe over een koemt met de leeringhe der propheten ende der apostelen, ende dat alle onse kerckendiensten ende ceremonien dienen tot uutroeyinghe des rijcx Satane in syne godloosicheyt, ende tot stichtinge des rijcx Christi in alle syne godvreesentheyt ende heylicheyt. Ende met de uutwendige miraculen soude onse leeringhe meer by de christenen voor suspect dan voor oprecht ghehouden worden, aengesien dat de heylige schrift merc[82ᵛ]kelicken spreeckt van de miraculen des antechrists ende valscher propheten, die in de leste tijden zijn souden. Christus seyt: 'Veel valsche christi ende valsche propheten sullen haer verheffen, die teeckenen ende wonderwercken doen sullen, dat se oock de uutverkorene verleyden, indien 't moghelick ware. Siet, Ick hebt u altemael van tevoren geseyt.'[2] Ende Paulus seyt dat de boosachtige syne aenkoemst aenrichten sal met allerley leughenachtighe krachten, ende teeckenen ende wonderheden.[3] Ende van het beest dat van der aerden opklimt wort gheseyt in de Openbaringhe Joannis, dattet groote teeckenen doet, also dattet oock vyer van den hemel doet vallen voor den menschen ende verleyt die opter aerden woonen, om der teeckenen wille die hem ghegheven zijn te doen.[4] Ende van den valschen propheet staet gheschreven dat hy teeckenen dede, door welcke hy verleyde die dat merckteecken des beests namen ende die dat beelt des beests aenbaden.[5]

---

1 2 Thes. 2:8.
2 Mat. 24:24-25; Mar. 13:22.
3 1 Thes. 2:9.
4 Op. 13:13-14.
5 Op. 19:20.

Waeruut dan te mercken is dat men met rechte gheen uutwendige teeckenen noch miraculen van ons en behoort te eysschene, om te bewijsen dat onse vergaderinghen oprecht zijn.

[83ʳ] Noch vint men der hedensdeachs eenen grooten hoop die alle uutwendige christelicke ghemeynten oft vergaderinghen onder den schijn eender 'inwendigher ende gheestelicker godsdiensts' seer kleyn achten ende verworpen, oft ymmers gheheel vrij stellen. 'Want de kercke Gods,' seggen sy, 'is onsienlick, aen gheen plaetse ghebonden, diewelcke God selve door synen Gheest ende inwendich woort inwendichlicken leert, voedt, regeert ende onderhoudt, sonder eenighe uutwendighe behulpingen.' Ende om dese haer leere te bevestighen, brenghen sy ghemeynlicken dese ghetuyghenissen uut de h[eylighe] schrift by.

In den eersten den spreucke Jeremie, daer hy seyt: 'Ick sal mijn wet in 't midden van haer geven, ende Ick sal se in haer herten schrijven; ende Ick sal haer God zijn, ende sy sullen mijn volck zijn. Ende niemant en sal den anderen, noch de een broeder den anderen, leeren ende segghen: "Kent den Heere." Want sy sullen My altesamen kennen, beyde kleyn ende groote, spreeckt de Heere. Want Ick wil haer hare misdaet verghven ende haerder sonden nimmermeer gedencken.'¹

Daerenboven oock hetghene datter in Ezechiel staet: 'Also spreect de Heere Heere: [83ᵛ] "Siet, Ick wil nu mijnder kudden selfs aennemen, ende die soecken, gelijck als een herder syne schapen soeckt als sy van der kudden verdwaelt zijn."'²

Ende korts daerna: 'Ick wil haer eenen eenigen Herder verwecken, diese weyden sal; te weten, mynen knecht David. Die sal se weyden ende sal haer Herder zijn.'³

Item, hetgene Moyses seyt: 'Dat woort is seer naby u, in uwen mont ende in uwer herten, dat ghij 't doet.'⁴

Noch allegeren sy dese spreucken Christi ende der apostelen:
'Het rijcke Gods is in u.'⁵
'Mijn rijcke en is van deser werelt niet.'⁶
'Sy sullen alle van Gode gheleert worden.'⁷
'Onse wandelinge is in den hemel.'⁸

---

1 Jer. 31:33-35. [cf.] Jer. 24:7; Hebr. 8:10; Jes. 54:13.
2 Ez. 34:11.
3 Ez. 34:23.
4 Deut. 30:14.
5 Luc. 17:[21].
6 Joh. 18:36.
7 Joh. 6:45; Jes. 54:13.
8 Fil 3:20.

'Hier na en kennen wy niemant meer na den vleesche. Al hebben wy oock Christum na den vleesche ghekent, nu nochtans en kennen wy Hem niet meer. Daerom isser yemant in Christo, so is hy een nieuwe creatuere. Siet, het is altemael nieu gheworden.'[1]

Hier by doen sy noch al hetghene datter over al by de propheten tegen de sacrificien ghelesen wordt. Als in Esaia: 'Wie eenen osse slacht, die is effen als die eenen man versloeghe. Wie een schaep offert, die is als die eenen hondt den hals brake.'[2]

Item in Osea: 'Sy sullen komen met haren schapen ende runde[84ʳ]ren, den Heere te soecken, maer niet vinden. Want Hy heeft Hem van haer gekeert.'[3]

Ende by Malachias: 'Ick en sal voortaen de offerhande niet meer aensien.'[4] Ende wat onse wedersegghers hier noch al meer by brenghen is desen al ghelijck, also dattet niet van nooden en is altemael op de rije te verhalen.

Wij sullen nu op d'een voor, d'ander na, ordentlicken antwoorden.

In den eersten, wy bekennen wel dat de kercke Gods in alsulcker manieren onsienlick ghenaemt mach worden, dat men van de warachtighe ende oprechte leden derselver na des vleeschs vernuft niet oordelen en kan. Ende dat deselve tot sommighe plaetsen van de tyrannen so jammerlicken verstoort ende verstroyt wort, dat men daer nauwelicx uutwendichlicken eenen voetstap meer af ghesien en kan. Gelijck men segghen mach dat de gloeyende kole doot is, die wel diep onder de asschen verborghen leyt. Item, dat een weynich korens, met veel kafs overdeckt, onsienlick mach ghenoemt worden. Gelijckerwijs den standt der christelicker kercken in Israël geweest is ten tijden des propheten Elie, als hy seyde: 'Heere, sy hebben dyne propheten gedoot ende dyne altaren om[84ᵛ]meghestooten, ende ick ben alleen ghelaten, ende sy staen my na mijn leven.'[5]

Maer dat onse wedersegghers segghen willen dat de kercke daerom onsienlick zy omdat se van alle uutwendighe ceremonien ghevrijdt zijnde niet ghesien en kan worden, is al te plompelicken ghesproken ende opentlicken der h[eyligheʳ] schrift gantsch contrarie.[AJ]

Christus ende de apostelen hebben haer kercken sienlick ende met sekere heylighe uutwendige teeckenen van andere kercken oft ghemeynten afgheteeckent ghehadt. Hy heeft oock synen apostelen sommighe uutwendighe dinghen ghegheven, die sy altijt onderhouden souden om

---

1 2 Kor. 5:16-17.
2 Jes. 66:3
3 Hos. 5:6.
4 Mal. 2:13.
5 1 Kon. 19:10; Rom.11:3.

de kercken te vergaderen ende oock t'onderhouden. Te weten, den dienst des woorts, der sacramenten ende der christelicker straffen. Ende waer 't sake dat de kercke tot allen tijden onsienlicken bleef, so moeste dat bevel Christi, 'segghet der gemeynten,'[1] heel teniete gaen. Oock waer 't tevergheefs gheweest, dat Paulus de huysghenooten des gheloofs afgescheyden hadde van deghene die buyten der gemeynten zijn.[2] God maect oock wel tegen des werelts danck dat zijn kercke oft ghemeynte een stadt op eenen hooghen [85ʳ] berch is, die van God ende van allen menschen aenghesien wort.[3]

Wy en zijn oock so buyten sinnen niet, dat wy de kercke Gods met hare warachtighe godsdiensten aen eenighen hoeck des werelts binden willen. Maer uuten woorde Gods achten wy datter plaetsen ende tijden zijn, also dat so waer het woort Gods reyn ghepredict wort, dat daer oock het huys ende de kercke Gods zy, ende dat God de Vader aldaer in den gheest ende in der waerheyt gedient ende aenghebeden wort. Niet om der uutwendiger plaetsen wille, die ons Gode niet aengenaem en maect, maer om de groote weldaet wille, dat aldaer den wille Gods geopenbaert ende verkondicht wort. Also worden sommige plaetsen in de h[eylighe] schrift heylich ghenaemt omdat God ende synen godlicken wille daer in sonderlinghe gheopenbaert worden.[4]

Wy bekennen oock gewillichlicken met onse wedersegghers dat God innichlicken met synen Gheest de syne leert, regeert ende vertroost; maer dat se daer noch by hanghen 'sonder eenighe uutwendighe behulpinghen,' dat versaken wy. Niet dattet God niet doen en kan, maer dattet Hem also niet belieft [85ᵛ] en heeft. Want haddet Hem also belieft, Hy en soude gheen uutwendighe ceremonien inghestelt hebben. Nochtans en willen wy hiermede niet segghen dat de Heylige Gheest onkrachtich zy, oft dat wy van de uutwendige ceremonien afgoden maken, maer wy begeeren dat eenen yegelicken na den woorde Gods zijn officie oft ampt onghekrenckt behoude; te weten, dat den uutwendighen godsdienst den uutwendighen mensch bewege, ende dat de heylighe Gheest oock inwendichlick 't herte aenroere, beweghe, optrecke ende buyghe, makende also dat de uutwendighe mensche met vermeerderinge der godsalicheydt door de uutwendighe ceremonien ende godsdiensten beruert ende beweecht worde.

---

1 Mat. 18:17
2 1 Kor. 5:12; Gal. 6:10.
3 Mat. 5:14; 1 Kor. 4:9.
4 Gen. 28:17; Ex. 3:5; Joz. 5:15; Ps. 138:2; Hand. 7:35.

De mensche hier opter aerden is van ziele ende lichaem tesamen ghevoecht. Ende gemerct nu, dat deselve met veel uutwendighe middelen door de uutwendighe sinnen tot sonden verwect ende ghetrocken wort, so heeft God, om dese menschelicke swackheydt door syne wijsheydt te helpen ende te ghemoet te komen, oock uutwendighe remedien ende middelen inghestelt (onder dewelcke de principaelste zijn de heylighe cere[86ʳ]monien der kercken), door dewelcke hy van de sonde afghetrocken ende tot de godsalicheyt des te meer verweckt mochte worden. Want God maect dat de uutwendighe godsdiensten door synen H[eylighen] Gheest in der menschen herten so krachtich zijn, dat sy ghevoelen (wanneer die oprechtelicken ende in den gheloove ghebruyct worden), dat hare herten inwendichlicken vermaect ende opghetoghen worden. De uutwendighe godsdiesten dan, ende de inwendighe aenblasinghe des H[eylighen] Gheests, wercken t'samen in den mensche ende komen oock seer wel over een. Daerom doen onse wederseggers seer qualicken die, onder den schijn des H[eylighen] Gheests, de h[eylighe] ceremonien van God inghestelt kleyn achten, oft uut de christelicke kercke sluyten willen.

Ende aengaende de sentencie uut Jeremia ghenomen, dat God zijn wet in der menschen herten schrijven wilt, also dat niemandt synen broeder noch synen naesten meer en sal leeren etc., dat en kan de onderhoudinghe der christelicker vergaderinghen niet te niete maken. Maer in dese beloftenisse, dewelcke niet tot alle menschen maer alleen totter christelicker ghemeynten toe[86ᵛ]behoort, wort alleenlick uutghedruckt, door een comparacie oft verghelijckinghe des ouden volcks by den nieuwen volcke, hoe groot de weerdicheyt ende vordeel des nieuwen volcx onder Christo zijn soude, so wel in 't onderhouden der gheboden Gods, als in de godsalighe kenisse Gods, by het joodtsche volck, dat onder Moyses was.ᴬᴷ Want onder het jootsche volck en konde de wet door den dienst Mosis anders niet dan de herten verschricken ende gramschap wercken, als Paulus seyt.¹ Maer in 't nieuwe volck gheeft Christus door synen H[eylighen] Gheest, denwelcken Hy rijckelicken uutghestort heeft, een bereyt ende vlijtich herte om den gheboden Gods ghehoorsaemheyt te bewijsen.

Ende gemerct dat de kennisse Gods (door dewelcke wy kennen dat Hy, onse God, onsen sonden ghenadich is)ᴬᴸ in 't oude testament seer duyster was, als alleen met bedeckte beloftenissen ende door sekere sacrificien die den volcke duysterlicken voorghestelt waren, die doetertijt de alderexcellentste mannen met seer groote vlijticheit oock nauwelicx

---

1 Rom. 4:25.

verstaen konden, deselve wort den geloovigen in 't rijcke Christi so klaerlicken voorgestelt ende beloeft, dat nie[87ʳ]mant – ja, ooc niet een van de alderminste leden der kercken – des onwetende zy, so dat hy daerna, als na een onbekende sake, behoeve te vraghen.

Hier toe dient 'tghene dat Christus tot syne discipulen seyde: 'Salich zijn de ooghen die sien de dinghen die ghy siet. Want Ick segghe u, dat veel propheten ende koninghen begheert hebben te sien hetghene dat ghy siet, ende en hebbens niet ghesien; ende te hooren hetghene dat ghy hoort, ende en hebbens niet ghehoort.'[1] So en wort dan in dese beloftenisse niet uutghesloten uuten rijcke Christi het uutwendich gebruyc des woordts ende der sacramenten, maer daer in wort uutghedruckt het eyghen ende onderscheyden ampt Mosis ende Christi, oft des ouden ende nieuwen testaments. Item, door een comparacie des meesten teghen het minste, de weerdicheydt ende excellencie der kercken Christi by de jootsche kercke, voor also veel als de onderdanicheydt des wets ende de kennisse des willen Gods aengaen mach. Ende daerenboven mach men seggen dat de propheet hier niet en spreeckt van de volmaecktte kennisse aller Godlicker dingen, maer alleen van d'eerste beginsselen der ken[87ᵛ]nissen Gods, door dewelcke men hem kendet: Dat Hy onse God is ende dat Hy onser sonden in Christo ghenadich zy. Als in Jesaia staet: 'Dat lant is vol der kennissen des Heeren, ghelijck als met water des meyrs bedeckt.'[2] Want daer staet merckelicken: 'Niemant en sal den anderen leeren etc.' Tot dewelcke aenvanghende oft beghinnende kennisse Gods wy noch de kennisse van veel Godlicke mijsterien ende verborgentheden behoeven, dewelcke kennisse door den dienst des woordts verkreghen ende bevesticht wort, gelijck oock dat eerste begintsel der kennisse Gods niet sonder voorgaende predicacie des woordts verkreghen en wort. Want het geloove koemt door het ghehoor.[3] Ende allen den gheloovighen, na de leere Pauli, wort bevolen toe te nemen ende te wassen door den dienst des woorts, totdat se tot een volkomen man worden, die daer zy in der maten des volkomen ouderdoms Christi.[4]

Noch moet men gade slaen in alle de prophecijen van de heerlicheyt des rijcx Christi, dat deselve hare volkomenheit niet hier opter aerden, dan alleen in den hemel hebben. Te weten, wanneer alle de vyanden Christi tot een voetbanck zijn[88ʳ]der voeten sullen ghemaeckt zijn.[5] 't Is wel waer dat se nu beginnen, van dien tijt af dat na de hemelvaert Christi

---

1 Luc. 10:23-24.
2 Jes. 11:9.
3 Rom. 10:17.
4 Ef. 4:12-13.
5 1 Kor. 15:25.

de H[eylighe] Gheest seer rijckelicken,¹ na de prophecije Joelis,² in de menschen uutghestort is, maer sy en komen noch tot hare volmaectheyt niet voor den uutersten dach des oordeels. Want wy en sien noch niet dat alle dinghen Christo onderworpen zijn.³ Maer alsdan sal wederghebracht worden al wat God gesproken heeft door den mont zijnder heyliger propheten van der werelt af.⁴ Daerom dat deel der prophecijen daer gheseyt wort: 'Niemandt en sal den anderen leeren', behoort eygentlicken tot de volkomenheyt des rijcx Christi. 'Want ons weten is nu stuckwerck ende ons propheteren is stuckwerck, maer wanneer dat volkomen sal komen, so sal dat stuckwerck ophouden.'⁵ Nochtans en heeft Paulus deselve prophecije in den brief totten Hebreën, tot twee reysen, den teghenwoordigen standt der kercken niet onbequamelicken toe gheeyghent; te weten, omdat se doe heeft begonnen vervult te worden, ghemerckt dat alsdoe in de christelicken ghemeynte de ghenade des Gheests ende der godsaligher leeringhen overvloediger was [88ᵛ] dan se daer tevoren in de Israelitische kercke geweest hadde. Ende door dien dat Paulus dese prophecije tot twee reysen verhaelt,⁶ daer en leert hy niet mede dat de vergaderinghen der gemeynten (item, den dienst des woordts ende der sacramenten) opgeheven zijn, ghemerckt dat hy selve met schriften ende met woorden den menschen den wille Gods geleert heeft, christelicke vergaderinghen aenghericht ende gesticht heeft, allen gheloovighen den dienst des woorts ende der sacramenten neerstelicken bevelende. Ende korts daerna in denselfden brief vermaent hy tot onderlinghe vermaningen ende tot onderhoudinge der christelicker vergaderinghen, schrijvende in deser manieren: 'Laet ons onder malcanderen onsselven waernemen, met verwecken totter liefden ende goede wercken, ende niet verlaten onse vergaderinghe, als sommighe pleghen, maer onder malcanderen vermanen. Ende dat so veel te meer so veel ghy siet dat den dach ghenaket.'⁷

Uut alle dese boven gheruerde redenen is 't wel klaer ende blijckelick, dat deser prophecijen meyninghe niet en is dat in desen loop des rijcks Christi alle onderhoudinghe der christelicker [89ʳ] vergaderinghen ophouden oft stille staen soude, ende dat men alleen der Godlicker inspiracien oft ingevingen soude behoeven, ghemerckt dat in de voor-

---

1 Joh. 7:39.
2 Joël 2:28; Hand. 2:16-17.
3 Heb.2: [8] [original: 2.d.39]
4 Hand.3:21.
5 1 Kor. 13:[9-10].
6 Hebr. 8; Hebr. 10:16.
7 Hebr. 10:24-25.

geschreven prophecije alleen beloeft wort een klaerder ende overvloedigher kennisse des willen Gods in 't rijcke Christi dan in de wet gheweest is; item, een volkomender ghehoorsaemheyt, welcke alle nochtans niet en sullen volbracht worden dan in 't toekoemende rijck Christi, in d'welck wy sien sullen aengesicht aen aenghesicht,[1] ende sullen God sien als Hy is.[2] Want alsdan salt God al in allen wesen,[3] als de apostel spreeckt.

Ende dese onse wedersegghers, die so veel teghen den uutwendigen dienst des woordts segghen willen, moeten noch selve wel bekennen dat se uut 'tselve woort veel gheleert hebben, ende noch daghelicx leeren. Ja, sy doen selve haer uuterste beste dat se hare eyghen leeringen den menschen met woorden, schriften ende boecken inbeelden. Ende 'tghene dat se in ons t'onrechte berispen, daer behelpen sy henselven mede.

Datter nu in Ezechiele staet dat God beloeft syne schapen selve te willen soecken, ende dat Hy over hen eenen Herder, synen knecht David (dat's [89ᵛ] te seggen Christum), verwecken wil, daer en dreycht Hy niet mede uut syne kercke te roeyen de ghetrouwe dienaers die onder Christum zijn, maer alleen degene die henselven ende niet hare schapen en weyden.[4] Want Christus selve en heeft niet alleen dienaers des woorts in syne kercke inghestelt,[5] welcke Hy so wel ghehoort wil hebben als Hemselven,[6] maer heeft oock bevolen, wanneer datter ghetrouwe dienaers ghebreken, dat wy alsdan den Heere des oogsts bidden souden, 'dat Hy wercklieden in synen oogst senden wil'[7].

Ende met dat woort Mosis, daer Hy seyt totten kinderen van Israël: 'Dat woort is seer naby u etc.'[8] daer en wort der kerckendienst niet mede teniete ghedaen, maer wordt er meer door versterct. Want met dese woorden wort den joden alle ontschuldinge benomen waerom sy de wet Gods niet weten en souden, aengesien dat se God in haren mont ghestelt heeft. Dat is, Hy heeft se hen opentlicken door Moysen geopenbaert. Ende heeft se daerna door de Leviten[9] ende priesteren[10] onder hen laten

---

1 1 Kor. 13:12.
2 1 Joh. 3:2.
3 1 Kor. 15:28.
4 Ez. 34:2.
5 Mat. 28:19-20; Joh. 20:23; 21:15; Rom. 12:7, 9; 1 Kor. 12:28; Ef. 4:11.
6 Luc.10:16; Joh. 13:20.
7 Mat. 9:38.
8 Deut. 30:14.
9 Deut. 33:10.
10 Mal. 2:7.

prediken, also dat se hen altijt in den mont wesen konde.[1] Ende alsdan wort het woort genoemt in de herten te wesen, wanneer men 't van binnen [90ʳ] in der herten door 't gheloove ontfangt. Ende als Paulus deselve woorden Mosis den evangelio toeeygent ende appliceert, seggende: 'Maer wat seyt (te weten, de gerechticheyt die uuten geloove is) dat woort is naby dy, in dynen mont ende in dijn herte,'[2] so en neemt hy niet wech uut de kercke Christi den uutwendighen dienst des Woorts (d'welck hy veel meer ter selver plaetsen seer sterckelicken bevesticht. 'Hoe sullen sy ghelooven,' seyt hy, 'van dien sy niet gehoort en hebben? Ende hoe sullen sy hooren sonder predicant?'[3] Ende korts daerna: 'So koemt dan 't gheloove door 't gehoor, ende 't ghehoor door het woort Gods'), maer geeft alleen te kennen dat alsulcken lof, die van Moyses der wet toegeschreven wort,[4] veel meer den evangelio toebehoort, omdattet niet alleen in den mont door de openbare predicacie, noch oock niet alleen in der herten door 't gheloove der geener die 't aengenomen hebben, en is, maer ooc mede omdattet ons vastelicken van de saliceit door Christum te verkrijgen, versekert. 'Want,' seyt hy, 'is 't dat du Jesum bekenst met dynen monde dat Hy de Heere zy, ende ghelooft in dijn herte dat Hem God van den dooden opgheweckt heeft, so wortst du salich.'[5]

[90ᵛ] Ende dat Christus totten phariseen seydt: 'Het rijcke Gods is in u,'[6] daer en wort niet mede gheleert dat de eyghen woonstadt des rijcks Christi in der phariseen herten zy, die doch Christum ende zijn rijcke haetteden, maer daer wordt alleen mede te kennen ghegheven dat se tevergheefs na den rijcke Gods vraechden, alsoftet seer verre van hen ghemerckt hadde; ghemerckt dat Hij 't selve onder hen verweckt ende door de verkondinge des evangeliums toegebracht hadde, hoe wel dat se daer geenssins op en letteden. Also schrijft Joannes van Christo: 'Hy is in zijn eygen gekomen, ende de syne en hebben Hem niet ontfanghen.'[7] Item: 'Hy staet in 't midden van u, dien ghy niet en kent.' Daerom 'binnen', oft 'in u', is also veel te seggen als 'by u is het rijcke Gods'. Ende oft nu tot deser plaetsen 'in u' beteeckende 'in het binnenste der herten hebben', daer en soude nochtans noch niet uut volghen dat de uutwendighe regeeringhe der kercken wech genomen is, aenghesien dat se de Heere selve ingestelt heeft, ende dat de menschen door deselve als metterhandt

---

1 Hand. 15:21.
2 Rom. 10:8.
3 Rom. 10:14.
4 Deut. 30:12.
5 Rom. 10:9.
6 Luc. 17:20.
7 Joh. 1:11.

gheleydt worden, opdat het rijcke des satans uut hare herten verdreven, ende het gheestelicke rijck [91ʳ] Christi daer in verwect, ghevordert ende bevesticht worde.

Item, als Christus seydt dat zijn rijck van deser wereldt niet en is,¹ daer en wilt Hy niet mede dat Hy gheen sienlicke kercke oft ghemeynte in dese wereldt hebben en soude. Want in dese werelt, ende van dese wereldt een rijcke ende een kercke te zijn, zijn verscheydene dinghen. Pilatus meynde dat het rijcke Christi te ghelijcken was met de andere rijcken deser werelt, voor also veel als den uutwendighen standt ende regeringhe desselfs aengaen mocht, d'welck Christus loochent. Aenghesien dat het rijcke Christi heel gheestelick te verstaen is, so wel in hemselven als in de maniere van hetselve te regeren. Want het rijcke Gods is gherechticheyt, ende vrede, ende vreuchde in den H[eylighen] Gheest.² Ende de forme der regeringe hier in de werelt is ghelegen in de onderhoudinghe des woorts, der sacramenten ende der christelicker straffen.

Ende dat Christus den Capernaiten uut de propheten allegeert: 'Sy sullen alle van God geleert worden,'³ daermede en verworpt Hy niet den uutwendigen dienst des woorts, d'welck Hy oock alsdoe vruchtbaerlicken by syne apostelen gebruycte, [91ᵛ] dewelcke tot Hem seyden: 'Heere tot wien sullen wy gaen? Du hebtst de woorden des eewighen levens.' Maer met dese woorden des propheten heeft Hy alleen willen te kennen geven, dat de uutwendighe leeringhe gheenssins by de vleeschelicke menschen, hoe scherpsinnich dat se oock zijn moghen, van weerden ghewesen en kan, tenzy dat se oock inwendichlicken van God geleert, getrocken ende door den H[eylighen] Gheest beweecht worden. Maer wie soude daerdoor den dienst des woorts willen verworpen, so verre hy ymmers noch eenich verstant hadde? Paulus seyt: 'Door God leven, rueren ende zijn wy,'⁴ nochtans en mach niemant daerom seggen ende achten dat het ghebruyck der sonnen, des regens ende der spijsen ons onnut ende tevergheefs zy.

Ende hoewel dat wy alletijt nadat hemelsche Jerusalem moeten haken, ende dat onse conversacie altijdt in den hemel behoort te wesen, daerom en moeten wy nochtans noch de uutwendighe christelicke vergaderingen niet versmaden, in dewelcke door de oeffeninghen van God inghestelt ende na zijn bevel uutghericht, wy alle tijdt meer ende meer tot de soete aenschou[92ʳ]winghe ende overdenckinghe der hemelscher dingen ghetrocken ende verweckt worden.

---

1 Joh.18:36.
2 Rom. 14:17.
3 Jes. 54:13; Joh. 6:45.
4 Hand.17:28.

Ende dat Paulus tot die van Corinthen schrijft: 'Van nu aen en kennen wy niemant na den vleesche etc.,'[1] daer mede en wordt uuter kercken oft ghemeynten niet wech ghenomen het gebruyck des uutwendighen dienst, d'welck hy selve in 'tselve capittel grootelicken prijst. 'Hy heeft ons ghegheven,' seyt hy, 'dat ampt, dat de versoeninghe predickt. Ende heeft onder ons opghericht dat woordt van der versoeninghen. So zijn wy nu boden in Christus stede, want God vermaent door ons. So bidden wy nu in Christus stede, laet u versoenen met Gode.'[2] Maer hy vermanet alleen de Corintheren teghen de leere der valscher apostelen, dat se niet meynen en souden dat de ware christenheyt ghelegen zy in eenige uutwendighe vleeschelicke privilegie, gelijckerwijs dat yemant met Christo in den vleesche dagelicx omgegaen hadde, maer dat se gelegen is in de wedergheboorte ende vernieuwinge des gemoets door den Geest Gods. Dewelcke vernieuwinghe niet alleen den uutwendigen kerckckendienst niet uut en sluyt, ja dat meer is, sy wil[*]^AM [92ᵛ] dat denselven alle tijdt meer ende meer ghedreven worde, ghemerckt dat wy oock door denselven eenichsins weder gebaert ende vernieut worden. Als de apostel totten Corinthen schrijft: 'Ick hebbe u weder gebaert in Christo Jesu door dat evangelium.'[3] Ende wederom totten Galaten: 'Mijn lieve kinderkens, ick bare u noch eens, totdat Christus in u een ghedaente krijghe.'[4] Ende tot Philemon van Onesimo schrijvende: 'Ick bidde,' seyt hy, 'voor mynen sone Onesimus, denwelcken ick in myne banden gebaert hebbe.'[5] So dwalen dan onse wedersegghers, dewelcke door den lof der nieuwer creatueren, oft vernieuwingen des Gheests, concluderen willen dat het gebruyck der kerckendiensten den geloovighen onnut ende onnoodich zy.

Ende ten laetsten, dat de sacrificien van Gode inghestelt somtijts in de h[eylighe] schrift verworpen worden, dat en geschiet daeromme niet omdat de onderhoudinghe derselver sacrificien van haerselven verboden oft onnoodich zijn (want sulcx soude teghen God wesen, diese selve bevolen heeft), maer dat het quaedt betrouwen verworpen wordt, d'welck de menschen daer in hadden, die de sacrificien sonder eenige boete, [93ʳ] gheloove oft warachtighe godvreesentheyt alleen na den uutwendighen schijn ende letter onderhielden. Wie en weet niet dat een doot lichaem den menschen gantsch onnut is, d'welck daer tevoren, als 't noch leefde, denselven seer nut ende profijtelick was?

---

1 2 Kor. 5:16.
2 2 Kor. 5:18-20.
3 1 Kor. 4:15.
4 Gal. 4:19.
5 Filemon: 10.

Dus is 't nu klaerblijckelick genoech dat door alle de bovenghenoemde passagien der h[eyligher] schrift die onse wedersegghers bybrenghen de uutwendighe vergaderinghe der christenen, noch de onderhoudinghe der uutwendigher ceremonien van God inghestelt, in haerselven niet verdoemt noch verworpen en worden, maer door deselve wort alleen gheleert dat by den uutwendigen godsdienst, als by den lichame, oock ghevoecht moet worden den inwendighen gheestelicken godsdienst, als den gheest oft de ziele, opdat God volmaectelicken t'samen met onse lichamen ende zielen gheeert mach worden.¹

Ende hoewel dat onse wedersegghers onse kercken oft christelicke vergaderingen so sterckelicken aenvechten, nochtans so komen sy selve wel by malcanderen, ende leeren somtijts oock malcanderen wel, so met schriften, so oock met de levende stemme. Ende en waren sy [93ᵛ] niet eerst uutwendichlicken van ander[en] gheleert ende onderwesen gheweest, sy en souden so veel ghetuyghenissen der heyligher schrift teghen ons niet weten te allegeren. Wat willen sy dan so grootelicken in ons beschuldighen hetghene dat sy selve wel doen ende navolghen? Daerom alle dese beuselinghen achterrugghe worpende, laet ons God also in den Gheest dienen dat wy gheen uutwendighe middelen van Hem inghestelt ende gheboden achterweghen en laten, als daer zijn: de neerstige ende christelicke onderhoudinghe des woorts, der sacramenten ende andere ceremonien der christelicker kercken oft ghemeynten; niet achtende wat oock de dwase ende onwijse wereldt (die nochtans seer neuswijs meynt te zijn) daer teghen morren oft rasen mach.

 So verre heeftet saligher ghedachten Martinus Micronius ghemaeckt.ᴬᴺ

Ende nu heeft David Joris, daer hierboven af vermaent is, tot de boven-verhaelde argumenten onser wederseggheren, tegen de onderhoudinge der christelicker vergaderingen noch daerby [94ʳ] ghehangen, dat het ghebruyck aller ceremonien van Christo inghestelt, door hemᴬᴼ is wech ghenomen. Daerom dat hy, als hy meynde, het ampt oft officie des heylighen Gheests volbrenghende, de syne in alle waerheyt leydet, voortbrengende hetghene dat volkomen oft volmaeckt is, ende also hetghene dat noch stuckwerck was wechnemende.² Ende ghemerct hy syne leere voor d'alder volmaeckste houdt, ende verre boven de leeringhe Christi prijst, also dat de leere Christi syne leere wijcken moet, al wat de

---

1 1 Kor. 6:20.
2 1 Kor. 13:9-10.

heylighe schrift van des menschen volmaectheyt in de toekoemste Christi getuycht, dat trect hy altemael so schandelicken tot hem ende tot zijnder leeringhen, dat hy hemselven ende den synen de heerschappie des gantschen werelts, de onsterffelickheyt ende de volmaecte gherechticheyt oock in desen vleessche beloefde (by de volmaeckte gherechticheyt verstaende een inwendighe beweghinge des herten, die van der sonden gantsch gheen gevoelen en heeft).[AP]

Maer de boumeester ende timmerman van het 'Huys der Liefden' ende 'Stadt des Vredes', die vergodede werckmeester van den 'Spieghel der gherechticheyt', siende dat de voorseyde David [94^v] den menschen noch gheen volle vrijheyt en beloeft, maer dat hy se noch aen synen persoon bindt, so beroemt hy hem een volkomender leere ghevonden te hebben dan Davids leere; te weten, dat so wie in 't Huys der Liefden woont ende tot de Stadt des Vredes ghekomen is, die is vrij – niet alleen van des Heeren Christi, maer oock van alle uutwendige religie ende manieren van ceremonien. Ende de liefde noemt hy een alsulcke beweghinghe des ghemoets te zijn, door dewelcke yemant noch in hemselven, noch in yemant anders eenige sonde oft quaet en siet, maer alle dinghen, hoe se dan zijn moghen, ten besten verstaet ende (als hy dat noemt) na der liefden beduydet.

Ende overmidts dien dat beyde deser antichristen leeringe niet alleen de godsalighe onderhoudinghe der vergaderingen, die in den naem Jesu Christi tesamen komen, gantsch teniete willen maken, maer benemen oock uut der menschen herten alle hope des toekomenden levens in Jesu Christo ende gheven tot alle sonden ende boosheden groote oorsake, so ben ick ghedwonghen my met luttel woorden teghen haer leeringhe te stellene.

In den eersten soude ick van haer bey[95^r]den wel eens begheeren te vragen oft se oock wel met ghetuyghenissen der heyligher schrift souden konnen bewijsen, dat de evangelische leere Jesu Christi noch eens te niete ghebracht moeste wesen, ende datter een ander noch volkomender moeste na komen. Ende so sy heeft moeten wech ghenomen worden, oft se alsdan met ghetuyghenissen der h[eylighe^r] schrift wel souden konnen doen blijcken, dat haer leeringe dan in de stede van de leeringhe Christi opgenomen moeste worden ende voort eeuwelicken dueren? Daer en boven gheve ick hen oock te bedencken oft se oock wel konnen volbrenghen hetghene dat de h[eylighe] schrift ghetuycht, dat van Jesu Christo den Heere in den dach des oordeels te volbrenghen staet. Maer aenghesien dat se sulcx met een letterken der h[eyligher] schrift niet en konnen bewijsen dan alleen by menschen die heel buyten sinne, ende met een begeerte tot de valsche vrijheyt betoovert zijn ('want niemant en kander eenich ander fundament gheleggen dan datter gheleyt is, d'welc is Christus Jesus'[1]), ende aenghesien ooc dat so lange alsulcx niet bewesen en is alle hare droomen moeten vallen, so volcht daeruut dat men de leeringhe [95ᵛ] Christi Jesu als de alder volmaectste in dit leven behouden moet, ende dattet een grousame lasteringe ende bedriegerie is, allent wat sy hoochmoedelicken ende ijdelicken van de groote volkomenheyt haerder leere boven de leere Christi Jesu roemen, ende allent wat se van de vrijheyt der christelicker vergaderinghen den menschen beloven.

Ende dat se nu seggen willen, datter eenen Heyligen Gheest van Christo beloeft is die de menschen in alle waerheyt leyden soude, dat en kan haer sake niet vorderlick ghezijn. Want de heylighe schrift, dewelcke getuycht datter eenen Heylighen Gheest beloeft is,[2] deselve ghetuycht dat alsulcke belofte in de discipulen Christi Jesu volbracht is.[3] Willen sy een deel der heyliger schrift aennemen, so moeten sy d'ander oock wel ghelooven.

Hetghene dat Christus Jesus over de 1500 jaren in zijn discipulen volbracht heeft, dat en sullen sy haer niet laten voorstaen dat Hij 't tot nu toe op haren tijt uutghestelt soude hebben.

De apostelen zijn door den Heyligen Gheest in alle waerheyt gheleydt gheweest, voor also veel als der meschen salicheyt van noode was. Ende deselve [96ʳ] waerheyt verseghelt ende bevesticht noch die selve Gheest in de herten der gheloovigher.[4] Oock so leert deselve h[eylighe] schrift, dat de H[eylighe] Gheest niet leeren en soude dan hetghene dat met de woorden Christi Jesu ende met zijn leeringe soude overeenkomen. Want also seyt Christus tot zijn discipulen: 'Dien Gheest der waerheyt, die van den Vader uutgaet, die sal ghetuyghenisse gheven van My.'[5] Ende wederomme: 'Hy sal u inghevan al hetghene dat Ick u gheseyt hebbe.'[6] Item: 'Hy sal My verklaren, want van den Mynen sal Hij 't nemen ende u verkondighen.'[7] Also noemt de apostel Petrus den Heylighen Gheest die God gheghevan heeft een ghetuyge Christi.[8] Paulus accordeert daer oock mede: 'Niemant,' seyt hy, 'door den Heylighen Gheest sprekende en vervloect Jesum, ende niemant en kan Jesum een Heere heeten dan alleen

---

1 1 Kor. 3:11.
2 Joh. 14:16, 17, 26; ende 15: 26; Hand. 1:8.
3 Hand. 2:4; ende 5:32; ende 8:17; ende 9:17; ende 10:44; ende 11:15.
4 Rom. 8:16; 2 Kor. 1:22; ende 5:5; Gal. 4:6; 1 Thes. 4:8; 1 Pet. 1:11.
5 Joh. 15:26.
6 Joh. 14:26.
7 Joh. 16:14.
8 Hand. 5:32.

door den Heyligen Gheest.'[1] Recht oft hy wilde seggen: 'Daeruut kan men wel gheoordeelen oft oock yemant van den Gheest Gods ghedreven is; te weten, so hy Christum ende syne leeringhe lief heeft ende soeckt te vorderen.' Het is dan tevergheefs dat men, onder den schijn des Heylighen Gheests, in de kercke Gods eenighe [96ᵛ] ander leeringhe wilt verhopen dan de leeringhe des Heeren Christi Jesu. Aengesien dattet des H[eylighen] Gheests ampts is van Christo Jesu ghetuygenisse te gheven, Hem te verklaren, syne woorden inne te gheven ende hetghene te verkondighen dat Hy van Christo Jesu ontfanghen heeft.

Willen nu onse weddersegghers by brenghen datter in de h[eylighe] schrift vermaent wordt van de volmaeckte ende onvolmaeckte leeringhe, ende dat de onvolmaeckte leeringhe den apostelen toegheschreven wordt, ende dat die selve noch in de toekomende tijden de volmeackte leeringhe wijcken soude, als daer geschreuen staet: 'Ons weten is stuckwerck, ende ons propheteren is stuckwerck, maer wanneer komen sal hetghene dat volkomen is, so sal dat stuckwerck ophouden.'[2] Item: 'Wy sien nu door eenen spieghel in een doncker woort etc.' Daerop antwoorden wy also: Dat de apostel Paulus gheen gelijckenisse en wilt maken der leeringhen oft wetenschap der apostelen met eenighe andere leeringhe, die der wereldt noch naemaels soude gheopenbaert worden (want in de leste daghen heeft ons God ghesproken door synen Sone.[3] Also dat den tijt [97ʳ] Christi Jesu wel terechte ghenoemt wort de laetste ure, den laetsten ende den uutersten tijt,[4] het eynde der werelt;[5] te weten, omdat door Hem in desen tijt de alderlaetste verklaringe des Godlicken wille gheschiet is), maer hy siet op den toekomenden tijt oft leven, die na de verrijsenisse der dooden in den hemel zijn sal. Aldaer, de sterffelicheyt afgeleyt zijnde, oock ophouden sal hetghene dat stuckwerc is (1. Cor. 13.b). Ende daeromme, de heylige schrift, sprekende van de volmaecktheyt des menschen, wijst ons op dien tijt in denwelcken Jesus Christus wederom uut den hemel tot ons komen sal.[6] Also de evangelist Joannes: 'Wanneer,' seyt hy, 'Christus verschijnen sal, so sullen wy Hem ghelijck zijn. Want wy sullen Hem sien gelijck Hy is.'[7] Ende Paulus schrijft totten Philippensen in deser manieren: 'Wy verwachten uuten hemel den salichmaker Jesum Christum den Heere, die onse nietighe lijf verklaren sal, dattet ghelijck

---

1 1 Kor. 12:2.
2 1 Kor. 13: 9-10, 12.
3 Hebr. 1:2.
4 1 Joh. 2:18; 1 Pet. 1:20.
5 1 Kor. 10:11
6 1 Kor. 13:9-10.
7 1 Joh. 3:2.

worde synen verklaerden lijve.'[1] Item, oock totten Colossensen: 'Wanneer Christus, u leven,[AQ] Hem openbaren sal, dan sult ghy oock openbaer worden met Hem in der heerlicheyt.'[2]

Ende in den brief totten Corintheren, [97ᵛ] disputerende van de heerlicheyt der gheloovigher, so beveelt hy haer op de toekoemst Christi te verwachten.[3] Ende opdat niemant meynen en soude dat de apostelen van eenighen andere tijdt spreken dan alleen van de uutersten tijden der laetster verrijsenissen, so schrijven sy dat se oock tot de volmaecte kenisse ende openbaringe Christi komen sullen. 'Alsdan,' seyt Paulus, 'sal ick Hem sien aengesicht aen aengesicht. Nu kenne ick stuckwijse, maer dan sal ick Hem kennen, gelijck als ick gekent ben.'[4] Item: 'Hy sal onse lichaem verklaren etc.'[5] 'Wy sullen hem sien gelijck Hy is etc.'[6] Hadden nu de apostelen op de tijden ghesien daert onse wedersegghers op bedieden willen, so en souden sy haerselven de volmaeckte wetenschap niet toegherekent, noch oock deselve niet verhoept hebben.

So dwalen dan onse wederseggers, die desen tijt der volmaectheyt (omdat se so langhe niet vertoeven en konnen) voorkomen[AR] ende tot desen onsen tijdt trecken willen.

Daerenboven dese volmaectheyt der kennissen, daer Paulus af spreeckt, en is van haerselven ende in der waerheyt der onvolmaecter kennissen oft weten[98ʳ]schap niet contrarie, maer het verschil is alleen gheleghen in 't verkrijghen oft begrijpen derselver kennissen. Want nu ter tijt behoeven wy veel behulps om de kennisse Gods te begrijpen, ende so langhe wy noch in desen vleessche zijn konnen wy daer inne meer ende meer toenemen. Maer in 't toekomenden eewighe leven en sal deselve kennisse, die wy nu hier uut zijn woort hebben, niet verandert worden in een ander kennisse, maer sal op een nieuwe maniere volmaeckt worden ende sal alleen gheleghen zijn in de aenschouwinghe des Godlicken wesens. So sal dan alleen het verschil gheleghen zijn in 't verkrijghen oft begrijpen derselver kennissen, ende dieselve sal alsdan volmaecktelicker gheopenbaert worden. Want alsdan salt God al in alle zijn.[7]

Ende dat de apostel totten Hebreën schrijft: 'Willen wy de leere van den beghinne des christelicken levens nu laten varen ende tot der volkomenheydt grijpen, niet noch eens grontlegghende van boete der

---

1 Fil. 3:21.
2 Kol. 3:4.
3 1 Kor. 15:[35-58]; 2 Thess. 4:16-18.
4 1 Kor. 13:9-12.
5 Fil.3:21.
6 1 Joh. 3:2.
7 1 Kor. 15:28.

dooder wercken, van den gheloove aen God, van den doop, van de leere, van handtoplegghinghe, van de verrijsenisse der dooden, ende van dat eewighe oordeel,[1] dat en seyt hy [98^v] niet dattet noch eens op dese wereldt gheschieden sal datter een volmaeckter leere gheopenbaert sal worden dan de leere Christi ende der apostelen, maer de leere van de geheele mysterie oft verborghenheyt des oppersten priesterdoms Christi noemt hy een volkomene oft volmaeckte leere, makende een ghelijckenisse oft comparatie deser leeringhen met de eerste ende kleynste beginsselen des catechismi, als daer zijn de belijdinghe van een beteringhe des levens, de summe des gheloofs van God, de leeringhe van den doop ende oplegginge der handen, het hooft artijckel van de verrijsenisse der dooden ende des toekomenden oordeels. Dewelcke zijn als de principaelste hooftstucken der christelicker religien, die ooc den kinderen in 't generael behooren bekent te wesen, aenghesien dat se niet alle de weerdicheyt van de opperste priesterschap Christi so wel en kennen. Daerom en wordt se hier niet t'onrechte van Paulus de volmaecktheyt ghenaemt, dewelcke hy syne navolghers, ende noch veel te min David Jorisen, oft andere niet en heeft achter ghelaten om uut te legghen ende te verklaren, maer hy beloeft dat hij 't selve doen wilt, als [99^r] hy oock in sommighe navolghende capittelen, tot het elfde cap[ut] toe, seer wel uutghericht heeft.[2]

Nu hebben wy klaerlicken bewesen dat de leeringhe Jesu Christi altijt in der kercken Gods blijft, als die oock de volmaeckste is, maer dat se in de gheloovighe (voor also veel als der openbaringhen ende der volmaecktheyt aengaen mach) in den hemel volbracht sal worden, als de Heere Christus alle syne vyanden Hem t'onderghebracht sal hebben. Item, wy hebben oock bewesen dattet een groote ijdelheyt is, dat onse wedersegghers haer veel van de volmaectheyt haerder leeringhen beroemen willen.

Ende is 't dat se noch hardtneckelicken willen houden staende datter een volmaecter leere te verwachten is dan de leere Jesu Christi, so begheere ick dat se my met goede merckelicke argumenten bewijsen dat haer leere deselve leeringe zy dier te verwachten was, na dewelcke geen andere volkomender te verwachten en is. David Joris heeft de syne voor d'alder volmaecste ghehouden. Ende de leeraer vant 'Huys der Liefden', na hem komende, schrijft alsulcx zijnder leeringhen toe, ende verworpt Davids leere. Ende voort mach er noch een ander ko[99^v]men, die ooc alsulcx wat droomen mach. Dus begheeren wy dan dat se met also klare ende stercke argumenten bewijsen dat haer leere de volmaectste is, als

---

1 Hebr. 6:1-2.
2 Hebre.6.a.3.

Christus syne leere bewesen ende bevesticht heeft. Ende so sy noch even wel niet aflaten en willen te seggen, dat de volmaectheyt die wy in de wederkoemste Christi Jesu verwachten van hem nu wederghebracht zy, so begeeren wy dat se al hetghene metterdaet uutrichten dat wy met een vast gheloove van Christo Jesu in zijn wederkomste verwachten. Te weten, dat haer lichamen heel verklaert zijn als 't lichaem Christi; dat se geestlick [en] hemelsch zijn ende niet meer eenighe katijvicheden[AS] (niet meer den hongher, den dorst, der moetheyt, kranckheyt, ouderdom, noch oock den doot) onderworpen; dat haer huysvrouwen sonder swaricheyt kinderen draghen ende kinderen baren; dat, alle ongerechticheyt wech ghenomen zijnde, alleen de gherechtigheyt regnere; dat se sonder eenich behulp der boecken, vermaninghen ende dierghelijcke dinghen (die se daghelicx ghebruycken), de volle ende volmaeckte kennisse der hemelscher dingen vercrijghen; ende ten laetsten, dat zij 't al restitueren ende op synen eersten standt bren[100ʳ]gen, dat wy in Adam verloren hebben. Maer ghemerct dat se dese noch diergelijcke dinghen niet en volbrengen, ghelijck sy se oock gheensins volbrengen en konnen, so blijcket klaerlicken dat het niet dan een vertoovertheyt – ja, niet dan een enckele uutsinnicheyt – en is, dat men sulcke gheesten gheloven wilt. Maer op dit pas hebben wy nu hier genoech af geschreven, nu moeten wy oock wat voort handelen van hetghene dat sommighe teghen de heymelicke christelicke vergaderingen in de papistische landen opworpen willen.

¶ Van de heymelicke christelicke vergaderinghen in de papistische landen.

Hetghene dat hier boven van de weerdicheyt, nutheyt ende nootsakelicheyt der christelicker kercken oft vergaderingen gheseyt is nemen sommige wel voor warachtich aen, maer sy en konnen gheenssins lijden noch voor goet, noch gheoorloeft houden, de vergaderingen die in de huysen heymelicken gheschieden. Derwelcker argumenten wy hier na ons vermoghen d'een voor d'ander na examineren willen.

In den eersten worpen sy voor het ge[100ᵛ]bot Christi: 'Hetghene dat Ick u in 't duyster segghe, dat spreeckt in 't licht. Ende hetghene dat ghy in de oore hoort, dat predickt op de daken.'[1] Maer hiermede en bewijsen sy noch niet dat Christus met alsulcken ghebot alle heymelicke oft particuliere vergaderingen gantsch verboden heeft. Want hiermede en heeft Hy anders niet willen te kennen gheven dan dat de leeringhe des

---

1 Mat. 10:27.

evangeliums, die eenen tijt lanck als verborgen in sommige hoecken des jootschen lants onder seer luttel menschen duysterlicken schuylde, eens in 't licht ghebracht ende overal in de wijde werelt door der apostelen predicatie verbreydt moeste worden, als oock daerna gheschiet is. Daer mede en wort nu den gheloovighen niet verboden, telcken alsser vervolghinghe voorhanden was, heymelicke ende particuliere christelicke vergaderinghen te houden. Ghelijckmen leest dat de apostelen met gheslotene deuren, uut vreese der joden, heymelick vergadert zijnde, gheseten hebben. Diewelcke heymelicke vergaderinge Christus selve eens oft tweemael met syne teghenwoordicheyt ende leeringe vereert heeft.[1] Desghelijcx oock de discipulen, die Christum ten hemel hadden [101ʳ] sien opvaren, bleven heymelick in 't opperste des huys binnen Jerusalem. Sy baden ende leerden aldaer, ende verkoren Matthiam tot een apostel.[2] Ende in deselve besonderde ende heymelicke vergaderinghe is daerna de Heylighe Gheest wonderlicken nederghedaelt.[3] Daerna dede Petrus een seer heerlicke predicacie door het bevel des Heylighen Gheests in 't huys Cornelii des hooftmans, die syne vrienden ende maechschap daertoe t'samen geroepen hadden.[4] Ende binnen Jerusalem warender sommige besondert ende heymelick in een huys vergadert die voor den ghevanghenen Petrum baden.[5] Paulus leerde oock by de stadt Philippi buyten aen 't water.[6] Deselve heeft oock besonderlick ende particulierlicken 't huysghesin des deurwachters gepredict.[7] Ende binnen Troas, daer de discipulen des nachts vergadert waren, heeft hy het broot gebroken ende voort totten dagheraet ghepredict.[8] Ditselve exempel der apostelen hebben ooc treffelicke ende christelicke mannen der eerster kercken in 't woeden der vervolginghen allessins nagevolcht. Plinius Secundus getuycht in eenen brief die hy aen Traianus den keyser schrijft, dat de christenen binnen synen tijden hare [101ᵛ] vergaderinghen des morghens, voor den dagheraet, ghehouden hebben (als geschreven staet by Eusebius in den derden boeck Eccles[iastica] Hist[oria] in 't 33. cap[ut][AT] ende Tertullianus Apol[ogeticum] cap[ut] 2[AU]). Item, men leest ooc dat dese ouderlingen, Maximus, Dioscorus, Demetrius ende Lucius heymelicken geseten, ende de broederen secretelicken besocht hebben (als ghetuycht

---

1 Joh. 20:19-22., 26.
2 Hand. 1:[15-26].
3 Hand. 2:1-4.
4 Hand. 10: [24, 34] [Original: 10: 11, 15.]
5 Hand.12:12.
6 Hand.16: 13.
7 Hand. 16: 31-33.
8 Hand. 20:7.

Euseb[ebius], 7 Lib[er] Eccles[iastica] Hist[oria] cap[ut] 11^(AV)). Ende ten tijden des tyrans Licinii, de christenen die in oriënten tot in Lybiën by Egypten woonden en dorsten niet opentlicken tesamen komen, noch hare christelicke vergaderinghen houden (Zosomenus, Hist[oria] Eccle[siastica] Lib[er] 1, ca[put] 2^(AW)). Ende ten tijden des tyrans Maximinus hielden hen de christenen so secreet, dat hoewel hy een gebot hadde laten uutgaen den christenen te voordeele, so en wasser nochtans niemant van den christenen so stout, dat hy in 't openbare soude gekomen hebben (Euseb[ius], Eccles[iastica] Hist[oria] Li[ber] 9, cap[ut] 9^(AX)). Ende waer 't sake dat de christenen ten tijden der vervolginghen altijt oft openbare vergaderingen oft gantschelicken gheene gehouden en hadden, ende nimmermeer heymelicke ende particulierlicken t'samen gekomen en waren, waertoe souden de holen in der aerden [102^r] dan ghedient hebben, die men noch hedensdaechs siet, in dewelcke sy hare vergaderingen uut vreese der tyrannen heymelicken gehouden hebben? Daerenboven en souden de christenen niet so lichtelicken van de heydenen beklaecht geweest hebben, als se nu na de getuygenisse Tertulliani (in Apol[ogeticum] ca[put] 9^(AY)) beklaecht zijn gheweest van dese grouwelicke sonden, als van onverscheyden byslapen onder hen, van kinderen ghedoodt te hebben ende van dat se de sacrificien oft offerhanden met menschen bloet verontreynicht souden hebben, waer 't datter onder hen gheen particuliere ende heymelicke vergaderinghen gheweest en hadden.

Maer ghemerckt dat de apostelen ende de christenen die de apostelen terstont na gekomen zijn alsulcke particuliere ende heymelicke vergaderinghen noyt aenghericht en hebben dan als sy daer van noots weghen toe gedrongen waren, maer hebben altijt ghesocht in 't openbaer te prediken, ende zijn tot allen tijden bereyt geweest van de leeringe met eenen yegelicken te handelen ende daer af te spreken, so en kan ooc niemant geseggen dat se teghen 't ghebot Christi van op de daken te prediken, eenichsins ge[102^v]sondicht hebben. Daerom oock, dewijle wy niet van selfs, maer door de vervolghinghe der tyrannen ghedwonghen zijnde, particuliere vergaderinghen der christenen aenrichten ende in 't heymelick prediken, anders bereyt zijnde openbaerlicken ende voor al de werelt van de leeringe met een yeghelick christelicken te handelen, so en heeft niemant ons na te segghen dat wy 'tselve gebot Christi overtreden.

Hier is nu oock goet uut te mercken hoe ongheschictelicken dat se ons voorschieten hetghene dat Christus geseyt heeft: 'Alle die quaedt doet, die hatet licht, noch en koemt oock in 't licht niet, opdat syne wercken niet ghestraft en worden. Maer wie de waerheydt doet, die koemt in het licht, dat syne wercken openbaer worden, want sy zijn in God gedaen.'[1] Aengesien dat wy niet uut haet des lichts, maer alleen om der tyrannen ghewelt wille, ons in 't verborghen houden; nochtans, niet lievers ter werelt wenschende dan dat wy in 't licht komen mochten. Ende wy souden 't ooc voor een groote weldaet Gods houden, waer 't dat der tyrannen gemoet sulcx eens toeliete, dat men deselve leeringe opentlicken ende voor al de werelt prediken mochte.

[103r^AZ] Ende soude men nu willen seggen, dat alle deghene die uut vreese der tyrannen heymelicke vergaderinghen maken het licht haten ende quaet doen, so soudender met ons noch veel moeten ghescholden worden. Want hier voortijden hebben de patriarchen byna allegader hare kercken in hare huysen ende familien ghehadt.[2] Ende onder de afgodische koninghen van Israël ende van Juda en konde men nauwe ergent eenigen voetstap der uutwendiger kercken oft ghemeynten gesien.[3] Veel gingen doe dolende met schaeps ende geyten vellen bekleedt die verlaten, benaut, beancxt werden; dewelcke de werelt versmadende, gingen in bosschen, wildernissen, geberchten, speloncken ende holen der aerden dolende. Ende hierboven hebben wy bewesen hoe dat de apostelen, ende die de apostelen in de eerste kercke naghevolcht zijn, uut vreese der tyrannen hare heymelicke vergaderinghen ghehadt hebben. Ja, de evangelisten ghetuyghen wel dat Christus de Heere selve, om der phariseen ende der herodianen tyrannije wille, dickwils heymelick, of thuys, oft op de bergen, wildernissen ende aen den oever van der zee ghepredict heeft.[4] De papisten sel[103^v]ve, wanneer sy tot sulcke plaetsen komen daer 't hen niet toegelaten en wort opentlicken ende voor al de werelt misse te doen, daer soecken sy wel eenighe verborghene hoecken om haer werck te doen. Nochtans en begeeren sy noch niet dat men van hen segghe dat se het licht haten, ende dat se qualicken doen. Daeromme en behoort men se gheenssins voor beminders der duysternissen ende haters des lichts te schelden die, uut vreese der aenstaender perijckelen, erghent hen heymelick ende in het verborghen houden, ende begeeren nochtans wel alle tijdt in het openbaer te wandelen, soecken daer alle middelen toe. Ende deselve gevonden hebbende, nemen sy se gheerne aen, ende zijn oock bereyt met eenen yeghelicken, tot allen stonden, vrij ende ongheveynsdelicken van haer leere te handelen. Maer deghene dien sulcx

---

1 Joh. 3:20-21.
2 Gen. 35:[14-15?].
3 1 Kon. 19:10; Rom. 11:3; Hebr. 11:36-38.
4 Mat. 13:1; ende 14:13; ende 15:21;
  Mar. 3:7; ende 4:1; ende 7:2[4];
  Joh. 3:2; ende 11:54.

wel ghebeuren mach, ende nochtans niet en willen aennemen, maer blijven evenwel in 't verborghen met gheveynsdicheyt ende huychelijen omgaende, ende altijdt oorsaecke ende onschult soecken waerom dat se niet tenvoorschijn komen ende met andere van de leere christelick spreken souden; oft deghene die opentlicken opten [104ʳ] stoel prediken, ende en willen hen geenssins der ghemeynten oordeel onderworpen, die haer leere alleen met ghewelt beschermen willen, schandelicken op deghene scheldende die vriendelicken met hen van de twistighe saken der religien begheeren te handelen (gelijckerwijs hier voortijdts waren de phariseen ende schriftgeleerden, ende hedensdaechs zijn de papisten ende mispapen ende veel andere hierin desen niet onghelijck), van die soude men moghen seggen dat se het licht haten, ende dat se quaet doen. Maer niet van ons, die niet in 't heymelick en leeren noch en leven dan daer toe ghedronghen zijnde, ende laten gheeren een yeghelick na den woorde Gods van onse leeringhe oordeelen; weygheren oock nimmermeer manierlicken met eenen yeghelicken van de religie te spreken, noch en weten oock ter wereldt niet lievers dan in het openbaer te leeren ende te wandelen.

Nu segghen sommighe dat men alle heymelicke vergaderinghen in 't generael, om oproer te verhoeden, niet alleen schouwen maer ooc van rechtswegen behoort te verbieden, aenghesien dat men ghemeynlick siet dat de muyte[104ᵛ]makers hare aenslaghen altijdt in verborghen maken ende besluyten. Soude men also willen oordeelen, so moesten alle de godsalighe christenen, de apostelen – ja Christus selve – oock al muytemakers gheweest hebben, ghemerckt dat hier tevoren ghenoech bewesen is dat se oock heymelicke vergaderingen gehouden hebben. 't Is wel waer, dat de boose menschen dickwils haer quaedt voornemen in schuylhoecken practiseren, maer daerentusschen doet men ons te kort, dat men ons onder dien hoop ooc rekenen wilt, van welcken wy in leven ende leere gantsch verscheyden zijn. Wy die niet dan ghedwonghen zijnde in 't heymelick te leeren, ende met onse leere de weerdicheyt des wereltlicken overheydts sterckelicken beschermen, ende in onse vergaderingen – so wel in de openbare als in de heymelicke – seer ernstelicken gebieden datter niemant yet voort en brenge dat tot oproer dienen mochte. Item, wy die het volck vermanen met alle vlijticheyt, dat se haer overicheydt ghewillighe onderdanicheydt, hoe suer dattet hen valt, van consciencie wegen schuldich zijn te bewijsen. Ende in onse predicacien niet en handelen van landen, steden, stercten ende castselen te bestor[105ʳ]men, maer leeren hoe den hemel door een vast gheloove ende een boetveerdich leven door Christum Jesum in te nemen is. Ende en kan men de overheydt van de suspicie oft achterdencken niet ghebrenghen, waermede sy ons, om der heymelicker vergaderingen wille, voor oproerische menschen schelden, so bidden wy hen vriendelicken dat se ons consent geven willen in 't openbaer onse vergaderinghen te houden. Ende is 't seacke dat ons dat oock niet ghebeuren en mach, ende dat men even wel niet af en laet ons voor oproerische ende muytemakers te scheldene ende te vervolgene, so moeten wij 't verduldichlicken verdraghen, denckende by onsselven dat de heylighe mannen – Moyses, David, Elias, de apostelen, ja, Christus selve – van de ondanckbare wereldt voor oproerders ende muytemakers gherekent gheweest hebben.[1]

Maer dese groote ongherechticheyt des overheyts teghen de godsalighe en sal in den dach des oordeels voor den rechterstoel Christi niet ongestraft blijven. Ja, sy wordt hier oock op dese wereldt ghenoech ghestraft. Want als sy ons verdreven hebben, die noch teghen de overheydt, noch teghen de [105ᵛ] wet Gods, door Gods ghenade, en misdoen, so schict God in onse stede tot een straffe boose menschen, die onder het decksel des vreedts, der ghehoorsaemheydt ende der godvreesentheyt also weten te huychelen ende hen te gheveynsen, so dat se nauwelicx van de godvreesende onderscheyden mogen worden, ende daerentusschen nochtans so zijn zijs schalckelicken onder malcanderen eens, ende en soecken niet alleen den ghemeynen vrede, maer oock de gantsche religie onder de voeten te brenghen. Ende eenen yeghelicken na goet ende leven staende, gheven sy hen onder het vendel oft van David Joris, oft van het Huys der Liefden, oft eenighen anderen dierghelijcken sectenmeester, verwachtende also een nieu rijck op dese werelt, in dewelcke alle godloosen (so sy segghen) verslaghen zijnde, sy alleen regneren ende triumpheren moghen. Alsulcke straffe Gods hebben deghene verdient die teghen God kloeck wesen, ende door een valsche vreese van oproer hare policijen onrechtelicken, met der gherechtiger bloet te storten, beschermen ende in vrede houden willen. Maer ghemerckt dat uut onse vergaderinghen, hoewel [106ʳ] dat se heymelick ghehouden worden, gheen perijckel van oproer onder de ghemeynte te vreesen en is, so bidden wy dat men ons sulcken schandelicken naem niet na en gheve, noch oock om alsulck valsch naghheven en verbiede christelicke vergaderingen in 't pausdom te moghen hebben.

Noch daer en wordt oock door onse heymelicke vergaderinghen in het pausdom gheen oorsaecke tot valsche leeringhen ghegheven, als sommighe segghen willen, maer de valsche leeringhen wordender meer mede gekrenct. Want aldaer groeyen sonder twijffel eerst alderhande

---

1 Ex. 5:[1-9]; 1 Sam. 22:[13]; 1 Kon. 18: [17]; Hand 16:20; ende 17:6-7; ende 21:28; ende 24:5; Luk. 23:2; Joh. 18:30; ende 19:12.

secten ende ketterijen, waer (nadat men de papistische afgoderijen ghekrenckt heeft) gheen christelicke byeenkoemste noch vergaderinghen ghehouden en worden, daer hen de christgheloovighe by voeghen moghen. Want 'daer de prophecije ophoudet, daer wordt het volck verstroyt.'[1]

Oock en sal hem niemandt daerinne erghreren dat terstondt alle secten ende valsche leeringhen door de christelicke vergaderinghen niet teniete gebracht en worden. Want de apostel, sprekende van de vergaderingen der ge[106ᵛ]loovigher, seyt in deser manieren: 'Daer moeten secten onder u wesen, opdat deghene die oprecht zijn openbaer onder u worden.'[2]

Sommighe segghen: 'Men moet de overheydt om der consciencien wille onderdanich zijn, als Paulus bevolen heeft.' Daerom concluderen sy uut krachte der princen decreten dat men alle heymelicke vergaderingen behoort te schouwen. Antwoort: Daer spreeckt Paulus van alsulcke overheyt die niet teghen het gheloove, noch teghen de liefde en ghebiedt, maer die haer draecht ende houdt, als een dienersse Gods toe behoort. Want der overheydt en is 't niet gheoorloeft allerley wetten te maken na haer welghevallen. De propheet roept: 'Wee denghenen die onrechte wetten maken, ende die onrechte oordeelen schrijven, opdat sy de saken der armer buygen, ende ghewelt gebruycken in den rechte der ellendiger.'[3] Waerom men oock al haer wetten sonder onderscheyt niet ghehoorsaem zijn en mach. Darius hadde een ghebot laten uutgaen in alsulcker formen: 'So wie yet begheert van eenighen god, oft van eenighen mensche, voor den dertichsten dach, dan alleen van den ko[107ʳ]ninck, die sal in der leeuwen kuyl gheworpen worden.' Ditselve ghebot, hetwelcke na de wet der Perssen ende der Meden onghekrenckt moeste ghehouden worden, heeft de heylige propheet Daniel overtreden, die te synen huyse drymael 's deachs God aenriep.[4] Daerom, dit exempel des heylighen propheten navolghende, wanneer de overheydt teghen de wet Gods verbiedt christelicke vergaderinghen te houden, so en sullen wy niet sondigen, al is 't dat wy na het exempel der heyligher mannen, die in den tijden der eersten kercken gheleeft hebben, ons tot eenighe particuliere ende heymelicke vergaderinghe oft ghemeynte voeghen, om God oprechtelick daer in te dienen. Want 'men moet Gode meer ghehoorsaem zijn dan den menschen.'[5] Aldus schrijft Hilarius in synen boeck teghen Auxentius oft teghen de Arianen van de apostelen des Heeren: 'Sy voedden ende

---

1 Spr. 29: 18.
2 1 Kor. 11:19.
3 Jes. 10:[1-2a].
4 Dan. 6:[8-14].
5 Hand. 5:29.

onderhielden henselven metten arbeyt haerder handen, ende byeenkomende in eetkameren ende in secrete plaetsen, hebben sy by na alle dorpen en vlecken, alle casteelen ende volcken te water ende te lande doorghereyst teghen de wetten ende [107ᵛ] decreten der overheden.'ᴮᴬ

Maer nu sullen de overheden van onsen tijden, van de papen haer lesse gheleert hebbende, by avontuerenᴮᴮ segghen, dat onse saecke met de saecke der apostelen hier inne niet overeen en koemt, ende dat om de valscheydt onser leeringhen wille. Hier op soude ick hen wel willen vraghen, waer 't dat wy in hetselve gheloove, dat wy heden ten daghe belijden, ten tijden der apostelen gheleeft hadden, oft ons de apostelen niet en souden verdraghen ende voor leden der ghemeynten Christi aenghenomen hebben? Willen se 'neen' daertoe segghen, dat se ons dan bewijsen uut de heylighe schrift dat onse leeringhe ende ceremonien, voor also veel als het wesen derselver aengaet, met der apostelen leere niet overeen en koemt. Ende ghemerckt dat se dat niet ghedoen en konnen, ende dat se daerom in haer consciencie ghedronghen worden te belijden (voor also veel als de leere aengaet) dat ons de apostelen oock voor leden der gemeynten Christi souden aenghenomen hebben, moeten se dan in henselven niet wel ghetuyghen dat se daeromme vyanden Christi ende der apostelen [108rᴮᶜ] zijn moeten, ghemerckt dat se ons so seer vervolghen om der leeringhen ende belijdinghe des gheloofs wille, die wy metten apostelen ghemeyn hebben?

Onse wedersegghers en konnen ons oock niet voorgheschieten dat der apostelen leeringhe, die eens goedt gheweest heeft, nu quaedt gheworden zy, oft dat se veranderlick zy, oft dat se tot allen tijden niet genoechsaem, noch oock niet sufficient en zy. Want deselfde leeringhe die van den beghinne goedt gheweest heeft, die en kan door lanckheydt van tijden niet quaet gheworden. Ende allenthalven vindt men veel ghetuyghenissen in de heylighe schrift dat de evangelische leere Jesu Christi ende der apostelen in der kercken onveranderlick ten eewighen daghen blijven moet. 'Hemel ende aerde sullen vergaen,' seydt Christus, 'maer myne woorden en sullen niet vergaen.'¹ Ende de apostel Paulus seyt: 'Niemant en mach er ander fundament legghen dan hetghene datter gheleyt is, dat is: Christus Jesus.'² Ende op een ander plaetse: 'Al waer 't oock dat wy oft een engel uuten hemel u een ander evangelium predicte dan dat wy u ghepre[108ᵛ]dict hebben, die zy vervloeckt. Als wy nu gheseyt hebben, so seggen wy oock nu noch eens. Is 't dat u yemant een

---

1 Mat. 24:35.
2 1 Kor. 3:11.

ander evangelium predickt dan dat ghy ontfangen hebt, die zy vervloect.'¹ Hier toe dient oock hetgene dat deselve apostel van de evangelsiche leere ghetuycht dat se niet ophouden en sal, als de wet, maer dat se tot allen tijden onverandert blijven sal.² Daerom is 't dat Paulus oock op een ander plaetse verbiedt te hooren deghene die een andere leere predickten dan hy ghepredict hadde.³ Ende hy beveelt Timotheum te blijven staende in 'tgene dat hy ontfangen hadde, noch en seydt hy niet datter een ander te verwachten zy.⁴ Ende Joannes de evangelist vermaent de christenen by de oude apostolische leere te blijven. 'Hetgene,' seyt hy, 'dat ghy van den beginne gehoort hebt, dat blijve in u. Is 't dat u blijft [in] hetgene dat ghy van den beginne gehoort hebt, so sult ghy ooc in den Vader ende in den Sone blijven.'⁵ Ende wederom: 'So wie uut God is, die hoort ons. Wie uut God niet en is, die en hoort ons niet. Daer aen kennen wy den Geest der waerheyt ende den gheest der dwalinghen.'⁶ Also vermaent oock Judas de apostel de gheloovighe, dat se om 't ghe[109r^BD]loove strijden dat den heylighen eens ghegheven is.⁷ Ende hetselve getuycht oock God de Heere in de Openbaeringhe Joannis, segghende: 'Is 't dat yemant daer wat toesettet, so sal God op hem toesetten de plaghen die in desen boecke geschreven staen. Ende is 't dat yemant daer wat afdoet van den woorden des boecx deser prophecien, so sal God afdoen zijn deel van den boeck des levens ende van der heyligher stadt.'⁸

Aengehsien dan, dattet uut alle dese boven verhaelde schriften blijckelick ghenoech is, dat de leeringhe Christi ende der apostelen warachtich, bestendich, tot allen tijden onveranderlick ende totter salicheyt genoechsaem is; item, dat men niet bewijsen en kan dat wy van deselve leere, noch in onse openbare noch in onse heymelicke vergaderingen afwijcken, so volcht daeruut dat onse wedersseggers, die ons oft om onser leeren oft om onser vergaderinghen wille verdrijven ende vervolgen, noch eens met alle andere vervolghers der christelicker gemeynten sullen ghestraft worden. Als de Heere oock van de schriftgheleerden ende phariseen ghetuycht heeft, dat op haer komen soude al dat rechtveerdighe bloet dat opter aerden [109ᵛ] uutghestort is, van den bloede af des rechtveerdigen Abels tot op het bloet Zacharie des

---

1 Gal.1:8-9.
2 2 Kor. 3:11.
3 Rom. 16:17.
4 1 Tim. 1:3-4; ende 6:3-5; 2 Tim. 4 [3?]:16.
5 1 Joh. 2:24.
6 1 Joh. 4:6.
7 Judas: 3.
8 Op. 22:[1]8-[1]9.

soons Barachie, dien sy ghedoot hebben tusschen den tempel ende den altaer.[1] Want de wreetheyt der vervolginghen en wort niet geacht na de bloote persoonen der godsaligher menschen, maer na de rechtveerdicheyt ende gelijckheyt der sake ende leere die sy drijven. Ende al degene die nu deselfde schult hebben, die sullen oock metter selver straffen ghestraft worden.

Ende dat nu sommighe seggen willen dat men om der christelicker vergaderingen wille hemselven in gheen perijckel en behoort te steken, aenghesien dat men wel sonder by deselve te komen salich worden mach etc., in der waerheyt sy en overleggen noch en verstaen niet wel terechte hetghene dat hier boven van de weerdicheyt, nutheyt ende noodicheyt der christelicker gemeynten oft vergaderingen geleert is. Want hoewel dat wy door het onderhouden der christelicker vergaderinghen niet salich ghemaeckt en worden (want door gheen van onse goede wercken, maer alleen door de barmherticheyt Gods in synen Sone Jesu Christo worden wy salich), daerom nochtans en is 't niet ghe[110ʳ]seyt dat men de ghemeyne vergaderinghen, om des perijckels wille, schuwen sal, dewijle sy van God bevolen ende seer nut zijn tot vorderinghe der menschen salicheyt. Ghelijckerwijs oock deselve na te laten ende te versuymen tot grooter schaden ende achterdeel der godsalicheyt ghedijet.

Wy en willen ontwijffelicken alle deghene niet verdoemen die in de uuterlicke christelicke vergaderinghen niet en komen noch en verkeeren, maer segghen dat deghene die uut enckelder verachtinghe, versuymelickheyt, onachtsaemheyt oft sorgheloosheyt, oft uut haet der christelicker straffen ende liefde des vrijen levens, oft uut vreese der menschelicker beschaemtheydt, oft om in eensaemheyt ende op haer selven te leven ende te ghelooven, oft om eenigerhande dierghelijcke oorsaken haer van de christelicke vergaderinge afscheyden, ende maken dat se ander lieden oock verachten ende haten, die segghen ende achten wy sonder twijffel groote schult te hebben ende swaerlicken te sondigen; ende tenzy dat se by God vergevinghe haerder schult verwerven, so staen sy grootelicken in 't perijckel haerder zielen. Ick rade oock dat een yeghelick hierin [110ᵛ] zijn eyghen consciencie neerstelicken ondersoecke, ende ghevoelt hy dat hem zijn consciencie wroecht, dewelcke so veel als duysent ghetuyghen is, dat hy terstont God om vergiffenisse bidde, zijn schult betere ende hem by de christelicke ghemeynte begheve.

Nu wy dan ghenoechsaemlicken bewesen hebben dattet den christenen niet alleen gheoorloeft maer oock grootelicken van nooden is dat se christelicke vergaderinghen maken ende deselve oock in 't pausdom

---

1 Mat. 23:35.

onderhouden (daer de valsche leeringhe ende de openbare afgoderijen hardtneckelicken verantwoort ende beschermt worden, ende daer men gheen behoorlicke t'samensprekinghen, handelinghe noch beproevinghe der leeren uut de heylighe schrift hebben en mach), so hebben wy hier oock wel by willen voeghen een korte vermaninghe van de manieren ende middelen die men behoort te ghebruycken om alsulcke heymelicke vergaderingen aen te richten, ende die selve oock aengericht zijnde, in haren standt te onderhouden.

¶ *Hoe men de heymelicke vergaderinghen aenrichten ende oock onderhouden sal.*

[111ʳ]In den eersten moet men nootsakelicken aenmercken, dat so waer eenen verdraghelicken standt der uutwendigher christelicker kercken is daer men noch de ghebreken, ofter eenighe waren, beteren mach ende daer een manierlicke christelicke beroepinghe ende ondersoeckinghe der leeren na der heyligher schrift bevel toegelaten wort, dat men aldaer gheen heymelicke vergaderinghe tot schade ende achterdeel des opentlicken diensts der kercken aenrichten noch hebben en mach, oft anders en souder der twisten ende seckten nemmermeer gheen eynde wesen, ghemerckt datter altijt hier in dese strijdende kercke eenich menschelick ghebreck gevonden wort. Want daer moet men dencken op 'tghene dat Paulus seyt: 'Vermaent de ongheschicte, troost de kleynmoedige, draecht de swacke, weest verduldich tegen alle man.'[1] Also en leert Paulus niet van de kercken der Galaten ende der Corintheren af te wijcken, hoewel datter nochtans sommighe ghebreken, ende die oock niet kleyn, inghedronghen waren, want in deselve kercken was 't noch gheoorloeft matichlicken ende metten woorde Gods alsulcke gebreken te straffen ende te beteren. Also hebben de apostelen in [111ᵛ] der joden synagogen ghepredict ende ghedisputeert, so lange als men daer manierlicken van de leere handelen mochte. Also heeft Apollo tot Ephesen in de synagoge gheleert.[2] Desghelijcx oock Paulus ende Barnabas in Salaminen,[3] tot Antiochien in Pisidien[4] ende tot Iconien.[5] Item, Sylas ende Paulus tot Thessalonia dry sabbathen langhe[6] ende tot Berrhea.[7] Ende Paulus heeft

---

1 1 Thes. 5:14.
2 Hand. 18:26.
3 Hand. 13:5.
4 Hand. 13:14.
5 Hand. 14:1.
6 Hand.17:2.
7 Hand. 17:10.

noch tot de andere plaetsen ghepredict, als tot Athenen,[1] tot Corinthen[2] ende tot Ephesien.[3] Maer daer Paulus ghevoelde dat hy tevergheefs in de synagoghen predicte hetghene dat den rijcke Gods aenghinck, ende dat syne wedersegghers verhardden ende en wilden niet ghehoorsaem zijn, maer spraken qualicken van den wech des Heeren voor de ghemeynte, daer weeck hy van haer ende versamelde de jongheren af, dagelicx leerende in eens heeren schole.[4]

Dus sondighen dieselve teghen alle billicheyt ende tegen de exempelen der apostelen, die heymelicke vergaderinghen tot alsulcke plaetsen maken willen daer den ghecruysten Christus, de boete ende verghevinghe der sonden in synen Name ernstlicken ghepredict [wordt], [112ʳ] de sacramenten (na den bevele des Heeren) om de weldaden Christi te verklaren uut ghereyct worden, ende daer het eenen yegelijcken vrij ghelaten is van de leere godvreesendtlicken ende heylichlicken, tot stichtinghe der gantscher ghemeynten, te moghen handelen. Alle welcke dinghen, aenghesien dat se by ons ende in onse ghemeynten, daerse opentlick zijn, door Gods ghenade also bevonden worden, so blijcket wel klaerlicken, dat se seer onrechtelick ende qualicken doen die tot schade ende achterdeel onses dienstes ende onser ghemeynten eenighe particuliere oft heymelicke vergaderingen maken.

Maer aenghesien dattet hierboven ghenoech bewesen is dat de roomsche kercke, so wel in de leere als in de regheringhe der kercken-diensten, veel onverdraghelicke ende ongeneselicke gebreken heeft, ende datter oock gheen hope van beteren onder haer ghesien wordt; item, dat men daer oock niet vrijelicken uut den woorde Gods van de leere handelen en mach, so en kan voorwaer niemandt ons daer in ghestraffen noch eenighe schuldt gheven, dat sommighe van den onsen oock in [112ᵛ] het midden des pausdoms heymelicke vergaderingen aenrichten in den name Christi, ende die selve oock ghetrouwelicken onderhouden ende beschermen.

Als wy dan van noots weghen ghedronghen worden heymelicke vergaderinghen te maken, so sullen wy in den eersten besorghen dat men in deselve vergaderinge, kercke oft gemeynte eenen godfruchtighen, ghetrouwen, wijsen ende neerstighen dienaer des woorts hebbe, die Christum ende syne gemeynte van herten meyne, die den goeden raedt ende vermaninghe syner broederen gheerne ghehoorsaem zy, die vyerich

---

1 Hand. 17:17.
2 Hand. 18:4.
3 Hand. 18:19; ende 19:9.
4 Hand. 19:9.

sy in den ghebede, ende die alle andere in heylicheyt ende vromicheyt des levens eenen spieghel zy. Also heeft Christus, siende dat de menschen verstroyt waren als schapen die gheenen Heerder en hebben, haer gheraden, segghende: 'Biddet den Heere des oogsts dat Hy wercklieden in synen oogst uutsende.'[1] Ende is 't datter terstont so gheenen voorhanden en is, ende dat men van de naestghelegehene ghemeynte gheenen sulcken bekomen en kan (want altijt sal men het woort Christi warachtich bevinden, daer Hy seyt: 'Den oogst is groot, maer de wercklieden weynich'[2]), so sal men [113r[BE]] alsdan uut het midden der ghemeynten eenen verkiesen, die so wel in zijn gheschickt leven, als in de suyverheyt der leeren den anderen eenen spieghel zy, ende die selve sal alsdan het volck leeren, totdat God van eenen, bequamelickeren, sal voorsien hebben.

Niemant en zy in desen onsen raedt gheerghert, want nu ter tijt en is den dienst des woorts niet meer aen eenich seker volck ghebonden, als ten tijden Mosis, maer hetzy ghenoech dat yemant van de gantsche gemeynte daer toe verkoren zy, so verre hy in zijn herte bevint hem van God daer toe gheroepen te zijn. Hetwelcke oock Jeronymus also van dese laetste tijden ghepropheteert heeft, schrijvende op het derde capittel des propheten Nahums in deser manieren: 'In de aenkoemste Christi ende des woordts Gods, ende der leeringhen der kerckcken, ende in de eyndinghe Ninive, der schoonder hoeren, sal het volck hem verheffen ende haesten (het welck daer tevoren onder de meesters in eenen diepen slaep lach) ende sal gaen tot de bergen der schriftueren. Daer salt vinden de bergen Mosen, Jesum den sone Nave,[BF] de berghen, [113v] d'welck zijn de propheten, de berghen des nieuwen testaments, als de apostelen ende evangelisten. Ende wanneert tot alsulcke berghen ghekomen sal zijn ende hem met het lesen daer in gheoeffent sal hebben, de wijle het niemant en vindt die hem leere (want den oogst is groot, ende de werclieden zijn weynich), so sal syne neersticheyt ghepresen worden omdat het tot aen de berghen geloopen is, ende de traecheyt ende versuymelickheyt der meesteren sal ghestraft worden etc.'[BG] Dus verre zijn 't de woorden Jeronymi.

Men sal oock de ghemeynte so dicwils by een vergaderen als 't bequamelicken sal moghen gheschieden. Ende overmidts dien dat ons Christus bevolen heeft ons voor de menschen te wachten, ende wijs te zijn als serpenten,[3] so sullen wy wel toesien dat wy niet onbedachtelicken noch

---

1 Mat. 9:38.
2 Mat. 9:37.
3 Mat. 10:16-17.

lichtveerdichlicken en handelen in 't vergaderen der gemeynten. Ende ghemerckt dat men hierinne lichtelicken oft door onverstandicheyt, oft onbedachtsaemheyt, oft oock door al te groote kloeckheydt ende neuswijsicheyt hem haest vergrijpen kan, so sullen wy God den Heere [114ʳ] ernstelicken bidden dat Hy in 't verkiesen der plaetsen tot de ghemeyne vergaderinghe (item, des tijdts ende der menichten des volcx) een serpentische wijsheyt oft kloeckheyt verleenen wil, die met duyven simpelheyt ghemengt zy. Ende alsdan sal ontwijffelicken de Heere, als eenen stercken muer, met bescherminghe zijnder enghelen, alsulcke christelicke ghemeynte omcinghelen ende beschutten.

Ende oftet nu somtijts ghebeurde, dat oft om der vervolghinghen, oft om andere treffelicke oorsaken wille, de ghemeynte niet in so groote menichte tesamen komen en konde, so sal men se op eenen andere bequameren tijt in des te grooter menichte by een roepen. Oft so dat niet gheschieden en mach, so sal men dickwils als nu dese, alsdan die broederen ende susteren onder andere vermenghen, opdat also de liefde by hen blijve ende onderhouden worde. Ende alsdan sullen haer de christenen met de soete belofte Christi vertroosten, daer Hy seyt: 'Daerder twee oft dry in mynen name vergadert zijn, daer ben Ick in het midden van hen.'[1]

Item, oft nu om des perijckels wil[114ᵛ]le de vergaderinghe des nachts gheschieden moeste, als de schrift ghetuycht dat de apostelen ghedaen hebben, so sal men wel toesien datter niet oneerlicx en gheschiede. Want het en is niet tevergheefs dat Lucas, daer hy seyt dat Paulus by nachte gheleert heeft, noch daerby schrijft datter veel lichten opten solder ware, daer se by een saten.[2]

Desghelijcx sal men oock in alle vergaderinghen hem wachten van ijdele woorden, van kijven, twijsten, achterklappen ende quaet spreken van deghene die niet teghenwoordich en zijn. Maer men sal den gheheelen tijdt overbrenghen met bidden, godsalichlicken te leeren, de sonden te straffen, met onderwijsen, stichten, beteren, troosten, ende met God te bidden, te loven ende te dancken. Alle curieuse ende neuswijsighe disputacien, die niet en dienen tot vorderinghe des geloofs oft der liefden, sullen neerstelicken uutghesloten worden, als Paulus oock radet. Ende het eynde van alle leeringen ende predicacien sy Christus Jesus, de glorie Gods, ende de liefde des naesten.[3]

---

1 Mat. 18:20.
2 Hand. 20:8.
3 1 Tim. 1:4; 4:7; 6:20. 2 Tim. 2:16; Tit. 3:9.

In alle predicacien behooren de toe[115r^BH]hoorders haer daer toe te bevlijtighen dat se beter, godvreesender ende gheschickter in de kennisse der waerheyt weder thuys keeren danse van huys ghegaen waren, ende dat se denghenen ghehoorsaem zijn die over de ghemeynte tot voorstanders ghestelt zijn, als daer zijn de predicanten ende de ouderlinghen, so verre sy alles na den bevele des godlicken woorts uutrichten. Sy en sullen ooc der weldadicheyt ende ghedeylsamheyt niet verghteten, maer daghelicx meer ende meer in de broederlicke liefde toenemen. Sy sullen met alle haer andere kercken oft ghemeynten een christelicke gemeynschap onderhouden, altijt in haer ghemoet totten cruyce ende tot het lijden bereyt zijnde.

Is 't dat wy in deser manieren ons leven aenrichten, ende onse kercken oft vergaderinghen onderhouden als boven gheseyt is, so sal ons God ontwijffelicken wel beschermen, diewelcke syne kercke oft ghemeynte in 't midden des gloeyenden ovens,[1] ende in der hongheriger leeuwenkuyl[2] door synen machtighen arm wel bewaren ende behoeden kan.

[115^v] Ende in ghevalle dat wy in dit heylich godvreesende voornemen van de tyrannen ghevanghen, ghespannen, ghepijnicht oft ghedoodt worden (hetwelcke door de ghehenghenisse^BI Gods gheschieden sal, sonder wiens wille een hayrken van onsen hoofde niet vallen en sal[3]), so sullen wy dat verduldichlicken verdraghen, wel versekert zijnde, dat wy door Christum een onverderfelicke kroone in den hemel voor ons bereyt hebben.[4] En heeft ons hooft Christus Jesus niet veel moeten lijden, eer Hy in zijn glorie ende heerlicheyt ingegaen is?[5] So en is 't dan niet te verwonderen, dat wy syne leden, door veel tribulacien in het rijcke der hemelen komen moeten.[6]

Nu bidden wy allen denghenen die God lief hebben, ende die den pausdom afgheweken zijn, om den Heere Christus ende om zijn heerlicke wederkoemste wille ten oordeele, dat se henselven in gheen perijckel en stellen om het verworpen van eenigher leeringhe, behalven om alsulcke leeringe die opentlicken teghen de heylighe schrift strijdet. Want is 't sake dat wy de leeringhen loochenen willen die in de heylige schrift [116^r] haren gront hebben, als het artijckel van de menschwerdinge Christi van den mensche, van de autoriteyt des overheyts in 't ghebruycken des sweerts, van den wettelicken behoorlicken eedt (die men by den naem

---

1 Dan. 3:[2]8
2 Dan. 6:22.
3 Mat.10:30-31.
4 1 Pet. 1:4.
5 Luk. 24:26.
6 Hand. 14:22.

Gods in ernstelicke saken doet), van den kinderdoop, ende andere diergelijcke artijckelen, so sal onder andere dit quaet daeruut komen dat onse wedersegghers daerdoor in haer afgoderijen sullen ghesterckt worden ende een oorsake grijpen alle andere dinghen te lachteren, waer inne wy van haer wel terechte verscheyden zijn.

Ende dat nu de voorghenoemde artijckelen met de meyninghe der heyligher schrift overeenkomen en dient alhier met veel woorden niet uutgeleyt noch gedisputeert te worden. Nochtans, om der eenvuldiger wille, moeten wy met een woordeken sulcx aen roeren.

Want en bewijst de schrift niet seer krachtich ende eendrachtich den oorspronc des vleeschs Christi te zijn uut den mensche, nadenmael dat se Hem noemt des menschen zaet,[1] spruyte,[2] bloeme,[3] vruchte[4] ende sone,[5] ende dat na den vleessche[6]?

[116ᵛ] Ende dat de overicheyt de macht heeft de misdadige oock metten sweerde te straffen ende te dooden, ghetuycht Paulus klaerlicken ghenoech in den brief totten Romeynen. Aldaer hy oock in 't eynde des briefs vermaent, dat men alle deghene schouwen sal de eenighe contrarie leere voeren.[7]

Ende den behoorlicken eedt in treffelicke groote saken hebben de propheten ende de apostelen neerstelicken ghepresen, bevolen, ende oock selve ghebruyct.[8] Maer dat men onbehoorlicken, lichtveerdichlicken, ende niet van rechtsweghen ghedreven zijnde, sweeren soude, heeft Christus ende oock de apostel Jacobus klaerlicken verboden.[9]

Ende ghemerckt datter nerghens in de heylighe schrift verboden en is de kleyne kinderkens te doopen, ende dat alle de passagien die daerteghen van onse wederseggers uut de schrift gheallegeert worden eygentlicken te verstaen zijn tegen de onboetveerdige, ongeloovige oude bejaerde[BJ] menschen die noch niet gedoopt en zijn, ende niet tegen de kinderen (item, dattet niet nieus en is in de kercke Gods aen de kinderkens de [117ʳ] sacramenten te bedienen, denwelcken Christus ooc so wel met woorden als met omhelsen een ghetuyghenisse gegheven heeft dat men

---

1 Gen.3:[15]; ende 22:[18]; ende 26:[3-4]; ende 28:[13-14]; 2 Sam. 7:[12].
2 Jer. 23:[5]; ende 33:[15].
3 Jes. 11:[1].
4 Ps. 132[:11]; Luc. 1:42.
5 Mat. 1:25
6 Rom. 1:3; Hand. 2:30.
7 Rom.16:17.
8 Deut. 6:[10]; ende 10:[20]; Gen. 21:[31]; Ps. 15:[4]; ende 6[3]:[12]; Jes. 65:[16]; Hebr. 6:16; Op. 10:6.
9 Mat.5: 34-36; Jac.5:12.

se van de uutwendighe teeckenen der ghenaden niet en behoort af te keeren, mitsdien dat haer den hemel toebehoort;[1] item, dattet leden des lichaems Christi ende zijnder kercken zijn, hebbende ghemeynschap metten Vader, metten Sone ende met den H[eylighen] Gheest, ende zijn ghewasschen ende wederghebaert metten blode Christi, als men genoechsaem uut veel verscheydene plaetsen der Schrift afnemen mach,[2] op alle welcke dingen de doope des waters is steunende), so konnen alle eenvuldighe wel daeruut verstaen, dat men se met gheenen rechte van den doop afweeren en mach, ende dat veel hedensdaechs al te lechtveerdelicken – den kinderdoop verworpende – de menschen totten wederdoop willen dwinghen.[BK] Het waer veel beter dat se, desen twist van de kinderdoop achterlatende, de oude bejaerde menschen, die in haer kindtsheyt ghedoopt zijn, neerstelicken vermaenden tot een vernieuwinge des doops des H[eylighen] Gheests, dewelcke totter salicheydt principalick van nooden [117ᵛ] is, daer wy ons gantsche leven lanck mede moeten ghedoopt worden, ende die oock het alderswaerste om aennemen is. Also lesen wy dat Moyses[3] ende de propheten[4] hier voortijden met de Israëliten, die tot haren jaren ghekomen waren, ghehandelt hebben. Te weten, dat se denghenen die in haer kindtsheydt eens besneden waren, alletijt de besnijdinghe des herten inbeeldden ende vermaenden. Daer soude ontwijffelicken veel meer goedts af komen, ende meer eenicheyts ende godsalicheydts der kercken mede inghebracht worden, dan met de curieuse disputacie van den kinderdoop.

Dit zy nu ghenoech, dese dinghen also met een woordeken kortelicken aengheruert te hebben. Alleen willen wy hier vermaent hebben denghenen die den pausdoms af ghevallen zijn, dat se gheene twisten noch gheen ghekijf teghen de wedersegghers aen en nemen, dan alleen om sulcke leeringhen die opentlicken der eeren Gods teghen zijn, oft die de liefde des naesten scheuren ende quetsen, als daer zijn, die hier voren overvloedelicken ghenoech aengeteeckent zijn.

[118ʳ] Nu wilde ick alle godvreesende dienaren Gods, dien der menschen salicheyt ende de eere Christi ter herten gaet, vriendelicken ghebeden hebben, telcken als den noodt der kercken in Babylonien sulcks eyscht, dat se hen dan niet te soecken en maken, maer dat se gheerne ende ghewillichlicken deselve besoecken, troosten, leeren ende vermanen; besunderlicken, wanneer dat se daer gesonden oft door het suchten

---

1 Mar. 10:14.
2 Joel 2:[16?]; Ef. 5:26; 1 Kor. 12:12-13; 2 Kor. 5:16 [17?]; Tit. 3:5.
3 Deut.10:[16].
4 Jer. 4:[4].

derselver kercken gheroepen worden. Gelijck oock ten tijden der apostelen de heylige dienaren Gods Timotheus, Titus, Apollos ende meer andere, om veel ende verscheyden ghemeynten te gaen troosten, leeren ende vermanen, dickwils sware reysen aenghenomen hebben.

Oock bidden wy alle deghene die het sweert voeren, alle princen, overheden, burghermeesters ende raetslieden, om den naem Christi wille, dat se met onse kercken oft christelicke vergaderinghen, daer Christus de Sone Gods het hooft af is, niet so wreedelicken noch tyrannichlicken om en gaen. Ende duncket hen dat onse saecke onrecht ende strafweerdich is, so bid[118^v]den wy hen, dat se de saecken wat beter insien ende terechte examineren willen, of se haer voornemen hier namaels voor den rechterstoel Christi oock wel sullen konnen verantwoorden, opdat se henselven niet schuldich en maken des rechtveerdighen, ontschuldighen uutghestorten bloedts. Ende is 't dat se noch den rechten gront onser saken niet wel ten rechten en verstaen, oft daer noch eenichsins in twijffelen, so bidden wy, dat se hen niet so seer en haesten die ontschuldige met een roeckeloos vonisse te verwijsen. Christus heeft van tevoren klaerlicken ghenoech ghepropheteert dat uut onwetentheydt de vervolginghe spruyten soude. 'Dese dinghen,' seydt Hy, 'sullen sy u doen, omdat se niet en kennen den Vader noch My.'[1] Sy en behooren gheens anders ooghen noch ooren te betrouwen, maer behooren hen in des Heeren wet te oeffenen, als hier voortijden den koninghen in Israel[2] ende den rechter Josue[3] bevolen werdt. So sullen sy daer innen vinden hoe swaerlicken sy hen met ons te vervolghen, teghen God vergrijpen.

Ende deghene die wel weten ende verstaen dat onse saecke oprecht ende [119r^{BL}] goet is, denselven willen wy om Gods wille ghebeden hebben, dat se niet Pilatum (die den keyser vreesende, den onnooselen Jesum ter doodt verdoemde),[4] maer veel meer den goeden raetsheer Joseph navolghen (die der joden raedt ende daet in Christum te veroordeelen, niet toestaen noch volghen en wilde).[5] Maer is 't dat se onse vermaningen verachtende, voorghenomen hebben teghen het Lam ende syne heylighen te strijden,[6] ende dat se in het verstooren der christelicker ghemeynten, in het berooven haerder goeden, in het verjaghen ende dooden der christgheloovigher hardtneckichlicken voortvaren willen, so sullen sy ten laetsten de rechtveerdighe straffe Gods, des wrekenden

---

1 Joh. 16:3.
2 Deut. 17:[18-20].
3 Joz.1:[7-8].
4 Joh. 19:12, 16
5 Luc. 23:50-51.
6 Op. 13:7.

rechters,[BM] over hen ghewaer worden, dewelcke alle de droppelen des uutghestorten onnooselen bloedts, ende de beroofde goeden zijnder christenen van hare handen wreedelicken eyschen ende wreken sal. Want God staet in de gemeynte gods, ende is rechter onder de goden.[1] De alderhoochste, o ghy princen, vorsten ende heeren, sal uwe wercken ondersoecken, ende Hy sal uwe raedtslaghen examineren.[2] Alsdan en [119v] sullen in der waerheydt uwe mispapen, doctoren, inquisitoren ende kettermeesters, bisschoppen noch pausen – die nu so stoutelicken hare zielen voor u te pande setten willen, ende die u alle goet beloven wanneer ghy dapperlicken ghenoech vervolghet – eenen van u uut des rechters handen niet konnen verlossen. 'Daerom laet u nu onderwijsen ghy koninghen, ende laet u tuchtighen, ghy rechters op aerden. Dient den Heere met vreesen, ende verblijdt u met beven. Kust den Sone, dat Hy niet toornich en worde ende ghy opten wech vergaet.'[3]

Nu bidden wy God onsen hemelschen Vader, dat Hy u de ghenade gheve dat ghy dese vermaninghe des konincx Davids aennemen moecht, ende dat ghy u wereltlick sweerdt alleen gebruycken en moecht in de vreese Gods tot bescherminghe der goeden, ende tot straffinghe der quader.

Ten laetsten bidden wy oock alle onse broeders ende susters om Christus wille, dat se standtfastelicken in de godsalicheydt ende bekende waerheyt totten eynde toe volherden, ende volgende de vermaninghe Pauli, dat se hare [120r[BN]] vergaderinghen niet en verlaten.[4] Item, dat se den korten ende onsekeren tijdt haerder pelgrimagien hier op aerden heylichlicken ende onstraffelicken over brenghen,[5] opdat onse wedersegghers, die ons als quaetdoenders ende boose menschen voor al de wereldt schelden, beschaemt moghen worden, ende dat onse hemelsche Vader, in de uutroeyinghe des pausdoms ende alle hoocheden, die haer teghen zijnder kennisse verheffen, eewichlicken ghepresen worde.[6] Amen.

Eynde deses Boecx.

---

1 Ps.82:[1].
2 Ps. 33:[10-16?].
3 Ps. 2:[10-12a].
4 Hebr. 10:24.
5 1 Pet. 2:11-12.
6 2 Kor. 10:5.

[O^r]^{BO}
**Een kort
register van hetgene
dat een yeghelick capittel in
dit boecxken principalicken
inhoudt.**

*Inhoudt des eersten
capittels.*

God de Heere heeft ghewilt, van den beginnen des werelts af, datter een uuterlicke ghemeynte der gheloovighen wesen soude, in welcke Hy na synen geopenbaerden wille ghedient ende aengeroepen worde. Fol. 3^v tot fol. 6^r

De ghelucksalige stand der gemeynte Gods in den beghinne bleef niet langhe ongheschendt.
 Fol. 6^r

God heeft zijn vervallen kercke in Abraham wederopghericht ende in zijn nakomelinghen trouwelicken [O^v] bewaert. Fol. 6^r tot 8^r

Christus heeft oock de vergaderinghen bevesticht ende daertoe veel dinghen verordent ende gheboden.   Fol. 8^v tot fol. 11^r

Een yeghelick moet ende behoort hem tot de onderhoudinge der vergaderinghe der ghemeynte Gods te begheven, ghelijck sulcx veelderley namen, waarmede de ghemeynte Gods in der schrift genoemt, klaerlicken betuygen. Fol. 11^r tot fol. 14^r; item, fol. 22, 23 etc.

Veel heylighe menschen des ouden ende nieuwen testaments hebben de heylighe vergaderinghen in veelderley periculen seer neerstelicken onderhouden ende gheleert. Fol. 14^v tot fol. 17^r

Hoe nutte ende profijtich dattet zy in de heylighe vergaderinghen [Oii^r] der ghemeynten daghelicx te zijn, ende hoe schadelick het is hem van deselfde af te trecken. Fol. 17^r tot fol. 25^r

*Inhoudt des anderen
capittels.*

Hoe een godvreesende mensche een onderscheyt tusschen d'een ende d'ander vergaderinghe maken sal, ende by wat teeckenen men de ware kercke van de valsche onderscheyden sal. Fol. 26^r tot fol. 30 etc.

*Inhoudt des derden
capittels.*

De oorsaken waerom de godsalighe, door de kennisse der waerheyt verlicht zijnde, ge[Oii^v]drongen werden van alle geselscha[p] ende gemeynschap der roomscher kercken af te wijcken. Fol. 31^r tot fol. 45^r

Welcke daerna door ghetuygenisse der schrift bevesticht ende met exempelen der heyligher mannen Gods bewesen wordt.
Fol. 45^v tot fol. 49^r

De principaelste argumenten van sommighe teghensprekers werden verhaelt ende nedergeleyt. Fol. 49^v tot fol. 67^r

Alle onse woorden ende wercken, ja alle onse leden, moeten den eenighen God te dienen toegheeyghent worden. Fol. 58^r tot fol. 60^v

Tegen deghenen die daer meynen dat hen alle uutwendighe belijdinghe ende verminginghe der valscher godsdiensten vrij zij omdat haer gemoet gantsche vrij is van alle ghedachten ende ghevoelen der afgoderijen.
Fol. 60^v tot fol. 64^v

[Oiii^r] Men moet na de uutwendige woorden oft wercken van de uutwendighe affectie des herten, sy zij goedt oft quaet, rechten.
Fol. 62

Teghen de grouwelicke dwalinge Davids Joris ende des boumeesters van het Huys der Liefden. Fol. 64^v tot 67^r; item, fol. 94^r tot fol. 100^r

Inhoudt des vierden capittels.

Bewijs dat een christen, van de roomsche kercke afgeweken zijnde, hem behoort ende moet tot eenighe christelicke ghemeynte oft vergaderinge begeven. Fol. 67^v tot fol. 69^v

Tweederley raet voor de christenen die in papistische landen woonen, daer gheen rechte godsdienst en is:

[Oiii^v] De eerste, dat se vertrecken tot alsulcker plaetsen daer de reyne godsdienst opentlick oft heymelick is, met wederlegginghe der swaricheden die men daer teghen plach op te worpen. Fol. 70^r tot fol. 76^r

De andere, so sulcx gheenssins of qualicken gheschieden kan, dat se alsdan daer se woonen onder hen christelicke vergaderingen maken ende onderhouden, met wederlegginge der teghenredenen die men daer teghen plach op te worpen. Fol. 100^r

Teghen dengenen die, om vrucht by den eenvuldighen te schaffen, met de papistische afgodrije uuterlick veynsen. Fol. 72^v etc.

De uutvluchten waerom sommige hen tot gheen christelicke vergaderinghen begheven willen worden wechghenomen. Fol. 76^v tot fol. 81^{r-v}

De kercke Gods en kan gantsch [Oiiii^r] sonder feylen niet zijn in deser werelt om de verdorvenheyt onser natueren. Fol. 77^{r-v}

Van alsulcke dienaers der ghemeynten Christi die ergherlick leven. Fol. 78 etc.

Teghen denghenen die de beroepinghe der predicanten ende de oprechticheit der gemeynte uut de wonderwercken ende miraculen af meten willen. Fol. 81^v etc.

De principaelste argumenten dergheender die alle uutwendighe christelicke vergaderinghen onder den schijn eender inwendigher ende gheestelicker godsdienst verworpen ende vrij stellen worden verhaelt ende nedergheleyt. Fol. 82^r tot fol. 93^v

Bewijs dat de leere Jesu Christi de volmaeckste is, die alletijt blijven sal, ende behalven welcke gheen andere te verwachten is. Teghens dat duyvels voorgheven van David [Oiiii^v] Joris ende de timmerman van het Huys der Liefden. Fol. 94^r tot fol. 100^r

De principaelste argumenten dergheender die de heymelicke vergaderinghen voor ongheoorloft houden worden verhalet ende nedergeleyt.
Fol. 100 tot fol. 110^v

Waer ende wanneer men de heymelicke vergaderingen aenrichten ende onderhouden mach, ende hoe men daer in handelen sal.
Fol. 111^r tot fol. 115^v

Vermaninge aen alle christenen die van het pausdom afgheweken zijn.
Fol. 115^v tot fol. 117^v; item, fol. 119^v

Vermaninghe aen alle dienaren des woorts. Fol. 117^v; 118^r

Vermaninghe aen alle overheden ende dienaren des sweerdts.
Fol. 118^{r-v}; 119^r

[Ov^r]
Register van sommighe plaetsen der schriftueren, die hierinne verklaert worden.

Deut. 30: 14	Dat woort is seer na by u, in uwen mont.	Fol. 89^v
2 Kon. 5:18, 19	Dat de propheet Elizeus Naaman van Syrien soude toeghelaten hebben in den tempel Rimmon te bidden.	Fol. 56^v
Jes. 66: 3	Wie eenen osse slacht, die is effen als die eenen man versloeghe.	Fol. 92^v
Jer. 31: 33 & 34	Ick sal mijn wet in 't midden van haer gheven, ende Ick sal se in haer herten scrhrijven, etc.	Fol. 86^r tot fol.89
Ezech. 34: 11 & 23	Siet, Ick wil nu mijnder kudden selfs aennemen ende die besocken. Item, Ick wil haer [Ov^v] eenen eygenen Herder verwecken, etc.	Fol. 89^r
Hab. 2:4	De gherechtighe sal uuten gheloove leven.	Fol. 64^r
Baruch 6:5	Van den raet Jeremie, den joden in Babylonien ghevanghen zijnde ghegheven.	Fol. 57r
Mat. 10:27	Hetghene dat Ick u in 't duyster segghe, dat spreeckt in 't licht, etc.	Fol. 100v, etc.
Mat. 23: 2	Op Moses stoel sitten de schriftgheleerde, etc.	Fol. 52^v, 53^r, etc.
Luc. 17:20	Het rijcke Gods is in u.	Fol. 90^v
Joh. 3:20-21	Wie quaet doet, die hatet licht.	Fol. 102^v
Joh. 6: 45	So sulle alle van God ge[Ovi^r]leert zijn.	Fol. 91^r

Joh. 14: 16-17 & 26 ende 15:26	Van den Heyligen Gheest, welcken Jesus den synen beloefde.	Fol. 95ᵛ, etc.
Joh. 18: 38	Mijn rijcke en is van deser werelt niet.	Fol. 91ʳ
Rom. 8:1	Daer en is gheen verdoemenisse denghenen die in Christo Jesu zijn.	Fol. 64ʳ
Rom. 8:28	Wy weten dat denghenen die God liefhebben alle dinghen, etc.	Fol. 64ᵛ
Rom. 13: 1 & 5	Een yeghelick zy onderdanich der overheyt, die macht heeft, etc.	Fol. 106ᵛ
Rom. 14: 14 & 22	Ick weet ende bens gewisse in den Heere Jesu, datter niet onreyn, etc. Item, salich is deghene die hemselven gheen consciencie, etc.	Fol. ⁶²ʳ⁻ᵛ etc.
[Oviᵛ]		
1 Cor. 13:9 & 10	Ons weten is stuckwerck, etc. Item, wy sien nu door eenen speighel, etc.	Fol. 96ᵛ tot fol. 98ʳ
2 Cor. 5:16 & 17	Hier na en kennen wy niemant meer dan den vleessche, [etc.].	Fol. 92ʳ
Fil. 3:20	Onse wandelinge is in den hemel.	Fol. 91ᵛ
Tit. 2:15	Den reynen zijn alle dingen reyn.	Fol. 61ʳ⁻ᵛ etc.
Hebr. 6: 1 & 2	Willen wy de leere van den beghinne des christelicken levens laten varen, etc.	Fol. 98ʳ⁻ᵛ FINIS

Endnotes

A The tekst is illegible. Some letters are vaguely discernable; however, they are too unclear to come to any certain reading. The ensuing 'de' is not part of the word. It is clear the basic idea is that Micron's Latin tekst has been translated into Dutch, hence the choice for 'overghelevert'.
B I.e. divided.
C Ezra
D Haggai
E In the original text there are brackets instead of quotation marks.
F Original: 'BethEel'.
G Hezekiah.
H Original: 'Fol. 3'.
I This must refer to God the Father (and not to the Holy Spirit) for Micron says: 'He… through His Son(…)'.
J Due to the large quantity of biblical references the original manuscript has marked them with letters. The use of footnotes makes these letters redundant. This also applies to folios 27^v, 28^r, 45^v, 47^r, 55^r, 68^r, 77^v, 89^v, 95^v, 96^v, 97^r, 111^v, 116^{r-v}.
K This is a complicated sentence. The basic sentence is: 'Ghelijckerwijs oock den anderen niet anders te verbeyden en staet dan na dit leven die eewighe verderfenisse.' Micron indicates two reasons how this could happen: 1) seeking salvation outside Jesus Christ; 2) Leading a sinful life without repentance.
L A word seems to be missing in this sentence. The original punctuation reads: 'Sy en overlegghen niet / hoe swaerlick een yeghelick van alle / in sonderheyt in een sulcke verderffenisse der natueren tot godvreesentheyt te trecken is.' The German translation reads: 'Sie uberlegen nit wie schwårlich ein jeder under uns allen / in sonderheit inn solcher grossen verderbung der natur / zu der Gottesforcht zu ziehen ist(…)' (39^v).
M 'Quansuys' means that the word is not applied correctly to the matter at hand (source: http:„www.wnt.inl.nl,iWDB,search?actie=article&wdb=WNT&id=M0359 46 [21-11-2017])
N Or: 'verderen'. The meaning of 'deden' is probably 'ontdeden'. It is unclear whether 'berderen' or 'verderen' is the right reading. 'Berderen' means 'wooden [plank]' and could be correct. However, how can a monk have a wooden face? On the other hand, how can a monk take off the 'rest of his face'? Engelbert Faber struggled with this sentence as well. In his German version he does translate 'berderen' with 'platten', yet changes the word order. Instead of 'kappen ende b/verderen aenghesichten' he translated: 'Welche [i.e. München] / so ire kutten / platten und Angesichte thete / viel geschickter weren hinder dem pflug zugehen (…)' (43v).
O We have not been able to discover the precise meaning of this word.
P I.e. lies, deceit.
Q I.e. Holy days.
R I.e. dare.
S I.e. paint over.
T A 'consilium' is an ecclestical council or gathering of the clergy to decide on matters of doctrine, liturgy, ceremonies and discipline.

U	I.e. Elisha. The form 'Eliseus' could be due to either the Latin Vulgate or Micron's original manuscript being written in Latin.
V	Libertine is probably Micron's synonym for various Nicodemitic groups and sects. On fol. 83^r Micron possibly refers to a Libertine remark. Cf., also, ch. 2.5; 8.1 of the study and the literature given there.
W	Original: veere.
X	Original: 'kercker.'Although this is not listed in the errata, the 'oft ghemeynte' which follows makes it clear 'kercken' was meant instead of 'kercker'.
Y	This word is illegible. The first letter might be a long 's' or a misprinted 'p'. The 'k' in the middle seems fairly sure. Thankfully the meaning of the sentence as a whole is still clear enough. The German translation reads: 'dann sie waren durch des Herren befelch an ein sicher ort unnd Leuitische Priester gebunden (…)' (62^v).
Z	Original: 55.
AA	Original: 53.
AB	The syntax of this sentence seems to be faulty. The main clause is: 'Aenghesien dan datter een so groot onderscheyt is tusschen de kercken van dien tijden…ende tusschen de Roomsche Kercke van onsen tijden…so en kan men etc.' The second part of the main clause could either be: 'so en kan men […] [uut] de comparacie oft ghelijckinghe van alsulcke kercken oft ghemeynten teghen een noch niet ghecon-cluderen etc.' or, 'so en kan men niet de comparacie oft ghelijckinghe van alsulcke kercken oft ghemeynten teghen een [maken], noch niet geconcluderen etc.' The German translation chooses the second option: 'Dieweyl dann so grosser underscheit ist zwischen der kirchen der Israeliten / der phariseer und der Corinther zu denen zeyten / und zwischen der Römsiche kirchen zu unsern zeyten / so viel die verfälschung und kirchendienst belangt / so kan man die comparation und vergleychung deren kirchen nit gegen einander halten / noch darauß schliessen das man vom der papistischen kirchen nit soll abweychen.' (65^v-66^r).
AC	The German version translates: 'demůt' (69^r).
AD	Possibly a reference to Lucian of Samosata.
AE	Punctuation is based on the German translation, which reads: 'Wolan / ich laβ sein das irer etliche / wiewol sehr wenig / von gůtem herzen also sprechen (…)' (84^v).
AF	Eusebius, *Ecclesiastical History, I*, ed. Jeffrey Henderson, Loeb Classical Library 153 (Cambridge, Massachusetts: HUP, 1926), 8.1.1-9 [*Ecclesiastica Historica*] (accessed via: Loeb Classical Library online).
AG	Cf. the German translation: 'Aber lieber saget mir (…)' (88^v).
AH	Punctuation based on the German translation, which reads: 'Darumb können wir / so wir die Bibel bey uns selbs lesen / unsere gebrechen darauβ nicht so wol erkennen (…)' (92^r).
AI	We interpret the 'hem' to be used as a reflexive pronoun, reading 'geen vleesch… beroeme [hem]'. This would be incorrect in contemporary Dutch, as 'beroemen' is a reflexive verb, demanding 'sich'. When 'hem' does not have the function of a reflexive pronoun, it would refer to God, making the 'voor Hem' later in the sentence redundant. Moreover, regarding 'hem' as a reflexive pronoun is a correct translation of the original Greek (ὅπως μὴ καυχήσηται πᾶσα σὰρξ ἐνώπιον τοῦ Θεοῦ. (majority text)) The German translation has: 'auff das sich vor im kein fleisch rhůme' (94^r).
AJ	The syntax of this sentence is not very lucid. The German translation is clearer: 'Aber das unsere Widersacher sagen wöllen / das die kirch darumm unsichtlich sey / das sie von allen auβwendigen Ceremonien gefreyet ist / und derhalben nit kan gesehen werden / ist viel zo grob geredt / und der h. Schrifft gantz zuwider.' (97^r).

AK The main clause in this elaborate sentence is: 'Maer in dese beloftenisse...wort alleenlick uutghedruckt...hoe groot de weerdicheyt ende vordeel des nieuwen volcx onder Christi zijn soude...[vergeleken] by het joodtsche volck.'
AL The original punctuation reads: 'Ende gemerct dat den kennisse Gods (door dewelcke wy kennen / dat Hy onse God / onsen sonden ghenadich is) in 't oude Testament seer duyster was (...)'. 'Hy onse God' is the subject of the subclause. For clarity sake we changed this into an appositional phrase.
AM The last letter of this word is misprinted and could be either a t or and l.
AN Nicolaus Carinaeus continued and finished the book.
AO I.e. David Joris.
AP The syntax of this sentence is unclear. It would appear that this is the best reconstruction of the main idea: 'Ende ghemerckt [dat] hy syne leere voor d'alder volmaeckste houd, [so] treckt hy altemael so schandelicken tot hem al wat de heylighe schrift in de toekomste Christi getuycht.' That, at least, is what the German translation suggests: 'Und dieweyl er seine lere für die allervolkomneste helt und weyt uber die lere Christi preyβt / also das die lere Christi seiner lere weychen müβ / so zeuhet er alles was die h. Schrifft von der volkommenheit der menschen inn der zukunfft Christi bezeuget so schåndlich zu sich und seiner lere (...)' (107ʳ).
AQ In the original 'u leven' is part of the subject.
AR 'Voorkomen' here means 'to let these things come before their time' and not 'to prevent'.
AS I.e., defectiveness, deficiency (source:http:„www.wnt.inl.nl,iWDB,search?actie=article&wdb=WNT&id=M030796 [3-1-2018]).
AT Eusebius, *Ecclesiastical History,* 3.33.1-3.
AU Tertullian, *Apology,* ed. Jeffrey Henderson, Loeb Classical Library 250 (Cambridge, Massachusetts: HUP, 1931), 10 [*Apologeticus*] (accessed via: Loeb Classical Library online).
AV Eusebius, *Ecclesiastical History,* 7.11.24.
AW Sozomen, *Ecclesiastica Historia,* ed. Jacques Paul Migne, Patrologiae Cursus Completus. Series Graeca 67 (Paris: Migne, 1864), 863-864.
AX Eusebius, *Ecclesiastical History,* 9.9.11.
AY Tertullian, *Apology,* 47-55.
AZ Original: Fol. 16(?)
BA Hilary of Poitiers, *Liber contra Arianos vel Auxentium* ed. Jacques Paul Migne, Patrologiae Cursus Completus. Series Latina 10 (Paris: Vrayet, 1845), 311.
BB I.e. 'perhaps'.
BC Original: Fol. [.]6. Due to a correction by a previous owner the first number is no longer legible.
BD Original: Fol. [.]6. Due to a correction by a previous owner the first number is no longer legible.
BE Original: Fol. 131.
BF I.e. Joshua the son of Nun.
BG Jerome, *In Naum liber unus* ed. Jacques Paul Migne, Patrologiae Cursus Completus. Series Latine 25 (Paris, Garnier, 1884), 1272. (We were unable to consult the edition by M. Adriaen (Corpus Christianorum Series Latine 76a).
BH Original: Fol. 133.
BI Ie.permission,dispensation(source:http:„gtb.inl.nl,iWDB,search?actie=article&wdb=WNT&id=M018065 [9-1-2018]).
BJ I.e. adult, not elderly.

BK This sentence is very poor from a stylistic point of view. The main structure is: Ende ghemerckt datter nerghens in de heylighe schrift verboden en is de kleyne kinderkens te doopen, ende [ghemerckt] dat alle de passagien die daerteghen van onse wederseggers uut de schrift gheallegeert worden eygentlicken te verstaen zijn tegen de onboetveerdige, ongeloovige oude bejaerde menschen…so konnen alle eenvuldighe wel daeruut verstaen dat men se met gheenen rechte van den doop afweeren en mach.

BL Original: Fol. 104.

BM In the original 'des wrekenden rechters' is part of the subject.

BN Original: Fol. 105

BO The indexes do not have folio page numbers. We therefore refer to the signature marks.

Index of Persons and Places

Considering that Micron is referred to on virtually every page of the book, he has been omitted from this index.

Alba	100.
Alkmaar	83, 84n168, 115.
Alting, M.	12, 77, 111n140.
Amsterdam	15n36, 27n2, 37, 38, 83, 84n168, 115, 131, 241.
Anastasius. See: Versteghe	
Anna, countess	77, 79, 93-96, 129, 238.
Anselmus of Canterbury	22n75.
Antwerp	47, 52, 55, 61, 113.
Aportanus, G.	90.
Arentsz. J.	115.
Aurich	89.
Backereel, H.	38, 39, 75, 133, 239,
Balthasar von Esen	7, 92, 237.
Basel	50n3, 53-56, 59, 209n3, 238.
Becker, J.	11, 18, 68n94, 105, 109, 126, 129-130, 217-218, 223.
Benninck, C.	83.
Berghe, N. van den	32, 33.
Beza, Th.	111n140, 131, 135.
Bibliander, Th.	58.
Block, H.	75.
Bocher, J.	65.
Boer, E.A. de	44-45n53, 249.
Faber de Bouma, Gellius	78, 89, 96-99.
Bourgogne, J. de	54, 55, 238.
Brass(ius), H.	78.
Bremmer, R.H.	110-112, 120, 122n211.
Brès, G. de	40n46, 228n144, 246-247.
Brun, H.	90.
Bugenhagen, J.	92.

Bullinger, H.	13-16, 35n30, 39, 44, 55-59, 70, 71, 80-82, 86, 121, 165n122, 178, 183, 209-213, 215-216, 218-220, 222, 224-227, 229, 230n163, 231-233, 236, 238, 242, 244-245, 252.
Buwo, B.	39, 132, 133, 135.
Calvin, J.	8n7, 14, 15, 17n43, 35n30, 36, 44-45, 54, 58-59, 76, 80-81, 86, 104, 111n140, 113, 117, 121, 123, 200, 209-213, 215-220, 222-224, 226n129, 230-236, 245, 252.
Carinaeus, N.	8, 24, 29, 33-34, 35n30, 36-37, 40, 41, 43, 46, 48, 49, 83-86, 87, 115, 132, 135, 146, 241.
Carter, Ch.	141-142.
Charles V	51-52, 71, 93, 96n51.
Christian III	72, 74.
Christophorus of Ewsum	84.
Coolhaes, C.	103, 111, 112n145, 120, 122, 126.
Cooltuyn, C.	83, 98, 115, 120.
Coornhert, D. V.	103, 122n121, 126, 249.
Cornelisz., A.	111, 237, 248-250.
Corput, H. van de	112.
Cranmer, T.	62, 63n64, 64, 66, 69n99, 71, 170n142, 201, 238.
Ctematius, G.	27-28, 31-34, 39, 41, 48.
Daneau, L.	111.
Dankbaar, W.F.	17-18, 69.
Datheen, P.	38-39, 40n46, 82, 100-101, 111, 115-116, 120, 122, 126-127, 131, 133-134, 239, 247-248.
David Joris / David Joristen	34, 37n36, 43, 45, 46, 48, 95, 131, 137, 138.
Decavele, J.	46, 50n5.
Delenus, W.	67, 71, 84-85, 115.
Delft	237, 248.
Dickens, Ch.	19.
Dieussart, J.	81.
Donteclock, R.	249-250.
Dordrecht	102, 111, 124, 128, 134, 246n5, 248.
Dordt. See: Dordrecht	
Dudley, A.	137.
Dudley, R.	139.
Duifhuis, H.	103, 112n145, 122n211, 126.
Dyrkinus, J.	34, 36, 37.
Edward VI	5, 32, 61, 63n67, 71, 104n104, 108, 178.

Edzard the Great	90.
Ehlers, C.	18.
Emden	12n19, 12n20, 12n22, 13, 17n42, 32, 33, 37-39, 74-75, 77, 81, 83- 84, 89, 90-94, 96, 98, 101, 102n81, 103, 108-116, 119-121, 125-127, 217n55, 240, 246-248.
Enno II	91-93.
Erven, G. van der See: Ctematius, G.	
Eubulaeo, K.	133.
Faber, E.	18, 24, 38-39, 131-136, 246, 248.
Faber (de Bouma), G.	78, 89, 96-99.
Fabri, P.	133.
Flekkerøy	72.
Fontaine Verwey, H. de la	34, 37-38, 41, 43, 45, 46n58, 135, 137n24.
Frankenthal	103, 111, 248.
Frankfurt	38-39, 79, 195n119, 131, 133.
Freudenberg, M.	115, 121.
Friedrich III	133-136, 246.
Frisius, V.	78, 81n154.
Gallus, R.	67.
Geneva	16, 210.
Gerretsen, J.H.	14-15, 17, 18, 31, 69.
Ghent	27, 28n6, 31, 46, 50-53, 61, 86, 238.
Gnapheus, W.	78.
Grell, P.O.	116, 118, 120n201.
Grey, Lady J.	71.
Grindal, Archbishop	141.
Grochowina, N.	88n2, 89n3, 94n35, 95, 97-98.
Groen van Prinsterer, G.	101-102, 113-114, 121, 239.
Haemstede, A.C. van	47.
Hamburg	17n47, 75-77, 202.
Heidelberg	12n19, 39, 82, 111, 112n145, 131, 133, 246, 248.
Heijden, G. van der	111, 113, 115.
Helsingør	72.
Henry VIII	61, 229n150.
Herberts, H.	103, 112n145, 122n211, 126.
Heijting, W.	69n99, 132n6, 135.

Hill, N. See:	
Berghe, N. van den	
Hilles, A.	55.
Hilles, R.	55.
Hoen, C.	78n139, 90.
Hofmann, M.	91.
Holtmann, A.	78, 82.
Hommius, F.	82.
Hooft, A. J. van 't	14-15.
Hooper, A. See:	
Tserclaes, A. de	
Hooper, J.	13, 16, 55-56, 59, 61, 64, 65, 66, 70, 71, 86, 178, 201, 203, 209-216, 218-224, 227-229, 233, 235-236, 238, 245, 252.
Hugo, V.	8n5.
Huss, J.	81.
Huysman, B.	75.
Jan of Nassau	134.
Janssen, G.H.	108n131, 119.
Janssen, H. E.	88n2, 90, 93-94, 96n52.
Janssen, K.	151n39.
Jennelt	84, 241.
Johann Cirksena	93.
Johann II of Rietberg	79.
Jud, L.	209, 212-213, 215, 218, 219, 220n76, 221n85, 231, 232n171.
Jürgens, H.P.	88n2, 93.
Kamphuis, J.	112.
Karel of Gelder	92.
Katelyne, Hoste vander	80, 106n117, 165n122.
Kempen	133.
Knewstub(s), J.	24, 136-142, 246
Koldingen	72.
Köln	132-136.
Kooi, Ch.	11, 49n1.
Krahn, C.	91, 95n47.
Kuper, A. de	37-38, 81 240.
Kuyper, A.	15n36, 69, 101, 102.

Lasco, J. à	5, 9-10, 12, 14-15, 17n42, 18, 32, 39, 44, 53n21, 64, 66-69, 71-72, 74, 79, 81-82, 86, 88n2, 89, 93-97, 116, 129, 183, 209-213, 215- 224, 228n144, 232, 234, 236, 238, 252.
Leer	89.
Lemsius, W.	77-78, 96, 99.
Lindanus, Bishop	134.
London	9, 12, 17n42, 23, 31-33, 38, 39, 48, 53, 61, 64, 65, 71, 76, 82n163, 83n164, 84-86, 93, 94, 103, 115, 136, 153, 180, 201, 206, 238, 241, 247.
Lübeck	74-76.
Luther, M.	51-53, 89, 90-92, 96, 129, 202, 209n2, 227, 237.
Lydius, M.	111.
Marshall, P.	61.
Marstrandt	72.
Mary of Hungary	52.
Mary Tudor	9, 16, 32, 71, 238.
Meiners, E.	12.
Middelburg	111, 125, 246n5, 248.
Mierdman, S.	32-33.
Moded, H.	100, 120, 122, 126.
Mönckeberg, C.	81.
Müller, J.	11, 105-109, 126, 129-130, 239.
Musculus, W.	80, 165n122, 209-211, 213-216, 221n82, 224n104, 233-234, 252.
Muylaert, S.	5, 18, 55n27, 56n32, 66, 68n95, 69n96, 71n106, 82n163, 85n176, 104n104.
Myconius, O.	54, 59.
Niclaes, H.	37n36, 38n39, 45n56, 139-141.
Nicolai, G.	39, 40n44.
Nijmegen	133n15, 134.
Nissen, P.	113.
Norden	7-9, 12, 24, 39, 48, 68n94, 69-70, 72, 77-82, 83n167, 87-92, 96-99, 129, 145, 161, 165, 237-238, 251-252.
Oberman, H.	10, 102, 116-117, 119, 121, 123.
Oecolampadius, J.	54.
Oldersum	90.
Panneel, M.	111.
Parker, M.	13.
Pellikan, C.	56n34, 58, 61, 216.

Pelt, J.	91.
Perussel, F.	67.
Pettegree, A.	10-11, 18, 33n24, 46n58, 63n68, 68n93, 72n114, 81, 83n167, 102, 110, 113-115, 118n187, 119, 121, 123.
Philips of Marnix, Lord of St. Aldegonde	121.
Pijper, F.	14.
Pistorius, J.	78n139, 90.
Plasger, G.	121, 220n78.
Pol, F. van der	247.
Reershemius, P.F.	13, 36n32, 50.
Reese, H.	90, 92.
Reitemeier, A.	88-89, 127, 129, 130, 237, 240.
Ridley, N.	65-66.
Rode, H.	78n139, 90, 92.
Roger, J.	140.
Rosendale, T.	63, 65.
Rutgers, F.L.	15.
Schatorjé, J.	18, 48n67, 131-136.
Schelven, A. A. van	16-17, 35n36, 85n181, 113.
Schilder, K.	22n75.
Schilling, H.	10, 83n167, 102, 116-121, 123.
Schreiber, T.	18, 39, 116, 190n250.
Selderhuis, H.J.	113, 219.
Siller, A.	115, 121.
Simons, M.	9n9, 17, 28, 32, 46, 50n4, 53, 75, 80, 94n38, 95, 165, 203.
Skinner, Q.	19.
Snelleart, F.A.	28-29, 31.
Sophie Quadt von Kinkelbach	133.
Spohnholz, J.	11, 100-105, 107, 109-110, 122, 124-126, 128-129, 239.
Stevens, J.	90.
Strasbourg	16, 55, 56, 59, 61, 209n2, 209n3.
Stumpf, J.R.	59, 61.
Taffin, J.	111, 115.
Terpstra, N.	110, 123-124, 158, 199, 214.
Thysius, A.	12, 102.

Timann, J.	91.
Trabius, IJ.	111.
Tserclaes, A. de	55-56, 61.
Utenhove, J.	9-10, 12, 14, 32, 36, 39, 53, 61, 66n86, 67, 69n96, 70-75, 81.
Vanlangenhove, F.	28.
Veen, M. van	11, 18, 56n58, 100-105, 107, 109-110, 116n170, 124-126, 129, 200, 239.
Velsius, J.	85, 126.
Venlo	133-134.
Vermigli, P.M.	44, 81-82 209, 211, 213, 218, 220, 221n82, 222n88, 223-224, 230, 232, 236, 245, 252.
Versteghe, G.	134.
Vincentius	75.
Vis, G.N.M.	84n168, 115, 120.
Weerda, J.R.	92, 94-95.
Wesel	100, 101n75, 102n81, 103, 116, 124-125.
Westphal, J.	17, 36, 46, 76, 77n133, 81, 151, 181, 202.
Wilhelm Quadt von Wickrath	133.
Wilkinson, W.	140.
Willems, W.O.R.	17-18, 50n8, 53n21, 74n122, 81n152, 151n37, 151n38, 188-189.
William of Orange	100, 121.
Wilson, R.P.	64, 223.
Wingen, G. van	36.
Wismar	75-76, 80.
Wolfsheim	133-134.
Wycliffe, J.	81.
Zijlstra, S.	95.
Zimmerman, J.	133.
Zurich	13-15, 18, 23-24, 55-59, 61-62, 67n86, 70, 86, 97, 121, 180, 209-211, 213-214, 220, 223-224, 227, 228n143, 229, 231-232, 236, 238, 244.
Zwingli, H.	54, 56n34, 57-58, 77, 81, 89n6, 122n210, 180, 202, 209, 211, 212n14, 227, 233n181.